The Age of
Global Dialogue

The Age of
Global Dialogue

Leonard Swidler

PICKWICK Publications • Eugene, Oregon

THE AGE OF GLOBAL DIALOGUE

Copyright © 2016 Leonard Swidler. All rights reserved. Except for brief quotations in critical publications or reviews, no part of this book may be reproduced in any manner without prior written permission from the publisher. Write: Permissions, Wipf and Stock Publishers, 199 W. 8th Ave., Suite 3, Eugene, OR 97401.

Pickwick Publications
An Imprint of Wipf and Stock Publishers
199 W. 8th Ave., Suite 3
Eugene, OR 97401

www.wipfandstock.com

PAPERBACK ISBN: 978-1-4982-0867-3
HARDCOVER ISBN: 978-1-4982-0869-7
EBOOK ISBN: 978-1-4982-0868-0

Cataloguing-in-Publication data:

Names: Swidler, Leonard J.

Title: The Age of Global Dialogue / Leonard Swidler.

Description: Eugene, OR: Pickwick Publications, 2016 | Includes index.

Identifiers: ISBN 978-1-4982-0867-3 (paperback) | ISBN 978-1-4982-0869-7 (hardcover) | ISBN 978-1-4982-0868-0 (ebook)

Subjects: LSCH: Religion—Relations. | Dialogue—Religious aspects.

Classification: BL410 S850 2016 (print) | BL410 (ebook)

Manufactured in the U.S.A.   10/31/16

To

Arlene Anderson Swidler
my beloved partner in life and beyond

Contents

Introduction | ix

1. Bases of Dialogue | 1
2. Religion (Ideology)—Its Meaning | 35
3. The "Inner" Dialogue | 82
4. The "Inter" Dialogue | 95
5. Dialogue in the World | 312
6. Dialogue Attempted | 366
7. Final Conclusion | 409

Index | 411

Introduction

In the late 1980s, when the Soviet Union and Communism were teetering on the edge of oblivion—but no one, including the KGB and the CIA, knew it—I finished writing my first rather comprehensive book on interreligious dialogue, *After the Absolute*, and it was published in 1990 with Fortress Press in Minneapolis. Sometime during 2004 my newly-found-on-the-web Chinese friend, Professor Lihua Liu in Beijing, asked if she might translate it into Chinese. I agreed, but only of a greatly revised and expanded version. She undertook the massive task, and the Chinese revised and expanded version—*Quanqiu Duihua de Shidai: The Age of Global Dialogue*—came out with China Social Science Press in Beijing in 2006. I have continued to revise and expand since then (I suppose that I will continue to do so until I run into my tombstone). Though I am now 86, I fortunately am in good health (though, as we all know, that could evaporate in a moment!), so perhaps I will be allowed to ride my bike (can't run anymore because of my knees) for a few more years. Perhaps there will, then, be a further expansion of my experience of and reflection on Deep-Dialogue and Critical-Thinking—*Deo volente* (the Latin Christian phrase, "God willing," which Muslims match with *Inshallah*).

At this point I think that it would be helpful to provide a little historical and autobiographical background on how I came to be involved in ecumenical, interreligious, interideological, intercultural dialogue long before it became the almost faddish thing it threatens (happily!) to morph into in 2015.

Nothing in human history appears *ex nihilo*. There are always roots that go back into the mists of history. However, since the tragic events of September 11, 2001, it is clear to everyone reading the daily newspapers that a rising tide of interreligious dialogue is afoot, and for most people it seems strikingly new. I would suggest that the very obvious interreligious dialogue movement of today can point to its conscious beginning at the first World's Parliament of Religions at the 1893 Chicago celebration of the four-hundredth anniversary of Columbus's discovery of America.

It grew gradually after that and was given a significant shove forward with the launching of the Christian ecumenical movement in 1910—for turning away from an inward gaze that insisted that "my" Christian denomination is the only correct one, to an outward turn toward other denominations—carries with it its own unstoppable outward momentum to engage in dialogue with an ever-widening circle. This ecumenical movement was thus launched by Protestants, who sought Orthodox and Catholic institutional participation. They quickly formally gained the former, but not the latter.

Nevertheless, Catholics did eventually join in the dialogue, though against very heavy Vatican resistance. Over a half-century ago (1957), when I started researching the ecumenical dialogue, I found this early and persistent Catholic involvement in what became known as the *Una Sancta* Movement between Catholics and Protestants starting already just after World War I in Germany, the Land of the Reformation.[1] Then came Vatican Council II (1962–65) of the Catholic Church (with its 1.3 billion members!), which reversed its resistance to dialogue and embraced it fully.

The pages of the *Journal of Ecumenical Studies* (*JES*) serve as an excellent bellwether marking the progress of the interreligious dialogue movement. It was in the middle of Vatican II that my wife Arlene Anderson Swidler and I launched *JES* (it was her brilliant idea!). The first issue appeared in 1964, carrying articles by today's most famous living Catholic theologians, Hans Küng and Joseph Ratzinger (now Pope Benedict XVI, *emeritus*). Already in the late 1960s *JES* was found in a worldwide survey by the Centro Pro Unione in Rome to be the most important publication in the world devoted to ecumenical and interreligious dialogue.

The first volume of *JES* (1964) carried the subtitle "Protestant, Catholic, Orthodox," but already in 1965, we dropped it, as we took on our first non-Christian Associate Editor, Rabbi Arthur Gilbert. In the next three years *JES* continued to expand the dialogue (adding Muslim, Hindu, Buddhist, etc., Associate Editors) so that the initial dialogue among Christians quickly spread to dialogue among all religions and beyond to all ideologies, cultures, and societal institutions—including, in 1968, the Christian-Marxist

---

1. See Leonard Swidler, *The Ecumenical Vanguard* (Pittsburgh: Duquesne University Press, 1965), where I detailed the history of the *Una Sancta* Movement.

dialogue.² In 1978, I established the outreach arm of *JES*, the Dialogue Institute: Interreligious, Intercultural, International.

Thus, what I had started to study as a graduate student in the 1950s, namely, the dialogue between Catholics and Protestants, naturally moved on to Jewish-Christian dialogue, then Jewish-Christian-Muslim trialogue, and further to dialogue with Hinduism, Buddhism, Confucianism, and even Marxism (by 1968). As part of this wave, I then began to reflect about dialogue itself. In 1989, the Berlin Wall came down, and, as noted, the Soviet Union suddenly disappeared. Shortly afterward in 1993, Samuel Huntington argued that the world had settled back into a "Clash of Civilizations."

He was right. There was/is a "Clash of Civilizations," but that nomenclature did not, and does not, describe all of the contemporary global scene. The world also dramatically began to move into the "Age of Global Dialogue."³ As a personal reflection of this huge tsunami shift, I as just one scholar published in that same time period, between 1990 and 1992, twelve books dealing with interreligious dialogue.⁴ Soon the very term "dialogue" became extremely popular (but not always the reality), so much so that it was at times applied indiscriminately or even deceptively.

Hence, it is important to be clear about how the term "dialogue" is used, especially in the area of interreligious/interideological dialogue. Clearly, serious use of the term today is not understood in some "light-headed" fashion but as something much deeper than mere conversation, as something life-transforming. Here is the definition used in the first version of the "Ground Rules for Interreligious Dialogue":⁵ "By dialogue is meant a

---

2. For a detailed history, see Leonard Swidler, "Christian-Marxist Dialogue: A Historical Overview and Analysis," in Leonard Swidler and Edward Grace, eds., *Catholic-Communist Collaboration in Italy* (Lanham, MD: University Press of America, 1988), 7–26.

3. In 2000, Paul Mojzes and I used the term in our book, *The Study of Religion in an Age of Global Dialogue* (Philadelphia: Temple University Press, 2000), and in a 2006 book I changed "*an* Age" to "*the* Age": *Quanqiu Duihua de Shidai: The Age of Global Dialogue*, tr. Lihua Liu (Beijing: China Social Science, 2006).

4. Leonard Swidler, (1) *After the Absolute: The Dialogical Future of Religious Reflection* (1990); (2) *Death or Dialogue. From the Age of Monologue to the Age of Dialogue* (1990); (3) *Bursting the Bonds? A Jewish-Christian Dialogue on Jesus and Paul* (1990); (4) *Attitudes of Religions and Ideologies towards the Outsider: The Other* (1990); (5) *A Bridge to Buddhist-Christian Dialogue* (1990); (6) *Christian Mission and Interreligious Dialogue* (1990); (7) *Human Rights: Christians, Marxists, and Others in Dialogue* (1991); (8) *Der umstrittene Jesus* (1993); (9) *Muslims in Dialogue: The Evolution of a Dialogue over a Generation* (1992); (10) *The Meaning of Life At the Edge of the Third Millennium* (1992); (11) *Die Zukunft der Theologie im Dialog der Religionen und Weltanschauungen* (1992); and (12) *Introduzione al buddismo: Paralleli con l'etica ebraico-cristiana* (1992).

5. The first version of just four ground rules was published as "Ground Rules for

conversation between individual persons and at times through them, two or more communities or groups, with differing views, the *primary* purpose of which is for each participant to learn from the other so that she or he can change and grow and thereby the respective groups or communities as well." Subsequently, I came to perceive dialogue as much deeper, much more pervasive, in our human, and indeed, cosmic realty. From the middle-1990s I increasingly used the term "Deep-Dialogue" and essentially linked it with "Critical-Thinking," and eventually "Competitive-Cooperation"[6] and "Emotional-Intelligence," and most recently, "Spiritual"-Aikido.

Hence, this first English publication of the expanded/emended version of my 1990 *After the Absolute* and the 2004 Chinese version, *The Age of Global Dialogue* will in many sections be mainly as it was first written in the late 1980s, in some, with the newly written material from up to 2004, and in yet others, still newer material or references. Clearly, then, this book is a 2015 snapshot of my understanding of life, and especially interreligious, interideological dialogue.

Since neither I nor anyone else can view reality from a "nonposition" position, I wish to acknowledge here that I am writing as a Catholic Christian thinker. I try to be as "objective" as I possibly can be, but, in so doing, I recognize that complete objectivity is impossible. Further, I also sometimes specifically address Christian issues in these pages. I do so, however, for all of my readers, but for different reasons. Clearly, for Christians I wrestle with some issues specifically from a Christian perspective. For example, "What should Christians as Christians make of the claims of Muslims to have received a revelation after Jesus?" However, the issue underlying that question—"What do I make of claims after the close of my religious canon?"—is one that most, if not all, religions must deal with. What I do here as a Christian I hope will serve as one example of a helpful stimulus.

Interreligious Dialogue," in the *Journal of Ecumenical Studies* 15 (1978) 413–14; and expanded to "The Dialogue Decalogue: Ground Rules for Interreligious Dialogue," *JES* 20 (Winter, 1983) 1–4; from 1984 onward the title was "Dialogue Decalogue: Groundrules for Interreligious, Interideological Dialogue." It has been reproduced in at least 39 different publications in dozens of different languages; see http://dialogueinstitute.org/dialogue-principles/ or the growing number of translations. These commonsense guidelines were named "Dialogue Decalogue" for mnemonic pedagogical reasons: Members of the Abrahamic religions—Judaism, Christianity, Islam—will all recognize and easily remember the term the "Decalogue," the "Ten Commandments"; in addition, the alliteration of D/D also aids recall.

6. See Leonard Swidler, "Deep-Dialogue/Critical-Thinking/Complementary-Cooperation," *JES* 40 (2009) 465–66.

1

Bases of Dialogue

Definition of Religion

Let me begin by giving my understanding of the term "religion" in very brief fashion:

> Religion is an explanation of the ultimate meaning of life, based on a notion and experience of the transcendent, and how to live accordingly; and it normally contains the four "C's": Creed, Code, Cult, Community-structure.

Creed refers to the cognitive aspect of a religion; it is everything that goes into the "explanation" of the ultimate meaning of life.

Code of behavior or ethics includes all the rules and customs of action that somehow follow from one aspect or another of the Creed.

Cult means all the ritual activities that relate the believer to one aspect or other of the Transcendent, either directly or indirectly, prayer being an example of the former and certain formal behavior toward representatives of the Transcendent, such as priests, of the latter.

Community-structure refers to the relationships among the believers; this can vary widely, from a very egalitarian relationship, as among Quakers, through a "republican" structure as Presbyterians have, to a monarchical one, as with some Hasidic Jews vis-à-vis their Rebbe.

Transcendent, as the roots of the word indicate, means "that which goes beyond" the everyday, the ordinary, the surface experience of reality. It can mean spirits, gods, a Personal God, an Impersonal God, Emptiness, etc.

Especially in modern times there have developed "explanations of the ultimate meaning of life and how to live accordingly" that are not based on a notion of the transcendent, for example, Marxism or Atheistic Humanism. Although in every respect these "explanations" function as religions traditionally have in human life, because the idea of the transcendent, however it is understood, plays such a central role in religion, but not in these "explanations" as was discussed above, for the sake of accuracy it is best to give these "explanations" that are not based on notion of the transcendent a separate name; the name often used is "ideology." Much, though not all, of the following discussion will, *mutatis mutandis* (Latin: "changing what needs to be changed"), also apply to ideology even when the term is not used. More about this below.

Meaning of Dialogue

I am here focusing on the current customary meaning of dialogue, namely, the Dialogue of the Head (more about this distinction and others of dialogue below), and especially dialogue in the religious—and ideological—area. It is important to realize that Dialogue of the Head is not simply a series of conversations. It is a *whole new way of thinking*, a way of seeing and reflecting on the world and its meaning.

If I were writing just for Christians, I would use the term "theology" to name what I am largely talking about here. But, the dialogical way of thinking is not something that is peculiarly Christian, though Christians for a variety of historical reasons are today at the forefront in employing it and promoting its use. Dialogue, however, is a way for all human beings to reflect on the ultimate meaning of life. So, whether one is a theist or not, whether one is given to using Hellenistic thought categories as Christians have been wont to do in their "theologizing" or not, dialogue is ever more clearly the way of the future in religious—and ideological—reflection on the ultimate meaning of life and how to live accordingly.

In this book I try to think beyond the absolutes that I as a Christian—and others in their own ways—have increasingly found deabsolutized in the modern thought world. I try to reflect on the ways all of us humans need to think about the world and its meaning, now that more and more of us, both individually and even at times institutionally, are gaining enough maturity to notice that there are entire other ways of integrating an understanding of the world than the way in which we and our forebears grew up.

In this new situation I sense the need for consciously developing a common language we can use effectively to communicate with each other so that we can learn about these other ways of seeing the world, both to appreciate our neighbors and to enrich ourselves. I call this common language "Ecumenical Esperanto," because it should serve as a common language without replacing any of the living languages, that is, the languages of our religious and ideological traditions.

Of course, such thinking anew about the world and its meaning must necessarily mean thinking anew about all of our religious beliefs, and for me as a Christian this preeminently includes my central teaching, the meaning of Jesus the Christ, Christology. Hence, I here attempt to begin thinking through again the meaning of Christology—but this time, in dialogue.

My dialogue partners in this new paradigm of understanding the world, of thinking, are all the world's ways of understanding the world and its meaning—the world's religions and ideologies. So, I here attempt to engage in dialogue with at least the world's major religions and ideologies, reflecting on what we—in this case, Christian and non-Christian—can learn about and from each other. But, beyond all these dialogue partners is the often unconscious but always pervasive dialogue partner, for me and an ever increasing number of contemporaries, of modern critical thought, Modernity.[1]

Precisely those of us who are open to dialogue, that is, those of us who are open to going beyond our prior absolutes to learning from each other, live in a deabsolutized, a relationized, a modern, critical-thinking thought-world, a thought-world wherein we no longer can live on the level of the first naiveté but are at least striving to live on the level of the second naiveté. On this level we see our root symbols and metaphors *as* symbols and metaphors and, hence, do not mistake them for empirical, ontological realities, but also we do not simply reject them as fantasies and fairy tales. Rather, because we see them as root symbols and metaphors, we correctly appreciate them as indispensable vehicles to communicate profound realities that go beyond the capacity of our everyday language.

Here again it is becoming clear that in the attempt to communicate and receive the understandings and insights gained in reflecting dialogically on our root metaphors, we need a common language—one of course that never will be adequate but will always be growing, one that will never replace the "primary" living languages of our root metaphors growing out of our origins and traditions but that nevertheless will become increasingly indispensable in the future: "Ecumenical Esperanto." It is in that language that I attempt at the end of this volume to do an exegesis of a key Christian scripture—dialogically after the absolute.

In the past, from the very beginning of humankind, we have always talked with ourselves, that is, we always spoke with persons who thought as we did—or who should! We spoke always in monologue. In the past century-and-a-half, as we have slowly moved in the direction of a deabsolutized

---

1. See my book, *Club Modernity: For Reluctant Christians* (Philadelphia: Ecumenical Press, 2011).

understanding of truth, we have slowly begun to realize that no one person or community, culture, religion, or civilization can express all there is to know about any particular reality, especially Ultimate Reality. Hence, we are beginning to realize that we must be in dialogue with those who think differently from us, not to teach them the truth, but to learn more about reality that we cannot know from ourselves alone. We are unavoidably moving into dialogue, into Deep-Dialogue.

In short, humanity is now painfully leaving the Age of Monologue, where we have been since the dawn of *Homo Sapiens Sapiens*, and are moving, with blinking, blurry vision yet, into the Age of Global Dialogue.

Hence, beyond the absolute way of understanding the world and its meaning for us, beyond the absolute way of thinking, we humans are beginning to find a much richer, "truer," way of understanding the world—the dialogical way of thinking. It is to this dialogical way of thinking, particularly in the area of religion and ideology, that I turn now in greater detail.

Thomas Kuhn revolutionized our understanding of the development of scientific thinking with his notion of paradigm shifts. He painstakingly showed that fundamental "paradigms" or "exemplary models" are the large thought-frames within which we place and interpret all observed data and that scientific advancement inevitably brings about eventual paradigm shifts—from geocentrism to heliocentrism, for example, or from Newtonian to Einsteinian physics—that are always vigorously resisted at first, as was the thought of Galileo, but that finally prevail.[2] This insight, however, not only is valid for the development of thought in the physical sciences but also is applicable to all major disciplines of human thought, including the systematic religious and ideological reflection that Christians, and now some others as well, call "theology."

A major paradigm shift in systematic religious and ideological reflection, that is, in "theology" then means a major change "in the very idea of what it is to do theology."[3] For example, the major Christian theological revolution that occurred at the first Ecumenical Council (Nicaea, 325 CE) did not so much resolve the battle over whether the Son and Father were of "the same substance," *homoousion*, important as that was, but rather that, "by defining '*homoousion*,' tacitly admitted that here were issues in theology that could not be solved simply on the basis of recourse to the language of

---

2. Thomas Kuhn, *The Structure of Scientific Revolutions*, 2nd ed. (Chicago: University of Chicago Press, 1970).

3. Quentin Quesnell, "On Not Negotiating the Self in the Structure of Theological Revolutions," typescript, January 3–11, 1984, Honolulu conference on "Paradigm Shifts in Buddhism and Christianity: Cultural Systems and the Self," 2.

the Scriptures."[4] In the next several centuries a flood of new answers poured forth to questions being posed in categories unused by Jesus and his first (Jewish, of course) followers—in this case, in Greek philosophical categories of thought.

As the paradigm within which the data of what Jesus taught, and wrought and how his Jewish followers responded was perceived and understood shifted from the Semitic, concrete biblical thought world to a Hellenistic, largely abstract, philosophical one, the questions asked and the terms in which they were asked shifted accordingly, and of course so did the answers. As always, when a new major paradigm shift occurs, old answers are no longer helpful, for they respond to questions no longer posed, in thought categories no longer used, within a framework that no longer prevails. It is not that the old answers are now declared wrong; it is simply that they no longer apply. Aristotle's answers in physics and chemistry in terms of the four elements of air, fire, water, and earth, for example, simply do not speak to the questions posed by modern chemists and physicists. Tenth-century Christian theologians answering that Mary remained a virgin while giving birth to Jesus (that is, her hymen was not broken) were answering a question that no modern critical-thinking Christian theologian would pose, for it presupposed a thought-world that placed a high value on physically unbroken hymens. That thought-world is largely gone. Hence, the old answer is not only *non*pertinent, but perhaps even *im*pertinent.

Today we are in the midst of another fundamental paradigm shift in our approach to what it means to do "theology." This book will try to spell out some of the dimensions of this shift but will focus mainly on one of the major aspects: the turn to dialogue. The old paradigms of doing theology in splendid isolation, of hostile polemic, or the allegedly loving proselytizing of religious or ideological "outsiders" is more and more being found wanting. Instead, dialogue within and without is seen as the way forward beyond religious and ideological isolation, polemic, and enmity-breeding proselytization. I want to argue in these reflections, then, that, as part of this shift, dialogue, and very especially interreligious and interideological dialogue, is the most appropriate matrix within which to carry out systematic reflection on the "explanations of the meaning of life and how to live accordingly," which Christians call "theology."

First, a word about terminology: In the past most "explanations of the meaning of life and how to live accordingly" have entailed a belief in that which "goes beyond," "*trans*cends," humanity and the world, traditionally termed the divine or the transcendent—Theravada Buddhism is a clear

---

4. Ibid., 3.

exception—and in recent centuries they have been called "religions" in the West. Those most recent "explanations of the meaning of life and how to live accordingly" that do not include a belief in the transcendent, such as atheistic Marxism and atheistic Humanism, have at times been called "ideologies," as in the World Council of Churches' "Dialogues with Peoples of Living Faiths and Ideologies." I am here adopting that terminology.

The reasons why in this controverted area of the definition of religion I have been led in this direction are the following:

The generic term is "worldview and way," of which there are two main species: religion and ideology. A "worldview and way" is an "explanation of the meaning of life and how to live accordingly." It will always include the four "C's": *Creed* (belief system), *Code* (ethical system), *Cult* (celebratory system), and *Community*-structure (social system). If the "explanation of the meaning of life and how to live accordingly" is based ultimately on something that "goes beyond," "transcends," humanity and the world, it belongs to the species "religion"; if it does not, but is ultimately "innerworldly" in its explanation, it belongs to the species "ideology."

There is, of course, something problematic with the term "ideology"—and also its possible alternatives. Despite the fact that etymologically "ideology" means something like the systematic study of an idea (as biology is the systematic study of living things), often is understood to have a pejorative connotation. Thus used, an ideology would be a system of thought that, like a Procrustean bed, forces all data within its structures, even if it means distorting them grossly. However, ideology is also understood in a neutral fashion, meaning simply a systematized body of thought, as, for example, in a reference to Marxist ideology, which also includes a code for behavior flowing from the theoretical analysis.

"Philosophy" is a possible alternative here to the term "ideology" in a neutral sense, but it has the disadvantage of including Christian philosophy, Hindu philosophy, and other "religious" philosophies. Hence, it could lead to confusion if it were used without a modifying adjective to refer *solely* to a system of thought and action that does not include the notion of the transcendent. The difficulty with using the term "worldview" (*Weltanschauung*) alone instead of "ideology" is that it usually does not denote a spelled-out thought structure, which the term "ideology" does but, rather, suggests a general, somewhat vague attitude toward life—and that surely does not describe Marxism, for example, as formerly practiced in the Soviet Union and satellites and still practiced in North Korea and Cuba. Hence, the neutral, more nearly root etymological, understanding of "ideology" seems to be the least problematic term to use to describe an "explanation of the meaning of life and how to live accordingly" that does not include the element of the transcendent. Moreover, it is a self-description that has also been used by at least some Marxists, and it has the additional practical advantage of having been part of the official terminology used by the World Council of Churches. Consequently, its usage in this manner will probably gain in consensus and thus create further clarity in communication.

Another key term in these reflections that will need to be clarified further is "dialogue." It has of late become the "in" thing; consequently, the term has come to be used in a number of conflicting ways. After a description of what is meant by "dialogue," I will sketch briefly the recent process of deabsolutizing our understanding of reality and of truth and how this has led to the possibility, and even necessity, of dialogue. Then, I will look more in detail at the meaning of religion/ideology, human nature, and Ultimate Reality. Following that, I will look at the several "circles" of dialogue, starting with the innermost, dialogue within an individual institution, with Catholicism as the example. The next concentric circle is that of the individual religion or ideology, with Christianity as the example because the dialogue there is the furthest advanced.

The fullest demands upon and the greatest benefits from dialogue are seen in the next circle: interreligious, interideological dialogue. This will be the heart of the book: an attempt to show the way forward, not in "practical" and "spiritual" areas, each of which warrants separate full treatment, but in the "cognitive" area. In my later writings, I referred to these divisions of dialogue as the Dialogue of the Head ("cognitive"), Dialogue of the Hands ("practical"), and Dialogue of the Heart ("spiritual"). One central thesis will be that a common language, an "Ecumenical Esperanto," must be developed to supplement, though not supplant, the various religious and ideological languages. Some major interreligious/interideological dialogues will then be looked at briefly to ask what might be hoped for from them.

Next will follow a series of reflections on how dialogue could/should be applied in some of the major areas of human life: human rights, politics, economics, law, ethics, and education. Finally, I will undertake two Christian experiments in "Ecumenical Esperanto," which I hope will stimulate others to do something similar in their religion, so that together we can move on in the third millennium, the Age of Global Dialogue, thereby aligning ourselves with the "Cosmic Dance of Dialogue."

The Universe Is a Cosmic Dance of Dialogue

Dialogue—in its broadest, deepest understanding, *the mutually beneficial interaction of differing components*—is at the very heart of the Universe, of which we humans are the highest expression: from the basic interaction of *matter and energy* (in Einstein's unforgettable formula: $E=mc^2$—energy equals mass times the square of the speed of light), to the creative interaction of *protons and electrons* in every atom, to the vital symbiosis of *body and spirit* in every human, through the creative dialogue between *woman and man*, to the dynamic relationship between *individual and society*. Thus, the very essence of our humanity is dialogical, and a fulfilled human life is the highest expression of the "*Cosmic Dance of Dialogue.*"

In the early millennia of the history of humanity, as we spread outward from our starting point in central Africa, the forces of *di*vergence were dominant. However, because we live on a globe, in our frenetic divergence we eventually began to encounter each other more and more frequently. Now the forces of stunning *con*vergence are becoming increasingly dominant.

In the past, during the Age of Divergence, we could live in isolation from each other; we could ignore each other. Now, in the Age of Convergence we are forced to live in One World. We increasingly live in a Global Village. We cannot ignore the Other, the Different. Too often in the past we have tried to make over the Other into a likeness of ourselves, often by violence, but this is the very opposite of dialogue. This egocentric arrogance is in fundamental opposition to the "Cosmic Dance of Dialogue." It is not creative but destructive. Hence, we humans today have a stark choice: dialogue, or death!

Dialogues of the Head, Hands, Heart, and the Holy

For us humans there are four main dimensions to dialogue—*the mutually beneficial interaction among those who are different*—corresponding to the structure of our humanness: Dialogue of the *H*ead, Dialogue of the *H*ands, Dialogue of *H*eart, and Dialogue of the *H*oly.

The Cognitive or Intellectual: Seeking the Truth

In the *Dialogue of the Head* we mentally reach out to the Other to learn from those who think differently from us. We try to understand how they see the world and why they act as they do. The world is far too complicated for any of us to understand alone; we can increasingly understand reality only with the help of the Other, in dialogue. This is very important, because how we *understand* the world determines how we *act* in the world.

The Illative or Ethical: Seeking the Good

In the *Dialogue of the Hands* we join together with Others to work to make the world a better place in which we all must live together. Since we can no longer live separately in this One World, we must work jointly to make it not just a house but a home in which all of us can live. Stated otherwise, we join hands with the Other to heal the world. The world within us, and all around us, always is in need of healing, and our deepest wounds can be healed only together with the Other, only in dialogue.

The Affective or Aesthetic: Seeking the Beautiful, the Spiritual

In the *Dialogue of the Heart* we open ourselves to receive the beauty of the Other. Because we humans are body and spirit or, rather, body-spirit, we give bodily-spiritual expression in all the arts to our multifarious responses to our encounters with life: joy, sorrow, gratitude, anger, and, most of all, love. We all try to express our inner feelings, which grasp reality in far deeper and higher ways than we are able to put into rational concepts and words; hence, we create poetry, music, dance, painting, architecture—the expressions of the Heart. All the world delights in beauty, wherein we find the familiar that avoids sameness and diversity that avoids distastefulness. It is here that we find the easiest encounter with the Other, the most available door to dialogue, for everyone delights in a thing of beauty, and through the beauty of the Other we most easily enter into the Other. Here, too, is where the depth, spiritual, mystical dimension of the human spirit is given full rein. As seventeenth-century mathematician/philosopher Blaise Pascal said, "*Le cœur a ses raisons que la raison ne connaît point*" (The heart has its reasons, which reason knows not).

Holiness: Seeking the One

We humans cannot long live a divided life. If we are even to survive, let alone flourish, we must "get it together." Indeed, this is what the religions of the Western tradition mean when they say that we humans should be Holy. We *H*umans (another *H*!) are not *dis*integrated beings. Rather, we can be truly *H*uman only if we bring our various parts together in *H*armony, if we integrate our being *H*olistically. Therefore, we are authentically *H*uman only when our multiple elements are in dialogue with each other and we in turn are in dialogue with the Others around us—within the entire "Cosmic

Dance of Dialogue." We must dance together the *Dialogue of the Head*, the *Dialogue of the Hands*, and the *Dialogue of the Heart—Holistically*.

The Meaning of Dialogue of the Head

Today, when we speak of dialogue between religions or ideologies, we mean something quite definite. In the broadest sense—and here we are speaking of the *Dialogue of the Head*—it means a two-way communication between persons, not one-way lecturing or speaking. However, there are many different kinds of two-way communication: for example, fighting, wrangling, debating, etc. Clearly, these are not dialogue. At the other extreme is the communication between persons who hold precisely the same views on a particular subject. We also do not mean this when we use the term "dialogue"; rather, we might call that something like encouragement or reinforcement but not dialogue. If we look at these two opposite kinds of two-way communication that are *not* meant by the word dialogue, we can learn quite precisely what we *do* mean when we use the term.

Looking at the last example first, the principle underlying "reinforcement" is the assumption that both sides have a total grasp on the truth of the subject and simply need to be supported in their commitment to it. Since this example and its underlying principle are excluded from the meaning of dialogue, dialogue must include the notion that neither side has a total grasp of the truth of the subject, but both need to seek further.

The principle underlying "debating" is the assumption that one side has all the truth concerning the subject and that the other side needs to be informed or persuaded of it. Since both that example and its underlying principle are excluded from the meaning of dialogue, this implies that dialogue means that no one side has a monopoly on the truth about the subject, but both need to seek further.

It may turn out in some instances, of course, that after a more or less extensive dialogue it is learned that the two sides in fact agree completely on the subject discussed. Naturally, such a discovery does not mean that the encounter was a nondialogue, but rather that the dialogue was the means of learning the new truth that both sides agreed on the subject; to continue from that point on, however, to speak only about the area of agreement would then be to move from dialogue to reinforcement.

Hence, to express at least the initial part of the meaning of dialogue positively, dialogue is a two-way communication between persons who hold significantly differing views on a subject, with the purpose of learning more truth about the subject from the other.

This analysis may to some seem obvious and, hence, superfluous, but I believe it is not. Dialogue has become a faddish term that is sometimes, like charity, used to cover a multitude of sins. Sometimes, for example, it is used by those who are quite convinced that they have all the truth on a subject but feel that in today's climate, with "dialogue" in vogue, a less aggressive style will be more effective in communicating to the ignorant the truth that they already possess in full. Therefore, while their encounters with others still rely on the older nondialogue principle—that they have all the truth on a subject—their less importuning approach will now be *called* "dialogue." This type of use would appear to be merely an opportunistic manipulation of the word.

Maybe some of those people, however, truly believe that they are engaging in dialogue when they employ such a "soft sell" approach and encourage their interlocutors also to express their own views on the subject—even though it is known ahead of time, of course, that they are false—for such a "dialogue" may well make the ignorant person more open to receiving the truth that the one side knows it already has. In that situation, the "truth-holders" simply had a basic misunderstanding of the term "dialogue" and mistakenly termed their "convert-making" dialogue. Therefore, the above clarification is important.

Dialogue is conversation between two or more persons with differing views, the primary purpose of which is for each participant to learn from the other so that he or she can change and grow. In addition, both partners will also want to share their understanding with their partners. Minimally, the very fact that I learn that my dialogue partner believes "this" rather than "that" changes my attitude toward her or him; a change in my attitude is a significant change—and growth—in me. We enter into dialogue, therefore, primarily so that *we* can learn, change, and grow, not so that we can force change on the other.

In the past, when we encountered those who differed with us in the religious and ideological sphere, we did so usually either to defeat them as opponents or to learn about them so as to deal with them more effectively. In other words, we usually faced those who differed with us in a confrontation—sometimes more openly polemically, sometimes more subtly so, but usually with the ultimate goal of overcoming the other because we were convinced that we alone had the truth.

However, that is not what dialogue is. Dialogue is *not* debate. In dialogue each partner must listen to the other as openly and sympathetically as possible in an attempt to understand the other's position as precisely and as much from within as possible. Such an attitude automatically assumes that at any point we might find the partner's position so persuasive that, if we were to act with integrity, we ourselves would have to change. That means that there is a risk involved in dialogue, that old positions and traditions may be found wanting. But, as the Hindu scholar R. Sundara Rajan remarked, "If it is impossible to lose one's faith as a result of an encounter with another faith, then I feel that the dialogue has been made safe from all possible risks," to which Anglican scholar Lesslie Newbigin added, "a dialogue which is safe from all possible risks is no true dialogue."[5] Even the Vatican has an incredibly strong statement supporting that position: "Doctrinal discussion requires perceptiveness, both in honestly setting out one's own opinion and in recognizing the truth everywhere, even if the truth demolishes one so that one is forced to reconsider one's own position, in theory and in practice, at least in part."[6]

Until quite recently in almost all religious traditions, and certainly very definitely within Christianity, the idea of seeking religious or ideological wisdom, insight, or truth through dialogue, other than in a very initial and rudimentary fashion, occurred to very few people, and it certainly had no influence in the major religious or ideological communities. The further idea of pursuing religious or ideological truth through dialogue with other religions and ideologies was even less thinkable. As recently as 1832, Pope Gregory XVI wrote:

> We come now to a source that is, alas! all too productive of the deplorable evils afflicting the Church today. We have in mind indifferentism, that is, the fatal opinion everywhere spread abroad by the deceit of wicked men, that the eternal salvation of the soul can be won by the profession of any faith at all, provided that conduct conforms to the norms of justice and probity ... From this poisonous spring of indifferentism flows the false and absurd, or rather the mad principle [*deliramentum*] that we must secure and guarantee to each one liberty of conscience.[7]

Today the situation is dramatically reversed. In 1964 Pope Paul VI's first encyclical focused on dialogue: "dialogue is *demanded* nowadays ... is *demanded* by the dynamic course of action that is changing the face

---

5. R. Sundara Rajan, "Negations: An Article on Dialogue among Religions," *Religion and Society* 21 (December 1974) 74; Lesslie Newbigin, *The Open Secret* (London, 1979), both cited in Kenneth Cracknell, "The Ethics of Interreligious Relationships," *World Faiths Insight*, n.s. 9 (Summer 1984) 23.

6. Secretariat for Unbelievers, *Humanae personae dignitatem*, August 28, 1968, quoted in full in Austin Flannery, *Vatican Council II* (Collegeville, MN: Liturgical, 1975) 1010.

7. *Mirari vos*, 1832, quoted in Leonard Swidler, *Freedom in the Church* (Dayton, OH: Pflaum, 1969) 47.

of modern society. It is *demanded* by the pluralism of society and by the maturity man has reached in this day and age. Be he religious or not, his secular education has enabled him to think and speak, and to conduct dialogue with dignity."[8] Further official words of encouragement came from the Vatican secretariat for dialogue with atheists: "All Christians should do their best to promote dialogue . . . as a duty of fraternal charity suited to our progressive and adult age."[9] Moreover, this secretariat spoke not solely of "practical" matters but also recommended a focus on theology and doctrine without hesitation or trepidation: "Doctrinal dialogue should be initiated with courage and sincerity, with the greatest of freedom and with reverence. It focuses on doctrinal questions that are of concern to the parties in dialogue. They have different opinions but by common effort they strive to improve mutual understanding, to clarify matters on which they agree, and if possible to enlarge the areas of agreement. In this way the parties to dialogue can enrich each other."[10]

We are, of course, in this context speaking about a particular kind of dialogue, namely, interreligious dialogue in the broadest sense, that is, dialogue on a religious subject by persons who understand themselves to be in different religious traditions and communities. If religion is understood as an "explanation of the ultimate meaning of life and how to live accordingly," then that would include all such systems even though they customarily would not be called religions but, rather, ideologies, such as atheistic Humanism and Marxism; hence, it is more accurate to speak of both interreligious and interideological dialogue (more about this below).

Who Should Dialogue?

One important question is: Who can, who should, engage in interreligious, interideological dialogue? There is clearly a fundamental communal aspect to such a dialogue. For example, if a person is neither a Lutheran nor a Jew, she or he could not engage in a specifically Lutheran-Jewish dialogue. Likewise, persons not belonging to any religious or ideological community could not engage in interreligious, interideological dialogue. They might of course engage in meaningful religious, ideological dialogue, but it simply would not be *inter*religious, *inter*ideological—between religions or ideologies.

Who, then, would qualify as a member of a religious community? If the question is of the official representation of a community at a dialogue,

---

8. *Ecclesiam suam*, no. 9; emphasis added.
9. *Humanae personae dignitatem*, in Flannery, *Vatican Council II*, 1003.
10. Ibid., 1007.

then the clear answer is those who are appointed by the appropriate official body in that community: the congregation, bet din, roshi, bishop, Central Committee, or whatever. However, if it is not a case of official representation, then general reputation usually is looked to. Some persons' qualifications, however, can be challenged by elements within a community, even very important official elements. The Vatican Congregation for the Doctrine of the Faith, for example, has declared that Professors Hans Küng and Charles Curran were no longer to be considered Catholic theologians. In both these cases, however, hundreds of Catholic theologians subsequently stated publicly in writing that both those professors were, indeed, still Catholic theologians.

In the end, however, it seems best to follow the principle that each person should decide for her or himself whether or not they are members of a religious community. Extraordinary cases may at rare times present initial anomalies, but they inevitably will resolve themselves. Furthermore, it is important to be aware that, especially in the initial stages of any interreligious, interideological dialogue, it is very likely that the literally *eccentric* members of religious, ideological communities will be the ones who will have the interest and ability to enter into dialogue; the more centrist persons will do so only after the dialogue has proved safe for the mainline, official elements to venture into.

Likewise, it is important to note that interreligious, interideological dialogue is not something to be limited to official representatives of communities. Actually, the great majority of the vast amount of such dialogue that has occurred throughout the world, particularly in recent decades, has not been carried on by official representatives, although that too has been happening with increasing frequency.

What is needed then is (1) an openness to learn from the other, (2) knowledge of one's own tradition, and (3) a similarly disposed and knowledgeable dialogue partner from the other tradition. This can happen on almost any level of knowledge and education. The key is the openness to learn from the other. Naturally, no one's knowledge of her or his own tradition can ever be complete; each person must continually learn more about it. One merely needs to realize that one's knowledge is in fact limited and know where to turn to gain the information needed. It is also important, however, that the dialogue partners be more or less equal in knowledge of their own traditions. The larger the asymmetry is, the less the communication will be two-way, that is, dialogic.

Hence, it is important that interreligious, interideological dialogue *not* be limited to official representatives or even to the experts in the various traditions, although they both have their irreplaceable roles to play in the dialogue. Dialogue, rather, should involve every level of the religious, ideological communities, all the way to the "persons in the pews." Only in this way will the religious, ideological communities learn from each other and come to understand each other as they truly are.

Mutuality, Relationality, and Dialogue

Why this dramatic change? Why should we pursue the truth in the area of religion and ideology by way of dialogue? There are many "external" factors that have appeared in the past century and a half that have contributed constitutively to the creation of what we today call the "global village." In the past the vast majority of people were born, lived, and died all within the village or valley of their origin. Now, however, in many countries hundreds of millions of people have left their homes not only once or a few times but have done so frequently—consequently experiencing customs and cultures other than their own. Even when we are in our homes, the world comes to us. It is difficult for a reading people to imagine what a dramatic change it was from the past to have the constant flood of information about others throughout the world in the form of newspapers, books, magazines, and even for the illiterate in the form of the radio, television, and unending electronic devices. Until the twentieth century, for the masses of people other cultures and religions could not even be imagined, or, perhaps even worse, they were imagined; today they come into "Everyman's" living room on the TV and in "Everywoman's" hand-held device.

In the past, economic self-sufficiency was often a reality for nations and cultures, and even well into the twentieth century it was a desideratum for some nations (for example, Nazi Germany), but today economic interdependence is for most an accepted assumption. For the first time in human history even our wars have become global, and even the "small" ones threaten to become global. This fact has led to the establishment of a global politics never before seen—frustrating and unsatisfactory as it may be: the League of Nations after World War I and the United Nations after World War II. Now even the space around our Earth is slowly becoming "global" through cooperation and joint space ventures.

All these "externals have made it increasingly impossible for Westerners, and then gradually everyone, to live in isolation. We need "the other" willy nilly, and after two catastrophic world wars, a world Great Depression, and a worldwide Great Recession we are learning that our meeting can no longer be in indifference, for that leads to encounters in ignorance and prejudice, which is the tinder of hostility and then violence. But, if this violence leads to World War III, it will be the end of human history. Hence, for the sake of survival, meeting in dialogue and cooperation is the only alternative to global disaster.

The mid-twentieth-century global catastrophic events also had a profound impact on the Christian churches. Stanley Samartha, the first director of the World Council of Churches' division on interreligious dialogue, noted that, "It is not without significance that only after the second world war (1945), when, with the dismantling of colonialism, new nations emerged on the stage of history and asserted their identity through their own religions and cultures, that both the Vatican and World Council of Churches began to articulate a more positive attitude toward the peoples of other religious traditions."[11]

Paralleling the rise of these extraordinary "external" factors was the rise of "internal" ones, which might be described succinctly as the even more dramatic shift in the understanding of the structure of reality, and especially the understanding of truth, that has taken place in Western civilization and even beyond, throughout the nineteenth and twentieth centuries, and now into the third millennium. This shift has made dialogue not only possible but also necessary. Where such words as immutability, simplicity, and monologue had largely characterized the Western understanding of reality in an earlier day, in the past 150 years mutuality, relationality, and dialogue have come to be understood as constitutive elements of the very structure of our human reality. This substantive shift has been both very penetrating and broad, profoundly affecting both our understanding of what it means to be human and our systematic reflection on that meaning—in traditional Christian terms, our "theologizing." It is important, therefore, to examine this enormous sea-change in our understanding of reality and truth, this fundamental paradigm shift—and the implications it has for our systematic reflection.

Metaphysics: From Statics to Dynamics

In the philosophical world inherited by the West, Greek philosophy was dominant, and by the Middle Ages the "substantive" thinking of Aristotle, transmitted greatly through the writings of Thomas Aquinas *et al.*, came to predominate. The universe was thought of in terms of substance and accident. This very structure of reality tended toward a static view of things. All

---

11. Stanley Samartha, "The Cross and the Rainbow: Christ in a Multireligious Culture," in John Hick and Paul F. Knitter, eds., *The Myth of Christian Uniqueness: Toward a Pluralistic Theology of Religions* (Maryknoll, NY: Orbis, 1987) 79.

reality was said to be made up of combinations of substances and accidents. Substances could not be perceived. For example, there exists the substance of a particular chair in which such varied accidents as its size, shape, color, and hardness inhere. The accidents can change, can go out of and come into existence, as the chair is painted, reupholstered, and the like, but the substance will persist as the underlying reality within which the various accidents come and go. This philosophical structure clearly tends toward the static.[12]

In the post-Enlightenment period of the past two hundred years, the dominant Western understanding of reality has moved from static to dynamic, from a center-and-periphery dependence of the passing accidents on the persisting substance to a pluralistically mutual and relational conception. Even the relationships of the internal elements of a being within itself and their relationship to the various elements of its context are now seen as part of the being itself. Nothing exists in isolation; the relationship of things to one another is essential to both. In theoretical physics Einstein taught us the relativity of the whole cosmos, and in nuclear physics we learned that our very physical reality is so dependent upon the most exquisite interplay of such *sub*atomic elements as forces, anti-forces, electrons, protons, neutrons, quarks, and gluons that, if one or another element were to be modified or eliminated, our whole material reality would change radically or perhaps even disappear into the equivalent of an astronomical "dark hole." Though not all critical Western thinkers conceive of reality as process—many do, of course—they do, however, think of it at least as being constituted in mutuality, relationality.

Epistemology: Deabsolutizing Truth

From a certain perspective, how we conceive the ultimate structure of the universe—as either static or dynamic, for example—is the most fundamental dimension of our human thought. Everything else is built upon and stems from it. Even those who claim to have no ultimate view of the universe, no

---

12. There is a myriad of books on Greek and Scholastic philosophy. An excellent and standard history of philosophy that deals thoroughly with both is Frederick Copleston, *A History of Philosophy* (New York: Doubleday, 1962–), multiple volumes in paperback. It should be noted that at least some neo-scholastic philosophers try to overcome this structurally rather static quality by insisting that substance is a dynamic reality. For example, see Henri Renard, *The Philosophy of Being* (Milwaukee, WI: Bruce, 1943) 204. Despite such insistence, however, substance/accident metaphysics overwhelmingly tended toward a static understanding of reality.

metaphysics, do in fact have the most elusive kind of metaphysics, a covert one.

However, from another perspective, that of origin and development, it is how we understand our process of understanding and what meaning and status we attribute to our statements about reality—in other words, our epistemology—which is primary. It will profoundly determine how we conceive our view of the ultimate structure of reality, our metaphysics: what value we place on it and how we can use it. The same is true of everything else we perceive, conceive, and think of, and how we subsequently decide on things and act. For this reason, the revolutionary changes in our understanding of our understanding, in our understanding of truth, that is, in our epistemology, that have occurred in the West since the Enlightenment have been extremely pervasive and radically influential. They must, therefore, be examined in greater detail.

Whereas our Western notion of truth was largely absolute, static, and monologic or exclusive up to the nineteenth century, it has since become *de*absolutized, dynamic, and dialogic—in a word, "relational." (Already two millennia and more ago some Hindu and Buddhist thinkers held a nonabsolutistic epistemology, but that fact had no significant impact on the West; because of the cultural eclipse of those civilizations in the modern period and the dominance of the Western scientific worldview, these ancient non-absolutistic epistemologies have until now played no significant role in the emerging global society—though in the context of dialogue, they should in the future.)[13] This "new" view of truth came about in at least six different, but closely related, ways. In brief they are:

1. *Historicism*: Truth is deabsolutized by the perception that reality is always described in terms of the circumstances of the time in which it is expressed.

2. *Intentionality*: Seeking the truth with the intention of acting accordingly deabsolutizes the statement.

3. *Sociology of knowledge*: Truth is deabsolutized in terms of geography, culture, and social standing.

4. *Limits of language:* Truth is expressed in various "languages," legal, abstract, practical, metaphorical, etc.; talk about the transcendent is

---

13. Since the mid-nineteenth century, Eastern thought has become increasingly better known in the West and proportionately influential. This knowledge and influence appears to be increasing geometrically in recent decades. It is even beginning to move into the hardest of our so-called hard sciences, nuclear physics, as evidenced by the popular book of the theoretical physicist Fritjof Capra, *The Tao of Physics*, 2nd ed. (Boulder, CO: Shambhala, 1983).

especially deabsolutized because the object of the talk "goes beyond" or transcends words.

5. *Hermeneutics:* All truth, all knowledge is seen as interpreted truth, knowledge, and thus is deabsolutized by the observer who is always also interpreter.

6. *Dialogue*: The knower engages reality in a dialogue in a language the knower provides, thereby deabsolutizing all statements about reality.

In short, our understanding of truth and reality has been undergoing a radical shift. This new paradigm that is being born understands all statements about reality to be historical, intentional, perspectival, partial, interpretive, and dialogic. What is common to all these qualities is the notion of *relationality*, that is, that all expressions or understandings of reality are in some fundamental way related to the speaker or knower. It is while bearing this paradigm shift in mind that we must now proceed with our analysis.

Before the nineteenth century in Europe, *truth, that is, a statement about reality*, was conceived in quite an absolute, static, exclusivistic, either-or manner. If something was true at one time, it was always true; not only empirical facts but also the meaning of things or the oughtness that was said to flow from them were thought of in this way. For example, if it was true for the Pauline writer to say in the first century that women should keep silence in the church, then it was always true that women should keep silence in the church; or if it was true for Pope Boniface VIII to state in 1302, "we declare, state, and define that it is absolutely necessary for the salvation of all human beings that they submit to the Roman Pontiff,"[14] then it was always true that they need do so. At bottom, the notion of truth was based exclusively on the Aristotelian principle of contradiction: A thing could not be true and not true in the same way at the same time. Truth was defined by way of exclusion; A was A because it could be shown not to be not-A. Truth was thus understood to be absolute, static, and exclusivistically either-or. This is a *classicist* or *absolutist* ("absolute" comes from the Latin "*ab-solvere*," "to loose from" all limitations or conditions, so "absolute" means complete, unlimited) view of truth.

Historicism

In the nineteenth century many scholars came to perceive all statements about the truth of something as partially the products of their historical

---

14. Boniface VIII, "Unam sanctam," no. 875, in J. Neuner and J. Depuis, eds., *The Teaching of the Catholic Church* (Dublin: Mercier, 1972) 211.

circumstances. Those concrete circumstances helped determine the fact that the statement under study was even called forth, that it was couched in particular intellectual categories (for example, abstract Platonic, or concrete legal, language), particular literary forms (for example, mythic or metaphysical language), and particular psychological settings (such as a polemic response to a specific attack). These scholars argued that, only if the truth-statements were placed in their historical situation, their historical *Sitz im Leben*, could they be properly understood. The understanding of the text could be found only in *con*text (this modern sense and study of history was launched in the early nineteenth century, particularly by such German scholars as Leopold von Ranke). To express that same original meaning in a later *Sitz im Leben* one would require a proportionately different statement. Thus, all statements were now seen to be deabsolutized in terms of time.

This is a *historical* view of truth. Clearly at its heart is a notion of *relationality*: any statement about the truth of something has to be understood in relationship to its historical context.

Intentionality

Later thinkers such as Max Scheler added a corollary to this historicizing of knowledge that concerned not the past but the future. Such scholars also saw truth as having an element of intentionality at its base, as being oriented ultimately toward action, praxis. They argued that we perceive certain things as questions to be answered and set goals to pursue specific knowledge because we wish to do something about those matters; we intend to live according to the truth that we hope to discern in the answers to the questions we pose, in the knowledge we decide to seek. The truth of things was thus seen as deabsolutized by the action-oriented intentionality of the thinker-speaker.

This is an *intentional* or *praxis* view of truth, and it, too, is basically *relational*: A statement has to be understood in relationship to the action-oriented intention of the speaker.

Sociology of Knowledge

Just as statements of the truth of things were seen by some thinkers to be historically deabsolutized in time, so too, starting in the twentieth century with scholars such as Karl Mannheim, such statements began to be seen as deabsolutized by such things as the culture, class, and gender of the thinker-speaker, regardless of time. All reality was said to be perceived from the perspective of the perceiver's own worldview. Any statement of the truth of something was seen to be perspectival, "standpoint-bound," as Mannheim put it, and thus deabsolutized.

This is a *perspectival* view of truth and is likewise *relational*: All statements are fundamentally related to the standpoint of the speaker.

Limitations of Language

Following Ludwig Wittgenstein and others, many thinkers have come to see that any statement about things can be at most only a partial description of the reality it is trying to describe. Although reality can be seen from an almost limitless number of perspectives, human language can express things from only one, or perhaps a few, perspectives at once. If this is now seen to be true of what we call "physical scientific truths," it is so much more true of statements about the meaning of things. The meaning of "meaning" is that something has a purpose or goal. We say that something is meaningless, if there is no point to it, no purpose. Hence, the very fact of dealing with of the "meaning" of something indicates that the knower is essentially involved, and thus reflects the perspectival character of all such statements. A statement may be true, of course—it may accurately describe the extramental reality it refers to—but it will always be cast in particular categories, language, concerns, etc., of a particular "standpoint," and in that sense will be limited, deabsolutized.

This also is a *perspectival* view of truth and therefore is also *relational*.

This limited and limiting, as well as liberating, quality of language is especially clear in talk of the transcendent. The transcendent is by definition that which goes beyond our experience. Any statements about the transcendent must thus be deabsolutized and limited far beyond the perspectival character seen in ordinary statements.

Hermeneutics

Bernard Lonergan, Hans-Georg Gadamer, and Paul Riceour recently led the way in developing the science of hermeneutics, which, by arguing that all knowledge of a text is at the same time an *interpretation* of the text, further deabsolutizes claims about the "true" meaning of the text. However, this basic insight goes beyond knowledge of texts and applies to all knowledge.

Some of the key notions here can be compressed in the following mantra (a mantra often is a seven-syllable phrase that capsulizes an insight): "Subject, object, two is one." The whole of hermeneutics is here *in nuce*: All knowledge is interpreted knowledge; the perceiver is part of the perceived; the subject is part of the object. When the object of study is some aspect of humanity, the obvious fact that the observer is also the observed "deobjectivizes," deabsolutizes, the resultant knowledge, truth. But, the same thing is also fundamentally true of all knowledge, of all truth, even of the natural sciences, for the various aspects of nature are observed only through the categories we ourselves provide, within the horizons we establish, under the paradigms we utilize, in response to the questions we raise, and in relationship to the connections we make—a further deabsolutizing of truth, even of the "hard" sciences.

"Subject, object, two is one." Knowledge comes from the subject's perceiving the object, but since the subject is also part of its object, as described above, the two are in that sense one. In knowing also the object in some form is taken up into the subject, again the two are one. Yet, there is also a radical twoness there, for it is the very *process* of the two *becoming* one—or the two being perceived as one, or, even better, the becoming aware that the two, which are very really two, are also in fact on another level very really one—that we call knowing.

This is an *interpretive* view of truth. It is clear that *relationality* pervades this hermeneutical, interpretative, view of truth. (It is interesting to note that one dimension of this interpretive understanding of truth can already be found in St. Thomas Aquinas, who stated that "things known are in the knower according to the mode of the knower."[15]

Dialogue

A further development of this basic insight is that I learn not by being merely passively open or receptive to, but by being *in dialogue* with, extra-mental reality. I not only "hear" or receive reality, but I also—and, I think, first of all—"speak" to reality. I ask it questions and stimulate it to speak back to me, to answer my questions. In the process I give reality the specific categories and language in which to respond to me. The "answers" that I receive back from reality will always be in the language, the thought categories, of the questions I put to it. It can "speak" to me, can really communicate with my mind, only in a language and categories that I understand.

When the speaking, the responding, grows less and less understandable to me, if the answers I receive are sometimes confused and unsatisfying, then I probably need to learn to speak a more appropriate language

---

15. Thomas Aquinas, *Summa Theologiae*, II–II, Q. 1, a. 2 ("*cognita sunt in cognoscente secundum modum cognoscentis*").

when I put questions to reality. If, for example, I ask the question, "How far is yellow?" of course I will receive a non-sense answer. Or, if I ask questions about living things in mechanical categories, I will receive confusing and unsatisfying answers. Thus, I will receive confusing and unsatisfying answers to questions about human sexuality if I use categories that are solely physical-biological; witness the absurdity of the answer that birth control is forbidden by the natural law—the question falsely assumes that the nature of humanity is merely physical-biological.

This is a *dialogic* view of truth, whose very name reflects its *relationality*.

With this new and irreversible understanding of the meaning of truth, the critical thinker has undergone a radical Copernican turn. Just as the vigorously resisted shift in astronomy from geocentrism to heliocentrism revolutionized that science, the paradigm or model shift in the understanding of truth statements has revolutionized all the humanities, including theology-ideology. The macro-paradigm or macro-model with which critical thinkers operate today (or the "horizon" within which they operate, to use Bernard Lonergan's term) is characterized by historical, social, linguistic, hermeneutical, praxis, and dialogic—*relational*—consciousness. This paradigm or model shift is far advanced among thinkers and doers, but, as in the case of Copernicus and even more dramatically of Galileo, there are still many resisters in positions of great institutional power.

It is difficult to overestimate the importance of the role in the "understanding of reality and how to live accordingly" played by the conceptual paradigm or model one has of reality. The paradigm or model within which we perceive reality not only profoundly affects our theoretical understanding of reality but also has immense practical consequences. For example, in Western medicine the body is usually conceived of as a highly nuanced, living machine; therefore, if one part wears out, the obvious thing to do is to replace the worn part—hence, organ transplants originated in Western, but not in Oriental, medicine.

However, in Oriental medicine, the body is conceived of as a finely balanced harmony: "Pressure" exerted on one part of the body is assumed to have an opposite effect in some other part of the body—hence, acupuncture originated in Oriental, but not in Western, medicine.[16]

Furthermore, obviously some particular paradigms or models for perceiving reality will fit the data better than others, and they will then be preferred—for example, the shift from the geocentric to the heliocentric model in astronomy. But, sometimes differing models will each in their own

---

16. I am grateful for this exemplary comparison to Henry Rosemont, Fulbright Professor of Philosophy at Fudan University, Shanghai, 1982–84.

ways "fit" the data more or less adequately, as in the example of Western and Oriental medicines. The differing models are then viewed as complementary. Clearly, it would be foolish to limit one's perception of reality to only one of the complementary paradigms or models. Perhaps at times a more comprehensive model, a *mega*-model, can be conceived to subsume two or more complementary models, but surely it will never be possible to perceive reality except through paradigms or models; hence, *meta*-model, *beyond*-model, thinking is not possible, except in the more limited sense of meta-*mono*-model thinking, that is, perceiving reality through multiple, differing models that cannot be subsumed under one mega-model but must stand in creative, polar tension in relationship to each other. Such might be called multi-model thinking. This pattern in fact has been characteristic of physics for decades, as it uses both particle and wave descriptions of subatomic matter.

With the deabsolutized view of the truth, we come face to face with the specter of relativism, the opposite pole of absolutism. Unlike *relationality*, a neutral term that merely denotes the quality of being in relationship, *relativism*, like so many "isms," is a basically negative term. If it can no longer be claimed that any statement about reality is absolute, totally objective, because the claim does not square with our experience of reality, it is equally impossible to claim that every statement about reality is completely relative, totally subjective, for that also does not square with our experience of reality, and of course it would logically lead to an atomizing isolation that would stop all discourse, all statements to others.

Our perception, and hence description, of reality is like our view of an object in the center of a circle of viewers. My view and description of the object, or reality, will be true, but it will not include what someone on the other side of the circle perceives and describes, which will also be true. So, neither of our perceptions and descriptions of reality is total, complete—"absolute" in that sense—or "objective" in the sense of not in any way being dependent on a "subject" or viewer. At the same time, however, it is also obvious that there is an "objective," doubtless "true" aspect to each perception and description, even though each is relational to the perceiver-"subject."

At the same time that the always partial, perspectival, deabsolutized view of all truth statements is recognized, the common human basis for perceptions/descriptions of reality and values must also be kept in mind. All human beings experience certain things in common. We all experience our bodies, pain, pleasure, hunger, satiation. Our cognitive faculties perceive such structures in reality as variation and symmetries in pitch, color, and form. All humans experience affection and dislike. Here, and in other commonalities, we find the bases for building a universal, fundamental epistemology, aesthetics, value system. Although it will be vital to distinguish carefully between those human experiences/perceptions that come from nature and those that come from nurture, it will at times, however, be difficult to discern precisely where the distinction lies. In fact, all of our "natural" experiences are more or less shaped by our "nurturing," because all of our experience and knowledge are interpreted through the lens of our "nurturing" structures.

But, if we can no longer hold to an absolutist view of the truth, we must take certain steps so as not to be forced logically into the silence of total relativism (if *everything* were relative, then we would not even have a common language by which to, mistakenly, claim that we have nothing common). First, besides striving to be as accurate and fair as possible in gathering and assessing information and submitting it to the critiques of our peers and other thinkers and scholars, we need also to dredge out, state clearly, and analyze our own presuppositions—a constant, ongoing, always challenging task. Even in this, of course, we will be operating from a particular "standpoint."

Therefore, we need, secondly, to complement our constantly critiqued statements with statements from different "standpoints." That is, we need to engage in dialogue with those who have differing cultural, philosophical, social, and religious viewpoints so as to strive toward an ever fuller perception of the truth, of reality. If we do not engage in such dialogue, we will not only be trapped within the perspective of our own "standpoint," but we will now also be *aware* of our lack. Then we will no longer with integrity be able to remain deliberately turned in on ourselves. Our search for the truth, of reality, makes it a necessity for us as human beings to engage in dialogue. Knowingly to refuse dialogue today could be an act of fundamental human irresponsibility—in Judeo-Christian-Islamic terms, a sin.

Paul Knitter noted much the same thing concerning the shift from the former exclusivist either-or model of truth to the dialogic or relational model: "In the new model, truth will no longer be identified by its ability to exclude or absorb others. Rather, what is true will reveal itself mainly by its ability to *relate* to other expressions of truth and to grow through these relationships: truth defined not by exclusion but by relation. The new model reflects what our pluralistic world is discovering: no truth can stand alone; no truth can be totally unchangeable. Truth, by its very nature, needs other truth. If it cannot relate, its quality of truth must be open to question."[17]

---

17. Paul F. Knitter, *No Other Name?* (Maryknoll, NY: Orbis, 1984) 219.

Psychology: Developmental and Relational

Because the sharpening focus on mutuality, relationality, and dialogue in the science of the human psyche has provided another foundation stone for interreligious, interideological dialogue, it is important to reflect here on what we have learned in recent decades about the structure and growth of the human self, particularly through the work of developmental and relational psychology. The pioneers of the former were Jean Piaget and Erik Erikson; one of the important thinkers of the latter is Ivan Boszormenyi-Nagy. Piaget's and Erikson's work was applied to the area of the development of the moral self and the believing self, especially by Lawrence Kohlberg and James Fowler. Key philosophical and theological thinkers in this field include Bernard Lonergan and H. Richard Niebuhr.

The reality of mutuality, of relationality, of dialogue is at the very foundation of our human self. The self does not come into existence full blown at birth. None of us mere mortals were born like the goddess Athena, full grown from the forehead of Zeus. We are all born from our mothers' wombs as tiny animals with the potential of developing into conscious selves. If left to ourselves we would soon physically perish. If simply fed automatically—say intravenously—without human contact, we would not physically perish, but we would also never become human.

In the beginning there is no distinction between "me and what is not me"; there is just a continuum of various sensations, good and bad. Only gradually does the new potential human being learn to distinguish between its own body and the world around it. This we all know simply from observing the growth of our own infants. However, what is not so immediately obvious, but nevertheless equally true, is that the human, conscious selves of children come into existence and develop only in relationship to other selves. H. Richard Niebuhr put the matter succinctly when he wrote: "To be a self in the presence of other selves is not a derivative experience but primordial. To be able to say that I am I is not an inference from the statement that I think thoughts [here, Niebuhr was obviously rejecting Descartes's *cogito, ergo sum*] nor from the statement that I have a law-acknowledging conscience [here, he was rejecting Kant's starting points of the starry skies above and the inner law of conscience]. It is, rather, the acknowledgment of my existence as the counterpart of another self" [here, he was affirming the foundational "I-Thou" relationship of authentic humans posited by Martin Buber].[18]

---

18. H. Richard Niebuhr, *The Responsible Self* (New York: Harper & Row, 1963) 65.

Just how fundamental mutuality, relationality, and dialogue are to developing human beings is illustrated very clearly by some comments of Fowler. He divided human faith development into six stages, plus what he called a pre-stage, infancy and early childhood. Speaking of the origin of the images of God that are being formed in this initial period, he wrote: "Particularly they are composed from our first experiences of *mutuality*, in which we form the rudimentary awareness of self as separate from and dependent upon the immensely powerful others, who were present at our first consciousness and who 'knew us.'" He then went on to say of this pre-stage of faith: "The quality of *mutuality* and the strength of trust, autonomy, hope and courage (or their opposites) developed in this phase underlie (or threaten to undermine) all that comes later in faith development. The emergent strength in this stage is the fund of basic trust and the *relational* experience of *mutuality* with the one(s) providing primary love and care. The danger or deficiency in this stage is a failure of *mutuality*."[19]

Although it would not be appropriate here to describe and analyze the various stages of psychological development as presented by Piaget, Erikson, and others, there are several points that will be helpful to note. First, as the cognitive faculties develop—as, for example, the individual learns to distinguish the self from what is not the self, to discern discrete objects, to relate them, to make formal generalizations—the capacity for affectivity, that is, the search for values, develops in parallel fashion, as does the capacity for moral judgment. Becoming more intelligent does not automatically mean a person will become proportionately more loving, more moral, but, if the cognitive self does not develop adequately, the affective and moral self also cannot develop adequately. Kohlberg summed up the point: "Cognitive maturity is a necessary, but not a sufficient condition for moral judgment maturity. While formal operations [the ability to make cognitive generalizations] may be necessary for principled morality, one may be a theoretical physicist and yet not be able to make moral judgments at the principled level."[20]

Thus it became apparent that, although not all humans continue to grow into fully mature persons, there clearly are stages of development in both the cognitive and affective-moral judgment areas and that the two areas are intimately related, with the cognitive, up to a point, being a prerequisite, but not automatic, cause of the affective-moral. It became further clear that, as in the cognitive area the child comes to distinguish its own self from the world and other selves around it, so in the moral area the child

---

19. James W. Fowler, *Stages of Faith* (New York: Harper & Row, 1981) 121; emphases added.

20. Lawrence Kohlberg and Carol Gilligan, "The Adolescent as a Philosopher: The Discovery of the Self in a Postconventional World," *Daedalus* 100 (Fall 1971) 1071.

moves from external moral direction to internal principles. According to Kohlberg, this more advanced moral stage is followed by an "orientation not only to actually ordained social rules but to principles of choice involving appeal to logical universality and consistency."[21] He also noted that, "the general direction of maturity of moral judgment is a direction of greater morality,"[22] of greater inclusivity: loving your neighbor means loving first those closest to you, then all your relatives, members of your "tribe," your nation, the whole human race, all living things, all reality, and finally the Source of reality.

It is possible, of course, to have a very restricted scope of who to love and then immediately include the Source; one can love immediate friends and God but no one in between. The New Testament notes pertinently that whoever says they love God whom they cannot see but does not love their brother/sister whom they do see is a liar—1 John 4:20. Such persons can be called liars in that their restrictive actions at least unconsciously belie the ontological, and hence moral, implications embedded in the very notion of the Source of *all* reality.

The motor that moves the human person through these several stages of development, cognitive and affective-moral, is the drive for self-transcendence, the desire to go beyond oneself. We are commonly aware of this by our everyday experience of always wanting to know more—why else read this book, for example?—of always wanting to do better. But, of course, at the very heart of the notion of self-transcendence are mutuality, relationality, and dialogue, for we transcend ourselves by seeking the other. Walter Conn noted that "it is clear that Erikson is telling us that one becomes one's truly and fully human self only insofar as, and to the extent that, one reaches out beyond oneself to others, that, in short, *self-realization is self-transcendence.*"[23]

Piaget made a converse point when he wrote: "Through an apparently paradoxical mechanism . . . it is precisely when the subject is most self-centered that he knows himself the least, and it is to the extent that he discovers himself in the universe and constructs it by virtue of that fact"[24]

---

21. Lawrence Kohlberg, "Education for Justice: A Modern Statement of the Platonic View," in Nancy F. Sizer and Theodore R. Sizer, eds., *Moral Education* (Cambridge: Harvard University Press, 1970) 72.

22. Lawrence Kohlberg, "Moral Education in the Schools: A Developmental View," *The School Review* 74 (1966) 21.

23. Walter E. Conn, *Conscience: Development and Self-Transcendence* (Birmingham, AL: Religious Education, 1981) 79.

24. Jean Piaget, *The Construction of Reality in the Child*, trans. Margaret Cook (New York: Ballentine, 1971; original French, 1937) xii.

that he knows himself most. If the drive toward reaching out is blocked, even the possibility to be one's own self is blocked: The only way to self-realization is through self-transcendence, through knowing and loving the other. Catholic philosopher and theologian Bernard Lonergan arrived at the same conclusion: "Just as it is one's own self-transcendence that enables one to know others accurately and to judge them fairly, so inversely it is through knowledge and appreciation of others that we come to know ourselves and to fill out and refine our apprehension of values."[25]

If self-realization comes through the self-transcendence of knowing and loving the other, it reaches a high point in knowing and loving another self, another person. Erikson wrote, "*We are what we love.*"[26] Conn further stated, "In the love of intimacy, then, self-transcendence is radically 'personified' insofar as the very meaning of identity is transformed to include in it the other to whom one reaches out."[27]

Growth, then, is a series of interconnected levels of development in self-realization/self-transcendence. The critical move of self-transcendence on each level so radically alters our horizon of reality that everything within it has to be re-ordered, turned around into a new constellation. Hence, it is rightly called a conversion, a turning around of things toward a new center. Lonergan spoke of an intellectual conversion as a new perception of "truth attained by cognitional self-transcendence," not unlike the paradigm shift change in our views of truth discussed above, and of moral conversion "to values apprehended, affirmed and realized by real self-transcendence,"[28] where actions are decided on the basis of internalized principles.

An even more radical and comprehensive self-transcending conversion is that of falling in love. As Lonergan noted, when one falls in love, "one's being becomes being-in-love," for the mere "capacity for self-transcendence [becomes] achievement when one falls in love."[29] "Such a being-in-love brings about a transformation of one's horizon, one's world, one's very being, and so a transformation of the source of all one's discoveries, decisions and deeds. Such being-in-love, then, is a real and basic conversion."[30] (It should be noted parenthetically that with each new stage arrived at, with each conversion experienced, whether cognitively, morally, or affectively,

---

25. Bernard Lonergan, *Method in Theology* (New York: Herder & Herder, 1972) 253.
26. Erik Erikson, *Identity: Youth and Crisis* (New York: Norton, 1968) 138.
27. Conn, *Conscience*, 71.
28. Lonergan, *Method*, 241.
29. Bernard Lonergan, "Faith and Beliefs" (mimeographed paper presented at the Annual Meeting of the American Academy of Religion, Newton, MA, October, 1969) 9, as quoted in Conn, *Conscience*, 186.
30. Conn, *Conscience*, 187.

the attainments of the previous stages are not rejected but subsumed in the new stage.)

The final conversion that Kohlberg, Fowler, and Lonergan have spoken about is called "religious conversion." This does not refer to becoming a Christian, a Muslim, a Hindu, or the like, although, to be sure, Christians, Muslims, and Hindus can experience the religious conversion they speak of. Rather, as Conn put it, it is "the radical reorientation of one's entire life that occurs when God is allowed to move from the periphery to the center of one's being... (which) is possible only for the person who has totally fallen in love with a mysterious, uncomprehended God, for the person who has been grasped by an other-worldly love and completely transformed into a being-in-love... such radical transformation might be best understood as a conversion from religion to God."[31]

I agree with what Walter Conn has so perceptively stated here, especially when one bears in mind that each new stage or conversion does not mean the rejection of but, rather, taking up and radically intensifying what was attained in the previous stages. However, we run a grave risk of confusing ourselves when we use the word "God." For theists God tends to become *a* person—the source and goal of all truth and goodness, to be sure—but still the person who is this huge, unfathomable, infinite source of values. Nevertheless, I do not love another human person radically differently, radically more intensely, because I have also come to love this best person of all, God. No, the religious conversion means coming to know and love, and therefore truly to become one with, all Reality, not quantitatively, but qualitatively; that means becoming one somehow with its very Structure, its Principle. Perhaps we theists should consider—at least for a period of a healthy moratorium—not calling the Source of reality "God," not out of reverence for the name "God," but out of reverence for that toward which it points, lest we distort it, her, him, which we try to name. We might also come to appreciate more the nonpersonal dimension of divinity (more about that below).

The Japanese Seiichi Yagi made a similar point:

> God is not a being alongside of humans. The human being knows God when s/he loves. But the encounter with God also means that in the [Christian] word of the proclamation we perceive God. God on the one hand is the one who loves through me. On the other hand God is the one whom I encounter in the word of the proclamation. God is, then, on the one hand

---

31. Walter E. Conn, "Conversion: A Developmental Perspective," *Cross Currents* 32 (Fall 1982) 326–28.

the deepest Subject of me, and on the other is simultaneously the Over-against (*das Gegenüber*) who addresses me through humans. Transcendence is, so to speak, that Field of Force (*Wirkungsfeld*) ... The human being is thus in the Field of Force of Transcendence.[32]

In any case, such a religious conversion does not in any way deflect our love of human persons. I believe that through it we come to love each person more intensely, physically and emotionally, as well as spiritually. (Persons less advanced in virtue, (w)holiness, often have to love unlikable persons by an act of the will without the support of the emotions. Holy persons—saints, arahats, bodhisattvas, etc.—are those who *see* the lovableness in every person, and therefore respond with emotional support in love.) In a fundamental way, concern for the good of persons—conscious, loving selves—cannot be surpassed, only expanded. Doubtless, that is why Jesus, standing in the heart of the Jewish tradition, quoted from it, urging us not only to follow the commandment that we should love God with all our heart, but "like unto it" (*homoia aute*—Matt 22:39), we should love our neighbor. Jesus, and the best of the world's religious wisdom, perceived that we come to the full love of all reality and its Source and Goal through the love of human persons—and we never leave the love of them behind, if we would be fully human, truly religious—authentically Christian (or Jewish, Muslim, Hindu, etc.).

A similar point is touchingly made in an Italian folk song about Francis of Assisi, who is in love with nature and human beings:

One day Francis crying said to Jesus:

"I love the sun, I love the stars,
I love Clara and the Sisters,
I love human hearts,
I love all the beautiful things.
Oh my Lord, I must excuse myself,
For I should love you alone."

Smiling, the Lord responded to him thus:

"I love the sun, I love the stars,
I love Clara and the Sisters,
I love human hearts,

---

32. Seiichi Yagi, *Die Front-Struktur als Brücke vom buddhistischen zum christlichen Denken* (Munich: Kaiser, 1988) 74. E.T. in Seiichi Yagi and Leonard Swidler, *A Bridge to Buddhist-Christian Dialogue* (New York: Paulist, 1990) 119.

I love all the beautiful things.
Oh my Francis, cry no more,
For I love what you love."[33]

As a link between this section and the next, let me recall the last half of the second greatest commandment of Judaism and Christianity: "Love your neighbor *as yourself*." We cannot love our neighbor except, and to the degree that, we love ourselves. This is the moral acme of mutuality.

Ethics: A Focus on Mutuality, Relationality, and Dialogue

Since a religion or ideology is an "explanation of the meaning of life *and how to live accordingly*" it is important that we look at least ever so briefly at the penetration of the notions of mutuality, relationality, and dialogue into the field of ethics. To do this we will follow the route of the discipline of relational psychology. Relational psychology sees human development as taking place within a context of many relationships, which by their very nature are always mutual. There is no such thing as a one-way relationship. You cannot always give and never receive, nor can you always receive and never give, without the relationship's becoming gravely distorted and destructive. Margaret Cotroneo, a Catholic theologian and practicing family therapist (and in this, a colleague of Ivan Boszormenyi-Nagy), believes that it is inherent in the structure of things to demand a balance of give and take in all sustained relationships. "This notion of an intrinsic order of justice

---

33. Piangendo Francesco disse un Giorno a Gesu:

"Amo il sole, amo le stelle,
amo Chiara e le sorelle,
amo il cuore degli uomini,
amo tutte le cose belle.
O mio Signore, mi devi perdonare,
perche te solo io dovrei amare."

Sorridendo il Signore gli rispose cosi:

"Amo il sole, amo le stelle,
amo Chiara e le sorelle,
amo il cuore degli uomini,
amo tutte le cose belle.
O mio Francesco, non devi piangere piu,
perche io amo quel che ami tu."

(Sung by Bernardino Greco, OFM, at the Institut für ökumenische Forschung, Tübingen, June 22, 1985.)

is the ontological ground of relationship. It begins with the fact that we are born in need of care and nurture. Whether or not we were given what we rightly deserved helps to shape our ethical stance toward relationships."

The ethical model of mutuality is built upon the possibilities of a just exchange. If we do not directly experience justice in human exchange, our will to extend to others due consideration weakens and is changed into a lack of personal accountability because there is no basis upon which to examine one's own part in a relationship. Personal accountability does not arise in a vacuum. It is elicited when we confront the needs and expectations of others. Interpersonal injustice is like a magnet that draws to itself future doubt, mistrust, and resentment. To the degree that people remain fixed in injustice, whether intentionally or unintentionally, they are not free to trust and care for others. Instead, they turn to other people as if they were objects in the service of righting their own past hurts and disappointments. "Thus they predispose themselves to more failure and disappointment in relationship. When failures and disappointments predominate in one's relational world, options to give and receive consideration are gradually diminished and may be closed off entirely."[34]

We have here the first element of what relational psychology can contribute in the field of ethics: From the beginning of our human lives, the relationships we enter into are formative of our human selves; but no relationship can be one-way—mutuality is of the essence. Even in a harmful relationship there are not sheer victims and sheer victimizers; each plays both roles vis-à-vis the other, though one role may well dominate on one side or the other.

But, what does one do when difficulties develop in a relationship, as they inevitably do? The first step is to "return to the source of the injury or injustice," restoring some trust from at least one side and opening up the possibility of dialogue. "The dialogue context requires that each partner be able to state his or her needs and expectations to the other in terms of the present. It is a process of mutual accountability. Reestablishing a dialogue on this basis in an injured relationship is a form of giving." By asking for something, the persons say they continue to care enough about the relationship to risk rejection. They are extending trust in order to open up the possibility of rebalancing a "ledger" of exploitation by the reciprocal giving of the other. "Giving through asking is a claim on the other for reciprocal consideration of one's own needs and expectations. Because the claim is in the form of asking, it is an acknowledgment of the other's capacity for

---

34. Margaret Cotroneo, "A Contextual Catholic Ethics," PhD diss., Temple University, Philadelphia, PA, 1983, 213.

trustworthy giving. Asking is the fundamental 'I' position (trust initiative) in dialogue because it invites the partner to respond."[35] In this dialogue new trust options are created that can set the relationship aright again.

These, then, are the two key notions that relational psychology offers to ethics: mutuality must be recognized to be present in all relationships; when it is not sufficiently recognized, the way out of the impasse is dialogue.

Summary

Thus, our new understandings of the ultimate structure of reality, of truth-statements, of the development of the human self and its ethical behavior, which see mutuality and relationality at their very bases, point ineluctably to the need for dialogue. Without it, ethical behavior becomes frozen and eventually shatters; the self remains dwarfed, never becomes fully humanized; and the perception and expression of reality is fundamentally skewed by one perspective absolutizing itself as the only true one. The search for the truth of the meaning of things must lead to dialogue—or a living death.

If this is true for all human beings in the search for the truth of the meaning of things, it is most intensely so for religious persons and those committed to ideologies, such as Marxism. Religions and ideologies describe and prescribe for the whole of life; they are holistic, all-encompassing, and thus tend to blot out (either convert or condemn) outsiders even more than other institutions that are not holistic—thus, the need for due modesty in truth-claims. Complementarity for particular views of the truth is most intense in the field of religion.

---

35. Ibid., 248

2

Religion (Ideology)—Its Meaning

Deeper Definition of Religion

General "Western Definition" of Religion

I have all along been using the term "religion" and provided a rather shorthand description of it above—the four "C's." Let me reiterate and spell out in a little more detail what I stated about the meaning of "religion" in the Introduction, and I will start with the etymological roots of the Western term "religion," even though it turns out not to be particularly helpful. We say in English that we "ought" to choose good and avoid evil; we speak of being "obliged" to choose the good. Our English word "obliged" comes from a Latin root, "*ob-ligare*," "to be bound to" (*ligare*, "to bind," has an English cognate, "ligament," the muscles that "bind" together our leg bones, etc.). Hence, we are bound to, obliged to, do good. The Latin root of the term "religion" is fundamentally the same as that of "oblige," that is, "*re-ligare*," "to be bound back." This word root is really more helpful in another way that we use the term "religious," as when we say, "One follows one's routine religiously, meaning that one is "bound" to it. That regular commitment may at times, or even often, be a part of what we normally name religion (the third "C," Cult, our relations, our "binding" to, the Transcendent, such as prayer, fasting, etc.), but it surely is not its core, which is to live a good human life.

    Scholars writing about the meaning of religion often start by stating that it is not possible to give a definition of religion, and then often follow that up with quotations of a number of "descriptions" by other scholars, ending up, nevertheless, offering their own "description" or perhaps tentatively a "working definition." I am more optimistic about the possibility of giving a definition and offered one earlier, and repeat it here: *Religion is an explanation of the ultimate meaning of life, based on a notion and experience of the transcendent, and how to live accordingly; and it normally contains the four "C's": Creed, Code, Cult, Community-structure.*

Creed refers to the cognitive aspect of a religion; it is everything that goes into the "explanation" of the ultimate meaning of life.

Code of behavior or ethics includes all the rules and customs of action that somehow follow from one aspect or another of the Creed.

Cult means all the ritual activities that relate the believer to one aspect or other of the Transcendent, either directly, such as prayer, or indirectly, such as "appropriate" formal behavior toward representatives of the Transcendent, such as priests, rabbis, etc.

Community-structure refers to the relationships among the believers; this can vary widely, from a very egalitarian relationship, as among Quakers, through a "republican" structure such as Presbyterians have, to a monarchical one, as with Hasidic Jews vis-à-vis their Rebbe.

Transcendent, as the roots of the word indicate, means "that which goes beyond" the everyday, the ordinary, the surface experience of reality. It can mean spirits, gods, a Personal God, an Impersonal God, Emptiness, etc.

Especially in modern times there have developed "explanations of the ultimate meaning of life and how to live accordingly" that are not based on a notion of the transcendent, for example, Marxism or Atheistic Humanism. Although in every respect these "explanations" function as religions traditionally have in human life, because the idea of the transcendent, however it is understood, plays such a central role in religion, but not in these "explanations." For the sake of accuracy, it is best to give these "explanations" that are not based on a notion of the transcendent a separate name; the name often used is "ideology."

It is clear that when we say religion provides an explanation of the "meaning" of life, all religion is, therefore, by its very nature related to humans; it is to provide *our* understanding of life. (The great Swiss Protestant theologian Karl Barth agreed with this idea when he argued that all religions are *human* creations—and therefore will necessarily be finite, and therefore misleading—but he then went on to insist that Christianity was not a religion, for it alone was created by God, by the Transcendent, and therefore it alone was not misleading. I am persuaded that he is mistaken in this judgment.)

Also apparent in my definition above is that religion offers an explanation of the "ultimate" understanding of life, not just part of it. It is an attempt to "get it together," as the American expression of the 1960s had it. Religion does not just attempt to explain the meaning of physical life, as "bio-*logy*" does, or just psychic life, as "psycho-*logy*," or life in community, as "socio-*logy*," or the earth on which we live, as "geo-*logy*," etc. Rather, it is an explanation of the meaning of Ultimate Reality and how Ultimate (Infinite) Reality relates to all finite reality and most especially to us humans. Perhaps the best way in Western languages to speak of Ultimate Reality as Ultimate Reality relates to us is to follow the Greek linguistic tradition reflected in the other "ologies" above: "theo-*logy*." The ancient Greeks spoke of Ultimate Reality as *Theos*, God. Hence, theology basically means the study of *Theos* and the relationship of the rest of reality, especially humans, to *Theos*.

As I noted earlier, I am aware that the term "theology" is not only culturally a Western term, and therefore has severe limitations, but also that it is a term that has come to mean Ultimate Reality understood in "personal" terms, and therefore is still more restricted. Concerning the latter, I do not want to claim that religion must have a personal understanding of Ultimate Reality in order to qualify as religion; that is a matter that is a potentially fruitful subject of dialogue between theists and nontheists.

Concerning the former restriction, the fact is that no term from whatever culture can possibly be without its limitations. Hence, the best we can do is consciously to choose terms that we think will be the most helpful—and then always bear in mind their cultural and other limitations. Only thus can we avoid on one hand being condemned to silence, because we cannot find any words to describe reality that will not be limited and hence distorting, and on the other hand being guilty of "idolatry," that is, mistaking our words, the "idols" (that is, the images, the symbols, the "finger pointing to the moon") for the reality they are supposed to describe or image.

There is much more to reflect on concerning the various explanations of Ultimate Reality and the relation of humans to Ultimate Reality, all of which religion is supposed to provide. Therefore, I mean to return to that subject later.

The Way

I noted in the Introduction and again just above that those "explanations of the ultimate meaning of life and how to live accordingly" that are not based on a notion of the Transcendent will be termed "ideologies." Also, the term "philosophy" was found to be too exclusively cognitive to serve as a generic term embracing both religions and ideologies, and *Weltanschauungen* (worldviews) too vague. I suggested that a combination, "worldview and Way" might serve as such a generic term. Let me here detail a bit more about the importance of the term the "Way."

Religion is much more than just an intellectual explanation of the ultimate meaning of life—absolutely vital to religion though that theoretical dimension is. Religion is also "how to live according" to that explanation. It is a "way" of living, of life. This is reflected in the interesting fact that many major religions of the world have the very term "way," or some variation of it, at the heart of their self-understanding.

For example, in the three "Semitic" or "Abrahamic" religions—Judaism, Christianity, and Islam—all the following terms mean the "Way":

Central to Judaism, the Hebrew word *Halacha*, "the Way," has come to mean the rabbinic teachings, the "legal" decisions to be followed, in order to lead a life according to the Torah, that is, as "instructed" by God (the Hebrew word "*Torah*" means "instruction").

At the beginning of Christianity the followers of Jesus (*Yeshua*, in Hebrew) were not called Christians, but followers of "the Way" (*Hodos*, in the Greek of the New Testament—Acts 9:2; 19:9, 23; 22:4; 24:14, 22) that "Rabbi" Yeshua taught and exemplified.

In Islam the traditional way to live a correct life was to follow the *Shar'ia*, an Arabic term for "the Way"—specifically the path to find water in the desert; it also, analogous to *Halacha* in Judaism, came to mean the myriad "legal" decisions that should be followed by the devout Muslim.

Much the same is also true for the major religions coming out of India—Hinduism and Buddhism:

In Hinduism there are three major "Ways," *Marga*s in Sanskrit, to attain the goal in life: *Moksha* (Sanskrit for "liberation"), namely, the Way or *Marga* of knowledge (*Jnana*), the *Marga* of works (*Karma*), and the *Marga* of devotion (*Bhakti*).

In Buddhism the key term meaning "Way" is *Magga*, in Pali (a language "descendant" from Sanskrit), and refers to the Noble Eightfold *Path* (the fourth of Gautama's fundamental Four Noble Truths) to be followed in order to reach *Nirvana*, the goal of life; moreover, Gautama himself in his first, fundamental, sermon, and Buddhism after him, described his way as the Middle *Way* (*Majjhima Patipada* in Pali) between harsh asceticism and loose sensuality, which will lead to the goal of life.

For the major religions of the Far East too, the term was also central: The very name of Chinese Taoism places the Way, *Tao*, at the center, at the foundation of the entire religion, the goal of which was to discern the *Tao* of the universe and live in harmony with it. This notion of the Way, the *Tao*, was also central to the doctrine of Confucius, who taught that "The Way of Humanity" (*Ren-Tao*) is to follow "The Way of Heaven" (*T'ien-Tao*)—for Confucius Heaven, *T'ien*, was largely "personal," *Theos*, though eventually, and especially for the Neo-Confucians of the Song Dynasty (960–1279 CE) and afterwards, *T'ien* became largely nonpersonal.

Japan's native religion, Shinto, likewise has embedded in its very name the term "the Way," namely, *To*, "The Way of the Gods," *Shin-To*. The term was taken from the Chinese with the same meaning, *Shen-Tao*, to distinguish the original Japanese religion (which in pure Japanese was called the "Way of the *Kami* or Gods," *Kami-no Michi*) from that religion of India, Buddhism, which came to Japan by way of China through Korea, also known in Chinese as "the Way of Buddha," *Butsu-Tao*.

The Second Axial Period[1]

It was the German philosopher Karl Jaspers who over a half-century ago in his book *The Origin and Goal of History*[2] pointed to the "axial" quality of the transformation of consciousness that occurred in the ancient world. He called the period 800–200 BCE the "Axial Period" because "it gave birth to everything which, since then, man has been able to be." It is here in this period "that we meet with the most deepcut dividing line in history. Man, as we know him today, came into being. For short, we may style this the 'Axial Period.'"[3] Although the leaders who effected this change were philosophers and religious teachers, the change was so radical that it affected all aspects of culture, for it transformed consciousness itself. It was within the horizons of this form of consciousness that the great civilizations of Asia, the Middle East, and Europe developed further. Although within these horizons many developments occurred through the subsequent centuries, the horizons themselves did not change. It was this form of consciousness that spread to other regions through migration and explorations, thus becoming the dominant, though not exclusive, form of consciousness in the world. To this day, whether we were born and raised in the culture of China, India, Europe, or the Americas, we bear the structure of consciousness that was shaped in this Axial Period.

---

1. In this section I am especially indebted to Ewert Cousins's essay, "Judaism–Christianity–Islam: Facing Modernity Together," *Journal of Ecumenical Studies* 30 (1993) 417–25.

2. Karl Jaspers, *Vom Ursprung und Ziel der Geschichte* (Zurich: Artemis, 1949) 19–43.

3. Ibid., 19; Michael Bullock, trans., *The Origin and Goal of History* (New Haven: Yale University Press, 1953) 1. For the ongoing academic discussion of Jaspers's position on the Axial Period, see "Wisdom, Revelation, and Doubt: Perspectives on the First Millennium B.C." *Daedalus* 104 (Spring 1975); and S. N. Eisenstadt, ed., *The Origins and Diversity of Axial Age Civilizations* (Albany: State University of New York Press, 1989).

What is this structure of consciousness and how does it differ from pre-Axial consciousness? Prior to the Axial Period the dominant form of consciousness was cosmic, collective, tribal, mythic, ritualistic—the characteristic consciousness of primal peoples. It is true that between these traditional cultures and the Axial Period there emerged great empires in Egypt, China, and Mesopotamia, but they did not yet produce the full consciousness of the Axial Period.

The consciousness of the tribal cultures was intimately related to the cosmos and to the fertility cycles of nature. Thus, there was established a rich and creative harmony between primal peoples and the world of nature, a harmony that was explored, expressed, and celebrated in myth and ritual. Just as they felt themselves part of nature, so they experienced themselves as part of the tribe. It was precisely the web of interrelationships within the tribe that sustained them psychologically, energizing all aspects of their lives. To be separated from the tribe threatened them with death, not only physical but psychological as well. However, their relation to the collectivity often did not extend beyond their own tribe, for they often looked upon other tribes as hostile. Yet, within their tribe they felt organically related to their group as a whole, to the life cycles of birth and death and to nature and the cosmos.

The Axial Period ushered in a radically new form of consciousness. Whereas primal consciousness was tribal, Axial consciousness was individual. "Know thyself" became the watchword of Greece; the Upanishads identified the *atman*, the transcendent center of the self; Gautama charted the way of individual enlightenment; Confucius laid out the individual's ethical path; the Jewish prophets awakened individual moral responsibility for powerless persons. This sense of individual identity, as distinct from the tribe and from nature, is the most characteristic mark of Axial consciousness.

From this flow other characteristics: consciousness that is self-reflective and analytic and that can be applied to nature in the form of scientific theories, to society in the form of social critique, to knowledge in the form of philosophy, and to religion in the form of mapping an individual spiritual journey. This self-reflective, analytic, critical consciousness stood in sharp contrast to primal mythic and ritualistic consciousness. When self-reflective *logos* emerged in the Axial Period, it tended to oppose the traditional *mythos*. Of course, mythic and ritualistic forms of consciousness survive in the post-Axial Period even to this day, but they are often submerged, surfacing chiefly in dreams, literature, and art.

Following the lead of Ewert Cousins, if we shift our gaze from the first millennium BCE to the latter part of the twentieth century, we can discern another transformation of consciousness, which is so profound and far-reaching that he called it the "Second Axial Period."[4] Like the first, it is happening simultaneously around the earth, and like the first it will shape the horizon of consciousness for future centuries. Not surprisingly, too, it will have great significance for world religions, which were formed in the First Axial Period. However, the new form of consciousness is different from that of the First Axial Period. Then it was individual consciousness; now it is global consciousness.

This global consciousness, which is generated on a "horizontal" level through the worldwide meeting of cultures and religions, is only one of the global characteristics of the Second Axial Period. The consciousness of this period is global in another sense, namely, in rediscovering its roots in the earth. At the moment that the various cultures and religions are meeting each other and creating a new global community, our life on the planet is being threatened. The very tools we have used to bring about this convergence—industrialization and technology—are undercutting the biological support system that sustains life on our planet. The future of consciousness, even life on the earth, is shrouded in a cloud of uncertainty.

Cousins was not suggesting a romantic attempt to live in the past but, rather, that the evolution of consciousness proceeds by way of "recapitulation." Having developed self-reflective, analytic, critical consciousness in the First Axial Period, we must now, while retaining these values, reappropriate and integrate into that consciousness the collective and cosmic dimensions of the pre-Axial consciousness. We must recapture the unity of tribal consciousness by seeing humanity as a single tribe.

Further, we must see this single tribe related organically to the total cosmos. This means that twenty-first-century consciousness will be global from two perspectives: (1) From a horizontal perspective, cultures and religions must meet each other on the surface of the globe, entering into creative encounters that will produce a complexified collective consciousness; and (2) from a vertical perspective, they must plunge their roots deep into the earth in order to provide a stable and secure base for future development. This new global consciousness must be organically ecological, supported by structures that will insure justice and peace. The oppressed must be heard and heeded: the poor, women, and racial and ethnic minorities. These groups, with the earth itself, can be seen as the prophets and teachers of the Second Axial Period. This emerging twofold global consciousness

---

4. For a more comprehensive treatment of Cousins's concept of the Second Axial Period, see Ewert Cousins, *Christ of the 21st Century* (Rockport, MA: Element, 1992).

is not only a creative possibility to enhance the twenty-first century; it is absolutely necessary for us to survive.

Globalization

Since the sixteenth-century European "Age of Discovery," the earth has tended more and more to become, as Wendell Wilkie put it in 1940, "One World." This increasingly happened in the form of "Christendom," which dominated and colonized the rest of the world. In the nineteenth century, however, "Christendom" became less and less "Christian" and more and more the "secular West," shaped by a secular ideology, or ideologies, alternative to Christianity. Still, the religious and ideological cultures of the West, even as they struggled with each other, dealt with other cultures and their religions in the customary manner of ignoring them or attempting to dominate, and even absorb, them—though it became increasingly obvious that the latter was not likely to happen.

As the twentieth century drew to a close, however, all of those ways of relating became increasingly impossible to sustain. For example: What happened in other cultures quickly led young men and women of the West to die on the volcanic ash of Iwo Jima or the desert sands of Iraq. But, more than that, the "West" could no longer escape what was done in the "First World," such as the production of acid rain; in the "Second World," such as the Chernobyl nuclear accident; or in the "Third World," such as the mass destruction of the Amazon rain forest, "the world's lungs."

At the same time the world has been slowly, painfully emerging from the millennia-long "Age of Monologue" into the "Age of Dialogue." As noted above, until beginning a century or so ago, each religion, and then ideology—each culture—tended to be very certain that it alone had the complete "explanation of the ultimate meaning of life and how to live accordingly." Then through the series of revolutions in understanding, which began in the West but ultimately spread more and more throughout the whole world, the limitedness of all statements began to dawn on isolated thinkers, and then increasingly on the middle and even grassroots levels of humankind: The epistemological revolutions of historicism, pragmatism, sociology of knowledge, language analysis, hermeneutics, and, finally, dialogue.

Now that it is increasingly understood that the Muslim, Christian, secularist, Buddhist, etc., perception of the meaning of things is necessarily limited, the Muslim, Christian, secularist, etc. increasingly feels not only no longer driven to replace, or at least dominate, all other religions, ideologies, cultures, but even drawn to enter into dialogue with them, so as to expand, deepen, enrich each of their necessarily limited perceptions of reality and the meaning of things. Thus, often with squinting, blurry eyes, humankind is emerging from the relative darkness of the "Age of Monologue" into the dawning "Age of Dialogue": Dialogue is understood as a conversation with someone who differs from us so *we* can learn, because we now realize that our understanding of reality is necessarily limited, and therefore we hope to learn more about reality and its meaning through someone else's perception of it.

The Age of Global Dialogue

Cousins basically affirmed everything that Hans Küng described as the newly emerging contemporary paradigm shift, but, as noted, Cousins saw the present shift as much more profound than simply another in a series of major paradigm shifts of human history. He saw the current transformation as a shift of the magnitude of the First Axial Period that will similarly reshape human consciousness. I, too, want basically to affirm what Küng has seen as the emerging contemporary "Major Paradigm Shift," as well as with Cousins that this shift is so profound as to match in magnitude the transformation of human consciousness of the Axial Period, so that it should be referred to as a "Second Axial Period."

More than that, however, I am persuaded that what humankind is entering into now is (1) not just the latest in a long series of major paradigm shifts, as Küng has so carefully and clearly analyzed.[5] I am also persuaded that it is (2) even more than the massive move into the consciousness transforming Second Axial Period, as Cousins so thoroughly demonstrated. Beyond these two radical shifts, though of course including both of them, humankind is (3) emerging out of the "from-the-beginning-till-now" millennia-long "Age of Monologue" into the newly dawning "Age of Dialogue."

The turn toward dialogue is, in my judgment, the most fundamental, the most radical and utterly transformative of the key elements of the newly emerging paradigm that Küng has so penetratingly outlined and that Cousins also perceptively discerned as one of the central constituents of the Second Axial Age. However, that shift from monologue to dialogue constitutes such a radical reversal in human consciousness, is so totally new in the history of humankind from the beginning, that it must be designated as literally revolutionary, that is, it turns everything absolutely around. In brief, as noted above: Dialogue is a whole new way of thinking in human history.

---

5. See, among others, Hans Küng, *Theologie im Aufbruch* (Munich: Piper, 1987) especially 153–54.

To sum up and reiterate: In the latter part of the twentieth century, humankind is undergoing a Macro Paradigm Shift (Küng). More than that, at this time humankind is moving into a transformative shift in consciousness of the magnitude of the Axial Period (800–200 BCE) so that we must speak of the emerging of the Second Axial Period (Cousins). Even more profound, now at the beginning of the third millennium humankind is slipping out of the shadowy "Age of Monologue," where it has been since its beginning, into the dawn of the "Age of Global Dialogue" (Swidler). Into this new Age of Global Dialogue Küng's "Macro Paradigm Shift" and Cousins's "Second Axial Period" are sublated, that is, taken up and transformed. Moreover, as Cousins already detailed, humankind's consciousness is becoming increasingly global. Hence, our dialogue partners necessarily must also be increasingly global. In this new Age of Global Dialogue, dialogue on a global basis is now not only a possibility but also a necessity. As I noted in the title of a recent book—humankind is faced ultimately with two choices: Dialogue or Death!

Goals of Religion (Ideology)

The goal, or goals, of religion have been described in many different ways. At times the goal seems to be quite crude, and at others it appears to be quite sublime. For example, on a rather primitive level, one goal might be to gain a self-benefitting power or to deflect an injurious power. Here religion tends to merge with magic—or emerge from magic. However, on a higher level one goal of religion might be to engage in selfless praise of Beauty, Truth, Goodness, or to pour one's self out for another. The Beatific Vision of Christianity would be an example of the first; the Bodhisattva of Mahayana Buddhism, an example of the second.

Popular Religion—Reflective Religion

This wide variation in goals underlines the importance of bearing in mind the distinction between "popular-level religion" and "reflective-level religion." In popular religion the degree of reflexive consciousness, of self-awareness, is quite low. It is rather like that of a child's experiencing something. The child is not very aware of its experiencing something but, rather, tends to be exclusively focused on the thing experienced. We thus say that the child is *naive*, that is, its mentality is still close to the way it was when it was born, *natus*. Things tend to be understood by the child in a fashion that is rather literal, straightforward, *im*mediate, that is, with no *inter*mediate element, with no mental distance between the thing experienced and the one experiencing.

But, as a child grows through puberty into adulthood, it gains a certain distance on the things it learned when it was young—and on itself. It becomes reflexive, reflective. It becomes aware not only of the things it encounters, that it experiences, but also increasingly aware of its experiencing of things. It often becomes critical of the things it had previously learned, at times rejecting them because it judges that they could not possibly be literally true, as it had earlier understood them to be.

If the process of maturation continues as it should, the young adult will gradually move to the stage of a "second naivete," as Paul Ricoeur named it. Now the adult realizes that often those things it understood when it was a child as literally true, and rejected as not literally true when it was a young adult, are in fact true—far *more true* than the child thought, who took them literally, or the adolescent who rejected them in the same way. Now they are seen for what they truly are—and they often are metaphors, symbols, images pointing to a much deeper reality than can be expressed in literal language.

Matters of deep human import are far too weighty for prose to carry them adequately; poetry—metaphor, symbol, image—must be brought into play to carry such a message, even partly adequately. For example, a prose description of one's beloved (blond hair, blue eyes, so tall, etc.) is much too feeble to express the object of such an important human experience as being in love; hence, the world is full, not of love prose, literal description, but of love poetry, which bursts with metaphors, symbols, images.

However, all this is true of the development not only of individuals but also of whole communities and ultimately of the entire human race. We see the breakthrough to the level of "reflective religion" particularly in what Jaspers called the "Axial Age," a period in human development when the major world religions in several different cultures were born. Humankind in general moved through a kind of "communal puberty."

Thus there will be individuals, regardless of age, whose religious consciousness is on a quite naive level and those whose religious consciousness is on a very reflective level—and persons everywhere in between. There will also be whole communities of the different types; for example, certain Protestant Christian churches tend to be "fundamentalist" (naive) and others tend to be "liberal" (from the critical to the "second-naivete" level).

Some communities may even to a large extent be officially on the "second-naivete" level, but with much of its leadership still largely, or at least to a significant extent, on the "pre-critical" level; this is true at present of the Catholic Church with its Second Vatican Council (1962–65) official commitments to a historical, dynamic, dialogical, collegial, freedom-oriented, turn-toward-this-world self-understanding on the one hand, and the static, pre-Vatican II, fortress mentality of Pope John Paul II and his then chief adviser, Cardinal Ratzinger, now Pope Benedict XVI *emeritus*, and many of the bishops the two of them appointed over the past thirty-five years, on the other hand. Pope Francis, however, has brought in a dramatically more open spirit, giving hope that perhaps Sisyphus in fact will reach the mountain top.

It is also important to keep in mind that one can hardly expect that the level of a person's religious consciousness will be higher than her or his general human consciousness; so, a person who in general is rather naive would also tend to be religiously rather naive. However, perhaps because religious institutions frequently are so old, and hence often very traditional and conservative, it is far too often true that many people's level of religious consciousness is below that of their general consciousness, especially in modern society with its rapidly expanding educational system, which tends to raise the general level of consciousness of whole populations. Fowler, for example, judges that American churches and synagogues tend to cultivate their congregants at a level significantly below their level of moral and faith ability.[6]

Terms Used

There are many different terms used in the religions of the world to describe the goal of religion. These terms reveal an understanding of human nature, and of Ultimate Reality to which it is related, that is held by at least part of that religion's tradition. Hence, it will be revealing for us to analyze, however briefly, some of the most prominent of these terms—perhaps in the end thereby permitting us to conclude with a consensus understanding of the goal of religion in general:

"Redemption" is a term used in the Abrahamic and other religions—very prominently in Christianity—that etymologically means "buying back," "ransom." At times, however, both in the Hebrew Bible and in the New Testament, it simply means the "liberation" of humans. Although it is not always clear in the Hebrew biblical texts what humans are liberated from, both there and in the New Testament it usually is liberation from "sin," meaning from the condition of being in thralldom to the power of evil resulting from humans' having committed evil acts. Humans are prevented

---

6. See Fowler, *Stages of Faith*, 107; also see Leonard Swidler, *After the Absolute: The Dialogical Future of Religious Reflection* (Minneapolis: Fortress, 1990) 195–99.

by sin from attaining their goal, which ultimately is living in harmony or union with Ultimate Reality, that is, for monotheists, with God.

"Liberation" (*Moksha* in Sanskrit) is a Hindu term describing the goal of life in negative fashion, that is, the freeing of the individual human self or soul (in Sanskrit, *atman*, "breath," which linguistically is related to the Greek word for breath, *atmo*—as in the English word "atmosphere") from a constant round of new physical lives (*samsara*, Sanskrit for "passing through," or "transmigration"). Some (in fact, Buddhism as well as Hinduism uses the term *samsara*) describe this samsaric ring as being within a single human lifetime, but traditionally it meant a series of lifetimes that a single *atman* passes through until it attains liberation, *Moksha*, so that it can thereby accomplish its desired end, that is, union with Ultimate Reality—in Hinduism called *Brahman*. It is clear that there is a close resemblance between the largely Hindu term "liberation" and the largely Judeo-Christian term "redemption." Both are a freeing of the inner "spirit" (which is simply a Latin-rooted word for "breath," *spiritus*) from that which prevents the self, the soul, from reaching its goal, which in both traditions is fundamentally the same: union with Ultimate Reality. How that Ultimate Reality is understood and what "union" with it means is variously explained—but more of that later.

"Enlightenment" is a term most often found in Buddhism to describe the goal of life. Indeed, the very name of Buddhism contains the term Enlightenment: *Bodhi* in Sanskrit means "enlightened," and Siddharta Gautama (563–487 BCE) was a *Buddha*, an "Enlightened One." At bottom, Enlightenment means the perception of reality, including preeminently one's self, as it truly is. Hence, Enlightenment is a human state of being that can be attained in this life. Theravada Buddhism teaches that only a few can attain Enlightenment (or *Nirvana*, to be discussed further below)—hence, it is called by those who disagree with it, *Hinayana*, or "small Vehicle"— whereas *Mahayana*, "Great Vehicle," Buddhism claims that many, or even all, humans can attain Enlightenment (or *Nirvana*). Japanese Zen Buddhism refers to this Enlightenment as *Satori*, and, according to one sect, Rinzai Zen, it comes suddenly, whereas according to another, Soto Zen, it comes gradually. It should also be noted that this knowledge, this "Enlightenment," is not a theoretical kind of knowledge but an experiential one that utterly transforms all subsequent experience.

Nirvana is another term Buddhism uses (as do Hinduism and Jainism from about the same time as the rise of Buddhism and Jainism, that is, the fifth century BCE, though in somewhat different ways) to describe the ultimate goal of human life. Literally, in Sanskrit it means "blown out." What is blown out is the *Tanha*, the distorting "craving or clinging" that causes the *Dukkha*, "suffering," that humans experience throughout life (because they unrealistically attempt to "cling to"—*Tanha*—things, even though all life is in reality transient, *Anicca*). When that state of *Nirvana* is attained, a person is then in a condition of blissful calm. However, as already noted, *Nirvana* can be arrived at only by perceiving reality, and most of all one's self, as it truly is. To some extent, this is like the view of the slightly later Greek thinker, Socrates (470–399 BCE), who taught that ignorance is the source of human evil.

"Heaven" as the final goal of human life is a term that has been prominent in the Judeo-Christian-Islamic tradition. In fact, however, the term appears in many religions, coming from more primitive times when the heavens above were seen as the source of light, heat, and life, and hence the abode of the gods—whither humans then also wanted to migrate. In popular religions of all kinds—not just the three Abrahamic ones—heaven became a place of bliss where humans went after death; the same localizing misunderstanding of heaven also happened to the Buddhist notion of *Nirvana*—in popular Buddhism it too became a place of bliss where humans went after death.

On the reflective level, however, as Jesus stated, "The kingdom of God [or, "heaven"][7] is not here or there; it is *within* you (*entos hymon*—Luke 17:21). Clearly, for Jesus and subsequent reflective Christianity (and the same is true for reflective Judaism and Islam), heaven as the ultimate goal of life is not a place to go to after death, but a "state of being" to be attained in this life—which, however, does not cease at the grave. In fact, the customary English translation of the New Testament *Basileia tou Theou* as "Kingdom of God" is really a mistranslation, reflecting the localizing tendency of popular religion. It is more accurately translated as the "*Reign* of God," that is, the state of being wherein one lives entirely in harmony or union with God, which state of being should exist now and continue after death.

Medieval Christianity combined this understanding with Aristotelian philosophy and described the ultimate goal of human life as holiness in this life and complete union with God after death, when humans will be "face to face" with God, utilizing to the fullest their highest human capacities, the intellect and will, in knowing and loving *The* Truth, Goodness, Beauty, Being (which are various aspects of the Infinite Ultimate Reality of God) in what Thomas Aquinas called the *Visio Beata*, the "Beatific Vision."

---

7. The rabbis of Judaism spoke similarly in Hebrew of the *Malkut Shomaim*, the "Kingdom (or better, Reign) of Heaven" (Heaven is a euphemism for the name of God), and this is reflected in use of "the Reign of *Heaven*" by Matthew, the most "Jewish" of the evangelists.

"Communism" is the "final" state humanity is expected to arrive at in the historical future, according to Karl Marx and his subsequent theorists. In that situation there will be the "withering away of the State" because the new "Soviet Man" will have evolved and the force of the State will no longer be necessary; then will be fulfilled the "communist" goal wherein everyone will "give according to his ability and take according to his needs." Before that time the penultimate condition, Socialism, will have to be enforced through the "dictatorship of the proletariat." Whether Marx himself held this position literally or not has been debated by subsequent Marxists, but clearly most of the "orthodox" variety (that is, those who took power under Lenin and Stalin and maintained it in the Marxist world until recently) did hold such a position, despite obvious contradictory evidence in Marx's writings. Thus, except to naive "orthodox" Marxists, it is evident that the condition of "communism" lies beyond human history, as an always receding horizon.

"Nonorthodox" Marxist thinkers argued this cogently from Marx's writings, as, for example, Roger Garaudy when he was a member of the Politburo of the Communist Party of France in the 1960s: "Yes, man will always be capable of an always greater future. For us, Communism is not the end of history, but the end of pre-history, man's pre-history that is made up of the jungle-like encounters common to all class societies. 'This social formation,' Marx writes in his *Contribution to the Critique of Political Economy*, 'constitutes . . . the closing chapter of the prehistoric stage of human society.'"[8]

"Salvation" is a term that is widespread especially in the Abrahamic religions, but it is also one that can be used in regard to the final goal of humans in most, if not all, religions. It should be noted, however, that "salvation" is used both in its primary and secondary senses in religions. Its primary meaning is literally living a "whole, healthy" life. The term comes from the Latin *Salus*, "health," whence a number of English and Romance language cognates are derived, all fundamentally referring to health: salutary, salubrious, salute, salutation. The Germanic counterpart is *Heil*, "salvation," and as an adjective, *heilig*, "holy," whence the English cognates: health, hale, heal, whole, holy. To be "holy" means to be "(w)hole."

The secondary meaning of salvation is "saving," that is, as when a "savior" rescues someone in danger of losing his or her "health," as, for example, when "saving" a person from drowning—whether in water or in "sin." Thus, even in its secondary meaning, the term "salvation" ultimately means

---

8. Roger Garaudy, *From Anathema to Dialogue: A Marxist Challenge to the Christian Churches*, tr. Luke O'Neill (New York: Herder & Herder, 1966 [orig.: *De l'anathème au dialogue* (Paris: Plon, 1965)]) 90–91.

attaining, preserving, or restoring a healthy, holy, whole human life—however understood.

Some religions emphasize the secondary meaning in claiming that "wholeness," "(w)holiness," can be attained only through the help of the "savior." For example, in traditional Protestant Christianity, a person can be saved only thus: *sola fide*, "by faith alone," *sola gratia*, "by grace alone," through *solus Christus*, "Christ alone"; in Pure Land Buddhism calling on the name of Amida Buddha is the only, and certain, way for *anyone* to attain *Nirvana: Namu Amida Butsu*, shortened to *Nembutsu*, "Praise to Amida Buddha." This way of being saved is described in Japanese as *Tariki*, "Other-power," in contrast to *Jiriki*, "self-power."

Faced with the generally human religious question of whether humans are "saved" by either *Jiriki or Tariki*, it appears to me that here the traditional Protestant principle of *sola*, "alone," is not appropriate, but rather the Catholic principle of *et/et,* "both/and" is: On the other hand, we can become as authentically and wholly human as is possible for us only if we persistently and wisely make the necessary effort. But, we can attain success in this lifelong endeavor only to the extent that we have been given the wherewithal: If we had not been born, we could not become (w)holy human; if we die too young, if we did not have loving care in infancy, or if we did not have a good education and training, encouragement, love, moral example, inspiration, and on and on, we could not become (w)holy human according to our inborn potentialities. So, we become (w)holy human by both *Jiriki* and *Tariki*, but we must remember that when we speak of these two "powers" we are speaking on two different levels of causality. As a consequence, there can be no clash—only complementarity.

What it means to be authentically and wholly human, and the best way to attain such, however, is precisely where the greatest, most fundamental, divergences among religions appear to be found. As a consequence, it is important to reflect, however briefly, on the major ways of understanding what it means to be human. I will approach this question by looking at the foundational ways of understanding human nature: human nature is (a) fundamentally good, (b) fundamentally corrupt, (c) fundamentally mixed. Then I will offer (d) a resolution of my own, after which (e) an excursus on a contemporary understanding of human nature will be added. Many examples could be proffered, but it will be sufficient to allude to only one or two representatives of each foundational view of human nature.

Human Nature

Human Nature is Fundamentally Good

In the ancient Far East, one of the strongest proponents of the idea that humans by their nature are good was the Confucian, Mencius (Meng Tzu in Chinese, 371–289 BCE). He argued that humans commit evil only because they forget their original good nature. The human who does evil is like a hillside that was covered with trees (that is, with virtue, with instinctive goodness), which has been deforested by saw-toothed vice. That is, that person has been so abused by vice that she or he even can no longer discern her or his own instinctual spontaneous tendency toward altruism and justice—for example, anyone seeing a child about to fall into a well would instinctively rush to prevent it.

In the modern eighteenth century, West Jean-Jacques Rousseau represents well the optimist tradition. For him humans, born good, are corrupted by "civilization": "Man is born free, and everywhere he is in chains!" According to Rousseau, humanity's problems would be solved if the education of the young were such as to "lead out" the goodness inherent in the child, as the very term "education," "*e-ducere*," suggests, and keep the corrupting influences of "civilization" at bay.

Human Nature Is Fundamentally Evil or Corrupt

In the ancient East a much younger contemporary of Mencius, the Confucian Hsün Tzu (c. 313–238 BCE), took the exact opposite position of his elder and argued that "the original nature of humans is evil."[9] He was very detailed in his description of the innate evil tendency of humans: "Man, by his nature, at birth lusts for profit . . . is envious and hateful . . . and because he follows these tendencies, impurity and disorder result."[10]

In the post-medieval West, the sixteenth-century Protestant Reformers stressed the fundamental corruption of human nature after its sinful "Fall" in the "mythic" paradise of Eden. Fallen humanity's state is so dismal, according to Luther and Calvin, that it can do nothing at all to attain its true

---

9. Burton Watson, tr., *Hsün Tzu–Basic Writings* (New York: Columbia University Press, 1963) 157.

10. See Homer H. Dubs, tr., *The Works of Hsün Tzu* (Taipei: Confucius, 1983). There has recently been a somewhat more nuanced revision of this customary view of Hsün Tzu's understanding of human nature as evil. See Chang-shin Jih, "Human Nature: A Comparative Study of Xunzi and Augustine," doctoral dissertation, Religion Department, Temple University, 2003.

goal, union with God. It can be "saved" only by God's free gift, *sola gratia*; and that comes, as noted above, only by faith in Christ, *sola fide, solus Christus*. Humanity's inability to do anything for itself was so thoroughgoing for Luther that he taught that humans have no free will, and for Calvin, that he taught that each human's ultimate fate was predetermined, predestined, ahead of time by God, regardless of what the individual allegedly freely chose to do.

Human Nature Is Fundamentally Both Good and Evil

For Catholic Christianity, humanity was created good (following the biblical Genesis story of creation, where the Hebrew original says that, when God looked over God's creative handiwork on the sixth day of creation, God saw that it was all *mod tov*, "very good"), but, through humanity's disobedience in the Garden of Eden, it fell into a state of "Original Sin," that is, its intellect was darkened, its will was weakened, and it developed an inclination toward evil.

Concerning the posing of the problem as Luther, and particularly Calvin, did, namely, asking about the relationship between God's omnipotence or complete foreknowledge—Providence—Thomas Aquinas, and Catholicism following him, steered between Scylla and Charybdis thus: "All things are subject to divine providence, but rational creatures are so in a superior way. For they are under divine providence by participating in it, for they are called to in some way *be* divine providence for themselves and for others."[11]

Thus, Catholicism taught that human nature was originally fundamentally good, but had been so stricken that it needed a "savior"; at the same time, however, each person must also freely collaborate with God's freely offered help, grace. Hence, humans attain the goal of life, union with God, not through faith alone, but through "faith *and* good works."

Human Nature: Love of Self and Others Mutually

As "balanced" as the Catholic "both-and" position appears in comparison to the Protestant "only," the terms in which the question to be answered were posed caused Catholics endless logical problems (not to mention the immense intellectual antinomies Protestants ran into).

For example, how can one affirm both an Absolute Ultimate Reality, an Ultimate Uncaused Cause of everything—and at the same time a radically

---

11. Thomas Aquinas, *Summa Theologiae*, I–II, Q. 91, a. 2.

free human will (which of course must be the cause of its own decisions; otherwise it would not be free)? The difficulty, it seems to me, is the result of posing the question badly. If I ask, for example, How far is yellow? of course I will receive a non-sense response. Here, too, Christian thinkers in this matter were actually doing something even more irrational.

They were dealing with two elements, both of which by definition cannot be rationally "comprehended," namely, God (the Infinite cannot be "comprehended," by the finite), and the free human will (if it could be "rationally" understood, it would then be "determinable" by reason—and therefore not radically free); then they had the *hubris* to ask how they were to understand the relationship between these two elements, neither of which they could understand. This is like trying to solve a mathematical equation with three unknowns—and no knowns!

I would like to offer an alternative description of human nature as found in its beginning and development in each human being, which I hope will be both true to our universal human experience and at the same time avoid the antinomies that the above traditional solutions ineluctably run into as a result of how they pose the issue.

What differentiates us humans from all other living beings is the fact that we are animals with the ability of abstract thought, who therefore can become reflexive and, as a result of this capacity, possess the ability of free choice (also called "love"). All our faculties of knowing—our cognitive faculties, mainly our senses and abstract intellect—present us reality under the aspect of "the true." All our faculties of desiring—our appetitive faculties, mainly our physical and emotional "drives" and our will—relate us to reality under the aspect of "the good."

The cognitive faculty moves outwardly and then inwardly, reaching out and drawing the outside world to itself by *knowing* it and thereby "becoming one" with it; the appetitive faculty also moves outwardly and then inwardly, reaching out and drawing the outside world to itself by *loving* it and thereby "becoming one" with it. To restate the latter: The nature, the very structure, of the appetitive faculty is to reach out toward what the cognitive faculty presents as true and good and to draw it to itself, thereby becoming one with it; thus, the fundamental meaning of the term "love" is, having perceived the good, to reach out and to draw it to oneself.

When a human is born, it does not even know itself as different from the rest of reality but learns to know itself only by coming to know "the other," as, for example, the infant's coming to know its own fingers as different from the flame when it comes to know the flame by touching it. Thus, as the child develops, it gradually becomes increasingly aware of its own self and of others.

There is a similar mode of mutuality that operates in the appetitive, the love, area. The infant begins by perceiving the good—its mother's breast, for example—and naturally draws it to itself, and in that sense "becomes one" with it. When it perceives the good, it will identify with it in one way or another—the natural manner for the appetitive faculties to operate. If in the process of growing up it receives much love, the child will necessarily perceive the one loving it, its "lover," as the source of pleasure, as good, and will therefore reach out to it, identify with it; its "lover" will also become its "beloved."

When the sense of identity with the beloved becomes strong enough, we speak of an "other self," an *alter ego*. Then in the natural process when a person's appetitive faculties perceive the good and draw it to its self, to its *ego*, she or he will also tend to draw the good to its *alter ego*. If the love identification of the "*primus ego*" with the *alter ego* is strong enough, more and more of the perceived good will be drawn to the *alter ego* rather than the *primus ego* (for example, the father gives food to his child rather than keeping it for himself), possibly even to the extreme of "giving up one's life for one's friend"; and, as Jesus said, "greater love than this has no one" (John 15:13).

Thus, the very nature of humans is to love the good as it is presented to them, and their "greatest good" (because it is the most "human," the most "humanizing") is to have others act in a loving way toward them—with which "other" they would then naturally identify, making the other to a greater or lesser extent *alter ego*s, "other selves," thereby drawing the perceived good to them as well as—or even, instead of—themselves.

It should be noted that there is operating here something like a psychical version of the physical law of inertia: "A body at rest remains at rest, unless moved by another body already in motion." Humans would not perceive other loving humans as their "greatest good" were they not first loved by those other humans. That is, they would "remain at rest" were they not first "moved" by the "motion," the loving action, of the other, and hence in turn find them good—and therefore love them in return.

But, how does it all get started? Ultimately, "Ultimate Reality" has to be ultimate not only as a goal, a final cause (a *telos*), but also as a beginning (a *protos*), an efficient cause (*causa efficiens*). Process philosophers speak of Ultimate Reality as this initial efficient cause by its acting as a lure, a "Divine Lure." The New Testament says much the same when John remarks, "We love because God first loved us" (1 John 4:19). It is, of course, the very same with the human infant: I learn to love by responding to my mother's first love for me.

It is doubtless the awareness of the humanly natural movement from the *primus ego* to the *alter ego* that has led the great religious traditions to phrase their fundamental principles accordingly. For example, for both Judaism and Christianity the second of the two "great commandments," and the main way the first one is *de facto* observed, is "to love your neighbor *as yourself*" (Leviticus 19:18; Matthew 22:38). One begins with an authentic self-love, which then extends to the neighbor, the *alter ego*.

It must also be remembered that it is precisely by this mutual knowing and loving that humans develop their humanity ever more fully. It is the nature of humans to be potentially open to all being, cognitively and appetitively, as far as their faculties can reach—and they can always reach farther. Humans are by nature "open-ended." In other words, humans fulfill their nature by a *process* of constant self-transcendence, a going beyond themselves, knowing and loving ever more "being"—and a convinced theist would add, ultimately knowing and loving "Infinite Being," the "Ground of Being," "Being Itself," called God.

Excursus: Golden Rule

The same principle of mutuality that starts from the center and moves outward is phrased in another way in most of the world religions in the various forms of the "Golden Rule":

1. *Zoroasterism:* Perhaps the oldest recorded version—which is cast in a positive form—stems from Zoroaster (628–551 BCE): "That which is good for all and any one, for whomsoever—that is good for me . . . what I hold good for self, I should for all. Only Law Universal is true Law" (*Gathas*, 43.1).

2. *Greece:* The Greek Thales of Milet, around 600 BCE, asked: "How can we conduct the best and most righteous life? By refraining from doing what we blame in others."[12]

3. *Greece:* Pittakos, a contemporary of Thales's, advised: "Don't do yourself that others make you angry at!"[13]

4. *Confucianism:* Confucius (551–479 BCE), when asked "Is there one word which may serve as a rule of practice for all one's life?" said: "Do not to others what you do not want done to yourself" (*Analects*, 12.2 &

---

12. H.-U. Hoche, "Die Goldene Regel. Neue Aspekte eines alten Moralprinzips," *Zeitschrift für philosophische Forschung* 32 (1978) 371.

13. Ibid., 372.

15.23). Confucius also stated in a variant version: "What I do not wish others to do to me, that also I wish not to do to them" (*Analects* 5.11).

5. *Taoism:* A contemporary of Confucius was Laozi, the founder of Taoism, which taught: "Consider your neighbor's happiness and suffering as your own happiness and suffering and strive to increase his well-being as your own."[14]

6. *Jainism:* The founder of Jainism was Vardhamana, known as Mahavira ("Great Hero"—540-468 BCE); the various scriptures of Jainism, however, derived from a later period: "A man should wander about treating all creatures as he himself would be treated" (*Sutrakritanga* 1.11.33). "One who you think should be hit is none else but you . . . Therefore, neither does he cause violence to others nor does he make others do so" (*Acarangasutra* 5.101-2).

7. *Buddhism:* The founder of Buddhism was Siddhartha Gautama, known as the Buddha ("Enlightened One"—563-483 BCE); the various scriptures of Buddhism also derived from a later period: "Comparing oneself to others in such terms as 'Just as I am so are they, just as they are so am I,' he should neither kill nor cause others to kill" (*Sutta Nipata* 705). "Here am I fond of my life, not wanting to die, fond of pleasure and averse from pain. Suppose someone should rob me of my life . . . If I in turn should rob of his life one fond of his life . . . How could I inflict that upon another?" (*Samyutta Nikaya* v.353)

8. *Greece:* Herodotus (484-425 BCE), the Father of History in Greece wrote: "For what I reproach the neighbor, I won't do to the best of my ability."[15]

9. *Hinduism:* The Hindu epic poem, the third-century BCE Mahabharata, states that its "Golden Rule," which is expressed in both positive and negative form, is the summary of all Hindu teaching, "the whole Dharma"; "Vyasa says: Do not to others what you do not wish done to yourself; and wish for others too what you desire and long for for yourself—this is the whole of Dharma; heed it well" (*Mahabharata*, Anusasana Parva 113.8).

10. *Israelitism:* In the biblical book of Leviticus (composed in the fifth century BCE, though some of its material may be more ancient) the Hebrew version of the "Golden Rule" is stated positively: "You shall love your neighbor as yourself" (Lev 19:18).

---

14. K. O. Schmidt, *Das Geheimnis der Goldenen Regel* (Munich: Drei Eichen, 1972).
15. Hoche, "Die Goldene Regel," 372.

11. *Judaism:* The deuterocanonical biblical Tobit was written around the year 200 BCE and contains a negative version—as most are—of the "Golden Rule": "Never do to anyone else anything that you would not want someone to do to you" (Tob 4:15).

12. *Judaism:* The major founder of Rabbinic Judaism, Hillel, who lived about a generation before Yeshua, though he may also have been his teacher, taught that the "Golden Rule"—his version being both positive and negative—was the heart of the Torah; "all the rest was commentary": "Do not do to others what you would not have done to yourself" (*B. Talmud*, Shabbath 31a).

13. *Christianity:* Following in this Jewish tradition, Yeshua stated the "Golden Rule" in a positive form, saying that it summed up the whole Torah and prophets: "Do for others just what you want them to do for you" (Luke 6:31); "Do for others what you want them to do for you: this is the meaning of the Law of Moses [*Torah*] and of the teachings of the prophets" (Matthew 7:12).

14. *Islam:* In the seventh century CE, Mohammed is said to have claimed that the "Golden Rule" is the "noblest religion": "Noblest religion is this—that you should like for others what you like for yourself; and what you feel painful for yourself, hold that as painful for all others too." Again: "No man is a true believer unless he desires for his brother that which he desires for himself."[16]

15. *Sikhism:* Guru Angad (1504–52 CE) recommends to the Sikhs: "Treat others as you would like to be treated yourself."[17]

16. *Yorubism:* The "Golden Rule" is likewise found in some nonliterate religions: "One going to take a pointed stick to pinch a baby bird should first try it on himself to feel how it hurts"[18]

17. *Aufklärung:* The eighteenth-century Western philosopher Immanuel Kant provided a "rational" version of the "Golden Rule" in his famous "Categorical Imperative," or "Law of Universal Fairness": "Act on maxims which can at the same time have for their object themselves as

---

16. Hadith: Muslim, chapter on iman, 71–72; Ibn Madja, Introduction, 9; Al-Darimi, chapter on riqaq; Hambal 3, 1976. The first quotation is cited in Bhagavan Das, *The Essential Unity of All Religions* (1934) 298.

17. N. J. Hein, "Goldene Regel. 1. Religionsgeschichtlich," in *Religion in Geschichte und Gegenwart* (1958) col. 1688.

18. A Yoruba Proverb (Nigeria), cited in Andrew Wilson, ed., *World Scripture* (New York: Paragon, 1991) 114.

universal laws of nature . . . Treat humanity in every case as an end, never as a means only."[19]

18. *Baha'ism:* The late-nineteenth-century founder of Baha'ism, Baha'ullah, wrote: "He should not wish for others that which he doth not wish for himself, nor promise that which he doth not fulfill."[20]

19. *Won Buddhism:* In 1915 a new version of Buddhism, Won Buddhism, was founded in Korea by the Great Master Sotaesan. In the teachings he left behind are found variants of the "Golden Rule": "Be right yourself before you correct others. Instruct yourself first before you teach others. Do favors for others before you seek favors from them." "Ordinary people may appear smart in doing things only for themselves, but they are really suffering a loss. Buddhas and *Bodhisattvas* may appear to be stupid in doing things only for others, but eventually they benefit themselves."[21]

It is clear that the core of the world's major religions, the Golden Rule, does not attempt the futile and impossible task of abolishing and annihilating egoism. On the contrary, it makes egoism the *measure* of altruism: "Do not foster the *ego* more than the *alter;* care for the *alter as much as* for the *ego.*" To abolish egoism is to abolish altruism also; and *vice versa.*[22]

Authentic egoism and authentic altruism then are not in conflict with each other; the former necessarily moves to the latter, even, as noted, possibly "giving one's life for one's friend." This is the last and highest stage of human development, the stage of the (w)holy person, the saint, the arahat, the bodhisattva, the sage. Such a stage cannot be the *foundation* of human society but the *goal* of it. The foundation of human society must first be self-love, which includes moving outward to loving others. Not recognizing this foundation is the fundamental flaw of those idealistic systems, such as communism, that try to build a society on the *foundation* of altruism. A human and humanizing society should *lead* toward (w)holiness, toward altruism, but it cannot be built on the assumption that its citizens are (w)holy and altruistic to start with. Such altruism must grow out of an ever developing self-love; it cannot be assumed, and surely it cannot be forced (as has been tried for decades—with disastrous dehumanizing results).

---

19. Immanuel Kant, *Critique of Practical Reason,* A 54; and *Groundwork of the Metaphysics of Ethics,* BA 66–67.

20. Shoghi Effendi, tr., *Gleanings from the Writings of Baha'u'llah,* 2nd ed. (Wilmette, IL: Baha'i Publishing Trust, 1976).

21. *The Scripture of Won Buddhism,* rev. ed. (Iri, Korea: Won Kwang, 1988) 309–10.

22. Das, *Essential Unity,* 303.

Ultimate Reality

Because religion (and ideology) provides an explanation of the ultimate meaning of life, two key elements in this explanation are the understanding of human nature and the understanding of Ultimate Reality, for only after at least vaguely grasping these can one hope to explain the relationship of the two—being careful not to fall into the trap of trying to explain the two elements and their relationship in the rationalistic manner that so many Christian theologians of past centuries fell into when trying to explain the relationship of an omnipotent God and a radically free human will, referred to above.

Having looked at the major understandings of human nature, it is necessary to turn to an investigation of the understandings of Ultimate Reality. Because the conceptions of Ultimate Reality in the three Semitic, religions (Judaism, Christianity, Islam) appear so strikingly different from those of the Eastern religions (Hinduism, Buddhism, Confucianism, and Taoism) it will be helpful to look at those understandings by comparing the Eastern and Western notions; that will be followed by a comparative look at a Marxist (as a chief representative of an ideology) understanding of Ultimate Reality.

Hindu and Semitic Understandings

There are some extremely interesting disparities *and* similarities between the Judæo-Christian-Islamic and the Hindu understandings of Ultimate Reality: First, both traditions distinguish between Ultimate Reality, "God," in self, *in se*, and God related to, perceived by others, *ad extra*. God is said to be infinite, so any perception of God by something other than God, that is, by something finite, is by the very nature of the knowing receptacle bound to be finite. ("Things known are known according to the mode of the knower," as Thomas Aquinas said.) Hence, God, the infinite, is not known directly. God is not known *in se*, but only as God relates to non-God, that is, *ad extra*.

This distinction was very clear in the Hebraic tradition as between God, *Yahweh*, whose "face no one can see and live," on the one hand, and the Spirit (*Ruach*) of God, who moves over the waters in creation, and Wisdom (*Hokmah*), through whom all things were created, on the other.[23] An

---

23. In the early rabbinic period (around the beginning of the Common Era) a third term was also employed to denote God vis-à-vis humanity, God's presence (*Shekhinah*). Wisdom was further identified with another extremely important expression of the divine *vis-à-vis* humanity, namely, *Torah* (see Sirach 24:1–3); the Rabbis made the identification even closer (see *Genesis Rabbah* 1; 8[6a]).

interesting aspect of these depictions (including *Shekhinah* and *Torah*) of the divine *ad extra* is that they are feminine, and not only in grammatical gender, but also in general imagery. This is matched to some extent by the Hindu distinction between *Brahman*, analogous to God *in se*, and the feminine *Shakti*. *Shakti*, like the Hebrew *Ruach* and *Hokmah*, is understood as, "the Divine *Sakti* penetrating everything and manifesting God, disclosing him in his immanence and being present in all his manifestations—this Spirit of God."[24] That the Spirit of God, *Ruach*, was understood as feminine was reflected in Christian depictions of God the Holy Spirit as feminine:

A Statue in the Eggfelden, Bavaria parish church, from the first half of the fifteenth century—the Holy Trinity crowning Mary Queen of Heaven. The Holy Spirit is depicted as a woman because in Hebrew (and other Semitic languages) the word for "spirit" (*ruach*) is feminine. Author photo.

In the Christian tradition the feminine figure of Wisdom, *Hokmah*, was in many instances assimilated in its traits into the Christ figure. *Christos* is simply the Greek form of the Hebrew *Meshiach*, the Anointed One, but in Christian tradition it quickly took on the much more far-reaching

---

24. Raimundo Panikkar, *The Unknown Christ in Hinduism*, rev. ed. (Maryknoll, NY: Orbis, 1981) 9.

characteristics of *Hokmah*. This is seen perhaps most strikingly in the Prologue of John's Gospel (John 1:1–4) where the talk is about the Thought or Word, the *Logos*. However, it must be borne in mind that the Jewish Scriptures had already identified God's Word (*Dabar*) with Wisdom (cf. Psalm 119; Sirach 24:1–3, 9, 23; also Wis 9:1–2), and many Christian Scripture scholars today suggest that in this Prologue *Logos* was simply substituted for *Hokmah/Sophia* in a previously existing hymn to Wisdom.[25] Thus, in the Christian tradition *Christos* and *Logos* are very like the Hebraic figure *Hokmah*, that is, the creative aspect of God, God *ad extra*, and both are like the Hindu *Shakti*, and even more prominently (as will be discussed below) the masculine Lord, *Ishvara*.

Ultimate Reality is not only variously named but also variously conceived, in both West and East. Although the proper Hebraic name for Ultimate Reality, Yahweh (which was long understood to mean, "I am who I am," as the Latin Vulgate translates it, but now is usually thought to be more accurately understood as something like the more dynamic, "I will be who I will be"), does seem largely to describe divinity *in se*, the Bible and most subsequent Jewish and Christian writings speak almost exclusively of God *ad extra*—not so in Hinduism.

The preferred term there for Ultimate Reality is *Brahman* (occasionally referred to as *Atman*, written with a capital "A"). *Brahman* is not exactly divinity *in se*, but at times is understood in a way close to that concept. In that case it is *Brahman* without attributes, *Nirguna Brahman*, as opposed to *Brahman* with attributes, *Saguna Brahman* (this latter being largely identified with the Lord, *Ishvara*). In any case, *Brahman* usually is not thought of as personal, but rather like Paul Tillich's "Ground of Being"—"Pure Potency," in Aristotelian terms (quite the opposite of God in the West, who would be thought of rather as "Pure Actuality"). This contrasts with the Judeo-Christian-Islamic understanding of divinity as personal. Hence, the Greek term *Theos* (related to the Latin *Deus*, both of which are rendered in English as "God"), including as it does the notion of *personal* divinity, leads to the concept of "theism" as affirming a personal God. In brief, it can be said then that the notion of "God" is personal, theistic, whereas the notion of *Brahman* usually is nonpersonal, nontheistic.

A related teaching in Hinduism is that at the absolute inner foundation of the human person is the authentic self, or *atman*, and this individual self was seen by the Shankara Advaita (nondualistic) Hindu tradition to be identified with *Brahman* (sometimes this is expressed: *atman* is *Atman*).

---

25. Gerhard Kittel, ed., *Theological Dictionary of the New Testament*, vol. 4 (Grand Rapids: Eerdmans, 1968) 133–34.

Since *Brahman* is the innermost "breath" of everything (as was seen, *atman* fundamentally means "breath"), it is best understood in terms of immanence, the "within" of things—and God in terms of transcendence, the "beyond" all things. The former stresses unity and the latter otherness.

Indian speculation for the most part is inclined to search for identity; Semitic speculation, on the other hand, characteristically emphasizes the uniqueness of each being and differences between beings. "The first kind of mind, typically Indian, probes the depths of being to find the truth; the second kind of mind is directed upwards, looking for the truth in the most sublime heights . . . the conception of Brahman scarcely coincides at all with the conception of God; the two conceptions are almost as opposed as pure potentiality to pure actuality."[26]

However, neither religious tradition was content with affirming its "traditional" conception of Ultimate Reality. The West did try to speak of God *in se*, as, for example, in the Jewish Kabbalah's term *En Sof* (Infinite), from which come Ten Lights, the last of which is the *Shekhinah*, that is, the manifestation of God to humanity. Of course in Christianity there is the development of the doctrine of the Trinity, which is an attempt to describe God *in se*. The Christian mystic theologian Meister Eckhart in the thirteenth/fourteenth centuries distinguished between the Godhead, which he called *Deitas* (God *in se*) and God, which he called *Deus* (God *ad extra*). In modern times Tillich spoke of "the God above the God of theism."[27] Alfred North Whitehead and subsequent process theologians have distinguished between the primordial nature of God (*in se*) and the consequent nature of God (*ad extra*). It should be added that the Muslim Sufi term *al Haqq* as the underlying "abyss" below the personal *Allah* and the Taoist *Tao Te Ching*'s comment that "the Tao that can be expressed is not the eternal Tao"[28] are both references to similar distinctions in other major religious traditions.

Although this stress on God *in se*, on divinity in itself, has been relatively less in the Judeo-Christian-Islamic traditions than in the Hindu, every major religious tradition eventually must deal with, reflect, both dimensions: Ultimate Reality *in se* and *ad extra*. How it is done is a question of emphasis.

Though the emphasis in Hinduism has been on Ultimate Reality *in se*, on *Nirguna Brahman*, the notion of God as perceived by humanity, God "for us," *ad nos*, did develop and took a form that has some extraordinary

---

26. Panikkar, *The Unknown Christ in Hinduism*, 140.

27. Paul Tillich, *The Courage to Be* (New Haven: Yale University Press, 1952) 190.

28. Cited in John Hick, *God Has Many Names* (Philadelphia: Westminster, 1982) 92.

parallels to the Jewish, and even more, the Christian tradition. In Hinduism, *Brahman* acting *ad extra* is referred to as Lord, as *Ishvara*:

> Brahman is absolutely transcendent and in a sense beyond being and non-being. It is pure silence and utter nothingness, truly absolute, i.e., unrelated. It can thus perform no external function, and it is for this that the figure of Isvara appears ... In other words Brahman is devoid of relations, and it is precisely Isvara who provides for them ... He is properly speaking, the revelation of Brahman, the first issue, so to speak, of the unfathomable womb of Brahman. Isvara is God. Brahman cannot be a person, for if it were it would have to relate to others (things or persons), which would compromise its absoluteness. Isvara is the personal aspect of Brahman ... Brahman *as such* cannot be creator of the World, again because of its absolute transcendence. Isvara, therefore, is that "aspect" of Brahman responsible for the creation of the World ... Brahman is so immutable and unmanifest, beyond every capacity for action, that Isvara has to take over its functions in relation to the universe and to souls.[29]

Despite the differences, the similarities of *Ishvara* to *Ruach*, *Hokmah*, and *Shekhinah* in the Hebraic/Jewish tradition and the *Pneuma* (Spirit), *Logos*, and *Christos* in the Christian are striking. Important differences are there also, to be sure: *Hokmah* in the Hebraic tradition is not associated with a historical person, whereas *Christos* is associated with Yeshua of Nazareth; there are "incarnations," "*Avatars*" of *Ishvara* (*Vishnu*) in Hinduism, for example, *Rama* and *Krishna,* but these are not true historical figures. However, according to the *Bhagavata Purana*, another *Avatar* is Buddha, who was a historical figure.

Buddhist and Semitic Understandings

The fundamental difference in approach to the basic question of the meaning of life between the Rabbis, Yeshua (as Jesus was called in his native Semitic tongue), and the Muslim Ulema on the one hand, and Gautama on the other, and consequently between Judaism-Christianity-Islam and Buddhism, can be summed up in one word: God. In the theistic tradition God is understood in a most positive sense, whereas in Buddhism some of the basic terms—for example, *Nirvana*, *Sunyata* or emptiness—are either understood in a totally negative manner, or at least are misunderstood thus by many. Since, however, there has been a growing tendency among both Buddhist

---

29. Panikkar, *Unknown Christ*, 152–53.

and Western scholars either to claim that Gautama's original meaning was ultimately positive and, therefore, to give a positive meaning to terms like *Sunyata*—in any case, to make that latter move—the question arises as to whether even in this bedrock difference there might not be the common ground for a fruitful dialogue. Catholic theologian Küng thus wrote:

> It has already been indicated how the concept of emptiness in Mahayana has increasingly turned into something positive ... For on the highest level of mystical experience the human person recognizes that "emptiness"—beyond all concepts and words—is the expression of the deepest reality, of the Absolute, of that which Christian theology calls "God." ... as an expression of the "*ineffabilitas*" of the Godhead ... *Nirvana* is understood positively as a happy final goal of unshakable calm, of definitive peace and inexpressible blessedness (instead of *Dukkha*, *Sukkha* [happiness]) ... the presentation of *Nirvana* then is very like the Christian presentation of "eternal life,"[30]

which for Christians starts not after death, but "now," as also in the teaching of Gautama. Küng then asks the following pointed question: "Would the conclusion be disallowed that that which Christians call 'God' is likewise present under very different names in Buddhism insofar as it does not in principle completely disallow all positive statements? ... Against the background of what has been developed here, I would like to attempt the answer in a single sentence," which Küng then capsulates as follows:

> If God truly is the Absolute, then he is *all these in one*:
>
> *Nirvana*, insofar as he is the goal of the path of liberation;
>
> *Dharma*, insofar as he is described as the law of the cosmos and humanity;
>
> *Emptiness*, insofar as God constantly escapes all affirmative specifications;
>
> *Primordial Buddha*, insofar as he is the origin of all that is.
>
> Could one not, after all the explanations of emptiness, nirvana and dharmakaya in comparison with the Christian understanding of the Absolute, despite all the divergences, also speak of *convergence between Christianity and Buddhism*?

---

30. Hans Küng et al., *Christentum und Weltreligionen* (Munich: Piper, 1984) 492, 491.

Küng then points to the writings of the Japanese Mahayana Kyoto school and the Theravada Thai monk Buddhadasa for contemporary Buddhist substantiation of his position.[31]

It is not only Christian or Western thinkers who have been concerned with trying to express the understanding of Ultimate Reality in ways that will take into account both the various theistic affirmations and the nontheistic affirmation of much of Buddhism. For example, the Zen Buddhist of the Kyoto school, Masao Abe, recently attempted to build such a bridge between the theistic notion of "God" and Buddhist "Emptiness," "*Sunyata*."[32] To do so he made use of the Mahayana doctrine of the threefold body, the *Trikaya*, of the Buddha, that is, of Ultimate Reality. In this "trinitarian" doctrine the three bodies are named; first, the manifestation body, *Nirmana-kaya*; second, the heavenly body, *Sambhoga-kaya*; and third, *Dharma-kaya*, in ascending order, as it were. The *Nirmana-kaya* is like the various human manifestations of Ultimate Reality, for example, Moses, Yeshua, Buddha, Mohammed. The *Sambhoga-kaya* is like the several personal Gods affirmed by the various traditions, for example, Yahweh, the Holy Trinity, Allah, Ishvara, Amida (of Pure Land Buddhism), who have various virtues, characteristics, names, etc. At the highest point is Ultimate Reality itself, *Dharma-kaya*, which Abe described as "Formless Emptiness or Boundless Openness."

In many ways this suggestion is reminiscent of the earlier discussion comparing the Semitic and Hindu notions of the Ultimate. On the Hindu side there was the distinction made between *Brahman* without attributes (*Nirguna Brahman*) and *Brahman* with attributes (*Saguna Brahman*, later identified with *Ishvara*), and on the Semitic side the various expressions of the distinction between God *in se* and *ad extra*. It seems that the Semitic, Hindu, and Buddhist notions of Ultimate Reality are similar in that they all affirm that the Ultimate is boundless, infinite, unutterable in itself, and that various aspects of it are encountered, perceived by humans. John Hick, in commenting favorably on Abe's suggestion, likened this distinction to that of Kant's distinction between the *noumenon*, the thing in itself, which we do not perceive, and the *phenomena*, which we do.[33]

It is not difficult for thinkers of the Semitic religious traditions and the theistic strand of the Hindu traditions to accept a *theologia negativa*,

---

31. Ibid., 551–52.

32. Masao Abe, "A Dynamic Unity in Religious Pluralism: A Proposal from the Buddhist Point of View," in John Hick and Hasan Askari, eds., *The Experience of Religious Diversity* (Hants, UK: Gower, 1985) 163–90.

33. John Hick, "Religious Diversity as Challenge and Promise," in Hick and Askari, *Experience of Religious Diversity*, 19.

an apophatic theology, that acknowledges that the grandest proclamations about God are like whispers in the face of the Infinite Hurricane. It is true that the theistic traditions would tend to speak of God more in terms of Pure Act, *Pleroma*, Fullness, rather than Pure Potency, *Sunyata*, Emptiness. However, there might not be the contradiction involved here that appears on the surface, for, just as the theistic notion of God as Pure Being is conceived as the very opposite of *Stasis*, namely, as *Dynamis*, so also the nontheist notion of the Ultimate, namely, Nothingness—*das Nichts* (an alternative term of Meister Eckhart's for *Deitas*), Emptiness, *Sunyata*—is also thought of not in static but in dynamic terms: "This Emptiness is not a static state of emptiness, but rather a dynamic activity constantly emptying everything including itself. It is formless formlessness, takes various forms deeply by negating its own formlessness. This is the reason that 'Formless Emptiness' or 'Boundless Openness' is here regarded as the ultimate ground which dynamically reveals itself both in terms of personal 'Gods' and in terms of 'Lords' that are historical religious figures."[34]

Where a more serious difficulty does come in, however, is that the theist tradition is reluctant to give up the affirmation that Ultimate Reality is ultimately personal, and accept that it is "Formless Emptiness" in the sense that negates, or even "goes beyond," the personal in a way that obviates it. The Hindu Santosh Chandra Sengupta was probably speaking for the theistic tradition in general when he wrote: "In the upanishadic view there is no negation of the personality of the ultimate. There is no need for the transcendence of personality, for the personality, which the ultimate is, is free from the limitations of human personality."[35]

Perhaps a resolution of the apparent contradiction lies in an analysis of how the human mind and language works. When theists state that the Ultimate is personal, they mean to affirm something positive about it. But, by the very fact of making an affirmation, the theist necessarily asserts certain limitations, even when she or he immediately rushes in with a "not this, not that," *neti, neti*, disclaimer, asserting that all limitations are automatically to be rejected.

For example, when asserting the positive characteristic of personality, the theist will necessarily, if not reject, at least temporarily ignore, the possible characteristics of the Ultimate as Energy, Force, etc. The theist might then hurry to assert: Of course, all the positive characteristics of Energy, Force, etc., are also to be attributed to God, but this task goes on endlessly

---

34. Abe, "Dynamic Unity," 184.

35. Santosh Chandra Sengupta, "The Misunderstanding of Hinduism," in John Hick, ed., *Truth and Dialogue in World Religions: Conflicting Truth Claims* (Philadelphia: Westminster, 1974) 97.

or, as Abe might say, with "Boundless Openness." This the theist would gladly grant but would want to add that this "Boundless Openness," far from eliminating or negating the positive affirmations of Personality, Energy, etc., in fact gives them a Boundless Depth, Dynamism, Openness—with which perhaps Abe and much of Buddhism might also agree, and perhaps Taoism as well with its notion of "Dynamic Vacuity," *Kung Ling*.[36]

Exactly what is understood by *Sunyata*, Emptiness, warrants a little more probing. It can be said that Emptiness is another name for the Buddhist doctrine of *Pratitya samutpada*, Dependent Origination, which in short means that nothing exists as a self-subsisting, isolated thing. Rather, everything is ultimately a net of relationships and consequently is always in flux, is "becoming." This of course is not a new thought to the West; it was expounded by the ancient Greek Heraclitus (536–470 BCE), a near-contemporary of Gautama's (563–483 BCE).

However, this relational understanding has received greater prominence in the West in recent times. It is largely from the second-century CE Nagarjuna, the second patriarch of Mahayana Buddhism, that the doctrine of *Sunyata* comes. He clearly denied that there are any self-subsisting substances but insisted that whatever "is" at any moment of space-time consists of conditions or relationships, and these too are dependently co-originated: "The "originating dependently" we call "emptiness." "Emptiness *is* dependent co-origination."[37]

It should also be noted that how one describes Ultimate Reality is, among other things, dependent upon one's culture. What is thought to be of greatest value in a culture will be attributed to Ultimate Reality; the fact that Ultimate Reality is so described will, of course, in turn dialectically reinforce that value in the culture.

For example, when females were thought to be the sole source of life, and hence, power, divinities were described in female terms—which in fact is how divinities first turn up in human cultures, as we know from archeological excavations at the most primitive layers. However, when it was discovered that males also played a role in producing new life, male divinities slowly began to appear and develop. As cultures became patriarchal—and practically all cultures did by the time humankind arrived at the historical period of development (around 3000 BCE, when writing was first invented in Sumer)—it became less and less acceptable to refer to the

---

36. See Tang Yi, "Taoism as a Living Philosophy," *Journal of Chinese Philosophy* 12 (December, 1985) 408.

37. Nagarjuna cited in Paul O. Ingram, "Buddhist and Christian Paradigms of Selfhood," typescript paper delivered at January 3–11, 1984, conference in Honolulu on "Paradigm Shift in Buddhism and Christianity: Cultural Systems and the Self."

divinity as female. Hence, for example, God became almost exclusively a male, father God in the Semitic traditions; it would have been denigrating and blasphemous to refer to God in female terms, because women were of lesser value in the culture.

So it was also for a long time in Western culture concerning the notions of "being," "substance," "stability," and the like. These were high values in the culture, so naturally they were attributed to the Ultimate Reality. However, now in the West immutability, substance, status quo, etc., are increasingly less valued as compared with change, relationality, evolution. Hence, earlier in the West it would have been difficult to speak of Ultimate Reality as being in constant change, in complete relationship, etc., for it would have seemed to be saying that the Ultimate Reality was less than ultimate—with the recent cultural shift, to speak thus seems to be more and more appropriate. Consequently, a Methodist theologian, for example, could publish an article titled, "Can God Be Change Itself?" and conclude in the affirmative, insisting that this was more in keeping with the original genius of the Hebrew God—whose very name, Yahweh, as noted above, means "I will be who I will be"—is always changing.[38]

But, what about the apparently opposite trend in the modern Judeo-Christian tradition, namely, the emphasis not on the Emptiness of Ultimate Reality, of God, but on God's passion, commitment, involvement in history, and particularly on the side of the oppressed—the talk of God as the "God of the Oppressed"? This tradition grew out of the line of the Hebrew prophets, continued in Judeo-Christian history and expanded in the nineteenth century as the Western awareness of the influence in human life of social structures grew—that religion had to be concerned about changing them for the better if the individuals were to be changed for the better. This led in the last hundred years, for example, to the Jewish passion for social justice, the Jüdischer Bund, Christian Socialism, the Social Gospel, and the several contemporary "liberation" theologies. One Christian answer has been that "liberation theologies can themselves learn from Buddhism that the "God of the Oppressed" to whom they point is also a "God who is empty." . . . in a Buddhist sense, referring to that absence of self-subsistence and, hence, that radical relationality of which all beings are exemplifications. To say that God is "empty" is to say that God, too, is relational. It is to affirm (1) that the efficacy of God's action in the world depends partly on worldly response, and (2) that the world's sufferings are God's own."[39]

38. Jung Young Lee, "Can God Be Change Itself?" *Journal of Ecumenical Studies* 10 (1973) 752–70.

39. Jay McDaniel, "The God of the Oppressed and the God Who Is Empty," *Journal of Ecumenical Studies* 23 (1985) 687.

Confucian and Semitic Understandings

There of course was religion in China before Confucius (c. 552–479 BCE) and the legendary founder of Taoism, Lao-tzu (perhaps fifth century BCE), but they gave it a classical, highly developed form or, rather, forms, for Confucianism and Taoism, though they influenced each other considerably, are very different from each other.

Julia Ching (1934–2001) noted, "From his own account of spiritual evolution, it might also be inferred that Confucius was a religious man, a believer in Heaven as personal God, who sought to understand and follow Heaven's Will."[40] Her own understanding of religion, she said, includes a consciousness of a dimension of transcendence that "I perceive as present in Confucianism from the very beginning, even though this has not always referred to a belief in a personal deity . . . The very insistence upon the priority of the 'way of Heaven,' and the quest itself for the discovery and fulfillment of such within the way of man, point to a movement toward self-transcendence," and consequently Confucianism "remains religious at its core, on account of its spiritual teachings of sagehood or self-transcendence."[41]

Closely connected to this question is the understanding and even the name of the transcendent in Confucianism. Careful research has shown that already in the Shang period (1766–1123 BCE) the term *Shang-Ti* (Lord on High) or *Ti* (Lord) was used to refer to the highest of the gods and eventually to a transcendent being, perhaps even a creator god. In the Chou period (1122–249 BCE) the term most often used for God was *T'ien* (Heaven), symbolized by a large human head. After the Chou conquered the Shang, both *Ti* and *T'ien* were used to refer to God, understood as a personal God.

The nineteenth-century English Protestant missionary and translator of many of the Chinese religious classics, James Legge, found in his research the name for the highest God, *Shang-Ti*. "There was, then, before Confucius and many of the sage kings, a monotheistic religion: *the* Confucian religion"[42] Of course even earlier, in the sixteenth century, the great Catholic scholar, scientist and missionary to China, Matteo Ricci, learned much the same about Chinese, and especially Confucian, religion as Legge later did, and wrote accordingly.

Though many traditions see the transcendent and the immanent as opposites, the twentieth-century Confucian Mou Tsung-san "sees the Confucian as joining the ethical and religious dimensions in an effective unity

---

40. Hans Küng and Julia Ching, *Christentum und chinesische Religion* (Munich: Piper, 1988) 95.

41. Ibid., 116.

42. Ibid., 42.

of lived experience . . . There is no ultimate separation of the subjective and objective, the inner and outer, the immanent and the transcendent."[43]

Already in the writings of Mencius (371–289 BCE) we find the tendency to speak less in terms of a personal God, or in terms of the Transcendent as *ganz anders*, completely other, but more in terms of the Transcendent, Heaven, being reflected in the human heart: Who knows his or her own heart and nature also knows Heaven.[44] Hence, the Transcendent, instead of being "out there," more and more was found within, immanent. Such an understanding, of course, is very congenial to a very important strand in the Judeo-Christian tradition, starting already with the creation story, where it is said that humanity is made in God's image.

It is in this relationship between the Transcendent and the Immanent or between Heaven and Humanity that Confucianism's special characteristic comes to the fore. The core of Confucianism is humanism, but a humanism which, as the contemporary Confucian Tu Wei-ming put it, includes *"a faithful dialogical response to the transcendent."* He goes on to say that "the mutuality of Heaven and man (in the gender neutral sense of humanity) makes it possible to perceive the transcendent as immanent." In other words, "the Confucians advocate a humanism which neither denies nor slights the transcendent . . . Humanity is Heaven's form of self-disclosure, self-expression, and self-realization."[45] Already in 1958 a number of Chinese scholars in Taiwan issued "A Manifesto for the Reappraisal of Sinology and Reconstruction of Chinese Culture," in which "the harmony of the 'way of Heaven' (*T'ien-tao*) and the 'way of man' (*Ren-tao*) is extolled by those who signed it as the central legacy of Confucianism."[46]

Again, in this conceptualization there are certain parallels to a Christian theology of the *Imago Dei*, or of an incarnational theology; perhaps most of all it is like Hegel's notion of *Welt Geist*—this latter parallel especially offers to Western, including Christian, thinkers many possibilities, as well as problems. However, Hegel's thought and all modern historical, dynamic, processive, immanentist thought stands in severe tension with

---

43. Mou Tsung-san, *Chung-kuo che-hsüeh t›e-chi* [The Uniqueness of Chinese Philosophy] (Taipei: Student Book Co., 1974), as cited by John Berthrong, "Adjustments: Dual Transcendence and Fiduciary Community," a paper delivered at the Hong Kong International Christian-Confucian Conference, June 8–15, 1988.

44. *Book of Mencius*, 7a, 1.

45. Wei-ming Tu, "On Confucian Religiousness," paper delivered at a June 8–15, 1988, Hong Kong international Confucian-Christian conference.

46. Carsun Chang, *The Development of Neo-Confucian Thought*, vol. 2, Appendix (New York: Bookman, 1963), as cited in Küng and Ching, *Christentum und chinesische Religion*, 123–24.

much of traditional Christian philosophy and theology because, as noted previously, the older tradition gave Being, *Stasis*, Non-change the pride of place, whereas much of contemporary thought holds up Becoming, the Dynamic, Change as the highest value, seeing the static as the mode of death.

Nevertheless, as I have argued earlier in these pages, the stress on the dynamic is clearly the mode of thought of more and more critical-thinking persons, including Christian theologians—witness subsequent Catholic and Protestant theology, despite various inevitable temporary backlash movements. Hence, here is a very promising contemporary basis for Christian, and other, dialogue with Confucianism: Because "being religious, in the Confucian perspective . . . means being engaged in the *process* of learning to be fully human,"[47] and learning to become "human is the real informing characteristic of all authentic Confucian religious sentiment. This *process* of 'humanization' has no limits and is therefore called a transcendent reference . . . the *process* is unending in its scope and completely moral in its intention, while transcendent in ultimate reference."[48]

If for Confucianism, and Christianity, becoming human is an unending process that aims at an ever-receding horizon of Heaven, God, the Transcendent ("Our inborn ability to respond to the bidding of Heaven impels us to extend our human horizon continuously so that the immanent in our nature assumes a transcendent dimension"),[49] Confucians make clear that it is a process that is engaged in by self-transcendence, self-effort: "The Confucian faith in the perfectibility of human nature through self-effort is, strictly speaking, a faith in self-transcendence."[50] Mou Tsung-san spoke in similar terms, stressing the centrality of creativity in being human: "For him the heart of being human is creative reason, the capacity to transform self and relate in a meaningful and humane way to others. The essence of being human is hence the creation of new values."[51]

Taoist and Semitic Understandings

Tao of course means "Way," though it also has the meaning of "Word" or "saying." It implies that humans are to follow the "Way," but it is quite the opposite of the Jewish and Muslim analogues, *Halacha* and *Shar'ia*. These latter two, as seen above, came to have a specialized meaning of the legal

47. Tu, "On Confucian Religiousness," 2.
48. Berthrong, "Adjustments," 11.
49. Tu, "On Confucian Religiousness," 8.
50. Ibid.
51. Berthrong, "Adjustments," 46.

decisions of the proper Way to live. For Taoism, following the Tao essentially means "doing nothing" (*wu wei*) in the sense of being unattached to any particular thing, thereby living in harmony with Ultimate Reality, which is also named Tao.

Tao as Ultimate Reality, however, is the all-embracing first and last principle, indefinable, unutterable, and indescribable, the "Ground of all worlds before all worlds," which existed even before heaven and earth. It is the mother of everything; and it calls all things into being, without action, in stillness. It is the "power" (*Te*) of Tao that is working in all creation, all unfolding, and all preservation of the world. It is the *Te* of Tao in all appearances that makes them what they are, but the Tao with its power is nowhere tangible or available. Tao is a "not-being" in the sense of "not-being-thus": It is "empty," without any characteristics that are perceptible to the senses. If, however, everything that exists is the Tao, then it would seem that the Tao is identical with *Being*, that is, not "Being" understood in a static Greek sense, but rather in the dynamic modern sense—"Being" understood as "Being in Becoming."

However, if Tao can be understood as "Being," as "Being in Becoming," then is it not ultimately identical with God? Of course, this cannot be meant in a primitive anthropomorphic or in an ontological, pantheistic sense, but in the differentiated way of the Western philosophical-theological tradition from Augustine through Thomas to Nicholas of Cusa: as "Being Itself" (*Ipsum Esse Subsistens*, as Thomas Aquinas put it. Note, the "infinitive," that is, limitless, unparticularized, form of the verb "to be" is used—*esse*) to which the being of all contingently existing beings refers. In fact, there is an extraordinarily dynamic character reflected in the very form of our English word "being." The noun is in a gerundive form, be*ing*, indicating its processive, dynamic character.

Küng asked, "If *nothingness* is the *veil of being* through which being reveals itself, then could the *being* in which humanity participates not also be understood as the *veil of God*?" His response is that "the being of what exists in becoming covers over the "Being Itself" that can rightly be called God." Conversely, "the Tao can be identified with the original and final reality."[52] "It can be identified with ultimate transcendent reality ([Henri] Maspero)."[53] Hence, there is a possible parallel in structure in the concepts

---

52. Hans Küng and Julia Ching, *Christianity and Chinese Religions* (New York: Doubleday, 1989) 174. I am particularly grateful to Küng in this section for insight into Taoism.

53. G. H. Dunstheimer, *Histoire des religions*, ed. H. C. Puech, vol. 3 (Paris: Gallimard, 1976) 389.

of Tao, Being, and God that could be of great importance to the understanding of Ultimate Reality that would bridge cultures and religions.

One more important point needs to be looked at here. During the Han dynasty (206 BCE–220 CE), *yin-yang* thinking began to be absorbed into both Confucianism and Taoism. Although a superficial reading of the Taoist material might give one the impression that the claim is made that Ultimate Reality is somehow a combination of opposites, *yin* and *yang*, dark and light, good and evil, such a reading would indeed be superficial, for in the *Tao-te ching* itself the Tao is *prior* to heaven and earth, that is, before duality.

Küng noted: "Indeed, the Tao is before the one and the two, is the origin of the world before all worlds, and is thus the origin of the polarity, not the polarity itself" and adds: "No, an ultimate reality that is both double-sided and contradictory is part of neither the great Chinese nor the great Western tradition. Only penultimate reality is double-sided and contradictory."[54]

Thus, one can say that Tao is unchanging "Being" behind all reality—like the early Chinese understanding of the "Lord-on-High," *Shang-ti* (God *in se*), but it later also takes over the active aspect of "Heaven," *T'ien* (God *ad extra, ad nos*), for it is then also understood as a "divine" pattern for humans to follow (not unlike the Jewish *Torah*).

In the end, on the basis of their tradition of mystical and negative theologies, Christians can appreciate completely why Taoists refuse all definitions of the Tao, whether positive or negative. Even that giant of Christian speculative theology, Thomas Aquinas, insisted that God's proper essence remains inaccessible to human reason and concurred with the mystic Pseudo-Dionysius when he wrote: "Wherefore man reaches the highest point of his knowledge about God when he knows that he knows him not, inasmuch as he knows that which is God transcends whatever he conceives of him."[55]

Marxist and Christian Understandings

At first blush one might assume that Marxists would have no notion of Ultimate Reality, but if the term is not filled ahead of time with theistic content, the matter is not so simple. For example, Garaudy, as representative of Marxist thinkers who, in the several decades just before the collapse of the Soviet Union in 1990, were in serious dialogue with Christians,[56] saw—in

---

54. Küng and Ching, *Christianity and Chinese Religions*, 177.

55. Cited in Thomas Aquinas, *De Potentia*, q. 7, a. 5. E.T.: *On the Power of God*, vol. 3 (London, 1934) 33.

56. See, e.g., Swidler, *After the Absolute*, chapter on "Dialogue with Ideologies:

the positive attitude toward matter, evolution, the immanent force within matter that rises unendingly to the level of consciousness and beyond, as expressed pre-eminently in the thought and writings of the Jesuit scientist-theologian Pierre Teilhard de Chardin—a Copernican turn in Christian thought that enabled Marxists not only to join with Christians in "building the earth," as Teilhard put it, but also to learn something from them in their efforts to relate the immanent and transcendent in the universe. As Garaudy cited Teilhard: "The synthesis of the [Christian] God of the Above and the [Marxist] God of the Ahead: this is the only God whom we shall in the future be able to adore in spirit and in truth."[57]

This Teilhardian idea is also much like Karl Rahner's notion that the Ultimate of humankind is the Absolute Future, the ever receding, ever beckoning Horizon, as Bernard Lonergan expressed it, within which humankind lives and moves forward. Garaudy, as noted above, understood Marxism to see the future of humankind similarly: "Yes, man will always be capable of an always greater future."

A popular-level version of Marxism has thought of humanity as determined by great social forces, especially economic, in a way that submerged the individual human person and forecast the inevitable triumph of Marxism through the inexorable development of a classless society that will have gone through the phases of the dictatorship of the proletariat, socialism, and, finally, communism, as described above. Such a crass understanding, however, is not the way a careful Marxist understanding of what it means to be human is presented by "nonorthodox" Marxist thinkers.

In the 1960s philosopher and French Communist Party Politbureau member Garaudy stressed that Marxism is not static or predetermined, but dynamic, relational, and unendingly so:

"The individual for Marx is defined by the whole of his social relations just as the object is defined infinitely, inexhaustibly by its relations with the totality of other objects. The reality with which the physicist has to deal is already, as Lenin wrote, inexhaustible. How much more inexhaustible is the human reality which with life, conscience, society has crossed so many other thresholds of complexity!"[58]

Such a "relational" understanding of human nature became more and more widespread in twentieth-century philosophical thinking and became increasingly prominent among Christian thinkers. It is also very like the

---

Marxism," 165–89.

57. Garaudy, *From Anathema to Dialogue*, 54.

58. Ibid.

Buddhist notion of "Dependent Co-origination" and, hence, of *Sunyata*, which will be discussed below.

Garaudy also stressed the dynamic, nondetermined core of reality in his emphasis on the Marxist notion that *praxis* is the fountain of history and truth. He cited Marx as saying that "men make their own history," and went on to ask, "How, in spite of such insistence, has it been possible to ascribe to Marx a supposed "economic determinism" which is so contrary to the basic spirit of his doctrine?" He answered that, "superficial disciples or excessively hasty or ill-intentioned opponents have frequently mistaken the true originality of Marx's materialism . . . understanding "scientific" history to mean a history in which the future has already been written. This is a distortion of the very spirit of Marxism which is essentially a *methodology of historical initiative*."[59] Garaudy secured the validity of his interpretation by a citation of Engels (Marxism will be treated in greater detail below): "Marx and I are ourselves partly to blame for the fact that younger writers sometimes lay more stress on the economic side than is due to it. We had to emphasize this main principle in opposition to our adversaries, who denied it, and we had not always the time, the place or the opportunity to allow the other elements involved in the interaction to come into their rights."[60]

Writing in 1965, Garaudy argued that for a quarter of a century there had been an "intellectual hardening of the arteries within Marxism," but then there was a "vigorous reappearance of the problems of subjectivity, choice, and spiritual responsibility." He insisted that "this development has occurred because of the inescapable abandonment of old values and the birth-pangs which accompany the creation of new ones" but granted that "to the extent that Marxism has failed to answer these questions adequately, youth has turned elsewhere to seek the answer which it is our job today to seek, though we may not yet fully discover it." He emphasized that in seeking for answers to these critical human questions Marxism, at least in part, could not evade the quest for what it owed to Christianity as a religion of the absolute future and as a contributing factor in the exploration of the two essential dimensions of human beings: subjectivity and transcendence. "We cannot," he wrote, "without impoverishing ourselves, forget Christianity's basic contribution: the change in [the human's] attitude toward the world, preparing a place for subjectivity."

Moreover, he claimed that he was not alone in "this realization of the Christian contribution to civilization and culture, and of the revolutionary potential of the faith," which he said had been "operative not only within

---

59. Ibid., 73.
60. Ibid., 75 (subsequent quotes from Garaudy are from this same source).

the French Communist Party since the great step forward in 1937 but also within all . . . those countries where progressive movements were taking shape within the Catholic Church," meaning especially Italy and Spain.

Garaudy claimed that Marxism had an interest in the questions raised by women and men "about the meaning of their life and their death, about the problem of their origin and their end, about the demands of their thought and their heart," and granted that there is much that "Marxists must assimilate from the rich Christian heritage." However, he went on to claim that although the greatness of religion is displayed by its awareness and concern for these fundamental human questions, its weakness is in its fixing of its once-given answers as always-given answers, despite humanity's advances in thought and ways of understanding. Marxism and Christianity, he stated, both live under the same exigencies, but they differ in their answers:

He began by saying, "If we reject the very name of God, it is because the name implies a presence, a reality, whereas it is only an exigency which we live, a never-satisfied exigency of totality and absoluteness, of omnipotence as to nature and of perfect loving reciprocity of consciousness." Then he added, "We can live this exigency, and we can act it out, but we cannot conceive it, name it or expect it. Even less can we hypostatize it under the name of transcendence. Regarding this totality, this absolute, I can say everything except: It is. For what it is is always deferred, and always growing."

Garaudy, then, wanted to stake out a claim for Marxism of both a doctrine of subjectivity and of transcendence, an unendingly self-transcending future for humanity: "I think that Marxist atheism deprives man only of the illusion of certainty, and that the Marxist dialectic, when lived in its fullness, is ultimately richer in the infinite and more demanding still than the Christian transcendence." But, "it is undoubtedly such only because it bears within itself the extraordinary Christian heritage, which it must investigate still more," and in the end it "owes it to itself in philosophy to work out a more profound theory of subjectivity, one which is not subjectivist, and a more profound theory of transcendence, one which is not alienated."

Most Christian theologians will today admit that the old arguments for the existence of God do not have the rational force of a demonstration that they were once thought to have had. Many will with Küng claim that in the end it is reasonable to affirm the existence of God, not ineluctably so, but in fundamental trust, although in the very affirmation one is confirmed in the reasonableness of one's affirmation.[61] The transcendental theologians and philosophers, such as Rahner and Joseph Marechal, however, have

---

61. Hans Küng, *Does God Exist?* (1980; reprinted, Eugene, OR: Wipf & Stock, 2006).

argued that the very presence of the open-ended thirst for knowledge, for being, found in the inner nature of humankind, demands that there be an open-ended Source and Goal of that spiritual drive. Garaudy took that idea up when he said that "my thirst does not prove the existence of the spring."

But, ultimately, does it not? Is it conceivable in this world as we know it that there could develop a being that has a need for something—say, water—if there were no such thing as water? No, it would die aborning, but humankind has not died aborning.[62]

In any case, Garaudy took seriously the Teilhardian-Rahnerian notion of God as no-*thing*, as the unendingly, infinitely creative, absolute future (again reminding one of Buddhism's "Boundless Openness," *Sunyata*): "In such a perspective God is no longer a being nor even the totality of being, since such a totality does not exist. Being is totally open to the future to be created. Faith is not the possession of an object by cognition." He then added that "the transcendence of God implies its constant negation since God is constant creation beyond any essence and any existence. A faith which is only assertion would be credulity. Doubt is part and parcel of living faith. The depth of faith in a believer depends upon the force of the atheist he bears in himself and defends against all idolatry."

For his part, of course, Garaudy did not find what theists call a divine presence, but only its absence. Still, he was aware that his affirmation of absence was also not an ineluctable rational affirmation, but likewise a choice of his whole being, and in that sense, a "faith": "We thus reach the highest level of the dialogue, that of the integration in each of us of that which the other bears in himself, as other. I said earlier that the depth of a believer's faith depends upon the strength of the atheism that he bears in himself. I can now add: the depth of an atheist's humanism depends on the strength of the faith he bears in himself."

More than twenty years later the Hungarian Marxist Pal Horvath made a similar point when he said "that the existence of God cannot be theoretically proved or denied . . . Whoever sees the essence of Marx's atheism in this is mistaken." He then quoted another Hungarian Marxist, Tamas Nyiri, saying: "Until a communist society without religion has developed, the Marxist theory pretending that religion is essentially a false form of consciousness, cannot be considered as proved. It is just one of several potential theories to be verified or refuted by historical-social practice." After all, Horvath said, "When we turn to the question of whose ultimate hypotheses

---

62. See Anthony Matteo, "Joseph Marechal and the Transcendental Turn in Catholic Thought" (PhD diss., Temple University, 1985).

of a cosmic nature will prove true, I am convinced that an answer can only be expected in a perspective of world history."[63]

Garaudy in the end pleaded—to both sides obviously—for the dialogue to continue and deepen—both the ideological and practical dialogue. He said that it would be one of the tragedies of history "if the dialogue between Christians and Marxists and their cooperation for mutual enrichment and for the common building of the future, the city of man, the total man, were still longer to be spoiled, perhaps even prevented, by the weight of the past." He was not asking for "conversion" of one side to the other, but rather, "we offer a dialogue without prejudice or hindrance. We do not ask anyone to stop being what he is. What we ask is, on the contrary, that he be it more and that he be it better." He then added that "we hope that those who engage in dialogue with us will demand the same of us."

All this was rather stunning stuff, coming as it did from a Marxist philosopher and French Politburo member of such prominence and profundity. Garaudy admonished, however: "Let us be clearly aware of the fact that we are still only at the start of a great turning point in the epic of man. The turning point itself will not be reached until we have graduated from the meetings of a few lonely scouts, possibly even suspect in their own communities, to the authentic dialogue of the communities themselves." Then in words that were much too painfully prophetic he continued: "The road is heavily ambushed and . . . we must confess that present political conditions do not make any the easier the requisite clarification of the problems."[64] That was 1965. Then came the 1968 Soviet crushing of the "Prague Spring," against which Garaudy spoke out vigorously, and Garaudy's expulsion from the Communist Party in 1970, and similar retrenchments elsewhere, which nearly destroyed the dialogue between Christians and Marxists for a number of years.

Decades later the Yugoslav Marxist philosopher from the "Praxis" group, Professor Zagorka Golubovic, argued along a similar line, insisting that according to Marx "the uniqueness of being human cannot be expressed by a definition based on a selection of one of the distinctive traits."[65] Rather,

---

63. Pal Horvath, "Changes in the Evaluation of Religion and the Churches in the Last Decade in Hungary and the U.S.A.," paper delivered at the Christian-Marxist dialogue held in the Law School of the University of Budapest, June 20–25, 1988.

64. Ibid., 120.

65. Zagorka Golubovic, "A Marxist Approach to the Concept of Being/Becoming Human," a paper delivered at the Christian-Marxist dialogue, "Christian and Marxist Views on the Meaning of Being Human," in Granada, Spain, August 23–27, 1988, sponsored by the New Ecumenical Research Association. Other citations below from Professor Golubovic all come from this paper. See also her essay, "Philosophical Basis of Human Rights in Marxism," Leonard Swidler, ed., *Human Rights: Christians Marxists*

"the very fact that men persistently create and recreate themselves speaks against a definition of man in terms of a fixed set of traits." For Marx, a key notion was that of praxis, which helps us understand "that human beings do not exist as "determined objects," or as "unambiguously free subjects," but as the conscious agents who both construct the world by their actions, and are conditioned and limited by the world they themselves have created."

Golubovic developed this notion of humans as conscious agents, rejecting the vulgarized Marxist concept of economic, or other, determinism: "One cannot speak strictly in terms of determinism when human processes are concerned because the many-sided interactions taking place in the sphere of human conduct are not explainable by the categories of causality." Rather, one must go beyond the usual causal categories; "a new kind of *teleological causality* should be applied when trying to understand human activity and man's relation to his world." As a consequence, "Men's developments depend not only on the given conditions and opportunities, but also on the choices and decisions they have to make . . . in their conscious goal-directed actions."[66]

In the end, Golubovic offered her own description of the constitutive elements of being human, with a strong stress on freedom and the "spiritual" dimensions—not what one usually expected from alleged atheistic dialectical materialists:

> a) an evolved psychic structure which is unique to man (which may be named as "spiritual nature," expressing a network of many-dimensional psychic traits and abilities);
>
> b) a new mode of human-environment relationship (taking freedom as a paradigm which explains how the human breaks through natural determinism and causal relations and changes the world); and
>
> c) self-actualization as an essential expression of individual existence, which links human characteristics and abilities evolved

and Others in Dialogue (New York: Paragon, 1991) 71–84.

66. Golubovic called attention at this point in a footnote to a very important distinction between what Marx himself thought and what most so-called "orthodox" Marxists taught: "Marx was aware of the fact that social laws appear merely as tendencies, unlike natural laws which have a causal structure and determine the effects. This is a very significant distinction which the Orthodox Marxists failed to make, thanks primarily to a greater influence of Engels' 'dialectics of nature.' However, when the necessary distinction is made it becomes possible to speak of man's freedom as an important component of a specific kind of social determinism which involves the 'teleological causality.'"

in the course of sociocultural evolution of humankind with the process of personalization.

Conclusion

Thus, although the dialogue did revive slowly in the late 1970s and into the 1980s, it quite suddenly became largely moot with the "Great Transformation" in Eastern Europe in 1989–90, which left very few reputable thinkers overtly espousing Marxist ideology. (In China, the one remaining major Marxist stronghold, there do not seem to be any Marxist thinkers, only political ideologues.) Still, the serious Marxist thinking by reflective philosophers such as Garaudy in the 1960s, Golubovic in the 1980s, and others offers an approach to the questions of Ultimate Reality by a very important and influential ideology in human history. Moreover, Atheistic Humanism, of which Atheistic Marxism was for a time the most powerful example, has not disappeared and will not disappear. The dialogue between Theism and Atheism begun here needs to go forward.

Interim Conclusion I

If these reflections are at all close to the mark in trying to discern the meaning of religion (and ideology), then I would like to draw them together in kind of summary of what religion means and what its purpose is. The definition of religion I began with in fact was my conclusion after much study and reflection. Hence, I would simply paraphrase it here, stressing its various elements with the help of the four "C's" and "T" (the "Transcendent"):

Religion is an *explanation* (*Creed*) of the ultimate meaning of life and *how to live* (*Code* and *Community-structure*) accordingly, which is based on the notion of the *Transcendent* (*Cult*). Because religion is an explanation of the *ultimate* meaning of life, it provides a code of behavior in the fullest possible sense, including all the psychological, social, and cultural dimensions of human life, and is hence a "Way of Life"—for *humans*. The "Way of Life" that religion tries to provide, however, is not just *any* more or less acceptable way of life, but it is an attempt on the basis of its "explanation" and experience to put forth the best possible "Way of Life."

As has been described, there are many different ways of describing the best possible "Way of Life" that will lead humans most effectively to the goal of life, which is also variously described according to the various religious "explanations" of the ultimate meaning of life. What they all surely have in common, however, is that they aim at providing *humans* with the best possible way to live so as to attain the goal of their lives. Hence, it can be concluded that all religions aim ultimately at making humans as authentically and wholly human as possible—that is, they aim to provide "salvation," however it is described, for humans, however they are understood.

There are also a variety of ways of understanding Ultimate Reality, with a major distinction between the theist, personal understanding, on the one hand, and the nontheist, nonpersonal on the other. Still, the theistic understandings of Ultimate Reality also make room for nonpersonal understandings—without forfeiting their personal understanding. Also, some versions of the nonpersonal understanding, especially in dialogue, also stretch to make room for a "personal" understanding of God, as for example in the writings of the Zen Buddhist Masao Abe, who has been deeply involved in dialogue with Christians. There is promise of a deeper, richer understanding of Ultimate Reality by both theists and nontheists in pursuance of dialogue. The dialogue, temporarily largely in abeyance, between adherents of religion and of Ideology also gives promise of leading to a further understanding of what it means to be human.

3

The "Inner" Dialogue

Intrainstitutional Dialogue: Catholicism

General Reflections

With whom must dialogue happen? We must be in constant dialogue with all reality and its Source, which theists call God. This reality and its Ultimate Source is found both within ourselves and our various communities. In listening for the Ultimate within ourselves we must learn to trust our life—our needs, our yearnings, our fears. A basic trust in reality and ultimate trust in the Source of reality will rid us of the ancient dualism, antithetic to authentic religion, which for centuries undermined this basic trust. In reappropriating this trust in our inner selves, we must also learn to be healthily critical of our inner selves, to avoid becoming self-centered. This requires delicate balancing, avoiding extremes. However, given the centuries of distrust and even self-hate, especially in Christian history, it is the basic trust in our inner selves that must be stressed. Our inner self is one key place where we enter into dialogue with the Ultimate, with God.

The other present gate to enter into dialogue with God lies *within* the various communities where we live; they, too, are an essential part of the human reality that God in the Semitic tradition created and saw as not just good but very good. We must learn to be sensitive to the signs of the times as reflected in our communities, both secular and religious. We must welcome and appreciate the different streams within religious and secular society, expecting and embracing their pluralism, listening carefully so as to draw every bit of insight and wisdom we can from them. At the same time, merely celebrating the secular city and simply rejoicing in "theological" and religious pluralism without engaging in careful and mature critiques of all they have to offer would, of course, be naive and irresponsible. Again, it is that delicate balance of maturity, the ongoing work of life, which must be our goal.

Yet, as human beings we are substantially products of our past; hence, we must enter into serious dialogue with our history and heritage if we are to lead full human lives. In addition, Christians have a very special reason to enter into dialogue with their history, for Christianity, like Judaism, is a historical religion. It finds God at work and speaking in the events of history, not only in the present but also in the past. The specifically Christian understanding of life is that God speaks through the events of history in general, and more specifically through the history of the Jewish people, the "People of God," particularly as expressed in the Hebrew Bible and even more specifically in the person of Yeshua of Nazareth, particularly as expressed in the New Testament. For Christians he is the focal point; everything revolves around him. All subsequent Christian theory is simply trying to plumb and live out in particular circumstances what Christians understand to be God's action in Jesus, in Yeshua, as God's special sign—God's revelation of how to lead full human lives.

Here religion returns us to the present, to ourselves, and to the Catholic Church. It is within these concentric contexts that all institutions, including the leadership of the Catholic Church, are to be placed and engaged in serious dialogue. There can be no complete disjuncture between the Church as *magisterium* and as *fideles*, between the teaching and learning church, the *ecclesia docens* and the *ecclesia discens*. Rather, the Church must, according to the primordial Christian tradition, be understood as the *ecclesia in dialogo*. But, is this understanding of the Church, the Catholic Church, even a theoretical possibility today? I think it is.

Vatican Understanding of Dialogue

What does the Vatican understand the purpose of dialogue to be? One official explanation comes from the Vatican Secretariat for Unbelievers: The purpose of dialogue is to attain "a greater grasp of truth . . . to reach an agreement, to be established in the realm of truth . . . and the achievement by common effort of a better grasp of truth and an extension of knowledge."[1] The pope himself also publicly recognized the propriety of pursuing the truth by dialogue. Pope Paul VI in 1964 stated that "dialogue is *demanded* nowadays . . . It is *demanded* by the dynamic course of action which is changing the face of modern society. It is *demanded* by the pluralism of society and by the maturity man has reached in this day and age."[2]

---

1. *Humanae personae dignitatem*, 1005.
2. Pope Paul VI, *Ecclesiam suam*, no. 79; emphasis added.

Years later, the Vatican Committee for Religious Relations with the Jews wrote, "From now on real dialogue must be established."[3] Already in 1968 the Vatican Secretariat for Unbelievers had forcefully expressed the idea that "all Christians should do their best to promote dialogue . . . as a duty of fraternal charity suited to our progressive and adult age." It linked a commitment to dialogue with a commitment to Church renewal: "The willingness to engage in dialogue is the measure and the strength of that general renewal which must be carried out in the Church, which implies a still greater appreciation of liberty." That being the case, such renewal-related dialogue should be pursued not only by people whose views are fairly similar but, rather, "dialogue is of greater importance . . . when it takes place between people of different and even sometimes opposing opinions. They try to dispel each other's prejudiced opinions and to increase, as much as they are able, consensus between themselves."[4] It is ironic that this impressively open and generous document was issued by a Vatican agency for relations with unbelievers and not from one for internal relations among other Catholics.

Dialogue, the "search for truth," as the assembled Catholic bishops of the world taught at Vatican II, "must be carried out in a manner that is appropriate to the dignity of the human person and his social nature, namely, by free inquiry with the help of teaching or instruction, communication and dialogue."[5] According to the Vatican this dialogic search for truth is by no means limited to "practical" matters, but in a central way it is to focus on theology and doctrine, and without hesitation or trepidation. "If dialogue is to achieve its aims, it must obey the rules of truth and liberty. It needs sincere truth, thus excluding manipulated doctrinal discussion, discussion which is undertaken for political ends . . . [I]n discussion the truth will prevail by no other means than by the truth itself. Therefore the liberty of the participants must be ensured by law and reverenced in practice."[6]

To be sure, there is risk involved in dialogue—to be really open to what is being said is to reckon with the possibility that the partner will prove to be persuasive on any particular point. The Vatican admits as much in these words: "Doctrinal discussion requires perceptiveness, both in honestly setting out one's opinion and in recognizing the truth everywhere, even if the

---

3. Committee for Religious Relations with the Jews, *Guidelines on Religious Relations with the Jews*, December 1, 1974, in Flannery, *Vatican Council II*, 744.

4. *Humanae personae dignitatem*, 1003, 1005.

5. *Declaration on Religious Liberty*, December 7, 1965, no. 2, in Flannery, *Vatican Council II*, 801.

6. *Humanae personae dignitatem*, 1010.

truth demolishes one so that one is forced to reconsider one's own position, in theory and in practice, at least in part."[7]

Unfortunately, however, 1979 saw the beginning of an extraordinary return to the pre-Vatican II defensive model by the Congregation of the Doctrine of the Faith, yet subsequently there were public verbal commitments to intellectual freedom of inquiry by Pope John Paul II.

"The Church needs her theologians, particularly in this time and age ... The Bishops of the Church ... all need your work, your dedication and the fruits of your reflection. We desire to listen to you and we are eager to receive the valued assistance of your responsible scholarship ... We will never tire of insisting on the eminent role of the university ... a place of specific research which must apply the highest standards of scientific research, constantly updating its methods and working instruments ... in freedom of investigation."[8] He even went so far as to comment, "Truth is the power of peace ... What should one say of the practice of combating or silencing those who do not share the same views?"[9]

Recommendations for Dialogue

In line with these counciliar, papal, and curial quotations, the function of religious leadership vis-à-vis reflection by the faithful on the meaning of their faith—that is, theology—should be a positive one. The function, for example, of the Vatican's Congregation of the Doctrine of the Faith should be to promote dialogue among theologians of varying approaches so that the most enlightening and helpful expression of theology can find acceptance. Thus, 100 American Catholic theologians sent the following to the Vatican, in the Fall of 1979:

> We call upon the Congregation of the Doctrine of the Faith to eliminate from its procedures "hearings," and the like, substituting for them dialogues that either would be issue-oriented, or, if it is deemed important to focus on the work of a particular theologian, would bring together not only the theologian in question and the consultors of the Congregation of the Doctrine of the Faith, but also a worldwide selection of the best pertinent theological scholars of varying methodologies and approaches. These dialogues could well be conducted with the collaboration

---

7. Ibid.

8. Pope John Paul II, "Address to Catholic Theologians and Scholars at Catholic University," October 7, 1979.

9. Reported in the *Washington Post*, December 19, 1979.

of the International Theological Commission, the Pontifical Biblical Commission, universities, theological faculties, and theological organizations. Thus, the best experts on the issues concerned would work until acceptable resolutions were arrived at. Such a procedure of course is by no means new: it is precisely the procedure utilized at the Second Vatican Council.[10]

If dialogue is seen as the preferred instrument for arriving at an even deeper understanding and expression of the truth about reality and our Christian faith, it must also be recognized that authentic dialogue can take place only between equals, *par cum pari*, as the Decree on Ecumenism puts it. Although Catholics are usually aware of their various responsibilities, they are woefully unaware of their rights. Not until those rights have been promulgated and secured by practice and law can true dialogue flourish in the Catholic Church. Hence, Catholics aware of the need for dialogue and for spelling out and securing their rights in the Church have founded such organizations as the Association for the Rights of Catholics in the Church (ARCC) and attempt to promote dialogue on all levels in the Catholic Church. To this end they have produced a "Charter of the Rights of Catholics in the Church" and the theological underpinnings for it: *A Catholic Bill of Rights*.[11] Later ARCC, in conjunction with other American, European, and Asian Catholic reform organizations, produced a *Proposed Catholic Constitution*.[12]

The general atmosphere within the Vatican changed dramatically on the very Spring, 2013, night that Francis was chosen pope—he immediately engaged in dialogue the Catholics waiting for his appearance. In fact, just a few weeks later when traveling in South America he told a huge crowd of Catholics that, whenever difficulties arise, they should: "Dialogue, dialogue, dialogue!"

Intrareligious Dialogue: Christianity

Dialogue within one's "home" community is the most fundamental. To paraphrase a folk saying, "Dialogue begins at home," and to rephrase a

---

10. Quoted in full in Leonard Swidler, *Küng in Conflict* (New York: Doubleday, 1981) 514–17.

11. For information on the Association for the Rights of Catholics in the Church, see arcc-catholic-rights.net. See also Leonard Swidler and Herbert O'Brien, eds., *A Catholic Bill of Rights* (Kansas City, MO: Sheed & Ward, 1988).

12. See Leonard Swidler, *Toward a Catholic Constitution* (New York: Crossroad, 1996); and http://arcc-catholic-rights.org/, for the various translations of the proposed constitution.

Judeo-Christian principle, "You dialogue with your neighbor as you dialogue with yourself." Obviously, however, the drive toward dialogue must reach beyond this innermost concentric circle of partners toward ever wider circles of potential partners. Clearly, for Catholics, as for other Christians, the next obvious dialogue partners are their fellow Christians from whom they are separated. In fact, the massive contemporary intra-Christian dialogue has had a huge impact on the self-understandings of and relationships with not only the Christian churches but other religious and ideological institutions as well.

Divisions in Christianity

To begin with, the "founder" of Christianity, Jesus of Nazareth, was not a Christian. He was a Jew. He was Rabbi Yeshua. His first followers, both during his lifetime and after the resurrection event, also thought of themselves as Jews. However, the majority of Jews living at that time did not choose to become followers of Rabbi Yeshua. This decision constituted the first major separation or "division" in the history of the followers of "The Way" of Rabbi Yeshua, which eventually came to be called the Christian Church. While this centrifugal force was at work within nascent Christianity, the followers of Rabbi Yeshua strove to retain unity by a balancing centripetal force. These two forces of unity and division have continued to vie for dominance within the history of Christianity, as in all human institutions.

The next major division in Christianity resulted from the major universal or Ecumenical Councils from the fourth through the eighth centuries. Those who accepted the decisions of the Councils described themselves as orthodox, and those who did not were labeled heterodox by the "winners," though to be sure they did not so describe themselves. A number of these ancient so-called "nonorthodox" Christian churches, such as the Coptic Church of Egypt, still exist today.

The fall of the Roman Empire in the West eventually led to another major division, that between Eastern and Western Christianity, both understanding themselves to be adherents of orthodox Christianity. This division took place gradually in the latter centuries of the first millennium CE and was "fixed" in the year 1054 with the mutual excommunications of the leaders of both Eastern and Western Christianity. Western Christianity was torn once again in a major way in the sixteenth century with the Protestant Reformation.

There were, of course, many futile attempts all along the way to avoid the disastrous divisions, just as there were many futile attempts to bridge the breaches once they had occurred. The force of division seemed to be growing ever stronger. In many Christian quarters unity did not even seem like a virtue or an attractive goal; ideals such as liberty, independence, and "the" truth (mine, of course) were preferred. As to the question of whether there ought to be one or many Christian churches, the response often seemed to be "the more the better." By the twentieth century, as a consequence, there were hundreds of Christian churches in existence.

Toward Christian Unity

In the nineteenth century, however, doubts began to arise about the value and the validity of division in the Christian church. Ever since the sixteenth century the Catholic Church had been heavily involved in missionizing those parts of the world newly discovered by Spain, Portugal, and France. Protestants seemed to have little interest in such work until the nineteenth century, when they too began to evangelize the non-European world with a huge outpouring of funds and resources. As the nineteenth century passed into the twentieth, Protestant missionaries increasingly found that the division within the Christian church was a scandal, a stumbling block, to the acceptance of the Christian gospel by non-Christians.[13] Hence, the modern Christian movement toward unity, the "ecumenical movement," began at the 1910 World Missionary Conference in Edinburgh, Scotland. It was there that the intention to found an organization to work for Christian unity was publicly declared by Episcopal Bishop Charles H. Brent. From that initiative came the "Movement for Faith and Order" which strove to overcome the divisions which it saw to be founded on disagreements over belief and church structure, that is, over "Faith and Order."

A second great arm of the ecumenical movement, started by Swedish Lutheran Bishop Nathan Söderblom, was called the "Movement for Life and Work." It was founded on the notion that the Christian churches cannot wait until the divisions caused by differences in belief and church structure are overcome but must begin to work in harmony on the issues of contemporary "Life and Work"; from working and living together would flow deeper unity.

From the beginning, both groups tried to include Protestant, Catholic, and Orthodox (Eastern) Christian churches. In reality, only Protestant

---

13. Most of the data in this section are substantiated in Robert McAfee Brown, *The Ecumenical Revolution* (New York: Doubleday, 1967); and Margaret Nash, *Ecumenical Movement in the 1960's* (Johannesburg: Ravan, 1975). See also the *Journal of Ecumenical Studies*, from 1964 on.

churches participated at the start. The first world conference of the "Life and Work Movement" was convened at Stockholm in 1925, and in 1927 the first world conference of the "Movement for Faith and Order" met in Lausanne. The spirit of unity had its effect on the two movements themselves, which decided to hold both their next world conferences in Britain during the Summer of 1937, at which time a proposal for merger was put forth and agreed to. The formal initiation of the merged ecumenical organization was postponed because of World War II—just as the first two world conferences had been postponed by World War I—with the result that the World Council of Churches first came into formal existence at the Amsterdam Conference in 1948.

At that first General Assembly of the World Council of Churches (WCC), there were 351 official delegates from 146 churches. The smaller Eastern churches were represented, but neither the Orthodox Church of Russia nor the Orthodox churches from Eastern Europe sent delegates—nor, of course, did the Catholic Church. The second General Assembly of the WCC took place in Evanston, Illinois, in 1954, followed by New Delhi in 1961, Uppsala in 1968, Nairobi in 1975, and Vancouver in 1983. By then the number of participant churches had more than doubled, to over three hundred, and the number of delegates had multiplied to over three thousand. Since then Assemblies were held about every eight years in Canberra, Australia in 1991; Harare, Zimbabwe in 1998; Porto Alegre, Brazil, in 2006; and Pusan, South Korea, in 2013.

Paralleling the international WCC are national structures. In the U.S. there is the National Council of the Churches of Christ in the U.S.A., a federation of Christian churches, with its national headquarters in New York for many years, now in Washington, DC, which functions like the WCC international headquarters in Geneva. In addition, almost every state has a council of churches, and every sizeable city has its equivalent of a city council of churches. A metropolitan area will even have scores of regional "ministeria" where the local clergy can engage in dialogue and cooperation. Besides this, local churches, colleges and universities, and other Christian institutions often join their neighbors in ecumenical projects.

Though the centrifugal forces of church division far outstripped the centripetal forces of church unity into the twentieth century, in recent decades the trend has been reversed. The U.S. alone has seen some twenty-six church unions between 1900 and 1968. The most ambitious church merger attempt was a several-decade effort to bring together ten U.S. churches with a total of over thirty million members: the Consultation on Church Union (in 2002, becoming the Churches Uniting in Christ). The impetus toward church union continues; 1983 saw the initiation of two more major church unions in the U.S.—between the northern and southern Presbyterian churches, and among three of the four major Lutheran churches. The same sort of thing has been going on elsewhere in the world. Some of the most dramatic have taken place in India; in 1947 a new Church of South India brought together the Episcopal, Methodist, and Presbyterian churches of that area, while a similar union, the Church of North India, subsequently occurred in the north of India. In addition, there are serious conversations under way to unify these two churches, along with other Protestant and Orthodox churches in India that have not as yet joined either of the two.

In addition to these conversations with merger explicitly on the agenda, there have been many official theological conversations between churches, sometimes on a bilateral, and sometimes on a multilateral, basis. In 1975 the WCC reported on fourteen such major bilateral dialogues on the international level, and an additional thirty-two on the national or regional levels. Since these conversations are not necessarily directed toward merger, the partner churches are at times quite disparate in their theology and structure. This may be why they have tended to be immensely creative in new theological understanding.

For example, the three U.S. bilaterals between Catholics on the one side and Reformed Christians, Lutherans, and Anglicans on the other each independently took up the questions of baptism, the eucharist, and ministry. After a great deal of intense research and dialogue, all three independently arrived at basically the same positions, advocating mutual recognition of the authenticity of the baptism, eucharist, and ministry in one another's churches.

The extremely fruitful results of the bilateral dialogues have helped the multilateral theological conversations, often sponsored by the Commission on Faith and Order of the WCC, to make significant progress. The most hopeful advance has been the document on baptism, eucharist, and ministry passed by Faith and Order at its meeting in Lima in 1982. It was accepted by the hundred theological representatives of all the participating churches, which included the great majority of both Protestant and Orthodox churches, along with active voting observers from the Catholic Church. As a consequence, this document—which deals with some of the most fundamentally divisive, and at the same time potentially unifying, issues in Christian teachings—was studied, discussed, and acted upon by all the involved churches. A liturgy based upon that document was used at the 1983 Vancouver General Assembly of the WCC with immense success. Many participants found it the outstanding experience of an outstanding world assembly.

Catholic Ecumenism

Because Catholics outnumber the rest of the Christian world, the degree of participation by Rome in the ecumenical movement is extremely important.[14] Like so many of the Protestant churches, the Roman Church was also involved in an effort to reunite Christianity toward the latter part of the nineteenth century, although in its own distinct style. The Oxford Movement within the Anglican Church in the mid-nineteenth century had created a strong interest on the part of both high-church Anglicans and some Catholics, especially in England, to bridge the gulf between the two churches. Their efforts began to be productive in the final quarter of the nineteenth century, after the death of Pope Pius IX—perhaps the most reactionary pope of modern times—in 1876. Unfortunately, these efforts led by Lord Halifax on the Anglican side and Abbe Portal on the Catholic were shattered in 1893 when, contradicting the findings and recommendations of scholars he himself had appointed, Pope Leo XIII issued a document declaring that Anglican priestly orders were "utterly null and void."

Nevertheless, some thirty years later, in the early 1920s, Lord Halifax and Abbe Portal once again tried to move Rome and Canterbury on the road to unity through the Malines Conversations, meetings that took place during the pontificates of Benedict XV and his successor Pius XI, under the direct protectorship of Cardinal Mercier of Malines, Belgium. Fruitful as far as they went, the conversations unfortunately ended with the death of Cardinal Mercier in 1926.

Following World War I, Germany was the scene of significant Catholic-Protestant theological dialogue, doubtless spurred on by the developments in the 1920s that led to the 1925 Stockholm and 1927 Lausanne world conferences described above. However, Pope XI's very restrictive 1928 encyclical, *Mortalium animos*, dampened enthusiasm for Catholic-Protestant ecumenism in Germany. Nevertheless, partly because of the pressure of Nazi persecution, the Una Sancta Movement arose in Germany in the 1930s, led by Father Max Metzger, a reform thinker and activist who had founded a world Catholic peace organization during World War I that smuggled Jews out of Nazi Germany. He eventually was beheaded by the Nazis in 1944 for his peace work.[15] After the war was over, the Una Sancta Movement in Germany suddenly blossomed into a popular movement, bringing Catholic and Protestant clergy and theologians together on public

---

14. Most of the data in this section are found in Leonard Swidler, *The Ecumenical Vanguard* (Pittsburgh: Duquesne University Press, 1966).

15. Leonard Swidler, *Bloodwitness for Peace and Unity: The Life of Max Josef Metzger* (Denville, NJ: Dimension, 1977).

platforms and in each other's churches, until the impetus was once again dampened by a Vatican *Monitum* in 1948. The *Monitum*, too, turned out to be only a temporary setback, for the momentum of Catholic-Protestant dialogue soon resumed, especially in Germany, but also in France, though to a much lesser extent, under the inspiration of Paul Couturier, until it received full Vatican approbation at Vatican II.

A major link between the German Una Sancta Movement and the endorsement of ecumenism at Vatican II was that the newly established Secretariat for Christian Unity was set up under the presidency of Augustin Bea, a German Jesuit theologian, who was created a cardinal for this purpose by Pope John XXIII, the convener of the Council. Most of the important theologians involved in promoting ecumenism were German.

Vatican II, a major turning point in the history of the Catholic Church, also marks a great divide in the history of the ecumenical movement. Beforehand, Rome had always refused to join in the ecumenical movement, reminding its Protestant initiators that reunion was always possible only by a return to Rome. The Vatican also repeatedly forbade Catholic involvement in ecumenism except under the strictest conditions. Then in 1964 Vatican II, consisting of the Catholic bishops of the world, including the bishop of Rome, passed the solemn "Decree on Ecumenism," which said of the Christian Church, "Division openly contradicts the will of Christ, scandalizes the world, and damages that most holy cause, the preaching of the Gospel to every creature."[16] From forbidding or restricting Catholic involvement in ecumenism, the Fathers of Vatican II turned to exhorting "all the Catholic faithful to recognize the signs of the times and to take an active and intelligent part in the work of ecumenism . . . In ecumenical work, Catholics must assuredly be concerned for their separated brethren . . . making the first approaches toward them . . . The concern for restoring unity involves the whole Church, faithful and clergy alike. It extends to everyone."[17]

At Vatican II the Church also shrugged off the siege mentality prevalent since the second quarter of the nineteenth century. Admitting that "men of both sides were to blame" for the divisions in the church, the Council no longer spoke of the Catholic Church in triumphalist terms, but rather as a church which "makes its pilgrim way," which is called by Christ, "as she goes her pilgrim way unto that continual reformation of which she always has need." This essential link between self-reform and the task of Christian unity was made explicit in the Decree on Ecumenism: "All are to examine their own faithfulness to Christ's will for the Church and, wherever

---

16. Flannery, *Vatican Council II*, 452.
17. Ibid., 456–58.

necessary, undertake with vigor the task of renewal and reform . . . Catholics' . . . primary duty is to make a careful and honest appraisal of whatever needs to be renewed and done in the Catholic household itself . . . Church renewal therefore has notable ecumenical importance."[18]

Vatican II opened the floodgates of ecumenism for Catholics. Catholic dioceses around the world began to set up offices for ecumenical dialogue. In the U.S., for example, each diocese has at least one professional person responsible for ecumenical dialogue; together these officials form the organization known as the National Association of Diocesan Ecumenical Officers (NADEO). The American bishops also set up a national Bishops Committee on Ecumenical and Interreligious Affairs (BCEIA), which is responsible for launching and overseeing national bilateral dialogues. These include Consultations with Episcopalians, Reformed and Presbyterian Christians, Lutherans, Methodists, Baptists, Disciples of Christ, Orthodox, and Non-Chalcedonian Eastern Christians, as well as Jews and Muslims.

Of all these bilaterals, the most productive has been the Lutheran-Catholic Consultation which has already published more than seven volumes of creative and respected theological research and joint statements on such neuralgic subjects as baptism, eucharist, ministry, papal primacy, infallibility, Mary, and justification. Although involvement in such bilateral consultations may not be as broad in other countries, since both resources and the spectrum of potential partners are much more limited, fruitful conversations nevertheless continue around the world.

Much more happens on the grassroots level. To begin with, there is official recognition of the validity of non-Catholic Christian baptism. Collaboration has advanced so that is is now possible for a marriage between a Catholic and a Protestant to take place before a Catholic priest, a Protestant minister, or both jointly. There are occasional pulpit exchanges between Catholics and Protestants, as well as joint worship services, all officially approved. The number of joint projects, ranging from the sharing of buildings and educational projects through a wide variety of social-justice concerns, seems almost unending. In a growing number of instances neighborhood ecumenical collaborations are ratified by "covenants": Mutual commitments are formalized in a document, which is then solemnly ratified by the laity and clergy of both churches and sometimes also by both dioceses or judicatories.

Innovations in the area of ecumenical theological education have been especially imaginative. In 1970 the Vatican Secretariat for Christian Unity, a permanent part of the Vatican bureaucracy since the end of Vatican II,

---

18. Ibid., 457.

issued a "Directory Concerning Ecumenical Matters—Part Two: Ecumenism in Higher Education." "Ecumenism" it said, "should bear on all theological disciplines as one of its necessary determining factors," although separate courses on ecumenism were also encouraged. It noted that joint retreats with non-Catholics are to be recommended and that experts from other religious traditions should be invited to teach about their own traditions. In vigorous support of the teaching of ecumenism, the Directory stated that bishops, religious superiors, and "those in authority in seminaries, universities, and similar institutions should take pains to promote the ecumenical movement and spare no effort to see that teachers keep in touch with advances in ecumenical thought and action," and urged that there "be cooperation between institutions of higher education and relationships on various levels between teachers and students of different churches and communities."[19] This has been happening in large numbers of instances with the sharing of both faculty and students. In the intra-Christian dialogue today's centripetal forces far outweigh the centrifugal ones so long dominant. Dialogue, of course, has been the key to this shift, as it will continue to be in the future, no matter what the eventual form of Christian unity may be or how long it may be delayed.

---

19. Ibid., 520, 526, 527.

4

The "Inter" Dialogue

General Reflections

Once Christians shifted from looking inward to looking outward, it was inevitable that their dialogue partners would no longer be limited to members of their own church or even to Christians of other churches. If it began to seem appropriate for a Lutheran to enter into dialogue with a Presbyterian, or a Catholic with a Lutheran, then the appropriateness of entering into dialogue with members of the religion from which Christianity sprang, Judaism, would naturally suggest itself. The next step was dialogue with members of Islam, the religion so intimately related to both Judaism and Christianity, and then with the other world religions, and beyond that with people who are not adherents of any religious tradition. Gradually, the attitude of triumphalistic superiority toward non-Christians common in the initial stages of *intra*-Christian dialogue began to change. Christians engaged in dialogue with non-Christians also more and more experienced the effect of interreligious dialogue on the theological statements they composed jointly with other Christians. The ramifications of interreligious, interideological dialogue have been immense.

Just because religions and ideologies are "holistic," and because mass communications and our high level of mobility increasingly allow us to experience "others" as living holistic, "holy" lives, not in spite of, but because of their religion or ideology, the need for dialogue in religion and ideology grows. When I as a Christian come to know Jews as religious persons who are leading whole, holy, human lives out of the fullness of their Judaism, I am immediately confronted with a question: What is the source of this holiness, this wholeness? Obviously it is not Christianity. Unless I really work at duping myself, I cannot say that it is unconscious or anonymous Christianity; if there is any religion which has for two thousand years consciously and publicly rejected Christianity, that religion is Judaism. Clearly, the only possible answer is that the source of the holiness, the wholeness, of the Jew is the Jewish religion—and the God who stands behind it, the God of Abraham, Sarah, Isaac, Rebecca, Jacob, Rachel, and Jesus.

In traditional theological language, Christianity, like Judaism, is a religion that believes that divine self-revelation comes to us through events and persons. If we are to learn God's message, God's Torah, good news, gospel, we Christians must seek to listen wherever and through whomever God speaks, which means that we must be in dialogue with persons of other religions to learn what God is saying to us through them.

Ground Rules for Interreligious, Interideological Dialogue

In true interreligious, interideological dialogue, it is not sufficient to discuss a religious-ideological subject, that is, "the meaning of life and how to live accordingly." The partners must come to the dialogue as persons significantly identified with a religious or ideological community. If I were neither a Christian nor a Marxist, for example, I could not participate as a partner in a Christian-Marxist dialogue, though I might listen in, ask some questions for information, and make some helpful comments.

Below are some basic ground rules for authentic interreligious, interideological dialogue. These are not theoretical rules from an ivory tower. They have been learned from hard experience; to ignore them is to diminish or destroy the dialogue.

First, an essential precondition, as formulated by Eric J. Sharpe:

> A willingness and a readiness to listen to the other *as other*. We may not listen in order to prepare our next words of approach, proclamation or attack, but with the awareness that Christ [members of other religions will make appropriate substitutions here and below] speaks to us from the other. Far from expecting to despise or belittle what we hear we will be set to appreciate. To listen means therefore far more than simply to stop talking; it demands a silence in oneself in order to understand the non-Christian brother [/sister] as he understands himself, a "putting into brackets" of my own explicit Christian convictions. The moment will come in real dialogue when the Christian will speak and when that comes it will not be a prefabricated answer but a word to a partner who has been understood.[1]

---

1. Eric J. Sharpe, "The Goals of Inter-Religious Dialogue," in Hick, ed., *Truth and Dialogue in World Religions*, 83–84.

This responding not with a pre-set answer but with a "word to a partner who *has been understood*" is a key notion in the dialogical understanding of truth, as has been aptly pointed out by Klaus Klostermeier:

> Classical science was linked with a classical, linear understanding of causality: this has become the model for "explanation" adopted by the social sciences and followed by many writers in religious studies. Linear causality has been found insufficient to explain the physical aspects of the world opened up by relativity and quantum theory. The interconnectedness of all objects in the universe, the mutuality between object and subject and between cause and effect, the holistic nature of the universe—all have been recognized fairly universally by now. A new model of causality has been introduced: the feedback loop, the self-regulating cybernetics of systems. This is the model of the process of dialogue: dialogue is a "feedback loop"—a statement made by a dialogue partner after having entered into dialogue does reflect the other's viewpoint and proceeds from there. It is not simply a logical development of the first proposition or an analysis of the partner's proposition from "the only true perspective."[2]

The following, then, is my "Dialogue Decalogue,"[3] basic ground rules or "commandments" of interreligious, interideological dialogue, which must be observed if dialogue is actually to take place.

First Commandment: *The primary purpose of dialogue is to learn, that is, to change and grow in the perception and understanding of reality and then to act accordingly.* We come to dialogue so that we ourselves may learn, change, and grow, not so that we may force change on the *other*, our partner, as the old polemic debates hoped to do. On the other hand, because in dialogue both partners come with the intention of learning and changing themselves, each will in fact find the partner has changed. Each partner will also have taught the other—but only because teaching was not the primary purpose of the encounter. Thus the alleged goal of debate, and much more, is accomplished far more effectively by dialogue.[4]

---

2. Klaus K. Klostermaier, "Interreligious Dialogue as a Method for the Study of Religion," *Journal of Ecumenical Studies* 21 (Fall 1984) 758. For a full description of these developments in the understanding of modern physics and its parallels with Eastern religious philosophies, see Fritjof Capra, *The Tao of Physics*, 2nd ed. (Boulder, CO: Shambhala, 1983).

3. *Journal of Ecumenical Studies*, 1984, rev. 2003. The earliest version appeared in *JES* 15 (1978) 413–14.

4. Gadamer made a series of similar points: "If dialogue (*Gespräch*) means allowing the participants to seek a fuller understanding of what is being discussed, then the art of dialogue is the art of questioning by which the solidity of opinion is opened up to

Second Commandment: *Interreligious, ideological dialogue must be a two-sided project*—within each religious or ideological community and between religious or ideological communities. Because interreligious, interideological dialogue is corporate, and because its primary goal is for all partners to learn and change themselves, it is necessary that all the participants enter into dialogue not only with their partners across the faith line—the Catholic with the Protestant, for example—but also with their coreligionists, with their fellow Catholics, to share the fruits of the interreligious dialogue. In this way the whole community can eventually learn and change, together gaining ever more perceptive insights into reality.

Third Commandment: *Each participant must come to the dialogue with complete honesty and sincerity.* It should be made clear in what direction the major and minor thrusts of the tradition move, what the future shifts might be, and even where the participants have difficulties with their own traditions. False fronts have no place in dialogue.

Conversely, each participant must assume the same complete honesty and sincerity in the other partners. A failure in sincerity will prevent dialogue from happening, but a failure to assume the partner's sincerity will do so as well. In brief: no trust, no dialogue.

Fourth Commandment: *In interreligious, interideological dialogue we must not compare our ideals with our partner's practice,* but rather our ideals with our partner's ideals, our practice with our partner's practice.

Fifth Commandment: *Each participant must define her or himself.* Only the Jew, for example, can define from the inside what it means to be a Jew; the rest of us can only describe what it looks like from the outside. Moreover, because dialogue is a dynamic medium, as each participant learns, she or he changes and hence continually deepens, expands, and modifies her or his self-definition as a Jew, being careful to remain in constant dialogue with fellow Jews. Thus it is mandatory that each dialogue partner define what it can mean to be an authentic member of that tradition.

Conversely, the side interpreted must be able to recognize itself in the interpretation. This is the golden rule of interreligious, interideological hermeneutics often reiterated by the "apostle of interreligious dialogue," Raimundo Panikkar. For the sake of clarity, the dialogue participants will

---

new possibilities of meaning. A person who possesses the art of questioning is a person who is able to prevent the suppression of questions by the dominant opinion. A person who possesses this art will . . . seek for everything in favor of an opinion. Dialectic consists, not in trying to discover the weakness of what is said, but in bringing out its real strength. Dialogue requires not the art of arguing but the art of thinking whereby what is said is strengthened by reference to the subject matter being discussed" (Hans-Georg Gadamer, *Wahrheit und Methode* [Tübingen: Mohr/Siebeck, 1965], 349).

naturally attempt to express for themselves what they think is the meaning of the partner's statement; the partner must be able to recognize her or himself in that expression. The advocate of "a world theology," Wilfred Cantwell Smith, would add that the expression must also be verifiable by critical observers not involved.

Sixth Commandment: *Each participant must come to the dialogue with no hard-and-fast assumptions as to where the points of disagreement lie.* Both partners should not only listen to one another with openness and sympathy, but also try to agree as far as is possible while still maintaining integrity with their own tradition; where they absolutely can agree no further without violating their own integrity, precisely there is the real point of disagreement—which most often turns out to be quite different from what was assumed beforehand.

Seventh Commandment: *Dialogue can take place only between equals*, or *"par cum pari,"* as Vatican II put it. Both must come to learn from each other. This means, for instance, that between a learned scholar and an uninformed person there can be no authentic, full dialogue but at most a gathering of information as in a sociological interrogation. Or, if a Muslim views Hinduism as inferior, or a Hindu views Islam as inferior, there will be no dialogue. For authentic interreligious, interideological dialogue between Muslims and Hindus, both partners must come mainly to learn from each other; only then will they speak "equal with equal," *par cum pari*. This rule also indicates that there can be no such thing as a one-way dialogue. The Jewish-Christian discussions begun in the 1960s, for example, were on the whole only prolegomena to interreligious dialogue. Understandably and properly, the Jews came to these exchanges only to teach Christians, and the Christians came mainly to learn. But, for authentic interreligious dialogue between Christians and Jews the Jews must also come to learn; only then will the conversation be *par cum pari*.

Eighth Commandment: *Dialogue can take place only on the basis of mutual trust*. Although interreligious, interideological dialogue has a kind of "corporate" dimension in that the participants must be involved as members of a religious or ideological community—for instance, as Marxists or Taoists—it is also fundamentally true that only *persons* can enter into dialogue. But, a dialogue among persons can be built only on personal trust. Hence it is wise not to tackle the most difficult problems in the beginning but to seek those issues most likely to provide some common ground and establish a basis of human trust. Then, as this personal trust deepens and expands, the more thorny matters can gradually be undertaken. As Lao Tzu has said: *Tu nan yu yi* (Hard work must have its beginnings in the easy).[5] Just as in learning we move from the known to the unknown, in dialogue we proceed from commonly held matters—which, given our mutual ignorance resulting from centuries of hostility, will take us quite some time to explore—to matters of disagreement.

Ninth Commandment: *As we enter into interreligious, interideological dialogue we must learn to be at least minimally self-critical of both ourselves and our own religious or ideological tradition.* A lack of such self-criticism implies that our own tradition already has all the correct answers. Such an attitude not only makes dialogue unnecessary but even impossible, since we enter into dialogue primarily so *we* can learn—which obviously is impossible if our tradition has never made a misstep, if it has all the right answers. To be sure, participants in interreligious, interideological dialogue must stand within a religious or ideological tradition with integrity and conviction, but their integrity and conviction must include, not exclude, healthy self-criticism. Without it there can be no dialogue—and, indeed, no integrity.

Tenth Commandment: *Each participant eventually must attempt to experience the partner's religion or ideology "from within."* A religion or ideology is not merely something of the head, but also of the spirit, heart, and "whole being," individual and communal. John Dunne here spoke of "passing over" into another's religious or ideological experience and then coming back enlightened, broadened, and deepened.[6] While retaining our own religious integrity, we need to find ways of experiencing something of the emotional and spiritual power of the symbols and cultural vehicles of our partner's religion—and then come back to our own, enriched and expanded, having experienced at least a little of the affective side of our partner's.

Interreligious, interideological dialogue operates in three areas: the practical, where we collaborate to help humanity; the depth or "spiritual" dimension, where we attempt to experience the partner's religion or ideology "from within"; and the cognitive, where we seek understanding and truth. Dialogue also has three phases. In phase one, which we never completely outgrow, we unlearn misinformation about each other and begin to know each other as we truly are. In phase two we begin to discern values in our partner's tradition and wish to appropriate them into our own. In the Buddhist-Christian dialogue, for example, Christians might learn a

---

5. Lao Tzu, *Tao Te Ching*, chap. 63, quoted in Tang Yi, "Taoism as a Living Philosophy," 399.

6. Cf. John S. Dunne, *The Way of All the Earth* (New York: Macmillan, 1972).

greater appreciation of the meditative tradition, and Buddhists might learn a greater appreciation of the prophetic, social-justice tradition—both values strongly, though not exclusively, associated with the other's community. If we are serious, persistent, and sensitive enough in the dialogue, we may at times enter into phase three. Here we together begin to explore new areas of reality, of meaning, of truth—aspects of which neither of us had even been aware before. We are brought face to face with these new, still unknown dimensions of reality through questions, insights, probings produced in the dialogue. We will experience for ourselves that dialogue patiently pursued can become an instrument of new "re-velation," a further "un-veiling" of reality—on which we must then act.

Between phase one and phases two and three there is a radical difference. No longer do we simply add on another "truth" or value from our partner's tradition. Now, as we assimilate it within our own religious self-understanding, it transforms our self-understanding proportionately. Since our dialogue partner is in the same position, we now can witness sincerely to those valuable elements in our own tradition that our partner's tradition may find profitable to assimilate. All this sharing and transformation is done with complete integrity on each side, with each partner remaining true to the vital core of his or her own religious tradition. Yet, that vital core will now be perceived and experienced differently under the influence of dialogue. Still, if the dialogue is carried on with both integrity and openness, the Jew will remain authentically Jewish or the Christian authentically Christian, not despite the fact that Judaism and/or Christianity have found and adapted something of deep value in the other tradition, but because of it. There can be no talk of a syncretism here, for syncretism means amalgamating various elements of different religions into some kind of a *(con)* fused whole without concern for the integrity of the religions involved—which is not the case with authentic dialogue.

Dialogue in Practice

Religions and ideologies are not only explanations of the meaning of life, but, as has been seen, also *ways* to live according to that explanation (the term "way" is key in many religions, as *Hodos* in New Testament Christianity, *Halacha* in Judaism, *Shar'ia* in Islam, *Marga* in Hinduism, *Magga* in Buddhism, *Tao* in Taoism and Confucianism and *To* in Shintoism). For example, the Buddhist is not only to seek interior liberation but also to practice such virtues as justice, honesty, and compassion. In Judaism the prophetic tradition of social justice is even encoded into specific laws in the Talmud. Jesus said that those are saved who feed the hungry, clothe the naked, and house the homeless. St. John said that whoever says he loves God but hates his brother is a liar; St. James said that faith without works is dead. Marxism also offers not just a social theory but likewise a social program and practice.

Some human problems are so urgent that they call forth social action from many different religions and ideologies: peace, hunger, discrimination, social justice, human rights. Often the joint action that is recognized as more effective than separate or parallel efforts also breaks down barriers between the religions and ideologies and leads to conscious dialogue about the self-understanding and motivations underlying the commitment of the different religions and ideologies involved. For example, the Christians and atheistic humanists who in the 1960s ended up in the Selma, Alabama, jail together after marching with Martin Luther King, Jr., for equal rights for blacks in America entered into dialogue to learn how their differing faiths and ideologies led to the same radical action.

Dialogue in the practical area, "where we collaborate to help humanity," began to develop in earnest in the West only in the nineteenth century. Until that time efforts to help disadvantaged human beings were mostly done on a remedial individualistic basis. "Charitable" institutions were founded—actually in quite extraordinary richness. The situation began to change drastically, however, with the coming of the Industrial Revolution in England in the late eighteenth century and elsewhere in Europe and America starting in the nineteenth century; the old guild and feudal systems no longer functioned for the increasing millions caught in the transfer of populations to the cities. Whereas most people had died quite young, and a much smaller population lived in relative social and geographical stability before the nineteenth century, suddenly a massive and exploding population problem burst upon the world for which neither civil society nor religion was prepared. Individual acts of charity and charitable institutions were increasingly swamped in the growing flood of social misery that rose as the nineteenth and twentieth centuries wore on.

At the same time, the structures of society and their workings were being studied. Plans on how to shape and reshape those structures were laid and tested, adjusted and retested. Such awareness, planning, and action also took place within Western religion. One need only remember the large number of Jews involved in the history of socialism, starting with Marx, and the labor movement, including Jewish social-justice organizations from the *Jüdischer Bund* to Israeli Kibbutzim. Christian socialism started in England with such people as Kingsley and in Germany with such people as Bishop von Ketteler; in France religious social-justice work was led by activists such as de Mun, Tour de la Pin, and Sagnier; in America, there were Terence Powderley and the Knights of Labor and Walter Rauschenbusch and his highly influential "Social Gospel" message. Even the popes moved in this direction: Leo XIII issued *Rerum novarum* in 1893; Pius XI, *Quadragesimo anno* in 1933; John XXIII, *Pacem in terris* in 1963; and Paul VI, *Populorum progressio* in 1968.

The most recent developments include European Political Theology, Latin American Liberation Theology, North American Black Theology and Feminist Theology, and Korean *Minjung* or People's Theology. Around the globe Christian churches spend hundreds of millions of dollars annually on social-justice issues, a significant portion of which is aimed at changing the structures of society to benefit more people. The notion has spread among Christians that the mission of the church is to preach the Good News of the gospel to all humanity, not just quantitatively in terms of individual persons, but also qualitatively in terms of every aspect of the human being—and the human patterns one lives in are an essential part of one's humanity. The message of *relationality* has struck home here.

From the beginning, Islam has had a deep concern for social justice. The paying of *Zakat*—a tax on all Muslims destined mainly for the poor—is one of the "five pillars" of Islam, and today's movement toward Islamization, in both its fundamentalist and more moderate forms, includes a concern for the structures of social justice based on both religious and secular reasons.

Religions of the East, such as Buddhism, have always considered such virtues as compassion essential, and that has doubtless had an ameliorative effect on much human misery; yet, the religions of the East, probably even more than the Semitic religions, have often been closer to being what Marx called "the opium of the people," an "escape" or consolation in this vale of tears that must be endured rather than changed. In any case, in the East, as in the West, individual compassion and charity have increasingly been found inadequate to cope with the rising tide of modern social change; some of the Eastern religions, therefore, have recently begun to see social justice and just structural social change as religious responsibilities. In Bangkok Dr. Sulak Sivaraksa, a Therevada Buddhist layperson, is extremely active in organizing a wide range of social-action projects arising out of his Buddhist commitment.[7] In Hong Kong Buddhist monks who came from the mainland in 1949–50 after the Communist revolution have recently turned to social-justice issues, partly, it is clear, as a result of their encounter with the social-justice orientation of the Christian churches. Something similar is happening within traditional Buddhism in South Korea. More striking

---

7. Lecture at the University of Tübingen, June, 1985, by Dr. Sulak Sivaraksa.

is Won Buddhism, founded in Korea in the second decade of the twentieth century. Won Buddhism works to combine the principles of Gautama Buddha with an affirmation of modern science and technology in working for the betterment of men and women, individually and collectively; hence, it is not surprising that the Won Buddhists also have a very strong commitment to interreligious dialogue.

The Catholic theologian and Buddhologist Aloysius Pieris noted that "The social dimension of Buddhist ethics is being reclaimed from oblivion and reexpressed as the Buddha's vision of a just political order for today, so that social justice is regarded at least as an inevitable by-product of Buddhist soteriology."[8] For example, some low-caste Hindus sought freedom from their social lot in conversion to Buddhism and have produced a "Literature of the Oppressed." The following verse from a poem to Buddha is an example of this contemporary social-liberation image of Buddha:

> I see you
> Speaking and walking
> Amongst the humble and the weak
> In the life-threatening darkness
> With torch in hand
> Going from hovel to hovel.
>
> Today you wrote a new page
> of the *Tripitaka* [early Buddhist scripture][9]

Pieris commented, "This indeed is a new interpretation of the Buddha's soteriological role. The belief in his cosmic lordship is hermeneutically extended to the sociopolitical structures whose radical transformation is believed to be possible under the Buddha's soteriological influence. Undoubtedly, this is 'a new page in the *Tripitaka*,' as the poet declares."[10]

Even in Taoism, where one might least expect it, a concern for social-justice issues is at least beginning to arise in both theory and practice. It has been recently pointed out by a Chinese scholar from Beijing that, in Taoism, Lao Tzu, who like Gautama advocated "desirelessness," "ultimate vacuity," "dynamic vacuity," and "true tranquility," also was said to have been "decidedly on the side of the common people" and to have had "a deep reverence

---

8. Aloysius Pieris, "The Buddha and the Christ: Mediators of Liberation," in Hick and Knitter, *Myth of Christian Uniqueness*, 168.

9. Dayar Powar, "Siddhartha," *Panchasheel* (October 1972) 7; E.T. quoted in J. B. Gokhale-Turner, "*Bhakti* or *Vidroha*: Continuity and Change in *Calit Sahitya*," *Journal of African and Asian Studies* 15 (1980) 38.

10. Pieris, "The Buddha and the Christ," 169.

for ecological and cosmic equilibrium. If nature is in dynamic harmony, why not human society?" As Lao Tzu said of the sage, "he thinks and feels with the common people . . . the sage should save the people so that no one is abandoned." The sage says "I have three treasures which I keep and cherish. The first is Great Love." It is clear that Lao Tzu "is committed to a strong sense of social responsibility. The sage who is out to save the people so that no one should be abandoned is not a fairy-hermit who lives a carefree life on morning dew and pine nuts."[11] Concerning practice, in 1986 I visited a large and flourishing Taoist temple in Hong Kong that is actively involved in various social projects, for example, homes for the aged, schools, and other educational projects.

I mentioned earlier the two separate world organizations founded early in the twentieth century: the movement for Faith and Order that focused on the issues of belief and church order or structure that divided the churches, and the movement for Life and Work that helped the divided Christian churches to collaborate on matters of everyday living and work. Because it became so obvious that thought and action are intimately interrelated, the two organizations integrated and formed the World Council of Churches. Perhaps something similar for all the religions of the world lies in the not-too-distant future; already there is a World Conference on Religion and Peace. One of its meetings was in Beijing, in June, 1986.

Attention should also be given here to the effort of scholars such as Knitter who would almost seem to make the praxis of the "preferential option for the poor and the nonperson" of liberation theology the only authentic entry into interreligious dialogue.[12] As the earlier Christian ecumenical movements (for example, "Life and Work" *and* "Faith and Order") bear out, "liberation praxis" surely is an authentic way to enter the dialogue, but there are *de facto* also other ways to enter the dialogue—for example, the cognitive, spiritual, and esthetic. However, as insisted from the beginning, the dialogist must then *live* according to her or his new knowledge, and, since full human life is both individual and communal, the new insights flowing from the dialogue must be reflected on both levels.

Knitter, however, wants to make the social-justice praxis dimension of interreligious specific, namely, as mentioned, the "preferential option for the poor and the nonperson." At times I feel slightly uneasy about a possible zealotry in this urging. To be sure, structures of dominance must be unmasked and dismantled wherever they are to be found, and that demands a

---

11. Tang Yi, "Taoism as a Living Philosophy," 410, 412–13.

12. Paul F. Knitter, "Toward a Liberation Theology of Religions," in Hick and Knitter, *Myth of Christian Uniqueness*, 178–200.

constant searching within and without. But, at the same time, it is important to be aware that it is not possible for the "haves" in a material sense to eliminate the material poverty of the "have-nots" simply by "external" changes, such as modifying the social structures, or heavier taxes, or lowering their own material standard of living. Some or all of these may be necessary, but they are not sufficient.

It is not mainly in the direction of "giving up things" on the part of the "haves" that the "poor and nonpersons" will be liberated but, rather, in the direction of doing more, both qualitatively and quantitatively. We have learned in the last two centuries that material wealth is not limited, static; it is essentially linked with "spiritual wealth," with mental creativity, which is dynamic, unending. It is essentially, though not only, this spiritual wealth that needs to be expanded, shared; material wealth will then follow. This lesson was learned the hard way by such formerly Marxist countries as Hungary: "Our existing socialism had to realise that *structural changes either in the economy or in the very society itself do not involve automatic changes in the mentality* of the people."[13]

I would like to suggest that the "other" toward whom our "altruistic" ethical action should reach might be named simply the oppressed, the unfree in any dimension—and who is completely free? Logic, of course, also directs that those in greatest need should receive the greatest attention, but it likewise directs that each should contribute according to her or his gifts, and in a preeminent, though not exclusive, way to those before them *now* in need, whether that need be material, spiritual, social, esthetic, or whatever: producing good material things for both the well-to-do and the poor, teaching both the poor and the well-to-do, making democracy work better for both the well-to-do and the poor. Allowing (out of three hundred million Americans) forty million to be "poor" must be eradicated, but at the same time the various spiritual poverties of the 260,000,000 "well-to-do" must likewise be diminished. This "preferential option for the unfree" in no way rules out the "preferential option for the poor." Rather, it includes it—in eminent fashion—but expands it.

It seems to me that the question of timing is also all-important. Both Christianity (as well as other religions) and Marxism have in practice far too often sacrificed the present generation to the past and the future. Because of its age, Christianity has been much more guilty than Marxism of sacrificing the present to the past (tradition!), but both are equally guilty of sacrificing the present to the future: Christians have often been taught to accept their

---

13. Laszlo Lukacs, "Changing Forms of Religiosity in a Changing Society," unpublished paper prepared for a Christian-Marxist dialogue between Americans and Hungarians in Budapest, held in June, 1988.

lot as God's will, not to try to change the social structure of things but to look forward to a future "heavenly" reward (popularly expressed: pie in the sky, bye and bye). Populations in Marxist countries were often told that they ought not try to change the economic order of things but to give up "consumer goods" so future generations could benefit from their development of "heavy industry" (leading to their subsequent economic mess wherein neither consumer goods nor heavy industry were adequately developed, which resulted in either their collapse, as in the Soviet system, or their utter abandonment of economic Marxism, as in China).

Here again, Marxist Hungary years ago learned this lesson the hard way (but it learned it!): "What is more, individual persons are not only citizens to be governed, but also autonomous living beings with specific needs and rights. Their basic needs and rights cannot be neglected for a long period without considerable damage even to society, and in consequence to the state . . . The socialist system in Hungary aimed to achieve social justice . . . But in the recent past the fact had to be faced and acknowledged that a *new type of poverty* emerged: . . . *in the financial sense* . . . *in a moral and human sense*."[14] Each person, each society must find the delicate balance whereby the past is properly appreciated and revered, the future responsibly cared for, and the present lived as fully and intensely as possible, *now*.

Perhaps another way to express the needed integration of the several essential elements of the Christian commitment to "practical interreligious, interideological dialogue" can be found in the Enlightenment and the American and French Revolutions. Surprising as it may be to many Christians, the slogan of the French Revolution really encapsulates the essence of the fundamental Good News of Jesus: *Liberté, fraternité, égalité*. The essence of the love of neighbor is freely (*liberté*) to treat *all* men and women as brothers and sisters (*fraternité*—today we would eliminate the sexist language and probably say *solidarité*), especially the powerless of society (*égalité*).

The conclusion is that interreligious, interideological action that does not eventuate in dialogue will grow mindless, ineffective. Interreligious, interideological dialogue that does not eventuate in action will grow hypocritical, ineffective. Neither can survive singly.

Depth or "Spiritual" Dialogue

In depth or "spiritual" dialogue we experience the partner's religion or ideology "from within." Raimundo Panikkar spoke of this when he said, "Religious dialogue must be genuinely *religious*, not merely an exchange of

14. Ibid.

doctrines or intellectual opinions... Dialogue must proceed from the depths of my religious attitude to these same depths in my partner."[15] He says of himself, "I 'left' as a Christian; I 'found' myself a Hindu; and I 'returned' as a Buddhist, without having ceased to be a Christian."[16] Such double or multiple "belonging" may not be possible for most religious persons, for most religious thinkers, or those ideologically committed, but some experience of another's religion or ideology "from within" is possible at least to some extent for all of us. John Dunne's "passing over" is one very effective means for doing so: "Passing over is a shifting of standpoint, a going over to the standpoint of another culture, another way of life, another religion. It is followed by an equal and opposite process we might call 'coming back,' coming back with new insight to one's own culture, one's own way of life, one's own religion."[17]

Here, imagination plays a key role. After entering into the feelings of my partner and permitting the new symbols and stories to stimulate images in my own mind, I must allow these images to live and develop, leading me where they will, so that eventually I will return to my own tradition greatly enriched. In Dunne's words: "The technique of passing over is based on *the process of eliciting images* from one's feelings, attaining insights into the images, and then turning insight into a guide of life. What one does in passing over is to try to enter sympathetically into the feelings of another person, become receptive to the *images* which give expression to his feelings, attain insight into those images, and then come back enriched by this insight to an understanding of one's own life which can guide one into the future."[18]

Knitter noted that, although passing over is mainly the work of the imagination, it also requires hard intellectual homework, confirming that while one never attains a final answer, one can come to more answers, real answers. "The imagination is persistently excited; new insights are born; the horizon of knowledge expands. Interreligious dialogue, like all life, is seen not as a nervous pursuit of certainty but a freeing, exciting pursuit of

---

15. Panikkar, *Intrareligious Dialogue*, 50.

16. Raimundo Panikkar, "Faith and Belief: A Multireligious Experience," *Anglican Theological Review* 53 (1971) 220.

17. Dunne, *The Way of All the Earth*, ix. Another creative approach might be by way of Ira Progoff's "process meditation." See his *The Practice of Process Meditation* (New York: Dialogue House Library, 1980).

18. Dunne, *The Way of All the Earth*, 53. For further use of the technique of "passing over" by John Dunne, see his *A Search for God in Time and Memory* (Notre Dame: University of Notre Dame Press, 1977); and *The City of the Gods* (Notre Dame: University of Notre Dame Press, 1978).

understanding."[19] He also pointed out that David Tracy's *The Analogical Imagination* "might be read as a hand book of guidelines on the nature of dialogue with other traditions and the pivotal role of the imagination in such dialogue."[20] Tracy confirmed "the possibilities of approaching the conversation among the religious traditions through the use of an analogical imagination . . . If I have already lived by an analogical imagination within my own religious and cultural heritages, I am much more likely to welcome the demand for further conversation."[21]

A Universal Systematic Reflection (Theology) of Religion-Ideology

But, what of the cognitive area, where perhaps the greatest challenge to interreligious, interideological dialogue lies? How can we proceed beyond mutually informative lectures? Perhaps the question can be phrased as follows: In reflection upon my own belief—in "theologizing," to use Christian terminology—how can I speak so that, on the one hand, I maintain my own religious, ideological integrity and, on the other, allow my dialogue partner to understand and recognize herself or himself in my language? How can I as a Christian speak about the central insights of my faith in such a way that the Jew or the Marxist will be able to say, "Yes, that sounds like familiar territory. I feel somehow included in those concepts and words, although I might not use precisely them in reflecting or 'theologizing' on my own tradition"?

Panikkar noted, "This seems to be a major challenge in our times; lacking an authentic Philosophy of Religion we shall be able to understand neither the different world religions nor the people and the cultures of this earth, for religion is the soul of a culture."[22] He went on to say that "a genuine Philosophy of Religion in our times . . . has to be critically aware that no single individual nor any single religious tradition has access to the universal range of the human experience. It must then pull together the findings, experiences and data coming from the four directions of the earth: It has to be dialogical and like a net encompass the different religious experiences of [hu]mankind."[23]

---

19. Knitter, *No Other Name?*, 215.
20. Ibid., 216.
21. David Tracy, *The Analogical Imagination* (New York: Crossroad, 1981) 451.
22. Panikkar, *Intrareligious Dialogue*, 67.
23. Ibid., 69.

To put the problem concisely, we who are convinced of the advantage and even the necessity of interreligious, interideological dialogue must work together to forge a *"universal systematic reflection (theology) of religion-ideology."* Of course, whenever we put a name on a project with such a comprehensive scope, serious difficulties arise. There is no way that we can speak of anything—can name things—except within a particular cultural framework, no matter how broad it may be. Regardless of how expansive a cultural framework is, it is still particular and it automatically differs from all other particular cultural frameworks; the writer must justify choosing that cultural framework rather than another. Actually, the choice of *this* particular cultural framework is not essential. What is essential is simply the choice of *some* particular cultural framework. In these reflections I have chosen the cultural framework with which I am most familiar with, the one in which I can speak most clearly and precisely.

"Theology" here simply means a systematic, reasoned reflection upon the convictions—religious or ideological—held by one or more persons. The term "philosophy" is inadequate here, for it often deliberately excludes sources of wisdom in a tradition outside of ratiocination. Though "theology" is largely a Christian term—invented, however, by the pre-Christian Greeks—it has the advantage of including both reasoning and the other wisdom sources in a tradition: "sacred" books, for example—whether the Bible, the Qur'an, the Vedas, or *Das Kapital*. So, despite its theistic and Christian particularity, and until a better term is found or forged, I shall utilize the shorthand "theology" to refer to the systematic reasoned reflections on the religious and ideological convictions held by human communities.

Although Panikkar in one place speaks of a Philosophy,[24] in another he thinks better of the term: "in the philosophy, or rather the theology, of religion."[25] Hick also wrote of "The Philosophy of World Religions"[26] but likewise wrote elsewhere that "the possibility opens up of what might be called (for want of a better term) a global theology."[27] Wilfred Cantwell Smith unabashedly titled his last book *Towards a World Theology*, commenting: "The fact that this term comes primarily from a Christian background, and that we have no word, either in Western language or in oriental, for the

---

24. Ibid., 65–66.

25. Panikkar, *Unknown Christ*, 66–67.

26. John Hick, "The Philosophy of World Religion," *Scottish Journal of Theology* 37/2 (1984) 229–36.

27. Hick, *God Has Many Names*, 23. See also a more recent book on the subject: Leonard Swidler, ed., *Toward a Universal Theology of Religion* (Maryknoll, NY: Orbis, 1987).

new concept that is being born, constitutes a problem—and illustrates our challenges."[28]

A universal theology of *religion-ideology* is a phrase meant to indicate all the insights of a faith or ideology that attempt to explain the "meaning of life and how to live accordingly"—whether that includes the notion of "*Theos*" or not. What makes it *universal* is that the categories of reflection are such that they can be understood and embraced by people of all religions or ideologies, not just one, or even a particular group such as the Abrahamic religions or theistic religions. This universal theology of religion-ideology has been said to have a basis in one Ultimate Reality to which all humans in their various religions respond—a principle expounded, for example, by the Sufi Muslim Frithjoh Schuon.

But such a position is merely stipulative and is not demonstrated or agreed to by all of the religions and ideologies in the world. Rather, it is our human condition and situation that we all share that provides the common ground for a universal theology of religion-ideology:

> The ontological explanation of the agreement [between the different religions in the world], i.e., an explanation on the assumption that the different religions are responses to one divine reality, is not tenable, since it is question-begging. It is necessary to establish that the reality is divine and that there is one divine reality. It is only on the basis of the belief in a common religious situation that we can legitimately talk of a common religious discourse and of the possibility of a philosophy of religion that presupposes a common religious discourse.[29]

If that is the task, the way forward, I believe, is for the thinkers in each religious and ideological tradition to attempt to express their reflections, or theologizing, in categories, terms, and images that others not only can understand but also in which they will feel included.

The task may seem impossible. How can Christians, for example, speak of the insights into the meaning of human life they have received from the Christian tradition in any categories, terms, or images other than Christian ones? Yet, it seems to me that sometimes Christians already do something of that sort. Christians very often speak a language that is extremely familiar to Jews. As Jesus was not a Christian but a Jew, and all his first followers were Jews (and Samaritans—see Jn. 4:41), and as the majority of Christian liturgical prayers come from the Hebrew Bible, such a fact is not surprising.

---

28. Wilfred Cantwell Smith, *Toward a World Theology* (Philadelphia: Westminster, 1981) 129.

29. Sengupta, "Misunderstanding of Hinduism," 107.

The fact that Mohammed also looked upon the Hebrew Bible and the New Testament as sacred books means that much of Christian language will likewise be familiar to Muslims, as well. Christians, then, might try to do some of their reflecting using only a vocabulary that is familiar to the other two Abrahamic religions. This is precisely the sort of thing that can reasonably be attempted within the framework of a Trialogue.[30]

However, modern critical thinkers immediately see a problem even in such a relatively limited step toward "a universal theology of religion-ideology." Much of the language of the Jewish and Christian traditions no longer finds a clear resonance among many Jews and Christians who have been bred in the atmosphere of modern critical thought. (Of course, modern critical thinkers are not automatically somehow less religious or committed than "pre-critical" thinkers. Moses, Jesus, and Mohammed were, after all, extremely "critical" thinkers in the religious sphere in their time; in fact, it was their "critical" thinking that made them the fountainheads of new religious streams.) Such critical thinkers demand language that will effectively communicate the authentic insights of the religious tradition in ways that will find true resonance in understanding and life.

"Ecumenical Esperanto"

It is precisely this challenge from within the Western Jewish and Christian traditions, this demand for a language and a way of understanding ancient religious insights in terms of modern thought, that can point to us the way forward as we try to forge a "universal theology of religion-ideology." We must build our theological language, terms, categories and images on our common humanity, which we all—the traditional Jew, Christian, Muslim, the modern critical thinker, Hindu, Buddhist, Marxist—share in common. To the extent that we can formulate our religious, ideological insights in such humanity-based language, we will be building a "universal theology of religion-ideology."

In other words, we must attempt to cast our religious and ideological insights in language "from below," from our humanity, rather than "from above," from the perspective of the transcendent, the divine. To use a different image, we must attempt to develop a theological language that is "from

---

30. See Leonard Swidler, Reuven Firestone, and Khalid Duran, *Trialogue: Jews, Christians, and Muslims in Dialogue* (New London, CT: Twenty-Third, 2007); and a history, starting in 1978, of the International Scholars Abrahamic Trialogue (ISAT)—Leonard Swidler, "Trialogue: Out of the Shadows into Blazing 'Desert' Sun!" *Journal of Ecumenical Studies* 45 (Summer 2010) 493–509.

within," not "from without." We must try to speak a language of immanence, not of transcendence. This is not to say that religious persons should no longer speak of, let alone believe in, the transcendent, but that this particular task of forging a universal theology of religion-ideology demands that we speak of the transcendent in immanent terms, imagery, and categories. This new theological language "from below," "from within," might helpfully be called a theological-ideological "Esperanto," for, like Esperanto, it is intended as an intercultural language that borrows from various living languages but is so simplified, so "reasonable," so "generally human," that anybody with the knowledge of one's native tongue and a slight smattering of others will easily be able to master it.

Until quite recently it was largely thought that transcendent meant "supernatural," something other than and entirely outside of our day-to-day and scientific experience. Now we increasingly recognize that the transcendent is imbedded in our everyday and scientific experience and language. We simply need to become aware of it and develop thought categories and a language to reflect on and speak of it with more penetration, precision, and purpose. Fundamentally, the transcendent or "religious" dimension appears when we come up against "limit" situations such as the death of a loved one or something as simple as the appearance of our first gray hairs, leading to an existential awareness of our own personal finitude or "limit"; we are led to recognize our own "limit" or "grounding" understanding, such as the value of existence, the trustworthiness of our senses and intellect.

In everyday life and in modern science human beings are constantly engaged in—or at least attempting—acts of self-transcendence, of going beyond their present status, whether by learning more, acting more efficiently, or behaving more ethically. Ultimately, every human, every scientist, is ineluctably led to ask what the conditions and the ground are that make possible this unending process of self-transcendence. They are led to "reflect upon each level of self-transcending inquiry to understand what horizon or dimension it presupposes . . . [The scientist] can also ask such limit-questions as . . . Can these answers work if the world is not intelligible? Can the world be intelligible if it does not have an intelligent ground? . . . The question can be described as a religious-as-limit question."[31]

What is especially important to note here is that this transcendent dimension is not something alien to our everyday human experience and language but is imbedded in it or, conversely, is the bed within which all else lies and is spoken of. It is this fact that we must become increasingly conscious of and articulate about, not only to understand ourselves ever

---

31. David Tracy, *Blessed Rage for Order* (New York: Seabury, 1979) 98.

more profoundly, but also to understand others ever more fully. The basis of this knowledge of self and others is our common humanity, which is imbedded in this transcendence—hence, the pressing need for developing a humanity-based "language" that will articulate the transcendent in terms of immanence, an "Ecumenical Esperanto."

There is of course much in the past heritage of the various great traditions of thought both East and West that contribute to the development of an "Ecumenical (universal) Esperanto." A further step forward toward its development was taken in the European Enlightenment of the eighteenth and nineteenth centuries, with its stress on our common human reason and the cosmopolitan citizen. Its universality was fed by Europe's contact with the rest of the world as it both received from and imparted information and impulses abroad. The ideas of the Enlightenment, at first somewhat naive, were then chastened, sifted and deepened in the later nineteenth and twentieth centuries by the critiques from such movements as historicism, hermeneutics of suspicion, and cross-cultural analysis. It is this ever-widening, penetrating, worldwide, dialogic Enlightenment that made possible today's development of an "Ecumenical Esperanto." The social sciences—psychology, sociology, anthropology—founded and expanded in the past hundred years, help to provide the thought categories and vocabulary of a language that is "humanity-based," "from below," "from within," "immanent." Before their development it would have been almost impossible even to conceive the possibility of such an "Ecumenical Esperanto," but it is now possible.

An "Ecumenical Esperanto" cannot consist solely of a rational verbal vocabulary: it must include symbols, aesthetic expressions, actions. Of course, a completely culture-free vocabulary can never be devised, but, if the structuralists among the anthropologists and the Jungians among the psychologists are not completely mistaken, there are certain elements in humanity that are pervasive and perennial. It is upon these that an "Ecumenical Esperanto Symbolics" will have to be built.

At the same time it should be remembered that Esperanto itself was developed to facilitate communication on a broad international, intercultural level. It was never intended to replace all or even any of the world's living languages but to function merely as an international supplementary language. As such, however, it could be of immense value.

David Lochhead has also pled for both recognition of the uniqueness of each religious tradition—just as each language—and the need to become "bilingual." Applying Wittgenstein's notion of "language games," he wrote that we might "think of the different religious traditions as distinct language games . . . ultimately not reducible to the language of the others . . . then dialogue is more like the process by which one becomes bilingual."[32]

A word of caution here: "All analogies limp," *Omnis analogia claudet*. Analogies can be helpful devices to assist us to grasp new ideas by likening them to things known. Basically analogies say that the unknown, A, is *like* the known, B. The operative word is *like*, that is, A is the same as B in *some* ways, but different in others. Hence, if analogies are to be helps rather than hindrances, they must be followed *only insofar* as they point to commonalities, and not to differences, not to the point where they begin "to limp." To "push an analogy too far" is simply to misunderstand the speaker and (deliberately?) distort her or his intention. All this should be borne in mind when speaking of Ecumenical Esperanto, for it is clearly an analogy.

It is at this point, I believe, and hope, that the analogy of Ecumenical Esperanto breaks down. The language Esperanto has not, in fact, been a success. Perhaps only twenty million people throughout the world know Esperanto; hence, it can hardly fulfill its stated function. Further, it is based only on an Indo-European language culture. The Ecumenical (universal) Esperanto of a universal theology of religion-ideology must gain adherents beyond the relatively small coterie of theological-ideological thinkers in various contemporary traditions. If it does not do so, it will suffer the same fate as Esperanto has in the linguistic world. We must learn from history.

Of course, a vision of an ultimately all-comprehensive, and therefore unchanging, single humanity-based "language" would be illusory. Because all knowledge is interpreted knowledge, perceived from a particular perspective, every knower knows reality somewhat differently from everyone else. Yet, the very recognition that we come to know reality differently from others presumes a certain commonness which we share only partially. It is precisely that commonness of human experience that provides the basis for each of our several cultural languages, for example, English, German, Catalan, etc. Because of a variety of particular historical, geographical, and other reasons, our sharing of the commonness of human experience is limited such that the various cultural languages result. However, despite the unending variety of human languages—reflecting of course the variety of human knowledge of reality—there is at the same time the commonness of their all being precisely human languages. Thus, there will always be variety in the human perception and expression of reality, but there will also be the commonness of the (varying, perspectival, etc.) *human perception and expression* of reality.

---

32. David Lochhead, *The Dialogical Imperative* (Maryknoll, NY: Orbis, 1988) 68–69.

Although there is no one, all-comprehensive, undifferentiated, unchanging English language, there is nevertheless a sufficient commonness to allow us to speak of the variations of the English language and, what is more important, to communicate through it. So, too, with our Ecumenical Esperanto and universal theology of religion: Epistemologically, as well as linguistically, there will always be both an ultimate pluralism *and simultaneous* commonness sufficient for humans to see that they perceive reality in various ways. For this reason, Ecumenical Esperanto and the ecumenical consciousness that it expresses and molds are like the universal theology of religion, never-ending, never-end*able*, projects, which draw us as human beings ever forward to seek and understand reality, even if in unendingly differing ways.[33]

We probably can find a little more help in the analogy of learning a foreign language when speaking about developing a "universal theology of religion-ideology." One of the first things to do in approaching a new language is to learn to "hear," to discern the new sounds, or those sounds that at least seem new to us. This usually becomes more difficult as we grow older and more accustomed to and steeped in the sounds of our own language, or, to use our analogy, accustomed to and steeped in our own particular religious or ideological language with its own categories, terms, images, and stories. An additional problem is that all our religious traditions have grown up and developed in an era that tended to speak from above, from without, from the perspective of the transcendent, of God. Now we must attune our theological, our religious ears to hearing the same message in the new and alien sounds of that other language that is so strange to our traditions—that Ecumenical Esperanto, from below, from within, of immanence rather than transcendence, or, perhaps better, *transcendence within immanence*. However, such ideologies as Marxism, for example, may have greater difficulty discovering the depth or spiritual dimension.

We all in fact have before us not only the gigantic task of developing a new language, an Ecumenical Esperanto, but also at the same time the even more challenging task of forging a "new consciousness" capable of hearing and understanding this new Ecumenical Esperanto. Clearly this task is not one that can be performed in two sequential steps, one after the other.

---

33. See Knitter, "Toward a Liberation Theology," especially where he wrestles with Panikkar's more recent rejection of a common religious language or "common ground" of religions (see Raimundo Panikkar, "A Universal Theory of Religion or a Cosmic Confidence in Reality?" in Swidler, ed., *Toward a Universal Theology of Religion*, and that of some other Western scholars. Knitter rightly notes that all these scholars, in an apparent self-contradiction, nevertheless proceed to strive to talk in what they presume to be a commonly understood language—otherwise, why talk?

Rather, it must be carried out in dialectical fashion, with a constant dialogue between the forming of the new language, the Ecumenical Esperanto, and the new consciousness, the "ecumenical consciousness." However, what could be more fitting as a method of carrying out the task of providing a "theology" for worldwide interreligious, interideological dialogue?[34]

Because interreligious interideological dialogue is always necessarily a two-sided project—within each religious or ideological community as well as between religious and ideological communities—one further step is necessary. Just as each participant in an interreligious, interideological conversation must enter into dialogue not only with her or his partner across the faith-ideology line, but also with her or his coreligionists, co-ideologists, to share with them the fruits of the dialogue, so, too, in making use of Ecumenical Esperanto and forging a new ecumenical consciousness to hear and understand that new universal theology of religion-ideology, it is necessary all along the way to make the connections between the newly formed Ecumenical Esperanto and each of the traditional religious languages: When we say "X" in Ecumenical Esperanto, that corresponds to "A" in Christianity, "B" in Judaism, "C" in Marxism, etc., and then we can begin to talk to and understand each other through the "translation" of our traditional languages into Ecumenical Esperanto. Panikkar pointed in the same direction when he said, "We need a common symbolics not only to check the translation and establish two-way communication, but also even to make the translation."[35]

At the same time, we must note that, just as in the linguistic area, no translation is precisely the same as the original. Although "X" may be essentially and fundamentally the same as "A," "B," or "C," no two will be precisely the same. This, of course, is not to be deplored but greatly appreciated. All

---

34. The same notion of the contemporary need of a new consciousness in both intra- and interreligious, interideological dialogue was expressed by Ewert Cousins when speaking of Raimundo Panikkar as a pioneer in its formation: "When Christian consciousness opens to global consciousness, a new type of systematic theology can be born. This new theology calls for a new kind of theologian with a new type of consciousness—a multi-dimensional, cross-cultural consciousness characteristic of mutational man. I believe that Raimundo Panikkar is such a new theologian and that he has already begun to develop such a Christian systematic theology" (Ewert Cousins, "Raimundo Panikkar and the Christian Systematic Theology of the Future," *Cross Currents* 29 [Summer 1979] 146.

35. Panikkar, *Intrareligious Dialogue*, 67. Comparative philosopher Henry Rosemont made the same point: "We must begin to develop a common language to take the place alongside the other languages of the world . . . My thrust here is similar to that of Alisdair MacIntyre in his recent *After Virtue* (South Bend, IN: Notre Dame University Press, 1981) ("Against Relativism," an unpublished manuscript for a lecture delivered at Temple University, and elsewhere, Spring, 1985).

life is complicated and human life most of all. To express and understand all its complexities, a person would have to be as comprehensive as all humanity: past, future, and potential. Add to this the infinite complexity of the transcendent related to all this actual and possible humanity, and it is clear that only a fully "divine" person could utter such an all-comprehending notion—or even understand it. Obviously this we cannot do—hence, the absolute necessity of our attempting to gain an ever fuller insight into the meaning of human life by a dialogue with an ever fuller set of expressions of that meaning. In other words: Variety, yes, even to infinity, but with an access to that variety by way of an adequate simplicity that will facilitate and not obfuscate understanding.

Ecumenical Esperanto should not be thought of as some sort of pale, reductionist, least-common-denominator kind of theological expression. It must not be more superficial than our present particular theologies but, rather, more profound, going even more deeply into our psyches, individual and communal. Ecumenical Esperanto must not be a superficial Enlightenment rationality warmed up again. No, it must go far beyond that and also include all the intellectual advances made in our understanding of knowledge in history, sociology of knowledge, limitations of language, hermeneutics, plus ideology critique, praxis dialectics, and paradigm shift. Of course all these new insights from Western culture point up the fact that they themselves are necessarily culture-bound. To be truly "humanity"-based, the religious-ideological thinker must incorporate all insights into what it means to be human, including those from outside Western culture. The "we" implicit in the terms "from below" and "from within" must be as broad a "we" as possible, in fact an *ever increasingly* broad "we." This can be accomplished only by moving beyond—without abandoning—Western culture, beyond Judaism, Christianity, Western humanism, and Marxism, to absorb the insights of Islam, Hinduism, Buddhism, etc. This can be done only by hard study of, "passing over" into the inner heart of, patient and profound dialogue with, other religions, ideologies, and cultures.

To introduce a practical note: If anything like this is to be realized, religiously committed persons must not only study their own tradition deeply but must also seek teachers in other traditions who are not only trained in but also stand in those traditions so that they might learn that tradition "from within."

If one understands the term "ecumenism" to include dialogue with all religions and ideologies, one finds strong support for this recommendation in both the documents of Vatican II and subsequent Vatican documents:

We *must* become familiar with the outlook of our separated brethren. Study is *absolutely* required for this, and it should be pursued in fidelity to the truth and with a spirit of good will. Catholics . . . need to acquire a more adequate understanding of the respective doctrines of our separated brethren, their history, their spiritual and liturgical life, their religious psychology and cultural background. Most valuable for this purpose are meetings of the two sides—especially for discussion of theological problems—where each can treat with the other on an equal footing (*par cum pari*).[36]

The "Directory Concerning Ecumenical Matters," issued by the Secretariat for Christian Unity of the Vatican in 1970, made the point more concretely: "All Christians should be of an ecumenical mind . . . hence, the principles of ecumenism sanctioned by the Second Vatican Council should be appropriately introduced in all institutions of advanced learning . . . Bishops . . . religious superiors and those in authority in seminaries, universities and similar institutions should take pains to promote the ecumenical movement and *spare no effort* to see that their teachers keep in touch with advances in ecumenical thought and action.[37] Surely, these reflections are valid not only for Christians, but for all religious and ideological communities.

In the area of Christian missiology a similar point is made by Knitter, who argued that, in order to "promote the Kingdom," Christians of course must witness to Jesus. "All peoples, all religions, must know of him in order to grasp the full content of God's presence in history. Here is part of the purpose and the motivation for going forth to the ends of the earth." However, in the new ecclesiology and model for truth, "one admits also that all peoples should know of Buddha, of Muhammed, of Krishna"—one might also add Socrates, Marx, etc. "This, too, is part of the goal and inspiration for missionary work: to be witnessed to, in order that Christians might deepen and expand their own grasp of God's presence and purpose in the world. Through this mutual witnessing, this mutual growth, the work of realizing the Kingdom moves on."[38]

---

36. Vatican II, *Decree on Ecumenism*, no. 9; emphasis added.

37. *Spiritus domini*, 1970, nos. 64 and 79, quoted in full in Flannery, *Vatican Council II*, 515, 526.

38. Knitter, *No Other Name?*, 222.

Purposes and Problems of Interreligious, Interideological Dialogue

A number of things have already been said about the purposes of interreligious, interideological dialogue: Participants are to learn so as to grow, to know the other, to discern and appropriate values, to encounter new dimensions of reality, to witness and be witnessed to, etc. Nevertheless, it would be helpful at this point to try to summarize systematically what the goals of interreligious, interideological dialogue are, and are not.

First, a distinction must be made between "intra" dialogues (within a religion) on the one hand and "inter" dialogues (between religions) on the other. The goal of the former is some kind of overarching, "organic," yet pluralistic, unity. The goal of interreligious, interideological dialogue, however, can be said to be made up of a continuing search for (1) self-knowledge, (2) an authentic understanding of the other, and (3) a way of life consonant with these.

Self-knowledge

We come to know ourselves largely by contrast, by encountering the other. To be concrete, I discovered dimensions of my American cultural heritage as a result of living in Europe for several years, and, somewhat later, I recognized new elements of my Western cultural heritage by living in the Orient. Through dialogue we bring to consciousness our own inner selves with all of their consistencies and contradictions, their admirable and abhorrent aspects. Our dialogue partners will serve as mirrors for us, showing us our true selves. Such a prize alone is worth the price of frustration in dialogue.

Authentic Understanding of the Other

We come to know our partners not simply as objects over against ourselves, but—whether as an individual or a group—in dialogic fashion, in relationship to ourselves. While we deepen our knowledge of what we hold in common—which, as we know already from experience, will be almost immeasurably more, and deeper, than we had previously even imagined was possible, we also learn to know our true differences (obviously, we are not all essentially the same; if we were, there would be no dialogue, only monologue—the death of all human intercourse). These differences may be complementary, as, for example, a stress on the prophetic rather than the mystical; analogous, as, for example, the notion of God in the Semitic religions and of *Sunyata* in Theravada Buddhism; or contradictory, where the acceptance of one entails the rejection of the other, as, for example, the Judeo-Christian notion of the inviolable dignity of each individual person and the now largely disappeared Hindu custom of *suttee,* widow-burning.

Complementary authentic differences will indeed be true differences, but not such that only one could be valid. Furthermore, our experience tells us that the complementary differences will usually far outnumber the contradictory. Likewise, learning of these authentic but complementary differences will not only enhance one's knowledge but also may very well lead to the desire to adapt one or more of the partner's complementary differences for oneself. For, as the very term indicates, the differences somehow complete each other, as the Chinese Taoist saying puts it: "*Xiang fan xiang sheng*" (contraries complete each other).[39]

Just as we must always be extremely cautious about "placing" our differences, lest in acting precipitously we misplace them, so, too, we must not too easily and quickly place our true differences in the contradictory category. For example, perhaps Hindu *moksha,* Zen Buddhist *satori,* Christian "freedom of the children of God," and Marxist "communist state" could be understood as different, but nevertheless analogous, descriptions of true human liberation. In speaking here of true but analogous differences in belief or values, we are no longer talking about discerning teachings or practices in our partner's tradition that we might then wish to appropriate for our own tradition. Indeed, that does, and should, happen, but then we are speaking of something that the two traditions ultimately hold in common and has perhaps been atrophied or suppressed in one—something that is an authentic but complementary difference.

However, if it is perceived as analogous rather than contradictory, it will be seen to operate within the total organic structure of the other religion-ideology and to fulfill its function properly only within it. It could not have the same function, that is, relationship to the other parts, in our total organic structure and, hence, would not be understood to be in direct opposition, in contradiction to the "differing" element within our structure. At the same time, it needs to be remembered that these real but analogous differences in belief or values should be seen not as in conflict with one another but as parallel in function and, in that sense, analogous.

Still, at times we can find contradictory truth-claims or value-claims presented by different religious-ideological traditions. That happens only when they cannot be seen as somehow ultimately different expressions of the same thing (a commonality) or as complementary or analogous. But,

---

39. Cited in Tang Yi, "Taoism as a Living Philosophy," 410.

when it happens, even though it be relatively rare, a profound and unavoidable problem faces the two communities: What should be their attitude and behavior toward each other? Should they remain in dialogue, tolerate each other, ignore each other, or oppose each other? The problem is especially pressing in matters of value judgments. For example, what should the Christian (or Jew, Muslim, Marxist) have done in face of the now largely suppressed Hindu tradition of widow burning (*suttee*)? Try to learn its value, tolerate it, ignore it, oppose it (in what manner?). Or, the Nazi ideology's tenet of killing all Jews? These are relatively clear issues, but what of a religion-ideology that approves slavery, as Christianity, Judaism, and Islam did until a century and a half ago? Perhaps that is clear enough today, but what, for example, of clitorectomy, or of sexism—or only a little sexism? Or, the claim that only through capitalism—or socialism—human liberation can be gained? Deciding on the proper stance becomes less and less clear-cut.

It was eventually clear to most non-Hindus in the nineteenth century that the proper attitude was not dialogue with Hinduism on *suttee* but opposition, but apparently it was not so clear to all non-Nazis that opposition to Jewish genocide was the right stance to take. Further, it took Christians eighteen hundred years to come to that conclusion concerning slavery. Many religions and ideologies today stand in the midst of a battle over sexism, some even refusing to admit the existence of the issue. Finally, no argument need be made to point out the controversial nature of the contemporary capitalism-socialism issue.

Clearly, important contradictory differences between religions-ideologies do exist and at times warrant not dialogue but opposition. We also make critical judgments on the acceptability of positions within our own traditions—such as Christians' burning heretics, or Muslims' stoning sexual offenders—and, rather frequently, within our personal lives. Surely, this exercise of our critical faculties is not to be limited to ourselves and our tradition; this perhaps most human of faculties should be made available to all—with all the proper constraints and concerns for dialogue already detailed at length. It must first be determined on what grounds we can judge whether a religious-ideological difference is in fact contradictory and, if it is, whether it is of sufficient importance and a nature to warrant active opposition.

Since all religions and ideologies are attempts to explain the meaning of human life and how to live accordingly, it would seem that those doctrines and customs that are perceived as hostile to human life are not complementary or analogous but contradictory, and that opposition should be proportional to the extent they threaten life. What is to be included in an authentically full human life must then be the measure against which all elements of all religions-ideologies are to be tested as we make judgments about whether they are in harmony, complementarity, analogy, or contradiction with that measure—and then act accordingly.

Because the human being is by nature a historical being, what it means to be fully human is evolving both in terms of basic capabilities and in terms of a growing recognition of what in fact exists. At basis, everything human flows from the essential human structure, that is, being an animal who can think abstractly and make free decisions. Only gradually has humanity come to the contemporary position where claims are made in favor of "human rights," that things are due to all humans specifically because they are human. This position has not been held always and everywhere. In fact, it was for the most part hardly conceived of until recently. Less than a century and a half ago, for example, slavery was still widely accepted and even vigorously defended and practiced by high Christian church leaders, not to speak of Jewish and Muslim slave traders. Yet, this radical violation of "human rights" has today been largely eliminated both in practice and law. No thinker or public leader would today contemplate justifying slavery, at least in its directly named form of the past (see the *Universal Declaration of Human Rights* by the U.N. in 1948, art. 4). Here is a glaringly obvious example of the historical evolution of the understanding of what it means to be fully human in terms of *recognition* of what was always the case, that is, that human beings are by nature radically free.

However, the human right to private property (*Universal Declaration* art. 17: "*Everyone* has the *right* to own property alone."), perhaps first publicly acknowledged in the West in seventeenth-century John Locke's phrase, "life, liberty and property," had been unthinkable until the requisite previous development of control over matter. The same is true of the twentieth-century claim to the right to work (*Universal Declaration* art. 23): "The development of this new control over nature—first over external nature and increasingly also over human nature . . . has made possible entirely new dimensions of human self-development, and its apparently illimitable expansion leads to the expectation, at least in the developed countries, that it can release a sufficient potential so that everyone can participate in them—and consequently has a right to participate therein."[40] Here are clear examples of the historical evolution of the understanding—if not always the practical realization—of what is means to be fully human in terms of the expansion of the basic *capabilities* of humanity.

---

40. Johannes Schwartländer, ed., *Modernes Freiheitsethos und christlicher Glaube* (Munich: Kaiser/Grüne-wald, 1981) 11.

What has been acknowledged fundamentally in the twentieth century as the foundation of being human is that human beings ought to be autonomous in their decisions—such decisions being directed by their own reason and limited only by the same rights of others: "All human beings are born free and equal in dignity and rights. They are endowed with reason and conscience and should act toward one another in a spirit of brotherhood" (*Universal Declaration* art. 1). This autonomy in the ethical sphere, which Thomas Aquinas recognized already in the thirteenth century,[41] expanded into the social, political spheres in the eighteenth century—well capsulated in the slogan of the French Revolution: Liberty, Equality, Fraternity (as noted earlier, contemporary consciousness of sexist language would lead to a substitute such as "Solidarity" for "Fraternity"). In the term "Liberty" would be understood all the personal and civil rights; in the term "Equality" is understood the political rights of participation in public decision-making; in the term "Solidarity" is understood (in an expanded twenty-first-century sense) the social rights.

The great religious communities of the world, though frequently resistant in the past, and too often still in the present, have likewise often and in a variety of ways expressed a growing awareness of and commitment to many of the same notions of what it means to be fully human. One such joint, global-level expression reflecting the thought and *engagement* of leaders of all the major world religions (over a thousand persons, including 219 full delegates) was issued by the World Conference on Religion and Peace at Kyoto, Japan, in October, 1970:

> As we sat down together facing the overriding issues of peace we discovered that the things which unite us are more important than the things which divide us. We found that we share:
>
> A conviction of the fundamental unity of the human family, and the equality and dignity of all human beings;
>
> A sense of the sacredness of the individual person and his conscience;
>
> A sense of the value of human community;

---

41. As already noted above on page 52: "All things are subject to divine providence, but rational creatures are so in a superior way. For they are under divine providence by participating in it, for they are called in some way to *be* divine providence for themselves and for others" ("Inter cetera autem rationalis creatura excellentiori quondam modo divinae providentiae subiacet, inquantum et ipsa fit providentiae particeps, sibi ipsi et aliis providens," *Summa Theologiae*, I–II, Q. 91, a. 2).

A realization that might is not right; that human power is not self-sufficient and absolute;

A belief that love, compassion, selflessness, and the force of inner truthfulness and of the spirit have ultimately greater power than hate, enmity, and self-interest;

A sense of obligation to stand on the side of the poor and the oppressed as against the rich and the oppressors;

A profound hope that good will finally prevail.[42]

Thus, through dialogue humanity is painfully, slowly creeping toward a consensus on what is involved in an authentically full human life. The 1948 U.N. Declaration of Human Rights was an important step in that direction. Of course, much more consensus needs to be attained if interreligious, interideological dialogue is to reach anything approaching its full potential.

In other words: Since humanity is open-ended in its development, not only is humanity oriented toward an ever-expanding consensus on what it means to be authentically human, but likewise the reality of human life is expanding in an unending fashion—ever transcending itself toward an always receding but ever beckoning Horizon of Being.

A Life Consonant with Points 1 and 2

Not much argumentation need be mounted about the third goal of interreligious, interideological dialogue: "to live ever more fully according" to the fuller grasp of truth obtained in the dialogue. As indicated in the very definition of dialogue, the whole point of the enterprise is "to learn, that is, to change and grow." The inner transformation of one's self-understanding and the consequent shift in one's way of life in self-transcendence is the final purpose of the dialogue—again, always remaining aware of the need to share the fruits of the dialogue with the other members of one's own religious or ideological community, so the whole can participate in the deepening and transforming of its self-understanding and way of life.

A number of growing fundamental problems remain, however. From the very definition of dialogue given above in rule one—that its primary purpose is for each participant to learn from the partner—it would seem clear that people must have an at least somewhat deabsolutized understanding of truth in order to engage in what is called dialogue. If they do not,

---

42. Homer A. Jack, ed., *Religion for Peace* (New Delhi: Gandhi Peace Foundation, 1973) ix.

they of course will have no motivation to enter into dialogue, other than to gain new information quantitatively, which would not significantly affect their understanding of reality.[43] If it in fact did begin significantly to affect their understanding of reality, that would mean that they had to that degree begun to "deabsolutize" their understanding of truth. In the beginning there doubtless would be an inability or unwillingness to admit this consciously, but the process would have begun and thereby would increasingly make genuine dialogue possible—and eventually even consciously necessary.

Some have accused the advocates of dialogue of being "elitist," of allowing only those who already share the same "liberal" epistemology into the exclusive club of dialogue. But, that is a strange sort of accusation,[44] for, as noted, until recently no one really wanted to enter into dialogue with someone who was religiously/ideologically different, that is, to talk with them primarily to learn from them. If we were convinced we had the truth, we simply wanted to converse with them to "convert" them, to persuade them to accept our position. But, the whole point of using the word "dialogue" in this context today is to name a *different* reality, namely, a conversation whose primary purpose is to learn, not to teach—and that clearly can happen only if one admits that there is something to learn that is not already known, or at least that there could be something. However, if one is convinced otherwise, if one is convinced that one already has all ultimate truth, then one will not be able to, indeed one will not even want to, come to a conversation to learn, to dialogue. Dialogue will not be seen as a virtue, but as a vice, and some fundamentalist groups say this clearly, for they see the "dialogists" as traitors to their own heritages and communities.

---

43. Much the same insight was expressed already over a generation ago by Catholic philosopher Leslie Dewart when he wrote: "Evidently, if one supposes not merely that one's belief is wholly true, but also that it is the whole of an unchanging truth, one cannot hope to deepen and extend the truth of one's belief, even by oneself, least of all cooperatively" ("Introduction: From Dialogue to Co-operation," in Garaudy, *From Anathema to Dialogue*, 14).

44. Lochhead made a relevant comment in this connection: "The groups that [John] Cobb cites with whom dialogue is not appropriate, the Nazis and the Ku Klux Klan, are both groups whose behavior can be described in terms of psychological pathology. For a start, both groups are paranoic. A case could be further made that both groups are psychotic, out of touch with reality. The relevance of psychological categories is that they remind us of the fact that there are some individuals and groups who are not capable of dialogue. This is not because we, from the perspective of our morally superior insight, categorize prospective dialogue partners into 'good guys' and 'bad guys.' Rather it is because certain groups and individuals behave in a way that continually subverts the dialogical process. The problem is not that we could have dialogue with groups but choose not to. The problem is that dialogue itself is impossible" (Lochhead, *Dialogical Imperative*, 75).

There are, of course, those who adopt the term "dialogue" as camouflage, consciously or unconsciously, in order to carry on more effectively their old polemic and proselytization. The Protestant Indian theologian Stanley Samartha remarks that, "Evangelicals' recent talk about 'dialogue' with its *seeming* openness to members of other faiths is misleading,"[45] with deliberateness implied: In "true" dialogue "we seek both to disclose the inadequacies and falsities of non-Christian religions and to demonstrate the adequacy and truth, the absoluteness and finality of the Lord Jesus Christ."[46]

However, there are many others who are not so single-mindedly zealous or fanatic and who either somehow sense to some degree that the dialogic approach toward those who differ from them in this fundamental area of religion-ideology is more human, more Christian, more Islamic, etc.—in short, better—than the old polemic approach; they move to identify at least somewhat with the term "dialogue."[47] In both instances this is partly because of the relative popular-level success of the "dialogists." However, this very success carries with it its own special problem: term inflation. Once the term "dialogue" has become "in," not only does everyone want to use it; they often also overuse it. As good and "virtuous" as dialogue is, it is not the only proper human action in all circumstances; it is not the only virtue that should exist in the human character—that is, as noted, one does not enter into dialogue with a "witch-burner" (Christian)[48] or a "widow-burner" (Hindu) or a Nazi genocidist; one opposes them.

If it is then the case that only those with an at least minimally deabsolutized understanding of truth can enter into authentic dialogue—that is, those who realize that because they cannot perceive and express all ultimate reality in their religion or ideology, they are open to, and need to, enter into dialogue—then what should be the attitude of the "dialogists" toward

---

45. Samartha, "The Cross and the Rainbow: Christ in a Multireligious Culture," in Hick and Knitter, *Myth of Christian Uniqueness*, 71.

46. John Stott, "Dialogue, Encounter, Even Confrontation," in Gerald H. Anderson and Thomas F. Stransky, eds., *Faith Meets Faith: Mission Trends* 5 (New York: Paulist, 1981) 168.

47. Lochhead, with a rather "worst-case scenario" retains at least a "hope against hope": "We might choose to converse with the Ku Klux Klan, for example. Our conversation would not be dialogue. At best it would be long-term therapy which, if one were to be very optimistic, might one day become dialogue" (Lochhead, *The Dialogical Imperative*, 75).

48. "It is computed from historical records that nine millions of persons were put to death for witchcraft after 1484, or during a period of three hundred years, and this estimate does not include the vast number who were sacrificed in the preceding centuries upon the same accusation" (Matilda Joslyn Gage, *Women, Church, and State* [New York: Arno, 1983] 272).

those who do not share more or less their deabsolutized view of truth? On the basis of time and energy and pressing need priorities, they might be ignored, but surely not in principle, for that would mean deliberately leaving a possible avenue to a fuller grasp of reality uninvestigated. To make that move on principle would be to fly in the face of the experience of our humanness, that is, our potential openness to all reality, cognitively and affectively. Hence, we will in principle want to enter into dialogue with all other religions and ideologies—at least to the point of truly learning that they are life-threateningly contradictory to our understanding of an authentic human life.

As was seen above, however, a human relationship cannot forever remain one-sided without becoming destructive. Likewise dialogue cannot forever remain one-sided. If the potential partners are incapable of and uninterested in dialogue because they hold an absolutized view of truth, it would seem that one has but two possible courses of action, other than ignoring them, which in principle is ruled out for the person with a deabsolutized view of truth. It seems clear that the "dialogist" should (1) enter into sympathetic contact with them to the degree possible, not only to learn from them, but also to (2) encourage in them the development of an at least minimally deabsolutized understanding of truth. This latter can of course take place over an extended period of time and in a limitless number of ways.

Given the ineluctably mutual character of a healthy human relationship, if the "dialogist" is in fact in sympathetic contact with "absolutists" and is in fact learning from them, it would seem that this state of affairs could not go on indefinitely without the "absolutists" also beginning to learn from the "dialogists." As that slowly happens the "absolutists" will proportionately move toward a deabsolutization of their understanding of truth—as mentioned, at first quite unconsciously, but then eventually necessarily consciously (of course, the relationship may be derailed or cut off before this happens). If the mutuality does not develop, then in fact the "dialogist" will begin to cease learning from the "absolutists," and the relationship will gradually slip, at best, into a sort of suspended animation, "at medium," into the old "splendid isolation," and at worst, into polemics and possibly even violence. Naturally, in the concrete, situations will not always follow these pure "textbook" stereotypes, but it would seem that they are the built-in tendencies of our human structures.

In any case, those two steps might well be called *prolegomena* to dialogue, rather than dialogue itself, and in many instances they will have to be gone through before authentic dialogue can be arrived at. To affirm so is not to admit defeat, or to be "elitist" (must that always be a bad thing?—I would like to have only an "elite" surgeon operate on me!). It is to take reality the way it is and deal with it accordingly—surely the proper human, religious, way to act.

There is also a difficulty that arises in connection with Dialogue Decalogue rule five, that is, that "each participant must define [him or] herself." What if, for example, the Jewish dialogue partner knows a great deal more about Christianity than the Christian partner does? Does that mean that the dialogue must be carried on at the relatively misinformed level of the Christian? How could this benefit anyone? In fact, in this case the Jewish partner might learn something about a more popular, relatively uninformed Christianity, but this clearly would be of limited value. It is probably more accurate to assert that no authentic dialogue in the full sense can take place in these circumstances, for dialogue rule seven, that "dialogue can take place only between equals," is not being observed. Such an interchange as here described might well be humanly and religiously quite worthwhile, but it just would not have the characteristics of a dialogue—and that is all right. We have to keep recalling that not every good thing has to be called a dialogue!

A variation on this problem is the question of what role critical scholarship and critical thinking should play in interreligious, interideological dialogue. If a group of Jews and Muslims get together on the congregational level, for instance, they could, and should, have dialogue. Must dialogue, however, remain only on the more popular level? It is clear that the answer is, no. What about, however, critical-thinking Christian scholars who want to have dialogue with Muslims, for example—must they limit themselves to the traditional, pre-critical type of Islam as a source of dialogue partners? Or, could they, indeed, should they, not push to find Muslim scholars who are their equal in critical scholarship and thought? Is that in fact not the only way they can enter into a full, authentic dialogue, *par cum pari*? The answer would seem to have to be a resounding, yes, even though such thinkers, perhaps even on both sides, would as yet represent only a small minority of their respective memberships.

Surely, no one would want to—or at least, no one should want to—restrict thinking as such to the popular level. That would run counter to the very structures of our humanity and would be inimical to the welfare of humankind. But the whole argument of this book is that dialogue is a preeminently important way of thinking today, within whose matrix all systematic reflection in the area of religions and ideology must be carried out. If that thesis is ultimately agreed to, then clearly dialogue must be carried on at all levels of humanity, including certainly on the highest possible level, for it is precisely at that level that many of the breakthroughs have occurred and will continue to occur, which then will greatly liberate the dialogue at the other levels.

Full Human Life

If the language of a "universal theology of religion-ideology" is to be "from below," humanity-based, there need to be articulations both of what a minimally acceptable human life, "by right," is and of what an authentic, *full* human life is. Only as we become increasingly more explicit, penetrating, conscious about what it means to be fully human will we be able to live that ever fuller human life (a never-ending task both for the individual and for humanity as a whole), and only thus will a humanity-based theological-ideological language become available to us. Let me try, then, to articulate *an* understanding of full human life in terms that should be understandable to all sensitive humans, theist and nontheist, religious and nonreligious.

One possible way to view full human life that I believe can be helpful is in the three relatively distinct but closely connected areas referred to before: the cognitive, practical, and depth or "spiritual." In the cognitive area we seek to understand and articulate in various conscious, intellectual ways our perceptions of the world and experiences of life. In the practical area we act and make things; we seek not to understand the world, but to *affect* and *effect* it. In the depth or "spiritual" area we discern the deeper meanings of our experiences and the world. This depth dimension of human life is where our imagination and feelings and the more synthetic aspect of the intellect come more into play; it is characteristic of this area that it brings the potent images, emotions, connections of our inner life to the conscious level. Each of these areas needs to be ever more fully developed as life progresses. Furthermore, it is also absolutely necessary that they be interconnected, integrated, so that they might mutually energize each other and produce a holistic life.

In nineteenth- and twentieth-century Western civilization there has been a decided tendency to down-play the "spiritual," the depth, dimension to the point where it has very seriously atrophied. Moreover, as mentioned before, the traditional Judeo-Christian images and structures—the four "C's," Creed, Code, Cult, Community-structure—have been increasingly incapable of effectively illuminating the life experiences of modern critical-thinking "Westerners," from whatever part of the globe they come. Consequently, it is often precisely the "Western" intellectual who needs first to be awakened to even the existence of the "spiritual," depth dimension of full human life and then be assisted in its cultivation. (In most recent times this has begun slowly to happen.) As contact is made with the inner process of one's life, as its images and feelings are acknowledged and allowed their proper effect, as meanings beyond rational expressions are discerned and connections between portions of life are made and larger integrations formed, this "spiritual" dimension of life will, at first slowly and subtly but eventually profoundly affect the other two areas of life. It is, however, especially vital that the various depth experiences of modern persons be brought to the conscious level so their power can be fully developed and also be made available to the other two areas of life.

As these depth experiences are raised to the conscious level, they will not only provide a deeper meaning to the rational expressions of the cognitive area of life, but they will also make demands for a rearticulation of those newly discerned meanings in intellectual categories and expressions that more adequately reflect the contemporary intellectual world. This step, too, is vital, lest the "spiritual" dimension come to be perceived as fairy-tale-like and eventually again be rejected—to the disastrous loss of the full human person. In turn, of course, as the conundrums of life, on all levels, are increasingly more fully and richly analyzed and articulated, the cognitive area of life will also in turn spill its newly released energies over into the "spiritual" area, providing it more adequate means to raise the depth experience to the conscious level and make the integrative connections in terms that "make sense" in contemporary critical language.

One of the strengths of modern Western civilization has been its stress on effective human action, both individual and corporate. The West has been nothing if not "practical" and activist, and this dimension has often been closely linked with the cognitive dimension. However, if the depth dimension is seriously atrophied, the practical and cognitive dimensions will be more limited, shallower than they could or should be. As our action becomes more effective, however, our cognitive life will be stimulated to understand the new circumstances, new realities that are created by our action—which will also generate the need to discern still further insights and integrations in our "spiritual" dimension.

A special danger in the intensification of the "spiritual" life that must particularly be guarded against is what can be called privatizing. An extremely important insight into human reality that the West has generated in the last two centuries is the recognition of the penetrating power of social structures. All humans are pervasively formed by the structures of the society in which they live. Even when the few "rise above" those societal structures, they are immensely influenced by them—in this case largely negatively by being forced to "overcome" them, though of course they are never completely "overcome."

The West then went on to understand—and partially to act on that understanding—that if the lot of humans is to change significantly, the social structures must be changed (and they can be); most persons will not have their lives profoundly altered simply on a one-by-one basis. Put somewhat colloquially: The world cannot be "saved" simply by trying to "save" individual persons; the social structures within which individual persons live must also be "saved." It is absolutely vital to a full human life that this precious insight be preserved, magnified, and acted on as the "spiritual" dimension of life is reactivated and intensified; that "insight" from the "practical" dimension must pour its energies into not only the cognitive dimension of life but also the "spiritual," and in turn be energized by the other two.

A key, if not *the* key, to a full human life is the maximizing of awareness in all dimensions. Acting, making, reasoning, feeling—all increasingly suffused with awareness in expanding depth, breadth, and interconnectedness—is, I believe, a proper description of a full human life.[49] For example, acting with spontaneity is a human good. But, without eliminating the spontaneity, also becoming aware that I am acting with spontaneity, of what that feels like, of what significances it has for other aspects of my life, for other persons and things I am related to, etc.—all clearly are an enrichment of my life, making it a fuller human life. The fact that when life is reduced to unreflective action we usually describe such life as unhuman, or even inhuman, robot, or machine-like (and if reflective life is further reduced, as in a coma, the person is said merely to be vegetating) clearly indicates negatively that awareness is of the essence of human life. As awareness approaches zero, life ceases, and death is approached; conversely, as awareness expands toward infinity, human life intensifies, moving toward the bursting of all bounds—for which all religions and other worldviews have specific terms: for example, *moksha* or liberation (Hindu), *nirvana* or "reality" (Buddhist), *basileia theou* or Reign of God (Christian). It is that Omega point of total awareness toward which all human life tends.

To summarize, the greatest dangers to a full human life are the severe atrophication of any of the three dimensions of life, and their existing in unconnected, unaware, fashion—a *dis*integrated life. Stated positively, in a full human life all three dimensions continue to grow maximally, become ever more fully conscious, aware, and are closely integrated so they mutually fecundate each other, producing an always increasing unity, a *holos*.

---

49. The Japanese Protestant Seiichi Yagi expressed the same idea: "Human life is the life that is conscious of itself, understands itself, that is, the life that brings its essence, its being into the light. Life and light belong together" (Seiichi Yagi, *Die Front-Struktur als Brücke vom buddhistischen zum christlichen Denken* [Munich: Kaiser, 1988] 70).

It should be recalled here that Christians have often spoken of the goal of life as "salvation," in the sense of being "saved" from the outside, like someone being "saved" from drowning. However, this word "salvation" has to a large extent been significantly altered in the Christian tradition from its meaning in Israelite religion and its root meaning in Greek and Latin. For the most part, it has been given its restricted meaning since the third century CE, namely, that when believers in Jesus Christ die, if they have remained faithful, they will go to heaven. However, that is not at all what the word basically means. In its Latin form, *salvatio*, it comes from the root *salus* (the Greek form is *soterion/soteria* from *saos*), meaning wholeness, health or well-being—hence, "salutary" and "salubrious" in English. A similar derivation is true of the Germanic word for salvation, *Heil*, which adjectively also means whole, hale, healed, healthy. In fact, this is also where the English word "holy" comes from. Being holy means being whole, leading a whole, a full life. If we lead a whole, full life, we are holy; we attain salvation, wholeness.

Results of Interreligious, Interideological Dialogue

What results of the dialogue among religions and ideologies can be looked for? In general we can expect not only a proportional drop in violence—physical, verbal, economic, etc.—but also a burst of creativity. It is obvious that the diminishing of hostility in the world will automatically raise the level of "happiness" in the world. But, beyond that, it is also true that the energy—particularly psychic and intellectual energy—otherwise poured into polemics, overt and covert, will then be released for constructive rather than destructive purposes. Will these newly freed forces not be turned to other wasteful or even destructive uses? It is possible.

However, the overwhelming likelihood is that they will be focused on a creative expansion of the individual's authentic self, which very much includes relations with others—other persons, animals, inanimate things, and, finally, Ultimate Reality. The reasons for this are several.

Dialogue Partners Serve as Mirrors

First, in dialogue the partners also serve as mirrors for each other. The same basic human law of becoming more wholly human through mutuality referred to above operates very centrally here in dialogue. Every person entering dialogue will have a certain self-understanding. However, in the dialogue they will not only learn more about the partners that they did not know before, they will also learn how the partners have perceived them.

Even if the first dialogue partners claim that the second have misunderstood them—which to a greater or lesser extent normally happens—the first partners will learn how they *de facto* have been seen by at least some others—and this "relationship" of being perceived by others is also very much a part of their own reality. Relationships are essential constitutive elements of each human (of every being, for that matter). Humans live not as atomized "monads" but in groups; as Aristotle noted, humans are gregarious animals (as in the Latin *gregis*, "flock"). Through their dialogue partners humans learn an additional piece of "how they are in the world," as Heidegger might put it.

Since in dialogue people come primarily to learn from the other and then to change accordingly, this learning to know how others perceive them will also tend to have a transformative effect on the first partners. For example, if the first partners understand themselves to be tolerant, but they frequently learn that others perceive them as intolerant, they will perhaps try to change their way of acting so as to communicate what they believe is their authentic self. Or, they may be forced, after reflection, to admit to themselves that they in fact were not as tolerant as they thought they were and then either move to change their inner reality and become more tolerant, or change their understanding of tolerance, or perhaps decide they are being as "tolerant" as they believe they, with integrity, ought to be (for example, they judge they should not be "tolerant" of racism).

Shift from Inward to Outward Gaze

Second, entering into serious interreligious, interideological dialogue entails shifting from a kind of inward staring—whose concomitant move is to sally forth to persuade or attack the outsider—to a looking outward. This is a fundamental, radical shift that normally will utterly transform the dialogue partners. The outside religious world is now no longer perceived as essentially hostile and the locus of evil and error or, at best, sometimes only of ignorance, as it always has been throughout the Age of Monologue. Rather, the outside religious and ideological world is now perceived as a possible source of knowledge, wisdom, insight, inspiration, edification—though of course one does not naively think that everything in other religions and ideologies is inspiration and wisdom. But, by approaching the outside world with positive expectations, the dialogue partners are inevitably amazed at the extraordinary quantity and quality of inspiration and wisdom that is found there. They both were there all along; the monologists were deaf to them, but the dialogists—as Jesus observed of the authentic seekers among his listeners—now "have the ears to hear" (Matt 13:9).

Dialogical "Chain Reaction"

Third, the turning of one's gaze from inward to outward toward a dialogue partner creates a kind of "chain reaction." For example, the Catholic Church long was stolidly engaged in "navel gazing" until Vatican II. In the early 1920s Pope Benedict XV refused to join with those Protestant and Orthodox Christians who invited him and Catholicism to help form the Ecumenical Movement, a movement of dialogue among Christians to work for Christian unity. His successor, Pope Pius XI, forbade Catholics to participate in the first world meeting of the Faith and Order Movement (for Christian unity) in 1927, and his successor Pope Pius XII did the same sort of thing again in 1948 and 1954.

However, his successor, "Good Pope John," Pope John XXIII, in 1959 called for Vatican II "to renew the Catholic Church so it could work for Christian unity." The Council went on to insist officially on the absolute necessity of Catholics' entering into dialogue not only with Protestants and Orthodox Christians, but also with Jews, Muslims, Hindus, Buddhists, and other religionists and also nonbelievers.

Once the turn to dialogue with the first logical partners for Catholics—Protestants and Orthodox—was made, the inner logic of that turn continued the dialogic move to each next "logical" partner: If inspiration and wisdom can be found in dialogue with non-Catholic Christians, should that not also be possible with Judaism, Christianity's "source"? Why not, then, the other Semitic religion, Islam? Why not the religions of the East—Hinduism, Buddhism, Confucianism, Taoism, etc.? Why not "All men of good will," as John XXIII put it in his moving encyclical *Pacem in terris*?

The spiritual "fission/fusion" that has occurred as a result of this "chain reaction" in the Catholic Church has indeed been nothing short of "nuclear." The Council itself stated that "All Christians should do their best to promote dialogue . . . as a duty of fraternal charity suited to our progressive and adult age."[50] In his very first encyclical (1964), Pope Paul VI wrote: "Dialogue is demanded nowadays . . . It is demanded . . . by the maturity man has reached in this day and age."[51] In 1968 the Vatican Secretariat for Dialogue with Unbelievers wrote, "Doctrinal dialogue should be initiated with courage

---

50. Vatican II, *Decree on the Apostolate of the Laity*, no. 7.
51. Pope Paul VI's encyclical *Ecclesiam suam*, 1964, no. 79.

and sincerity, with the greatest freedom," and added these stunning words: "Doctrinal discussion [must] recognize the truth everywhere, even if the truth demolishes one so that one is forced to reconsider one's own position, in theory and in practice."[52]

Adapt Elements from Our Dialogue Partners

Fourth, as noted earlier, in dialogue we will not only learn to know our partners more accurately but also often find things in their tradition that we find admirable, even to the point that we will want to adopt certain elements from our partners for ourselves. For example, some Buddhist traditions of meditation have made a strong impression on many Christians. Conversely, some Buddhists have been greatly impressed by the Christian commitment to social justice, even to the point of going to prison or dying for social justice. The result has been that some Christians have taken up meditation methods they learned from Buddhists, and some Buddhists have become deeply involved in social-justice actions.

However, interreligious dialogue should not, as already stressed, lead to a kind of syncretism in the sense of an eclectic mixture of elements from here and there. Rather, dialogue should, and does, lead one to "adapt" rather than simply "adopt" elements from our dialogue partners. This means that the adapted element is modified to fit with integrity into the first partner's tradition. For example, a Christian does not become a nontheist by adapting Zen meditation; a Buddhist does not engage in social-justice action despite her or his being a Buddhist, but because of it!—as was vigorously stated by the Theravada Buddhist Sulak Sivaraksa from Bangkok.

Dialogue Must Result in Practice

Fifth, dialogue must result in joint action in the practical area. Such joint religious action began to develop in earnest in the West only in the nineteenth century. Until that time efforts to help disadvantaged human beings were pretty much done on a remedial individualistic basis. "Charitable" institutions were founded—actually in quite extraordinary richness. The situation began to change drastically, however, with the coming of the Industrial Revolution in England in the late eighteenth century and elsewhere in Europe and America starting in the nineteenth century; the old guild and

---

52. *Humanae personae dignitatem*, 1007, 1010.

feudal systems no longer functioned for the increasing millions caught in the transfer of populations to the cities.

Whereas most people had died quite young, and a much smaller population lived in relative social and geographical stability before the nineteenth century, suddenly a massive and exploding population problem burst upon the world for which neither civil society nor religion was prepared. Individual acts of charity and charitable institutions were increasingly swamped in the growing flood of social misery that rose as the nineteenth and twentieth centuries wore on. At the same time, the structures of society and their workings were being studied. Plans on how to shape and reshape those structures were laid and tested, adjusted and retested. Such awareness, planning, and action also took place within Western religions.

Around the globe today Christian churches and Jewish synagogues spend hundreds of millions of dollars annually on social-justice issues, a significant portion of which is aimed at changing the structures of society to benefit more people. The notion is spreading among Christians that the mission of the church is to preach the good news of the gospel to all humanity, not just quantitatively in terms of individual persons, but also qualitatively in terms of every portion of the human beings—and the human patterns one lives in are an essential part of one's humanity. The message of the *relationality* of all reality—very much including humankind—has struck home here.

A similar phenomenon is also beginning to take place in some dimensions of Buddhism. One very striking example is Won Buddhism, which sprang up in Korea early in the twentieth century. Clearly Won Buddhism works to combine the principles of Gautama Buddha with an affirmation of modern science and technology in working for the betterment of men and women, individually and collectively; hence, it is not surprising that the Won Buddhists also have a very strong commitment to interreligious dialogue.

There is a like development in Japan, namely, in some of the so-called "new religions" that are Buddhist-based. For example, the Rissho Kosei-Kai, founded in the 1930s by Nikkyo Niwano, was initially very much an individualistically oriented branch of Buddhism, but in recent decades—significantly as a result of dialogue with Catholics, and in particular a meeting with Pope Paul VI in 1965—it has moved to a strong commitment to social justice and interreligious dialogue.

At the same time, I would like to reiterate my prior emphasis that joint religious action should not be limited to helping those who are in material need. Rather, as I have suggested, the "other" toward whom our joint "altruistic" ethical action should reach might be named simply, the oppressed, the unfree in any dimension—remembering at the same time both that those in greatest need should receive the greatest attention, and that each should contribute according to her or his gifts, and in a preeminent, though not exclusive, way to those before them *now* in need, whether that need be material, spiritual, social, esthetic, or whatever.

In conclusion, Interreligious, interideological action that does not eventuate in dialogue will grow mindless, ineffective. Interreligious, interideological dialogue that does not eventuate in action will grow hypocritical, ineffective. Neither can survive singly.

Probe New Questions Not Raised Before

Sixth, patiently pursued dialogue will eventually cast up new questions that neither of the dialogue partners had thought of on their own. Here is the area of the greatest potential creativity in dialogue. Of course, we will not know what the creative questions will be ahead of time. If we did, they would not be new, not be fully creative. Still, let me offer two examples of such questions that have already begun to arise from the Buddhist-Christian dialogue in one case and the Christian-Muslim in the other.

What are the effects of describing Ultimate Reality? Earlier, I laid out something of my understanding of Christian (and one could perhaps also add here, Jewish and Muslim) and Buddhist understandings of Ultimate Reality. I, along with some other Christians engaged in dialogue with Buddhism, suggested that the Christian penchant for describing Ultimate Reality in positive terms (*Being, Pleroma*) and the Buddhist tendency to describe it in negative terms (*Emptiness, Sunyata*) need not be understood as mutually exclusive contradictions but, perhaps, more like complementary descriptions.

Now, if this position is more or less accepted, it becomes extremely interesting and enlightening to investigate whether, and then how, these different descriptions of Ultimate Reality "make a difference in the world." Is the patent fact that the Semitic religions over the centuries have invested huge energies in trying to improve the human lot *in this world*, and that Buddhism institutionally has been relatively uninterested, connected with their descriptions of Ultimate Reality? Is the other indisputable fact that at least two of the Semitic religions have consistently over centuries been considerably more aggressive, intolerant, and violent than has Buddhism also connected with their particular—affirmative, negative—descriptions of Ultimate Reality? If there is a connection, what are its mechanisms? What, if anything, can, or should, be done about it? These, I believe, could be extremely critical questions for the future of humanity, of the religions in questions, and their mutual relationships. A further discussion on this is found below.

What of human rights and separation of religion and state? It was mentioned above that the biblical notion of the equal dignity of all human beings because each was created by the one God as an *Imago Dei* was one of the pillars of what is known today as human rights, as are enshrined in the U.N. 1948 *Declaration* and subsequent documents. Two other pillars are the Greek concept of the political rule of the people, democracy, and the highly developed Roman system of universal law. It took a long and circuitous evolution of human history before Western civilization was able to establish on the foundation of these three pillars the modern concept and growing reality of human rights. However, particularly after the American and French Revolutions at the end of the eighteenth century, human rights began to become a conscious reality—unfortunately often resisted by the Christian Church until recent decades, when it has become a vigorous promoter of human rights.

One of the essential elements in the advances of Western civilization in the area of human rights, as well as in science, politics in general, and economic prosperity, the like of which was never before experienced in human history, is the separation of state and religion—and "religion" here of course includes any ideology that functions like a religion, as, for example, atheistic Marxism.

Christendom in the Late Middle Ages began reaching the cultural level of the earlier Greek and Roman and the then contemporary Islamic civilizations. All historical data strongly suggest that Christendom would have plateaued at that approximate level for a longer or shorter period of time, and then gone into decline—as had all other civilizations before then, and as eventually the Islamic civilization did as well. That did not happen, however. Why? One very fundamental reason is that, starting with the Renaissance, religion and the state slowly and very painfully began to be separated. This separation broke the forced quality of religion (ideology) and consequently freed the human spirit and mind to pursue its limitless urge to know ever more, to solve every problem it confronts. This resulted in a series of what historians call revolutions: the commercial revolution (sixteenth–seventeenth centuries), scientific revolution (seventeenth century), industrial revolution (eighteenth century), political revolution (epitomized in the American and French Revolutions, eighteenth century), and on into the nineteenth, twentieth, and twenty-first centuries with myriads of revolutions of all sorts occurring at geometrically increasing speed and magnitude.

With the formal and growing separation of religion (in this case, specifically Christianity) from the *power* of the state, there emerges what we no longer term "Christendom" but Western civilization. With these "exponential" advances in capabilities, of course, the possibilities of destructiveness increased correspondingly—as the medieval philosophers said: The corruption of the best becomes the worst, *Corruptio optimae pessima*. Nevertheless, because freedom is of the essence of being human, even though we may well destroy ourselves if we do not learn wisdom and live virtuously, we can never turn back to an unfree stage of human development.

Hence, those societies that try to reunite religion/ideology with the power of the state are doomed always to be third-class societies. That is why, for example, I am convinced that the present attempt of "Islamists" to reestablish the Muslim law, the *Shar'ia*, in the Muslim world will condemn those countries *always* to be behind the West. And, given the Islamists' memory of the past medieval cultural glory and superiority of Islam over Christendom, it is precisely the present inferiority in every way of all Islamic countries vis-à-vis the West that infuriates them.

When they argue that Islam is different from Christianity because, unlike Christianity, it is a holistic religion that includes politics as well as all other aspects of life, they need to be reminded that Christendom was exactly the same for well over a millennium—the Constantinian Era. It is only when the West broke out of that mischievous marriage of religion/ideology and state that it embarked on the path of human freedom with its limitless possibilities of creativity (and destruction).

Dialogue for a Global Ethic

Seventh, dialogue must lead to the building of a consensus on a *Global Ethic*. Bilateral dialogues, vital as they are, are no longer sufficient for the world of today and tomorrow. By "Ethic" here is meant the fundamental attitude toward good and evil and the basic principles to carry that attitude into action. See below, where this critical matter will be dealt with in detail.

Seven Stages of Deep-Dialogue/Critical-Thinking

The following are *Seven Stages of Deep-Dialogue/Critical-Thinking* that a person can go through if one persists in the project.[53]

---

53. The text of these stages was initially drafted by Ashok Gangadean and then with Leonard Swidler somewhat modified; this version has been further adapted by Leonard Swidler.

Stage 1: Radical Encountering of Difference; Self Faces the Other

This first encounter comes with a certain shock, with a realization of an Other, a different way of life, a different worldview, an alien Other that resists, interrupts, disrupts my settled way of interpretation. With this initial encounter there is a new realization that my habits of thinking cannot make sense of this Other. This radical encounter with Difference—a different world, a different way of making sense of and experiencing the world—is disconcerting, sometimes threatening, and it evokes a vulnerability to this alien presence. I have a new sense of delimitation, and I feel challenged to change, to revise my way of relating to this Other. I realize now that my habit of translating the Other into *my* pattern of thinking, of appropriating the Other to *my* worldview, is dysfunctional. I am forced toward a *self-critical Deep-Dialogue/Critical-Thinking*. So, I face a sudden silence, pause, opening—an open horizon of uncertainty and risk. I must make a decision to move forward—or draw back.

Stage 2: Crossing Over, Letting Go, and Entering the World of the Other; Self Transformed through Empathy

After the initial shock and realization that I now face an alien world, a worldview very different from mine, I feel challenged to inquire, investigate, engage, enter this new world—to engage in reflective Deep-Dialogue/Critical-Thinking. As I open my Self to this Other, I realize that I need to stand back and distance myself from my former habits and patterns of perceiving the world. I begin to realize that this other world organizes and processes the world very differently from my way. I realize that I must learn new habits and ways of interpretation to make sense of this different world. I must learn a "new language." Indeed, I must translate myself into a different form of life that sees the world differently. This involves a bracketing of my assumptions.

Stage 3: Inhabiting and Experiencing the World of the Other; Self Transformed into the Other

I begin to feel a new and deep empathy for my new habitat; I want to let myself go—free myself to enter, experiment, learn and grow in this new way of being—to embrace *Deep-Dialogue/Critical-Thinking*. I hold on to my prior views as much as I can, but I advance in a conservative fashion. Still, I experience an excitement in discovering, in inhabiting a new and different worldview. I have a new realization of an-Other, an alternative reality and form of life, but in the end I realize this is not really my home.

Stage 4: Crossing Back with Expanded Vision; Self Returns Home with New Knowledge

I now cross back, return to my own world, bringing back new knowledge of how to think and act—self-reflective *Deep-Dialogue/Critical-Thinking*—and may even wish to adopt/adapt some of it for myself. As a result of this encounter with the world of the Other, I now realize that there are other ways of understanding reality. I am therefore open to rethinking how I see myself, others, and the world. I encounter myself and my culture anew, with a newly opened mind. My encounter with radical difference now challenges my former identity, and everything begins to appear in a new light. There now begins a dramatic deepening of my sense of myself, my identity, my ethnicity, my life-world, my religion, my culture, etc. There is no return to my former unilateral way of thinking.

Stage 5: The Dialogical/Critical Awakening—A Radical Paradigm Shift: Self Inwardly Transformed

As a result of this new encounter with Self, when I cross back from my deep encounter with an Other I begin to experience a profound shift in all aspects of my world—my inner experience, my encounter with others, my relating to the world. I begin to realize that my encounter with the Other has shaken the foundation of my former worldview, my former identity. Now that I am aware of the living reality of other worlds, other perspectives, I can no longer return to my former identity and forget this living presence of the Other. Indeed, I now begin to realize that there are many other worlds, other forms of life, other perspectives that surround me. I now open to a plurality of other worlds and perspectives, and this irrevocably changes my sense of Self. I feel transformed to a deeper sense of relation and connection with my surroundings. I feel more deeply rooted in this experience of relationality and community. I now see that my true identity is essentially connected with this expansive network of relations with Others. This is the ignition of the Deep-Dialogue/Critical-Thinking awakening.

Stage 6: The Global Awakening—The Paradigm Shift Mature; Self Related to Self, Others, and the World

In my transformed Deep-Dialogue/Critical-Thinking awakening, I discover a deeper common ground between the multiple worlds and perspectives that surround me. I have a new sense that Self and Others are inseparably bound together in a limitless interrelational web. I realize that multiplicity and diversity enriches myself and my world. I now see that all worlds are situated in a common ground of reality and that radical differences are nevertheless also situated in a field of unity. I experience three related dimensions of Global Deep-Dialogue/Critical-Thinking awakening:

a. An ever deepening discovery of Self: I become aware of a deep inner Deep-Dialogue/Critical-Thinking within myself. I discover a rich multiplicity and diversity of perspectives within my own inner world. In this inner Deep-Dialogue/Critical-Thinking I feel increasingly more deeply rooted and grounded in my world. My identity is enriched with multiplicity, and I experience a more powerful sense of my uniqueness as I celebrate my expanded world of relationality with Others and with my surroundings.

b. A dynamic dialogue opens with Others in my community: As my new inner Deep-Dialogue/Critical-Thinking evolves I find myself in a new and transformed relation with others who share my world, tradition, religion, culture. This new phase of relations with my peers can be disorienting and disconcerting, for as I now grow more deeply in my identity I find myself in an estranged distance from many of my peers, even as I discover a deeper affinity and embrace of my community. I face a new turbulence—miscommunication and misunderstanding with my colleagues—and challenging and dialogue unfold.

c. A global awakening emerges in all aspects of my life: As this inner and outer Deep-Dialogue/Critical-Thinking matures, I realize that my understanding of my world is suffused with a new "global" light: I realize that I am surrounded with many worldviews. I enter a global horizon and a global consciousness in which interreligious, intercultural, interideological, interdisciplinary, interpersonal dialogues abound in all directions. I now have a new globalized sense of reality—a Deep-Dialogue/Critical-Thinking domain in which multiple alternative worlds are situated in dynamic, ever-deepening relations. With this understanding comes a new attitude toward life and ethics.

Stage 7: Personal/Global Transforming of Life and Behavior; Self Lives and Acts in a New Global Deep-Dialogue/Critical-Thinking Consciousness

As this paradigm shift in me matures, I realize that there is a deep change in all aspects of my life—a new moral consciousness and practice. As my new Deep-Dialogue/Critical-Thinking consciousness becomes a habit, a virtue, it deepens into a way of life, and I find that my behavior and my disposition to Self and Other have been utterly transformed. I feel a new sense of communion with myself, with Others, and with my surroundings. I realize that the deepest care for myself essentially involves my care for Others and the "environment." I have a deeper sense of belonging to my world, to my community, and, with this, a limitless sense of responsibility in my conduct. I now realize that I am transformed in the deepest habits of mind and behavior. I find a deeper sense of self-realization, fulfillment, and meaning in my life and my relations with others and the world around me and with its Source and Goal, however understood. I embrace and am embraced by the virtue, the way of Deep-/Dialogue/Critical-Thinking—*Dia-Logos*!

Interim Conclusion II

In conclusion, humankind needs an "explanation of the ultimate meaning of life and an ethics of how to live accordingly." Every religion tries to provide such an explanation and ethics based on a notion of the Transcendent; an ideology attempts to do the same not based on a notion of the Transcendent.

While the inherent variety of humankind, stemming from human freedom, assures that there will always be a variety of "explanations and ethics," a variety of religions and ideologies, these religions and ideologies can no longer continue to exist in hostility toward, or isolation from, each other. Rather, they all need to expand and deepen their understanding of reality, including Ultimate Reality, by learning from each other, by being in dialogue. Most pressing of all is the need for this dialogue to focus on the building of a Global Ethic.

Christological Imperative to Dialogue

Up until now my general line of argument has been: The need of people searching for the meaning of things to engage in dialogue with persons with views other than their own is becoming ever more pressing, and especially so for religious persons. This is doubtless true for persons who have experienced the above-described developments in "Western" culture regardless of their religion, but for particular historical reasons it is most valid for Christians: for good or ill—or rather, with its good and ill—Christians in large measure have created Western culture.

However, Christians specifically as Christians have a special imperative to engage in dialogue: the christological imperative. This constitutive Christian need of dialogue flows from Christianity's "filial-sibling" relationship with Judaism. The hyphenated term "filial-sibling" is not a result of uncertainty on my part. Rather, it is a result of certainty that Christianity is at the same time an offspring of that Judaism that grew out of the biblical Israelite religion and reached a highly developed form in the century or so before the Roman destruction of Jerusalem in 70 CE, and a sibling of Rabbinic Judaism, which, like Christianity, emerged from that turbulent period. If Christianity had remained dominantly Semitic in its development, the grounds for dialogue with Judaism would have been largely other than they in fact are. However, because Christianity in many ways developed more within the Hellenistic rather than the Semitic cultural world, it tended to forget, or even suppress, its Semitic origins. In so doing, it forgot or suppressed its own roots. Hence, if Christians are going to be able to dialogue with anyone, they first will have to get clearer about their own identity, and that identity is Jewish at its source: Jesus the Christ.

Christianity's Jewish Roots: Jesus (Yeshua) the Jew

The "cornerstone" of Christianity, of course, is Jesus of Nazareth, *Yeshua ha Notzri*. It must be remembered, however, that Jesus, Yeshua, was not a Christian; he was a Jew,[54] and not only racially, ethnically, but also religiously. That meant that in a very central way he was committed to the Law,

---

54. This point was made with lapidary clarity over eighty years ago by Julius Wellhausen: "Jesus was not a Christian; he was a Jew" (Julius Wellhausen, *Einleitung in die Drei Ersten Evangelien* [Berlin: Reimer, 1905] 113).

the *Torah* (better translated as "instruction," God's instruction on how to live a proper human life). Recalling this will perhaps be a shock for many Christians, for they have been taught that Jesus, Yeshua, often violated the Law, placed himself above it, changed it—in short, released himself and his followers from having to follow it. Often Christians have also been taught that it was this setting aside of the Law by Yeshua that so earned him the ire of the Jewish leaders of the time that he was put to death; hence, freedom from the Law was an essential mark of the follower of Yeshua.

Nothing can be farther from the facts. From Yeshua's own words it is clear that he was committed to the keeping of the Law, the Torah, "as long as heaven and earth last!" and "whoever breaks even the smallest of the commandments, and teaches others to do the same, will be least in the Reign of heaven" (Matt 5:18-9). There was no notion whatsoever of setting aside the Law in his words: "Do not think that I came to destroy the Law or the prophets; I came not to destroy but to carry out" (*plerosai*, literally, "to implement"; Matt 5:17-9).[55]

Despite this and other clear documentary evidence, Christian scholars over the centuries have maintained Yeshua's opposition to the Law. A major problem with this claim, from a scholarly point of view, however, was that the vast majority of these Christian scholars did not know the Law as interpreted by the rabbis—and Yeshua was a rabbi, as the Gospels make clear time and again—in their original sources. Even more, they did not know the Judaism of the time of Yeshua.

This latter, in fact, is only in recent time beginning to be recovered. The contemporary Christian New Testament scholar who does know the rabbinic material first-hand and who is the most recognized authority in this field is the Protestant E. P. Sanders, and he makes it clear that he is convinced that Yeshua did not stand in opposition to the Law: "Opinions range from this extreme all the way to another: there is no violation of the law at all or none worth much mention. In this case, one of the extremes must be judged to be correct: the second one."[56]

55. A word has many possible meanings; the one intended can be known only in relation to its context, as was in this case again pointed out by Gerhard Delling: "The meaning of *pleroo* cannot be deduced ... it must be based on the context ... According to Mt. 5:17a this [mission of Yeshua] is primarily fulfillment of the Law and prophets ... Jesus does not merely affirm that He will maintain them. As He sees it, His task is to actualise the will of God made known in the OT" (Gerhard Kittel, *Theological Dictionary of the New Testament* (Grand Rapids: Eerdmans, 1968) 6:293-94. For a thorough discussion of the meaning of *plerosai* and the attitude of Yeshua toward the Law see Franz Mussner, *Traktat über die Juden* (Munich: Kösel, 1979) 185-93; E.T.: *Tractate on the Jews*, tr. Leonard Swidler (Philadelphia: Fortress, 1984) 115-21.

56. E. P. Sanders, *Jesus and Judaism* (Philadelphia: Fortress, 1985) 264.

Often Christians have contrasted Christianity and Judaism, Yeshua and the Rabbis, by stating that the latter teach a religion of law and the former a religion of love—and of course the religion of love is far superior. The quintessential text-proof for this Christian claim is from the three synoptic Gospels where Yeshua speaks of the whole Law's being summed up in the two great commandments, loving God with one's whole heart, mind, and soul, and loving one's neighbor as oneself.

The difficulty with this evidence is manifold. First, the two commandments given by Yeshua are in fact quotations from the Hebrew Bible: Deut 6:5, which, indeed, is a portion of the opening of the Jewish daily prayer, the *Shema*: "Love the Lord your God with all your heart, with all your soul, and with all your strength," and Lev 19:18: "Love your neighbor as you love yourself." In fact, the linking together of these two commandments and the summing up of the Law in them was also not something new or special to Yeshua. According to Luke 10:25–8, it was an "expert in the law" (*nomikos*) in the crowd who spoke of the twofold command of love; Yeshua merely agreed with him.

Moreover, perhaps two hundred years before Yeshua was born, other Jewish writers stated much the same sentiments. They are found in various of the Pseudepigrapha (noncanonical Jewish writings in Greek): "Love the Lord and the neighbor" (Testament of Issachar 5:2); "I loved the Lord and every human being with my whole heart" (ibid., 7:6); "Love the Lord in your whole life and one another with a sincere heart" (Testament of Daniel 5:3); "Fear the Lord and love the neighbor" (Testament of Benjamin 3:3); "And he commanded them to keep to the way of God, do justice, and everyone love his/her neighbor" (*Jubilees* 20:9); "Love one another my sons as brothers, as one loves oneself . . . You should love one another as yourselves" (ibid., 36:4–6).

Precisely the same summing up of the Law, *Torah*, in the double commandment of love was expressed by a slightly older Jewish contemporary of Yeshua, Philo of Alexandria (c. 20 BCE–50 CE). In the tractate, "Concerning Individual Commandments," II, 63, he wrote: "There are, so to speak, two fundamental teachings to which the numberless individual teachings and statements are subordinated: in reference to God the commandment of honoring God and piety, in reference to humanity that of the love of humanity (*philanthropia*) and justice."

Phillip Sigal noted that "The rabbi par excellence of the 1st century, Akiba, far from denying that the love command is a significant criterion by which all action should be measured, insisted upon it," and gives the rabbinic references, as well as several other supporting rabbinical citations in addition to those given above.[57]

Of course, much like Hillel and Shammai, founders of great "rabbinic" schools before him, Yeshua developed his own way of how to interpret and apply the Torah to life—not at all a simple matter, as the dozens of volumes of the Talmud indicate. A great deal of Yeshua's Torah interpretation, his *halachot*, can be found imbedded in the Gospels, though perhaps often in redacted form—so, too, of course are the other rabbis' *halachot* redacted in the Talmud. In thus interpreting and applying the Torah, Yeshua followed good rabbinic practice and in no way thereby moved outside Judaism, despite what might be considered by some Jews his "liberal" handling of the Torah—in this he was much more like the liberal Hillel than the conservative Shammai.

If Yeshua applied the Law to concrete life, it would, of course, seem apparent that he was in favor of the Law. But, a traditional Christian maneuver here has been to point out that he abrogated parts of the Law, indeed even the written Torah—something a rabbi would never do. However, as Sigal pointed out, "the abrogation of specific precepts of the written Torah is not unusual for Jesus' milieu," and noted that the tannaitic (the period from about two hundred years before and after the birth of Yeshua) sage R. Nathan stated that, when "one must act for the Lord, annulment of provisions is allowed. He maintains this in reference to either Torah, the written or the interpretative . . . no 'law' is absolute. What stands above all is the will of God,"[58] which is applied though the interpretative wisdom of the rabbi. One example of many such rabbinic abrogations of parts of the written Torah is the rescinding of the trial by ordeal of the suspected adulterous wife (Num 5:11–31) by the contemporary of Yeshua, Rabbi Yohanan ben Zakkai.[59]

A frequent example offered by Christian scholars of Yeshua's "sovereign abrogation" of a central written Torah obligation that supposedly set him outside the rabbinic tradition is Yeshua's statement found in Mark 2:27: "The sabbath was made for human beings, not human beings for the sabbath." However, a very close paraphrase is also found in an early rabbinic writing: "The Sabbath is committed to you; you are not committed to the Sabbath" (*Mekilta* 31:13). In fact, Sigal argues that, "During his brief ministry Jesus was a proto-rabbi (his term for the pre-70 predecessors of the Rabbis of Rabbinic Judaism) whose views influenced his contemporaries

---

57. Phillip Sigal, *The Halakhah of Jesus of Nazareth according to the Gospel of Matthew* (Lanham, MD: University Press of America, 1987) 18.

58. Ibid, 16.

59. *Mishnah*, Sotah 9:9.

and possibly entered tannaitic literature as the views of others . . . A classic example of a view enunciated by Jesus that is attributed to later tanna R. Simon B. Menasia" is the Mekilta statement about the Sabbath.[60] Either way, Yeshua in this regard was in the center of the rabbinic tradition—as being either paralleled or plagiarized.

Sometimes almost in desperation to make Yeshua different, to separate him from Judaism, Christian scholars point out that a number of times Yeshua cites the Torah and then says, "but I say to you," *ego de lego hymin*, arguing that as an ordinary rabbi he could not do such a thing in contradiction to the word of God; he therefore must have divine sovereignty over the Torah. Again, a lack of knowledge of the rabbinic materials has betrayed such Christian scholars. Language of this sort by Yeshua "should not be regarded as evidence of anything more than proto-rabbinic insistence upon one's own view even when it contradicts and abolishes earlier teaching. It is found used by the first/second-century sage, R. Simon b. Yohai, at T. Sot. 6:6–11 . . . It is self-evident that people 'marveled' at Menahem b. Sungai (T. Ed. 3:1) as they did at Jesus (Mt. 7:28)."[61]

Thus, far from being different because of his strong teaching style in regard to Torah, Yeshua fit very well into his intellectual and cultural environment on its account. Later, of course, after 70 CE, the custom developed of deciding on the correct way, the *halacha*, by a majority vote among the rabbis—but that was not yet the case before 70 when Yeshua taught.

The question should also be raised concerning what place Yeshua held among the various Jewish groups of his time that were vying for recognition as *the* correct way to lead a proper human life according to God's Torah. Indeed, the Palestinian Talmud records that at the time of the destruction of the Temple in 70 CE there were twenty-four branches of Judaism![62] There were at least six major groups discernible during the lifetime of Yeshua: (1) The Sadducees, largely patricians who recognized only the written Torah; (2) the Zealots, the ancient equivalents of the Zionists, who sought to reestablish the kingdom of Israel by throwing out the Romans; (3) the Essenes, who were hyper-strict on ritual purity and whose core group lived in monasteries along the Dead Sea; (4) the Hellenists, the vast majority of the then-living Jews who lived in the Roman Empire outside Judea and tried to integrate the Jewish religion with Hellenistic culture; (5) the Pharisees, who first appeared in history a century and a half before the birth of Yeshua and

---

60. Sigal, *Halakhah of Jesus*, 159.

61. Ibid., 81–82.

62. *Palestinian Talmud*, Sanh. 29c, as cited in Phillip Sigal, *Judaism: The Evolution of a Faith* (Grand Rapids: Eerdmans, 1988) 67.

emphasized the twofold Torah, the written and the oral; and (6) the proto-rabbis, who, according to Sigal, were the true predecessors of the post-70 CE. Rabbis of Rabbinic Judaism, and who in their day were independent-minded teachers/sages commanding, like Yeshua (who Sigal says was also a proto-rabbi), significant followings.[63]

Ironically, it is the Pharisees who have most often in Christian history been portrayed as the main enemy of both Yeshua and of Christianity. I say "ironically," because many scholars today are convinced that the Pharisees were in fact the group that Yeshua stood closest to. I have elsewhere gone into some detail about what we know of the Pharisees today and their relationship to Yeshua,[64] but it would be important at least to summarize that material here.

The almost totally negative picture of the Pharisees that Christians have from the Gospels is recognized by many Christian scholars—who assume that the Pharisees were the predecessors of the post-70 Rabbis—to be grossly one-sided and therefore unhistorical. Exactly who and what the pre-70 Pharisees were, however, and their relationship to the post-70 Rabbis as well as to Yeshua is the object of intense research and debate. We do know that there were two major schools of interpretation before 70: the liberal one following Hillel, and the conservative one following Shammai. The Shammai school, it would appear, was largely dominant before 70, that is, during the lifetime of Yeshua, and the Hillel school after 70.[65] Many scholars at-

---

63. See the very important writings of Sigal, which unfortunately have received too little attention. In addition to the two referenced above, see Phillip Sigal, *The Emergence of Contemporary Judaism*, vol. 1, *The Foundations of Judaism*, part 1: *From the Origins to the Separation of Christianity*, Pittsburgh Theological Monograph Series 29 (Pittsburgh: Pickwick, 1980).

64. Leonard Swidler, *Yeshua: A Model for Moderns* (Kansas City, MO: Sheed & Ward, 1988). See also Louis Finkelstein, *The Pharisees*, 2 vols. (Philadelphia: Jewish Publication Society, 1962); R. Travers Herford, *The Aim and Method of Pharisaism*, republished as *The Pharisees* (Boston, MA: Beacon, 1962); Asher Finkel, *The Pharisees and the Teacher of Nazareth* (Leiden: Brill, 1964); Jacob Neusner, *The Rabbinic Traditions about the Pharisees before 70*, 3 vols. (Leiden: Brill, 1971); and John Bowker, *Jesus and the Pharisees* (London: Cambridge University Press, 1973). For updating articles, see Michael Cook, "Jesus and the Pharisees: The Problem as It Stands Today," *Journal of Ecumenical Studies* 15 (Summer 1978) 441–60; Leonard Swidler, "The Pharisees in Recent Catholic Writing," *Horizons* 10 (Fall 1983) 267–87; Lewis Eron, "Implications of Recent Research on the Pharisees for Jewish-Christian Dialogue," in Leonard Swidler, ed., *"Breaking Down the Wall" between Americans and East Germans, Jews and Christians—Through Dialogue* (Lanham, MD: University Press of America, 1987) 131–60.

65. Cf. Gerd Theissen, *Sociology of Early Palestinian Christianity* (Philadelphia: Fortress, 1977) 83: "The result was that in the first century AD they [the Pharisees] split into two schools . . . Thus the Shammaites required strict separation from the Gentiles. In eighteen halachoth, there were prohibitions against various Gentile foods, the Greek

tribute the negative image of the Pharisees in the Gospels largely to the fact that they were written after 70 in a polemic context vis-à-vis a simultaneously emerging rabbinic Judaism. Some would stress the dominance of the conservative Shammaites during Yeshua's lifetime as a source of the polemic between the liberal Yeshua and the Pharisees.[66]

In any case, the picture of the Pharisees that is tentatively emerging from contemporary scholarship—assuming that the Pharisees were really the predecessors of the post-70 Rabbis, and therefore that the early rabbinic attitudes could also be credited to them—is a much more positive one than the dark, legalistic one of the much of the Gospels. Ellis Rivkin, a major scholar in the field of research on the Pharisees,[67] described the heart of

language, Gentile testimony, Gentile gifts, sons and daughters-in-law (j.Shab.3c 49–50). They even used force against the Hillelites to carry through these intensified norms (j.Shab.3c 34–35). Only after the catastrophe of AD 70 did the more moderate Hillelites succeed in gaining the upper hand."

66. E.g., Harvey Falk, *Jesus the Pharisee* (New York: Paulist, 1985).

67. Ellis Rivkin, *A Hidden Revolution* (Nashville: Abingdon, 1978). Rivkin's method is to analyze separately the three bodies of early literature that deal with the Pharisees: The New Testament, late first century CE; the Jewish historian Josephus, late first century CE; early rabbinic writings, e.g., Mishnah, codified late second century, but including materials going back to 200 BCE. He concludes that they all come out with fundamentally the same image of the Pharisees.

Until recently, almost all Christian scholars have simply been ignorant of rabbinic literature. Even now many are reluctant to admit its helpfulness in understanding the New Testament. Christians have often been so bent on insisting on Yeshua's difference from his contemporary fellow Jews that they discount the validity of Mishnaic materials when they produce rabbinic parallels to teachings or actions of Yeshua. It is true that much work remains to be done on the form-critical analysis and dating of these rabbinic writings (Jacob Neusner and his students have been hard at work on the task for years). Nevertheless, if the Mishnah, or even the two Talmuds (Jerusalem and Babylonian, codified at the end of the fourth and fifth centuries, respectively), attribute a teaching to a predecessor or contemporary of Yeshua, the logical assumption should be to accept its accuracy until some counter-evidence challenges it. Such rabbinic documentation would not, of course, be the strongest possible documentary evidence, for the later redactors of the Mishnah and Talmuds reshaped the cited material for their contemporary purposes. It would be stronger, however, than the simple *a priori* assumption that it is not valid merely because it appears in a later codified document. The burden of proof is on the "rejectionist" Christian scholar, not the one who carefully uses rabbinic documents.

A Christian scholar of the targumic literature, Martin McNamara, who has made a study of its relevance to the New Testament, not only said much the same but went farther: "We are still left with the delicate task of how to approach rabbinic material for New Testament studies. Authors, as already noted, differ on the point and most probably will continue to do so. A legitimate, and probably wise approach would appear to be the following: accept rabbinic tradition as the continuation of the Pharisaic tradition of New Testament times and earlier, and regard both as being in the same spirit. Even if a given formulation of rabbinic tradition may be later, it is to be presumed as the Pharisaic teaching in terms of a triad as follows: "(1) The singular Father God so loved the individual that he (2) revealed, through Moses, his twofold Law [that is, the written Law, the Scriptures, and the oral, the rabbinic commentaries and application of the written Law] that, if internalized and steadfastly adhered to, (3) would gain for such an individual eternal life for his soul and the resurrection of his body."[68]

Rather than the Pharisees' being legalistic and formal in their relationship with God, Rivkin's research led him to argue that the opposite was true. He found that the source of the attractive power of the Pharisees was the relationship they established between the one God and the singular individual: "The Father God cared about *you*; He was concerned about *you*. He watched over *you*; He loved *you*; and loved *you* so much that He wished *your* unique self to live forever." For the Pharisees "The Heavenly Father was ever present. One could talk to Him, plead with Him, cry out to Him, pray to Him—person to Person, individual to Individual, heart to Heart, soul to Soul. It was the establishment of this personal relationship, an inner experience, that accounts for the manifest power of Pharisaism to live on ... *Internalization* is the only road to salvation."[69]

---

being in the spirit of earlier Pharisaism. We may freely have recourse to the rabbinic tradition for New Testament studies because of this. Since later development in the rabbinic tradition cannot be denied, however, care must be taken to ascertain the date of each rabbinic tradition used in New Testament studies . . . The problem of dating will always remain with us in the use of this material, and the efforts being made to refine our methodology in its use must continue. But the problems in assigning an exact date to individual pieces of rabbinic tradition are amply offset by the realization that the tradition as a whole has every appearance of continuing the form of Judaism with which Christ and his followers had the closest contact" (Martin McNamara, *Palestinian Judaism and the New Testament* [Wilmington, DE: Michael Glazier, 1984], 177, 204).

The Jewish scholar Geza Vermes, as an expert in both the Jewish literature and the New Testament, categorically supports this position: "Rabbinic literature, skillfully handled, is still the richest source for the interpretation of the original gospel message, and the most precious aid to the quest for the historical Jesus" (Geza Vermes, *Jesus and the World of Judaism* [Philadelphia: Fortress, 1983], 125).

68. Rivkin, *Hidden Revolution*, 293.

69. Ibid., 310; emphasis in the original. The Christian scholar Joachim Jeremias in a number of places has argued that Yeshua's addressing God as *Abba*, Father, was unique and indicated an extraordinarily intimate relationship between Yeshua and God. However, as Rivkin argued, to address God as Father was already something traditionally Pharisaic. Of course God was referred to as Father in the older Hebrew Bible numerous times. In addition, God is addressed as Our Father, *Abinu*, in Jewish, i.e., Pharisaic-Rabbinic, prayers, carefully traced back to the years 10–40 CE by Louis Finkelstein in his *Phariseeism in the Making* (New York: Ktav, 1972) 259–60. There is also evidence that the ancient hasidim—devout Jews living in Palestine before the birth of Yeshua— "spent an hour (in recollection before praying) in order to direct their hearts towards their Father in heaven," from the *Mishnah* Ber. 5:1. There is even evidence that precisely

THE "INTER" DIALOGUE   153

Some scholars, such as Harvey Falk, would place Yeshua close to, though not a formal member of, the Pharisees, especially the Hillel school. Sigal placed Yeshua among the "proto-rabbis," whom, as mentioned, he designates the predecessors of the rabbis. Another proto-rabbi, according

---

the child's term of endearment for father, *Abba*, was used by the first-century Palestinian Jew Hanan to refer to God in prayer: "When the world was in need for rain, the rabbis used to send school children to him, who seized the train of his cloak and said to him, *Abba, Abba*, give us rain! He said to God: Lord of the universe, render a service to those who cannot distinguish between the *Abba* who gives rain and the *Abba* who does not" (*Bab. Talmud* Ta'an 23b). Since here the structure of the whole story is formed around the fact that Hanan referred to *God* in prayer with the same term for father (*Abba*) used by the children to address him, Hanan, the use of the term *Abba* could not be a retrojection into the story from the time of the codification of the Talmud. And, Hanan was a grandson of Honi the Circle-maker, who we know was an adult before Jerusalem fell to Pompey in 63 BCE (see Geza Vermes, *Jesus the Jew* [Philadelphia: Fortress, 1973], 72, 210–11). So, the events of this story probably occurred some years before the birth of Yeshua.

Vermes added to the arguments against Jeremias' "*Abba*" claim in a later book: "Jeremias understood Jesus to have addressed God as 'Dad' or 'Daddy', but apart from the *a priori* improbability and incongruousness of the theory, there seems to be no linguistic support for it. Young children speaking Aramaic addressed their parents *a abba* or *imma* but it was not the only context in which *abba* would be employed. By the time of Jesus, the determined form of the noun, *abba* (= 'the father'), signified also 'my father'; '*my* father', though still attested in Qumran and biblical Aramaic, had largely disappeared as an idiom from the Galilean dialect. Again, *abba* could be used in solemn, far from childish, situations such as the fictional altercation between the patriarchs Judah and Joseph reported in the Palestinian Targum, when the furious Judah threatens the governor of Egypt (his unrecognized brother) saying: 'I swear by the life of the head of *abba* (= my father) as you swear by the life of the head of Pharaoh, your master, that if I draw my sword from the scabbard, I will not return it there until the land of Egypt is filled with the slain.'" (Vermes, *Jesus and the World of Judaism*, 42).

Although Georg Schelbert in "Sprachgeschichtliches zu 'abba,'" in Pierre Casetti, et al., eds., *Mélanges Dominique Barthélemy*, Orbis Biblicus et Orientalis 38 (Fribourg: Editions Universitaires Fribourg, 1981) 395–447, confirmed that "the word play with '*abba*' certainly belongs to the original form of the tradition" of the Gospel story being analyzed, he argued that it is not possible to be certain that the text as we have it is verbatim from before the time of Jesus. Nevertheless, as a result of his thoroughgoing analysis of all the pertinent Aramaic texts and inscriptions, he concluded that, "In the Aramaic language of the time of Jesus, there was absolutely no other word [than *Abba*] available if Jesus wished to speak of or address God as father. Naturally such speaking of and addressing thereby would lose its special character, for it is then indeed the only possible form!" (396). He noted that Jeremias' claim of "special character" for the use by Yeshua—and worldwide popularization of that claim—was not only unwarranted but that this error was also recognized by others (e.g., such recognized scholars as H. Conzelmann, D. Flusser, E. Käsemann, E. Hänchen), and later even partly by Jeremias himself, although "the consequences were really not drawn in his text," nor were the contradictory opinions of the other scholars "hardly really taken account of" (396). Moreover, Schelbert showed in great detail that the Mishnah "without any doubt manifests an extremely intimate relationship to God as 'Father in heaven'" (419).

to Sigal, was Yohanan ben Zakkai. Sigal even made a personal link between Yeshua and the post-70 Rabbis of Yavneh by claiming that the founder of Yavneh and "Rabbinism," Yohanan ben Zakkai, was not only a contemporary of Yeshua but, since he spent twenty years in Galilee, including before and during the time of Yeshua's public ministry, probably was also a colleague of Yeshua:

> Jesus was first a disciple and then a colleague of proto-rabbis in Galilee. The most celebrated of those was Yohanan b. Zakkai. My conjecture is that Jesus and Yohanan were the same age and ultimately were colleagues in Galilee. Jesus would have been a mature disciple and colleague of proto-rabbis during the decade 20–30 when Yohanan b. Zakkai was in Galilee and Jesus was in his formative period. Both probably studied at both the schools of Hillel and Shammai and both took independent directions . . . During Yohanan's period of leadership at Yavneh, no action was taken against Christians.[70]

The deaths of Hillel and Shammai are placed around the years 10 CE and 30 CE, respecttively, and the birth of Yeshua around 4 BCE. If these dates are reasonably accurate, it is even possible that Yeshua sat at the feet of either Hillel or Shammai themselves or both, especially when one recalls that Jewish lads came of age religiously and otherwise at the age of twelve. That Yeshua was already steeped in religious learning by that age is recorded in Luke 2:40–52, where it is said that Yeshua was filled with wisdom and that he spent three days with the rabbis discussing religious matters with them and astonishing them with his answers. (*Didaskalon*, "teachers," which is the term Luke uses here, is what "*rabbi*" came to mean and is doubtless the Greek translation for *rabbi* used throughout the Gospels in general.) In any case, Yeshua probably studied with the rabbis during his youth in Galilee, as did also Yohanan ben Zakkai. It would appear quite unlikely that two such brilliant rabbinic students living and working in the same confined area of Galilee would not have learned of each other's teachings. Further, it seems quite likely that they would have sought each other out for extended discussion, as Sigal suggested. Of this, of course, we have no documentary proof, and so we are left with likelihood.

Some scholars, such as Geza Vermes, have likened Yeshua to the wandering charismatic, wonder-working devout ones (*hasid*) from Galilee, who were popular at that time.[71] His scholarship is very persuasive.

---

70. Sigal, *Halakhah of Jesus*, 248–49.
71. Vermes, *Jesus and the World of Judaism*, 168.

Thus, perhaps the best way to see Yeshua within the context of the Judaism of his time is as a wandering, wonder-working teacher (*rabbi*) from Galilee, a *hasid*, who in many ways was similar to Hillel (whose teaching eventually came to prevail generally over Shammai's in Rabbinic Judaism), and whom some scholars would also see as having had a close relationship to the Pharisees centered in Jerusalem—whom he nevertheless criticized and who in turn criticized him. Sigal would see him as a Galilean *hasid* and a proto-rabbi who, like Yohanan ben Zakkai both before and after 70, severely criticized the Pharisees. I am persuaded that Sigal has provided the most accurate and comprehensive description of Yeshua's place in the Jewish life of his time.

What, then, was special about the teaching of Yeshua? Was there anything at all special? As seen before, the great commandments of love were already there in the Judaic heritage. The notion of freedom from the Law was something that Paul, not Yeshua, expressed (and then only for the gentile followers of Yeshua, not the Jewish; see Romans 9–11).

Of course, there was something special about the teaching of Yeshua. First of all, the specific extraordinary constellation of teachings is a mark of the creative genius of Yeshua. As the Jewish New Testament scholar David Flusser has pointed out, although one may fundamentally be able to reproduce the Gospel out of citations from the many volumes of rabbinic writings, one would first have to have the Gospels before one in order to do it. Further, given the fact that the interpretation and application of the Torah was greatly in flux at the time of Yeshua, his own interpretation "according to the spirit," as Paul later put it (Rom 2:29),[72] was just that, his own, even though it lay in the direction of his great predecessor, Hillel.

However, Yeshua was not satisfied with teaching that the whole of the Torah should be carried out according to its spirit. He went beyond it in holding out the ideal of a self-emptying (kenotic, as Paul said in Phil. 2:6)

72. Ibid., 68. Vermes noted on the one hand that "Jesus . . . more than once expressly urges obedience to the purely ritual and cultic precepts in sayings all the more historically credible in that they are peripheral to the gospel narrative and actually run counter to the essential antinomianism of Gentile Christianity." But, he added that, "the chief distinction of Jesus' piety lies in his extraordinary emphasis on the real inner religious significance of the commandments . . . Philo and Josephus did the same. So did many of the rabbis, and the Qumran sectaries . . . Interiority, purity of intention, played a greater part in Jesus' thought . . . because of his natural bias towards the individual and personal rather than the collective" (Vermes, *Jesus and the World of Judaism*, 47). Jacob Neusner, in his three-volume work *The Rabbinic Traditions about the Pharisees before 70* (1971; reprinted, Eugene, OR: Wipf & Stock, 2005), argued that the Pharisees were essentially *haberim*, a small pacifist party concerned with purity. Rivkin rejected this, as Sanders did also: "His [Neusner's] analysis of the rabbinic texts is unpersuasive and is made especially dubious by the evidence from Josephus" (Sanders, *Jesus and Judaism*, 188).

love for one's friends, one's neighbors, even one's enemies—as seen especially in the Sermon on the Mount (Matthew 5–7). The Rabbis had a phrase for halachic decisions that went beyond the demands of the Torah, *lifnim meshurat hadin* ("beyond the requirements of the court"): "Proto-rabbis sometimes encouraged going beyond the strict requirement of law or the literal reading of a text. In this way they inspired some to sacrifice their monetary or property right under law in order to extend equity to others. This is how we are to understand Mt. 5:40 ['And if anyone sue you at law and take away your coat, let him have your cloak as well.']."[73]

However, what was most special about Yeshua was that he *lived* not only according to the Torah but also according to his supererogatory kenotic ideal, *lifnim meshurat hadin*—even to the point of agonizingly dying for the sake of his friends: "Greater love than this has no one, but that he gives his life for his friends" (that is, for those loved by him, *ton philon autou*, Jn. 15:13). As Vermes put it, "the heart of Jesus' message" was its "stress on interiority and supererogation."[74]

Thus, what apparently struck many of Yeshua's contemporaries about him and made them his disciples must have been his inner wisdom and love, which shone through his teaching the fulfillment of the whole Torah according to its spirit. He presented an ideal of kenotic love that went beyond it, and lived and died accordingly in his *whole* person. What Yeshua "thought, taught, and wrought," that whole, that life (and death) is what made Yeshua special—for many, a human transparency of the divine.

For Yeshua it was not a question of living by the Law, the Torah, *or* the spirit but, rather, by living the whole Law (Torah) according to its spirit; he thought, taught, and wrought a life that was open to and showed forth the Source and Goal of the Torah—*YHWH*: "Be perfect as my heavenly Father is perfect." Not freedom *from* the Law but freedom *through* the Law *and beyond* to kenotic love, *lifnim meshurat hadin*. Augustine put it: "Love, and do what you will," "*Ama, et fac quod vis*," for your love will lead you not contrary to the Law, but to it, and beyond.

Despite Yeshua's uniqueness, however, he did not step outside the pale of Judaism of his time. His later followers' beliefs about him are what eventually moved outside of Judaism. It is clear, nevertheless, that, however contemporary Christians understand themselves, if they want to be attached to their cornerstone, they need to recover an understanding of Yeshua—and he was through and through Jewish.

---

73. Sigal, *Halakhah of Jesus*, 79.
74. Vermes, *Jesus and the World of Judaism*, 55.

Christianity's Jewish Roots: The Jewish Christian Church?

Not only was Yeshua thoroughly Jewish, but so, too, was the band of his first followers, the incipient Christian Church. Like Yeshua, it was in many ways—more than I can spell out here—close to Phariseeism. To paraphrase Rivkin, it was not only Yeshua who was nurtured in the triadic teaching of the Pharisees; the same was also true for nascent Christianity: Stunned by the crucifixion, Yeshua's disciples reached out to the Triad and experienced Yeshua risen from the dead. The promise of the Scribes-Pharisees was a true promise indeed! God does raise from the dead. The Son of Humanity lives on. The Messiah reveals his authenticity by witnessing to God's power to quicken the dead, just as the Pharisees had time and again proved from the Scriptures. The Resurrected Christ was the living truth of a central element of Pharisaic teaching. The Triad was reinforced, but with a modification: God had revealed in addition to the twofold Law, Yeshua as the Christ; Christ must be *internalized* if the promise of eternal life and resurrection and the coming of the Reign of God was to be fulfilled. Thus for both the Pharisees and the Christians the Triad was: (1) the Father God, (2) the revelation of God's will (twofold Law for the Pharisees, Christ for the Christians), (3) eternal life and resurrection. "The middle term is the crux. It was here that the Christians parted company with their teachers."[75]

Even Paul, the sometimes alleged fabricator of Christianity, was not only thoroughly Jewish but also specifically a Pharisee—and that of *Bet Hillel*, for he noted that he was brought up in Jerusalem as a disciple of Gamaliel, the son of Hillel (Acts 22:3). Moreover, Paul not only *was* a Pharisee (Phil 3:5: "I was a Pharisee"; Acts 26:5: "I lived as a Pharisee"), but even long after his "conversion" experience he stated "I *am* a Pharisee," *ego Pharisaios eimi* (Acts 23:6). For Paul, as for Yeshua and his disciples, that apparently meant strict adherence to the twofold Torah, for he claimed that he was "blameless in the Law," *en nomoi genomenos ameptos* (Phil 3:6); note, the tense is not past, but present), and that up to the moment of his trial before the Roman Festus he had not sinned "against the Law of the Jews" (Acts 25:8).

---

75. Rivkin, *A Hidden Revolution*, 303–4. On p. 308, Rivkin added an interesting note: "The Pharisaic and Christian revolutions seeded still a third spiritual revolution when Muhammad revealed his own version of the Triad. For him, as for the Pharisees and for the Christians, God was the Father who had revealed the way to eternal life. The Triad, as form, is thus identical. What Muhammad altered was the middle term: God's will was made known to Muhammad in its purest form; and it is this will that the true Muslim must internalize. The teachings of the Koran displaced the twofold Law; the words of Muhammad, Christ. Islam emerged as living witness to the power of Pharisaism and to the power of Christ. Pharisaism thus generated two blooming offshoots: Christianity and Islam."

It is also clear that Paul, like Yeshua, intended that not only he should continue to observe the Torah, but so also should all born Jews: "Behold, I Paul tell you that if you are circumcised Christ will profit you nothing. I testify again to every man who receives circumcision that he is bound to keep the whole law" (Gal 5:2–3); "For neither circumcision counts for anything nor uncircumcision . . . Everyone should remain in the state in which he was called" (1 Cor 7:19–20). There is also evidence that Paul and the other followers of Yeshua in Jerusalem agreed that the gentiles were not obliged to follow the Torah but, rather, the Noahide Commandments (the seven basic ones are prohibitions of idolatry, blasphemy, killing, stealing, sexual sins, eating the limb of a living animal [cruelty to animals], and the command to establish courts of justice)—an abbreviated list is given in Acts 15:20, 29.

Note should also be taken of the statement of the Hillelite Gamaliel, made before 85 CE, presumably during the leadership of Yohanan ben Zakkai (post-70), Yeshua's contemporary (and colleague?), throughout which period no negative action was taken by the "Rabbis" against the followers of Yeshua, which lends further credence to Sigal's claim that Yohanan ben Zakkai and Yeshua had known each other. It also appears to support Rabbi Emden and Rabbi Falk's claim that disciples of Yeshua followed in the footsteps of *Bet Hillel* in launching a religion for the gentiles and that Gamaliel did not wish to block their efforts:[76] "But a Pharisee in the council named Gamaliel, a teacher

---

76. Falk wrote: "What emerges from this study is a new scenario of the times of Jesus, Paul and the Apostles. The Romans had conquered the land of Israel during the century before Jesus' birth. The Jewish People knew from an ancient prophecy that their Temple in Jerusalem would be destroyed by the Gentile enemy." However, Falk argued that *Bet Hillel* believed that reaching out to the Gentiles was the correct approach. "They maintained that righteous Gentiles merit salvation just as Jews do, and it was their hope that a mission to the Gentiles could avert the destruction of their land. *Bet Shammai*, however, looked down upon the Gentile world, holding that not even the most righteous Gentile could merit a share in the World to Come" (Falk, *Jesus the Pharisee*, 8). Following this line of thought of the famous eighteenth-century talmudist, Rabbi Jacob Emden (see Harvey Falk, "Rabbi Jacob Emden's Views on Christianity," *Journal of Ecumenical Studies* 19 [Winter 1982] 105–11), Falk argued that Yeshua was influenced by the *Bet Hillel* teaching and action to launch a ministry to "create a religion for the Gentiles based on the Noahide Commandments" (Falk, "Rabbi Emden," 106). In offering evidence, he wrote: "I discovered a passage in the Jerusalem Talmud recording that Menahem the Essene and one hundred and sixty disciples had left the Jewish community about 20 BCE on a mission to the Gentiles . . . This Menahem had served as a vice-president of the Sanhedrin under the sage Hillel some thirty years before Jesus' birth. The Mishnah makes quite clear that Menahem subjected himself totally to Hillel's authority" (Falk, *Jesus the Pharisee*, 6). Falk likewise argued that Yeshua "never wished to see his fellow Jews change one iota of their traditional faith. He himself remained an Orthodox Jew to his last moment. He only wished to see his people return to the teachings of the School of Hillel, which stressed love, humility, and the salvation of all mankind" (Falk, *Jesus the Pharisee*, 158).

of the law, held in honor by all the people . . . said: 'Men of Israel . . . keep away from these men and let them alone; for if this plan or this undertaking is of men, it will fail; but if it is of God, you will not be able to overthrow them. You might even be found opposing God!'" (Acts 5:34–9).

Although Jewish scholars have customarily perceived Paul as an apostate who deserted Judaism—Christian scholars also agreed that he left Judaism behind, but saw that as a great advance—that misperception is just now beginning to change. Christian scholars such as W. D. Davies[77] and Sanders[78] have begun to change the Christian anti-Jewish understanding of Paul, but so too have Jewish scholars such as Lester Dean,[79] Nancy Fuchs-Kreimer,[80] and Sigal. Sigal, for example, wrote: "Paul's teaching was not antithetical to Judaism . . . Paul (or Saul as he was originally called) was a proto-rabbinic disciple of Gamaliel I, a leading proto-rabbi . . . This schism [Judaism and Christianity] was not the work of Paul or the result of his theology . . . Paul's theses of early Christian theology are basically Judaic, and under normal circumstances would have made only for differentiation within Judaism . . . It cannot plausibly be argued that in the years 45–65 CE Paul's teaching would be considered either heretical or un-Jewish."[81]

Thus, Yeshua and nascent Christianity grew out of not only the Hebraic religion of the Hebrew Bible but even also partially right out of the root of its sibling Proto-Rabbinic-Pharisaic Judaism. Christianity and Rabbinic Judaism in the beginning were simply two different ways of being Jewish. In fact,

---

I have argued in these pages in favor of this description of Yeshua's positive attitude toward the Torah and his fellow Jews. However, the argument that Yeshua, and not first Paul and other disciples, moved to launch a Noachide commandments-based religion for Gentiles is not sustained by sufficient evidence, I believe. Sanders was correct, I am convinced, when he wrote that "Jesus does not seem to have made a definite gesture in favour of including gentiles in the kingdom, although he may well have envisaged their inclusion at the eschaton. The evidence to be discussed below will show Jesus not to have been *directly* concerned with the Gentiles." He later added that "although we need not think that Jesus imparted to his disciples any view at all about the Gentiles and the kingdom . . . the overwhelming impression is that Jesus started a movement which *came to see the Gentiles mission as a logical extension of itself*" (Sanders, *Jesus and Judaism*, 68, 221, 220).

77. W. D. Davies, *Paul and Rabbinic Judaism*, rev. ed. (New York: Harper & Row, 1965).

78. E. P. Sanders, *Paul and Palestinian Judaism* (Philadelphia: Westminster, 1977).

79. Leonard Swidler, et al., *Bursting the Bonds: A Jewish-Christian Dialogue on Jesus and Paul* (Maryknoll, NY: Orbis, 1990).

80. Nancy Fuchs-Kreimer, "The Essential Heresy: Paul's View of the Law according to Jewish Writers, 1886–1986," unpublished PhD diss., Temple University, Philadelphia, 1990.

81. Sigal, *Judaism*, 76–80.

that was even the first name for Christianity, The Way *(hodos* in the Greek of the Acts of the Apostles). St. Luke argued that Christians embodied a proper "*understanding and practice of Pharisaic Judaism.* Judaism and the Christian movement are not two separate religions. Rather, Christ's church must be thought of as that 'Way' that takes up the law, prophets, and the traditions of Judaism into itself."[82]

Pharisaic-Rabbinic Judaism was also a "way" of being Jewish, for its adherents were taught to follow the *halachah*, Hebrew for "way"; the fact that the term for the Christian was Greek and for the Jew was Hebrew was also prophetic of these two ways of being Jewish: Christianity was early deluged with Hellenism, both in membership and in thought patterns, and, although this deluge brought much of value, it also brought much that was problematic, most profoundly the almost total rejection of its Jewish roots.

Yeshua: Messiah or Christ?

If Yeshua taught that the Torah should be observed, should his followers then observe the Torah? Put that way, the answer seems an obvious "Yes." And that is precisely what all his first followers thought, too, and they acted accordingly. Peter and the other disciples and followers went to pray at the Temple and synagogue and observed the Torah. But, after a while as their teaching spread, there arose the problem of the gentiles. Could they also become followers of the Way? The first answer was "Yes." The Jews had already been doing it for scores of years. These gentile converts to Judaism were called proselytes; they were circumcised and took on the full observance of the Torah.

But, in the synagogues outside of Israel there were not only born Jews and proselytes, but also the so-called "God-fearers" (*phoboumenoi ton theon*), who apparently were much more numerous than the proselytes. The God-fearers were gentiles who accepted the teachings, ethics, scriptures, and main cultic practices such as the Sabbath, but they were not circumcised and did not follow all the ritual laws of Judaism. From among them came many of the first followers of the Way outside of Israel. At first they were often told they had to become full-fledged Jews in order to be followers of the Way (to be Jewish), to be followers of Yeshua. It made sense, but not complete sense to all. The scores of thousands of God-fearers in the Roman Empire had earlier decided to throw in their lot with Judaism, but not including circumcision and the full observance of the Torah. Why should

---

82. John Koenig, *Jews and Christians in Dialogue* (Philadelphia: Westminster, 1979) 119.

they change that decision in order to be associated with one particular Way of being Jewish?

The obvious direct way to solve that problem was to inquire what Yeshua had to say on the matter. Unfortunately, he had said nothing. As we read over the Gospels it appears that Yeshua felt himself sent "only to the lost sheep of the people of Israel" (Matt 15:24), as he told his disciples, and that, when he sent out the Twelve to preach the Good News, he said to them, "Do not go to any Gentile territory or any Samaritan towns. Go instead to the lost sheep of the people of Israel" (Matt 10:5). However, when gentiles came to him, he responded to them—he healed the child of the Syro-Phoenecian woman and of the centurion. Thus, it would seem that the teachings and actions of Yeshua did not speak directly to his later followers' problem, a situation that is bound to occur frequently in every movement.

Hence, the early Jewish followers of Yeshua had to solve their problem by applying the spirit of the teaching and life of Yeshua—what he thought, taught, and wrought—to their contemporary situation. They decided, after a struggle between Peter and Paul, along the lines of the God-fearers' solution: Those who were born Jews had received the privilege and burden of the Torah and should, as Yeshua himself taught and did, continue to observe it; those who were not should simply accept the Jewish teachings, Scriptures, ethics, and main cultic customs as focused through Yeshua, but they did not have to take on circumcision and the full obligation of the Torah, especially the ritual customs.[83]

But, something else very critical happened in this early gestation period of the Christian religion. Yeshua had taught his followers to live a life that was intensely, interiorly, and in prophet-like concern for the oppressed, faithful to God's Torah. His followers also thought after a while that he was the promised "anointed one" of God, the *Meshiach*, the Messiah, who was to overthrow Israel's yoke of Roman occupation and become king. Yeshua told them often that his kingdom was not to be a political one, but they nevertheless set their hearts wildly on the imminent in-breaking of God's reign under the religious and political leadership of the *Meshiach*, who they believed was Yeshua. This was not unheard of in the Judaism of that time, as it languished under the foreign oppression of the Roman Empire. There were many messianic claimants. For example, a hundred years after the death of Yeshua, Rabbi Akiba, who is highly revered in the Jewish community to

---

83. See Theissen, *Sociology*, 58: "The Jesus movement found doors opened to them in the Hellenistic cities because they could offer prospects of a resolution of the tensions between Jews and Gentiles: theirs was a universalistic Judaism, which was open to outsiders."

this very day, proclaimed that the anti-Roman Jewish freedom fighter Bar Kochba (who went down to defeat in 135 CE) was the *Meshiach*.

Those high, wild-hearted hopes were crushingly dashed on Good Friday. All seemed destroyed. They said, "This man was a prophet, and was considered by God and by all the people to be mighty in words and deeds. Our chief priests and rulers handed him over to be sentenced to death, and they nailed him to the cross. And we had hoped that he would be the one who would *set Israel free*" (Luke 24:19–21). However, as we know, it did not all end there. Three days after Good Friday was Easter, the Resurrection event. The followers of Yeshua experienced him now not only as the charismatic teacher who was ignominiously executed but also as the one raised up to a new life by God.

How is this extraordinary event described in the New Testament? In some ways, not very precisely, which is not surprising since it is said to be a unique event—there was nothing else exactly like it to compare with. It is clear from the New Testament what is *not* meant: The claim is *not* that the cadaver of Yeshua was simply resuscitated. The Risen One is described as having characteristics other than a normal human body. It was unrecognizable as Yeshua by Mary Magdalene in the garden (John 20:14) and by his disciples on the road to Emmaus (Luke 24:16); it appeared in various forms, including as a blinding light to Paul on the way to Damascus (Acts 3), and is cryptically described by Paul as a body "raised in glory . . . a spiritual body" (1 Cor 15:43–4). In any case, the New Testament describes the Risen One as not less real than the historical, pre-Good Friday Yeshua, but as the same Yeshua now "really" living *on another level*.

However, many scholars are not convinced that the Easter experience was just something that happened in the minds and hearts of Yeshua's followers, although obviously something very profound did happen there. Many historians looking at subsequent developments wonder how the psychologically crushed, relatively ignorant fishers, farmers, and women could have so turned themselves around, as the evidence shows they obviously did, simply on the basis of a mass psychological experience. At any rate, Christians scholars will have to content themselves with saying that something extraordinary called the resurrection happened that called forth a proportionate *teshuvah, metanoia*, conversion, turning around, in the disciples.

Something else very important to bear in mind in regard to the resurrection of Yeshua is the nature of language and particularly metaphorical language. It was earlier noted that not only is all language necessarily limited in its ability to capture and reexpress reality, but that it is most especially so concerning religious language, which attempts to deal with the meaning of things "beyond" the everyday level, the "transcendent." Hence, religious and ideological language must often move to metaphor to point to that which "goes beyond" or "transcends" the everyday. This metaphorical use of language naturally reaches its highest point when referring to the most comprehensive elements of the meaning of life. Also, each of these chief ultimate metaphors is culture-specific, culture-bound.

For example, for Indian culture the "self" is central, whether in the Hindu version where the prescribed ultimate meaning of life is the total union of the "self," *atman*, with its source, *Brahman*, or the Buddhist version where the true "self," *atman*, is described in terms of the "no-self," *anatman* (in Sanskrit, or *anatta* in Pali—more on this below). In Hellenistic culture the major metaphor of the ultimate meaning of life was the immortality of the spiritual, substantial soul, the *psyche*. In the Hebraic culture, the major metaphor that developed, particularly with the Pharisees and subsequently, was that of the resurrection of the body. The deepgoing difference between these latter two major meaning metaphors was why Luke reports that Paul was laughed out of the Areopagus by the Greeks in Athens when he tried to teach them about Yeshua and his resurrection: "When they heard Paul speak about a raising from death, some of them made fun of him" (Acts 17:32).

Thus, in the Buddhist culture to say the uttermost about someone would be to state that one had attained *nirvana*, literally a "blowing out" of all the false selves until the awareness of the final true self, expressed paradoxically as "no-self, *anatta*," was reached. In Greek culture someone would be said to have attained "immortality," that is, one's *psyche* was said to be immortal. But, those were not the major meaning metaphors in Jewish culture, where the ultimate that could be said of someone was that one had been bodily raised up by God. Since all the first followers of Yeshua were, like Yeshua himself, Jews, the only way they could say the uttermost about him and the meaning he had for their lives was to use their own major meaning metaphor, bodily resurrection.

In light of the extraordinary, energizing Easter experience, the followers of Yeshua began to reflect on everything he had said and done. They thus began to see things they were unaware of at the time. More and more they were convinced that God had been doing great things in Yeshua. As they reflected, they tried to name these great things, and so Yeshua was retrospectively given various titles: Lord, Savior, Son of Humanity, Son of God, etc. One title, *Meshiach*, was still attributed to him, as perhaps it was during his historical life, but now inwardly transformed, spiritualized. It comes down to us from the New Testament Greek as *Christos*, Christ. Thus, it is more accurate to say that Christians claim that Yeshua, crucified and raised up, is not the *Meshiach*, Messiah, as promised in the Scriptures—among other things a king who would liberate the nation Israel and bring universal peace was promised—but is the Christ, now spiritualized to mean somehow a meeting point of the human and divine.

Thus, in short order Yeshua, the Christ, becomes the door through which the gentiles enter into the knowledge (not just of the head but also of the heart, and not just individually but also into a community) of the one God, the Creator, the Source and Goal of all being, and of how they should live according to God's design, God's Torah. Because many gentiles came to the one true God through Yeshua the Christ, they called themselves Christians, but most born Jews in effect said: "Yeshua, yes—Messiah or Christ, no. Yeshua clearly did not fulfill the promises of the *Meshiach*, and we are not in need of a Christ to bring us to the one true God—we know God already."

As is familiar, later Christian tradition has tended to follow one school of thought in the New Testament, represented by Mark, and especially Matthew, namely, that "since we have been saved by Jesus, the *person* of Jesus as savior becomes as important as the *message* of salvation. In sum, the eschaton is historicized and the preacher becomes the preached" (although some recent theological thought argues that "Matthew's soteriology is based upon Torah; while it is Jesus who brings salvation, by interpreting the Law, it is finally the Law itself that is the efficient means of salvation, and not any kind of vicarious atonement . . . Rightly-interpreted Torah would indeed seem to be the actual basis of salvation").[84] However, Luke's Gospel offers a different theology: "For Luke, the historicized eschatology was not borne out in the lived experience of the early Christian community. Salvation had not been accomplished in any final sense." Thus, to call Yeshua the Messiah in any final sense would seem inappropriate. "The glimpse provided by Yeshua, and provided by God at other times throughout human history, allows all people to hope together that the Messiah will come and will make the end-time permanently part of history. Thus we see that the Messiah-event is not yet complete." Rather, Jesus began the restoration, "but Jesus is only the Messiah in an anticipatory way. All humanity, Jews and Christians, are still waiting."[85]

---

84. See Joseph G. Kelly, "Lucan Christology and the Jewish-Christian Dialogue," *Journal of Ecumenical Studies* 21 (Fall 1984) 691, for the first quotation; the second is from Russell Pregeant, *Christology beyond Dogma* (Philadelphia: Fortress, 1978) 61, 72. In analyzing Matt 5:17–20, Pregeant said that "the complex of vv. 17–19 draws the reader toward a recognition of the abiding validity of the Torah itself as the means of entering the Kingdom . . . In the background stands the assumption of God's continuing history of self-revelation to his people Israel."

85. Ibid., 691, 707–8.

Though it is through Yeshua, the *Christos*, that gentiles entered into the knowledge of the one true God, it was not just as individuals but as participants in a community of persons with such knowledge. This community (*qahal* in Hebrew, and *ekklesia* and *synagoge* in its two Greek translations) is the people Israel, the Jewish people, for they were the worshipers of the one true God who was revealed as the God of Abraham, Sarah, Isaac, Rebecca, Jacob, and Rachel. Gentiles became fellow members of this community of believers through the Jew Yeshua by becoming his followers, his imitators. They became members of the people of Israel by adoption. The Catholic Church acknowledges this when, echoing Paul (Gal 3:7), it states that all Christians are Abraham's children according to the faith and that the Christian *qahal* "draws sustenance from the root of that good olive tree [the Jewish people] unto which have been grafted the wild olive branches of the Gentiles (cf. Rom 11:17–24)."[86] It is to this adoption that Pope Pius XI was obviously referring when he remarked that Christians are all spiritual Semites.

Christians are not the new Israel. No such term was used by Yeshua or any of the New Testament writers. There is only one people Israel, the worshipers of Yahweh, the one true God, the God of Abraham, Sarah, Isaac, Rebecca, Rachel, and Jacob (also known as Israel). This is the primary meaning of the term, "the people Israel." Ethnicity and politics were and are important elements in the notion of the people Israel, but not the most fundamental. The basic unity of Israel is religious; Israel is the people of Yahweh. The term "Israel" was claimed by the nation under David and Solomon; then it went to the Northern Kingdom alone, after whose destruction the term was transferred to the Southern Kingdom, Judah. But, although the state of Israel was destroyed for almost two millennia in 70 CE, the people Israel continued to exist. In fact it had already existed mostly outside of the land of Israel for centuries before that. Moreover, there were many, many converts to the religion of Yahweh, most of whose adherents no longer spoke Hebrew long before the beginning of the Common Era, but none of these political and ethnic changes of the first magnitude could destroy the fundamental unity of the people Israel, as long as they believed in Yahweh and followed Yahweh's Way—recall, for the followers of the Pharisees that Way was *halacha*, and for the followers of Yeshua it was *hodos*.

---

86. Vatican II, "Declaration on Non-Christian Religions" ("*Nostra aetate*") no. 4.

Yeshua and His Disciples Thought Jewishly

We now come to an extremely crucial and delicate point following from the Jewishness of Yeshua and his first followers, the founders of The Way of Christianity. Because they were all Jews, they thought and talked like Jews. Consequently, if we are to understand correctly what Yeshua and his first followers meant when they spoke, we will have to perceive their statements in their Jewish categories and thought patterns. Not to do so would be to read *our* foreign meaning into their statements and actions rather than to draw out *their* intended meaning. We would be engaged in *eis*egesis instead of *ex*egesis. The Catholic systematic theologian Edward Schillebeeckx stressed this when he wrote: "Jesus was a Jew; and his close friends and disciples also thought as faithful Jews would think. It was as Jews that they were to interpret Jesus."[87]

The Catholic exegete, Prelate Franz Mussner, made the same point very strongly: "Jesus . . . thought and spoke in 'Jewish categories.' That, however, brought with it consequences of worldwide and world-historical magnitude . . . The Gentiles learned and learn to think and speak in 'Jewish categories.' The world became 'Jewish' through Jesus of Nazareth, and it belongs to the work of the Antichrist to again 'dejudaize' the world, especially in the area of language."[88] An American Catholic theologian, Bernard J. Lee, argued similarly: "It is my judgment that when Jesus is allowed to speak from the world in which he lived, it is a Jewish interpreter we hear."[89]

Those Christians who have gone the route of seeking out interpretations of the words and actions of Yeshua and his first followers that are different than Jewish understandings have obviously turned away from Yeshua and the founders of Christianity. To be sure, there were disputes among the Jews themselves about the correct meaning of many things, but these disputes all took place within an accepted framework of meaning.

It is within that broad Jewish framework of meaning that Yeshua and the founders of The Way thought and acted. Consequently, it is also the framework within which subsequent followers of Yeshua will have to understand Yeshua and his followers first if they are to grasp their message, their "good news," correctly. Of course, ways of thinking other than Jewish can be of great value, and Christians certainly are to be encouraged to embrace everything of value. Non-Jewish ways of thinking, however, will not be of value in understanding what Yeshua and his first followers said and did. In

---

87. Edward Schillebeeckx, *Jesus* (New York: Seabury, 1979) 527.
88. Mussner, *Tractate on the Jews*, 113–14.
89. Bernard J. Lee, *The Galilean Jewishness of Jesus* (New York: Paulist, 1988) 116.

fact, they can be extremely misleading and even fundamental hindrances to the "good news," the gospel of Yeshua and his first followers, if so applied.

Küng has also made a similar point by referring to the beliefs of the first believers in Yeshua, the Jewish-Christians: "The later, Hellenistically-influenced Gospel of John quotes Jesus as speaking of the glory that he had with God before the world began (17:5), which even conservative exegetes do not hold to be the words of the historical Jesus; the first three Gospels know nothing of a preexistence of Jesus." (He added that the first gospel, Mark, also knows nothing of a virgin birth.) In addition, "while right up to the account of the passion, the Gospel of John presents Jesus almost excessively as god-like as he roams the earth (but yet clearly distinguished from God!), the synoptic Gospels still present him as wholly Son of Man, through whom God acts."

Küng then noted that exegetes point especially to the monologues of the Acts of the Apostles, in which Luke uses an old tradition that has Jesus totally subordinate to God. "Clearly Jesus is spoken of as the servant *of God*, the Messiah, the Christ *of God*, the chosen one *of God*: God acts through him, God was with him, he was killed according to the plan of God, but God raised him from the dead and made him Lord and Christ, appointing him Son of God." Then Küng asked: "Do not all these statements of Luke—colored as they are by an 'adoptive' perspective—still have a certain place within the framework of a strict Jewish or Islamic faith [Küng was trying here to build a theological, christological bridge from Christianity to Judaism, and, especially, Islam] in one God? Yet this was the faith of Christians—of Jewish Christians!"[90]

As noted above, such a principle of understanding—in the jargon of today, such a principle of hermeneutics—of course will not solve those problems that were not addressed directly by Yeshua or his first followers, but it will provide a boundary outside of which solutions cannot be sought and still claim to be authentically Christian, namely, the correct understanding—that is, within the Jewish framework of meaning—of what Yeshua and his first followers said and did.

Such a principle of understanding appears quite straightforward and simple, but the grasp of this simple principle depends on perceiving all statements about the meaning of things to be relational, that is, properly understood only when seen in relation to the persons who made the statements, the contexts in which they made them, the patterns of thought and speech they used, etc. Such a perception is standard fare, as we have seen,

---

90. Hans Küng, "Christianity among World Religions: The Dialogue with Islam as One Model," *Harvard Divinity Bulletin* 15 (December, 1984–January, 1985) 8.

for a contemporary Western scholar—post historicism, sociology of knowledge, and linguistic analysis. This was not so, however, in the past.

Once the principle of understanding the Gospel relationally—that is, within the Jewish framework of meaning that Yeshua and his first followers embraced—has been raised to the conscious level, it is no longer possible with integrity for Christians so conscienticized not to follow it, for they would know that they were not following Yeshua. Moreover, following such a principle of understanding, simple and obvious as it seems to many today, will occasion in many instances a radical rethinking of Christian teaching to bring it in line with the thought of Yeshua and his first followers, the founders of The Way, Christianity—to bring it in line with their Jewish way of understanding. This is also true in regard to the central teaching of Christianity, upon which everything else depends: Christology, the teaching about the meaning of Christ.

It is clear that Yeshua's followers thought of him during his lifetime as the *Meshiach*, with all its political implications. Judging from contemporary scripture scholarship, it is unlikely that Yeshua himself ever claimed to be the *Meshiach*.[91] But, even if he did think of and claim himself to be the *Meshiach*, it was in very transformed, spiritualized fashion; the same was also true of his followers after the crucifixion and resurrection event. In any case, Jews never thought of the *Meshiach* (Christ—and who else thought of a *Meshiach* but a Jew?) as being divine in an ontological sense. The *Meshiach* was called "a son of God" by Jews, but never in an ontological sense. For the Jews this language was always understood in a nonontological sense, and Yeshua and his first followers were Jews. They thought and spoke as Jews. Consequently, when speaking of Yeshua as *Meshiach*, or even in the transformed, spiritualized sense of *Christos,* these Jews were not speaking ontologically. It was not the Jews but the Greeks who developed the ontological framework of thinking. Pouring ontological meaning into the nonontological Jewish language of Yeshua and his first Jewish followers, again is to engage not in *ex*egesis but in *eis*egesis.

What about the christological dogmas of the Councils of Nicaea (325), Constantinople (381), and Chalcedon (451)? Are they not full of ontological meanings? Whatever they are, surely they should be understood in light

---

91. Cf. Edouard Schweizer, *Jesus Christus* (Hamburg, 1972) 19–20; Ernst Käsemann, *Das Problem des historischen Jesus—exegetische Besinnungen* (Göttingen, 1960) 1:187, 205. The Professor of New Testament on the Protestant faculty of the University of Bern, Switzerland, Ulrich Luz, made the point even more sharply: "Not only did Jesus not declare himself to his people as the Messiah; more than likely he did not even consider himself to be the Messiah" (in Pinchas Lapide and Ulrich Luz, *Jesus in Two Perspectives* [Minneapolis: Augsburg, 1985] 129).

of what Yeshua and his first followers understood themselves to be teaching—and they understood themselves Jewishly, that is, nonontologically in these matters.

The whole question of understanding religious language was insightfully analyzed by the religious philosopher Alfred North Whitehead. He pointed out that a problem arises when readers of any language misunderstand its nature—"specifically, when they take it to be literal rather than analogical." "When a religion takes its faith-statements as dogmas, as denoting the content of faith in a direct, precise, literal fashion, then it distorts the relationship between language and faith (see Alfred North Whitehead, *Religion in the Making* [New York: Macmillan, 1927], 145). Properly understood, religious statements (like all other statements) are primarily lures for feeling."[92]

Küng raises the same issue and responded in a similar fashion: "As a European Gentile Christian I can quite well understand the Hellenistic development of Christology; I can accept the truth of the great christological councils of Nicaea through Chalcedon; [note this important following norm, however—emphasis added] its great intentions and substance can *in light of the New Testament* be completely affirmed."

But, he added, in the ecumenical context he must ask: "How can I make understandable to a Muslim (or a Jew) why Christians believe in this Jesus as the Christ, the revelation of God?" In answer he insisted, "I have complete right to refer to the original christological option which was forced to the edge and covered over," which he stated is nevertheless completely legitimate, "the one on the basis of which the disciples of Jesus and the oldest Jewish Christian communities proceeded and which for hundreds of years was carried further by the Jewish-Christian communities scattered in Transjordan and probably as far as Arabia, and thus ultimately were likewise handed on to Mohammed." Finally, he asked "whether possibly here already are the categories which make this Jesus as the revelation

---

92. Pregeant, *Christology beyond Dogma*, 38–39. In discussing the language of the Tome of Pope Leo the Great, which became so influential in the christological language of the Council of Chalcedon, Monika Hellwig remarked: "Throughout this document, Leo argues directly from the language of worship and piety to the abstract formulations that came to dominate the Council of Chalcedon. There is, of course, no reflection on the nature of religious language . . . one is compelled to ask whether there may have been a misperception of literary genre. The poetic language of piety seems to be used as though it were a simple historical record of the already self-critically nuanced language of a systematic exposition" (Monika Hellwig, "From the Jesus of Story to the Christ of Dogma," in Alan T. Davies, ed., *Antisemitism and the Foundations of Christianity* [New York: Paulist, 1979] 123). For a further discussion of this matter, see below.

of God more understandable to Jews and Muslims than the Hellenistic two-nature doctrine."[93]

Is there not a clear logic in contemporary Christians' taking as a basic standard of the meaning of Yeshua the explanation given by the chief of the Apostles, Peter (presumably his testimony would be very weighty with his "successor," the pope, and the more than a billion Catholics): "Jesus of Nazareth, a man (*andra*) attested to you by God with . . . signs which God did through him . . . God raised him up . . . This Jesus God raised up . . . God has made him both lord and Christ" (Acts 2:22, 24, 32, 36)? It is clear that Peter thought of Yeshua as a man (*andra*) in whom God was manifested through "mighty works and wonders and signs," who was killed and then raised to a new life as "lord and Christ" by God. If the first followers of Yeshua, after the resurrection event (led by no less a figure than Peter, according to Luke), held such a "low" Christology, should such a position not enjoy the greatest of respect? Such a "low" Christology is not simply "lifted up," by a "high" Christology that speaks of Yeshua as man and God; it is "swallowed up" and changed from a Jewish to a Hellenistic way of thinking.

Is this simple principle of understanding (that Yeshua must first and fundamentally be understood "Jewishly") then a thing of revolution? If revolution means a turning around, as it does, then the question should be answered, "Yes," and that is what Yeshua was all about: *metanoia, teshuvah*.

Development of Christology

At least two types of change or growth can be seen taking place in the formation of religious doctrinal positions.

One begins either at the very start of a religious idea or at some early stage that authentically and quite directly expresses the nuclear event and/or insight. Then the growth of the original idea moves in the direction of expansion and extrapolation that is other than, foreign to, and even in opposition to the nuclear event and/or insight. An obvious example might be the legend-building expansion of the image of the child Yeshua in its spare outline in Luke's Gospel to the wonder-working, self-impressed child Jesus of some of the apocryphal Gospels. A negative example of this sort of development within the canonical Gospels that continued this "expanding" move is the image of "the Jews" in Mark, where it is rather mixed, to a highly negative one in John; this anti-Jewish trajectory continued in ever-expanding fashion with the early Fathers and much of subsequent Christian tradition, almost to the present.

---

93. Küng, *Christentum und Weltreligionen*, 197.

A second type of change occurs by way of "evolution," that is, an explicitation of what was implicit in the initial event and/or insight, or at least a development of it in a way that is in keeping with the nuclear event/idea, that is, by responding to new circumstances and demands within the inspiration of the initial principles. For example, Yeshua's almost exclusive preaching of the Good News to his fellow Jews was understood by some early Christians—for example, Barnabas and Paul—to imply that gentiles ought to have the Good News preached to them by others, by Yeshua's followers, thus explicitating what they perceived to be implicit in Yeshua's preaching. In the kindred matter of not requiring all gentiles to take on the full responsibility of the Torah, those Christians (with Paul again in the lead) moved the doctrinal development "beyond" or "away from" the position taught by Yeshua by responding to the new circumstances within the inspiration of what they perceived to be the initial principles embodied and expressed by Yeshua—by what he thought, taught, and wrought.

In studying the growth of the doctrine about the significance of Yeshua, that is, Christology, one has to decide whether that growth in all or some instances is type A or B, or both, or neither—the only four possibilities.

The act of decision is unavoidable. The initial event cannot simply be "repeated." It must somehow be assimilated by the now-living person(s); otherwise, it does not become a "doctrine," a teaching. It simply remains a past fact that has no effect on anyone's life. Hence, it is not possible simply to point to or repeat the initial event or fact and claim that that is the teaching or doctrine. A living person or persons must somehow perceive the initial event and state, at first internally, its significance. It is that internal understanding, and perhaps eventual outward statement, that transmits and determines the direction and form of the power of the initial event in the lives of living persons. A number of persons might perceive the same event with some reacting with total indifference and others reacting positively or negatively in a great variety of ways. It is that "reaction to," understanding of, statement to, oneself and perhaps eventually others about the significance of the initial event that is the power-transmitting and shaping instrument. It is usually called doctrine or teaching.

Hence, when speaking of the doctrine of Christology it is not sufficient to attempt to point to or "repeat" the Yeshua-event. In fact, as seen, it is impossible to do so. Living persons must somehow perceive or apprehend the Yeshua-event and respond to it with something more than indifference in order to produce a doctrine (Christology) that will have an effect on their lives. Thus, there clearly are two poles involved in any doctrine: the initial event and the living person, and the relationship between the two. It is, then, no invention on the part of Küng, Schillebeeckx, or other contemporary theologians[94] to speak of the two poles or sources of Christian doctrine and their relationship. Rather, it is in the very nature of things. The source of the differences between Küng, Schillebeeckx, and like-minded Christian thinkers and, say, pre-Vatican II Catholic thinkers (and many still live after 1965) is in the assessment of what precisely the two poles and their relationship are. For Christians, this dispute comes to a critical head in the doctrine of Christology.

In Christianity many persons have somehow perceived the Yeshua-event and have reacted to it vigorously. It produced a deep effect on their lives, but not all actual "reactions to" the Yeshua-event or doctrines of Christology have been or are accepted by all committed Christians. No concerned Christian can affirm both the world-fleeing Christologies of some Gnostic Christians and the world-affirming Christologies of the Synoptic Gospels. Somewhere these Christians have a measuring stick by which to judge a "correct" (coming from "*rectus*" in Latin, meaning "straight"—in Greek it is *ortho*, "straight," and hence, "orthodoxy," "straight teaching") Christology. For some, it is contemporary church authority (*magisterium*). For others, it is some past church authority (*traditio*), either in whole or in part (for example, the first seven ecumenical councils). For still others it is the scriptures (*sola Scriptura*), although many Protestants now recognize that scripture itself is really the earliest set of traditions.

Today, historically minded Christian thinkers are putting forth a christological method that attempts to go behind tradition (whether *magisterium, traditio,* or *Scriptura*) and locate the initial event fundamentally not in any foreshortened "reaction to" or doctrine about the Yeshua-event but in the Yeshua of history. The living Christian(s) today, and tomorrow, must as best as possible apprehend and "react to" this Yeshua of history, that is, the Yeshua of Nazareth who lived in Israel two thousand years ago. It is no longer sufficient in a world that is historically conscious for a Christian to "react to" earlier "reactions to," doctrines about, the Yeshua-event. A historically conscious person wants to base her or his judgments and actions as much as possible on the primary facts; the Catholic experience with Galileo, the American experience of Watergate, and other similar experiences drive contemporary Christians in this direction.

94. See particularly Hans Küng, *On Being a Christian* (New York: Doubleday, 1978); Schillebeeckx, *Jesus*; and Edward Schillebeeckx, *Die Auferstehung Jesu als Grund der Erlösung* (Freiburg: Herder, 1978). Schillebeeckx spoke more recently of two poles within one source of Christian belief so as to emphasize the overarching mutuality and unity of how Christians arrive at their beliefs (in a lecture upon his formal retirement from the University of Nijmegen, February 19, 1983). Fair enough. The dialogic character of how not only Christians but all persons arrive at their beliefs is an extremely important lesson to be learned, one that can hardly be overstressed.

In a way the sixteenth-century Reformation attempted such a move by trying to go behind the *magisterium* and *traditio* to where it thought the initial event lay, the *Scriptura*, and in some ways that instinct was right. However, it had two shortcomings. First, it tended to act as if human communities could exist without developing a *traditio*, which is an impossibility. Second, it did not (indeed, at that time, could not) know that the New Testament, including the Gospels, was already a series of *traditiones*, doctrines, "reactions to," the Yeshua-event. This perception of the *Scriptura* arose only with the development of the historical-critical method and particularly with form and redaction criticism in the twentieth century.

The Yeshua of History

Although I will later nuance the standard Christian claim of the universal significance for salvation of Jesus Christ, I want to argue here that the historical person Yeshua of Nazareth must be the primary standard for what is Christian. Protestant theologian Ulrich Luz, among others, made the same point abundantly clear when he wrote: "*Christianity must appeal to Jesus if it wants to endure* without allowing itself to be transformed willy-nilly by anyone and by every historical epoch. It *must* appeal to Jesus, as long as it continues to affirm that God acted historically in Jesus and not merely in our momentary faith experiences and ideas." He added that he was "convinced that appealing to Jesus cannot be painless and without consequences for us in the present; rather, it demands that our churches modify their theology and practice."[95] The historical Yeshua naturally includes the Hebraic and Judaic traditions as they developed up to his time with the particular interpretation he gave them, but equally naturally it does not include later "Christian" reflections about him unless they agree with this primary measure, this *Urstandard*.

With the help especially of the historical-critical method, we are now able to perceive the major outlines of the Yeshua of Nazareth of two

---

95. Lapide and Luz, *Jesus in Two Perspectives*, 159. This position is likewise taken by Küng, Schillebeeckx, and many other prominent Catholic and Protestant theologians; see Leonard Swidler, ed., *Consensus in Theology?* (Philadelphia: Westminster, 1980). E.g., Küng: "And for the Catholic Christian too this criterion can be nothing but the Christian message, the *Gospel* in its ultimate concrete form, *Jesus Christ himself*, who for the Church and—despite all assertions to the contrary—also for me is the Son and Word of God. He is and remains the norm in the light of which every ecclesiastical authority—which is not disputed—must be judged: the norm by which the theologian must be tested and in the light of which s/he must continually justify her/himself in the spirit of self-criticism and true humility" (Küng, *On Being a Christian*, 163).

thousand years ago who had such a massive impact on his followers. This perception will continue to be refined, but the essential elements are already reasonably sure. (Other critical methods also contribute to our fuller, deeper—and never-endingly so—apprehension of the historical Yeshua, such as literary-critical and psychological-critical methods.)

We must bear in mind that it was only at the beginning of the nineteenth century that a sense of history as we now understand it developed in any civilization. One consequence was that Christian thinkers and scholars began the search for the "historical Jesus," the Yeshua of Nazareth who lay behind the many conflicting things said about him in the past two millennia. Up until that time his teachings, contained in the Gospels, were known as those of all the figures of antiquity are known, namely, as transmitted by his disciples.

Early in the twentieth century with the development of certain critical tools it was perceived that the sources of our image of the historical Yeshua, the Gospels, were not primarily historical documents—four different modern biographies—but, rather, four separate faith statements based on historical reminiscences. The Gospels communicated what various early followers of Yeshua understood and believed to be of the greatest importance about him, his teachings and actions, and his final "exaltation in glory."

For several decades beginning about 1918—although the tendency went back to S. H. Reimarus (d. 1768)—there was great skepticism among New Testament scholars concerning the possibility of getting behind the "Christ of faith" to the "Yeshua of history." That astringent phase is now largely over, so it is possible to state with confidence: "It is today a broadly held consensus that, though because of the nature of the sources it is impossible to produce a biography of Jesus, the description of the irreplaceable fundamental characteristics of his proclamation, his action and his fate, on the other hand, is very much possible."[96] This is the statement of Catholic systematic theologian, Hans Küng, who here quite accurately reflects the view and work of a growing number of New Testament exegetical scholars—Catholic, Protestant, and Jewish.

One of them, Sanders, referred to the works of ten of his most prestigious colleagues, including Martin Hengel, Paul Winter, Joachim Jeremias, Eduard Schweizer, C. H. Dodd, and Vermes, writing that "the dominant view today seems to be that we can know pretty well what Jesus was out to accomplish, that we can know a lot about what he said, and that those two things make sense in the world of 1st-century Judaism."[97] Vermes ar-

---

96. Küng, *Christentum und Weltreligionen*, 451.
97. Sanders, *Jesus and Judaism*, 2.

gued that "we can manage to perceive his ideas, the *ipsissimus sensus*, even without the actual words in which they were formulated."⁹⁸

It is that Yeshua of history, the one who lived then and there in Israel two thousand years ago (whatever else he might be), who must be the touchstone for all "reactions to" and doctrines about him, including the various ones in the New Testament itself. It cannot be objected that the image of the historical Yeshua produced by the help of the historical-critical method is simply a contemporary "image" and can make no more claim to allegiance by Christians than any other "image" of Yeshua, as, for example, that of Paul, who never knew Yeshua, or a Gnostic Christian, or the Council of Chalcedon (451 CE), for there is nothing in a living person's mind that is not an "image." But, there is a fundamental difference between the image formed of a person from the words and actions of the person him or herself and the image of what someone else thinks of that person.⁹⁹

I am aware of the grave difficulties of arriving at an authoritative, clear image of the historical Yeshua, but, to the extent that we can, that is the standard. Of course all of the subtle difficulties involved in the "history of effects," the *Wirkungsgeschichte,* of two thousand years of the Christian tradition will prevent our ever arriving at a completely "objective" image of Yeshua—but that is true of everything. Every fact is relativized by the perceiver, as I argued at length above. It is also true that we can come to a fuller grasp of a fact if we have perceptions of it available to us from several different standpoints—the whole argument in favor of dialogue. It is the original datum, the *Urtatsache,* that we are trying to grasp so that we can somehow relate it to ourselves; this latter part of course again relativizes the original fact, that is, puts it in relation to us (and this relationship is

---

98. Vermes, *Jesus and the World of Judaism*, 81.

99. Schillebeeckx noted the distinction between the historical Yeshua and our apprehension of him and states that the former is the ultimate Christian norm: "It is not the historical image of Jesus, but the living Jesus of history who stands at the beginning and is the source, norm and criterion" (Schillebeeckx, *Auferstehung*, 44). "The constant factor in Christianity is that Christians determine the final or ultimate meaning of their concrete history by reference to Jesus of Nazareth." Things are said to be Christian "with the same proviso that they are judged to conform to the yardstick of this historical reality that is Jesus himself" (Schillebeeckx, *Jesus*, 61–62). He went on, however, to make historical-critical research the means by which the earliest "reactions to," i.e., the original Christian beliefs, measure up to the final standard, "the living Jesus of history": "historical critical research can clarify for us the Jesus of history" (Schillebeeckx, *Auferstehung*, 44). In other words, our apprehension, by whatever methods, of the historical Yeshua will always fall short of apprehending him fully, but the very best "penultimate" image of the real historical Yeshua is the very best "temporary" final norm we can have for what is authentically Christian—until a fuller image of the historical Yeshua is developed.

further complexified and relativized by the whole history of effects between the original fact and our perception of it), but it is the *Urtatsache* that we are trying to grasp and relate to us. We now know that we can never fully clearly grasp it as it "objectively" originally existed (analogously to modern physics, wherein we now realize that to pass light or electrons, or whatever, through an object so as to "observe" it already changes it). Still, with that now-chastened knowledge that we can never attain a completely "objective" image of something, like the Parmenidian/Zenoian continuum, we can always strive to come closer. It is this I believe that we should do in regard to the historical figure of Yeshua.

Then, with due modesty and openness, it seems to me that the best image of the historical Yeshua that we are able to attain at a given moment has priority over all explanations as to his meaning. *What Yeshua thought, taught, and wrought*[100] *is the Yeshuanic, if not the "Christian," Gospel,* even though we learn that only through what others have told us that he thought, taught, and wrought. If communicating that had been the primary purpose of the Gospel writers, perceiving it would be much easier for us, but they primarily wanted to tell what they and their sources believed were the most important "meanings" of what he thought, taught, and wrought—and that makes this task more difficult, but not impossible.

Further, the "pull" that the whole history of the understanding of statements (Gadamer et al.) about Yeshua doubtless exerts on the contemporary Christian thinker may skew the image of the historical Yeshua. However, that history of understanding *(traditio)* can also be extremely enlightening. It would be foolish to pass up such insights and disastrous to attempt to skip over that history—because it is impossible! It is already in some form, often badly distorted in our heads, for we are the product of all that has gone before us. What makes us specifically human, of course, is not simply action, but conscious, knowing, and freely willed action. Hence, the more we learn our history (including here the history of the understanding of Yeshua), the more precisely we are able to make distinctions, decisions, and knowing free affirmations about it.

Still further, each person stands in a particular historical context (von Ranke et al.*)* and a particular place in the world so that all perceptions are fundamentally influenced by that fact (Mannheim et al.), including perceptions of historical-critical images. Again, an awareness of this limitation will allow the human being to avoid naive absolute certitude on the one hand and total skepticism on the other. Yet further, as we have seen, we are now

---

100. Long after coining this phrase, I came across the same idea in different words: "Our interest must be fixed on what Jesus said, thought and did" (Sanders, *Jesus and Judaism*, 129).

becoming aware that human language is both a liberating and a limiting instrument (Wittgenstein et al.). A growing awareness of its limiting as well as liberating powers will enable humans to proceed with modesty and also security, always being open to new evidence, insights, perspectives, and, hence, change. Of course, all this proper modesty is appropriate not only for the image of the historical Yeshua that is derived from the "primary data" but *a fortiori* also for all images of the "reactions to" him.

In a way we Christians are in a somewhat difficult position as far as our name, "Christian," is concerned. If our name had something to do with Yeshua or Jesus, my argument that the historical person Yeshua of Nazareth ought to be the primary standard for what is Christian would have at least a *prima facie*, etymological, plausibility. Unfortunately, the one common word, in English at least, that is derived from the name Jesus has come to mean quite the opposite of what the historical Jesus supposedly stood for: Jesuitical. Nevertheless, I still believe that all who call themselves Christians claim to center their religion on Yeshua, and therefore anything that is said about the meaning of Yeshua (Christology) must in fact not run counter to what Yeshua thought, taught, and wrought (to be concrete, but magnificently overbrief, it had long puzzled me how Yeshua could be God and yet not know it—and the latter was obviously the case as seen in numerous New Testament sayings). Of course, many things have developed in the Christian tradition that are called "Christian" and that did not come from Yeshua—for example, veneration of martyrs, religious orders, religious reading of the New Testament, etc. Thus, even though they cannot be attributed to Yeshua, if they do not run counter to what he thought, taught, or wrought, and if they have been incorporated into the Christian tradition, it is perfectly proper to call them "Christian" in that extended or secondary sense.

What does a contemporary Christian do with the historical fact that in the development of Christianity the "teaching Yeshua" quickly became the "taught *Christos*," even within the time of the writing of the New Testament? Clearly, the resurrection experience was a transforming one for the followers of Yeshua. However one understands the New Testament reports of the empty womb, as related to the followers of Yeshua, the resurrection experiences had a profound impact. As mentioned, his followers doubtless began to perceive things about Yeshua that they had not been conscious of when they were with him. Clearly, however, the Yeshua they knew was not transformed into some kind of magic figure or totem for them so that, merely by their waving of this magic wand or figure, salvation would be accomplished (though later and too often this "magical" use or, rather, misuse of Yeshua did take place in the history of Christianity). Rather, in the resurrection experience the followers of Yeshua were first of all inwardly confirmed in their pre-crucifixion experience of the encounter with the divine through Yeshua, through what he thought, taught, and wrought.

The Teaching Yeshua, Not the Taught Christ

New Testament scholar Thomas William Manson remarked: "We are so accustomed, and rightly, to make Jesus the object of religion that we become apt to forget that in our earliest records he is portrayed not as the object of religion, but as a religious man."[101]

Thus, in teaching (about) Yeshua, his followers attempted to teach what they had learned from him. However, what they learned from Yeshua could not be limited to what he put into words (what Yeshua "taught"); they obviously were deeply struck by his inner self, which appeared to be so full of wisdom and effective love (what Yeshua "thought"), and how this exuded into his every action (what Yeshua "wrought"), as is evident in the synoptic reportage. Yeshua's whole person was the source of this utterly transforming "learning" experience for his followers, and this transformation was so profound, so pervasive, that, rather than being shattered by the shattering of Yeshua on the cross (its agony both for Yeshua and for his followers proved to be the crucible in which their "enlightenment" and love were purified, strengthened, transformed), they were enabled, in Pauline symbolic language, to go down into the tomb with him and rise with the reconfirmation of their pre-crucifixion experience of him. In other words, their experience of him was true, authentic. After all, he really was—is—the source of true life; he lives on!

Thus the "taught Yeshua" (the taught or proclaimed *Christos*) was first of all the fullest way to hand on the "teaching Yeshua," that is, what he thought, taught, and wrought in his *whole* person. Hence, any move to understand the proclaimed *Christos* as someone, something, other than the "teaching Yeshua" can easily become problematic; any move to understand the "proclaimed *Christos*" in contrast to the "teaching Yeshua," to what he "thought, taught, and wrought" in his whole person, would be to play false with not only Yeshua but also his first disciples.

The theology of the Gospel of Luke is even clearer in its insistence that it is primarily what Yeshua preached, rather than Yeshua himself, that should be preached by Christians. The Catholic scripture scholar Joseph G. Kelly noted that, according to Luke, "Jesus always points not to himself but to God. As a result, the preacher cannot become the preached . . . The disciples are not called upon to preach the person of Jesus. What they must do is preach

---

101. Cited in Vermes, *Jesus and the World of Judaism*, 44.

the message of Jesus . . . Jesus shows Christians the Way and Christians see themselves on the Way." Therefore, Kelly says, what Christians must now preach is the Way that Yeshua preached: that is, repentance and the forgiveness of sin—release (*aphesin*, liberation, Lk. 4:18). This Way is to be preached in the name of Yeshua and followed by Yeshua's disciples because Yeshua was the one who accomplished this Way. But, for Luke, "Jesus is not the 'Way.' The Way is what Jesus taught must be done. The message is not Jesus, but release [liberation]. Jesus did not glorify himself, but lived in such a way as to give glory to God. This resulted in God's glorifying Jesus. Jesus did not proclaim himself, but said that his person and life made God known." Kelly added that "every time that the reign breaks in at a moment of release, one can glimpse God. God is the end and the goal. One of the ways to find God is to follow the Way of Jesus, but Jesus' Way is not the only way."[102]

At the same time, it should be remembered that not everything true, good, and beautiful comes from Yeshua or Christianity. So, claiming that Yeshua is the primary standard for what is Christian does not mean that Christians cannot appropriate true, good, and beautiful things from elsewhere—this whole book argues that they should—but that they should not be called Christian in a primary sense unless they are found in what Yeshua thought, taught, or wrought, nor Christian in a secondary sense if they have not been assimilated into the Christian tradition. It is conceivable that a Christian would find it necessary to espouse a position that runs counter to Yeshua—people claiming to be Christians, including priests, bishops, popes, and the like, have been being so for centuries—they simply should not say that such a position is Christian.

At one point in the first half of the twentieth century some Christian New Testament scholars (Bultmann et al.) gave up the search for the historical Yeshua and focused on the early "reaction to" him, the proclamation (*Kerygma*) about him, so that merely "that" Yeshua had existed was all that was seen as important about the historical Yeshua. "What" Yeshua's life consisted of was not important. The proclamation about Yeshua was perceived as God's instrument (*Scriptura*) to challenge contemporary humans to respond to God's message of the meaning of life. This approach would seem to fall into the category of neither A nor B in reference to Christology, that is, if Christology is conceived of as having something substantively to do with Yeshua. In any case, it has tended to fade from dominance as New Testament scholars again gained confidence, though chastened, in the project of the search for the historical Yeshua. Furthermore, this disjuncture between the historical Yeshua and the proclamation about him, the "Christ of faith,"

---

102. Kelly, "Lucan Christology," 693, 704, 708.

was felt by the vast majority of Christians to be fundamentally off the mark. The post-Bultmannian Protestant theologian Gerhard Ebeling stated the point clearly: "In regard to Christology nothing may be said about Jesus which is not grounded in the historical Jesus himself and which does not limit itself to expressing who the historical Jesus is."[103]

Imbedded in the Gospels of Matthew and Luke is a prior document that New Testament scholars refer to as "The Sayings of Jesus," or "Q" (from the German word *Quelle*, source). Analysts of Q, which is "one of the earliest writings, if not the earliest writing in Christianity,"[104] find in these reflections of perhaps the first Christians an understanding of Yeshua "almost entirely different from what we find in Paul, and its [Q] view of Christianity challenges us to rethink the very beginnings of Christianity itself."[105]

These scholars also note that in Q Yeshua the proclaimer does not become the proclaimed, "but in Q he remains the proclaimer," and "this is the very heart of Q's understanding of the way of salvation. Jesus himself is the very means of salvation, but it is not through his redeeming death, which is nowhere mentioned in Q, rather, in his revealing of God's reign and the way to share in that kingdom."[106] In other words, salvation, authentic human life, is to be found by following what Yeshua taught. Moreover, when Yeshua says in Q "whoever rejects me rejects him who sent me" (Luke 10:16), "of course, the sending from the Father does not refer to the incarnation of Jesus, but to Jesus' call to be a prophet."[107]

Most Christians over the centuries—gnosticizing minorities aside—have understood the historical Yeshua, what he thought, taught, and wrought, to be centrally important. It has for the most part been argued that a particular teaching about Yeshua was right, orthodox, because it ultimately really fit with the historical Yeshua who lived two millennia ago. True, some teachings may well have been directly based only on some later

---

103. Cited in Pinchas Lapide, *Ökumene aus Christen und Juden* (Neukirchen-Vluyn: Neukirchener, 1972) 72. Küng made the same point: "No contradiction can be permitted between the Jesus of history and the Christ of faith. We must be able to identify the Christ of faith as the Jesus of history" (Küng, "Toward a New Consensus in Catholic (and Ecumenical) Theology," in Swidler, *Consensus in Theology?*, 7). Schillebeeckx does likewise: "Moreover the phrase 'the Jesus of history' is often placed in an improper opposition to 'the Jesus of faith' . . . For Christians precisely the Jesus of history is the Jesus of faith" (Schillebeeckx, *Auferstehung*, 42).

104. Ivan Havener, *Q: The Sayings of Jesus* (Wilmington, DE: Michael Glazier, 1987) 11.

105. Ibid.

106. Ibid., 71. Lee, in *Galiliean Jewishness of Jesus*, 140, said almost the very same thing: "In Q Jesus is always and only the proclaimer."

107. Havener, *Q*, 71.

traditio, but then the claim was at least implicit that such a procedure was a sure way to link up with the real, historical Yeshua. There would be few Christians who would be willing to affirm the statements about Jesus Christ in the Council of Nicea (325 CE) or Constantinople (381 CE) if they could not be said of the historical Yeshua of Nazareth.[108]

The difficulty that historically conscious scholars point to in this situation is that the "reactions to," the statements about, Yeshua, whether past (*traditio*) or present (*magisterium*), tend too often to be the yardstick for understanding the historical Yeshua, when it should be the other way around. To realize that this is not just a dispute about some abstract theory, recall how a growing number of Christian scholars[109] perceive that the histori-

---

108. In a more recent book that has a great deal to recommend it in its expansive and balanced view and lucidity of presentation, Catholic theologian William M. Thompson (*The Jesus Debate* [New York: Paulist, 1985]) alluded to the "historical Jesus" and rejected him as "a final form of Christian revelation and theology" (104). One reason offered for this rejection is that our knowledge of the Jesus of history "must ultimately rely upon the kerygma" (104). The assertion is true, but how does that not make the historical Yeshua the ultimate standard? Of course, as noted above, for us it is *our apprehension* of the historic Yeshua, derived from a critical analysis of the kerygmatic text, that *de facto* is our final form, but that is *also true* of the kerygmatic Yeshua, the "previously 'reacted to'" Yeshua—only one step still further removed from the historical Yeshua. Mark, Matthew, Paul, Chalcedon, etc.—all believed and averred that they were communicating something very important about the historical Yeshua. They did not want their readers to accept it because they said it but because it told them something important about the real, historical Yeshua (which would lead them to live a full human, i.e., "saved" life). For a subsequent Christian to claim that their statements, their kerygma of, preaching about, reactions to, the historical Yeshua are the ultimate norm (or one pole thereof, along with contemporary experience) of what is authentically Christian is either to miss or reject the very essence of what they were saying. To be sure, the Gospels are the final documentary sources we have for our knowledge of Yeshua. But, the point to be noticed here is that they are "documents," i.e., "teachings," and teachings are of or about something and/or someone—in this case, Yeshua. The "documents" are merely the pointers to, images of, *eidola* of, the historical reality referred to. To stop short finally at the *eidola* rather than move on toward that to which the *eidola* point is *(e)ido-latria*, idolatry.

It would *seem* that David Tracy moved in a similar direction when he wrote that the best image of the historical Yeshua can and should correct the tradition," but not "replace it"; it cannot provide what he calls the "constitutive rather than corrective truth" ("Particular Questions within General Consensus," in Swidler, *Consensus*, 39). If Tracy is saying that Christians must appropriate the meaning of the Good News of Yeshua in their own concrete lives both individually and in community (one pole of Christian faith) and that this Good News of Yeshua comes to them through the entire Christian tradition (the second pole), but that the tradition is ultimately "corrected" by the best available image of the Yeshua of history—then I believe he is in basic agreement with Küng and Schillebeeckx and me.

109. E.g., Gerard Sloyan, *Is Christ the End of the Law?* (Philadelphia: Westminster, 1978); and Mussner, *Tractate on the Jews*.

cal Yeshua continued to affirm and carry out the Torah, Law, through the whole of his life and to teach his followers to do the same, that he set up no opposition whatsoever between Law and grace, that he in no way rejected his people the Jews—in fact, he felt himself to be sent to the Jews (cf. Mark 7:24–30)—all of which was discussed above.

Contrast that image of the historical Yeshua's emerging from careful historical-critical analysis with the "reactions to" Yeshua developed by Paul in the letters to the Galatians and Romans, as interpreted by traditional Christian triumphalism, and later Christian thinkers who set up varying oppositions between the Law and grace in Yeshua leading to the "replacement" of the Jewish people by the Christian Church as the People of God. This in turn provided the setting for the horrors of the Antisemitism that reached its abyss in my own lifetime. Thus, it is obvious that our Christian *traditio* about the Jewish people must be "corrected" by the image of the historical Yeshua the Jew emerging from historical-critical research—if for no other reason than to draw back from our previous *reductio ad horrorem*.

This very example highlights the limitation of the historical-critical method. It was precisely Protestant German New Testament scholarship that developed the historical-critical analysis of the scriptures, yet it was from Germany that the greatest cataclysm and Antisemitism came. It is clear that the historical-critical method by itself cannot solve the crucial problems of Christology and doctrine in general. In other words, to attain the most accurate picture of human reality today the historical-critical method is a necessary, but not sufficient, method. It is here that contemporary experience must play a balancing role.

For example, it now appears clear that the Protestant distortion of the image of the Jews, Yeshua's attitude toward the Law, and even Paul's attitude toward the Law and the Jewish people were twisted in its negative direction by the Protestant desire—with very little exception, for example, Julius Wellhausen—to carry on the sixteenth-century polemic of faith-works against Catholics. There were no work-righteous Catholics in the New Testament to contrast with faith-righteous Protestants, and so the Jews stood in for the Catholics and the "Christians" for the Protestants.[110] The contemporary sensitivity to our cultural, including religious, limitedness in all of our perceptions of reality is leading to a proper humility and openness to and even desire for dialogue with persons of other cultures and religions and theologies. The former Catholic-Protestant, Christian-Jew, etc., hostilities are shrinking, and consequently the distortions in historical-critical scholarship due to them are also shrinking.

---

110. Cf. Sanders, *Paul and Palestinian Judaism*.

Thus, in doing Christian theology today there are at least three new elements that must be formative: (1) The historical-critical method and other critical methods that gradually are providing us with an ever clearer image of Yeshua (the Jew) of history to which our "reactions to," our doctrines, our Christology ought to conform—no disjuncture between the Yeshua of history and the Christ of faith. (2) An awareness of the limitedness of our knowledge: historically limited (historicism); culturally, socially, and individually limited (sociology of knowledge); linguistically limited (linguistic analysis); and hermeneutically limited (all knowledge is interpreted knowledge—hermeneutics)—no doctrinal statement is ever complete, is not in need of "correction." (3) Because of the limitedness of our knowledge, we need to be "in dialogue" with others constantly to compensate as best we can for our limitations—no "going it alone" by any individual or group has any credibility today.

Moreover, the partners with whom we Christians need to dialogue are our contemporaries in other cultures, religions, theologies, etc., but not only they. We must also be in dialogue with our "source," the Yeshua of history, reached through the *Scriptura*; with all the other Christians who have ever lived, *traditio*, for their lessons of both what to believe and do and what not to believe and do are invaluable; with the contemporary *magisterium*, for that is the believing community within which we must live out our Christian lives, from whom we receive nourishment and whom we in turn nourish. However, this *magisterium* is not just a small group of hierarchs; rather, it includes the whole community in various ways as it believes, prays, and lives, and thus teaches.

Yeshua: Human and Divine

But, again, what of the christological dogmatic formulas hammered out in the ancient ecumenical councils to which assent was demanded under pain of excommunication (Whoever does not believe . . . *anathema sit*)? If accepted, do they not wipe out the above "low Christology" and require a specific "high Christology," namely, according to Chalcedon (451 CE), that Yeshua is "truly God and truly a human being" (*theon alethos kai anthropon alethos* in Greek, and *Deum verum et hominem verum* in Latin)? If one has internalized a deabsolutized understanding of truth statements, obviously an old-style, catechism-like yes or no answers—is not appropriate. One must first get clear about precisely what the Chalcedonian formula meant. To do that it is not sufficient even to come to understand the meanings of the various terms and images used in that intellectual milieu, especially in this instance, for the authors were dealing in part with that which "goes beyond" our experience, the "transcendent."

If taken literally, their language was non-sense; it spoke of a nonthing, or no-thing, for they spoke of Yeshua's being a "limited unlimited," a "finite infinite." Obviously, they did not mean to say nothing—even deliberately paradoxical language does not intend to communicate literal non-sense, but attempts to point to some reality beyond the apparent non-sense of the contradictory terms juxtaposed. The reader here then has the first task of discerning what meaning the authors were pointing to beyond and by way of the seeming non-sense of the juxtaposed mutually exclusive terms *homo* and *Deus*. I say "mutually exclusive" because *Deus* was understood in the monotheistic sense, that is, infinite, etc., and not in the polytheistic sense, that is, finite, whereby there could then be many "gods."[111]

To begin with, there is no reason to assume that the way the ancient Christian authors expressed the meaning they were attempting to communicate was necessarily the best, the clearest, the most helpful, etc. The very fact that the ancient Christians had to go back into council time and again over the same basic question (Nicaea 325, Constantinople 381, Ephesus 431, Chalcedon 451) amply demonstrates this point. I believe these ancient Christians were trying to express in Greek philosophical, ontological terms the Christian experience of the overwhelming confluence of the human and divine in *Yeshua ha notzri*.

As noted above, the ontological question was not one that excited the Semitic world. Jews tended to ask axiological questions rather than ontological questions—not questions of being, but of doing. "What must I *do* to gain eternal life?" not "What must I *be* or *believe* to gain eternal life was asked of Yeshua the Jew. This is seen reflected in the entire history and structure of Judaism; it is not the creed or doctrine that holds pride of place but the *halacha*, the rules of ethics, of just action.

Hence, Philo, a contemporary of Yeshua who fused Greek thought with Judaism, might well have been lost from Jewish memory were it not for Christian tradition and scholarship. When the great Maimonides in the twelfth century blended Judaism with specifically Aristotelian philosophy, he unleashed a great controversy and found relatively few followers among

---

111. Paul Tillich made the same point, writing that the statement "God has become man" is not paradoxical but "nonsensical," because "it is a combination of words which makes sense only if it is not meant to mean what the words say. The word 'God' points to ultimate reality, and even the most consistent Scotists had to admit that the only thing God cannot do is to cease to be God. But that is just what the assertion that 'God has become man' means" (Paul Tillich, *Systematic Theology* [Chicago: University of Chicago Press, 1957] 2:94).

Jews. The excommunication of the Jewish philosopher Spinoza in the seventeenth century reflects this general Jewish aversion for systematically raising ontological questions. To this very day "theology," understood as a systematic philosophical reflection on religious beliefs, is almost a noncategory in Judaism. It might be pointed out that the famous Muslim Arab (also Semite) philosophers of the Middle Ages (for example, Al-Farabi, Ibn Sina, and Ibn Rushd) also suffered condemnation within Islam, where again the big question is: What must I, not *be* or *believe* (the very brief *Shahada* answers that), but *do*? The *shar'ia*, which looms large in Muslim life, answers that question. Moreover, "the central concern of the Qur'an is the conduct of man . . . teaching of the Prophet and the Qur'an is undoubtedly *for action in this world*."[112]

If it can be granted that the Christians meeting at Chalcedon might not have communicated their meaning in the most helpful and clearest possible language for all time, I would then want to move from that subjunctive to the indicative mood. I am convinced that they did not express themselves as clearly and helpfully as possible for all ages to come. (Again, the very existence of several traditionally sequentially known and accepted creeds—for example, "Apostles," Nicene, Athanasian, Constantinopolitan, Chalcedonian—demonstrates the judged inadequacy, at least in some regard, of the previous creeds.)

It is within this context that I want to offer a suggestion that is intended not to reject the teaching of the Christian tradition as found in the Council of Chalcedon and elsewhere but to discern more precisely and meaningfully to Christians today what it was trying to express. In the twenty-first century most critically thinking Christians do not live in a world that perceives reality in the "substantialist" categories of the largely Aristotelian thought world of the Chalcedonian Fathers. They live in a post-Kant, -Wittgenstein, -Gadamer, etc., philosophical world that requires a probing of the *intentio* of the Council Fathers and a translation of it in contemporary thought categories. It is toward that end that the following endeavor is made. Its success will of course be variously judged, but its attempt cannot be responsibly avoided.

I would suggest that the meaning of Chalcedon would be better expressed by using adjective rather than noun forms, that is, instead of saying Yeshua is "truly God and truly a human being," it would be clearer to say that Yeshua is "truly divine and truly human," *vere divinus et vere humanus*. The paradoxical quality of the first statement is retained in the second in that the two terms, human and divine, appear to go in opposite directions,

---

112. Fazlur Rahman, *Islam and Modernity* (Chicago: University of Chicago Press, 1982) 14.

but the juxtaposition of the two does not result in non-sense; it is conceivable that someone could in some way be truly human and truly divine. In what way not only *might* this be, but in what way *was* this affirmed to be true of Yeshua?

There is no question that not only in the earliest layers of the Christian "good news" is Yeshua portrayed as and understood to be truly human but even the "highest" orthodox Christian christological formulas (like that of Chalcedon) insisted on that. The followers of Yeshua, especially upon post-resurrection-event reflection, perceived God working in and through him in an extraordinary manner.[113] To them, God appeared to be manifesting Godself through him. It seemed to them that Yeshua was so completely open to all dimensions of reality, of being (as all human beings, as intellectual cognitive beings, also are *in principle*), that he was totally suffused with an inpouring of being in a "radical," that is, in a "to the roots," way, that included the "Root," the Source of all being—in theistic language, God. Thus, one could meaningfully say that Yeshua was fully, truly divine. That is, because he was fully open to all being and the Source of being, there was no part of him that was not permeated with the Source of being. Now, it would seem that at this point many ancient Hellenistic Christians made the linguistic move of saying that because Yeshua was permeated with the Source of being, with God, he therefore could also meaningfully be said to *be* truly God.

But, linguistically, that was a confusing rather than a clarifying move, because such language inadvertently also suggested that God is co-terminus with Yeshua. That is: God is infinite and unlimited, whereas human beings, as well as all other beings, are finite, limited. However, to say that Yeshua *is* God is to say that Yeshua, a human being and therefore finite, *is* not finite, but infinite. In other words, to form a sentence linking together with the nexus *is* the subject and predicate when both are nouns and at least one is exhaustive

---

113. Dutch Catholic theologian Ansfried Hulsbosch—who unfortunately died at a relatively young age—took the evolutionary thought of Teilhard de Chardin seriously and developed an insightful Christology. He argued that the divinity of Yeshua consisted precisely in the perfection of his humanity. He wrote that Yeshua "is the Son of God in that this man is in contact with God in a way that separates Him from ordinary men. But this can mean nothing other than a special way of being-man, since the whole actuality of the mystery lies precisely in the sector of the human." He then added, "The divine nature of Jesus is relevant to the saving mystery only insofar as it alters and elevates the human nature. And whatever that is, it must be called a new mode of being man" (Ansfried Hulsbosch, "Jezus Christus, gekend als mens, beleden as Zoon Gods," *Tijdschrift voor Theologie* [1966] 6:255. It is summarized, along with two other key articles by Piet Schoonenberg and Edward Schillebeeckx from the same special number of the *Tijdschrift*, in Robert North, "Soul-Body Unity and God-Man Unity," *Theological Studies* 30 (March 1969) 36–37.

of its category can only mean that the subject and predicate are co-terminus. For example, if there is only one President of the United States, the statement that "Barack Obama is President" means that there is no Barack Obama [that specific person] who is not President and no President that is not that specific Barack Obama; Obama and President are limited to each other. Similarly, "Yeshua is God" means that there is no Yeshua that is not God and no God that is not Yeshua; Yeshua and God are limited to each other.

That, of course, was not what was intended, for Christians did not wish to imply that the unlimited God was limited to Yeshua. Hence, to avoid this unintended non-sense, it would help to use the adjective form "divine" rather than the noun form "God," since the former term does not limit the Unlimited to the limited, while the latter term does. Schillebeeckx made a similar point when he wrote, "Since 1953 I have firmly opposed the formulation 'Christ is God and man' and also the confusing expression 'the man Jesus is God.' The proper formula would be: 'Jesus Christ is the Son of God *in humanity*.' The deepest sense of revelation is that God reveals himself in humanity. We cannot seek farther, above or beneath the man Jesus his being-God. The divinity must be perceptible *in* his humanity itself."[114]

To say that "Yeshua is God," if both the subject and the predicate, Yeshua and God, are understood as nouns, clearly means that Yeshua and God are coextensive, that there is no Yeshua that is not God and no God that is not Yeshua. That is obviously *not* what Christians, whether early or current, mean to claim. Hence, it would appear unavoidable to conclude that in this sentence although Yeshua is meant as a noun, *God is not meant as a noun* (for that would make God co-terminus with Yeshua) but as an adjective. To make that clearly implied but confusedly disguised meaning explicitly clear, it would therefore be helpful to make the predicate specifically adjectival in form: "Yeshua is divine." Such a sentence is not non-sense and appears to capture precisely what Christians mean to say with the confusing sentence, "Yeshua is God."

There is metaphorical language in the Bible that helps to clarify this explanation, especially when linked with a basic Buddhist concept. I am speaking of the biblical term "light" and the Buddhist term "enlightenment" (*Buddha*, the enlightened one). In the ancient Near East in general, light is proper to deity; the Hebrew Bible is full of this light imagery relating to God; God's self *ad extra* is called light: "Yahweh is *my* light" (*ori*; Ps 27:1, Mic 7:8). The language of the New Testament is not only *ad extra* but at times even *in se*: "God is light" (*ho Theos phos estin*; 1 John 1:5). Of course *all*

---

114. Schillebeeckx, "Persoonlijke openbaringsgestalte van de Vader," *Tijdschrift voor Theologie* (1966) 6:276–77.

this language is used in metaphorical fashion; the ancient Jews and Christians did not worship light as God; they were not sun worshipers, but a similar metaphor is used when it is said that a human being has opened him or herself to the depth of Reality with the result that all aspects of his or her life are pervaded and transformed by this new awareness of Reality, by this new seeing of Reality as a result of this enlightenment. To use the Buddhist term "enlightenment" and make the connection with both the biblical term "light" and the Christian understanding of the meaning of Yeshua's relation to God ("Light"), it might be said that Christians believed that Yeshua received en-*Light*enment in the fullest possible manner; he was suffused with Light (Light = God: *Theos phos estin*)—hence, he was a God (Light)-suffused man, "the true light that enlightens every human being" (*to phos to alethinon ho photidzei panta anthropon*—John 1:8).

Ulrich Luz made a similar point about the shift from the Jewish to the Greek way of thinking and its impact on Christology. He wrote that, "the confession of Jesus' divinity may have been unavoidable and quite pertinent for the Greeks and for Europeans of the previous centuries, whose thought processes had been shaped by Platonic metaphysics, even though the possibility of a conversation with Israel thereby became inevitably strained." He added that this confession always had been problematic in that it threatened to swallow the humanity of Jesus as well as the historical reality of his mission. "Theologically this is true in its monophysite form, but for me this is also largely true of its Chalcedonian, non-Antiochene form. In my opinion it is impossible for us to go on thinking as the Greeks once did, even though we have learned, and still can learn, much from them."[115]

But, what of those passages in the New Testament itself that seem to state clearly that Yeshua is God and have been traditionally so understood—Paul's Epistle to the Philippians (Phil 2:5–11) and the Prologue to John's Gospel? Can they just be waved aside as the Hellenizing of the original Jewish understanding of Yeshua?

Of course, if it is *assumed* ahead of time that the concept of Yeshua as the Incarnation of the Second Person of the Blessed Trinity existing from all eternity could have been in the mind of a Pharisaic Jew in the middle of the first century, then the words of the hymn that Paul recites in his letter to the followers of Yeshua at Philippi can be so understood.[116] However, that was

---

115. Lapide and Luz, *Jesus in Two Perspectives*, 165.

116. Jerome Murphy-O'Connor, OP, has argued in great detail that the common belief that Phil 2:6–11 speaks of Christ's pre-existence as God and his subsequent incarnation is "a presupposition rather than a conclusion" that is unwarranted (Jerome Murphy-O'Connor, "Christological Anthropology in Phil. 2:6–11," *Revue Biblique* 83 [1976] 30–31). See also James D. G. Dunn, *Christology in the Making* (Philadelphia:

three hundred years before the Council at Nicaea and four hundred years before the one at Chalcedon when this concept was hammered out—not by Jews, but by Hellenistic Christians who were triumphant over Jews and everyone else in the Roman empire. As Sanders has pointed out, "It is true that the early church came to believe that Jesus was a transcendent being ... But it would be foolhardy—or worse—to rush to the conclusion that the historical Jesus must have corresponded to such beliefs."[117]

Pre-existent Christ?

In fact, reasonable principles of interpretation would indicate that the words of Paul should be understood in the way he and his readers would have understood them, and Paul was a Jew, in fact, "a Hebrew of the Hebrews, according to the Law a Pharisee" (Phil 3:5).

Vermes pointed out: "To a Greek speaker in Alexandria, Antioch or Athens at the turn of the eras, the concept *huios theou*, son of God, would have brought to mind either one of the many offspring of the Olympian deities ... But to a Jew, the corresponding Hebrew or Aramaic phrase would have applied to none of these. For him, son of God could refer ... to a good Jew; or to a charismatic holy Jew; or to the king of Israel; or ... In other words *"son of God" was always understood metaphorically in Jewish circles.*" He went on to make the very interesting observation that, "If the medium in which Christian theology developed had been Hebrew and not Greek, it would not have produced an incarnation doctrine as this is traditionally understood."[118]

This position is supported by the Christian exegete James Barr, who argued that Paul and other Jews probably understood Paul's hyperbolic references to Yeshua in typically Jewish metaphorical fashion, but that as heard by Hellenist ears they probably were misconstrued in a nonmetaphorical sense: "It could be argued that this emphasis upon the Hebraic background of ideas may indeed have been present in the minds of instructed Jews like St Paul, but that the words which had this series of associations for him could for the most part be *understood* by Gentile Christian hearers, especially by the less instructed among them, in the normal Hellenistic sense of the words."[119] In fact, the Jewish-Christians, the so-called Ebionites, "became

---

Westminster, 1980) 114–15.

117. Sanders, *Jesus and Judaism*, 21.

118. Vermes, *Jesus and the World of Judaism*, 72.

119. James Barr, *Semantics of Biblical Language* (London: Oxford University Press, 1961) 250.

convinced that they were witnessing in the Hellenistic communities a fatal misrepresentation of Jesus, a betrayal of his ideals, and their replacement by alien concepts and aspirations."[120]

Further, according to the Acts of the Apostles, Paul founded the Christian church at Philippi, having first gone on the Sabbath eve to the "Jewish place of prayer" (Acts 16:13), where his first "converts" were made. Naturally, the persons he met there were either Jews or gentile "fellow-travelers," that is, gentiles who were attracted to the Jewish tradition and way of life (known in the Acts as "God-fearers," *phoboumenoi*, or "God-worshipers," *sebomenoi*, or simply "Greeks," *hellenei*), and thus it was these two groups who comprised the great bulk of the first Christian churches outside Palestine, including the one that Paul founded and wrote to at Philippi and that met at the house of the *sebomena* Lydia. Hence, Paul's words must be understood as coming from a strict Jew to prayerful Jews or pious gentiles who were knowledgeable about and committed to the Bible and Judaism. With that in mind, let us look again at the pertinent part of the hymn:

> Your attitude must be that of Christ Jesus.
>
> Though he was in the form of God,
>
> did not deem equality with God
>
> something to be grasped at.
>
> Rather, he emptied himself
>
> and took the form of a slave,
>
> being born in the likeness of human beings . . .
>
> Because of this God exalted him . . .

Many careful exegetes today see operating here an "Adam Christology," which was so prevalent at the time Paul wrote. Being "in the form of God" simply means the same thing as Adam's being "in the image of God" (Gen 1:26). Rather than "grasp at" that level of being, that is, "equality with God," before the Fall (which came because Adam wanted to "grasp at" being "as God"—Gen 3:5), he chose to follow completely the path of Adam so as to redeem him, humbling himself and taking the "form of a slave" (Adam after the Fall)—completing in the poem the symmetry that is constitutive of Hebrew poetry. Toward the end of the poem God (not a person of the Trinity, but simply, "the God," *ho Theos*) "exalted," not "restored," him; Christ did not "retake" his allegedly former divine place. Christ here clearly is for the

---

120. Vermes, *Jesus and the World of Judaism*, 26.

Jew Paul and his Jewish and semi-Jewish readers the "Second Adam," not the pre-existent "Second Person" of the Trinity.[121]

Logos Theology

What of the Prologue to John's Gospel where it says, "In the beginning was the Word, and the Word was with God, and the Word was God . . . and the Word became flesh" (John 1:1, 14)? Again, keeping in mind that this is a Jew writing largely for fellow Jews, it must be recalled that there were several figures and images used in biblical and early Jewish writings as literary images of the invisible God that made God perceivable to humans. There is the Spirit (*ruach*) of God who already in Gen 1:1 moves over the darkness in creation; Wisdom (*hokmah*) who is present at creation (Prov 8:22–3; Sirach 24:9); God's Word who in numerous biblical (*dabar*, Hebrew) and postbiblical (*memra*, Aramaic) texts expresses God to humanity, as does God's *Torah* (Law) in both biblical and postbiblical texts; as well as God's Presence (*Shekhinah*) in postbiblical Jewish materials. It is within the context of this plethora of Jewish imagery of God's visible side turned toward humanity that John wrote and that his Jewish readers understood him. But, these were all metaphors, not ontological substances, and that was likewise true of John's *logos*, the Word (*dabar*, *memra*).

For the Jews the Word of God was God's speaking: God spoke, and the world was created. The Torah was God's Word—indeed the Ten Commandments, the Decalogue, means God's "ten words." God spoke to Israel through the prophets for hundreds of years. In short, the whole Jewish experience of God was God's speaking, expressing self, offering self for a relationship with human beings. "This self-expression of God had been going on for a long time before Jesus. It went back as far as humankind could remember. It seemed that God had always been speaking, from the beginning of the world."[122] Thus, as with Wisdom and the Spirit, it seemed to the Jews that the Word had been with God from the beginning. Indeed, again like Wisdom and Spirit, God was as perceived by humanity; it "expressed God's own selfhood, and the one who encountered the word encountered God.[123]

---

121. See Sanders, *Jesus*, 21; Thomas N. Hart, *To Know and Follow Jesus* (New York: Paulist, 1984) 94–95; Schillebeeckx, *Jesus*; Piet Schoonenberg, *The Christ* (New York: Seabury, 1971); and Piet Schoonenberg, "'He Emptied Himself': Philippians 2:7," in *Who Is Jesus of Nazareth?* Concilium 11 (New York: Paulist, 1965) 47–66.

122. Hart, *To Know and Follow Jesus*, 98.

123. Ibid.

Why did those ancient Jews see Yeshua as God's Word become flesh? Their experience of Yeshua was that he was a diaphany of God: "Everything God has ever said is summed up in Jesus. It is all said here, every word. Not only are the teachings of Moses and the prophets summarized in the teaching of Jesus, everything God wants to reveal about who God is is shown in who Jesus is for us. Jesus is not just someone who has occasional words to say to us on God's behalf. He is in all the dimensions of his life God's self-revelation. Thus the word of God was enfleshed in a human life . . . This is the Johannine vision as scholars reconstruct it today."[124]

Long after I had written the above section on Christology, I came across a book by John Hick that spoke of alternative Christologies to that of the "substance" category Christology of Chalcedon being developed, namely, what he called "degree Christologies." By this he meant that, insofar as a human being is open and responsive to God so that God is able to act in and through that individual, "we can speak of the embodiment in human life of God's redemptive activity. And in Jesus this 'paradox of grace' . . . occurred to a startling extent. The paradox, or the inspiration, are not however confined to the life of Jesus; they are found, in varying degrees, in all free human response to God." My christological thought outlined above would also seem to fall in this category of degree Christology.

I also found a related position of mine reinforced by Hick. There have been at times complaints that interreligious dialogue has led to a watering down of Christian theology, and specifically of Christology: Christian "dialogists" are emptying Christology of its traditional meaning because they do not want to offend non-Christians. Not so. The difficulty with traditional Christology was that it more and more made no sense to modern critical-thinking Christians, who nevertheless found what Yeshua thought, taught, and wrought to be a source of life-giving meaning. It is to resolve that problem that these new Christologies have been developed. Hick made a similar point when he wrote that, "these modern degree Christologies were not . . . developed in order to facilitate a Christian acceptance of religious pluralism . . . [They] were developed as alternatives to the old substance Christology, in which so many difficulties . . . had become apparent." He went on to point out that they too "claim to be compatible with the teachings of Jesus and of the very early Church," and then added that "as an unintended consequence, degree Christologies open up the possibility of seeing God's activity in Jesus as being of the same kind as God's activity in other great human mediators of the divine."[125]

---

124. Ibid., 99.
125. John Hick, *Problems of Religious Pluralism* (New York: St. Martin's, 1985)

Dialogue Suggests a Resolution

I would like to offer here a possible resolution to the seemingly intractable problem between Christians and Jews over the Christian claim of the confluence of the human and the divine in *Yeshua ha Notzri* that has come out of interreligious dialogue. This dialogue, however, was not between Christianity and Judaism, but between Christianity and Buddhism.

As a result of his long dialogue with Buddhism, the Japanese Christian Katsumi Takizawa (1909–84) distinguished between what he termed the primary and the secondary contacts of God with the human self. The first contact is the unconditional fact that God is with each one of us and is the very ground of our selves. This "contact" is real even though we may be unaware of it. The second contact occurs when we are awakened to that primary fact, allowing "the self to live in conscious accord with the will of God." "According to Takizawa, Jesus was a man who was awakened to the primary fact—that is, he attained the secondary contact, and he did this so thoroughly and completely that he became a model for other selves . . . Jesus was the person who in Hebrew tradition played the same role as did Gautama Buddha in the Indian tradition. The ground of salvation is the primary contact of God with the self, and this is the common ground of both Buddhism and Christianity [and one might also add Judaism]."[126]

Utilizing this distinction, another Japanese Christian, Seiichi Yagi, analyzed the "I" in the words of Yeshua, arguing that Yeshua at times speaks in a way that clearly indicates the distinction between himself and God and at other times in a way that indicates a unity between him and God. This occurs in various places in the several Gospels, perhaps most clearly in John's Gospel. Yeshua speaks of the unity between himself and God, whom he calls the Father: "That all may be one as you Father in me and I in you . . . that they may be one as we are one, I in them and you in me" (John 17:21, 23); "Anyone who has seen me has seen the Father" (John 14:9); "Do you not believe that I am in the Father and the Father in me? The words I speak to you I do not speak of myself; but the Father who dwells in me does his works"

35–36. Hick named several such "degree Christology" authors: John Baillie, *The Place of Jesus Christ in Modern Christianity* (1929); Donald Baillie, *God Was in Christ* (1948); Norman Pittenger, *The Word Incarnate* (1957); John Knox, *The Humanity and Divinity of Christ* (1967); Geoffrey Lampe, *God as Spirit* (1977); and the authors of *The Myth of God Incarnate* (1977). See also William E. May, *Christ in Contemporary Theology* (Dayton, OH: Pflaum, 1970) 104, who also spoke of Norman Pittenger's "degree-Christology."

126. Seiichi Yagi, "'I' in the Words of Jesus," in Hick and Knitter, *Myth of Christian Uniqueness*, 117. Yagi here summarized this aspect of Takizawa's work and applied it to Yeshua and Paul with some additional help from the Zen Buddhist Shin-ichi Hisamatsu (1889–1980).

(John 14:10). Here, when Yeshua speaks, it is fundamentally the Father who is speaking through him. The secondary contact has been so complete that it is the language of the unity between God the Father and Yeshua that comes forth. Yet, there is a distinction between them, for Yeshua obeys the Father when he says: "For I have not spoken of myself; but the Father who sent me gave me a commandment, what I should say, and what I should speak" (John 12:49). "In John 14:10, Father and Son can be seen as two concentric circles in which the two centers coincide, whereas in John 12:49, Father and Son appear as two centers in an ellipse, the latter obeying the former . . . Christ is the Son of God insofar as the ultimate subject of the Son is the Father, but also insofar as the Father and the Son are distinguished from each other. They are paradoxically one."[127]

Yagi further noted that these two types of relationship between Yeshua and God, the elliptic and the concentric, remind him of the two major kinds of Christologies in the ancient church, the Antiochoean and the Alexandrian. The Antiocheans (elliptic) maintained that there were two centers in the person of Yeshua, the divine and the human, and the latter obeyed the former. The Alexandrians (concentric) insisted that both centers coincided. "The ancient church, therefore, maintained that both Christologies were true when, in the Council of Chalcedon, it declared that the divinity and the humanity of Christ were distinguishable but not separable."[128]

Such an explanation, I believe, makes sense out of the apparently conflicting language of the Gospels and helps to make the reality to which paradoxical language points available to a contemporary person; if the Council of Chalcedon can be understood to be saying something of the same, it also helps to translate that Hellenistic ontological language into terms that likewise find resonance in a contemporary person's experience and thought patterns. It should be noticed, however, that the Yagi explanation is largely in psychological rather than abstract metaphysical terms. Further, what is said to be true in Yeshua's case is that the secondary contact with God (enlightenment, *satori*) in principle can happen to every human being. Indeed, Yeshua obviously believed it could, and should, for his language was full of exhortations to follow him, imitate him, be one with him and the Father.

Ultimately, of course, this explanation is not entirely different from the one I offered above when I wrote: Yeshua was so completely open to all dimensions of reality—as all human beings are in principle—that he was totally suffused with an inpouring of being in a "radical" way that included the "Root" of all being, God. Thus, he was thoroughly human because he

127. Ibid., 121–22.
128. Ibid., 122.

was through and through divine—which is evidenced in what he thought, taught, and wrought.

"Ontologization" in Religions

The dialogue between Christianity and Buddhism has something further to teach us Christians in our understanding of our Christologies and, hence, also about our relationship to Judaism.

The "ontologization" of Yeshua into the "divine" Christ, which occurred in Christianity as it moved from the Semitic cultural world into the Hellenistic, was matched by a similar development with the "ontologization" of Siddharta Gautama into the "divine" Buddha ("Buddha," like "Christ," is not a proper name but a title; it means "the enlightened one") as it moved from the Indian cultural world into the Chinese and Far Eastern cultural world. Connected with this is the development from the "internal" understanding of "salvation" to the external," as discussed earlier. This again is like the movement from the "teaching Yeshua" to the "proclaimed Christ," from the religion *of* Yeshua to the religion *about* Yeshua the Christ, from the "Yeshua of history" to the "Christ of faith."

These shifts are also in many ways paralleled in Buddhism with the movement from the "internal" understanding of "salvation" (termed *jiriki*, "self-power," in Japanese) to the "external" understanding (termed *tariki*, "other power"), from the "teaching Gautama" to the "proclaimed Buddha," from the religion *of* Gautama to the religion *about* Gautama the Buddha, from "the Gautama of history" (*Shakyamuni*) to the "Buddha of belief" (*Maitreya Buddha* and *Amida Buddha*).

Seeing the same kind of developments occur in such disparate religious cultures (one being theistic and the other originally nontheistic) should make Christians ask themselves what deeper grasping toward an underlying insight is represented by these "ontologizing" movements. Perhaps one way to express this deeper insight is as follows:

For Christians Yeshua is the key figure through whom they get in touch with those dimensions of reality that go beyond, that transcend the empirical, the everyday. This is fundamentally what Christologies are all about. All are attempts through the figure Yeshua to come into contact with the transcendent, the "divine," with each Christology perceived, conceived, and expressed in its own cultural categories and images. Some do it better, even much better, than others; some do it even badly. Naturally, they are all culture-bound. Otherwise, they would not reflect and effectively speak to the people in that culture. Concomitantly, each Christology is proportionately limited in effectiveness in regard to other cultures, whether the cultural differences result from variations in geography, time, class, or whatever.

All Christians naturally can and should learn from the insights, and failures, of all other Christians' reaching out for the transcendent in their Christologies and other theological reflections, but what is "religiously specific" about Christians is that these Christologies, these theological reflections, are, or at least should be, intimately connected and compatible with the person Yeshua of Nazareth—though of course they are not limited to imitating him in cultural detail.

Thus, it should become clear that, in moving from talk about the "internal" to the "external," from the human to the divine, from Yeshua to Christ, we Christians, like the Buddhists and others, are attempting to express an experienced reality that transcends our everyday human experience and language. We assert that there is a deeper reality that goes beyond the empirical surface experiences of our lives, and for us Yeshua is the bond-bursting means to become aware of that deeper reality (as for Buddhists it is Gautama). For us Christians it is preeminently in Yeshua that we encounter the divine; therefore, our move to talk about the divine in Yeshua. Hence, our attempt to speak of the divine in Yeshua, of Christ, etc., is not a mistake, but rather the result of the need to try to give expression to transempirical reality.

At the same time, however, we must be aware that, when we attempt to speak of the transcendent, we naturally will have to use transempirical language, that is, metaphor, symbol, and the like. The mistake we must be cautious to avoid in this situation is erroneously to think that when we speak about the transcendent we are using empirical language. We are not. We can not. At the same time we must also be cautious to avoid being reductionist and erroneously think all talk about the transcendent is merely fantasizing, that since Yeshua was merely a human being and all later talk about the divine in him, etc., is simply romantic emoting with no referent in reality. As I have argued, the "ontologization" move in fact is a response to an experienced profound reality. It should not be dismissed, but held onto for the vital insight into the meaning of human life it strives for—but it must be correctly understood for what it is, lest it become an idol, an image falsely adored, rather than the Reality toward which it points. When it is thus correctly understood and affirmed, we will then have reached what Ricoeur called the "second naivete," that is, the state of awareness in which the affirmation of the symbol, understood correctly for what it is, further unlocks for us the deeper, transempirical reality.

If this line of thought, prompted by seeing the parallels in "ontologization" in Christianity and Buddhism, has any validity in explaining how

Christians are coming to understand their Christologies, then many of the disagreements between Christians, Jews, Muslims, and others in this area will disappear. Jews, Muslims, and other religious persons will not thereby become Christians, of course, for Yeshua for them is not the door to the divine that he is for Christians, but perhaps their charges of blasphemy and idolatry against Christians will thereby be dissipated. Most importantly, the Christian tradition will thereby much more likely "make sense" to many contemporary Christians.

To summarize, the foundation of Christianity is Yeshua, known to Christians as the Christ, but, in order to understand themselves, Christians must return to their root, Yeshua—the Jew. Hence, dialogue with Judaism is imperative. This, simply put, is the christological imperative to dialogue.

Jewish-Christian Dialogue

All of the reasons given up until now for Christians to enter into dialogue with Jews and Judaism have been fundamentally for the Christians' sake. There is another reason why Christians must turn toward Jews in dialogue that is only partly for their own sakes and partly other-directed.

Antisemitism and Jewish-Christian Dialogue

I am speaking of our heinous history of hostility and hatred toward Jews and Judaism for two millennia. Thank God there are a few spaces of light; Jewish culture, learning, and life did in fact flourish in Christendom in certain places and at certain times. Particularly, some Christian princes and bishops—and often the papacy—supported and defended the Jews, but, as can be seen from careful histories of the Jews, such as that of Catholic historian Frederick M. Schweitzer,[129] this was a minor theme in a symphony of destruction. There are whole libraries detailing the ignominy to which Christians have subjected Jews and consequently besmirched their own souls.

Let us recall only a tiny number of our most saintly antisemites. I would have thought that such reminders were completely superfluous today with the calling to consciousness of the horrors of the Holocaust, but just a short time ago at a Protestant-Catholic clergy retreat I found priests and ministers proclaiming the righteousness of the church in the history of

---

129. See Frederick M. Schweitzer, *A History of the Jews* (New York: Macmillan, 1971).

its relations with the Jews. Is such ignorance or perversity possible among present-day Christian clergy? Sadly, it is.

Recall the words of the "golden-tongued" St. John Chrysostom (344–407 CE), which were uttered not among a small gathering of learned clerics but flung from the pulpit in Antioch for all Christians to hear, both there in that heavily Jewish city and reverberating through all the subsequent centuries of Christian antisemitic preaching. He thundered that Jews are the

> most miserable of all men . . . lustful, rapacious, greedy, perfidious bandits . . . inveterate murderers, destroyers, men possessed by the devil . . . whose debauchery and drunkenness have given them the manners of the pig and the lusty goat. They know only one thing, to satisfy their gullets, get drunk, to kill and maim one another . . . They have surpassed the ferocity of wild beasts, for they murder their offspring and immolate them to the devil. As to Judaism, symbolized by the synagogue, it is an assembly of criminals . . . a den of thieves . . . a cavern of devils, an abyss of perdition . . . far from venerating the synagogue because of the books it contains, hold it in hatred and aversion for the same reason . . . I hate the synagogue precisely because it has the law and prophets . . . I hate the Jews also because they outrage the law.[130]

The early ninth century was the time of the Carolingian Renaissance in Western Christendom, at the height of which we find St. Agobard (779–840 CE), powerful Archbishop of Lyons, and known as "probably the most cultured man of his time." St. Agobard's words about the Jews sound as if he was standing in a St. John Chrysostom echo-chamber; Jews "are cursed and covered with malediction, as by a cloak. The malediction has penetrated them as water in their entrails and oil in their bones. They are cursed in the city and cursed in the country, cursed is their coming in and their going out. Cursed are the fruits of their loins, of their lands, of their flocks; cursed their cellars, their granaries, their shops, their food, and the crumbs of their tables."[131]

The official Church at the highest level also played out the same role of the antisemite. There was the twelfth Ecumenical Council, Lateran IV (1215 CE), which visited a number of disabilities on all Jews, including enjoining them from appearing in public during Easter time, barring them from holding public office, and declaring a moratorium on crusaders' debts to

---

130. The Chrysostom quotations are from his eight *Homilies against the Jews* in Migne, *Patrologia Graeca* 38, 843–942. An English selection is found in Edward H. Flannery, *The Anguish of the Jews* (New York: Macmillan, 1965) 48–49.

131. Agobard in Migne, *Patrologia Latina*, 104, 113; E.T. in Flannery, *Anguish*, 83.

Jews. Edward Flannery, in his pioneer history of Christian Antisemitism, remarked: "Thus far, there was nothing new in these enactments, which merely extended to the universal Church what earlier centuries had applied more locally. The unique and most extraordinary measure taken by the Council was the prescription of a distinctive dress for Jews and Saracens. (At a later date, heretics, prostitutes, and lepers were included.)"[132]

Raul Hilberg listed twenty-two conciliar or synodal decrees that were severely restrictive of Jews (from the fourth to the fifteenth centuries) and were paralleled by specific Nazi decrees. The list is as follows (only the first date of each measure is listed):

> 1. Prohibition of intermarriage and of sexual intercourse between Christians and Jews, Synod of Elvira, 306.
>
> 2. Jews and Christians not permitted to eat together, Synod of Elvira.
>
> 3. Jews not allowed to hold public office, Synod of Clermont, 535.
>
> 4. Jews not allowed to employ Christian servants or possess Christian slaves, 3rd Synod of Orleans, 538.
>
> 5. Jews not permitted in the streets during Passion Week, 3rd Synod of Orleans.
>
> 6. Burning of the Talmud and other books, 12th Synod of Toledo, 681.
>
> 7. Christians not permitted to patronize Jewish doctors, Trulanic Synod, 692.
>
> 8. Christians not permitted to live in Jewish homes, Synod of Narbonne, 1050.
>
> 9. Jews obliged to pay taxes for support of the Church to the same extent as Christians, Synod of Gerona, 1078.
>
> 10. Prohibition of Sunday work, Synod of Szabolcs, 1092.
>
> 11. Jews not permitted to be plaintiffs or witnesses against Christians in the courts, 3rd Lateran Council, 1179, Canon 26.
>
> 12. Jews not permitted to withhold inheritance from descendants who had accepted Christianity, 3rd Lateran Council, Canon 26.

---

132. Flannery, *Anguish*, 102.

13. The marking of Jewish clothes with a badge, 4th Lateran Council, 1215 CE, Canon 68 (copied from the legislation by Caliph Omar II, 643–44, who had decreed that Christians wear blue belts and Jews yellow belts).

14. Construction of new synagogues prohibited, Council of Oxford, 1222.

15. Christians not permitted to attend Jewish ceremonies, Synod of Vienna, 1267.

16. Jews not permitted to dispute with simple Christian people about the tenets of the Catholic religion, Synod of Vienna.

17. Compulsory ghettos, Synod of Breslau, 1227.

18. Christians not permitted to sell/rent real estate to Jews, Synod of Ofen, 1279.

19. Adoption by a Christian of the Jewish religion or return by a baptized Jew to the Jewish religion defined as heresy, Synod of Mainz, 1310.

20. Sale or transfer of Church articles to Jews prohibited, Synod of Lavour, 1368.

21. Jews not permitted to act as agents in the conclusion of contracts between Christians, especially marriage contracts, Council of Basel, 1432, Sessio XIX.

22. Jews not permitted to obtain academic degrees, Council of Basel, Sessio XIX.[133]

Then there are the scourging words of the father of the Protestant Reformation, Martin Luther, who shortly before his death wrote a violent diatribe, *About the Jews and Their Lies*, in which among other things he wrote that Jews "are thirsty bloodhounds and murderers of all Christendom, with full intent . . . they had poisoned water and wells, stolen children and hacked them apart, in order to cool their temper secretly with Christian blood."[134] His conclusion was that their synagogues should be burned and their books seized, that they should be forced to work with their hands, or

---

133. Raul Hilberg, *The Destruction of the European Jews* (New York: Octagon, 1961) 5–6. He stated that the list of church measures was taken in its entirety from J. E. Scherer, *Die Rechtsverhältnisse der Juden in den deutsch-österreichischen Länder* (Leipzig: Duncker & Humblot, 1901) 39–49.

134. Martin Luther, *Von den Jueden und Jren Luegen* (Wittenberg, 1543) 3; also found in *Luthers Reformations-schriften* (St. Louis, 1890) 20:1861–2026.

better still, be expelled by the princes.[135] "They should be forced to hardest labor as handymen of serfs only; they should not be permitted to hold services; every Christian should be admonished to deal with them in a merciless manner; if you suffer, strike them on the jaw; if I had the power, I would assemble them to prove to us that we Christians do not worship God, under penalty of having their tongues cut out through the backs of their necks."[136]

Is it any wonder that Christians with this long heritage of hatred allowed and even abetted the cataclysmic horrors of the Holocaust, with its choking of the air with the smoke and ash of incinerated living Jewish children?

Presumably, no readers of this book share a direct responsibility for that terror, but all of us Christians share gladly in the Christian heritage that made it possible. We cannot claim only the good of that heritage and pretend that the evil is not also there. That Christian heritage is now our heritage and, therefore, our responsibility. There is no way that we can exorcize the demon of Antisemitism from its past, present, and future unless we first become aware of it. We must study it and face it honestly—and then repent. We cannot undo the overwhelming injustices of the past, but we can and must acknowledge and repudiate them. Then, we must make whatever recompense we can in an attempt to redress the imbalance of justice between Christian and Jew—inadequate though this attempt must of necessity be. Moreover, we must not expect the Jews immediately to embrace us, forgiving and forgetting. We Christians have had a two-millennia-long history of tricking and betraying Jews. They are understandably suspicious about our motives and sincerity. We must be patient and prove ourselves not only with words but also with many deeds, then perhaps they will turn to us in a dialogue in which there is no hidden Christian agenda of conversion. We will then meet as equal partners, *par cum pari*, each coming to learn from the other.

The Message of the Jewish "No" to Christianity

Furthermore, we Christians very much need to hear the Jewish "no" to Christianity, to learn the obvious message that is embedded in it for us. If, as was in fact the case, the vast majority of Jews, starting two thousand years ago, rejected not Yeshua but Christianity, that is, what some of the followers

---

135. Ibid.

136. Martin Luther, *Shem Hamphoras* (Wittenberg, 1543), found in *Luthers Reformations-schriften*, 2029–2109; also cited in Dagobert Runes, *The War against the Jew* (New York: Philosophical Library, 1968) 116.

of Yeshua, and then their followers, etc., claimed about Yeshua and what they did with those claims, we Christians can no longer simply ascribe their action to Jewish knavery. Everything known about Jews and Judaism points to a people and religion that, relatively speaking, was extraordinarily good, which at the time of Yeshua and early Christianity, despite its shortcomings, moved from moral strength to strength—it was after all the wellspring of the three great monotheistic religions of the world: Judaism, Christianity, and Islam. To describe that wellspring as essentially evil, and as such the source of the Jewish "no" to Christianity, is to fly in the face of the axiom of sufficient cause.

There must be other reasons for the Jewish "no," reasons that are adequate to the magnitude of that negation—and those reasons clearly are to be found at least partly in Christianity itself. For our own sake, but also for the sake of our Jewish sisters and brothers, and for the sake of the whole world, whom Christians manifoldly affect, we Christians deeply need to learn the message of that fundamental Jewish "no"—again I repeat, not to Yeshua (as the modern and contemporary Jewish writing of the most positive and penetrating sort about Yeshua loudly declaims), but to the Christ of Christianity. Have Christians distorted not only Christianity but also even Yeshua? If so, in what ways, and what must be done about it? These are fundamental life and death questions that Christians may not and cannot avoid. To find the answers to them, Christians need to enter into profound, long-term dialogue with living Jews and Judaism.

If Christianity wishes to be authentic, if it wishes to be true to itself, it must find its way back to its Founder and its foundation—and they were both Jewish through and through. In other words, in order to know and be our authentic selves, we Christians must be in dialogue with Jews and Judaism.

We Christians have not only tended to cut ourselves off from our Jewish Founder and foundation, but we have also grossly distorted ourselves for almost two millennia by unconsciously, and at times even consciously, fleeing from and suppressing what we perceived as Jewish. Only by reappreciating Jewish values, practices, ways of viewing the world, conceptualizations, and expressions can we begin to rebalance the distortions we have inflicted on ourselves. This distortion and loss resulted not only from the polarization wrought almost at our origin as the church but also from having cut ourselves off from the creative developments in Judaism subsequent to the early break. For both cases the only way to begin to recover our heritage is to be in extended, deep dialogue with the Jews and Judaism, not just from the past, but especially with living Jews and Judaism, for it is only they who can say how it is with the living religion from within.

Why Should Jews Dialogue with Christians?

Jews also need to engage in dialogue with Christians. Although it is most proper for a Jew rather than a Christian to voice these reasons, let me at least cursorily report on some of those reasons I have heard some Jews express. First, there are all the reasons listed above for dialogue with any religion, but there are also several reasons why dialogue specifically with Christianity is important for Jews.

(1) The most famous and influential Jew in history was Yeshua. His life and teaching were quintessentially Jewish, as is being recognized by a growing number of both Jewish[137] and Christian[138] scholars today. Prof. Nicholas de Lange said:

> Jesus is the spiritual father of a vast race of righteous gentiles, who have voluntarily chosen to separate themselves, up to a point, from the gentile world and taken upon themselves not only the privileges but some (at least) of the burdens of the people of Israel. Through their faith, Jesus is alive today . . . So long as Christians are faithful to the memory of Jesus, we have a pledge that they will be faithful to the God of Abraham, Isaac and Jacob, and to the teachings of Moses and the Hebrew prophets. They are our younger brothers, and our fellow-workers in the same vineyard. Surely we must agree with the words of Franz Rosenzweig: "Before God, Jew and Christian both labor at the same task. He cannot dispense with either" (*The Star of Redemption*, 415).[139]

This most famous of all Jews is being welcomed home by a growing number of Jews—without becoming Christians; that is, he is being recognized as authentically Jewish by other Jews—Martin Buber, for example, refers to him as Jesus his brother, and Schalom Ben Chorin's major book is *Bruder Jesus*. Rabbi Leo Baeck wrote a book in the midst of the Nazi horror

---

137. For surveys of sympathetic Jewish writing on Jesus, see Shalom Ben Chorin, "The Image of Jesus in Modern Judaism," *Journal of Ecumenical Studies* 11 (Summer 1974) 401–30; and Pinchas Lapide, *Ist das nicht Josephs Sohn? Jesus im heutigen Judentum* (Stuttgart: Calwer, 1976).

138. For a survey of the growing Christian scholarship on the Jewishness of Jesus, see Mussner, *Trakat über die Juden*, 109–14; see also Leonard Swidler, "The Jewishness of Jesus: Some Religious Implications for Christians," *Journal of Ecumenical Studies* 18 (Winter 1981) 104–13.

139. Nicolas De Lange, "Who Is Jesus?" *Sidic* 12/3 (1979) 13.

on the Gospel as teaching the fundamentals of Jewish faith[140] in which he had the following startling things to say about the Jewishness of Yeshua:

> In the ancient Gospel which emerges in this manner a man with noble characteristics stands before us who lived, helped, worked, endured and died during disturbed, tense days in the land of the Jews, a man of the Jewish people, walking Jewish paths, living in Jewish faith and hopes, whose spirit dwelled in the Holy Scriptures, who composed poetry in them, and who proclaimed, taught the word of God because God had given it to him to hear and to preach. Before us stands a man who won his disciples from among his people who sought the Messiah, the son of David, the promised one, and then found him and held fast to him, until he himself began to believe in himself . . . We see a man before us in this ancient tradition who in all the lines and features of his being the Jewish image shines forth, who reveals in himself so authentically and clearly the pure and good of Judaism, a man who could come forth only from the soil of Judaism, which he did, and only from this soil could he recruit his disciples and followers, as they were.[141]

This is something Jews and Christians need to talk about.[142]

(2) Schalom Ben-Chorin argued that the two surviving ways of being Jewish are ineluctably directed toward each other: "We must come together in dialogue because we are asked about each other . . . The ancient covenant exists, and the new covenant exists. The ancient and new covenants have not dissolved each other, but rather they persist through time. And since it is the case that the covenants really exist, the bearers of the covenant are asked from the perspective of the existence of one about the existence of the other . . . The message which we both have to deliver, Jews and Christians, lead us to one another."[143]

(3) Judaism can come to know itself better by dialogue with its offspring. For example, Hellenistic Judaism, by far the largest and most flourishing of all the ways of being Jewish at the beginning of the Common Era, in a few centuries thereafter disappeared from the stage of history. In fact, however, Christianity, which fused Hellenism with Judaism, might well be

---

140. Leo Baeck, *Das Evangelium als Urkunde der jüdischen Glaubens Geschichte* (Berlin: Schock, 1938).

141. Quoted in Pinchas Lapide, *Er predigte in ihren Synagogen* (Gütersloh: Gerd Mohn, 1980) 23.

142. See Swidler et al., *Bursting the Bonds?*

143. Schalom Ben-Chorin, "Das Judentum im Ringen der Gegenwart," *Evangelische Zeitstimmen* (Hamburg) 22/23 (1965) 30, 33.

viewed as a peculiar variant of that vanished Hellenistic Judaism. If so, Jews might see something of themselves in the strange mirror of Christianity, although they would see only darkly, as that Hellenistic Jew, Paul of Tarsus, put it. Contemporary Jews would also see in Christianity—and I might also add, in Islam—the continuance of the universalist strand of the Hebraic-Jewish tradition that led to perhaps 8 percent of the entire so-called "civilized world," that is, the Roman Empire, being Jewish at the beginning of the Common Era. Only now is the Reform movement of Judaism in the U.S. beginning to reclaim that essentially Jewish universalist strand of actively welcoming converts—at least in part a result, I would contend, of its dialogue with Christianity.

(4) In a variation of (3), I submit that Judaism would be entering into a dialogue with a portion of itself in a dialogue with Christianity, especially insofar as it is based on its ancient Gospel tradition. Let me again cite Rabbi Leo Baeck in this regard:

> When this ancient tradition thus comes before our view, then the Gospel, this Jewish reality, which it originally was, becomes a book which is not minor in Jewish scriptures ... It is a Jewish book through and through because the pure air which fills it and in which it breaths is the Holy Scripture, because the Jewish spirit, and only it, reigns in it, because Jewish faith and Jewish hope, Jewish suffering and Jewish need, Jewish knowledge and Jewish expectation, they alone ring throughout it—a Jewish book in the midst of Jewish books. Judaism may not pass it by, fail to appreciate it, or here wish to enter a disclaimer. Here too Judaism must embrace its own, in order to know its own.[144]

(5) Martin Buber stated why he thought Jews needed to enter into dialogue with Christians in his own inimitable manner—in a dialogue with K. L. Schmidt on January 14, 1933, only a few days before Hitler seized power:

> In all this what binds together Jews and Christians is their common knowledge of a single thing, and from that we can reach across the deepest divide to each other; every genuinely sacred thing can acknowledge the mystery of another genuinely sacred thing. The mystery of the other is within him and cannot be perceived from without. No person outside of Israel knows of the mystery of Israel. And no person outside of Christianity knows of the mystery of Christianity. But even not knowing, we can acknowledge each other in the mystery. How it is possible

---

144. Quoted in Lapide, *Er predigte*, 23–24.

that there are mysteries along side of each other is God's mystery. How it is possible that there is a world as a house in which these mysteries dwell together is God's concern, for the world is God's house. It is not because we question anyone concerning the reality of his faith; it is not that we by some subterfuge wish to introduce collaboration despite differences, but rather it is because with the acknowledgment of the differences that in unconditioned trust we share with each other what we know of the unity of this house. We hope that we one day will feel ourselves filled with its unity, without walls of division around us. We serve divided and yet with one another, until one day we will be united in a common service, until we all will, as it says in the Jewish prayer on the feast of the New Year: "Be a single covenant for the sake of doing his will."[145]

Jewish-Christian-Muslim Trialogue

I would now like to turn to the question of why it is important for Jews and Christians to enter into dialogue with Muslims—beyond those general reasons for interreligious dialogue already discussed. As a prolegomenon to responding to this question it is important to list at least some of the major elements these three Semitic or Abrahamic religions have in common.

First, they all come from the same Hebraic roots and claim Abraham as their originating ancestor; the historical, cultural, and religious traditions all flow out of one original source, an *Urquelle*.

Second, all three traditions are religions of ethical monotheism; that is, they all claim there is one, loving, just, creator God who is the Source, Sustainer, and Goal of all reality and that S/He expects all human beings, as images of God, to live in love and justice. In other words, belief in the One God has ethical consequences concerning oneself, other persons, and the world. This is a *common* heritage of the three Abrahamic religions, which is by no means shared by all elements of the other major world religions.

Third, the three traditions are all historical religions, that is, they believe that God acts through human history, that God communicates through historical events through particular human persons, preeminently Moses, Jesus, and Muhammad. Historical events, like the exodus, crucifixion, and *hijrah*, and human persons do not at all play the same central role in many other world religions, as, for example, Hinduism and Taoism.

---

145. Recorded in K. L. Schmidt, *Neues Testament-Judentum-Christentum.* Kleine Schriften-Theologische Bücher 69 (Munich, 1981) 149–65.

Fourth, Judaism, Christianity, and Islam are all religions of revelation, that is, they are persuaded that God has communicated or revealed something of Godself and will in special ways through particular persons, for the edification, for the salvation—or said another way, for the humanization, which is also the divinization—of all humankind. In all three religions this revelation has two special vehicles: prophets and scriptures. Clearly, in Judaism the male prophets Isaiah, Amos, Hosea, Jeremiah, and the female prophets Miriam and Huldah, etc., are outstanding "mouthpieces" of Yahweh (*prophetes*, one who speaks for another), and the greatest of all the prophets in Judaism is Moses. For Christianity, Moses and the other prophets are God's spokespersons—but also numbered among the Christian prophets are Anna (Luke 2:36–38), the two daughters of Philip (Eusebius, *Eccl. Hist.* III.31), and, most of all, Yeshua—though most Christians later came to claim something beyond prophethood for him. For Islam all these Jewish and Christian prophets are also authentic prophets, God's revealing voice in the world—and to that list they add Muhammad, the Seal of the Prophets. For all three Abrahamic faiths, God's special revelation is also communicated in "The Book." For Jews the Holy Scriptures are the Hebrew Bible; for Christians it is the Hebrew Bible and the New Testament; and for Muslims it is those two plus the Qur'an, which is corrective and supplemental to them. Muslims, Jews, and Christians have the special name, "People of the Book."

There are many more things that these three faiths have in common, such as the importance of covenant, law, faith, and the community (witness in the three traditions the central role of the terms "People," "Church," and "Ummah," respectively). Just looking at the list of commonalities already briefly spelled out will provide us with an initial set of fundamental reasons why it is imperative for both Jews and Christians to engage in serious, ongoing dialogue with Muslims.

First, if Jews and Christians believe that there is only one, loving, just God in whose image they are and whose will they claim to try to follow, they need to face the question of why there are three different ways of doing that—obviously that question can be faced only in dialogue.

Second, if Jews and Christians believe that God acts through human history, that God communicates through historical events and particular human persons, they need to face the question of whether all religiously significant historical events and persons are limited to their own histories. Colloquially, do Jews and Christians really believe that they have God in their own historical boxes or that, by their own principles, God transcends all limitations, including even their sacred historical events and persons?

Third, if Judaism and Christianity believe that God communicates, reveals Godself to humans not only through things, events, and human persons in general, but also in special ways through particular events and persons, they are going to have to face the question of whether God's will as delivered through God's spokespersons, that is, prophets, and the recording in writing of their teachings and kindred material in what is known as Holy Scriptures is limited to their own prophets and scriptures. Concretely, Jews will have to reflect on whether Yeshua and the writings of his first—Jewish—followers have something to say about God's will for humankind to non-Christians (and themselves?). Jews and Christians will have to reflect on whether the prophet Muhammad and his "recitation," that is, "Qur'an," have something to say about God's will for humankind to non-Muslims (including themselves?).

Obviously, these questions and others of serious importance to the ultimate meaning of life can be addressed only in dialogue among Jews, Christians, and Muslims. Once this is recognized, however, it also immediately becomes clear that all the questions just listed that challenge the absoluteness and exclusivity of the three Abrahamic traditions' claims about having all the truth, about God's being found only in the boxes of their history, prophets, scriptures, and revelation also apply to the non-Abrahamic religions and ideologies, such as Hinduism, Buddhism, and Marxism.

Praxis

Pragmatically, however, one cannot engage in dialogue with all possible partners at the same time. Moreover, all the goals of one dialogue with a certain set of partners can never be fulfilled by another set of dialogue partners. For example, the goal of working toward denominational unity between the Lutheran Church in America and the American Lutheran Church would never have been accomplished if Catholics had been full partners in that dialogue with Lutherans. Or, again, Jews and Christians have certain items on their mutual theological agenda, for example, the Jewish claim that the Messiah has not yet come, that will not be adequately addressed if Muslims are added as full partners—and so it goes with each addition or new mix of dialogue partners.

There is a special urgency about the need for Christians to dialogue among themselves to work toward the goal of some kind of effective, visible Christian unity; the absurdity and scandal of there being hundreds of separate churches all claiming "one foundation, Jesus Christ the Lord," is patent. The need for intra-Jewish dialogue I will leave to my Jewish sisters and brothers to inform me about. However, for Christians, as indicated much earlier, dialogue with Jews has an extraordinarily high priority that cannot be displaced, and, where it has not been both initiated and continued, it needs to be undertaken with all possible speed and perseverance. This is true even for those Christian communities where there exists no Jewish community, for Christians will have difficulty in knowing themselves fully if they do not in some way engage in significant dialogue with the adherents of the religion of Yeshua, namely, Judaism.

Nevertheless, there is something like—though not precisely—a relationship of parent-offspring that compels Jews and Christians to enter into dialogue with Muslims. Moreover, today there are all the external reasons for Jewish-Christian dialogue with Islam that flow from the reality of the earth's now being a global village and the unavoidable symbiotic relationship between the Judeo-Christian industrialized West and the partly oil-rich, relatively nonindustrialized Islamic world.

Expectations from the Trialogue

A special word of caution to Jews and Christians who enter into dialogue with Muslims is in order. They will be starting such a venture with several disadvantages: (1) the heritage of colonialism, (2) ignorance about Islam, (3) a distorted image of Muslims, and (4) the culture gap.

(1) The Heritage of Colonialism: The vast majority of Muslims trained in Islamics are non-Westerners, which means they very likely come from a country that was until recently a colony of the West. Many Muslims are still traumatized by Western colonialism and frequently identify Christianity, and to a lesser extent, Judaism, with the West. Jewish and Christian dialogue partners need to be aware of this and move to diffuse the problem.

(2) Ignorance about Islam: Jews and Christians will need to make a special effort to learn about Islam beyond what was required for them intelligently to engage in the Jewish-Christian dialogue, for in the latter they usually knew at least a little about the partner's religion. With Islam they will probably be starting with a negative quantity compounded from sheer ignorance and massive misinformation.

(3) A Distorted Image of Muslims: Most often the current Western image of a Muslim is a gross distortion of Islam. Indeed, it is frequently that of some kind of inhuman monster, but the Ayatollah Khomeni or Osama bin Laden distortion of Islam is no more representative of Islam than the Rev. Ian Paisley of Northern Ireland was of Christianity in general or Richard

Nixon was of the pacifist Quaker tradition, or the Jewish murderer of Israeli Prime Minister Yitzak Rabin is of Judaism. More about this below.

(4) The Culture Gap: Most difficult of all is the fact that a huge cultural gap exists between the great majority of Muslims and precisely those Jews and Christians who are open to dialogue. In brief, Islam as a whole has not yet really experienced the "Enlightenment" and come to terms with it, as has much, although obviously not all, of the Judeo-Christian tradition. Only a minority of Muslim Islamics scholars will share the deabsolutized understanding of truth described above, which means that many efforts at dialogue with Muslims will in fact be prolegomena to true interreligious dialogue. Frequently, such attempts will be not unlike "dialogue" with many Orthodox Jews or evangelical Christians—or with Catholics before Vatican II. But, the prolegomena must be traversed in order to reach authentic dialogue. Surely the words of the Vatican and Pope Paul VI apply to all Christians and Jews, who "must assuredly be concerned for their separated brethren . . . making the first approaches toward them . . . dialogue is *demanded* nowadays . . . by the pluralism of society, and by the maturity man has reached in this day and age."[146] It is toward that end that all Christians and Jews must strive, first among themselves, then with each other, and then with their quasi "offspring," Islam.

Islamist Terror

Since September 11, 2001, the whole globe has been painfully aware of the worldwide attacks by Muslim terrorists on America and the West. We begin with some words about the basic terms used.

(1) Definition of Terror: Terror is violence, usually deadly, that is deliberately perpetrated against specifically innocent persons so as to strike terror into the host group. There have been and are today several terrorist groups around the world, for example, in the recent past, the Ku Klux Klan, the Red Army, the Weathermen, recent groups on both sides of the Northern Ireland conflict, Aum Shin Riki, and today Hamas, Islamic Jihad, Laskar Jihad, al Quaeda, and others.

(2) Connection of Terror with Islam: As some of the names above indicate, there are several contemporary terrorist organizations that allege a connection with Islam. However, the sources of Islam and the vast majority of the Islamic tradition and living Muslims find terrorism abhorrent. They see terror done in the name of Islam as a perversion of Islam (whose very name "Islam" has peace, "salam," as its basis), just as the vast majority

---

146. *Ecclesiam suam*, no. 78, quoted in Flannery, *Vatican Council II*, 1003.

of Christians find the terror perpetrated in Northern Ireland done in the name of Christianity a perversion of Christianity (whose founder is called the "Prince of Peace").

(3) Fundamentalism: This term was coined at the beginning of the twentieth century by a group of conservative Protestants who wanted to stress what they called the "fundamentals" of Christianity. Their ideals included a "literalist" understanding of the Holy Scriptures, an alleged unchanging understanding of "the truth," and consequently a restrictive policy on the public behavior of women ("should be in the home," "wives subject to husbands"). Subsequently, the term "Fundamentalism" has found rather wide application to persons and groups other than conservative Protestantism where a similar *mentality* is present, that is, a mentality that tends to be characterized by a literalist approach to some basic text; an absolutist attitude toward "the truth"—which they hold exclusively, and whoever differs is in falsehood and must expect the consequences; and a restrictive policy toward certain groups, especially women. Such a fundamentalist mentality can be found today in Hindu, Christian, Jewish, Marxist, Muslim, and other religious and ideological groups.

(4) Islamism: In the 1970s a number of fundamentalist Islamic groups began to develop a political ideology and strategy, which they claimed was based on Islam, and began to call themselves "Islamists" (not to be confused with "Islamicist," which means a person who is an expert in the study of Islam). Islamist, as a consequence, has tended recently to be used to refer to these groups rather than fundamentalist, though it still make sense to use fundamentalist when referring mainly to their mentality, and especially when linking Muslim Fundamentalists with other Fundamentalists. Islamism must not be thought of as just another political movement intending to make its special contribution to the welfare of the world. It is a neo-fascist—that is, anti-freedom, anti-human—political movement that aims to eliminate all other political forms in the world! It may seem fantastic, but carried to its extreme by someone like Osama bin Laden, Islamism has the same aims that Hitler and Stalin had before him: to control the entire world. Bin Laden was convinced that through him God destroyed one Super Power, the Soviet Union, in the Soviet-Afghan War. Then, God, having destroyed the World Trade Center (bin Laden on October 9, 2001, told the world that "God" destroyed those buildings), was going to destroy the last Superpower, the Infidel U.S., through Osama bin Laden.

(5) Jihadism: "*Jihad*" is an Arabic word meaning "struggle." From almost the beginning of Islam in the seventh century, *Jihad* has meant both the *internal* struggle against ungodliness within oneself and the *external* struggle against the oppression of true religions. The Islamists have stressed

almost exclusively the external notion, equating Jihad with a so-called "Holy War" of Islam against non-Islam. A number of Islamists have pushed the "War" aspect so strongly that they call themselves "Jihadists," meaning, those who follow a program of attaining their goal of political power by means of violence, *Jihad*. Some Jihadists draw the "logical conclusion," like Osama bin Laden and his many supporters, and move on to terror.

(6) Why do Islamist Terrorists Attack America, and Other Democratic Peoples? Islamist terrorists attack America and the West because they hate modernity and its values—freedom/responsibility, personalism, human rights (especially for women and minorities), democracy, dialogue—and aim to supplant it with their absolutist vision of the truth and how everyone in the world should live. Some have argued that the oppression of the Palestinians is the cause of Islamist terror. The hostility between Israel and the Palestinians has been a running sore on the globe's body politic for decades. It has not only caused millions untold pain and destruction, but also threatens to become the trigger of a larger world conflagration. Hence, attaining a just and lasting peace in the Middle East is a challenge that desperately needs to be met both for those living there and for world peace.

Can one then claim that the present Islamist/Jihadist-led terrorism is caused by the lack of a Middle East peace? The answer is clearly no. Bin Laden was not, nor are his fellow terrorists, focused on a just Mideast peace. The attack on New York and Washington was in the works for over a year before 9/11/01—but a year earlier Israel and Palestine were engaged in the most intense peace negotiations to date, along with great urging and support on the part of the U.S. (January, 2000, at the end of the Clinton administration). If attaining a peace acceptable to Palestinians were the goal of the terrorists, they would not have started plotting the 9/11 horror just then. Rather, they definitely did *not* want Middle East peace but wanted to prevent it and therefore started planning these terror attacks.

Some say that we should look to eliminate the feeding grounds of terrorism: poverty and its related effects. We all *should* pursue this goal of social justice ever more intensely, but poverty is not the reason for the growth of terrorism. The world's poorest area, sub-Saharan Africa, has not produced suicide bombers and terrorists. Further, the percentage of poor people in the world in past history has been vastly greater than it is today. This fact is obscured by the talk about the growing gap between the rich and the poor (which is also a fact). Those classified as poor in America today, for example, have vastly more material wherewithal than the poor in America 100 years ago. Huge numbers of Americans, and others, are no longer poor—not *despite* Bill Gates's becoming the richest person in the world, but *because* of it.

Is the lifting of the "floor" of the world's poorest people already accomplished sufficiently? Of course not. All persons of good will—and they are legion—are working to raise the "floor" ever higher. Moreover, we all could, and therefore should, do more. However, the twenty-first century's most notorious terrorist, bin Laden, did not grow up in poverty but in luxury; he inherited three hundred million dollars. (After he became a terrorist, his family renounced him: "We consider those acts an unspeakable contravention of the principles of our religion and they stand to be condemned by any and all religions and by humanity at large . . . the family of bin Laden renounces Osama's deeds and stratagems and has absolutely nothing to do with them."). Clearly, poverty is not the source of terrorism; otherwise, the world would have been even more overwhelmed by terrorism in the past when there was vastly more poverty. We must do all we can to reduce and eliminate poverty, but we should not be misled into thinking that attaining that goal will eliminate terrorism.

(7) What Should Be Done about the Islamist Terrorists? First, we can *always* find fault with *any* position or person. However, cynicism is as humanly destructive as is its opposite, naivete. We should use our critical-thinking capacities at all times, being ever vigilant to see that in the pursuit of the criminal terrorists we do not give them the ultimate victory by eroding the foundations of freedom and human dignity for all. At the same time, however, we should also be aware that being naive vis-à-vis terrorists can be as destructive as Chamberlain's "pacifism" vis-à-vis Hitler. His weakness in the face of Hitler's 1938 assault on Czechoslovakia simply encouraged Hitler and led to his 1939 attack on Poland, launching World War II.

Jingoism, no, but forming a global alliance that will use all tools—diplomatic, political, economic, educational, investigative, and, where appropriate, force—to pursue and root out the terrorist criminals and their supporters, yes. Political leaders must be won over to opposition to terrorist crime. Those who continue to support terrorist crime must be shamed by the world and isolated, and, if their support for terrorism is vicious enough, they should be subjected to force as any violent criminal would be. What should ordinary citizens do about terrorism? Most cannot lead a multipronged "police" action. Rather, ordinary citizens must encourage and direct the police. Beyond that, I make four suggestions:

Non-Muslims Need to Advocate and Practice Tolerance and Respect

Those who are not Muslim must denounce any and all harassing or denigration of our fellow citizens who are Muslim, or Arab—indeed, we must courageously and even preemptively condemn any and all denigration of Muslims or Arabs as such, anywhere in the world. Not only toleration, but full respect of all, and now especially of Muslims and Arabs, must vigorously be advocated and acted on by all non-Muslims and non-Arabs.

Muslims Need to Speak Out

Beyond that, those who are Muslim need to speak out, courageously condemning the hijacking not only of airliners but also of Islam, perverting the "*salam*" of Islam into a murder of innocents and blaspheming God "the merciful and compassionate One," twisting God into a murderer of innocents. This strong and continual condemnation of terror, of Jihadism, of Islamism will be not just a minor, but a major and challenging contribution that our Muslim sisters and brothers can make to Islam and humanity.

Support Moderate and Progressive Islam

Beyond both Muslims' condemning Islamism, Jihadism, and terror and non-Muslims' promoting and practicing tolerance and respect, all together should protect, support, and encourage the voices of moderate and progressive Islam. It has often been repeated that the majority of Muslims abhor Islamism, Jihadism, and terror. This majority of Muslims must not be a "silent majority" but must provide a strong echo for those Muslim thinkers who risk speaking out—some even risking their lives—giving them the strength and courage to continue on that truly dangerous path. Non-Muslims likewise need to protect, support, and encourage moderate and progressive Muslim thinkers. Learn who they are, invite them to speak, strive to give them jobs and positions where they can speak and provide leadership instead of being blackballed by Islamist forces, which have a great deal of financial power. Combat that power by financially supporting the moderate and progressive Muslim thinkers.

Education for Deep-Dialogue and Critical-Thinking

The special responsibility of "ordinary citizens'" is to work in the field of education in the broadest sense, the kind that must go from the cradle to the grave; it includes the school but encompasses all life. At the heart of this education is the fostering of a mentality of Critical-Thinking and Deep-Dialogue of the personally transformative kind, whereby we come to understand and respect ourselves and reach out to understand and respect the Other. Many are trying to do this, but we *all* need to find creative ways to expand our efforts.[147] This can be the major contribution by ordinary citizens to a future world where terrorism will be something studied only in textbooks on the sociopsychopathology of past history.

Muslim Critical Thinkers

Despite the culture gap and the fact that only a minority of Muslim Islamicists (not Islamists!) have a "deabsolutized" view of truth, there are today many more of them than is usually recognized, often living outside the Muslim world. Let me recall a personal experience exemplifying why this is the case.

Fathi Osman (1928–2010)

An Egyptian Muslim Islamicist who spent a number of years studying and teaching in America absorbed the historical-critical mentality and was very open to interreligious dialogue. During a graduate seminar on Christian-Muslim dialogue that we taught jointly, we spoke quite specifically about a "dialogic" article he wished to write for the *Journal of Ecumenical Studies* (*J.E.S.*), which I founded in 1964 with my wife Arlene Anderson Swidler and still edit. Most unfortunately, for family reasons he had to return to Egypt and shortly thereafter took a position teaching Islamics at a university in Jedda, Saudi Arabia. After two years of correspondence and coaxing, he wrote me in despair that he could not write the article we had worked out together as long as he was in the Arabian world; the intellectual atmosphere was just "too restrictive for him to be able to think the thoughts he would have to" in order to write the article.

---

147. For details on what has been and is being done and to learn more about and become involved in Deep-Dialogue and Critical-Thinking, see the web site of the Dialogue Institute, www.dialogueinstitute.org.

The Muslim scholar in question was Fathi Osman (1928–2010), who taught with me at Temple University in 1975–76, during which time he wrote a review article on Christology that was published in *J.E.S.* in 1977.[148] He subsequently returned to the U.S. and joined the Jewish-Christian-Muslim trialogue sponsored by *J.E.S.* and the National Conference of Christians and Jews—and was again his former liberated self—and then some.[149] He was for years the Scholar in Residence at the "Institute for the Study of the Role of Islam in the Contemporary World, Omar Ibn Al Khattab Foundation," in Los Angeles.

The same point was made poignantly by Fazlur Rahman: "Free thought and thought are synonymous, and one cannot hope that thought will survive without freedom . . . Islamic thought, like all thought, equally requires a freedom by [which] dissent, confrontation of views, and debate between ideas is assured."[150] Rahman, who until his death in 1988 was for many years a professor at the University of Chicago, knew well whereof he spoke. He was the Minister of Education of the then newly created Pakistan from 1947 to 1957, and from 1962 to 1968 he was Director of a newly formed Islamic Research Institute (established by President Ayub Khan). "But even as the institute was a little less than halfway through to the initial stage of its goal, it became the victim of a massive attack of the combined forces of the religious right and the opposition politicians. I resigned in September 1968 and the Ayub Khan government fell six months later, and, although this group of progressive scholars has done its best to maintain itself, it has since been overwhelmed by the forces of reaction."[151]

Smail Balic (1920–2002)

Nevertheless, critical thinking among Muslim Islamicists broke through. Bosnian Muslim scholar Smail Balic wrote that, "in regard to research into the real occasions for the individual revelations of the Qur'an, and the consequent legal philosophy, not enough is done seriously to distinguish the timebound elements from the enduring. The knowledge that the Qur'an is

---

148. Fathi Osman et al., "Jesus in Jewish-Christian-Muslim Dialogue," *Journal of Ecumenical Studies* 14 (Summer 1977) 448–65; also in Leonard Swidler, ed., *Muslims in Dialogue: The Evolution of a Dialogue* (Lewiston, NY: Edwin Mellen, 1992).

149. See Fathi Osman, "The 'Good' in the Sources of Islam and Its Conception and Implementation by Muslims," in Leonard Swidler, ed., *THEORIA → PRAXIS: How Jews, Christians, Muslims (and Others) Can Together Move from Theory to Practice* (Leuven: Peeters, 1998).

150. Fazlur Rahman, *Islam* (New York: Doubleday, 1968) 125.

151. Ibid.

in part also a collection of time-related documents from the early history of Islam has not yet been able to move beyond pure theory."[152]

Asaf A. A. Fyzee (1899–1981)

Indian Muslim Asaf A.A. Fyzee stated: "For me it is clear that we cannot "go back" to the Qur'an. Rather, we must go forward with it. I want to *understand* the Qur'an as the Arabs of the time of the Prophet did only in order *to interpret it anew*, in order to apply it to my living conditions and to believe in it insofar as it speaks to me as a human person of the 20th century."[153]

Mohammad Arkoun (1928–2010)

Professor of Arabic Language and Islamic Culture at the University of Paris and, for a time, Temple University, Muhammad M. Arkoun, at a Christian-Muslim dialogue in Bonn in 1981, severely criticized the kind of dialogue wherein the conservative and fundamentalist elements of each side simply reinforced each other; rather, he wanted modern critical scholarly thought brought to bear on both religions and their dialogue: "For this reason I demand in what concerns me a critically new reading of the Scripture (Bible, Gospels, Qur'an) and a philosophical critique of exegetical and theological reason."[154] Later, Arkoun argued this point even more forcefully and with great stress on the need to study religions together: "In this context where struggling ideologies are at work, it seems totally romantic, irrelevant, and useless to engage in debates between religions about traditional faiths, values, or dogmas. Positive and efficient initiatives should be taken in the field of education: primary and secondary schools, universities, the mass media, nongovernmental organizations and other private and public institutions, so as to promote a new teaching of history, *comparative* cultures, *comparative* religions, *comparative* philosophies and theologies, *comparative* literature and law."[155]

---

152. Smail Balic, *Ruf vom Minareth* (Vienna, 1979) 90.

153. Cited in Rotraud Wielandt, *Offenbarung und Geschichte im Denken moderner Muslime* (Wiesbaden: F. Steiner, 1971) 159.

154. Cited in M. S. Abdulla, ed., *Der Glaube in Kulture, Recht und Politik* (Mainz: Hase & Koehler, 1982) 142.

155. Mohammad Arkoun, "New Perspectives for a Jewish-Christian-Muslim Dialogue," *Journal of Ecumenical Studies* 26 (Summer 1989) 523–29; also in Swidler, *Muslims in Dialogue*, 345–52.

After spelling out in some detail how this comparative study should be carried out with the aid of modern critical scholarly tools, Arkoun concluded:

> This is, in very short allusive terms, my proposal as a Muslim scholar—not to contribute, I repeat to an encounter that would mean that we think and work within the framework of *I and we* vs. *you and them,* but to the creation of a new space of intelligibility and freedom. We need to be emancipated from inherited traditions not yet studied and interpreted with controlled methods and cognitive principles.
>
> Muslims are currently accused of being closed-minded, integrists, fundamentalists, prisoners of dogmatic beliefs. Here is a liberal, modern, humanist, Muslim proposal. I await the response of Jews, Christians, and secularists to my invitation to engage our thoughts, our endeavors, and our history in the cause of peace, progress, emancipation, justice through knowledge, and shared spiritual values.[156]

Fazlur Rahman (1919-88)

Perhaps the most thoroughgoing exponent of the historical-critical method's being indispensable to ascertaining the correct meaning of the foundation of Islam, the Qur'an, was Rahman, who clearly argued that the text can be understood only in context: "The Qur'an is the divine response, through the Prophet's mind, to the moral-social situation of the Prophet's Arabia . . . It is literally God's response through Muhammad's mind (this latter factor has been radically underplayed by the Islamic orthodoxy) to a historic situation (a factor likewise drastically restricted by the Islamic orthodoxy)."[157]

Like Asaf Fyzee, Rahman wished to get to the original meaning of the Qur'an so it could be applied, *mutatis mutandis,* now: "There has to be a two-fold movement: First one must move from the concrete case treatments of the Qur'an—taking the necessary and relevant social conditions of that time into account—to the general principles upon which the entire teaching converges. Second, from this general level there must be a movement back to specific legislation, taking into account the necessary and relevant social conditions now obtaining."[158]

---

156. Ibid.
157. Rahman, *Islam,* 5, 8.
158. Ibid., 20.

This is very much like the "two-pole" theology of many contemporary Christian theologians, such as Küng and Schillebeeckx.[159] From this there follows another logical step—again like that of many progressive Christian theologians, and similarly criticized from the respective bastions of orthodoxy—namely, that "the tradition will therefore be more an object of judgment of the new understanding [of the Scripture] than an aid to it."[160]

Moreover, Rahman rejected the notion that "any significant interpretation of the Qur'an can be absolutely monolithic . . . the Prophet's companions themselves sometimes understood certain Qur'anic verses differently, and this was within his knowledge."[161] Further, "It is obviously not necessary that a certain interpretation once accepted must continue to be accepted; there is always both room and necessity for new interpretation, for this is, in truth, an ongoing process."[162]

Mahmud Muhammad Taha (1909–85) and Abdullahi An-Na'im (1946–)

It is precisely this last point that was raised to the level of a critical hermeneutical-methodological principle in dealing with the Qur'an by Ustaz Mahmud Muhammad Taha from the Sudan. Taha was an engineer and a Sufi mystic who worked tirelessly for the reform of Islam both inwardly and outwardly. He was tragically executed at age 75 in January, 1985, in a final outburst of violence by General Gaafar Muhammad Nimieri before his overthrow a number of weeks later. However, Taha's thought continues in his followers, such as the jurist Abdullahi Ahmed An Na'im.

Taha argued that the shift from the earlier revelation of principles in Mecca to the later one in Medina is essentially reversible. The Mecca principles are fundamentally open, liberal, liberating principles, whereas the Medina principles are specific and restrictive. The shift was made because in the concrete circumstances—both the external ones and the then-internal capabilities of the Muslims—the Mecca principles could not yet be implemented in all their openness. They were the ideal, on the way to which Medina was but a way-station; it is now time for Muslims to leave the Medina way-station and move forward toward fulfilling the liberating Mecca ideal.

---

159. See Swidler, *Consensus in Theology?*
160. Rahman, *Islam*, 7.
161. Ibid., 144.
162. Ibid., 145.

This in brief is the heart of the teaching of Taha, filled out with qur'anic citations and argumentation, of course.[163]

Mohamed Talbi (1921–)

Mohamed Talbi of the University of Tunisia at Tunis has for years been active both nationally and internationally in dialogue with Christians, receiving the Lucas Prize for his contributions to interreligious dialogue from the Protestant Theological Faculty of the University of Tübingen in May, 1985 (the funding for which comes from the family of Rabbi Dr. Leopold Lucas, who had been a student at Tübingen). Representative of Talbi's self-critical, yet islamicly committed, thought are his reflections on "Religious Liberty: A Muslim Perspective":

> In short, from the Muslim perspective that is mine, our duty is simply to bear witness in the most courteous way that is most respectful of the inner liberty of our neighbors and their sacredness. We must also be ready at the same time to listen to them in truthfulness. We have to remember, as Muslims, that a *hadith* of our Prophet states: "The believer is unceasingly in search of wisdom; wherever he finds it he grasps it." Another saying adds: "Look for knowledge everywhere, even as far as in China." And finally, it is up to God to judge, for we, as limited human beings, know only in part. Let me quote: "To each among you We prescribed a Law and an Open Way. And if God had enforced His Will, He would have made of you all one people. But His plan is to test you in what He hath given you. So strive as in a race in all virtues. The goal of you all is to God. Then will He inform you of that wherein you differed" (Qur'an, V, 51) . . .
>
> At the heart of this problem we meet the ticklish subject of apostasy . . . the Qur'an argues, warns and advises, but never resorts to the argument of the sword. That is because that

---

163. See Abdullahi Ahmed El Naiem, "A Modern Approach to Human Rights in Islam: Foundations and Implications for Africa," in Claude Welch and Ronald Meltzer, eds., *Human Rights and Development in Africa* (Albany: State University of New York Press, 1984) 75–89; and Abdullahi An-Na'im, "Religious Freedom in Egypt: Under the Shadow of the Islamic *Dhimma* System," in Leonard Swidler, ed., *Religious Liberty and Human Rights in Nations and in Religions* (Philadelphia: Ecumenical, 1986) 43–62. An-Na'im has translated into English Taha's 1967 fundamental work, *The Second Message of Islam* (Syracuse: Syracuse University Press, 1987). Because An-Na'im was also imprisoned for years, the E.T. was published only in 1987. See also Abdullahi Ahmed An-Na'im, "Mahmud Muhammad Taha and the Crisis in Islamic Law Reform: Implications for Interreligious Relations," *Journal of Ecumenical Studies* 25 (Winter 1988) 1–21; also published in Swidler, *Muslims in Dialogue*, 59–85.

argument is meaningless in the matter of faith. In our pluralistic world our modern theologians must take that into account.

We can never stress too much that religious liberty is not an act of charity or a tolerant concession towards misled persons. It is a fundamental right of everyone. To claim it for myself implies *ipso facto* that I am disposed to claim it for my neighbor too.[164]

Hasan Askari (1932–2008)

Hasan Askari, Chairperson of the Sociology Department of Muslim University of Aligarh, India, and subsequently a Fellow at the Center for the Study of Islam and of Christian-Muslim Relations at Selly Oak Colleges, Birmingham, U.K., long espoused authentic interreligious dialogue, placing at the base of which a deabsolutized understanding of truth: "One who does not allow for alternatives within one's own religious tradition may not allow for more than one religious approach . . . [But we must] hesitate to absolutise any of the approaches within one or other plurality as the only true approach . . . All religions, and all approaches within each one of them, are relative to the Absolute Truth [God] . . . The worst of all defiance is to be locked up within one's own tradition and refuse to embrace each and every one, whatever his or her faith and creed."[165]

Khalid Duran (1939–2010)

Likewise deeply involved as a critical-thinking, committed Muslim in interreligious dialogue not only with Christians but also with Jews—and others—is the Moroccan Khalid Duran, was long at the Islamic Institute of Pakistan while Rahman directed it, then for many years at the Deutsches Orient Institut at Hamburg, and more recently at Temple University, the

---

164. From a lecture given at a conference sponsored by the *Journal of Ecumenical Studies* at Temple University, November 3–8, 1985: "Religious Tolerance and Human Rights within the International Community, within Nations and within Religions." An earlier version was delivered at the Second World Congress on Religious Liberty in Rome, September 3–4, 1984. Published as Mohamed Talbi, "Religious Liberty: A Muslim Perspective," in Swidler, *Religious Liberty*, 181, 187; also in Swidler, *Muslims in Dialogue*, 465–82.

165. Hasan Askari, "Within and beyond the Experience of Religious Diversity," in Hick and Askari, *Experience of Religious Diversity*, 191, 217. See also his article, "The Dialogical Relationship between Christianity and Islam," *Journal of Ecumenical Studies* 9 (Summer 1972) 477–87; also in Swidler, *Muslims in Dialogue*, 37–47.

American University, the University of California at Irvine, and the Foreign Policy Research Institute in Philadelphia.[166]

Duran was active for years in Jewish-Christian-Muslim Trialogue, first in England, then in Germany, and more recently in the U.S., where among other things he served as the Muslim Coordinator of the International Scholars Abrahamic Trialogue (ISAT). His thought and writings are a rich source for dialogic bridge-building. For example, on the complicated issue of Christian Mission/Muslim *Dawa*, from the Muslim side he insists that "Islamic religion or 'normative' Islam provided ample scope for a concept of mission adjustable to a pluralist society."[167] He centered this claim in the "central theme of Al-Qur'an, namely, humanity's responsibility for this world, its mission as God's vicegerent humanity as the administrator (Caliph) of the earth. This is a broader sense of mission and a more essential one than that of mere proselytizing." He noted:

"As such, there is no inherent inability in Islam to conceive of mission as something above and beyond proselytizing. The difficulty lies with an onerous historical legacy that has come to be misunderstood as Islam per se. It would be patently wrong to gloss over this formidable obstacle to pluralism. Muslims need to be made aware of the disparities between their faith and their practice. This will remain difficult as long as education remains the privilege of a few percent of the population, with the standards of religious education, moreover, on the decline."[168]

Duran then moved in the direction of strongly advocating the separation of religion and state in his promotion of what he referred to as "secularism," which he insisted is needed "as a means of protecting Muslims against themselves, or, more precisely, of protecting some Muslims against some others not to speak of secularism as a protection of non-Muslims from Muslims."[169] More recently, he published an outstanding book introducing Islam to Jews (in fact, it works as well for Christians).[170] When writing about current affairs, Duran recognized and analyzed carefully the difficulties

---

166. See, e.g., Khalid Duran, "Muslim Openness to Dialogue," in Swidler, ed., *Toward a Universal Theology of Religion*, 210–17. Also see Khalid Duran, "Religious Liberty and Human Rights in the Sudan," in Swidler, *Religious Liberty*, 61–78; and in Swidler, *Muslims in Dialogue*, 513–36.

167. Khalid Duran, "Muslims and Non-Muslims," in Leonard Swidler and Paul Mojzes, eds., *Attitudes of Religions and Ideologies toward the Outsider* (Lewiston, NY: Edwin Mellen, 1990) 97; also in Swidler, *Muslims in Dialogue*, 103.

168. Duran, "Muslims and Non-Muslims," 103–4.

169. Ibid., 108.

170. Khalid Duran, *Children of Abraham: An Introduction to Islam for Jews* (New York: Ktav, 2001).

many Muslims are having with modernity, including the place of women and Islamism—with stunning prescience concerning Osama bin Laden and al Qaida. This earned him a relentless attack from the Council on American Islamic Relations (CAIR)—until after September 11, 2001—as well as a *fatwa* by an extremist from Jordan against his life.[171]

Riffat Hassan (1943–)

Riffat Hassan, a Pakistani-American and Chair of the Religious Studies Program at the University of Louisville in Kentucky,[172] has been active in the trialogue in America since 1979 and recently established an ongoing Christian-Muslim dialogue in her native Pakistan. Hassan's writings also are a rich source of dialogue material with not only Christians and Jews, but also with all religious persons and all those of "good will." This is particularly clear in her reflections on Islam and human rights, for which as a general context she claims: "It is imperative that Muslims rethink their position on all vital issues, since we can no longer afford the luxury of consoling ourselves for our present miseries and misfortunes by an uncritical adulation of a romanticized past. History has brought us to a point where rhetoric will not rescue us from reality and where the discrepancies between Islamic theory and Muslim practice will have to be accounted for."[173]

Hassan insisted that "human rights . . . are so deeply rooted in our humanness that their denial or violation is tantamount to a negation or degradation of that which makes us human." Human rights, she wrote, "were created, as we were, by God in order that our human potential could be actualized." Because human rights are not a human invention, "I do not look for their origin or essence in books of law or history but in those books of scripture which contain God's eternal message and guidance to humankind."[174] She then spelled out at least seventeen specific human rights asserted in the Qur'an and penultimately ended her essay with severe criticism:

---

171. Duran also subsequently wrote a German best-seller, *Osama bin Laden und der internationale Terrorismus* (Munich: Ullstein, 2001).

172. See, e.g., Riffat Hassan, "Messianism and Islam," *Journal of Ecumenical Studies* 22 (Spring 1985) 261–91; and Riffat Hassan, "The Basis for a Hindu-Muslim Dialogue and Steps in that Direction from a Muslim Perspective," in Swidler, *Religious Liberty*, 125–42; also in Swidler, *Muslims in Dialogue*, 403–23.

173. Riffat Hassan, "On Human Rights and the Qur'anic Perspective," in Arlene Swidler, ed., *Human Rights in Religious Traditions* (New York: Pilgrim, 1982) 54; also in Leonard Swidler, *Muslims In Dialogue*, 449.

174. Swidler, *Muslims in Dialogue*, 450.

> If Muslims were to exercise all the human rights granted to humankind by God, they would create a Paradise on earth and have no need to spend their time and energy dreaming about the "*hur*" promised in the afterlife. Unfortunately, at this time the spectrum before us appears very bleak, as more and more human rights disappear under the pressure of mounting fanaticism and traditionalism in many areas of the Muslim world. I am particularly concerned about serious violations of human rights pertaining to the rights of women, the rights of minorities, the right of the accused to due process of law, and the right of the Muslim masses to be free of dictatorships.

However, ultimately, she ended with a "hope against hope": "In the end we have what seems to be an irreconcilable gulf between Qur'anic ideals and the realities of Muslim living. Can this gulf be bridged? To me, the answer is immaterial, because those of us who believe that human rights cannot be abandoned, even when they are being denied and aborted, will continue to strive and hope and pray for the securing of these rights—regardless of the chances of success or failure."[175]

It should be added that Hassan, besides being deeply involved in interreligious dialogue, is also a Muslim feminist. Amidst a life of many demands, she is striving to finish a major book on women in Islam. On the way to it she has published a number of essays on the topic[176] and has for years been running a vigorous website and campaign to eliminate the "honor killing" murders of Pakistani women and girls.[177]

The American Islamic Congress

The American Islamic Congress, a newly formed coalition of American Muslims, states that it is "dedicated to building interfaith and interethnic understanding. Our organization grew out of the ashes of September 11. We believe American Muslims must take the lead in building tolerance and fostering a respect for human rights and social justice at home and throughout the Muslim world." To that end they have also established centers and

---

175. Ibid. 463.

176. See, e.g., Riffat Hassan, "'Jihad Fi Sabil Allah': A Muslim Woman's Faith Journey from Struggle to Struggle to Struggle," 11–30; and "The Issue of Woman-Man Equality in the Islamic Tradition," 65–82, both in Leonard Grob, Riffat Hassan, and Haim Gordon, eds., *Women's and Men's Liberation—Testimonies of Spirit* (New York: Greenwood, 1991).

177. See http://ecumene.org/INRFVVP/.

projects in the Islamic world. See their website for details at http://www.aicongress.org/.

In general, they insist that *"Within the Muslim community*, we are building a coalition around the agenda of unequivocal denunciation of terrorism, extremism, and hate speech. Reaching out to all people of conscience, we promote genuine interfaith dialogue and educate about the diversity within Islam." They recalled, "The vicious terrorist attacks made many American Muslims realize that we had been silent for too long in the face of Muslim extremism. We believe American Muslims must take the lead in building tolerance and fostering respect for human rights and social justice. We have a responsibility to help our country rebuild from this attack, and we have a responsibility to our religion to reaffirm that we are moderate and peace-loving people."

The American Islamic Congress further declared that "Muslim Americans have a responsibility to denounce those who speak in the name of Islam and call for the death of Americans and innocent civilians in general, *including Israelis*. American Muslims must confront the extremism that is propagated in the name of our religion." Their "statement of principles" includes the following:

> —American Muslims must champion pluralism and condemn all forms of intolerance. American Muslims have a vested interest in the strength of religious freedom and democracy . . . We must censure intolerance, whatever its source.
>
> —American Muslims must be leading ambassadors to the Muslim world. America has been a haven for Islam. American Muslims must educate the Muslim world about the remarkable freedoms and coexistence we enjoy here.
>
> —All Muslims should enjoy the social and economic prosperity experienced by American Muslims. We owe our strength and success in part to classic American principles of individual rights and social justice . . . We should strive to improve economic conditions and individual freedom in the Muslim world.
>
> —American Muslims must champion the rights of minorities in the Muslim world. We know firsthand the importance of protecting the full rights of minority communities. One of our gifts to the larger Muslim world must be a new emphasis on considering and protecting the rights of minorities. This includes a painful reckoning with past and present episodes of intolerance in the Muslim world—and a commitment to progress in the future.

The International Scholars Abrahamic Trialogue (ISAT)

The Origin of ISAT

The International Scholars Abrahamic Trialogue—ISAT was preceded by a lengthy U. S. national trialogue of about twenty Jewish, Christian, and Muslim scholars held at the Kennedy Institute of Ethics at Georgetown University in Washington, DC, from 1978 through 1984, meeting every six months for three days at a time.[178] The first meeting largely tried to set a self-agenda for the near future, and the second meeting focused on how each tradition viewed the others. The main problems were that earlier traditions were traditionally seen as preludes to themselves, and later traditions as unnecessary, at best. The third meeting witnessed a beginning maturation of the Trialogue wherein it became increasingly clear that even many of the apparently shared basic concepts and terms such as revelation, salvation, and love were nuanced in different ways and, hence, needed careful dialogue.

The fourth meeting brought up the question of sexuality and the role of women. Here, a commonness was found in the "negative" treatment of women in the three traditions. This issue continued to be an ongoing study theme for the rest of the meetings. Subsequently, additional issues were approached, including such controversial ones as mission/*dawa* and conversion, as well as the ongoing joint study of each other's sacred texts. Eugene Fisher reported that in the second 1981 meeting, "We reaffirmed the need (with all due caution and prudence) for an international trialogue"; and thus the meetings continued until 1984. I continued thereafter to pursue the goal of establishing that International Trialogue. The need was clearly there; what was lacking was the funding.

"No peace among nations without peace among religions, no peace among the religions without dialogue among the religions." Thus started the February, 1989, address of Catholic theologian Hans Küng at the UNESCO Conference in Paris on world peace and dialogue among religions. It was precisely this concept along with the six-year experience of the American Trialogue that underlay the establishment of the Jewish-Christian-Muslim scholarly dialogue known then as the "International Scholars Annual Trialogue" (ISAT), which held its first annual conference in the spring of 1989 in Philadelphia, Pennsylvania.

The effects of such a long-term "fundamental research and dialogue" approach to the interrelationship among the three "Semitic" religions might be difficult to predict. We do know, however, that the long-term

---

178. See the detailed report by Eugene Fisher, "Kennedy Institute Jewish-Christian-Muslim Trialogue," *Journal of Ecumenical Studies* 19 (Winter 1982) 197–200.

"fundamental research and dialogue" approach to the interrelationship between Protestantism and Catholicism in Germany in the 1950s had a profoundly positive effect on the revolutionary changes that Protestant-Catholic relations have undergone since the early 1960s.[179] One cannot guarantee such positive results in the much more complex Jewish-Christian-Muslims relationship, but one can guarantee that, without such a "fundamental research and dialogue" approach in a long-term manner, positive developments in their relationship will *not* come about. This will also insure the continued undermining of the world peace process.

ISAT was composed of twenty-seven scholars, nine from each of the three Abrahamic religious traditions, Judaism, Christianity, Islam. The composition of ISAT remained basically the same, though different local participant-observers were also invited to each annual meeting. Every effort was made to include in ISAT representatives of the major divisions of each of the three religions and women scholars as well as men. The sponsoring body of ISAT is *J.E.S.* and it was also supported by the National Conference of Christians and Jews, until 1995.

The importance of having the same scholars meet regularly is that only after certain basic understandings have been achieved and personal trust has been won can dialogue move beyond the superficial level. That is what has been happening in this interreligious "think tank." "Basic research" is being done here. As in basic research in the physical sciences, immediate applicability is not the primary focus, but laying the necessary foundation for any future practical developments. The ISAT scholars come (originally) from the U.S., England, Israel, Germany, former Yugoslavia, Greece, Austria, Morocco, Pakistan, India, France, Algeria, Spain, Tunisia, Egypt, and Turkey.

ISAT met every year from 1989, with a hiatus in the late 1990s, but resumed again in 2000. ISAT has on the one hand been careful not to try to force external results before they are mature, but on the other hand it attempts to do whatever it can to promote trialogue through both scholarly and more popular publications and through the mass media, particularly in the regions where it meets.

Initial Dialogues Test the Waters

If authentic dialogue is to occur—that is, each partner comes to learn from the other—then it is imperative that the invited dialogue partners be

---

179. For a history of this several-decades-long movement, see Leonard Swidler, *The Ecumenical Vanguard* (Pittsburgh: Duquesne University Press, 1965).

those who are open to learning from others. This is all the more so in a dialogue involving Jews, Christians, and Muslims, for there are so many barriers among the three that it is only the literally "*ec*centric" members of each tradition who are likely to be able to engage in such a Trialogue today.[180] After the pioneers have laid the groundwork—which doubtless will take years—then the more centrist members of each tradition will feel it is safe to tread the path of Trialogue. We know, for example, that it took decades of dangerous and often repressed and condemned dialogue between Catholic and Protestant pioneers before the breakthrough of the "Decree on Ecumenism" of Vatican II made it safe for the pope to venture forth on the ecumenical journey.

ISAT's first meeting (generously funded by a Presbyterian layperson, J. William Robinson, from Atlanta, Georgia) lasted three days in April, 1989, at St. Raphaela Mary Catholic retreat house in Haverford, a suburb of Philadelphia, a city whose very name means "Brotherly-Sisterly Love." Because it was vital at the beginning of our project that we began to get to know each other as persons, set an irenic and high scholarly tone, and decide on our own agenda, a very "low-key" initial program was planned. We distributed ahead of time three published essays, one by one of our colleagues in each of our traditions, which focused on some aspect of interreligious dialogue to serve as launching pads for our discussions. Assuming that the three papers were read ahead of time by all, commentators from each of the other two traditions were assigned for each paper, and ample time for free dialogue was provided.

Though all of us had had a good deal of experience in dialogue, nevertheless, given the relative newness of this three-way dialogue for many of us and our often widely differing backgrounds, we believed it was wise to stress from the very beginning the need for all of us to strive consciously to be as thoroughly dialogic in our participation as possible. We were successful, and an irenic but frank tone was set from the very beginning.

For the second meeting (generously funded, as were most of the subsequent meetings, by Mormon layperson James Sorenson), held in January, 1990, in Atlanta, the theme of the assigned papers was "The Understanding of Revelation in the Three Traditions." The third meeting, in Orlando, Florida, took up the theme, "The Dilemmas of Human Dignity and Tradition" and also spent time on exegeses of the Torah, New Testament, and Qur'an.

---

180. See Swidler, *Muslims in Dialogue*, iii–xviii.

Jews-Christians-Muslims Pass Impasse

"We are at an impasse. Each of our traditions, Judaism, Christianity, Islam, has at its core a central 'absolute,' which is nonnegotiable and blocks the possibility of genuine dialogue: The Chosen People/Promised Land, The Christ, The Qur'an." Thus the situation was described at the end of the third ISAT, and consequently it was decided to make those three "absolutes" the focus of intense research; nine papers were prepared on the respective "absolutes" as found in each tradition's scriptures, history, and contemporary thought.

These papers were the basis of the dialogue in January, 1992, at Emory University in Atlanta. By then a deep trust among the participants had developed that allowed them to be self-critical even in front of the "outsiders" and to accept constructive critiques offered by them. "We have long since passed the stage of 'ecumenical politeness,'" remarked Pinchas Lapide, a Jewish participant from Germany/Israel, "and can now proceed to remove both the beam from our own eye and the speck from our brother's or sister's."

The "Chosen People" with its intimate connection to the "Promised Land" has been understood by Jews on one extreme to mean that the Jewish people are uniquely privileged by God and that the Holy Land (stretching from the Nile to the Euphrates, that is, from the heart of Egypt to the heart of Iraq) has been eternally committed by God to their complete possession. More commonly the "Chosen People" concept has been understood to mean that the Jews—now scattered in the "diaspora"—have been chosen to make known to the "nations" God's ethical laws (Ten Commandments, etc.). Some Jews even spoke of possessing, that is, living in, the Holy Land without necessarily having sovereignty. In modern times the idea of the Chosen People has been quasi-rejected by some Jews, as reflected in the humorous verse: "How odd of God to choose the Jews," and even directly repudiated by others, for example, Mordecai Kaplan and the Reconstructionists. Even Zionism is understood by some Jews to mean that the state in the Holy Land should include fully non-Jews as well as Jews. Clearly, the Chosen People/Promised Land is only a "relative absolute," given to constant reinterpretation and negotiation.

Concerning the Christian nonnegotiable "absolute," Jesus the Christ, the variation in interpretation over the centuries has been as great. The first followers of Jesus experienced him as a great teacher and spokesperson, or prophet, of God: a "Rabbi" and "Nabi." Some of his followers also saw him as the "Messiah," that is, the "Anointed One of God" who would expel the hated occupiers of the Holy Land, reestablish the Kingdom of Israel, and bring peace throughout the world. Because of his execution, however, Jesus was not perceived by most Jews thereafter as the Messiah, but for the gentile followers the Hebrew "Messiah" was greatly spiritualized into the Greek *Christos*, "Christ."

The largely metaphorically oriented Semitic thought pattern, and hence language, of the New Testament was later increasingly understood by the then mostly Hellenistic followers of Jesus as if it were Greek abstract metaphysical language—thus in the early Ecumenical Councils claiming divinity as well as humanity for Jesus. This meant that Jesus the Christ was "absolute"; all truth and goodness was to be found in him. Thus, there was no point to dialogue with non-Christians, since they could communicate no truth or value that the Christians did not already possess in their founder, Christ.

However, today there are many committed Christian scholars who are convinced of the rightness of the view of the first followers of Jesus: Jesus is experienced as a great teacher and model of how to live an authentic human, indeed, "divine" life; moreover, Jesus was divine for he was totally open to and permeated by all reality, including Ultimate Reality, God. However, because Jesus' humanity was filled with divinity does not mean that divinity did not also permeate other beings, including other religious figures. Clearly, the nonnegotiable "absolute," the Christ, has been interpreted not only in the traditionally exclusivistically absolute manner but also both in initial and contemporary Christianity in a "relatively absolute" manner, that is, as absolutely the best teacher and model of life for Christians, who also provides a model for all humans, divinity "enfleshed," without excluding the possibility of other religious figures' being teachers and models of life as well, also "enfleshing" divinity in themselves.

For traditional Islam (the term means "to submit" to God), its nonnegotiable absolute, the Qur'an, is the very word of God dictated verbatim to Mohammed by the angel Gabriel—correcting the previous revelations of God found in the Bible, but distorted there by the Jews and Christians. Thus, not to follow the Qur'an is not to follow God's correct word, not "to submit" to God. However, in contemporary Islam an increasing number of scholars and educated laity understand the Qur'an as God's message, and therefore absolute, but necessarily communicated to limited humans in a human, and therefore limited, language. Moreover, the Qur'an itself makes clear that God does not expect all people to follow the religion of Islam, that as long as people follow their consciences they will be blessed. Thus Islam's "nonnegotiable absolute" likewise is also often understood in a nonabsolute way.

Thus, a general major conclusion of the intense discussions of this Trialogue was that it is obvious that each of the three "nonnegotiable absolutes" have been subject to an immense amount of interpretation and "negotiation" within each tradition. Hence, they do not block dialogue, though they make it difficult at times—but also enriching!

The Graz Trialogue

The fifth annual Trialogue was held in January, 1993, in Graz, Austria and was locally sponsored by the Akademie Graz, Afro-Asiatisches Institut Graz, and Pro Oriente-Sektion Graz. We spent two days in closed sessions and four papers were prepared for this dialogue. Three were on the common topic: "How to Conceive and Implement the Good: A Self-Critical Reflection"—Jewish (Professor Arthur Green), Christian (Professor Paul Mojzes) and Muslim (Professor Fathi Osman). A fourth paper was prepared by Professor Leonard Swidler, "Towards a Universal Declaration of a Global Ethic," all of which issued in a scholarly book.

One session was devoted to hearing about the situation in Bosnia from Mojzes, Dr. Jure Kristo, Balik, and Duran, all from or closely connected with Bosnia. One free day was spent on a tour of Graz. The fourth day was a public day with an extraordinarily sensitive and moving liturgy for peace in the morning—with music, readings from the three traditions, and symbolic gestures (reuniting the altar that had been broken into four pieces). The afternoon was devoted to a public panel discussion by Professors Pinchas Lapide, Gordon Kaufman, and Riffat Hassan, followed by a press conference and a reception by the mayor of Graz.

Several Austrian newspapers from both Graz and Vienna covered the dialogue over several days. Austrian Radio also held a panel discussion with several ISAT participants, and Austrian Television carried an hour-long discussion. In addition, Dr. Jochen Klicker of Radio RIAS in Berlin was a fulltime participant-observer and conducted taped interviews with six ISAT participants; a month later he produced an hour-long discussion on Bosnia with Duran, as well as several other radio presentations by him on Islam in a dialogical context. A Cairo newspaper reporter caught up with Osman in Vienna and did a lengthy interview with him, and Mag. Gudrun Harrer of the leading Viennese newspaper *Der Standard* published a full-page overview of the dialogue along with lengthy interviews with Duran and Professor Abderrahmane Lakhsassi of Morocco.

A selection of the scholarly work of the Trialogue was published in a book titled *THEORIA → PRAXIS: How Jews, Christians, Muslims (and Others) Can Together Move from Theory to Practice*.[181] Nearly a hundred copies of the book were distributed to the international and local scholars at the, Jakarta, Indonesia Trialogue in 2000.

On January 12, 1993, four of our members, Professors Swidler, Lapide, Knitter, and Duran, conducted a day-long Trialogue Symposium on "Auf

---

181. Swidler, *THEORIA → PRAXIS*.

dem Wege zu einem gemeinsamen Weltethos" ("Toward a Universal Global Ethic") in Munich, Germany, sponsored by the Katholisches Institut für missionstheologische Grundlagenforschung. It was extremely successful both qualitatively and quantitatively; concerning the latter, the hall held 130 places, all of which were sold out ahead of time, and an additional eighty persons had to be turned away. There was coverage by the Bavarian press and an extended conversation interview with the four of us was taped by the Bavarian Radio and aired later. Bavarian Television was also present and active, taping for a later large program.

"This Year in Jerusalem!"

Two topics were chosen for 1994, namely, "Women in Judaism, Christianity and Islam," and a continuation of the issue "Toward a Universal Declaration of a Global Ethic." Plans to have the January, 1994, Trialogue in Los Angeles were far advanced when the revolution in the political situation in the Near East occurred. Quickly, plans were changed to hold the 1994 ISAT in Jerusalem. For this, two further topics were added that would be particularly apropos for the new place and situation: "The Relationship between Religion and Politics: Jewish, Christian and Muslim Views" and "Visions of Peace: Jewish-Christian-Muslim." This latter became the general theme of ISAT in Jerusalem.

All agreed that the December 31, 1993–January 5, 1994, Jerusalem ISAT meeting was a unique growth experience for everyone involved. Moreover, many dialogical encounters resulted in Israel-Palestine because of ISAT's presence there. We all had previously thought that a meeting in Jerusalem was many years in the future, but gathering in Jerusalem in the midst of the Peace Process was an extraordinary opportunity to be present when and where the tides of world and religious history were visibly shifting. We were always conscious of this during our short week in Yerushalaim-Jerusalem-Al Quds.

Thus, shortly after September 13, 1993, plans began to be developed to hold the annual trialogue *not* in Los Angeles but in Jerusalem. Great pains were taken to strike a balance among Jewish, Christian, and Muslim, and Israeli and Palestinian local involvement in terms of local scholars, local religious and political leaders, as well as Jewish, Christian, and Muslim (and Mormon) venues. Score upon score of faxes, e-mail messages, and long-distance and international phone calls and hundreds of person hours went into these preparations. Nine local participants were eventually invited to the Trialogue, but the de facto participation was only partial, apparently because of other commitments.

Efforts to meet with Jewish, Christian, and Muslim religious leaders of the area met with mixed results. Up until the last moments, various high-level political leaders, both Israeli and Palestinian, were scheduled to meet with ISAT, but unpredictable diplomatic and political developments prevented many of those meetings. Media coverage was fairly extensive, subject to the vagaries of last-minute breaking political developments. Thorough Austrian newspaper coverage was assured by the constant presence of the Arabist reporter for the Viennese daily *Der Standard* and the Viennese weekly *Die Furche*, Gudrun Harrer.

The Jakarta Trialogue

The main part of the events that took place in connection with the ISAT in Jakarta, Indonesia, February 14–19, 2000, start, of course, with the Jewish-Christian-Muslim Scholars' Dialogue—the Trialogue itself. The related activities were carried out by the Global Dialogue Institute (GDI), like ISAT, a spin-off of *J.E.S.*

By way of background, Jakarta 2000 had its seed in the early 1990s when Alwi Shihab from Indonesia was a graduate student in Temple University Department of Religion (TUDOR). During that period, his friend Abdurrahman Wahid (better known as Gus Dur) came several times to the U.S. for medical treatment for his eyes, and each time he visited Shihab and TUDOR, when I came to know him. Gus Dur and I decided to work together to hold ISAT in Jakarta in the near future. Plans were laid to hold it there in the Fall of 1998, under the auspices of the Ministry for Religious Affairs, but political developments, a stroke experienced by Gus Dur, and the Asian economic meltdown all conspired to postpone it. Eventually, we reset the date for early 2000 and, in the Summer of 1999, when Gus Dur once again visited the U.S., we spoke at some length and settled on the dual theme: "Religion-State Relations and Building Democracy." Then the unplanned-for happened: In October, 1999, Gus Dur was elected president and shortly thereafter appointed Shihab his Foreign Minister, asking him to carry the responsibility on the Indonesian side for preparing the Trialogue.

The approximately two dozen Jewish, Christian, and Muslim scholars, mostly from prior ISAT meetings, supplemented by new additions, were matched by a like number of Indonesian observer-participants. The Trialogue was formally opened by President Gus Dur on February 14, 2000, at the Presidential Palace before a large international gathering. The keynote address was delivered by Prince Hassan of Jordan.

The intense scholarly dialogues began that afternoon, Monday, on the two themes, "Religion-State Relations and Building Democracy" from the perspectives of each of the three traditions and continued through Tuesday and Wednesday. A third full day of dialogue on the themes was held on Saturday. However, Thursday was given over to invitations to the scholars to reach out to the public in a variety of ways. There were also extensive interviews with newspapers, and radio and TV stations. Friday was a day free for sight-seeing and shopping—except for myself and several colleagues, who ran from one important meeting to the next from 10 AM to 8 PM (more on that below).

There were, of course, many viewpoints about the specifics of the twin theme of the Trialogue, but it became crystal clear that there was the widest possible agreement among the scholars of all three traditions that, however defined, named, or nuanced, the State must not be united to religion in the sense that any one religion be preferred over the others. It was likewise clear that, even though nowhere in the history of the three traditions was democracy as understood today ever envisioned or promoted, each contained elements that were conducive to democracy and that democracy was in no way incompatible with any of the three religions. Further, all were convinced that democracy was the morally best human form of governance—to be striven for and promoted. Despite its shortcomings, there is no better alternative to democracy, and therefore all women and men of good will ought to seek and support it.

One of the concrete products of this ISAT meeting was a book from the many excellent papers prepared by the scholars. It was appropriately titled *From Theocracy to Democracy*.[182] Although the Trialogue took place before 9/11/01, the slightly later publication of the book gave the authors an opportunity to emphasize even more their points about the need for dialogue and the development of democracy in all the areas of influence of all the traditions.

When the dates of the 2000 Trialogue were definite, I sent a number of memos to Shihab, requesting meetings with various government ministers and others. One of the requests was to meet with the appropriate ministers concerned with economic matters and with business leaders, both Indonesian and international, to explore with them the concerns of the Dialogue Institute (DI) to link to business the basic skills of Deep-Dialogue and

---

182. Alan Race and Ingrid Shafer, eds., *Religions in Dialogue: From Theocracy to Democracy* (Hants, UK: Ashgate, 2002).

Critical-Thinking, as well as the "Global Business Ethic Project." Shihabi contacted American businessperson, Harvey Goldstein, who had worked in Indonesia for thirty years and had built a company with many contacts in the business community. With an extremely heavy outlay of funds and effort by Goldstein and his staff, and with the joint sponsorship of the DI, a whole-day conference was set up on "Business Ethics and Anti-Corruption Reform," which was attended by three hundred business leaders. John Dalla Costa, Ashok Gangadean, and I spoke for the DI, and fifteen ministers spoke, as did President Wahid himself. By any measure, the conference was a great success.

A second memo to Shihab was a request to meet with the Ministry of Education leadership. That semester I held a graduate seminar in conjunction with the DI colleague from Haverford College, Ashok Gangadean, and my colleague from the College of Education of Temple University, Steven Gross, on "Deep-Dialogue/Critical-Thinking: New Foundation for Education." The focus was to work out concrete ways to train teachers to transfer those technologies to the classrooms. Our DI team in Jakarta met for several hours with the Minister of Education, with the Director General of the Ministry, and with the Director of Secondary Education. The results were concrete plans to launch a program wherein the DI would assist the Indonesian Ministry of Education to train their teachers in the core human competencies of Deep-Dialogue/Critical-Thinking and how to make them real in their classes. That project was launched in addition in conjunction with UNICEF in the Fall of 2000.

All in all, much was attained during the week of the Trialogue in the heady atmosphere of the new democracy (the third largest in the world) in the largest Muslim country in the world. The week began with the dramatic firing by the President of the most powerful general (Wiranto), thereby taking a major step is establishing civilian rule after an army-led dictatorship of three decades.

At the Edge of Civil War: Skopje, Macedonia

During the Jakarta Trialogue, Mojzes received a call from President Boris Trajkovski of Macedonia, inviting ISAT to hold its next meeting in Macedonia. ISAT responded positively to the invitation and proceeded to lay plans and search for funding. The resulting original intention was to hold the Trialogue in Skopje in November, 2001, but the level of violence between ethnic Albanians and ethnic Macedonians (mostly Muslim and Orthodox

Christians, respectively) became so intense during the summer of 2001 that we were advised to postpone our conference.

Mojzes and I visited Macedonia in both June and November of 2001, to meet with all the religious leaders (Orthodox, Muslim, Catholic, Methodist, Jewish) as well as President Trajkovski and several NGOs, and other key persons. In November, 2001, plans were set to hold the Trialogue May 10–14, 2002, in Skopje. The theme settled on was "Confidence Building among the Churches and Religious Communities in Macedonia through Dialogue." Funding was obtained from a wide spectrum of sources, including the United States Institute of Peace (USIP); the Foundation Open Society Institute, Macedonia; Graf von der Groeben, Germany; the United States Agency for International Development; Christians Associated for Relationships with Eastern Europe, USA; Church World Service, USA; Board of Global Ministries, United Methodist Church, USA; and Global Ministries of the Christian Church (Disciples of Christ and the United Church of Christ, USA. Local arrangements were handled by the Macedonian Center for International Cooperation.

Our two initial visits to Macedonia, Mojzes's knowledge of the "Balkan mentality," and the World Conference on Religion and Peace's lack of success in influencing the Macedonian religious leadership to cooperate by bringing in a small group of outsiders all convinced us that an entirely different approach was necessary. Hence, we abandoned our own format of previous Jewish-Christian-Muslim trialogues (of an equal number of scholars from the three traditions) and decided to bring a very impressive group of international scholars in which the ratio of Jews, Christians, and Muslims would more nearly approximate the religious configuration of Macedonia and to involve local scholars much more heavily. This combination, we felt, would raise the level of awareness of religion as a peace-making agent.

We were worried, however, that we simply would not be able to attract enough religious leaders and scholars from Macedonia if we did not make a "splash." We found that, as long as we spoke to the Macedonian religious leaders in general terms, they did not commit themselves to any significant participation. However, when we sent them the list of international participants, predictably, they responded, feeling that if such an important international gathering was to take place in Macedonia, they had better match or exceed the number of guests. At first we were not successful in creating a local organizing committee, but we persisted. When finally the local organizing committee was created (which, as noted, was another first, as the religious communities had previously not cooperated on *any* local project), it was our list of internationals (and the promise to provide honoraria to local participants) that prompted them to invite the nearly fifty participants (about twenty Orthodox, seventeen Muslim, and three to five each from the Jewish, Catholic, and Methodist communities).

The benefits of the large conference were several: (1) It convinced the Macedonian religious leaders and participants that the dialogical approach to confidence-building is respected abroad. (2) They felt honored that such a gathering took place in their country and (3) that the President of the Republic of Macedonia came to both the opening and closing ceremonies. (4) They felt that from such an important event it was necessary to send a message to their members and the country, which they formulated with our help. (5) A press conference took place which drew about thirty journalists and media people, resulting in wide media exposure. (6) Meetings of a small number of key persons from the several religious communities and the internationals took place with Archbishop Stefan and Reis-u-Ulema Emini. Dr. David Smock of the financially supporting USIP, who was present, noted that these two meetings were crucial to the acceptance of the above mentioned commitments. However, the two meetings of the religious leaders would not have taken place, nor would the commitments have been made, had the large conference not impressed upon them the importance of such cooperation.

The conference had its very festive aspects in the formal opening session with formal greetings by President Trajkovski of Macedonia; the heads of the five major religious communities of Macedonia, who also delivered their welcoming speeches; and the emissary of Prince Hassan of Jordan. The basic pattern of the proceedings was that a major plenary address was given by a prominent Jewish, Christian, and Muslim international scholar with two responses by representatives of the two other religions to each of the addresses. On another day, five important representatives of the religious communities of Macedonia presented their perspectives on cooperation and dialogue.

On Monday morning, matters took an unexpectedly dramatically dialogic turn. The Orthodox Christian Theological Seminary suddenly invited the entire Trialogue to hold its morning session at the Seminary. Further, an invitation was extended to Dean Ismail Bardhi of the Islamic Theological Seminary to lecture at the Orthodox Christian Seminary (a first!). It was there that the two deans reached out and shook hands, promising to cooperate with each other and to teach understanding and greater knowledge of each other's tradition. On Tuesday morning, the invitation was reciprocated by the Islamic Theological Seminary, inviting the Trialogue to hold its morning session there—and inviting Dean Jovan Takovski of the Orthodox Christian Seminary to lecture at the Islamic Seminar (another first!). The final session was again visited by Trajkovski, who spoke at some length with the participants. There was also a press conference with the result that the media and the press reported about the conference to the wider public.

If the meetings to help plan the Trialogue were unprecedented, the Trialogue itself with its dialogic experience and additional meetings and commitments to interreligious cooperation that it triggered approached the level of a minor miracle when one recalls that just a few months earlier the drums of war were beating loudly, and religious leaders were doing little to muffle them. Three firm, and quite revolutionary, commitments were publicly made at the large press conference referred to above, namely: (1) to establish a Council for Interreligious Cooperation (CIC) appointed by the respective heads of communities; (2) for the heads of the religious communities, particularly the Orthodox and Islamic, to meet three or four times a year under the leadership of the country's President to discuss issues between the communities; and (3) for the Orthodox and Islamic Theological Schools to begin cooperating in teaching students about each other's religion.

There were several further results after the meeting. (1) Several days after our departure, as a result of the impression made by the large conference, Deans Takovski and Bardhi and the Methodist clergyperson Mihail Cekov were invited to be panelists on a program by Radio Macedonia on issues of religious cooperation and education, lasting over an hour. (2) Brief training was given to members of the Orthodox Christian and the Muslim theological faculties in Skopje in August, 2003, and a further substantial grant was given by the USIP to support and expand the work of the CIC, with the collaboration of the two seminaries.

(3) A series of lectures were delivered by Swidler, Mojzes, and others, on interreligious dialogue during three subsequent ISAT visits, particularly at the University of Skopje, at the Ted Herman Balkan Peace Center, while Swidler also held two lectures at a Women's Center in Skopje. During these subsequent visits, several ISAT participants also organized a panel discussion at the new University in Tetovo, which is predominantly Albanian in composition. (4) The two seminaries subsequently collaborated on both the faculty and students levels. (5) The CIC subsequently met, and very successfully undertook on its own to set up one-day joint training programs for the clergy in three different towns in Macedonia, including Tetova, a mainly Muslim town. (6) The leaders of the five religious communities continued to meet regularly, along with the Macedonian President. We spoke to the Muslim leaders and participants, urging them as European Muslims to espouse a modern, tolerant, and dialogical Islam.

(7) The papers from the Skopje conference were collected, edited, and published in English in a special issue of the *Journal of Ecumenical Studies*

in late 2003 (vol. 39, nos. 2–3) and in book form as *Interreligious Dialogue toward Reconciliation in Macedonia and Bosnia*. It also appeared in a single book in Macedonian and Albanian translation in 2004. (8) As a "bonus" consequence, the book, *The Study of Religion in an Age of Global Dialogue* by Swidler and Mojzes, was translated and published in Macedonian (*Gzuchuvanyeto na Ryeligiata vo Yerata na Globalniot Dialog*) by Slobodanka Markovska in 2005. (9) There were two important developments since the 2002 Trialogue in Skopje, one a cause for rejoicing and one tragic. Professor Mehmet Aydin, who has been a member of ISAT since 1990, was made State Minister for Religious Affairs and Education of Turkey in 2003. Tragically, in 2004, President Trajkovski was killed in a plane crash.

Trialogue in Philadelphia

ISAT joined with the 35th Annual Scholars' Conference on the Holocaust and the Churches, held at St. Joseph's University in Philadelphia (a Jesuit-run university), March 5–8, 2005, so that it became a Trialogue. The reason for the expansion of the decades-old Jewish-Christian Scholars' Conference was that the year before its Honorary Chair, Nobel Laureate Elie Wiesel, told the leadership that he thought it was time to bring in the third voice of the Abrahamic traditions, Islam. The 2005 conference, consequently, was initiated by a dialogue with Prince Hassan bin Talal of Jordan through video downlink. During that dialogue he issued an invitation to hold a Trialogue in Jordan, which eventuated in the 2008 ISAT meeting in Amman, Jordan.

In addition to the scholars of Jewish and Christian background, several Muslim scholars also read scholarly papers and participated in the Philadelphia conference, including: Khaleel Mohammed of San Diego State University; Aslam Syed of Quaid-I-Asam University of Islamabad, Pakistan; Ismail Bardhi, Dean of the School of Islamic Studies, Skopje, Macedonia; Sanaullah Kirmani, Towson University; and Mahmut Aydin, Ondokuz Mayis University, Samsun, Turkey. Other ISAT scholars also participated, including two Orthodox Christians—Ratomir Grozdanoski, Orthodox Theological Seminary, Skopje; and Peter Baktis, U.S. Army Chaplaincy, Columbia, NC; three Jewish scholars—Racelle Weiman, Hebrew Union College, Cincinnati; Reuven Firestone, Hebrew Union College, Los Angeles; and Nancy Fuchs Kreimer, Reconstructionist Rabbinical College, Philadelphia; and two Christian scholars—Paul Mojzes, Rosemont College, Rosemont, PA, and Leonard Swidler, Temple University, Philadelphia.

Hindu-Christian Dialogue

Potential Dialogue Partners

As deep as the differences are among Judaism, Christianity, and Islam, in some ways they are much more profound between those three and the religions of the Orient stemming from India and China. Even the modern secular ideologies or "explanations of the meaning of life and how to live accordingly" of the West, such as humanism and Marxism, are essentially derivative from the Judeo-Christian tradition and are thus closer to their Semitic-Hellenic roots than are the religions sprung from Asian cultures. There are also the religions of Africa and the Americas, which again are very different from the rest in that they tend to be much more oral than the others. That fact alone places definite limitations on the accumulation of religious reflection that occurs in those religions as compared to the so-called major world religions.

Of course, as seen above, once the view of the religious thinker has turned outward from a self-centeredness, dialogue with one's neighbors is a logical step. For Jews, Christians, and Muslims their closest neighbors are each other, but the logic of dialogue does not stop here. In the relationship among these three Semitic religions and the Asian religions, a converse logic takes over; because the Asian religions are so different and their perspective on reality is so other, they can contribute many new insights into reality that the Semitic religions would not of themselves attain—and *vice versa*. Hence, dialogue with them also becomes imperative.

I will not attempt to spell out the problems and promises of the dialogue of the West with all the religions of the world or even with all the major ones. Rather, I will limit myself to the major religions of Asia, those arising in the ancient centers of civilization, outside of the Near East and Southeastern Europe, namely, India and China, and will restrict myself even further within the framework of the major religions of India and China to Hinduism, Buddhism, and Confucianism. Even then, I will content myself with raising only a very few major points. That, however, ought to be enough to provide the glimmerings of a horizon within which the dialogues can fruitfully take place.

Hinduism, Buddhism, and Confucianism have developed many highly articulate spokespersons in the modern Western world, which Taoism has not done in the same way—nor indeed, have any of the other even populous religions of Asia, Africa, or the Americas. Hence, outside the Semitic religions, Hinduism, Buddhism, and Confucianism are the major—though not the only—logical interreligious dialogue partners for the West, for Jews, Christians, and Muslims.

Openness to Dialogue?

As with Islam, though perhaps to a lesser extent, Westerners must be ready to deal with the bitter legacy of colonialism when entering into dialogue with Hinduism or any of the other Asian religions. The Indian Christian Stanley Samartha recorded the reaction of one Hindu to the Christian invitation to dialogue:

> Do not think I am against dialogue . . . on the contrary. I am fully convinced that dialogue is an essential part of human life, and therefore of religious life itself . . . Yet to be frank with you, there is something that makes me uneasy in the way in which you Christians are now trying so easily to enter into official and formal dialogue with us. Have you already forgotten that what you call "inter-faith dialogue" is quite a new feature in your understanding and practice of Christianity? Until a few years ago, and still today, your relations with us were confined either merely to the social plane, or preaching in order to convert us to your *dharma* . . . For all matters of *dharma* you were deadly against, violently or stealthily according to cases.[183]

Perhaps the first thing to bear in mind when dealing with Hinduism is that it is not a single religion. Rather, it is a complex of religions, which, though culturally and historically related, can be quite sharply different from each other. They range from a radical monism to a radical dualism, from a rejection of the world as illusion to a commitment to social change, from a philosophers' religion to a popular devotional religion—so caution is in order when making statements about what Hinduism is and is not.

Hindu and Christian Understandings of Ultimate Reality

The discussion that would normally fit here was moved earlier in the section dealing with Ultimate Reality.[184] Because religion is concerned to provide an explanation of the ultimate meaning of life, two key elements obviously are the understanding of Ultimate Reality and the understanding of the nature

---

183. Stanley Samartha, *Courage for Dialogue* (Geneva: World Council of Churches, 1981) 9.

184. See above pg. 58.

of humanity, for only after at least vaguely grasping these can one hope to explain the relationship between the two. With regard to Ultimate Reality, there are some extremely interesting similarities and disparities between those of the Judeo-Christian-Islamic and Hindu traditions. The material for the next few pages is substantially repetitious of what I laid out earlier when dealing with comparisons of the major ways of conceiving Ultimate Reality. However, it is important to bring those concepts back to the conscious level when dealing with the dialogue between Hinduism and Christianity.

First, both traditions distinguish between God in self, *in se*, and God as related to, perceived by, others, *ad extra*. God is said to be infinite, so any perception of God by something other than God, that is, by something finite, is by the very nature of the knowing receptacle bound to be finite. ("Things known are known according to the mode of the knower," as was noted that Aquinas said.)[185] Hence, God, the in-finite, is not known directly. God is not known *in se*, but only as God relates to non-God, that is, *ad extra*.

This distinction was very clear in the Hebraic tradition as between God, *Yahweh*, whose face no one can see and live, on the one hand, and the spirit (*Ruach*) of God, who moves over the waters in creation, and wisdom (*Hokmah*), through whom all things were created, on the other. In the early rabbinic period a third term was also employed to denote God vis-à-vis humanity, God's presence (*Shekhinah*). Wisdom was further identified with another extremely important expression of the divine vis-à-vis humanity, namely, *Torah* (see Sirach 24:1–3); the Rabbis made the identification even closer (see *Genesis Rabbah* 1; 8[6a]). An interesting aspect of all these depictions of the divine *ad extra* is that they are feminine—not only in grammatical gender but also in general imagery. This is matched to some extent by the Hindu distinction between *Brahman*, analogous to God *in se*, and the feminine *Shakti*. *Shakti*, like the Hebrew *Ruach* and *Hokmah*, is understood as "the Divine *Sakti* penetrating everything and manifesting God, disclosing him in his immanence and being present in all his manifestations—this Spirit of God."[186] Compare these two images of God vis-à-vis creation, these Hebraic and Hindu depictions of Lady Wisdom:

> This (in the beginning) was only the Lord of the Universe.
> His word was with him. This word was his second.
> He contemplated.
> He said, "I will deliver this word so that *she*
> will produce and bring
> into being all this world." (*Tandya Maha Brahmana* XX, 14, 2)

---

185. Thomas "Aquinas, *Summa Theologiae*. II, II, Q.1, a.2
186. Panikkar, *Unknown Christ*, 57.

> Wisdom speaks . . . "I came forth from the mouth of the
> Most High and I covered the earth like a mist . . .
> From eternity, in the beginning, he created me,
> and for eternity I shall remain.
> I ministered before him . . . (Sirach 24:1, 3, 9, 10)
>
> She is a breath of the power of God,
> pure emanation of the glory of the Almighty . . .
> She is a reflection of the eternal light,
> untarnished mirror of God's active power,
> image of his goodness.
> Although alone, she can do all;
> herself unchanging, she makes all things new. (Wis 7:21–27)

In the Christian tradition the feminine figure of Wisdom, *Hokmah*, was in many instances assimilated in its traits into the Christ figure. *Christos*, as noted, is simply the Greek form of the Hebrew *Meshiach*, the Anointed One, but in Christian tradition it quickly took on the more far-reaching characteristics of *Hokmah*. This is seen perhaps most strikingly in the Prologue of John's Gospel where the talk is about the Word, the *Logos*. However, it must be borne in mind that the Jewish Scriptures had already identified God's Word (*Dabar*) with Wisdom (cf. Psalm 119; Sirach 24:1–3, 9, 23, and Wis 9:1–2), and many Christian Scripture scholars today suggest that in this Prologue *Logos* was simply substituted for *Hokmah/Sophia* in a previously existing hymn to Wisdom.[187] The text reads: "In the beginning was the Word (*Hokmah*), and the Word was with God (*Yahweh*), and the Word (*Hokmah*) was God. He (She) was with God in the beginning. Everything was made through him (her), and without him (her) no existing thing came into existence. In him (her) was life, and the life was the light of humans" (John 1:1–4). Thus, in the Christian tradition *Christos* and *Logos* are very like the Hebraic figure *Hokmah*, that is, the creative aspect of God, God *ad extra*, and both are like the Hindu *Shakti* and, even more prominently (as will be discussed below), the masculine Lord, *Ishvara*.

Ultimate Reality is not only variously named, but also variously conceived, both West and East. Although the proper Hebraic name for Ultimate Reality, *Yahweh* (which was long understood to mean, "I am who I am," as the Latin Vulgate translates it, but now is usually thought to be better understood as something like the more dynamic, "I will be who I will be"), does seem largely to describe divinity *in se*, the Bible and most subsequent Jewish and Christian writings speak almost exclusively of God *ad extra*. Not

---

187. Gerhard Kittel, *Theological Dictionary of the New Testament* (Grand Rapids: Eerdmans, 1968) 4:133.

so in Hinduism. The preferred term there for Ultimate Reality is *Brahman* (occasionally referred to as *Atman*), which is not exactly divinity *in se*, but at times is understood in a way close to that concept. In that case it is *Brahman* without attributes, *Nirguna Brahman*, as opposed to *Brahman* with attributes, *Saguna Brahman* (this latter being largely identified with the Lord, *Ishvara*). In any case, *Brahman* is not thought of as personal but, rather, like the Ground of Being—pure potency, in Aristotelean terms (quite the opposite of God in the West, who would be thought of rather as pure actuality). This contrasts with the Judeo-Christian understanding of divinity as personal. Hence, the Greek term *"Theos"* (related to the Latin *"Deus,"* both of which are rendered in English as "God"), including as it does the notion of *personal* divinity, leads to the concept of theism as affirming a personal God. In brief, it can be said then that the notion of God is personal, theisitic, whereas the notion of *Brahman* is nonpersonal, nontheistic.

A related teaching in Hinduism is that at the absolute inner foundation of the human person is the authentic self, or *atman*, and this individual self was seen by the Shankara Advaita (nondualistic) Hindu tradition to be identified with *Brahman* (sometimes this is expressed: *atman* is *Atman*). Since *Brahman* is the innermost "breath" of everything (*atman* fundamentally means "breath"—related to the Greek *atmo* [vapor] and the German *Atem* [breath] and the English "atmosphere"), it is best understood in terms of immanence, the "within" of things—and God in terms of transcendence, the "beyond" all things. The former stresses unity and the latter otherness. "Indian speculation for the most part is inclined to search for identity; Semitic speculation, on the other hand, characteristically emphasizes the uniqueness of each being and differences between beings. The first kind of mind, typically Indian, probes the depths of being to find the truth; the second kind of mind is directed upwards, looking for the truth in the most sublime heights . . . the conception of Brahman scarcely coincides at all with the conception of God; the two conceptions are almost as opposed as pure potentiality to pure actuality."[188]

However, neither religious tradition was content with affirming its "traditional" conception of Ultimate Reality. The West did try to speak of God *in se*, as, for example, in the Jewish Kabbalah's term *En Sof* (infinite), from which come ten lights, the last of which is the *Shekhinah*, that is, the manifestation of God to humanity. Of course, in Christianity there is the development of the doctrine of the Trinity, which is an attempt to describe God *in se*. Meister Eckhart in the thirteenth/fourteenth centuries distinguished between the Godhead, which he called *Deitas* (God *in se*) and God,

---

188. Panikkar, *Unknown Christ*, 140.

which he called *Deus* (God *ad extra*). In modern times Paul Tillich spoke of "the God above the God of theism."[189] Alfred North Whitehead and subsequent process theologians have distinguished between the primordial nature of God (*in se*) and the consequent nature of God (*ad extra*). It should be added that the Muslim Sufi term *Al Haqq* as the underlying abyss below the personal *Allah* and the Taoist *Tao Te Ching*'s comment that "the Tao that can be expressed is not the eternal Tao"[190] are both references to similar distinctions in other major religious traditions.

Although this stress on God *in se*, on divinity in itself, has been relatively less in the Judeo-Christian and Muslim traditions than in the Hindu, every major religious tradition eventually must deal with, reflect, both dimensions: Ultimate Reality *in se* and *ad extra*. How it is done is a question of emphasis. Though the emphasis in Hinduism has been on Ultimate Reality *in se*, on *Nirguna Brahman*, the notion of God as perceived by humanity, God *ad nos*, did develop and took a form that has some extraordinary parallels to the Jewish, and even more, the Christian tradition. In Hinduism, *Brahman* acting *ad extra*, is referred to as Lord, as *Ishvara*:

> Brahman is absolutely transcendent and in a sense beyond being and non-being. It is pure silence and utter nothingness, truly absolute, that is, unrelated. It can thus perform no external function, and it is for this that the figure of Isvara appears . . . In other words Brahman is devoid of relations, and it is precisely Isvara who provides for them . . . He is properly speaking, the revelation of Brahman, the first issue, so to speak, of the unfathomable womb of Brahman. Isvara is God. Brahman cannot be a person, for if it were it would have to relate to others (things or persons), which would compromise its absoluteness. Isvara is the personal aspect of Brahman . . . Brahman *as such* cannot be creator of the World, again because of its absolute transcendence. Isvara, therefore, is that "aspect" of Brahman responsible for the creation of the World . . . Brahman is so immutable and unmanifest, beyond every capacity for action that Isvara has to take over its functions in relation to the universe and to souls.[191]

Despite the differences, the similarities of *Ishvara* to *Ruach*, *Hokmah*, and *Shekhina* in the Hebraic/Jewish tradition and the Spirit, *Logos*, and *Christos* in the Christian are striking. Important differences are there also, to be sure: *Hokmah* in the Hebraic tradition is not associated with a historical

---

189. Tillich, *Courage to Be*, 190.
190. Cited in Hick, *God Has Many Names*, 92.
191. Panikkar, *Unknown Christ*, 152–53.

person, whereas *Christos* is associated with Yeshua of Nazareth; there are "incarnations," "*avatars*" of Ishvara (*Vishnu*) in Hinduism, for example, Rama and Krishna, but these are not true historical figures. However, according to the *Bhagavata Purana*, another *avatar* is Buddha, who was a historical figure.

Distortions: Pantheism and Illusion

Two gross misconceptions of the West concerning Hinduism ought to be addressed here, because they assume a chasmic distinction between the three theistic Semitic religions and Hinduism, which is fundamentally mistaken. Hinduism is often perceived in the West as fundamentally pantheistic or monistic in its understanding of Ultimate Reality and as viewing the world as illusory and therefore not worthy of serious attention. Though both notions are to be found in Hinduism, to make them characteristic of Hinduism in general is totally unwarranted from the evidence, both literary and sociological. However, seeing Hinduism as basically theistic and world-affirming will immediately provide a common ground on which the Semitic and Hindu religions can meet in dialogue.

The characterization of Hinduism as monistic or pantheistic is usually based on two hymns of the Rgveda, the negative passages of the Upanishads and the monistic philosophy of Shankara's Vedanta. However, "a closer study of the Vedas and the Upanishads and the consideration of the Bhagavad-Gita (which has a much greater influence on most Hindus than the Vedanta), indicates that the dominant Hindu conception of God has an essentially theistic character that is similar in certain respects to that found in Christian theism."[192]

Sengupta pointed out that, while there are indeed two hymns in the Rgveda (the oldest of the Hindu Scriptures, composed toward 1500 BCE) that point to the Ultimate as nonpersonal, there are four other hymns that refer to the Ultimate as *Visvakarma*, that is, the Maker and Lord of the Universe. Moreover, the Vedic notion of God developed from polytheism through henotheism to monotheism; in fact, in the Yajurveda (the second oldest Veda) God is addressed as *Pita*. Father: "Salutations to Thee, Father, Awaken us and cause us no harm."[193]

In the Upanishads (the third, and final, portion of the Vedas—the oldest composed between 800 and 300 BCE) there are both passages that describe the Ultimate as nonpersonal and others that describe it as personal—the

192. Sengupta, "Misunderstanding of Hinduism," 97.
193. Ibid.

former stressing the transcendent and the latter the immanent aspects of the Ultimate. Sengupta pointed out that

> the common upanishadic view is that the Supreme Reality is both impersonal and personal, transcendent and immanent. The personal character of reality is evident as we view it in relation to the world and the individual self. But there is no suggestion of a transcendence of the category of personality in the real in its ultimate state. The real is in its essence also personal. The attribute-possessing (*Saguna*) God and the attribute-negating (*Nirguna*) absolute are the same reality. Passages can be extensively quoted from the Upanishads to show how in the upanishadic view there is no negation of the personality of the ultimate. There is no need for the transcendence of personality, for the personality which the ultimate is, is free from the limitations of human personality.[194]

Further, though it is true that the teaching of the first great Vedanta philosopher, Shankara (788–820 CE), was a radical monism, or nondualism (*a-dvaita*, non-twoness), and that his teaching subsequently has been very influential, he was in fact vigorously opposed by other philosophers working from the Upanishads—as he also did. Philosophically, the opposite was Madhva (1197–1276 CE), who espoused a clear dualism between God on the one hand and the world and souls on the other. However, his subsequent influence has remained rather limited. Not so, however, for Ramanuja (1056–1137 CE) who developed a "qualified *advaita*." He became fully as influential as, if not more than, Shankara: "To be sure, as for Shankara so also for Ramanuja, Brahman is 'two-less' (*a-dvaitam*), but it is not attribute-less, without qualities, character; it is not impersonal. No, it is *identical with the personal God.* That is Ramanuja's decisive insight."[195]

Sengupta objected to the Western miscategorizing of Hindu religions as fundamentally under the dominance of Shankara's monism by arguing, first, that "indeed contemporary Hinduism is characterized by an opposition to Shankara-Vedanta" and, second, that "the Advaita view of ultimate reality, associated with Shankara, is not a religious view at all, for it considers religion as a matter of ignorance (*Avidya*) . . . Shankara maintains that God [not *Brahman* but *Ishvara*, that is, God *ad extra*] is not real from the ultimate standpoint."[196] Sengupta also noted that biased Westerners tend to overlook the significance of the *Bhagavad-Gita*, which is not only

---

194. Ibid.
195. Küng, *Christentum und Weltreligionen*, 299.
196. Sengupta, "Misunderstanding of Hinduism," 100.

thoroughly theistic, but also strongly stresses the moral qualities of God—the principle one of which is love: "God is in essence love (*Karuna*)"[197] (a description of God found in Ramanuja's theistic Vedanta as well as in the Gita). This is especially important since "the Gita is to the Hindus what the Bible is to the Christians and the Qur'an is to the Muslims."[198]

A similar argument is made concerning a widespread Western view that Hinduism basically teaches *Mayavada*, the doctrine of the unreality of the world: "*Mayavada* is alien to the scriptures—the Vedas, the Upanishads and the Gita . . . Five of the six systems of Hindu philosophy are world-affirming. The sixth system, that is, the Vedanta, as has been observed, admits of different types and only one of these is world-negating. The others are characterized by the rejection of *Mayavada*."[199] Hence, Sengupta vigorously concluded that "the common ground between Hinduism and Christianity [one might also add Judaism and Islam] renders obsolete the language of contrast between the Hindu and the Christian [and Jewish and Muslim] views of ultimate reality. It is equally misleading to contrast the Hindu view of the world with the Christian, or for that matter, the western view of the world."[200]

There are too many profound similarities here simply to be ignored. There clearly is much of deep religious significance underlying all of them—as well as of the differences. Much work, study, and deep dialogue must take place simply to sort out the various meanings of all involved. In the process all will have clarified and deepened their own self-understanding, and probably learned something of the complementarity and analogousness of the traditions of one's own and one's partner—and possibly also the contradictoriness. There is in all these doctrines of the Semitic and Hindu traditions the profoundly important concern about Ultimate Reality *in se*, the Source and Goal of life, God *ad extra*; about the nature of the world and humanity; and the bridge between the two. About this we can never learn too much, too deeply. To learn more and more deeply, we clearly need each other.

197. Ibid., 101.
198. Ibid.
199. Ibid., 103.
200. Ibid., 102.

Buddhist-Christian Dialogue

Buddhist and Christian Parallels

Buddhism has striking parallels with Christianity. Its relation to the religious matrix of India is analogous to that of Christianity (and Islam) to Judaism. It has shown a remarkable ability to assimilate other cultures, and it has flourished chiefly on foreign soil. Like Christianity, Buddhism points to a particular historical figure and "celebrates his work and his authority in canonized scriptures. Gautama, like Jesus, is often worshiped by his followers. The universalistic claims made for the truth and importance of Gautama's teachings by Buddhists are much like those made by Christians in respect to Jesus. The relation of Buddha to Gautama is analogous to the relation of Christ to Jesus."[201]

In the West, Christianity and Judaism (and a part of Islam) have been going through a deep crisis of demythologization. As we have seen, for modern, critically thinking Westerners the old language "from above" sounds too much like fairy tales to be convincing, and so the response of critically thinking Christian and Jewish theologians had been to rethink their traditions with categories and language "from below," "from within," that express the transcendent in terms of the immanent. Hence, it was argued, it is precisely this language "from below," "from within," "immanent," which in fact is humanity-based, that must be developed as interreligious dialogue moves beyond a bilateral basis, for that is the only kind of language that we can have in common. In terms of the Judeo-Christian-(Islamic)-Buddhist dialogue it is that humanity-based language that provides a most apt bridge between the Judeo-Christian-(Islamic) and Buddhist traditions not only because it is more and more the language of critically thinking Jews and Christians (and some Muslims) but also because it is likewise the language of much of Buddhism.

In terms of the conceptualization and expression of reality, much the same sort of misadventure overtook Judaism, Christianity, and Buddhism. All suffered the fate of an externalizing and ontologizing of the original, metaphorical, nonideological message of their founders. In this connection the very names of the latter two religious traditions are revealing. The institutions' names come not from the names of the founding persons, Siddhartha Gautama and Yeshua of Nazareth, but rather from their titles: Buddha (Enlightened One) and Christ (Anointed One). Here already is reflected the move from the interior to the exterior. One need only, on the one hand,

---

201. John B. Cobb Jr., *Christ in a Pluralistic Age* (Philadelphia: Westminster, 1975) 205.

compare the language that Yeshua uses to describe himself and his relationship to the ultimate source of reality, which he, in good Jewish Pharisaic fashion, called Father, with the language of the great christological councils of the fourth and fifth centuries to note clearly the move from metaphor to ontology and, on the other hand, make a similar comparison of the language of Gautama in the Buddhist scriptures with some of the doctrines of later Mahayana Buddhism. Externalization and ontologization occurred in both instances.

Hans Küng has sketched a similar picture:

> It is unmistakable that Buddhology has in many ways likewise developed far from the historical Gautama, as did Christology from the historical Jesus of Nazareth. In both cases not only did the proclaimer become the proclaimed, and the guide for his own group of followers become the supernatural bringer of salvation and universal savior of humankind, but in both cases that development also took on a specific cosmic dimension. History was endlessly expanded: into the protological-supratemporal one (Adi Buddha and primordial Buddha, the source of all Buddhas and higher beings) and into the eschatological-endtime one (the future Buddha Maitreya). [Christians need not be reminded of their developed doctrines of the preexistent and eschatological Christ.] In both cases dogmaticians attempt with endless effort to define and refine in detail the essence and attributes of the bringer of salvation.[202]

Return to Sources

What is necessary then, in both traditions, and in Judaism and Islam as well, is a *ressourcement*, a probing back to the sources, the original vital core, of each of the religious traditions, to the teachings embodied in both the words and lives of Yeshua and Gautama and the "rabbinical" founders of Judaism and the original Meccan revelations of the Qur'an. There are immense historical-critical problems in accomplishing this goal, but significant progress has already been made. When that is done, one finds startlingly similar messages being taught by the original founders, despite the radically different milieux.

When dealing with the dialogue between Christianity and the other world religions, Hans Küng, as we saw above, stated clearly: "*Back to the origins*. At the origins we Jews, Christians and Muslims are closer to each

---

202. Küng, *Christentum und Weltreligionen*, 607.

other."[203] However, for Küng, too, this is true not only for the Semitic religions, but also for Buddhism and Christianity: "What is really Christian, what is really Buddhist can be decided neither theoretically-abstractly nor simply empirically-experimentally, but only in the context of a historical return to the early Scriptures, the original teaching, indeed to the founding figure himself."[204]

This same key move of back to the sources is also advocated by contemporary Chinese thinkers in relation to their own Taoist cultural base. For example, Tang Yi of the Institute of World Religions of the Chinese Academy of Social Sciences in Beijing wrote of Taoism: "Chinese culture is the only continuous ancient culture in the world. An old culture like this will necessarily survive by constructing and reconstructing upon the patterns set by a great period of intellectual blossoming . . . Authentic wisdom never becomes a thing of the past but it has to be rediscovered and revived by each new generation . . . A close scrutiny is yet to be made to reveal its full [Taoism] force as a modern source of inspiration with its cosmic perspective, its deep humanism, its subtle wisdom."[205]

Teachings of Gautama, Yeshua, and the Rabbis

It will be worth pausing to look at a few of the teachings of Yeshua and the Rabbis (Yeshua was a rabbi, but, for the sake of clarity, the term here

---

203. Ibid., 190. Küng has subsequently developed his thought in regard to the "return to the sources" in a lecture given at Tübingen University June 20, 1985, "Was ist die Wahre Religion?" The E.T. appears in Swidler, ed., *Toward a Universal Theology of Religion*, 231–50. In the lecture he posited three criteria for a true religion, namely, the general-ethical criterion of the *Humanum;* the general-religious criterion of the origin (authoritative scriptures and figures); and for the Christians the specifically Christian criterion of the Bible and Jesus, what he taught and did (Muslims, Buddhists, etc., would have their own respective specific criterion). It is interesting to note that such an antipodal "believer" as the then-atheistic Marxist philosopher and member of the Central Committee of the Communist Party of France, Garaudy, iterated the same notion of *ressourcement*: "A dialogue of this kind demands of each of the participants [Christian and Marxist] a fundamental return" (Garaudy, *From Anathema to Dialogue*, 37).

204. Küng, *Christentum und Weltreligionen*, 450. Aware of the differing historiographical problems in the question of the authenticity of the teachings of Yeshua and Gautama, he later insisted that, not unlike the case of Yeshua, "the classical Buddhist texts of course do not give the teaching of the historical Buddha verbatim, but with a high probability do reproduce it correctly in substance" (Küng, *Christentum und Weltreligionen*, 450).

205. Tang Yi, "Taoism as a Living Philosophy," 413–14.

will normally not include him) to see just how close they are to those of Gautama.

Gautama teaches that at the heart of the human experience of life there lies a basic dissatisfaction, suffering (*dukkha*). His goal is to bring us to face that and liberate ourselves from it; ignorance of our lot is the cause of our slavery, and knowledge is the way to liberation. Yeshua's and the Rabbis' message is also one of liberation, a dialectic of slavery and liberation that comes about through truth. As a good rabbi concerned for his disciples, Yeshua said to his Jewish followers: "If you follow my teaching you will be true disciples of mine, for you will know the truth, and the truth will set you free" (John 8:31–2). He made his own Isaiah's words about "liberating" (*aphesin*) those in bondage, setting them "at liberty" (*en aphesei*), as Luke records (4:18): "His mission is to save, to bring about release . . . He has been anointed to preach a theology of liberation."[206]

Gautama rejected the idea that the true meaning of human life, salvation, was to be found first of all through religious rituals, the practice of asceticism, virtuous acts, or intellectual speculations—though some form of all these things have their proper place in human life—but in a deep interior wisdom that sets all things in their proper order. Fundamentally, this is what Yeshua and the Rabbis taught with the central image, the *Reign* of God. Unfortunately Christians have often been misled by the usual translation of the phrase *basileia tou theou*, as we have it in the New Testament Greek—Yeshua probably said *malkut shomaim* in Hebrew (literally "reign of heaven," a euphemism by Rabbis to avoid pronouncing the sacred name of God)—as the "*Kingdom* of God," as if Yeshua were speaking of a place, a realm.

In fact, some of Yeshua's contemporaries made the same mistake and were corrected by him: "Some Pharisees asked Jesus when the *basileia tou theou* would come. His answer was: 'The *basileia tou theou* does not come in such a way as to be seen. No one will say, "Look, here it is!" or, "There it is!"; because the *basileia tou theou* is inside of you [literally, both *inside* of an *among* you, *entos hymon*]'" (Luke 17:20–1). Equally unfortunately, in Judaism a similar fate befell the Rabbis' image, *malkut shomaim*. The authentic meaning is that the Reign of God is the situation wherein all things are rightly ordered according to their nature; God's will reigns.

It is extremely interesting to note how what is usually thought to be the very core of Yeshua's teaching, the Sermon on the Mount, is translated at its beginning by Protestant New Testament scholar, Bishop Ulrich Wilkens: "Blessed are those who are poor in their selves; theirs is the Reign of heaven [*basileia ton ouranon*, the Jewish euphemistic alternate to *basileia tou theou*,

---

206. Kelly, "Lucan Christology," 695.

the Reign of God]." He footnoted this translation: "Literally: 'poor in (his) spirit' [*ptochoi to pneumati*]. Not, however, in the sense of 'spiritually less gifted,' and also not, 'without possessing the spirit of God.' 'Spirit' here rather stands for the interior of the human beings, the 'ego self.'" Although Wilkens gave no indication whatsoever of having the teaching of Gautama or Buddhism in mind, his understanding of the central saying of Yeshua is extraordinarily close to that of Gautama's notion of *anatta*, the need to rid oneself of all false egos, false selves. Paraphrasing Gautama and Yeshua: "Blessed are those who have grasped *anatta* for theirs is *nirvana*." "Blessed are the *ptochoi to pneumati* for theirs is the *basileia tou theou*."[207]

Of course the Rabbis and Yeshua spoke in theistic terms: God was the ultimate source and goal of reality, so, if things were ordered according to their nature, their fundamental structure, they would naturally be ordered according to the will, rule, reign of God. Gautama did not speak of God, either to affirm or deny; he was satisfied with speaking of a right ordering of things according to their ultimate authentic structure. Clearly, there are differences here between the teachings of the Rabbis and Yeshua on the one hand and Gautama on the other, but there is an even more profound unity of their messages: Our liberation is to be found within us in the right ordering of all things according to their fundamental structure.

In many different ways, Yeshua and the Rabbis spoke of the Reign of God, the interior right ordering of things, the importance of seeking that first, and its relationship to other values. At one point Yeshua said: "Rather, seek first of all the Reign and its rightness (*dikaiosynen*), and all these things [he had been speaking of not worrying about what to eat or wear] shall be added to you" (Matt 6:33). In the Talmud this saying of the Rabbis is recorded: "Did you ever in your life see an animal or a bird that had a trade? And they support themselves without trouble. And were they not created only to serve me? And I was created to serve my master. Does it not follow that I shall be supported without trouble?"[208] Yeshua and the Rabbis, like Gautama, did not reject the values of the body, but saw them as good things to be enjoyed within the right ordering of things. One can then appreciate and enjoy all things for what they are, without any disordered clinging (*tanha* in the Pali of Gautama) but with a proper detachment, for as Yeshua said elsewhere: "Where your treasure is, there your heart will be also" (Matt 6:21).

207. Ulrich Wilkens, *Das Neue Testament* (Zurich: Benzinger, 1971) 26–27. "Selig, die arm in sich selber sind: Ihnen gehört das Himmelreich. Wörtlich: 'in (ihrem) Geist arm', also nicht: 'geistig minderbemittelt', auch nicht: 'ohne den Geist Gottes zu besitzen'. 'Geist' gezeichnet hier vielmehr das Innere des Menschen, das 'Ich-selbst.'"

208. *Kiddushin* 4.14 (*kiddushin T* 5.15 (343), cited in Morton Smith, *Tannaitic Parallel to the Gospels* (Philadelphia: Society of Biblical Literature, 1951) 137.

Just how focused the message of the Rabbis and Yeshua was on the interior right ordering of all things according to the structure of reality—and in the theistic mode that means on the source/goal of reality, God—can be seen in the summing up of the whole of religion in two great commandments: "You shall love the Lord your God with your whole heart (*kardia*), and with your whole soul (*psyche*) and with your whole understanding (*dianoia*). This is the great and first commandment" (Matt 22:37–38). Here, all the essential notions are interior ones: love, heart, soul, and understanding. That is the first and greatest commandment; all other things flow from it—the interior right ordering of all things. But, in the Jewish tradition—and Yeshua was a very devout Jew—one does not live isolated like a hermit, so Yeshua went on to make an essential link between that first commandment and the second, which he described as *like unto* the first (*homoia aute*): "The second is like unto it: You shall love your neighbor as your self" (Matt 22:39). Interior right ordering has immediate social-ethical consequences. According to Yeshua, one does not "save" oneself alone, but liberation carries with it the impulse to share itself with others (as the medieval philosophers would say: *bonum sui diffusivum est*, goodness is diffusive of itself). This is exactly what the whole Buddhist tradition of the Bodhisattva is all about: The liberated ones teach liberation to the unliberated ones.

It should be remembered that, in this summing up of religion in the two great commandments of love, Yeshua was not only quoting from the Hebrew Bible (Deut 6:5 and Lev 19:18), but was also following his Jewish predecessors in linking the two together as the sum of religion as expressed two hundred years earlier in *The Testaments of the Twelve Patriarchs* and elsewhere. In Luke's version of the encounter between Yeshua and the Jewish expert in the Law who asked about how to be "saved," it was the lawyer, not Yeshua, who summed up religion in the two great commandments of love; Yeshua simply agreed with him (Luke 10:25–28).

It is also important to discern that, in the second commandment of love, the Jewish tradition and Yeshua spoke of loving one's neighbor as one's *self*. There, indeed, is the standard, the authentic self, and there is the interior focus once again—which then has immediate outreach consequences. In another place Yeshua said: "But what does it profit a person to gain the whole world (*kosmon*) and suffer the loss of one's own *self (heauton)*" (Luke 9:25). Should we humans not enjoy the cosmos? Yes, but we can really do so only through an interiorly right-ordered Self.

In the sayings of Rabbi Nathan we find: "To whomever saves a single soul [Self] it is reckoned as if [one] saved the whole world . . . To whomever destroys a single soul [Self] it is reckoned as if [one] destroyed the whole world . . . From this you learn that one human is worth the whole of creation" (Aboth de Rabbi Nathan 31). One also finds, "Whoever kills an innocent human being, it shall be as if [one] has killed all humankind, and whoever saves the life of one, it shall be as if [one] had saved the life of all humankind" (Qur'an 5:32). The near identity in these two religions' "revelations" is amazing. It is the human Self, that follows in the Torah, and the Qur'an as well—God's teaching on how to order life rightly—that is worth, and worthy of, the whole of creation (33).[209]

One of the prime teachings of Gautama was that of concentration or focus of the mind—that to which the various techniques of meditation are aiming. One should live fully in the "now." Of course the fullness of "now" includes an awareness of the past and a looking forward to the future, but they both focus on and move out from the present, which is to be embraced fully and consciously (the Western medieval motto—which I learned as a twelve-year-old high school freshman—was: *Age quod agis*: "Do what you are doing"). The same message is found in the words of Yeshua: "Therefore, do not worry about things for tomorrow; tomorrow will worry about itself. Sufficient for the day is the evil thereof" (Matt 6:34). The importance of focusing on the present as "the time of salvation" is expressed especially strongly in the Gospel of Luke in a wide-ranging net of subtle ways. Speaking of the sudden inbreaking of the Reign of God, "the disciples should not wait for it, but rather concern themselves with what is happening every day in history . . . the disciples of Jesus must learn to interpret the *present time*. It is *now* that is important."[210]

In some of later Buddhism, *nirvana* has come to mean something like the notion of "heaven," a place where one goes to live happily after death. The same thing happened to *nirvana* that happened to the *basileia tou theou* and the *malkut shomaim*: It was "thingified" and localized. In fact, to Gautama *nirvana* was very much like Yeshua's *basileia tou theou* and the Rabbis' *malkut shomaim*: a state of soul (*psyche*) wherein things are rightly ordered. *Nirvana* literally means "blown out." What is blown out? All of the false selves that most people mistake for their true, deep selves—so deep is this true self according to Gautama that he refers to it as a "nonself" *anatta*, a nonself in the sense of what we have normally mistaken for our self. These pseudoselves are "blown out" in *nirvana*, as is all *tanha*, distorting craving, that is the source of the pseudoselves. What is then left is the authentic Self, at deep peace, because it is rightly ordered in accordance with the structure of reality.

---

209. Aboth de Rabbi Nathan 31, quoted in Paul Billerbeck, *Kommentar zum Neuen Testament aus Talmud und Midrasch* (Munich: Beck, 1922) 1:750.

210. Kelly, "Lucan Christology," 699, 701.

What was said above about one's true self being correctly understood only as *relational* should be recalled here. Knitter explicitly made the connection between that recently developed Western understanding of the self and Gautama's teaching of the nonself: Christian participants in the dialogue with Buddhism acknowledge that Buddhism opens up to the Christian the possibility to know and experience that the true reality of the human person does not consist in being an "individual," a given entity. The true self is much more radically, essentially, and constantly in relationship to another self and all reality; its "existence" is continually that of an ongoing "arising in dependence"; its existence is relational. Therefore, the true self is a selfless self that continually loses and finds its self in its relationship to others.[211]

It is extremely interesting to note a very similar pattern of thought in a twentieth-century American nuclear physicist, whose thought grew out of neither Christianity nor Buddhism nor, indeed, any particular religious tradition, but out of his observations and reflection on reality as a scientist and a sensitive, feeling human being: He described what he called an "Implicate Order":

"The implications of such a vision are staggering. It means the universe has infinite levels while still acting like one indivisible unit, that higher levels determine the nature of what exists at lower levels, and that everything is intimately interconnected as an organic whole. What happens in one locality affects what is happening on that entire level, and sets up infinitely complex chains of causation above and below—so complex and imperceptible that

---

211. Paul Knitter, "Horizons of Christianity's New Dialogue with Buddhism," *Horizon* 8/1 (1981) 45. Whereas the Greek notion of the self tended to be that of an enduring, unchanging "substance," as described in the reflections on metaphysics at the beginning of this book, the biblical and modern Western notion is more that of a constantly changing network of relationships; the two together have clearly formed the traditional understanding of the self including such notions as immortality of the soul. Buddhism, however, is more like the biblical and modern Western notion and focuses on the doctrine of the no-self, *an-natta*, which rejects a substance metaphysics that stressed enduring "being," in favor of a relational metaphysics, stressing the flux of "becoming." In fact, "both may be true reflections of reality . . . both paradigms express differing yet valid interpretations of the bipolar structure of the experience of self-identity though time . . . The Buddhist non-self paradigm over-stresses the experience of becoming at the expense of ignoring the experience of stability and permanency by explaining it away as a delusion, and the Christian self paradigm over-stresses the experience of permanence and stability while ignoring the experience of becoming . . . A more integrative interpretation of the relationship than either the traditional Buddhist non-self paradigm or the traditional Christian self-paradigm seems capable of developing separately" (Paul Ingram, "Buddhist and Christian Paradigms of Selfhood," typescript for a January 3–11, 1984, Honolulu conference on "Paradigm Shift in Buddhism and Christianity: Cultural Systems and the Self," 37).

nature can often have the appearance of chaos. But regardless of what we perceive, there is always a deeper order."

This kind of understanding eventually led to David Bohm's theory of the "implicate order." Whatever order we perceive is only on the surface of reality, the explicate order. Mechanical causes and effects, the appearance of distance and separation, and even the nature of time and space—are all enfolded in the implicate order of a cosmic holo-movement, the flowing processes and transformations of an organic whole. This holo-movement is infinite in its potential and gives rise to everything within and beyond our understanding, including consciousness and human observers themselves.[212]

Yeshua spoke a different language from Gautama but sent much the same message, distinguishing the authentic (his own) from the pseudo (the world's) peace: "Peace I leave you, my peace I give you, not as the world gives do I give you" (John 14:27). As a Palestinian Jew, Jesus spoke not Greek but Hebrew and Aramaic. Thus, the word he used for peace was doubtless "*shalom*," which means much more than the mere cessation of exterior hostilities but, rather, an interior right ordering of things that positively spreads throughout the surrounding world. The Rabbis had a similar message couched in Hebraic categories: "Peace [*shalom*] is great for it is set aside to be the portion of the just . . . Those who love the Torah have great peace [*shalom*] . . . Peace [*shalom*] is great for it will be granted to the gentle."[213] Thus, for Yeshua and the Rabbis a synonym for *basileia tou theou/malkut shomaim*—and for *nirvana*—would have been the pregnant word "*shalom*."

In the end, those persons who attain liberation, salvation (from the Latin *salus*, meaning vibrant health), who arrive at *nirvana*, at the *basileia/malkut*, at *shalom* (or, indeed, at Bohm's "Implicate Order") do not lead a grim, stoic life. Rather, only they are able to live life "to the hilt," for it is only they who, having things rightly ordered, can fully appreciate and enjoy them. Yeshua said as much in a stunning call to full life: "I have come that they may have life, and have it more abundantly!" (John 10:10).

Let this suffice here to indicate something of the profound similarity of the messages of Gautama, Yeshua, and the Rabbis. Of course, there are also differences, but it must be asked whether these differences are over essentials or cultural variations, whether they are contradictory or complementary, whether they concern primary or secondary matters. In addition there will be many more differences—and some similarities—when one

---

212. See Jim Belderis, "David Bohm, Compassion, and Understanding," *Sunrise Magazine* (August/September 1997).

213. Billerbeck, *Kommentar*, 1:216.

moves into a comparative study of the religious traditions that flowed from Gautama, Yeshua, and the Rabbis over the millennia.

God and "Sunyata"

The discussion that would normally fit here has been moved earlier in the section dealing with Ultimate Reality.[214]

Conclusion

The move to compare later developed Buddhist, Jewish, and Christian teachings and practices, of course, is important, but as in the very teachings of Gautama, the Rabbis, and Yeshua themselves, the right ordering of the original vital core of the religious tradition is primary, so that all the other developments can be seen in that light; therefore, the importance of the return to the sources, to the teachings of Gautama, the Torah (and the Qur'an), the Rabbis, and Yeshua (and Mohammed).

Naturally, such a *ressourcement* may not be done in a reductionist or primitivist manner, as if we were to play first-century Bible Land or fifth-century BCE India. Our contexts are different from that of the Rabbis, Yeshua (Mohammed), and Gautama, and thus their messages must be applied to our contexts; we must make the interpretations. That is precisely where the history of the institutions comes in creatively; millions of the disciples of Gautama, the Rabbis, and Yeshua (and Mohammed) also tried to understand the teachings of their teachers and interpret them and apply them to their existential contexts. Their examples and traditions can be of immense help to us, but we must also be aware that these examples and traditions can be negative as well as positive. The traditional must always be tested by the original vital core in interpreting and applying it to the present.

Fortunately for today, the language of both the original vital core of Buddhism, Judaism, and Christianity (the teachings and lives of Gautama, the Rabbis, and Yeshua, that is—what they thought, taught and wrought) and the language of modern critical thinkers (who are largely the ones interested in interreligious dialogue) is largely language "from below," "from within," the transcendent in the immanent—in short, humanity-based. Hence, a dialogue with Gautama the Enlightened One, will not only broaden and deepen our grasp of Reality but will also speak to our life in today's world.

---

214. See above pg. 58.

Confucian-Christian Dialogue

Chinese Religions

Besides the major world religions that stem from the Near East, Judaism, Christianity, and Islam, and the major world religions flowing from India, Hinduism, and Buddhism, two other major world religions, Confucianism and Taoism, arise from another central source of human cultures, namely, China. Just as Judaism, Christianity, Islam, and Buddhism have spread far beyond their geographical and cultural origins, so also did Confucianism and Taoism spread beyond the borders of China into the whole East Asian area, including Korea, Japan, and Southeast Asia.

Hans Küng, with warrant, has characterized this third major stream of world religions as "wisdom" religions, in contrast to the "prophetic" religions of the Near East and the "mystical" religions of India, realizing of course that all the religions contain elements of all three characteristics.[215] This characteristic of the sage as the great model being held up for all to strive toward is particularly true, of course, of Confucianism; Taoism, in fact, tends rather in a more mystical direction.

In any case, partly because Confucianism has been so dominant for so long in China and has wielded such a profound influence in the rest of East Asia, I will concentrate here on the Christian dialogue with Confucianism. Another reason for doing so is that Confucianism appears to be a more concrete, "organized" religious phenomenon than Taoism. Furthermore, a Christian-Confucian dialogue has been launched in a very self-conscious way.[216] Why should this be? Ching has said that she considers "Confucianism to be more compatible with Christianity than is Buddhism, because of a more pronounced, shared ethical concern. Besides, Confucianism does not lack spiritual depth . . . Like Christianity, Confucianism possesses both an 'inwardness' . . . [and] a definite vertical dimension, rooted in its openness to the transcendent."[217]

---

215. Küng and Ching, *Christentum und Chinesische Religion*, 11-12.

216. The first International Christian-Confucian Conference was held in Hong Kong, June 8-15, 1988. Well over a hundred scholars from China, elsewhere in East Asia and from the West attended, each having written a scholarly paper for the occasion. The conference was felt to be such a success that plans were immediately launched to continue the international conferences. See the details of the continuation of this dialogue in Liu shu-hsien, John Berthrong, and Leonard Swidler, eds., *Confucianism in Dialogue Today with the West, Christianity, and Judaism* (Philadelphia: Ecumenical, 2005).

217. Julia Ching, *Confucianism and Christianity* (Tokyo: Kodansha, 1977) xxiii.

It should also be recalled here that there are actually three major Chinese religions: Confucianism, Taoism, and Buddhism. Even though the latter was imported from India, perhaps beginning in the first century CE after several centuries of intense missionary work and major adaptations to the Chinese culture, Buddhism was accepted by a major part of the Chinese (Han) people. In this regard it was different from the other major religions that came into China from the outside, such as Judaism, Islam, and Christianity, for they were largely not accepted by the Han people. However, since Buddhism has just been treated in the previous chapter, I will leave it aside here.

In connection with the three "Chinese" religions, one more preliminary remark is in order. Many Chinese (and to greater or lesser extent other East Asians as well) in fact partake of all three religions, drawing on Confucianism for their morality, Taoism for their ritual, and Buddhism for their philosophy. This "harmonizing" tendency continued so much so to a "logical conclusion" that Ching could remark that, since the Ming period, all three religions had so interpenetrated each other that today in Taiwan and Southeast Asia Confucius, Lao-tzu (the "founder" of Taoism), and Buddha are venerated by the faithful in the same cult. "Despite all rivalries, the three religions could live together. This bespeaks a spirit of tolerance, harmony and reconciliation, which in general is an essential characteristic of Chinese culture."[218] In a nonsyncretistic manner she sees this threefold Chinese religion as presenting a challenge to understand religion anew "in light of a humanism that in its own way calls for a self-transcendence; self-transcendence not only in regard to one's fellow humans but also in regard to another reality: a highest of all (Confucianism), a deepest of all (Taoism), a last of all (Buddhism) reality.[219]

Christians, and others, might well ask themselves whether there is not much to learn about how to relate to other religions and ideologies in this history of the Chinese religious symbiosis.

The New Confucian Paradigm

Confucianism is very old, decrepit, and rigid, blocking the advance of modern thought, science, and democracy. That is why it was totally dismissed in the land of its origin, China, in the 1911 overthrow of the Ching Empire and the anti-Confucian May Fourth Movement (1919). This is true, but it is also true that, at precisely the same time, the New Confucianism

218. Küng and Ching, *Christentum und Chinesische Religion*, 243–44.
219. Ibid., 252.

Movement (though the name appears only in 1941) was launched.[220] It is now in its "third generation," even beginning to move on to its fourth. New Confucianism (to be distinguished from, though in continuity with, the Neo-Confucianism of the Sung [960–1279], Ming [1368–1644], and Ching [1644–1911] dynasties) aims at culling the deep, lasting values from the twenty-five-hundred-year Confucian tradition and bringing them into dialogue with Modernity, especially Western philosophical and scientific thought and democracy. New Confucianism wants to remake the Confucian tradition into a living, creative dialogue partner for the West and the Rest, bringing its own distinctive contribution as one of many human partners in this Age of Global Dialogue.

The third generation of New Confucian scholars, now at the peak of its creativity and productivity, is led by four scholars: Ying-shi Yu (1930–), Shu-hsien Liu (1934–), Chung-ying Cheng (1935–), and Wei-ming Tu (1940–). In addition, there are the "Boston Confucians," who prominently include two Christian theologians, Robert Neville and John Berthrong.[221] As Neville noted: "Boston Confucianism, especially in its members who are also Christian, is deeply committed to multiple religious identity, and to serious faithful conversation that can test its limits."[222]

The three generations of New Confucians represent more than a passage of time and biological generations. Even more importantly they also represent a significant, even radical, evolution of thought and goals.

The first generation, best exemplified in Hsiung Shi-li (1885–1968), indeed wanted to cleanse Confucianism from the stultifying encrustations that had destroyed its contemporary effectiveness, but they also thought that, when that has been accomplished, it would then come to the rescue of a badly corrupt Western thought. They realized that they had to learn from the West in the areas of science and democracy, but, that having been done,

---

220. Lin He (1902–92) first used the term "*Xin rujia*" (New Confucian) in *Sixiang yu shidai*, August, 1941. Amazingly, the revaluation of Confucianism began when anti-Confucianism was reaching its climax in 1918. One of the first to offer a revaluation was a person with no training in the Confucian Classics, a Christian and a rebel, Sun Yat-sen (1866–1925). See Wing-tsit Chan, *Religious Trends in Modern China* (New York: Columbia University Press, 1953) 21.

221. See Robert C. Neville, *Boston Confucianism: Portable Tradition in the Late-Modern World* (Albany: State University of New York Press, 2000) xxviii: "This is the group, or group of overlapping groups, of East Asians and non-East-Asians, of Sinologists and non-Sinologists that has entered the world culture of philosophy as Confucians, New Confucians, or Boston Confucians."

222. Ibid. 209.

their hubris led them to the conviction that Confucianism would once again reign supreme in the thought of the world.[223]

The second generation, represented most prominently by Dongmei Fang (1899–1977) and Tsung-san Mou (1909–95), were much better informed about Western philosophy and thought in general and felt that a purified Confucianism and Western thought would be equal partners in resolving the philosophical and cultural issues of the world.

The third generation, however, having lived for many years in the West as well as in their native Chinese culture, has dropped all such pretensions and is committed to making a renovated Confucianism a partner in a global dialogue addressing the problems of humankind. I will describe briefly where these New Confucian thinkers have brought the dialogue between the Confucian tradition and Modernity. First, I will set the historical context for the reader who is not very familiar with Confucianism, either past or present.

Confucian Beginnings

Chinese religion had a long "pre-Confucian" history, which might be conveniently named folk religion, with all the usual manifestations of shamanism, etc. It reached sufficient maturity by the time of Confucius that he was able to crystalize and shape it so that from that time on it is simply given his name: Confucianism. In speaking of Confucianism we should also bear in mind that it has gone through at least five major periods, which might be briefly described as follows:

> (1) Confucianism of the "classical" period: thought system of the thinkers Confucius (551–479 BCE), Mencius (372–289 BCE), and Hsün-tzu (298–238 BCE)
>
> (2) Confucianism of the Han Dynasty (206 BCE–220 CE)
>
> (3) Confucianism of the middle period, from the fall of the Han up to the Song dynasty (960–1279 CE)

---

223. Hsiung Shi-li wrote: "Humankind in our age is progressively going down the road to its self-destruction. This is the inevitable result of single-mindedly pursuing a scientific culture, of being unable to return to its nature and search for itself, of ignoring the heavenly nature living in them. If we want to save humankind, the only way is to proclaim Oriental Learning" (cited in Umberto Bresciani, *Reinventing Confucianism: The New Confucian Movement* [Taipei: Taipei Ricci Institute, 2001], 458).

(4) Neo-Confucianism—thought system from the Song through the Ming (1368–1644 CE) to the end of the Qing (1644–1911 CE) dynasties, when the Republic was founded.

(5) New Confucianism (in this case, not the same as the like-meaning term, Neo-Confucianism)—twentieth-century re-thinking and transformation of Confucian thought, whose "founder" was Hsiung Shi-li.[224]

Is Confucianism a Religion?

A question that usually arises at the beginning of any discussion of Confucianism is whether or not it should even be considered a religion or, rather, "an explanation of the meaning of life and how to live accordingly," which is not ultimately based on a transcendent, to use my "definition" of an ideology as over against religion.[225] Ching, however, noted, "From his own account of spiritual evolution, it might also be inferred that Confucius was a religious man, a believer in Heaven as personal God, who sought to understand and follow Heaven's Will."[226] Her own understanding of religion, she said, includes a consciousness of a dimension of transcendence that "I perceive as present in Confucianism from the very beginning, even though this has not always referred to a belief in a personal deity . . . The very insistence upon the priority of the 'way of Heaven,' and the quest itself for the discovery and fulfillment of such within the 'way of man,' point to a movement toward self-transcendence," and consequently Confucianism "remains religious at its core, on account of its spiritual teachings of sagehood or self-transcendence."[227]

Another contemporary Chinese scholar, who in no way is Christian, as was Ching (who understood herself as Confucian as well as Catholic), Tsung-san Mou, likewise argued vigorously in favor of understanding Confucianism as a religion: "If we consider religion to be a quest for ultimate meaning in life, an attempt to answer profound questions of human destiny, then surely Confucianism is a religion . . . This universe of 'facts' is

---

224. I am grateful for this division to John Berthrong, in "Adjustments: Dual Transcendence and Fiduciary Community," a paper delivered at the Hong Kong International Christian-Confucian Conference, June 8–15, 1988.

225. See Swidler and Mojzes, *Study of Religion*, 1–2, for a discussion of the definition of religion.

226. Küng and Ching, *Christentum und Chinesische Religion*, 95.

227. Ibid., 116.

shot through and through with values which give it a transcendent base."[228] Western Confucianist scholar William Theodore de Bary also commented: "I would assert that it is clear, both from the Confucian sense of the *Tao* and from its mission, that we are dealing with a 'religious' tradition."[229]

God and the Transcendent

Closely connected to this question is the understanding and even the name of the transcendent in Confucianism. As noted earlier, already in the Shang period (1766–123 BCE) the term *Shang-Ti* (Lord on High) or *Ti* (Lord) was used to refer to the highest of the gods and eventually to a transcendent being, perhaps even a creator god. In the Chou period (1122–249 BCE) the term most often used for God was *T'ien* (Heaven), symbolized by a large human head. After the Chou conquered the Shang, both *Ti* and *T'ien* were used to refer to God, understood as a personal God.[230]

The nineteenth-century English Protestant missionary and translator of many of the Chinese religious classics, James Legge, found in his research the name for the highest God, *Shang-Ti*. "There was, then, before Confucius and many of the sage kings, a monotheistic religion: 'the Confucian religion.'"[231] Unfortunately, Legge was largely rejected by most of his fellow Protestant missionaries, and subsequently Christianity in China mostly went the way of attempting to convert Chinese away from their heritage under the protection of Western colonial military and economic power—which led to a disastrous collapse with the success of the Communist revolution in 1949.

Even earlier, in the sixteenth century, the great Catholic scholar, scientist, and missionary to China, Matteo Ricci, learned much the same about Chinese, and especially Confucian, religion as Legge later did, and he wrote accordingly. Unfortunately, because he was Catholic, his work was automatically suspect and rejected by most Protestants in pre-ecumenical days. However, Ricci's careful bridge-building work did provide the basis for an inchoatively flourishing Chinese Catholicism: Just sixty years after Ricci's

---

228. Tsung-san Mou, *Chung-kuo che-hsüeh te te-chi* [The Uniqueness of Chinese Philosophy] (Taipei: Student Book Co., 1974), as cited in Berthrong, "Adjustments."

229. William Theodore de Bary, *Neo-Confucian Orthodoxy and the Learning of the Mind-and-Heart* (New York: Columbia University Press, 1981) xvi.

230. Cf. Ching in Küng and Ching, *Christentum und Chinesische Religion*, 42.

231. Lauren Pfister, "Orienting the Confucian-Christian Dialogue: Perspectives Drawn from the Works of James Legge (A.D. 1815–1896)," a paper delivered at the International Confucian-Christian Conference in Hong Kong, June 8–15, 1988, 26.

death in 1610 there were over a quarter of a million Chinese Catholics, and for another third of a century the Chinese Catholic Church grew vigorously.

Then, in 1704, in what can only be called a kind of fit of self-mutilating doctrinaire orthodoxy, the Vatican proscribed Ricci's adaptive approach to relating Confucianism and Christianity—with the result that Christianity was proscribed in China, Confucianism was made the state religion, and the number of Chinese Catholics sank to a meager few. Only in 1939 did Pope Pius XII reverse the 1704 condemnation of Ricci's position—too late, of course, to undo the damage of the previous three centuries of unnecessary and nihilistic hostility and too late to prepare for the crisis of post-1949.

Though many traditions see the transcendent and the immanent as opposites, the New Confucian Tsung-san Mou "sees the Confucian as joining the ethical and religious dimensions in an effective unity of lived experience . . . There is no ultimate separation of the subjective and objective, the inner and outer, the immanent and the transcendent."[232]

Confucian and Christian Humanism

Already in the writings of Mencius we find the tendency to speak less in terms of a personal God, or in terms of the Transcendent as *ganz anders*, completely other, but more in terms of the Transcendent, Heaven, being reflected in the human heart: Who knows his/her own heart and nature also knows Heaven.[233] Hence, the Transcendent, instead of being "out there," more and more was found within, immanent. Such an understanding is very congenial to a very important strand in the Judeo-Christian tradition, starting already with the creation story where it is said that humanity is made in God's image.

As noted previously, it is in this relationship between the Transcendent and the Immanent or between Heaven and Humanity that Confucianism's special characteristic comes to the fore. The core of Confucianism is humanism, but a humanism that, as the New Confucian Tu put it, includes "*a faithful dialogical response to the transcendent.*" He goes on to say that "the mutuality of Heaven and man (in the gender neutral sense of humanity) makes it possible to perceive the transcendent as immanent." In other words, "the Confucians advocate a humanism which neither denies nor slights the transcendent . . . Humanity is Heaven's form of self-disclosure,

---

232. Tsung-san Mou, *Chung-kuo*, 20, as paraphrased in Berthrong, "Adjustments," 13.

233. *Book of Mensius*, 7a, 1.

self-expression, and self-realization."²³⁴ Already in 1958 a number of New Confucian scholars in Taiwan issued "A Manifesto for the Reappraisal of Sinology and Reconstruction of Chinese Culture," in which "the harmony of the 'way of Heaven' (*t'ien-tao*) and the 'way of man' (*ren-tao*) is extolled by those who signed it as the central legacy of Confucianism."²³⁵

Again, there are certain parallels in this conceptualization to a Christian theology of the *imago Dei*, or of an incarnational theology; perhaps most of all, it is like Hegel's notion of *Welt Geist*—this latter parallel especially offers to Western, including Christian, thinkers many possibilities, as well as problems. Hegel's thought—and that of all modern historical, dynamic, processive, immanentist thinkers—stands in severe tension with much of traditional Christian philosophy and theology, because the older tradition gave Being, Stasis, and Nonchange the pride of place, whereas much of contemporary thought holds up Becoming, the Dynamic, and Change as the highest value, seeing the static as the mode of death.

Nevertheless, the stress on the dynamic is clearly the mode of thought of more and more critical-thinking persons, including Christian theologians—witness Vatican II and subsequent Catholic and Protestant theology, despite various inevitable temporary backlash movements. Hence, here is a very promising contemporary basis for Christian, and other, dialogue with Confucianism: Because "being religious, in the Confucian perspective . . . means being engaged in the *process* of learning to be fully human,"²³⁶ and learning to become "human is the real informing characteristic of all authentic Confucian religious sentiment. This *process* of 'humanization' has no limits and is therefore called a transcendent reference . . . the *process* is unending in its scope and completely moral in its intention, while transcendent in ultimate reference."²³⁷

If for Confucianism and Christianity becoming human is an unending process that aims at an ever-receding horizon of Heaven, God, the Transcendent ("Our inborn ability to respond to the bidding of Heaven impels us to extend our human horizon continuously so that the immanent in

---

234. Tu, "On Confucian Religiousness," 7, 8, 16, a revised and enlarged version of chapter five, "Centrality and Commonality: An Essay on Confucian Religiousness," in his book, *Centrality and Commonality: An Essay on Confucian Religiousness*, SUNY Series in Philosophy and Culture (Albany: State University of New York Press, 1989) 94; emphasis in original.

235. Carsun Chang, *The Development of Neo-Confucian Thought* (New York: Bookman, 1963), as cited in Küng and Ching, *Christentum und Chinesische Religion*, 123–24.

236. Tu, "On Confucian Religiousness," 2.

237. Berthrong, "Adjustments, 11.

our nature assumes a transcendent dimension,")[238] Confucians make clear that it is a process that is engaged in by self-transcendence, self-effort: "The Confucian faith in the perfectibility of human nature through self-effort is, strictly speaking, a faith in self-transcendence."[239] Tsung-san Mou speaks in similar terms, stressing the centrality of creativity in being human: "For him the heart of being human is creative reason, the capacity to transform self and relate in a meaningful and humane way to others. The essence of being human is hence the creation of new values."[240]

Confucian and Christian Notions of "Salvation"

Here is a potential clashing point with much of Christian tradition, and many Confucian thinkers are aware of it, namely, how is one "saved," how does one become a whole, (w)holy human—by one's own effort or from the outside? Tu commented: "To say that man, by self-effort, without a leap of faith, can become one with the Creator is novel, if not blasphemous, in the Judeo-Christian framework."[241] He is right concerning much of Christian tradition, but that stream of the tradition has tended to misconstrue the basic meaning of both the key term "salvation" and the message and example of Jesus. Moreover, the alternatives of *either* salvation by self-power *or* other-power (*jiriki* or *tariki* in Japanese) is an unwarranted forced choice. Here the "Protestant" "alone," *solo*, is definitely to be rejected in favor of the Catholic "both-and," "*et*/*et*."

Of course *we* can become as wholly (w)holy, human as is possible for *us* only if *we* persistently and wisely make the necessary effort. We can also attain success in this life-long endeavor only to the extent that we have been *given* the wherewithal: If we are not born, we cannot become (w)holy human. If we die too young, if we do not have loving care in infancy, if we do not have good education and training, encouragement, love, moral example, inspiration, etc.—we cannot become (w)holy human according to our inborn potentialities. So, we become (w)holy human by both *jiriki* and *tariki*, but we must remember that, when we speak of these two "powers," we are speaking on two different levels of causality. As a consequence, there can be no clash—only complementarity.

It is most unfortunate that in the history of Christian thought the thinker in favor of "self-power," that good Irishman Pelagius (whose Irish

---

238. Tu, "On Confucian Religiousness," 8.
239. Ibid.
240. Berthrong, "Adjustments," 46.
241. Tu, *Centrality and Commonality*, 9.

name was Morgan, "the sea," hence, Pelagius, Latin for sea) has been so maligned that the position attributed to him by his weighty opponent, Augustine of Hippo, has been termed the *heresy* of "Pelagianism," namely, we are "saved" by responding with our free will to God's freely given "grace." Christian theology reeled for centuries from the effects of that false choice: human free will—*or* God's omnipotence.

The hubris of the theologians of that time and much afterwards to imagine that they could answer the question—How precisely are the human free will and God's omnipotence related?—is staggering. By the very nature of the problem, finite humans (there is another kind?) can "rationally" understand neither free will (if it were "rationally" understood, it would be "rationally" determined and therefore not free) nor God's omnipotence (nor God's anything else fully—unless they were God). Yet, some theologians thought they could answer the question of how the two were related. This was rather like a mathematician trying to solve an equation with two unknowns and no knowns! What we have here is simply a badly framed question (rather like "How far is yellow?"), with the result—an impossible solution.

The "catholic" both-and approach to the question of "how" one becomes (w)holy human not only frees the Christian to recast the question in contemporary dynamic, immanentist thought categories but also to see Confucian humanism with more nonprejudiced, appreciative eyes and thereby to be more properly prepared for a promising dialogue with it.

Beyond this first layer of the question of humanism there is another promisingly fruitful point of dialogue. It can be found in the growing awareness among Western thinkers, including Christian theologians, of the human relationship with and responsibility toward nature and the world around us, and the similar concern expressed by Confucianism, especially as influenced by Taoism and its emphasis on the need for humans to be in harmony with the way, the *Tao*, of nature. Tu, for example, has written of an anthropocosmic vision: "Confucians see humanity as more than an anthropological concept but as an anthropo-cosmic idea. Since the value of the human is not anthropo-centric, the assertion that man is the measure of all things is not humanistic enough."[242] This thought, and even language, is very like that of the Catholic philosopher/theologian Raimundo Panikkar (like his younger colleague Tu, he also taught at Harvard), who years ago wrote of a cosmotheandrism (later changed to cosmotheanthropism when the consciousness of sexism in language arose).[243]

242. Tu, "On Confucian Religiousness," 15.
243. Also see Charles Wei-Hsun Fu, "A Universal Theory of Religion or a Cosmic

Subordinationism and Egalitarianism

Underlying the question of humanism, even in its expanded form, is the understanding of what is meant by loving others, which needs to be reflected upon here.

The central virtue for Confucianism is *ren*, kindness, compassion, or humaneness. In this connection Confucius formulated a negative version of the Golden Rule: What you yourself do not wish, do not do to others (*Conversations* 15, 23)—as did later also the Jew Hillel and the Jew Yeshua (the latter in positive form).[244] Mencius remarked that "the man who possesses *ren* loves others" (*Book of Mencius* 4B, 28). He even uttered something like Yeshua's startling mandate to love one's enemies when he said, "The good person treats the unloved as he does the loved" (*Mencius* 7B, 1).

However, at the same time, for Confucius an equally critical virtue was that of *li,* often understood as hierarchical order. At the heart of the Confucian understanding of what it means to be human has been the idea of the five hierarchical relationships: ruler and minister, father and son, husband and wife, older and younger brother, and friend and friend. The prime paradigm was the relationship of father to son; everything else was modeled after it. The essence of the relationship was that of superior-inferior. One was to love one's fellow human being, but in the proper manner, in the correct order.[245] In contrast to this understanding of *ren* was the view of Mo-tzu (fifth century BCE), who taught a love of all without distinction; however, his position did not prevail in the Chinese tradition.

There is clearly a great similarity between the Confucian *li* and the Hellenistic "Household Codes" ("subjects obey the emperor, slaves your master, wives your husbands, children your parents"). Though Yeshua is the acknowledged "founder" of Christianity, it is not his teaching and example alone, we know, that are found in the New Testament. There are also reflections of something of the "extreme dualism" that permeated the Persian and Hellenistic society of that time—and Western civilization since. This can be seen very clearly in those "Household Codes" that were said to have originated with Zeno, the founder of Stoicism at the end of the fourth

---

Confidence in Reality?" in Swidler, ed., *Toward a Universal Theology of Religion*, 154–61.

244. See Leonard Swidler, ed., *For All Life: Toward a Universal Declaration of a Global Ethic: An Interreligious Dialogue* (Ashland, OR: White Cloud, 1999) 19–21.

245. See Ze Hua Liu and Quan Ge, "On the 'Human' in Confucianism," *Journal of Ecumenical Studies* 26 (Spring 1989) 313–35, for a negative critique of Confucianism as a possible basis for a democratic society. They argued that because of the patriarchal, hierarchical nature of traditional Confucianism, it had to look outside, to the West, for the notion of *human* rights, which of course is what the New Confucianists have been doing. Both authors were professors at Nankai University, Tianjin, China.

century BCE They turn up in the New Testament in the deutero-Pauline and pseudo-Petrine epistles, taking the form of hierarchical relationships that include: God-Christ, Christ-church, ruler-subject, master-slave, husband-wife, father-son. This superior-inferior relationship is reflected most often in the New Testament's—though not Yeshua's—sexist patriarchalism, where the woman in a variety of ways is said to be subordinate to the man.

Thus, insofar as Christianity is based not on the teaching and example of the Jew Yeshua and what he thought, taught, and wrought, as the basic touchstone for all Christian belief and praxis, but on other parts of the New Testament, especially the above Stoic patriarchal hierarchism found in the deutero-Pauline and pseudo-Petrine letters, there is also a great similarity between traditional Confucianism and traditional Christianity as well. Confucianism will—as Christianity is struggling to do today, with slow, but growing success—have to move to replace its human subordinationism with egalitarianism (while still recognizing the real differences in persons), especially in regard to women.

However, it appears that the egalitarian Mo-tzu doctrine was successfully resisted in the development of the Confucian tradition in a way that the egalitarian Yeshua teaching was not successfully resisted in the Christian tradition, especially after the eighteenth-century European Enlightenment. Still, today there are vital signs that certain strains of "New Confucianism" are moving in directions that are attempting radically to transform *li* away from its initial and traditional structure toward a more fundamentally "liberal, solidary, and egalitarian form."[246]

For example, Tu has argued that "properly interpreted in the anthropocosmic perspective, the sense of rootedness reminds us that we are responsible not only for those who came before us and brought about our existence but also for those who are yet to come." He insists that Confucian principles are "not conservative ideas designed to maintain existing power relationships" but, rather, "their service of such political aims in the past was derivative of a more fundamental concern: the concern for the cosmos as a whole . . . ecological principles." In fact, "Filial piety and reverence are not conservative but conservationist ideas."[247]

Only the future will reveal the success of these efforts to incorporate into the Confucian "conservationist ideas" the modern Western turn

---

246. See, e.g., the work of Catholic Confucianist scholar William Theodore de Bary, *The Liberal Tradition in China* (Hong Kong: Chinese University Press, 1983), where he argues with great learning that the thought of a number of Confucians, and especially of the great Confucian medieval thinker Chu Hsi, is indeed in what the West would call the liberal tradition.

247. Tu, "On Confucian Religiousness," 24.

toward freedom and the individual. They will, among other things, have to take seriously the scathing criticisms of Chinese scholars such as Ze Hua Liu and Quan Ge who concluded, "Individuation is a necessary component of the full development of the human being, but Confucianists only provided the procedure of socialization . . . Following the Confucian way of human development, there was, and will be, no hope of establishing the position of the individual and his and her dignity, freedom, and independence."[248] In the end, as Ching insisted, "Confucianism can remain genuine and viable only as one value system among others, in a society where freedom and responsibility are esteemed."[249]

Self-love: The Foundation of Society

There is at the same time, however, likewise something quite positive, and especially needed in the contemporary world (particularly in view of Marxism's now drastically faded influence), to be found in the Confucian understanding of love, namely, that the foundation of all love is self-love. In Confucianism the context within which this issue is discussed is whether learning to be human—the essential human act according to Confucianism—is to be done "for the sake of others (*wei-ren*) or "for the sake of self" (*wei-chi*).[250] Tu has pointed out that, theoretically, learning to be human can be done for both reasons: "Indeed, this preference for the inclusive 'both-and' rather than the exclusive 'either-or' solution for conflicts between self and society is a distinctive feature of Confucian ethics."[251] However, Tu added that, although learning for the sake of others may appear altruistic, Confucius criticized it as inauthentic: "A decision to turn our attention inward to come to terms with our inner self, the true self, is the precondition for embarking on the spiritual journey of ultimate self-transformation. Learning for the sake of the self is the authentic way of learning to be fully human."[252]

Such an approach is in line with the Judeo-Christian tradition, based as it is on the "two great commandments" of the Torah, namely, loving God wholly, which is concretely carried out by loving one's neighbor *as* oneself. One can love one's neighbor only to the extent that one loves

---

248. Liu and Ge, "On the 'Human' in Confucianism," 335.
249. Ching in Küng and Ching, *Christentum und Chinesche Religion*, 115.
250. Confucius, *Analects*, 14, 25.
251. Tu. "On Confucian Religiousness," 40.
252. Ibid. 41. De Bary, *Liberal Tradition in China*, 21, also documents thoroughly that this is, indeed, the position of Confucius and the Confucian tradition.

oneself authentically. The "golden rules" of Hillel, Yeshua—and Confucius and other religious traditions—also start with a love of self as the basis for loving the other: "Do unto others as you would have them do unto you." If you do not truly love yourself, you cannot love others. As the Christian medieval scholars noted, you cannot give what you do not have, *Nemo dat quod non habet*.

Using abstract, largely Aristotelian terms, it can be seen that, just as the object of the intellect, the highest human cognitive faculty, is the True, the object of the will, the highest human appetitive faculty, is the Good. As the cognitive faculty moves outwardly-inwardly, reaching out and drawing the outside world into itself by knowing it, thereby "becoming one" with it, so, too, the appetitive faculty moves outwardly-inwardly, reaching out and drawing the outside world into itself by loving it, thereby "becoming one" with it. The nature, the very structure of the appetitive faculty is to reach out toward what the cognitive faculty presents as the True/Good, to draw it to itself, thereby moving to become one with it. The fundamental meaning of the term "love" is, having perceived the good, to reach out to draw it to oneself.

At the same time, loving oneself is only the first half of the basic move toward humanization, as I argued above when presenting mutuality as an essential element in self-transcendence, the becoming unendingly ever more fully human. Thus, true love of self for the human implies that she or he move endlessly toward becoming more fully her or himself, that is, more wholly human—which can be done only by moving beyond oneself, by knowing and loving the other. Consequently, just as I cannot love others if I do not truly love myself, so also I cannot truly love myself if I do not love others. If I do not move out to know and love others, I will not become fully human, and if I do not move to become fully human, I will not be truly reaching out for the greatest good for me as a human—I will not be loving myself.

To turn once again to more abstract Aristotelian terms: The nature of the will is to draw the good to itself, to identify with it. In this process I will become more or less identified with other centers of consciousness, with other persons. When this love identification becomes strong enough, we speak of the beloved's becoming my *alter ego*, my other self. Now my love also takes the form of drawing the good—not only to my "first" self (*primus ego*) but also to my *alter ego*, and, if the love identification is sufficiently intense, I might draw the good to my *alter ego* rather than my "first" ego so entirely that I might even give up the greatest good in my "first" ego for the sake of giving it to my *alter ego*: "Greater love than this has no one than one gives up one's life for one's friend." It should be obvious, however, that this "altruism" is not in conflict with an authentic "egoism," for in this case the "*alter*" is the "*ego*."

This, however, is the last, the highest stage of human development. It is the stage of the (w)holy person, the saint, the arahat, the bodhisattva, the sage. Such a stage cannot be the foundation of human society, but the goal of it. The foundation of human society must be first self-love, which includes moving outward to loving others. Not recognizing this foundation of self-love is the fundamental flaw of those idealistic systems, such as Communism, that try to build a society on the foundation of altruism. A human, humanizing society should lead toward (w)holiness, toward altruism, but it cannot be built on the assumption that its citizens are (w)holy, altruistic, to start with. Such an "altruism" must grow out of an ever-developing self-love; it cannot be assumed, and surely it cannot be forced, as has been tried for decades—with disastrous dehumanizing results.

In this foundation of self-love moving outward to loving others, Confucianism ("all men are brothers within the four seas")[253] and Christianity ("if you have done it to one of these least ones, you have done it to me")[254] are fundamentally at one and have much to discuss with and learn from one another.

Future of the Dialogue

Ching asked whether, in the end, Confucianism is still relevant today and answered that it is, if by Confucianism is meant "a dynamic discovery of the worth of the human person, of the possibilities of moral greatness and even sagehood, of one's fundamental relationship to others in a society based on ethical values, of an interpretation of reality and a metaphysics of the self that remain open to the transcendent." To this she added that Confucianism must be "the basis for a true sense of human dignity, freedom, and equality—then Confucianism is very relevant, and can remain so, both for China, and for the world."[255]

There are many more points of commonality and contrast between Confucianism and Christianity, but let this suffice to indicate where some of the possibilities and already begun realities of dialogue between the two are. As the Westerner Lauren Pfister of the Hong Kong Baptist College remarked, "The possibilities of a transformative dialogue between Confucians and Christians at this time appear, consequently, far more promising than

---

253. Confucius, *Analects*, 12:5.
254. Matt 25:40.
255. Ching, in Küng and Ching, *Christentum und Chinesische Religion*, 117.

at any other time in the history of their encounters."[256] The Shanghai-born Ching expressed a similar sentiment: Confucianism, like Christianity, has had to confront the challenges of science, technology, and the political and social challenges of a Marxist regime. "Recent indications point to an increasing recognition, on the part of this regime itself, of the vitality of Confucianism. The encounter between Marxism and Christianity began only a short while ago. The encounter between Christianity and Confucianism is not yet over."[257]

Contemporary Christianity's Contribution to the World

What can Christianity in particular offer to the world now at the beginning of the third millennium, as we are entering the Age of Global Dialogue? It has something at once very old and very new. In brief, what third-millennium Christianity has to offer is a result of a major paradigm shift that has taken place in Christianity in recent decades and is still going on. This is the shift, as we have seen to some extent, from a static, ideological, exclusivist view of religion and the world to one that is dynamic, pragmatic, dialogic. This has meant the embracing of modern critical methods of thinking as the essential means of reappropriating the tradition. As with all creative renewal movements, contemporary Christianity is also in the process of returning to its source, not in a romantic spirit, but as a necessary step to make its source once again vital in today's world. It is that Source—"revitalized," made newly, more profoundly available through contemporary methods—that Christianity can offer the world for the third millennium.

Return to Sources

As we have seen above, the source, the origin, of Christianity—despite its name—is not "the Christ," not the church, not the New Testament, but Jesus (Yeshua) the Jew, his thought, teaching, and living example, that is, what Yeshua "thought, taught, and wrought." Millions of Christians have for centuries, however, focused their main attention on something other than the source of Christianity. They focused on a religious/theological concept, "Christ," the "Anointed One," which was laden with all sorts of meanings beyond its original Jewish meaning of a man who was given special

---

256. Pfister, "Orienting the Confucian-Christian Dialogue," 21.
257. Ching, in Küng and Ching, *Christentum und Chinesische Religion*, 117.

responsibilities by God—and hence also powers to carry out those responsibilities. Or, they focused on the doctrinal teachings of the church as laid out in early universal (ecumenical) councils, or by the pope. Or, they focused on the writings of the Bible, especially the New Testament.

However, none of those are the source of Christianity. The source of Christianity is Yeshua of Nazareth (whose family name was not "Christ"), who himself was not a Christian, who did not read the New Testament, who indeed did not even found a church. Rather, he was a devout Jew whose "family name," if he had had one, would have been "Ben-Yosep" (Josephson) or "ha Notzri" (the Nazarene), who read the Hebrew Bible, and as a "Rabbi" gathered around him a band of Jewish followers to be sent to "the children of the House of Israel," as did other rabbis.

It is to that source, to Jesus of Nazareth, "Yeshua ha Notzri," that more and more Christians are turning at the present time, both as individuals—ordinary people and theologians—and as ecclesiastical institutions. It is also precisely that source, Yeshua, that has much to offer the world in the third millennium.

Yeshua: A Concrete Human Being

The first thing to notice about the source of Christianity, Yeshua, is that it is not an abstraction, not a set of ideas or teachings, not an ideology—but a concrete person. Of course ideas and wise teachings are important, even essential, but in unembodied form they have limited inspirational power by which women and men can set their lives. The thin power of an ideology by itself is borne out time and again by the examples of some of the seemingly most powerful ideologies desperately casting up human figures as the centers of inspiration—why else, for example, the wax-like preserved bodies of Lenin and Mao Zedong in Red Square and Tiananmen Square, to say nothing of the millions of pictures and statues of them scattered about?

The most fetching thing about Yeshua is that he lived—and died—his profound teachings. It is one thing to teach the love of one's neighbor as oneself, as is taught in the Hebrew Bible. It is quite something more to pour out one's life helping person after person, no matter how wretched and unattractive they are—even to love one's enemies to the point of dying with a plea of forgiveness for them on one's lips. This is the stuff of which enduring human inspiration is made. Such a person will be an inspiration, a model for life, as long as there are human beings and his life's story is placed in front of them.

This very strength, of course, automatically carries with it a great danger. In the warmth of that extraordinary life, people will want to give expression to the deep emotions it stirs within them. They will want to say the very best they can imagine about him, so many miraculous acts will often be attributed to him, and increasingly so. This can be seen happening in the four canonical Christian Gospels, and with even greater intensity and imagination in the later apocryphal gospels.

But these alleged preter- and supernatural dimensions attached to Yeshua are not what will be helpful to the contemporary world; they will serve, as they have in past Christian history, more as distractions, if they are taken literally. Rather, they need to be not simply thrown out but "demythologized" and brought up to the level of the "second naivete," where they will be appreciated for the deeply meaningful poetic metaphors and symbols that they truly are, thereby pointing to a deeper reality that cannot be captured in purely prose articulation.

It is already enough of a "mind-blowing" image to see a man who so takes to heart the profound Jewish insight into the meaning of living an authentic human life by "loving one's neighbor *as* oneself" that he lives it out minute by minute, person by person. Yeshua does that, but also more: It was noted before that just as the object of knowing, of the cognitive faculty, is the "True," so the object of loving, of the affective faculty, is the "Good," and that one thus wants to be united with the "Good" in some appropriate way, whether it is to eat a "good" ice cream cone, to have a "good," comfortable house, to be with a "good" person, as one's friend. In other words, love is a unitive force; when we love another person, that means that we become more and more one with the other person, the beloved, and we then also want to unite the other "goods" that we perceive in the world with our "other self," our *alter ego*, the beloved.

Now, as already pointed out, Jews and Christians are taught to love all human beings as themselves, but often they must do so, if they in fact do it, by a sheer act of the will: I know in my mind that I should love, should will the "good" for, this unattractive person before me. What comes across in the image of Yeshua, however, is that he truly "loved" even his enemies, that is, he was able to *see* the goodness in them, no matter how deeply it may have been covered over, and to move to draw other good to that person—not because he *believed* they held an inner goodness somewhere, but because he *knew* that goodness—and acted accordingly.

Here, then, is a person who will accept me regardless of my failures, no matter how low I sink morally, psychologically, physically, or however—not because I *presumably* possess some goodness, some lovableness, but because I really have it, even though I at times might despair of locating it. No matter what, here is someone with whom I am "at home" (it is said that "home" is where they have to take you in—no matter what!).

But, such a human "friend" with whom one can feel so at home necessarily motivates one to imitation. It is sometimes remarked that imitation is the highest type of compliment—and it is. It is also true that those we admire the most are automatically also the ones we try to imitate the most. Hence, the deep, open-to-all love felt in Yeshua necessarily moves the person thus loved to love similarly in an open-to-all manner. Such a force is of immense power in human life, and it is this force that Christianity has to offer the contemporary world: the concrete human Yeshua who *lived* his love of each person regardless of who they were.

Yeshua: Positive on Life

One of the banes of the two-thousand-year Christian tradition is the massive infection it has suffered from extreme dualism, that is, the view that says: Body is bad, and spirit is good. It can be found to some extent already in the later New Testament writings in its growing subordination of women, who soon thereafter were increasingly depicted in Christianity as "the devil's gateway" (Tertullian, second century), the "bringer of death into the world" (*Vita Adam et Evae*, second century).

The extreme Christian asceticism found in strength already in the second century was another reflection of this extreme dualism, which entered Christianity not from Yeshua or his Jewish religious culture but from Hellenistic culture, which was rife with extreme dualisms of all sorts. Even in Plato one can see the effects of this dualistic attitude: The body, which is mortal, is understood as the prison of the soul, which alone is immortal; our sense knowledge is only of a shadow of the true reality, the Idea.

Such an extreme dualist view, however, runs fundamentally contrary to the Bible's view of reality as it is laid out in its very beginning when the creation of the world is described. The Hebrews made an extraordinary breakthrough in human history in seeing the unity of the cosmos. They claimed that the various parts of reality did not come into existence under the aegis of various gods or spirits or disparate forces but, rather, all reality had a single source—Yahweh God, the only creator of all. The crown of God's creation was humanity (*ha-adam*, literally, "the earthling"), created from matter (*Adamah*, earth or soil) with a divine element, breath, or spirit (*Ruach*) from God, breathed into it. Hence, for the Hebrews a human was not two separate realities temporally juxtaposed, a body and a spirit, but an embodied spirit, or enspirited body—a "body-spirit."

Beyond that, the Hebrews also wrestled with the problem of evil in a creative way: In the Genesis story of creation (the whole story of course is properly understood as a profound myth explaining reality, and hence, if it is taken with true seriousness, it must be perceived as such—Ricoeur's level of "second naivete"), at the end of each day God saw that what God had done was good; at the end of creation, on the sixth day, God saw that all that God had done was very good.

There were no evil gods or spirits who created evil things, as was often explained by other ancient polytheistic or animistic peoples. Rather, evil came into the world by humanity's not following the structural laws Yahweh God had built into humanity at creation. In following the deception of the serpent, humanity freely chose to try to "be like God" in deciding what was good and evil (eating the forbidden fruit of the tree of the knowledge of good and evil). Here was the first "domino theory"—when humanity fell out of "order" in its relationship to Yahweh God, its relationship with the rest of creation also fell into disorder in a kind of chain reaction. This is the symbolic meaning of the "curses" leveled against Adam and Eve as they are driven from the Garden of Eden; the "curses" were not really punishments God visited on humans, but rather what humans did to themselves, such as degenerative diseases that result from environmental pollution.

The main point to observe here, however, is that everything is created by Yahweh God, and it is created *mod tov*. This is the Jewish tradition within which Yeshua and all his first followers lived. He enjoyed friends; he ate—even after the "resurrection event" He drank wine; he even made it. He was in this regard very different from Siddhartha Gautama, the Buddha, who taught his followers that fundamentally all life is suffering or sorrow, *Dukkha*. Rather, Yeshua said to his followers: "I have come that you may have life, and have it more abundantly!" (John 10:10).

To be sure, Yeshua did not live a suffering-free life. Where Gautama lived to old age and died of "natural" causes, Yeshua died a violent, ex*cruci*atingly (note the word: *crux*, cross) painful death, and he overcame it not by fleeing it but by accepting it fully and plunging through it to a fuller life (the "resurrection event") for himself and others.

Of course, in the teachings of Gautama the Buddha there is great wisdom and "salvific" energy. Rightly understood, Buddhist doctrine is not world-fleeing and pessimistic, as it might seem to be at first blush. Nevertheless, it must be granted that in trying to "sell" Buddhism—and a teaching that isn't "bought" by people surely is worthless to them—the beginning idea that "all life is *Dukkha*" would not exactly be an advertising manager's dream slogan! Perhaps, however, in a culture like India's with its massive population and even more massive poverty, such a "slogan" did find a deep resonance in reality, if not great enthusiasm.

To continue the comparison, Buddhism penetrated deeply into Chinese culture and life, but as it did, it in turn was also profoundly shaped by China, especially by China's sense of practicality and concern for correct action in this world. It is precisely this pragmatism and this-worldliness, this humanism, that provides a striking parallel with the fundamental optimism and ethics-orientation of the Jewish tradition, with Yeshua at the heart of it. We are not talking here of the Augustinian and subsequent misreading of Paul's teaching about being "saved by faith" but about the teaching and life of Yeshua, who among other things described the "Last Judgment" as based on whether a person has given food to the hungry, drink to the thirsty, clothes to the naked, etc., even when they are "the least important of people" (Matt 25:31–46).

To repeat: Without fleeing from suffering, Yeshua's view of life is thoroughly optimistic. God has created all humans good. Though they may have wandered into one kind or another of confusion or even slavery, they can find their way (which, as noted, is what the first followers of the teachings of Yeshua called themselves—not Christians, but followers of "the Way") back to a properly ordered life, to the "Reign of God," wherein the laws that God structured into humans are again followed. Further, the core of God's laws are the Two Great Commandments, love of God, which can be fulfilled only through love of one's neighbors as oneself—and one's neighbors most in need of love are the "least important of people."

Yeshua's Question: What Must I Do?

Yeshua was a Jew, and for Jews the big question was not "What must I think?" That was the big question for the Greeks, who invented the science of abstract rational thinking, as our vocabulary tells us: philosophy (*philo-sophia*), logic (*logos*), metaphysics (*meta-physikos*), ontology (*ontos-logos*). It was the Greek Christians who developed the highly speculative doctrines of Christianity: Christology, Trinity, etc. Indeed, it was they who spelled out the primary essence of Christianity in creeds, the long lists of the precise way members must think. Again, our vocabulary reveals this to us, for we speak of the members of Christianity as "believers," that is, those who believe, who think, a certain way. The technical term the Catholic Code of Canon Law uses to refer to Church members is just that, "Believers in Christ," *Christfideles*.

As a Jew, the big question for Yeshua was, "What must I do?" His great concern was not doctrine, but ethics. There are no "creeds" in Judaism. It has only the regularly repeated prayer, the *Shema Israel*: "Hear oh Israel! Yahweh our God is one" (Deut 6:4). The burden of Judaism is expressed in the phrase "ethical monotheism," for, if there is only one God who created everything, there is only one "order" or code of ethics that God has structured into all creation. Thus, it is the *Torah*, God's Instructions (often badly translated as Law), that holds the pride of place in Judaism.

As noted before, just as the early followers ("followers," not "believers") of Yeshua designated themselves as followers of the "Way" (*Hodos*) to live a proper human life as taught and exemplified by Yeshua, so also the followers of what became known as Rabbinic Judaism placed the "Way" (*Halacha*) at the center of their tradition, and the other Semitic religion, Islam, also placed the "Way" (*Shar'ia*) at its center—and likewise the Indian religions, Hinduism (*Marga*) and Buddhism (*Magga*), and the Chinese religions (*Tao*). In this regard the focus of Yeshua and Christianity fits well with and reinforces the heart of the other great religions of the world.

Yeshua's Focus: On Persons

First and last, primarily and ultimately, Yeshua was interested in persons, paralleling the Two Great Commandments, that is, loving the Ultimate Person, and all human persons. In this, Yeshua was once again quintessentially Jewish. Not only were all humans created by the one God, but they were also created as an image of God, *Imago Dei*, meaning that, like God, humans could know and freely decide/love. Thus, there was only one set of ethics by which one was to treat all humans, regardless of where they came from.

In the ancient polytheistic world, religion provided people with the ethics by which to treat their co-religionists, but people from other countries had a different religion, a different god, and hence were not treated by the ethics the first group received from their god. It was not so with the monotheistic Hebrews: There was only one God who created all humans and therefore only one ethics by which to treat all humans.

How were humans to be treated in the Hebrew tradition? With the greatest of reverence, because they were created not only from the earth but also because they had a divine element, the Spirit (*Ruach*) in them, and, even further, they are created in the image of God; they are all *Imagines Dei*. As noted before, here then is the foundational pillar of the modern notion of human rights; *all* humans are to be treated with the respect due to their dignity: "All human beings are born free and equal in dignity and rights.

They are endowed with reason and conscience and should act towards one another in a spirit of brotherhood" (*Universal Declaration of Human Rights*, U.N., 1948).

For Yeshua it is preeminently persons who matter. He spends the whole of his public life helping persons. He is obviously not interested in accumulating wealth or in building a political power base or in pursuing academic or scholarly interests for the sake of the abstract idea of knowledge or in establishing and furthering an institution. He spends his energy helping individual persons in their physical and spiritual infirmities. His time is taken up constantly either in healing or in teaching persons the wisdom of life—the latter particularly through the many stories he related.

He broke many taboos to help persons. For example, he healed on the Sabbath, though some legalists criticized him for thus violating the Sabbath rule of rest. His response was that "The Sabbath was made for humanity, not humanity for the Sabbath" (Mark 2:27)—that is, principles are for persons—not persons for principles.

Yeshua's Feminism

Again, when Yeshua once visited an important Pharisee, he permitted a woman of ill-repute to kiss his feet, out of remorse, and to wash them with her tears and wipe them with her hair—a shockingly scandalous allowance! But, Yeshua dismissed what he considered the pseudo-scandal by noting that the guilt of her past misdeeds was obliterated "because she has loved much" (Luke 7:47). It was not societal custom or one's public image that was important, but persons. Persons needed to be treated with respect and love—regardless of their place in society, for all were *Imagines Dei*.

This last example points to a very special and very active concern that Yeshua had for the largest of the world's oppressed classes in all cultures—women. Elsewhere I have analyzed in great detail the "feminism" Yeshua exhibited in a very patriarchal society.[258] The first extraordinary thing is that in the midst of his patriarchal society there is not recorded a single negative action or remark by Yeshua about women; the second is that there is a plethora of positive examples of Yeshua's treating women as at least the equal of men and of his often taking stands, breaking taboos, working to free women from the shackles that bound them in that culture.

---

258. See Leonard Swidler, "Jesus Was a Feminist," first published in *The Catholic World* (January 1971), and in at least thirty-two other places in at least six languages through 1987; idem, *Biblical Affirmation of Women* (Philadelphia: Westminster, 1979); and Swidler, *Yeshua*.

On this account traps were set to discredit him, either with the women he was championing or with the Jewish authorities, as in the account of the woman taken in adultery (John 8:2–11).[259] There is even documentary evidence that Yeshua was denounced to the Roman governor Pontius Pilate because "he was leading the women astray."[260] This teaching and this moving, lived example of concern for individual persons regardless of their place in society as the supreme principle of behavior can be a great gift to the world in the third millennium.

For Yeshua Ultimate Reality Is Personal: Implications

Most of us human beings simply live most of the time in the present and on the surface of experience. However, that is not when we are most human. Rather, practically all of us have times when we glimpse some meaning beyond the surface experience. We have many ways of talking about this perception. We speak of a deeper meaning, about higher goals, of the supernatural, of heaven above, about something beyond history, about eschatology, of a meaning below the surface. In brief, we are persuaded that there is something more to reality than what meets the eye; that is the whole meaning of "meaning"—relating empirical data to the knowing subject.

With maturation we become increasingly aware of the interrelatedness of things, including most meaningfully, relatedness with the Source and Goal of all things, Ultimate Reality, however understood. Some persons eventually reach what various Eastern religious traditions, as we have seen, call Enlightenment, Awakening, or Liberation or what in Christianity is sometimes referred to as Infused Contemplation.

It must be recalled that Yeshua lived in a culture that did not use abstract, philosophical thought categories and language. Rather, the ancient Semitic culture thought and spoke in "picture-language." Hence, we must not look for what is not there in the biblical texts, that is, an attempt at philosophical clarity.

---

259. The facts that this story cannot be found in the earliest manuscripts and that it obviously is linguistically out of place in its present place in John's Gospel—it really was torn out of Luke's Gospel and "wandered" about until it found a home in John—make it clear that the early Christian Church (which had become so full of extreme dualism and therefore was anti-sex and misogynist) had great difficulty in accepting such a positive attitude toward sex and women on the part of Yeshua.

260. Marcion (second century) attests to the text: *kai apostrephonta tas gynaikas*, cited in Eberhard Nestle, ed., *Novum Testamentum Graece et Latine* (Stuttgart, 1954) 221; and Roger Gryson, *The Ministry of Women in the Early Church* (Collegeville, MN: Liturgical, 1976) 126.

A Philosophical Analysis of Language

Moreover, as was pointed out before, even when more philosophically trained thinkers speak in the most precise categories and terms possible, when they speak of Ultimate Reality, their language always fall short. Human language is necessarily based on human experience, which is always limited—but in this case it is attempting to speak of the Unlimited. Adequacy and accuracy are obviously impossible.

Perhaps the closest one can come to speaking intelligibly about Ultimate Reality is consciously to speak in what Thomas Aquinas referred to as analogical language. Thus, one could speak of both John and Mary as persons; here, the term "person" is employed univocally, that is, with identically the same meaning. Before the consciousness of sexist language was raised, one could speak of John being a man and Mary being a man (meaning a human being), and also of John being a man and Mary not being a man (meaning a male); here, "man" is used equivocally, that is, with completely different meanings. One can speak of God as person, meaning that God has the qualities of those human persons we know (ability to know and love), but without any of their limitations; here, "person" is used analogously, that is, the divine person and human persons are neither identical nor completely different, but similar or analogous to each other.

This is perhaps not a terribly satisfactory way of speaking of something so terribly important, but, given our human limitations, it is probably the best we humans can do. At the same time, we must also be extremely cautious that we not fall into the trap of taking our statements about Ultimate Reality literally, thereby succumbing to idolatry—mistaking the *idol*, the image (here, the words) for the reality it is symbolizing or pointing to.

Nonpersonal Understanding of Ultimate Reality

Ultimate Reality for Yeshua, as a Jew, was not simply an impersonal principle or force. Rather, Ultimate Reality is Person, that is, knowing and freely deciding/loving Reality. This understanding has been largely held throughout Christianity and Judaism and Islam and many other religions as well, and is usually designated by the term "theism," that is, belief in God who is Person. However, there is also the strand in the Judeo-Christian tradition that speaks of God in nonpersonal terms. To begin with, there are various nonpersonal metaphors for God both in the Bible and in tradition. For example, God is the rock of my salvation, is a mighty fortress, etc. However, no one takes these metaphors to mean that God really is a rock or a fortress;

these are just symbols in a very primary sense, and the terms are used very nearly equivocally, though analogously also in a somewhat extended sense.

Nevertheless, there are also those Christians, especially the mystics, who likewise speak of God in nonpersonal terms, used in a quite primarily analogous manner. This is particularly true when some use either very abstract or negative terms. As we saw earlier, Meister Eckhart, for example, spoke of Ultimate Reality as *Deitas* (*Gottheit*, misleadingly transliterated into English as "Godhead," whereas it ought to be "Godhood"), as *das Nichts*, "Nothingness," and as the *Ungrund*, "Abyss." The latter two mean, at least, that Ultimate Reality is so completely limitless that it is unfathomable, bottomless. Thus, often the "Way" of the mystics is called a *Via negativa*, a "negative way." Such language seems to appear among Christian mystics only at the highest reaches, or the deepest recesses (depending on which directional image one wants to use), and appears to be a reflection of the experience of the finite encountering the Infinite. Concepts and language necessarily fall far short, and one is reduced to stuttering negatives.

This part of the Christian tradition fits quite well with the negative descriptions of Ultimate Reality as found in the East, especially in Buddhism and some forms of Taoism. Ultimate Reality is spoken of in Mahayana Buddhism as the Void, Emptiness, *Sunyata*. However, upon investigation it becomes clear that *Sunyata* is not meant as merely the absence of being but is understood in a much more dynamic sense, as the Zen Buddhist Master Abe, quoted earlier, indicated.

Perhaps recalling the earlier analogy will help here—as long as one remembers that it is just an analogy, and therefore is not to be followed where it no longer is helpful—*Omnia analogia claudet*. That Ultimate Reality is Emptiness, *Sunyata*, means that "ultimately" it has no specific form. Hence, it is like the energy (*Dynamis* in Greek) of electricity when it is still in the dynamo; it does not yet have any specific form: neither the form of light (as in lamps) nor heat (as in stoves) nor locomotion (as in trains). The unspecified electrical energy in the dynamo is like Ultimate Reality in that it is the source of the specific "being" or forms of electricity as light, heat, locomotion but is itself without any form. It is, as Abe put it, "Formless Emptiness" or "Boundless Openness."

Personal Understanding of Ultimate Reality

In any case, Christians can accept the nonpersonal manner of speaking of Ultimate Reality, but they are not likely to give up the personal way of speaking of Ultimate Reality in addition, for several reasons.

One is that it is so centrally and fundamentally fixed in the Christian tradition from the very beginning, in the words of Yeshua and the Jewish texts and tradition before him. A second is that the principle of sufficient cause recommends retaining it. That is, there must be a sufficient cause for the existence of something. For example, if a large crater were found, no one would be satisfied with the explanation that it resulted from the explosion of one gram of TNT; there would have to be a much larger amount, or its explosive equivalent, to account for and to provide a "sufficient cause," for the existence of the crater. Knowing and loving beings, persons, exist; therefore, there must be a source of such "perfection" of being that will be a sufficient cause, which will mean having at least the perfection of what humans know as "personhood." Hence, Ultimate Reality must be at least personal, or perhaps better said, suprapersonal or transpersonal—but not less than personal, and therefore not just nonpersonal.

A third reason is that the vast majority of humans seem psychologically to need to perceive and relate to Ultimate Reality as personal. This is very obvious in Buddhism, which although in its original teaching deliberately avoids speaking of God, nevertheless on almost all levels a personal divinity (for example, Amida Buddha) or multiple divinities or quasi-divinities (for example, Bodhisattvas) are brought back into the *de facto* practice of Buddhism. Some argue that such a need is simply a sign of the present immaturity of humanity, and that, as it matures, that need will disappear. Most evidence, however, seems to point in the opposite direction.

For example, immediately after the formation of the United States of America in 1789, when religious membership became completely voluntary, recorded church membership dropped to its true level of 13 percent of the population. By the latter third of the twentieth century that figure had risen to over two-thirds of the population, with more than 95 percent expressing belief in God—and this occurred precisely during the period of the massive expansion of public education and general secularization. So, the increase of education and secularization does not appear to carry with it a necessary decrease of religious commitment and belief in God; quite the opposite happens in a genuinely free society.

The Understanding of Ultimate Reality Makes a Difference

Bearing in mind the cautions about the use of language when speaking of Ultimate Reality, I want to probe further into the question about what effect the way one conceives and speaks of Ultimate Reality has on how one acts in the world. Christianity and Judaism and Islam and some non-Semitic religions tend to speak of Ultimate Reality, in contrast to Taoism and Buddhism. The contrast is not only between personal and nonpersonal categories but also between positive and negative language. In the West, Ultimate Reality is usually spoken of as Being, Fullness, *Pleroma*. The "definition" Thomas Aquinas gives for God is "Subsisting Being Itself," *Ipsum Esse Subsistens*, or, in Aristotelian terms, "Pure Actuality," *Actus Purus*. As we have seen, Buddhism tends to speak of Ultimate Reality as the Void, Emptiness, *Sunyata*; in Aristotelian terms it would be "Pure Potency," *Potentia Pura*.

However, if one understands the negative terms of Buddhism not as static, mere absence of being, but as dynamic, the source of all being—as Buddhist thinkers apparently do—then the two sets of categories need not be understood as mutually contradictory but, rather, complementary, something like the two sides of a coin. They are talking about the same reality but from two different perspectives or viewpoints. One can find such a reconciliatory position expressed by a number of Buddhist and Christian thinkers. For example, Küng wrote: "Could one not, after all the explanations of emptiness . . . in comparison with the Christian understanding of the Absolute . . . also speak of *convergence between Christianity and Buddhism*?"[261]

Nevertheless, as noted, there is a huge contrast between the way the Semitic religions on the one hand and Taoism and Buddhism on the other operate in the world. The former have put massive amounts of energy into changing this world in myriad ways for the sake of the humans living in it: schools, hospitals, orphanages, social work projects, agriculture, etc. In contrast, Buddhism and Taoism have invested relatively little energy in such projects. There are exceptions, of course (especially in some modern Buddhist sects), and there are the Buddhist virtue of compassion and the Mahayana tradition of the Bodhisattva, one who works to help others. But, the notion of ethics, especially social ethics, is largely underdeveloped in Buddhism, and, traditionally, the Bodhisattva is a rare individual and is devoted to helping others attain *Nirvana*, rather than doing anything about changing this world. It is only in the "new religions" growing out of Buddhism in the twentieth century, such as Won Buddhism in Korea and Rissho Kosei-Kai in Japan, that have begun to place a stress on social ethics.

It appears to me that this major difference in how one acts "in the world" is very probably connected to the way one conceives and speaks of Ultimate Reality. Quite naturally, the positive language of "Being" is much more likely psychologically to encourage action than is the negative language of "Nothingness." Even if one can reconcile the two differing ways of conceiving and speaking so as not to be forced to make an excluding choice

---

261. Küng, *Christentum und Weltreligionen*, 491–92.

of one or the other, the language of one is bound to tend to generate activity and the other passivity. It must be remembered that how one conceives and speaks of Ultimate Reality provides the ultimate goal and motivation for individuals and whole cultures in the living of their lives. Hence, the choice of the language about Ultimate Reality is quite literally a fateful choice. Therefore, Yeshua's and the whole of the Judeo-Christian-Muslim way of understanding and speaking about Ultimate Reality can make an extremely positive contribution to the world of the future.

Three Christian Doctrinal Problems for Moderns

As I have already noted, modern people more and more live in a "critical-thinking" mental world, a world wherein our knowledge of the universe is increasing with a geometric acceleration in seemingly endless fashion—though that very "open-ended" knowledge also appears to be drawing in its wake an increasingly even more unfathomable "mystery." This mystery concerns not only the "whence" and "whither" of this fantastic, intricate order being revealed before our awestruck eyes but also, and most of all, its "why?"

Increasingly, modern people are leaving behind the "naive" mental world in which most humans lived until not many decades ago and are moving into the second stage of maturation, the "rejectionist" stage—when, for example, the "naive" literal existence of Santa Claus is rejected. However, it is also true that an increasing number of moderns are maturing beyond the rejectionist stage to that of the "second naivete," wherein, for example, Santa Claus is reappropriated for what he truly is, a profound symbol of a selfless concern to bring joy to others—the essence of the Christmas message.

That means that many moderns are having grave difficulties with the traditional explanations of a number of teachings that have been considered central in Christianity. This would not be the appropriate place to attempt a full scholarly analysis of all such problematic teachings. That would require a new "*Summa Theologiae*," and I am no Thomas Aquinas—nor would my readers be so foolish as to expect a new "*Summa*" within the confines of this book. However, they can rightfully expect a few direction-pointing reflections on how at least two or three of the traditional Christian teachings that are most obviously problematic for moderns can be understood in a way compatible with the critical-thinking mentality. Furthermore, I believe that in each instance modern people will also find new light shed on these traditional teachings by entering into a dialogue with other religions that have similar teachings.

The three Christian doctrines most difficult for critical-thinking, contemporary Christians are: the Humanity/Divinity of Christ, Resurrection/Immortality, and the Trinity.

Yeshua: "God-Man" or "Human-Divine"?

Recall the problems raised earlier in the section on Christology. What can be said to those contemporary persons of good will and a "critical-thinking" mentality who, not misunderstandably, find talk about God's becoming man," that is, an Infinite-finite, literally a non-sense, a non-being, like a square circle—who point out that such contradictory words and realities can be placed alongside each other (for example, a square next to a circle) but cannot be merged into a single reality? Can nothing at all be said other than: "Believe, and do not ask questions"? If they still ask: Who thought up this "non-sense"? it cannot be said that Yeshua did, nor indeed that any of the biblical authors did. It must be admitted that it is the Hellenistic (mis)understanding of the typically Semitic picture-language used by Yeshua, his followers, and the biblical writers as if it were Greek ontological-language.[262]

What of those christological dogmatic formulas hammered out in the ancient ecumenical councils to which assent was demanded under pain of excommunication? If accepted, do they not wipe out any "low Christology" (emphasizing Yeshua's humanity) and require a specific "high Christology" (emphasizing Christ's divinity), namely, according to Chalcedon (451 CE), that Yeshua is "truly a human being and truly God" (*vere homo et vere Deus*)? These issues have already been detailed earlier in other contexts. After a thorough discussion, I suggested that I believe those Christians were trying to express that we humans encounter God through the human being Yeshua of Nazareth, and that that would be more clearly, less confusedly expressed by using adjective rather noun forms of the key terms involved. That is: Jesus was simultaneously Divine and Human, *vere humanus et vere divinus*.[263]

Resurrection of the Body, Immortality of the Soul, Nirvana?

Resurrection of the body (everyone's) is an article of faith that Christians have been reciting for over fifteen centuries almost every Sunday at the

---

262. For a more detailed discussion of the implications of Yeshua and his first followers' thinking and speaking Jewishly, see chap. 2 of my *Yeshua*.

263. For a more complete discussion, see above, pg. 185.

celebration of the eucharist in the formula of the Nicene Creed. But, of course, the resurrection of the body is most of all associated with the resurrection of Jesus three days after his crucifixion.

The first thing that should be noted is that the teaching of the resurrection of the body is a peculiarly Jewish doctrine and, even more specifically, a particularly Pharisaic one. We know that the Sadducees of the time of Yeshua rejected it (operating in that case, as in many others, as a minority in the Palestinian Jewish population) but that Yeshua, and Christianity following him, along with the majority of the Jewish population, accepted it. This fact is important to realize because the teaching of the resurrection of the body is a part of the Jewish heritage that was not suppressed in Christianity as it early passed into Hellenistic culture. This is especially striking since Christianity also accepted as its own a parallel but clearly different Hellenistic belief, namely, immortality of the soul. Of course, that teaching had already also been absorbed to some extent into Judaism by the time of Yeshua, as is witnessed to by the deuterocanonical Book of Wisdom (Wis 3:1)—but without in any way replacing the Pharisaic doctrine of the resurrection of the body.

At least five hundred years earlier, the Greeks had developed their teaching of the immortality of the soul. For the Greeks, at least from the time of Socrates, a kind of dualism that viewed the body as the prison of the soul predominated; it was the latter, the soul, that was of true, lasting value. Hence, in that culture, the greatest thing that could be said of one who at least some Greeks thought was their greatest *hero* (Greek "Demigod"), Socrates, was that his soul was immortal. Socrates eschewed escaping the death of the body, forced upon him in the form of the cup of hemlock, because by passing through the portals of bodily death his undying soul would return to the empyrean heavens whence it came. The Greeks could not imagine anyone would want to return their incorruptible soul to the prison of their corruptible body. St. Paul had that fact driven home to him in Athens when he held the attention of a Greek audience at the Agora when speaking of Jesus—until he began to talk of his resurrection. Then "they laughed him to scorn!" (Acts 17:32).

However, the basic Jewish understanding of humanity was that every human is a unity of an "enlivened body," a "body-soul," but the "breath of life" is something divine, coming as it did from the Creator God: "And God breathed into his nostrils the breath of life" (Gen 2:7). Hence, since God is just, the "unnatural" state of the human body, after death, no longer being "enlivened," "ensouled," is a condition that has to be rectified—so the Jewish logic ran—and this was to be done by the "resurrection" of the body at "the end of days." Hence, in that Jewish culture, the greatest thing that could be said of one who at least some Jews thought their greatest "hero," its Messiah (Hebrew, "Anointed One"), Yeshua ha Notzri, was that his body was "raised from the dead" by God even before the "end of days." A simple living on of only part of God's *Imago Dei*, even though it was the spiritual part, just would not have entered the Jewish imagination as the final resolution of each human's life. In an extended sense: "What God has joined together, let no man put asunder" (Matt 19:6).

If we look at another totally different culture we again find a different predication of its greatest "hero," Siddharta Gautama. In the Indian culture human life was seen as part of a continuum with all life. Further, there was an ineluctable structural balance built into the cosmos, called *Karma*. Hence, there developed the doctrine of "samsaric" reincarnation whereby one was constantly reborn according to the way one lived in the previous life. Thus, this constant circle of reincarnation, *Samsara*, was understood in near-Sysiphusian fashion, with the possibility, however, of a final break of that awful samsaric circle—called *Nirvana*. Hence, in that Indian culture, the greatest thing that could be said of one who at least some Indians thought their greatest "hero," its *Buddha* (Sanskrit, "Enlightened One"), Siddharta Gautama, was that he had entered *Nirvana*. Of course, the Indians could not imagine that someone would want to have their body (which one?) resurrected or even their soul continue to live, for they understood the karmic law of the universe to have condemned them to the samsaric circle of life until they could eventually break that ring in *Nirvana*. How that is understood varies, of course, from a variety of Hinduisms to Jainism and Buddhism, but in any case, "life" with its constant grasping for "more" was to cease.

Thus, at a very deep level what the doctrine of the resurrection of Jesus reflected was a Jewish version of the human desire to say the very best about the greatest, whether that be the immortality of the soul of Socrates, the entering into *Nirvana* of Gautama or, in this case, the bodily resurrection of Yeshua. Each religious culture praised its greatest "hero" with its cultural superlative. This is by no means all that can be said about the teaching of resurrection, or indeed of immortality or *Nirvana*. For example, bodily resurrection affirms the essential goodness of matter as well as spirit; immortality of the soul responds to the perhaps deepest of human urges, the drive for survival; and *Nirvana* answers to the profound human yearning for an endless inner peace. What implications are suggested by these comparative facts? Are there further questions underneath the separated but obviously related questions the three "end-situations" attempt to answer? Much more can, and therefore should, be found in each of these doctrines and their comparative relatedness. Thus, this reflection is only a beginning, but I hope it can be useful at least as that.

Ultimate Reality: One? Three? Or?

What of the Christian teaching of the Trinity? Is it to be simply rejected as another Hellenistic misunderstanding of the Semitic picture-language? It is true that in the Hebrew Bible, in addition to its insistence on monotheism ("Hear, O Israel, Yahweh our God is one," Deut 6:5), there is also much talk of God as Our Father (*Abinu*), and as we have already seen, of God's Word (*Dabar*), and of God's Spirit (*Ruach*). Again, it is also equally true that these three were never thought of as ontologically existent but, rather, as metaphorical images of aspects of Yahweh as encountered by the Jews. Once again, the fact that other religious, and nonreligious, traditions likewise speak of Ultimate Reality in terms of a trinity tells us that something very deep in our human experience is being expressed in these triadic images and language.

Besides the Hebraic trinity—albeit metaphorical—an ancient form of Hinduism depicted Ultimate Reality as One in Three, the *Trimurti*: *Brahma* (a creator god, not to be confused with *Brahman*, the "Absolute" spoken of above), *Vishnu*, *Shiva*. In Mahayana Buddhism, Ultimate Reality is also conceived of as triadic in the *Trikaya*, the Threefold Body of the Buddha: *Dharma-kaya, Sambhoga-kaya, Nirmana-kaya*, as discussed earlier. Taoism also sees Ultimate Reality as triune: *T'ai I* (Grand Unity), *T'ien I* (Heavenly Unity), *Ti I* (Earthly Unity). Even in modern Western philosophy, triadic thinking holds a prominent place, most evidently in Hegelian dialectical idealism and, in inverted fashion, Marxist dialectical materialism: thesis, antithesis, synthesis. There are many other examples of the triadic view of things, but perhaps the most basically human version is the triad of man, woman, child.

In the Christian tradition, there is a tendency to see the triadic form of things as reflective of the triune nature of God, epitomized in the *Imago Dei*, which naturally takes the form of the human family of man, woman, and child. Many modern psychologists, after Feuerbach and Freud, would tend to say that rather than humanity's reflecting the nature of God, the human description of God is a projection of human experience. Humanity is not an *Imago Dei*, but God is an *Imago hominis*. However, one does not need to make a choice. Both could well be understood as true—indeed as mutually necessary, though for asymmetrical reasons. Of course, humans speak of Ultimate Reality, of God, in human terms. What alternatives are there? To be sure, Ultimate Reality can be spoken of in impersonal terms. To many, this seems all right, but too little—on the principle of sufficient reason: Ultimate Reality must be at least as perfect as the most perfect finite being, so therefore at least "personal," though without the limitations we see in limited human persons. It also seems logical that the effect will be a reflection of its cause; for example, if there are only blond genes in both parents, it is expected the offspring will be blond; conversely, blond offspring imply blond genes in the parents.

So, it is "natural" that Christians, along with many other religious persons, perceive Ultimate Reality as somehow triadic, thereby giving rise to the doctrine of the Trinity: One God in three divine persons. Given the early move of Christianity into the Hellenist thought world, it is not all surprising that the prominent Jewish triadic imagery would give rise to the more philosophical reflections that developed the doctrine of the triune God. This is especially true since the teaching of the *Imago Dei* was also so strong in Judaism, for there is not only the fundamental physical triad in human biology (and in all higher animal biology) but, perhaps even more importantly, also in human psychology, wherein the quality of being a divine image is thought to reside mainly: Knowing the true, loving the good, acting freely.

Long before Martin Buber, Christians were aware that the human "I-thou" relationship is qualitatively far beyond an "I-it" relationship. One of the special characteristics about an I-thou relationship is that it creates a third reality: I am aware of (love) you; you are aware of (love) me; we are aware that we are aware of (love) each other. The relationship between the I and the thou becomes a third reality, as it does not in an I-it relationship. This human psychological triad is mirrored at its zenith in the mutual love between a woman and a man resulting in a third reality, a third person, the child.

This rather universal human experience of a mutual awareness (love) creating a third reality between persons gave rise to the development of the renowned attempt by St. Augustine to "explain" the Trinity in psychological terms: God the Father expresses Godself completely (the Word); in mutually contemplating complete perfection in each other, the Father and God's Word love each other completely; since this mutual love is perfect, it also is a third reality, called the Spirit. Whether one finds such an "explanation" very helpful or not, it should be apparent that the Christian doctrine of the Trinity—however it is "explained," whether in Augustine's psychological terms, the Council of Nicaea's Greek philosophical categories, or whatever—is an attempt, like the triadic doctrines of the other religions and philosophies, to point to a basic trinitarian form of reality, both finite and infinite.

These are three attempts to try to "make sense" in contemporary thought categories out of three representative traditional Christian doctrines that have become problematic for critical-thinking moderns.

Dialogue: A Key to the Future

What of Yeshua's attitude toward non-Jews? One would not usually think of Yeshua in connection with interreligious dialogue. On the one hand, he is recorded to have sent out the twelve apostles only "to the lost sheep of the people of Israel" (Matt 10:6). On the other, he is also recorded to have said to them that they "should tell the Good News to the Gentiles" (Matt 10:18), and that "the Good News must be preached to all nations" (Mark 13:10). Moreover, Yeshua himself did go into the gentile area of present-day Lebanon.

There is also clear evidence of openness on his part to the gentiles: When he was accosted by a Roman officer for help for his servant, Yeshua was shaken and said, "I have never found anyone in Israel with faith like this!" (Matt 8:10). When Yeshua was in the gentile country around Tyre and Sidon, and a Canaanite woman pleaded with him to help her afflicted daughter, he at first ignored her, then said that he was "sent only to the lost sheep of the people of Israel." She persisted, however, in an even brash manner. Yeshua was obviously stunned and, having been confronted with his narrow nationalistic view by this pagan woman, relented and complied with her request.

Much more evidence than this we do not have, largely because the life of Yeshua was brutally cut short early in his manhood, thirty to thirty-three years old. That this is all the evidence we have is also due to the fact that his followers were obviously bent upon spreading his "Good News" and were not particularly interested in his attitude toward other religions. However, we can draw some probable conclusions both from the evidence above of Yeshua's openness to gentiles (not all Jewish schools of that time were open to the value of gentiles—for example, the then-dominant school of Pharisees, the Shammaites, despised gentiles) and the fact that his followers almost immediately moved into gentile areas. Thus, there was clearly a universalist quality about the attitude of Yeshua and his followers—which reflected the long-existing universalistic strand in Judaism.

How this attitude would have developed had Yeshua lived a few decades longer, or what his response would have been had he then encountered a profound devotee of Buddhism (there is evidence that there were Buddhists in the Near East around that time), is something that one can only muse about: If the trajectory of an openness to learning from those of other religions evidenced in the scraps of Gospel evidence that we have held true to course, the world would probably have been the beneficiary of a profound religious dialogue that we are only beginning to approximate today.

What are the meaning and implications of dialogue today? One of the most dramatic elements of today's paradigm shift is the radical reversal by the majority of Christianity away from an imperialistic debate-oriented stance toward non-Christians to a dialogue-oriented one. This can be seen on all levels, scholarly, grassroots, and institutional—the latter, for example, in a number of official documents from various Protestant denominations, but in its most influential form in the documents of the Catholic Church at Vatican II and subsequently.

The Council stated that "Catholics are to be keen on collaborating with all [persons] of good will . . . They are to enter into dialogue with them, approaching them with understanding and courtesy."390 In his very first encyclical (1964), Pope Paul VI wrote: "Dialogue is demanded nowadays . . . It is demanded . . . by the maturity man has reached in this day and age."[264] In 1968 the Vatican Secretariat for Dialogue with Unbelievers wrote, "Doctrinal dialogue should be initiated with courage and sincerity, with the greatest freedom," and added these stunning words: "Doctrinal discussion [must] recognize the truth everywhere, even if the truth demolishes one so that one is forced to reconsider one's own position, in theory and in practice."[265] This is not the place to repeat my earlier reflections on interreligious, interideological dialogue.[266]

Dialogue as a key to an ever-expanding future of deepening knowledge of reality, including Ultimate Reality, is an insight that is sweeping through Christianity—and through it into all the religions and ideologies of the world. It is creatively transforming Christianity, and will do so even more profoundly in the future. Thus, Christianity has two unique gifts to offer the world in the third millennium, one formal and one substantive and personal. The first is "Dialogue," the key to a never-ending creative future, and, in that dialogue, Christianity's always vital and vitalizing Source: Yeshua.

---

264. Vatican II, *Decree on the Apostolate of the Laity*, no. 14.

265. *Humanae personae dignitatem*, 1007, 1010.

266. See, e.g., the *Journal of Ecumenical Studies*; Leonard Swidler, John Cobb, Jr., Paul Knitter, and Monika Hellwig, *Death or Dialogue? From the Age of Monologue to the Age of Dialogue* (Philadelphia: Trinity, 1990); and Swidler, *After the Absolute*.

Interim Conclusion III

In these brief sketches of what might be hoped for in the dialogue between Christians and five of the other major world religions (there are also other important major religious dialogue partners, such as Taoism, Primal Religions, to say nothing of more "regional" ones, such as Jainism, Sikhism, Shintoism), the stress has been on searching out possible areas of commonness. This is only appropriate, given humanity's long history of mutual antagonism or at least indifference. However, it must also be borne in mind that it is an ever fuller grasp of reality that is being sought in dialogue, not a sentimental projection of false togetherness. The differences must also be discerned—the *real* differences—for which a concomitant and dialectical discernment of commonalities is also needed, and it is precisely this that has been so predominantly lacking—hence, the warranted stress on it here.

The discernment of real differences is not something to be disparaged but, on the contrary, to be appreciated, if the differences are ultimately complementary or analogous, for they then will provide an enrichment, expansion, of our perceiving of reality, and living accordingly. It is only those differences that are ultimately seen as contradictory on fundamental issues of what it means to be fully human and are life-threatening that present pressing problems and cause deep concern—and demand proportionate decision and action.

Dialogue with Ideologies: Marxism

As indicated in the beginning, ideology is here understood in its value-neutral sense as an "explanation of the meaning of life and how to live accordingly," which is not ultimately based on a transcendental element. Such ideologies tend to be some kind of nontheistic humanism. Sometimes these will have an organized expression, as in ethical and humanist societies, and sometimes they will not. Clearly, the most organized, thought-out, and widespread such ideology is Marxism (even though since 1990 it has waned drastically), and thus dialogue with it will merit our attention here. However, with Marxism the situation is somewhat ambiguous in that there are many persons who have identified themselves as Marxists, and even very active and influential members of Communist parties, who did not espouse the atheistic philosophy of Marx and might even have been prominently practicing Christians. This complicated the situation for the "purists" of both the Marxist and the religious camps, but for the rest it presented a very interesting reality that offered a great deal of potential for creativity or destructiveness, depending on one's perspective.

There was in the past a substantial Christian-Marxist dialogue—though, as noted, many of the former actual or potential Marxist dialogue partners have disappeared from the scene in Eastern Europe. In some ways, this dialogue was similar to the interreligious dialogues, but in other ways it was quite different, one of the fundamental reasons for which was the fact that Marxism was essentially very intimately bound up with politics.

A Survey History of the Dialogue

What came to be called the Christian-Marxist dialogue began in 1964. Of course there were roots of the dialogue that went back earlier, but before that time conditions simply were not favorable to the growth of interideological dialogue between Christianity and Marxism. Things happened on both sides in the early 1960s that provided the atmosphere for a fruitful encounter wherein persons from both sides sincerely wanted to learn from each other—in short, an atmosphere conducive to dialogue: de-Stalinization and the development of "peaceful coexistence" on the one hand, and the pontificate of Pope John XXIII (1958–63) and Vatican II (1962–65) on the other. John XXIII's two encyclicals, *Mater et magistra* and *Pacem in terris*, both of which breathed a much more irenic attitude toward socialism and those who espoused differing ideologies, as long as they were "persons of good will," contributed significantly to the new, positive atmosphere. So did John's receiving of Soviet leaders and other sympathetic actions and statements. Vatican II had an immense positive impact on the attitude, first of all of Catholics, but indirectly also on many more Christians, and even non-Christians, toward interreligious and interideological dialogue. Three Vatican Secretariats were set up to foster dialogue: with fellow Christians, with members of other religions, and with nonbelievers.

It was this latter Secretariat for Nonbelievers that issued the extraordinary document on dialogue with nonbelievers that was partially quoted at the beginning of this book: its whole purpose was to encourage Christians to engage in serious dialogue with nonbelievers. It is worth recalling again some of its most salient points here:

> All Christians should do their best to promote dialogue between persons of every class, as a duty of brotherly and sisterly charity suited to our progressive and adult age . . . The willingness to engage in dialogue is the measure and the strength of that general renewal which must be carried out in the Church, which implies

a still greater appreciation of liberty ... recognizing the truth everywhere, even if the truth demolishes one so that one is forced to reconsider one's own position, in theory and in practice, at least in part ... In dialogue the truth will prevail by no other means than by the truth itself. Therefore the liberty of the participants must be ensured by law and reverenced in practice.[267]

As a consequence, in 1964 Christian-Marxist dialogue "broke out" almost simultaneously in a number of European countries: Czechoslovakia, Italy, West Germany, and France.

Joseph Hromadka, a theologian of the Evangelical Church of the Czech Brethren, was a pioneer of this dialogue on the Christian side. Already in the early 1930s he initiated a number of discussions on the relationship between Christianity and Marxism. The Czech Communist Party did not respond then; however, practical cooperation did ensue during the Nazi occupation period. After the Communist takeover of the Czech government in 1948, the oppressive mood of the Communists was too dominant to allow for any dialogue. Still, Hromadka took a largely positive attitude toward the virtues of socialism, as exemplified, for instance, in his 1958 book, *The Gospel for Atheists*, and his 1964 book *The Field Is This World*,[268] which also encouraged direct dialogue with Marxists.

Meanwhile, Marxist philosopher Milan Machovec of the Charles University of Prague began in 1957 to treat the work of outstanding Christian thinkers in his seminars—despite internal resistance. In the same year he wrote his *The Meaning of Human Life*, but he did not venture to publish it until 1965.[269] Face-to-face dialogues began in 1964, when Machovec invited prominent foreign Christian theologians to his seminars for dialogue, including Charles West of Princeton, Albert Rasker of Leiden, Heribert Braun of Mainz, and Gustave Wetter of Rome; such Czech Christians as Hromadka, Jan Lochman, Milan Opocensky, and others were also involved. "Machovec is one of the giants of the Christian-Marxist dialogue and per-

---

267. *Humanae personae dignitatem*, 1003, 1010.

268. Cited in Paul Mojzes, "Christian-Marxist Dialogue in Eastern Europe: 1945–1980," *Occasional Papers on Religion in Eastern Europe* 4 (July 1984) 31. In much of what follows in this section I am especially indebted to my colleague and co-editor of the *Journal of Ecumenical Studies*, Paul Mojzes, for his work in the above article, in the two special issues of *JES* devoted to the Christian-Marxist dialogue, namely, "Varieties of Christian-Marxist Dialogue," *Journal of Ecumenical Studies* 15/1 (Winter 1978); and "Is Atheism Essential to Marxism? Christian and Marxist Views," *Journal of Ecumenical Studies* 22/3 (Summer 1985); and Paul Mojzes, *Christian-Marxist Dialogue in Eastern Europe* (Minneapolis: Augsburg, 1981).

269. Milan Machovec, *Smysl lidskeho zivota* (Prague: Nakladetelstvi politicke literatury, 1965); German: *Vom Sinn des menschlichen Lebens* (Freiburg: Romback, 1971).

haps its most seminal thinker. His own intellectual productivity is one of the main reasons for the brightness of the meteoric stage of the dialogue . . . his most significant [book] is *A Marxist Looks at Jesus*, undoubtedly the best Marxist scholarly study of Jesus written to date."[270] A number of other Marxist scholars also began to get involved in the dialogue, perhaps the most prominent being Vitezslav Gardavsky, who published "one of the most profound Marxist series of essays on Christianity in *Literarny Noviny* (Prague)" during 1966–67.[271] The dialogue intensified rapidly, both qualitatively and quantitatively, as Czech society liberalized.

A high point was reached when, on April 27–30, 1967, an international dialogue was held in Czechoslovakia at Marianske Lazne (Marienbad), cosponsored by the Section for the Theory of Sociology of Religion of the Czechoslovak Academy of Sciences and the Paulus-Gesellschaft of West Germany and Austria. Some 170 of the most prominent Christian and Marxist scholars attended; in the lectures there was not only criticism but also appreciation of the dialogue partners, as well as self-criticism. Liberalization continued explosively as Alexander Dubcek came to power and the Czechs tried to create "socialism with a human face" in the "Prague Spring" of 1968. During that Spring, many Christian-Marxist dialogues took place, with thousands of participants. The first public dialogue was held in Prague on April 29, with twelve panelists participating. Mojzes reported that somewhere between twelve hundred and three thousand persons attended, and James Will of Evanston, Illinois, who was present, said the dialogue was "very open and spirited."[272] Other such public dialogues continued throughout the "Prague Spring," until August 21, 1968, when the invasion by Soviet and Warsaw Pact troops brought them to an end.

The invasion was a terrible blow to the dialogue not only in Czechoslovakia but also throughout the world. Nevertheless, despite the fact that Machovec was stripped of all his teaching functions and expelled from the Party, along with his like-minded Marxist colleagues, and that "it became clear that the devastating change would turn the country into the most oppressed Soviet satellite," a number of Czechs, both Christians and Marxists, continued the dialogue—mostly from exile.[273] Within the country silence and oppression reigned: "Many Christians and Marxists remember

270. Milan Machovec, *A Marxist Looks at Jesus* (Philadelphia: Fortress, 1971); quotation from Mojzes, "Christian-Marxist Dialogue," 31–32.

271. These articles were later published in book form in English: Vitezslav Gardavsky, *God Is Not Quite Dead* (Harmondsworth, UK: Penguin, 1973).

272. Mojzes, "Christian-Marxist Dialogue," 33.

273. E.g., the Marxist Jaroslav Krejci, who emigrated to England, and Jan Lochman, who then taught at the theological faculty of the University of Basel.

with longing the days when they carried out a mutual engagement in the spirit of constructive criticism . . . Such conditions would arise again almost immediately if the heavy hand of Soviet intervention were lifted. For the time being prospects for that are very bleak. It remains the destiny of the protagonists of the dialogue to suffer together."[274]

In Italy, too, the Christian-Marxist dialogue began in a public way in 1964, this time with the publication of a book *(Il dialogo alla prova)* with essays by five Christian thinkers and five Marxist thinkers, co-edited by a Marxist, Lucio Lombardo Radice, and a Christian, Mario Gozzini.[275] Lombardo Radice, a professor of mathematics and a member of the Central Committee of the Italian Communist Party, has been described as "one of the initiators and most vigorous promoters of the dialogue between Marxism and Christianity."[276] Among his many subsequent writings and lectures for this cause was the 1968 book he authored in conjunction with Milan Machovec and Garaudy, *Marxisti di fronte a Gesu* (Marxists Face Jesus).[277]

The roots of the dialogue go much farther back in Italy. To begin with, Antonio Labriola, "the father of Italian scientific Marxism who laid the theoretical basis for an original Italian Marxism," had already in a 1897 letter to George Sorel attacked "the sterile anti-clericalism of the radical Socialist and insisted strongly that the Catholic world be taken seriously."[278] The great intellectual of Italian Communism, Antonio Gramsci, also pushed the ideal of dialogue with Catholicism during the 1920s and 1930s, though with little success; that began to come only with the cooperation in the anti-Fascism/Nazism efforts during the war. There an extraordinary thing happened.

A group of young Catholic activists became involved in the resistance movement. In 1941 they founded the "Sinarchic Cooperative Party" (*Partito Cooperativista Sinarchico*). After a year they changed their name to the "Communist Christian Party," and after the fall of the Fascist government on September 8, 1943, they changed it once more to the "Communist Catholic Movement." Under intense pressure from the Vatican, they changed their name for a last time to the "Christian Left Party," but, even then, under the

274. Mojzes, "Christian-Marxist Dialogue," 34.

275. Lucio Lombardo Radice and Mario Gozzini, eds., *Il dialogo alla prova* (1964).

276. Vittorio Messori, *Ipotesi su Gesu* (Turin: Societa Editrice Internazionale, 1976) 14; remark by the editors—Lombardo Radice wrote the preface.

277. Lucio Lombardo Radice, Milan Machovec, Roger Garaudy, *Marxisti di fronte a Gesu* (1968).

278. Lecture by Alceste Santini at a Seminar on Ecumenism from Temple University led by Leonard Swidler, at the Centro Pro Unione in Rome in May, 1978, published as, "The History of a Dialogue," in Swidler and Grace, *Catholic-Communist Collaboration in Italy*, 69–77.

threat of excommunication by the Vatican—which of course would have made their party politically ineffective—they dissolved the party in December, 1945, and urged their members to join the Communist Party of Italy (PCI).[279]

In the national assembly of the PCI from December, 1945, to January, 1946, the following article was inserted into the constitution of the party: "All Italian citizens of 18 years of age can be members of the PCI, independently of their race, religious faith, and philosophical convictions, provided that they accept the political program of the party and bind themselves to work for its realization." Hundreds of thousands of practicing Catholics and Protestants since then joined the PCI. For example, the President of the Protestant Church of Italy in the early 1980s, the Rev. Sergio Aquilante, was a life-long member, as were his parents before him; Antonio Tató and Giglia Tedesco, husband and wife, were among the members of the above-described group of Communist Catholics who joined the PCI. In 1961 both became members of the Central Committee of the PCI; he also became the personal political secretary of Enrico Berlinguer, the Secretary General of the PCI until his death in 1983, and she was a Senator of Italy since 1962, and a Vice President of the Italian Senate (dying in 2007). In Italy, the dialogue continued.

In West Germany and Austria the dialogue was initiated and led by the Paulus-Gesellschaft under the leadership of the Catholic priest Erich Kellner. German Marxist Ernst Bloch spoke at the Munich conference of the Paulus-Gesellschaft in the Spring of 1964, and that Fall the Polish Marxist philosopher and member of the Central Committee of the Polish United Worker's Party (Communist), Adam Schaff, spoke at another of their conferences in Cologne. There were further conferences at Salzburg, Austria, in 1965; Herren Chiemsee, West Germany, in 1966; and Marianske Lazne, Czechoslovakia, in 1967. There was one Marxist participant at each of the first two conferences, but the Marxist participation steadily increased, reaching its highpoint at the 1967 conference. The Paulus-Gesellschaft also sponsored a youth congress in Bonn in the Fall of 1968, but, since that was just after the Soviet invasion of Czechoslovakia, Marxist participation dropped off dramatically. and the Paulus-Gesellschaft suspended meetings until 1975. That year they sponsored a conference in Florence, and in 1977 another one in Salzburg, but Marxist involvement was modest.

Politically, Marxism was more or less absorbed and significantly modified by the Social Democratic Party in West Germany; there were also

---

279. Lecture at above Seminar by Antonio Tatò, in "Catholic Communists 1938–1946," in ibid., 79–90.

various splinter communist parties, but they were politically ineffectual—much as in the U.S. Hence, the dialogue in West Germany was conducted largely by intellectuals on both sides.

In France, however, the Communist Party was a significant political force—the socialists even more so, of course, as was visible in the presidency of François Mitterand. In 1936 the then-Secretary General of the French Communist Party (PCF), Maurice Thorez, made a radio speech in which he said, "We stretch out our hand to you, Catholic worker, employee, tradesman, peasant; we who are laic stretch out our hand to you because you are our brother and you, like us, are burdened with the same cares."[280] However, because the PCF followed the Moscow line so closely in the years after World War II, this invitation was viewed with extreme skepticism.

With the new conditions of the early 1960s, however, French Marxists, particularly in the person of Garaudy, also joined in the public dialogue. Garaudy had been a Senator and a Vice President of the French National Assembly, Director of the Center for Marxist Study and Research in Paris, member of the Politbureau of the PCF, and Professor of Philosophy at the University Institute of Poitiers. He, along with Christian theologians Johannes Metz and Rahner, spoke at the 1965 Salzburg dialogue sponsored by the Paulus-Gesellschaft, and later that same year his lecture was published in greatly expanded form as a book, *De l'anatheme au dialogue*.[281] Also in 1965, Garaudy was invited to lecture at the Catholic university at Louvain, Belgium, and at St. Michael's College of the University of Toronto on the Christian-Marxist dialogue. For the next several years he carried on an intense dialogue with a number of Christian theologians on both sides of the Atlantic, including a dialogue with Paul van Buren of the Religion Department at Temple University in 1966 that I organized.[282]

However, despite his powerful position within the PCF, after the August, 1968, Soviet invasion of Czechoslovakia, Garaudy he was outspokenly critical of the Soviet Union and was expelled from the PCF. He continued to be active in the dialogue for a number of years thereafter, but of course with much less effectiveness, until in 1975 he ceased identifying himself as an atheistic Marxist. He eventually converted to Catholicism and finally to Islam. Nevertheless, his impact as a Marxist was massive, and his contribution was substantive, so it merits some reflection below.

---

280. Cited in Francis Murphy, "Milestones of Christian-Marxist Dialogue in France," in Mojzes, *Varieties of Dialogue*, 139.

281. Garaudy, *From Anathema to Dialogue*.

282. See Roger Garaudy, "Christian-Marxist Dialogue," *Journal of Ecumenical Studies* 4 (Spring 1967) 207–22.

In many ways Yugoslavia was the country where the most creative and continuous Christian-Marxist dialogue was carried on. The first "quasi-dialogue" took place on March 28, 1967, in the Student Center of Zagreb between the Catholic theologian Mijo Skvorc and the Marxist philosopher and author of the book *Philosophy and Christianity*, Branko Bosnjak, on the topic of his book. "About 2,500 people attended. Though the two speakers were polite to one another the conversation can be best described as a polemic. Yet the symbolic value of the meeting, attesting to the openness of Yugoslav society, was great."[283] A number of Christian and Marxist thinkers, however, subsequently attended some of the dialogues sponsored by the Paulus-Gesellschaft and learned there what a dialogue really should be like. Then, just as the Christian-Marxist dialogue closed down everywhere else in the world in the wake of the Soviet invasion of Czechoslovakia, a most creative dialogue was launched in Yugoslavia and lasted in its public, relatively unfettered form until 1972.

It should be noted that in the beginning it was the Marxists who initiated the dialogue, which, since they were in the position of power, was quite understandable. However, after 1972, when the dialogue was forced out of the public into the private sphere because of restraints placed on the Marxist participants by their Party—though it also continued to some extent in print—it was the Christians who showed a greater willingness to continue the dialogue. In this case they had less to lose by going counter to Party directives. Also important to keep in mind is the fact that, for all practical purposes, it was only the Catholic Christians who engaged in the dialogue. The Orthodox churches, comprising about 40 percent of the population, and the tiny Protestant churches, making up less than one percent of the population, avoided the dialogue.

Despite the various restrictions, the dialogue continued creatively in Yugoslavia and spilled over into the wider world, to a large extent through the efforts of Mojzes and the *Journal of Ecumenical Studies*. Mojzes noted that

> the Yugoslav dialogue has an astonishingly broad base among intellectuals . . . Though the dialogue is still dependent on the internal political situation it is by no means dead. It is agreed by nearly all participants in the dialogue that there are no lasting theoretical obstacles to it. Only political circumstances and historical encumbrances hinder it. The de-dogmatization of theology and of Marxist theory has largely taken place among thinkers, who, however, are not fully trusted either by the party

283. Mojzes, "Christian-Marxist Dialogue," 36.

bureaucracy or ecclesiastical hierarchy . . . Only through a long and protracted struggle will forces favorable to the dialogue have a chance to assert themselves and tilt the precarious dialogue in the direction of taking a firm hold as the main means of Christian-Marxist interaction.[284]

In Hungary after the Communist takeover in 1948, grave oppression of the churches followed for many years, including after the 1956 Soviet military's crushing of the political reform movement under Imre Nagy. This hostile spirit continued until the 1980s, when, as part of a general liberalization of Hungarian Marxism, relations with the churches also began to improve. The leading intellectual Marxist in this liberalization was philosopher Joseph Lukacs, who unfortunately died suddenly in 1987. His influence, however, along with other causes, had already had their irenic effect, so that in June, 1988, it was stated publicly by a group of Hungarian Marxist intellectuals that now 90 percent of Hungarian Marxist intellectuals (not to be confused with the *apparatchiks*) were of the liberal humanist sort—and all available evidence seemed to support the statement. It was this dramatic shift that led to the organizing of the Christian-Marxist dialogue in June, 1988, in Budapest on "Changes in the Evaluation of Religion and the Churches in the Last Decade in Hungary and the U.S.A." The effect of that dialogue was so positive that a subsequent dialogue was arranged for late in 1989 in Washington, DC, on "Christian and Marxist Views on Human Rights: An American-Hungarian-Yugoslav Dialogue."

I organized that Washington conference, which took place September 29–October 5, 1989.[285] However, by then the collapse of communism was already underway, and as a consequence the conference ended up having to be described as "between Christians of various persuasions" and "those raised and trained in Marxism . . . [for] being brought up and trained in a Marxist ideology does not mean that such scholars are automatically convinced Marxists."[286] Several of the "Marxists," once they got to Washington, no longer described themselves as Marxists.

The dialogue in the rest of the Eastern European Socialist countries was not sufficiently extensive to merit detailing here. In Poland, until the rise and demise of Solidarity in the early 1980s, there was a "carefully managed dialogue in order to facilitate cooperation in recognition of each

---

284. Ibid., 39.

285. See Leonard Swidler, ed., *Human Rights: Christians Marxists and Others in Dialogue* (New York: Paragon, 1991).

286. Leonard Swidler, "Introduction," in ibid., x.

other's strength,"²⁸⁷ but its future remained cloudy—until the extraordinary revolution in 1989 that brought Solidarity to power. In the other countries, besides Czechoslovakia and Yugoslavia, where true dialogue existed, no dialogue ever existed, that is, in the U.S.S.R., Bulgaria, Romania, or East Germany. The effect of Gorbachev's "openness," *glasnost*, and "restructuring," *perestroika*, policies not only on Christian-Marxist relations but also on the whole political-social situation in Eastern Europe was overwhelming and quickly led to the collapse of communism and the transformation of not only Eastern Europe but also the former Soviet Union.

There was also been some dialogue in Spain and England but not sufficient to warrant discussion here.

In China there has been no formal dialogue, although, with the rejection of strict Maoism starting under the leadership of Deng Xiaping in the 1980s, the then-tiny Christian population (six million?), along with Buddhists, Taoists, Muslims, etc., began to enjoy considerable religious freedom. The churches, temples, and mosques were/are jammed with people as they seldom are in Europe. The Director of the Institute of Religion of the Shanghai Academy of Social Sciences, Xian Zhitian, noted in 1986 that the Party and state had adopted a series of policies that included "implementing the policy of freedom of religious belief, resolutely rejecting any suggestion or practice of abolishing religion by administrative or other compulsory means and consistently protecting the right of citizens to religious freedom."²⁸⁸ (Nevertheless, restrictions continued to exist regionally and locally, depending on the bureaucrats involved.) However, for the first time, in August, 1987, at Igls, Austria, a Chinese Marxist philosopher, Che Ming Zhou, participated in a Christian-Marxist dialogue organized by Paul Mojzes.

Even before that, however, in 1984 one young Chinese scholar

> had the chance to take part in a project which was jointly sponsored by a university in Yugoslavia and my home university. The project brought together several students of Marxism and Confucianism to write a book on Marxist and Confucian views of being human. At that time Professor Leonard Swidler was

---

287. Mojzes, "Christian-Marxist Dialogue," 20. For further information on Christian-Marxist encounter, particularly in Yugoslavia, Poland, and East Germany, see Nicholas Piediscalzi and Robert G. Thobaben, eds., *Three Worlds of Christian-Marxist Encounters* (Philadelphia: Fortress, 1985).

288. Xiao Zhitian, "A Tentative Enquiry into the Problem of the Compatibility between Religion and Socialist Society in China," *SASS Papers*, ed. Editorial Board of *SASS Papers* of Shanghai Academy of Social Sciences (Shanghai: The Publishing House of Shanghai Academy of Social Sciences, 1986) 381.

invited to lecture at my university. The topic of his lecture was the Christian-Marxist dialogue on what it means to be human. To my knowledge, Dr. Swidler was the first Western philosopher to bring the subject of Christian-Marxist dialogue to the attention of the Chinese Marxists after the Cultural Revolution.

The reaction to the subject was dramatic. The official authorities at my university insisted that the goal of Marxism is to eliminate religion from society, and therefore no dialogue should be allowed. Fortunately, the officials who were in charge of censorship did not know English and so [X] and I managed to translate the title of Dr. Swidler's lecture into a less dangerous one in Chinese—"Current Issues in Christianity in the West"—while Dr. Swidler nevertheless lectured [quite oblivious to all this behind-the-scenes activity, I might add—*Swidler*] on the Christian-Marxist dialogue on human nature.

His lecture was very well received and opened up a new avenue of dialogue for the Chinese audience. Since then I have kept my hope alive for a free and open dialogue between Christianity, Confucianism and Marxism.[289]

Once the barrier to dialogue was breached, the inflowing of open conversation seemed to have begun. In 1985 a division of the University of Beijing was set up to teach the academic study of religion (already of course in the late 1960s, just before the onslaught of the Cultural Revolution, an Institute of World Religions was set up within the Chinese Academy of Social Sciences in Beijing; it was placed in "suspended animation" during the decade of the Cultural Revolution and then reemerged, along with similar institutes in Nanjing and Shanghai and lesser ones with a more regional outlook elsewhere throughout the country).

By the Summer of 1988, when I was sent to China on an exchange program by the American Academy of Sciences to lecture on religion, similar divisions for teaching the academic study of religion had been set up in at least four additional universities: the People's University of Beijing, Nanjing University, Fudan University in Shanghai, and Nankai University in Tianjin by 2006.

I lectured at all of those universities, as well as the Institutes of Religion in those cities and universally found an extraordinary interest in the serious study of religion by the faculty involved and even more so by the students. Everywhere I lectured, the room where I spoke, regardless of its size, was

---

289. At that time I wrote: "This Chinese scholar shall remain anonymous throughout these reflections for reasons of security. Freedom of expression has not progressed sufficiently far to allow otherwise."

always jammed with students and faculty to nearly double its capacity: extra chairs were brought in; students sat all around me on the floor of the podium and stood in every other available space and out into the hallway through open doors—and they sat or stood "pin-drop" still for three hours while I lectured and answered questions (everything had to be translated into Chinese). One of my former graduate students in philosophy at Nankai University was appointed an instructor in religion at the People's University of Beijing where in 1987 he offered for the first time an introductory course on religion; 100 students took the course. He offered it again in 1988, and three hundred took it!

In June, 1988, at Hong Kong, several Chinese scholars of Confucianism or Christianity participated in the first international conference on Confucian-Christian dialogue, and in August, 1988, the participation of Chinese Marxists in the Christian-Marxist dialogue, which took place in Granada, Spain, increased to two, Professor Che Ming Zhou again, and Professor Yin Lujun, both of Nankai University.

I was invited to lecture on modern religious thought in the philosophy department of Fudan University in Shanghai during the Summer of 1989, but was prevented from doing so because of the political turmoil that June resulting from the massacre at Tiananmen Square. However, I did return to Fudan for the Summer of 1990 but could lecture only to graduate students, not undergraduates. Since the flourishing of the amazing economic development in China in the twenty-first century, restrictions in the area of religion, among others, have been gradually significantly lifted. Already by 2010 several universities were producing their own reputable PhDs in religious studies.

In Latin America, there was indeed an encounter in the 1980s between Marxism and Christianity, but not so much in dialogue as in a certain amount of collaboration and the assimilation of Marxist social analysis without its atheistic philosophy by Christian theologians in Liberation Theology. All this took place in the wake of the European dialogue and, indeed, was clearly in part made possible by it. It is not irrelevant to note here that Gustavo Guttierez, Leonardo Boff, and other prominent liberation theologians were theologically trained in Europe. Also in Africa, the Christian-Marxist encounter was by way either of mutual opposition or practical collaboration, rather than dialogue.[290]

It remains to say something about the involvement of Americans in the Christian-Marxist dialogue. To begin with, the "Institut für

---

290. See Norman E. Thomas, "Black Africa," and Alice L. Hagerman and Paul Deats, "Cuba," in Zhitian, "A Tentative Enquiry."

Friedensforschung" of the University of Vienna (encouraged by the Catholic Theological Faculty and led by theologian Rudolf Weiler) and the International Peace Institute of Vienna (under the leadership of Vladimir Bruskov from Moscow) jointly sponsored a conference in Vienna in 1971. That was followed by conferences almost each year, usually alternating between socialist and nonsocialist countries. In 1977 this European dialogue branched out to include Americans for the first time. That year the conference took place at Rosemont College (near Philadelphia). Already since 1975 the leadership on the American side has come from Paul Mojzes, and was supported by "Christians Associated for Relationships with Eastern Europe" (CAREE) and the *Journal of Ecumenical Studies*, with conferences continuing to occur almost annually. The American participation in the international conferences (twelve between 1971 and 1984) was substantial, ever since they joined in 1977.

What is particularly interesting, indeed unique, about this series of dialogues is that Soviet participation was also heavy, between five and ten persons each time—most Marxists, but also a single representative of the Russian Orthodox Church. Mojzes described their involvement as follows: "The Soviet participants in these conversations are highly placed scholars or ecclesiastical leaders. They tend to explain their party or church position intelligently and straightforwardly. They do not try to dominate the meetings nor do they engage in surreptitious tactical moves. But their presentations rarely take into account the contributions of the partners beyond perhaps a few quotations used in a "proof-text" manner. They speak and they listen, they defend their positions when under attack, but they are never self-critical and show no independence from the official position [except sometimes in private after a few vodkas—*Swidler*]."[291]

After September, 1986, Mojzes organized an additional series of Christian-Marxist dialogues sponsored by New ERA, an ecumenical outreach organization of the Unification Church in the U.S.—this despite the fact that in general the Unificationists were strongly anti-Communist. The last one was the one I organized on human rights in Washington in the Fall of 1989.

Attitudes toward Dialogue

In the dialogues between Christians and Marxists, each participant has most often felt the need to defend his or her participation and describe what they thought they were doing and why. Thus, "dialogue" was the most discussed topic in the dialogue. Next most discussed was the one partner's

---

291. Mojzes, "Christian-Marxist Dialogue," 17.

reassessment of the other, that is, the Marxist analysis of religion and the Christian analysis of Marxism. Then came joint concern for the human being, followed by such topics as alienation and sin, theism and atheism, Jesus and Marx, history, creativity and freedom, immanence and transcendence, evolution and revolution of society, and the search for peace.

Some participants thought that dialogue should be only for the sake of practical cooperation, that is, ideological dialogue was to be excluded, whereas others believed both practical and ideological dialogue should take place. Still others, without denigrating the need for practical cooperation, saw the ideological dialogue as a constant need of both Christianity and Marxism.

The Czech Marxist Machovec clearly valued ideological dialogue very highly: "The way of truth takes the form of dialogue . . . truth itself consists in dialogue. It may be that the metaphysics of human existence can be realistically grasped only when it is expressed in terms of dialogue."[292] Yugoslav Marxist sociologist Esad Cimic similarly found that it is impossible for Marxists, or anyone else, to enjoy a continuous development of their thought if they do not engage in dialogue with those who differ from them, providing thereby the needed correctives and stimuli for a critical reevaluation of their own presuppositions and goals.[293]

The Hungarian head of the Research Group Studying the Theory of Religion at the University of Budapest, Horvath, stated that there was "no alternative to the dialogue, either in Hungary or anywhere else in the world," and not just on practical issues: "It is now obvious that an exchange of views on the basic questions of ideology . . . is an indispensable element of the dialogue in a broader sense between Christians and Marxists . . . Christian Marxology, or Marxist theory of religion can accomplish an in-depth clarification of its own theoretical position in this very climate of metaphysical dialogue."[294]

Another Yugoslav Marxist sociologist, Zdenko Roter, believed dialogue to be a creative act that leads to an ever richer growth in a dynamic system by providing continuous interaction, complementarity, and fecundation.[295]

292. Machovec, *A Marxist Looks at Jesus*, 38.

293. Esad Cimic, "Politicko i idejno suocavanje s religijskim fenomenon," in Vjekoslav Mikecin, ed., *Religija i drustvo* (Zagreb: Stvarnost, 1969) 186.

294. These remarks, and others below, by Pal Horvath come from his paper delivered in English at the Christian-Marxist dialogue on "Changes in the Evaluation of Religion and the Churches in the Last Decade in Hungary and the U.S.A.," held in the Law School of the University of Budapest, June 20–25, 1988, sponsored by the New Ecumenical Research Association.

295. Quoted in Mojzes, "Christian-Marxist Dialogue," 43.

Andrija Kresic, a Yugoslav Marxist philosopher, argued that dialogue must lead us beyond co-existence—which he found to be just a forced pause in what was ultimately a position of contra-existence—to what he calls pro-existence: "Pro-existence means finding common ways to transcend basic social contradictions by forming a true human community of persons regardless of their ideological or religious orientation."[296]

Czech theologian Jan Lochman argued that "the spirit of authentic Christianity and of authentic Marxism *is* the spirit of dialogue."[297] Bishop Joszef Cserhati of Pecs, Hungary, believed the purpose of the Christian-Marxist dialogue is to share values, to promote the happiness of the people, and to respect each other.[298] Archbishop Frane Franic of Split, Yugoslavia, saw no biblical or theological barrier to Christians—Marxist dialogue; he believed that if both Marxism and Christianity "work more selflessly for the people and live for the other, then there is more hope that some day, which is probably still far off, Marxists and Christians can reach full understanding and agreement."[299]

The anonymous Chinese scholar cited above even saw dialogue as a "way of life":

> Like the world in which Marx lived, our world is still a world of conflicts. However, unlike the world in which Marx lived, in our world dialogue as a desirable way of being human has become a powerful vision for the human future. Not only should dialogue be promoted as a fundamental social virtue and as a pluralistic capacity to enjoy differences and diversities, but, more significantly, dialogue itself is a way of life, a dynamic state of social peace in which differences are not eliminated but communicated without violence. Dialogue, in this sense, should become the social practice of all members of our society.

He insightfully noted that "the real issue is not whether the solutions that Marxism or Christianity offer to the old problems are right or wrong; rather, the real issue is to realize that we have before us the unfinished task of redefining the problems facing our changing world." He then indicated not a solution but a direction, namely, "free, open dialogue in which the

---

296. Andrija Kresic, *Kraljevstvo bozje i komumizam* (Belgrade: Institut za medjunarodni radnicki pokret, 1975) 145–46.

297. Jan Lochman, *Church in a Marxist Society* (New York: Harper & Row, 1970) 172.

298. Joszef Cserhati, "Open Gates," *The New Hungarian Quarterly* 18 (Fall 1977) 49–52.

299. Frane Franic, *Putovi dijaloga* (Split: Crkva u svijetu, 1973) 132.

promotion of humanization is not the practice of a single class, bourgeoisie or workers, a single religion, Christianity or Confucianism, a single social system, socialism or capitalism, but the practice of all of us, the Marxist, the Christian and all others."

It is clear, as the Marxist Kresic explicitly pointed out, that there can be no dialogue between dogmatic Marxists and traditionalist Christians, for they will only reinforce each other's prejudices.[300] As was noted, if there is no minimally deabsolutized understanding of truth, there can be no dialogue. Related to this insight is the observation made by the Marxist Zdenko Roter that, "for politicians, both ecclesiastical and societal, dialogue is treated as an instrument which is to be turned off when those in power perceive that it does not suit their interests."[301] One notorious example on the Christian side was that of Salesian priest Guido Girardi who, for his continued dialogue with Marxists, was fired from the Salesian University in Rome and in September, 1977, was expelled from the Salesian Society. A similar fate overtook Garaudy, Machovec, Adam Schaff, and scores of other Marxist scholars. Dialogue was obviously perceived by the power brokers as an activity dangerous to them—and correctly so!

As pointed out above, in the nineteenth and twentieth centuries a growing number of Christian theologians, church leaders, and activists moved to embrace varying elements of a program of social justice and societal reform, not despite their being Christians, but *because* they were Christians. To this extent they could be said to have embraced much of the program of Marxism and other kinds of socialism. With the massive growth of the influence of Marxist thought after 1917, the Marxist analysis of society and, to some extent, even its critique of religion itself, were taken more and more seriously by a growing number of Christian thinkers and activists.

But, did the dialogue produce any reflection on the part of Marxists that was prompted by what they encountered in Christianity? The answer is yes, at least for those Marxist thinkers who took the dialogue seriously—at considerable risk of course, especially, though not only, in Eastern Europe.

Conclusion

At the beginning of the third millennium there are for all practical purposes no serious Marxists with whom Christians or anyone else can dialogue. There are party power-holders in China, North Korea, and Cuba, and a

---

300. Andrija Kresic, "Marksizam u dijalogu," in *Marksizam i marksisticko obrazovanje danas* (Zagreb: Biblioteka centra, 1973) 39.

301. Cited in Mojzes, "Christian-Marxist Dialogue," 43.

number of power-seeking rebel groups around the world, as well as a number of "arm-chair" academic Marxists in universities of the West, but they are not potential serious intellectual dialogue partners. Many of Marx's ideas have been assimilated—and many found wanting. In any case, its drawing power in the world is waning fast.

Still, the experience of the Christian-Marxist dialogue served a number of purposes, including bringing much of Christianity into the contemporary marketplace of ideas, helping to train it in the value of dialogue even when the challenge is almost overwhelming, and, when the Marxist partners were really serious, such as Garaudy and Golubovic and others, much was learned on both sides. Perhaps the "ideology" dialogue partner of the future will no longer be Marxism but the physical sciences. There are already serious efforts in this direction, led by organizations such as the Zygon Center,[302] Metanexus,[303] and the John Templeton Foundation,[304] as well as Küng's excellent book on the subject, *Der Anfang aller Dinge: Naturwissenschaft und Religion* (Munich: Piper Verlag, 2005), in addition to the fact that Pope Benedict XVI, emeritus, is very interested in that dialogue.

---

302. See http://zygoncenter.org/ for detailed information.
303. See http://www.metanexus.net/ for detailed information.
304. See http://www.templeton for detailed information.

5

Dialogue in the World

In this section I wish to take up several major issues of how dialogue can and should function "in the world," that is, in at least some of the major areas of human endeavor. This will not be anywhere near an exhaustive treatment of an exhaustive list of the major areas of human endeavor. Rather, I hope that my reflections here will be of sufficient breadth and depth to give the reader a feel for how dialogue should profoundly impact our world. I will deal with five areas, namely, human rights, politics, law, ethics, and education—but, even then, only with certain aspects of those huge areas.

Human Rights: A Historical Overview

A human right is a claim to be able and allowed to perform an action because one is a human being—not because one is a citizen or is permitted in law or has a grant from the king or the pope or for any other reason. To claim a right simply on the basis that one is a human is already a revolutionary act. Just as revolutionary is the notion that what it means to be human is an unending developing process, which implies that those things which can be claimed as rights on the basis of one's humanity are not statically fixed. Because the human person is a historical being, and therefore changing, so, too, human rights are historical realities and therefore changing.

The idea of human rights as we understand it today is something that has developed in Western civilization. It is not that no other civilization has been concerned with the human. Confucianism, for example, can be said to be a kind of humanism *par excellence*, but even there the human being had rights only insofar as one occupied a certain position in society. The person had rights not as a human being as such, but as a son, father, brother, or whatever. The idea of human rights, however, is based on the affirmation of a certain level of individualism wherein the individual person would be valued for one's own sake, not just as a relationship to others.

The Pillars of Western Civilization—and Human Rights

Though it is only in modern times that our notion of human rights has developed, it has its foundations in the two pillars of Western civilization: Greco-Roman culture and Judeo-Christian religion.

Plato, Aristotle, the Stoics, and others in Hellenistic civilization developed the notion of a natural law, under whose jurisdiction the human fell. It was the Greeks who created the ideal and at least partial reality of democracy, wherein the citizen had certain fundamental rights simply by being born into the society. Nevertheless, the Stoics, starting with their founder Zeno, like the Confucians, also thought of humanity in hierarchical orders—which appear in the New Testament as the (in)famous Household Codes in the deutero-Pauline and pseudo-Petrine letters. At the bottom of society were the slaves, then came children, then women, then free male adults.

Perhaps the greatest contribution of the Romans to Western civilization was the fantastic development of law. However, as they absorbed more alien peoples into their empire they did not apply their Roman civil law to them but their own indigenous law as far as possible. This differentiation also turns up in the New Testament when Paul, though a proud Jew, claims the right to be tried under Roman civil law because he is also a Roman citizen. Nevertheless, the Romans found many fundamentals of law that applied across all nations, a *ius gentium*, or "common law of all humans," *commune omnium hominum ius*, as the third-century Roman jurist Gaius phrased it. Here, indeed, is a basis for claiming a right simply on the grounds of one's humanity, for at the foundation of all is nature, which can be discovered by reason—which only humans have.

The second pillar of Western civilization and essential foundation of the idea of human rights is the Judeo-Christian religion. It begins with the beginning of the Hebrew Bible, the story of creation. All ethnic groups have come up with their own creation stories, covering the largest imaginable range of possible explanations. What was special about the Hebrews' explanation of the origin of the world was their claim that everything came from one source. There were not many gods who were responsible for the various parts of the world about us, as the different kinds of polytheism explained. Rather, the Hebrews argued, there was just one Source, one God of all reality, and all reality flowing from God was good; the source of evil in the world—and its presence was as obvious to the ancient Hebrews as it is to us—was humankind.

An important point to notice here is the claim that, because there was only one Source of all reality, the order encoded into all reality would also be one, and that included humankind, God's crowning creation, God's "image," *imago Dei*. Humans would live in paradise, a well-ordered "garden of delight," if they would simply follow the instructions, the order, God had structured into their very being. That meant that all humans were to be treated with the same reverence and respect, because they were all created by the one God, and God created them all good and in God's image.

Unlike the other ancient nations, which were polytheistic, and hence had one set of rules by which to treat their own people and another set for other peoples, the Hebrews were committed, at least in theory, to treating all human beings by the same ethical rules. This is the burden of the phrase "ethical monotheism," which describes the unique place the Hebrew religion held among all the religions of the ancient world. Also key in the creation story is the description of humankind's being created in the image of God—hence, having infinite worth and dignity. Here, then, are the two elements of the Judeo-Christian root source of the modern notion of human rights—ethical monotheism and *imago Dei*.

Religious Liberty

Because in the ancient world, and in many instances even into late modern times, the nation and its religion were largely congruent, the degree of religious liberty granted is an important—though not only—touchstone of the advance of the notion of *human* rights. Also, because religion is such a foundational element of a person's humanity, granting persons the right to practice their own religion approaches granting them that right on the grounds of their humanity. This again makes religious liberty an important bellwether of the notion of human rights. In this context the Christian Church started out gloriously, only to slide into the mire of power corruption. In the pre-Constantinian era, Christian writers laid vigorous claim to religious liberty—and, from the fiery pen of Tertullian—even the term "human right": "It is a fundamental human right, a privilege of nature that all human beings should worship according to their own convictions; one human person's religion neither harms nor helps another. It is not proper to force religion. It must be undertaken freely, not under pressure."[1]

In a way, a high point of religious liberty, and thus much of the basis of human rights, was reached publicly with the universal declaration for the whole Roman Empire in the Edict of Milan (313 CE) by Emperor Constantine: "We should therefore give both to Christianity and to all others

---

1. *Ad scapulam*, Migne, ed., *Patrologia Latina*, 1:699.

free facility to follow the religion which they may desire."[2] This moment of freedom was, however, short-lived, for in 380 CE the Edict of Thessalonica was issued by Emperor Theodosius, stating, "It is our will that all the peoples who are ruled by the administration of Our Clemency shall practice that religion which the divine Peter the Apostle transmitted to the Romans."[3] Even that great theological light of the West, Augustine, wrote against following one's conscience, except when it was correct—and in religious/ethical matters Christianity of course had a monopoly on correctness. Fortunately that even greater theological light of the West, Thomas Aquinas, following his great teacher Albert the Great, argued in favor of always following one's conscience, even if the pope claimed it was erroneous.[4]

America's Contribution

After the demise of the Western Roman Empire and the slow emergence of Western European civilization, the long struggle for human rights took a major step toward modern reality in thirteenth-century England when the barons forced the power-hungry King John to grant them a series of rights written in the *Magna Charta* (1215 CE). Although many specific rights were here spelled out, perhaps the most fundamental was that no punishment could be imposed without due process of law. Obviously, human reason was the foundation stone, thereby providing a solid basis for the building of the full-blown idea of human rights. The sixteenth-century Protestant Reformation—particularly in its so-called Radical wing—moved agonizingly in the direction of religious liberty, with mainline Protestants eventually establishing religious liberty, though with some restrictions, in the Netherlands under William the Silent.

It was most of all in the "new world" that religious liberty developed. It appeared first in the 1632 Charter of Maryland and the practice of the Catholic Cecil Calvert, the second Lord Baltimore, to whom the Charter was granted. In 1663 under the leadership of the Baptist Roger Williams, the tiny colony of Rhode Island was formed with a charter including a guarantee of religious liberty—for all Protestants. This was followed by the

---

2. From the Edict of Milan as contained in *De mortibus persecutorum*, in Migne, ed., *Patrologia Latina*, 7:267–68.

3. *Codex Theodosianus*, XVI, I, 2, in Coleman J. Barry, ed., *Readings in Church History* (Westminster, MD: Newman, 1960) 1:142.

4. The above quotations and a detailed presentation of the question of religious freedom in the history of Christianity can be found in the excellent work, Pius Augustin, *Religious Freedom in Church and State* (Baltimore: Helicon, 1966).

1677 "Concessions and Agreements of West New Jersey" (most probably written by the staunch Quaker and freedom-lover William Penn), which provided for total religious liberty. In 1682 when William Penn founded his own colony, with its first settlement the "City of Brotherly and Sisterly Love," Philadelphia—Greek: *phila*, "love," *adelphia*, "siblings"), he of course included religious liberty in its "Frame of Government," as well as many expanded democratic principles and practices.

Shortly thereafter, events in England moved the cause of human rights forward. King James II became Catholic and was perceived as a threat by many Protestants in England. Consequently, he was deposed in 1688 in the so-called "Glorious Revolution," which brought William of Orange and his wife Mary of England to the throne on condition of granting the various rights listed in the 1689 "Bill of Rights." Although it provided religious liberty only for Protestants, it was a very positive and influential model for subsequent American bills of rights.

It was also at this time that the English philosopher John Locke wrote his influential "Two Treatises on Government," in which he spoke at length about the natural law (building particularly on the work of such scholars as Grotius and Pufendorf), the separation of governmental powers (Montesquieu later spoke of the three separate powers of government: executive, legislative, and judicial), and the right of all to "life, liberty, and property." Locke's two treatises were in a way a philosophical justification of the "Glorious Revolution" and "Bill of Rights" and had a strong influence on subsequent American political developments.

Human-rights matters moved relatively gradually until the last quarter of the eighteenth century. In 1774 the First Continental Congress of the thirteen American colonies issued its "Declaration and Resolves," in which for the first time the law of nature was explicitly made the foundation of rights: "By the immutable laws of nature . . . the following rights . . . life, liberty, and property." Then came the fateful year of 1776, with its "Declaration of Independence" with its paraphrase of Locke: "All men are created equal . . . with certain unalienable rights . . . life, liberty, and the pursuit of happiness."

However, even before the "Declaration of Independence," and formative of it, was the issuance of the "Bill of Rights" of the Constitution of Virginia on June 12, 1776, drafted largely by George Mason. Its words rang out: "All men are by nature equally free and independent, and have certain inherent rights, of which, when they enter into a state of society, they cannot by any compact, deprive or divest their posterity; namely, the enjoyment of life and liberty, with the means of acquiring and possessing property, and pursuing and obtaining happiness and safety . . . All power is vested in, and consequently derived from, the people."[5] Among the many human rights listed were complete religious liberty for all, choice of leaders, due process of law, and, for the first time in any document of constitutional import, freedom of the press. There quickly followed that same year constitutions or bills of rights of Pennsylvania, Delaware, Maryland, North Carolina (all largely patterned on Virginia's "Bill of Rights"), and, most importantly and influentially, the "Declaration of Independence," drafted by Thomas Jefferson, of Virginia.

After winning the War of Independence in 1781, the U.S.A. was governed by the Articles of Confederation, which proved inadequate; thus, in 1787 a new Constitution was drafted and adopted. However, in the process of its acceptance by the various constituent states, the appending of a Bill of Rights was demanded. One was consequently drafted by James Madison (also from Virginia) and submitted to Congress on July 28, 1789—almost simultaneously with parallel events in France—and adopted later that year as the first ten amendments of the U.S. Constitution, known as the American "Bill of Rights"—a succinct list of human rights as then understood.

Revolutionary events were also occurring in France in the latter part of the eighteenth century. Although many basic human rights were viciously violated in the quarter-century of turmoil that was unleashed with the storming of the Bastille on July 14, 1789, a landmark document in the history of human rights was forged almost at the very beginning of the French Revolution—the "Declaration des droits des hommes et citoyens," a French, but now for the first time universalized, version of the Enlightenment's notion of human rights, passed on August 27, 1789. The "Declaration" largely repeated the American and English precedents, as is clear even from the language used: "[It] proclaims, in the presence and under the auspices of the Supreme Being, the following rights of man and the citizen. 1. Men are born and remain free and equal in rights . . . preservation of the natural and inalienable rights of man; these rights are liberty, property, security, and resistance to oppression. 3. The source of all sovereignty resides essentially in the nation . . . Law is the expression of the general will . . . No man may be accused, arrested, or detained except in the cases determined by law, and according to the forms prescribed thereby." As German historian Martin Göhring noted, "It was not wholly without significance that the soldier of freedom, LaFayette, who had fought for the independence of America and

---

5. This citation and the documents previously and subsequently cited or alluded to are found in the extremely helpful work, Richard L. Perry, ed., *Sources of Our Liberties*, rev. ed. (Chicago: American Bar Foundation, 1978) 311.

had been present when the American declaration was proclaimed, was the first to propose a declaration of rights to the National Assembly."[6]

Nineteenth- and Twentieth-Century Developments

Despite the glorious language used in these English, American, and French human-rights documents of the seventeenth/eighteenth centuries, there were still many restrictions on who qualified as human. For example, nonproperty owners in America did not qualify as voters until the second quarter of the nineteenth century, Blacks not until the third quarter, women not until the twentieth century. Further, the understanding not only of "human" but also of "right" underwent a constant evolution—and doubtless will continue to do so. The newly developed twentieth-century claim to the right to work (U.N., 1948 "Universal Declaration of Human Rights," art. 23) is a good example: "The development of this new control over nature—first over external nature and increasingly also over human nature . . . has made possible entirely new dimensions of human self-development, and its apparently illimitable expansion leads to the expectation, at least in the developed countries, that it can release a sufficient potential so that everyone can participate in them—and consequently has a right to participate therein."[7]

Various steps in the expansion of the idea and reality of human rights were taken throughout the nineteenth century and into the twentieth. A major opportunity at the end of World War I was, unfortunately, passed up. In 1919, the U.S. President, Woodrow Wilson, drafted the Covenant of the League of Nations in person, using his own typewriter, incorporating a number of human rights. One of Wilson's proposals was to include an article on religious liberty in the Covenant, but it was scuttled as soon as Japan sought to link it with racial equality and the equality of states. Thus, the League of Nations Covenant contained no mention of human rights, though in fact the League did protect a number of them through the "Minority Protection Treaties."

The United Nations and the Universal Declaration

The next milestone in the internationalizing of human rights was also set down by an American president, Franklin D. Roosevelt, when he delivered

---

6. Martin Göhring, *Weg und Sieg der modernen Staatsidee in Frankreich* (Tübingen: Mohr-Siebeck, 1946) 280.

7. Johannes Schwartländer, ed., *Modernes Freiheitsethos und christlicher Glaube* (Mainz: Grünwald, 1981) 11.

his famous address to Congress on January 6, 1941, on the "Four Freedoms." In it he outlined the four essential freedoms upon which the whole world should be founded: freedom of speech and expression, freedom of religion, freedom from want, and freedom from fear: "Roosevelt was explicit in stressing that these freedoms were to be secured everywhere in the world, that is to say, on a universal basis. He made it clear that traditional freedoms of speech and of worship should go hand in hand with such wider human rights as economic and social welfare and peace and security for all peoples and persons."[8] It is rather striking how Roosevelt anticipated—and influenced?— the development of the so-called three generations of human rights: first generation, civil and political rights; second generation, social and economic rights; third generation, rights of world development and peace.

In January, 1942, the Allied Powers spoke of human rights globally when they claimed that "complete victory over their enemies is essential to defend life, liberty, independence and religious freedom and to preserve human rights and justice in their own lands as well as in other lands."[9] These two statements provided an immediate vision for the framing of the U.N. Charter in San Francisco in 1945. Among the purposes of the U.N., it stated, were: "To achieve international cooperation . . . in promoting and encouraging respect for human rights and for fundamental freedoms for all without distinction as to race, sex, language or religion."

One of the first acts of the U.N. General Assembly, in January, 1946, was to recommend "the formulation of an international Bill of Rights." A year later the newly created U.N. Commission on Human Rights chose Eleanor Roosevelt as its president and immediately set to work on the "Universal Declaration of Human Rights," which was adopted on December 10, 1948.

> It is noteworthy that one of those who played an important part in the formulation of the draft Universal Declaration of Human Rights was Monsignor Roncalli, as he then was, subsequently Pope John XXIII. Monsignor Roncalli was then Papal Nuncio in Paris . . . He often, in conversations with me, expressed the hope that the Universal Declaration would save humanity from another war.
>
> The eminent French jurist and Nobel Peace Laureate, the late René Cassin, has paid eloquent tribute to the assistance

---

8. Theo C. van Boven, "Religious Liberty in the Context of Human Rights," *The Ecumenical Review* 37 (July 1985) 347.

9. Sean MacBride (Nobel and Lenin Peace Laureate, recipient of the American Medal of Justice, and former Minister of Foreign Affairs, Ireland), "The Universal Declaration—30 Years After," in Alan D. Falconer, ed., *Understanding Human Rights: An Interdisciplinary and Interfaith Study* (Dublin: Irish School of Ecumenics, 1980) 8–9.

which Monsignor Roncalli then gave to the French Delegation. This may also possibly explain the fact that some fifteen years later in his Encyclical *Pacem in terris*, Pope John XXIII lays specific reference on the need for a Charter of Fundamental Human Rights.[10]

For eighteen years the U.N. struggled to translate the Universal Declaration into legally binding instruments, which together with the Declaration are known as "The International Bill of Human Rights," namely, the "International Covenant on Economic, Social and Cultural Rights," the "International Covenant on Civil and Political Rights," and the "Optional Protocol to the International Covenant on Civil and Political Rights"—all adopted in 1966. A number of countries have explicitly incorporated large elements of this "Bill of Human Rights" into their own foundational legal documents, and by now it has the force of law in international law (which, other than world opinion, unfortunately does not have an effective enforcing agency).

Many other declarations and conventions on specific dimensions of human rights have been issued since 1948 by the U.N. and regional bodies, such as the Council of Europe. Sadly, a spelled-out declaration on religious liberty did not, as expected, quickly follow the superb *Study of Discrimination in the Matters of Religious Rights and Practices* in 1959 by the U.N. Special Rapporteur Arcot Krishnaswami. It was only in 1981 that the "Declaration on the Elimination of All Forms of Intolerance and of Discrimination Based on Religion or Belief" was passed by the U.N. General Assembly. Nevertheless, it is clear that progress in human rights is—slowly and painfully, and often with a wide breach between theory and practice—being made.

The Catholic Church and Human Rights

The foundation of the claim for human rights is human reason and freedom; along with "animality," they are what make humans human. The search for truth, "which makes us free," is a legacy the Christian Church has from its founder, the Jew Jesus. In very many ways the church was largely true to this legacy in the beginning, but in also very many ways, especially after Constantine, it became largely untrue to this legacy. This was increasingly so in the reaction of much of the Catholic hierarchy to the Protestant Reformation, and most particularly so in its reaction to the Enlightenment and the concomitant human-rights movement. This is not the place to replay the

---

10. Ibid., 9.

dirge of Christian reaction. Let a few notes from the Catholic section alone suffice as a reminder.

As noted above, in 1832, Pope Gregory XVI described liberty of conscience as the "false and absurd, or rather mad principle (*deliramentum*), that we must secure and guarantee to each one liberty of conscience; this is one of the most contagious of errors . . . To this is attached liberty of the press, the most dangerous liberty, an execrable liberty, which can never inspire sufficient horror." His successor from 1846 until 1878, Pius IX, did not hesitate to repeat that massive condemnation at least twice and make it his own. Even as late as the 1950s the American Jesuit John Courtney Murray was silenced by Rome for arguing that there was another, more faithful, line in Catholic tradition.

It is interesting to compare in this regard the language of Gregory and Pius (it is difficult to imagine how it could have been made more *ex cathedra* and, hence, presumably "infallible") on the one hand, with that of Pope John XXIII's *Pacem in terris* and Vatican II's "Declaration on Religious Liberty" on the other: "Man has a natural right . . . to freedom of speech and publication . . . to worship God in accordance with the right dictates of his own conscience and to profess his religion in both private and public: Man is bound to follow his conscience faithfully . . . he must not be forced to act contrary to his conscience. Nor must he be prevented from acting according to his conscience, especially in religious matters . . . Religious freedom in society is in complete harmony with the act of Christian faith."

It is both in the person of John XXIII and Vatican II, which he called into existence, that we finally find the official Catholic breakthrough to religious freedom—and human rights in general. For over a century-and-a-half the papacy fought bitterly against the Enlightenment and the human-rights movement, but with "*Pacem in terris*" in April, 1963, issued only a few weeks before John XXIII's death, the papacy embraced the idea of human rights. John spoke with high praise of the U.N. and stated that "a clear proof of the farsightedness of this organization is provided by the Universal Declaration of Rights," which, as we heard above, he helped shape in 1947–48.

Then John's successor, Pope Paul VI, at the end of Vatican II (1965) called for the drafting of a Constitution for the Catholic Church, appointing a Commission that worked on it for seventeen years. He likewise strongly advocated democracy and rights in the world in general:

> There can be no true democracy without a recognition of every person's dignity and without respect for his or her rights . . . modern forms of democracy must be devised, not only making it possible for each man to become informed and to express

himself, but also by involving him in a shared responsibility. . . . Let each one examine himself, to see what he has done up to now, and what he ought to do. It is not enough to recall principles, state intentions, point to crying injustice and utter prophetic denunciations; these words will lack real weight unless they are accompanied for each individual by a livelier awareness of personal responsibility and by effective action.[11]

The theme of human rights turns up once again in a papal document with great positive stress in the first encyclical of Pope John Paul II, *Redemptor hominis* (1979) where, among a welter of detail, John Paul wrote: "We cannot fail to recall at this point, with esteem and profound hope for the future, the magnificent effort made to give life to the U.N. Organization, an effort conducive to the definition and establishment of man's objective and inviolable rights . . . There is no need for the Church to confirm how closely this problem is linked with her mission in the modern world. Indeed it is at the very basis of social and international peace, as has been declared by John XXIII." He continued in this vein, writing that "the free and responsible participation of all citizens in public affairs . . . is a necessary condition and sure guarantee of the development of the whole individual and of all people,"[12] and later added that the Church "values the democratic system inasmuch as it ensures the participation of citizens in making political choices, guarantees to the governed the possibility both of electing and holding accountable those who govern them, and of replacing them through peaceful means when appropriate"[13] In preparation for the new millennium, he stated: "Without the concerted and united action of all believers—indeed of all men and women of good will—little can be accomplished to make genuine democracy, value-based democracy, a reality for the men and women of the 21st century."[14]

In the same address, John Paul II made an explicit and strong plea for the democratic principle of "Subsidiarity":

> smaller social units—whether nations themselves, communities, ethnic or religious groups, families or individuals—must not be namelessly absorbed into a greater conglomeration, thus losing their identity and having their prerogatives usurped. Rather, the proper autonomy of each social class and organization, each in

---

11. Paul VI, *Octogesima adveniens,* Apostolic Letter, May 14, 1971.

12. John Paul II, *Sollicitudo rei socialis*, December 30, 1987.

13. John Paul II, *Centesimus annus*, May 1, 1991.

14. Message of the Holy Father John Paul II to the Participants in the Sixth Plenary Session of the Pontifical Academy of Social Sciences, February 23, 2000.

its own sphere, must be defended and upheld. This is nothing other than the principle of subsidiarity, which requires that a community of a higher order should not interfere in the internal life of a community of a lower order, depriving the latter of its rightful functions; instead the higher order should support the lower order and help it to coordinate its activity with that of the rest of society, always with a view to serving the common good (cf. *Centesimus Annus*, 48 [May 1, 1991]). Public opinion needs to be educated in the importance of the principle of subsidiarity for the survival of a truly democratic society.

Unfortunately, much of the credibility of John Paul II's frequent preaching of strong pro-human rights, shared responsibility, subsidiarity, and democracy in the secular sphere was severely undercut by his anti-human rights, anti-democracy practice *inside* the Catholic Church. This double standard, among other things, called into existence in 1979–80—a period of severe papal repression—such organizations as Christenrechte in der Kirche, Comité de défense des droits des chrétiens, and the Association for the Rights of Catholics in the Church (ARCC). ARCC produced a "Charter of the Rights of Catholics in the Church," extending the work of the "Universal Declaration of Human Rights" into the Catholic Church. Later, in conjunction with Catholics around the world, it offered a "Proposed Catholic Constitution."[15]

Positive American Catholic Contribution to Human Rights

In December, 1946, just a year and a few months after the end of the Second World War, the Administrative Board of the American Catholic Bishops' official agency, the National Catholic Welfare Conference (the Administrative Board was composed of ten bishops, with Cardinals Samuel Stritch of Chicago and Francis Spellman of New York at the head) issued in the name of the American Catholic episcopate a declaration, "Man and Peace." They argued that the fundamental problem of the post-war period was the understanding of what it meant to be human. They were critical of the practice of the victorious powers (mainly the U.S.S.R.) of not releasing prisoners of war and for forced labor practices and of the Western Allies for succumbing to the totalitarian pressure from the East to drive millions of Germans out of their homes. They called upon all the signatories of the U.N. Charter

---

15. See http://arcc-catholic-rights.org; Leonard Swidler and Herbert O'Brien, eds., *A Catholic Bill of Rights* (Kansas City, MO: Sheed & Ward, 1988); and Leonard Swidler, *Toward a Catholic Constitution* (New York: Crossroad, 1996).

"to work together in the establishment and fostering of respect for human rights and the fundamental freedoms for all, without regard to race, language or religion." They ended with a ringing commitment: "For us . . . it is impossible to remain self-satisfied and actionless while our brothers in the human family groan under tyranny and are hindered in the free exercise of their human rights."

One specific action followed immediately. In January, 1947, a committee made up of laity and bishops appointed by the National Catholic Welfare Conference issued nothing less than a "Declaration of Human Rights,"[16] almost two years before the U.N. proclaimed its "Universal Declaration of Human Rights." In fact, the American Catholic Declaration was handed over to the "Committee on Human Rights of the United Nations," chaired by Eleanor Roosevelt. A comparison of the American Catholic Declaration (which, with fifty articles, is more detailed than the U.N. Declaration's thirty) and that of the U.N. reveals amazing similarities, some passages of the latter being even verbatim that of the former. The Catholic document speaks of human "personal dignity . . . being endowed with certain natural, inalienable rights . . . The unity of the human race under God is not broken by geographical distance or by diversity of civilization, culture and economy."

After the General Preamble, there are four major parts, the first being "The Rights of the Human Person" (eighteen articles): "The dignity of man, created in the image of God . . . is endowed as an individual and as a member of society with rights which are inalienable," which include life, liberty, religion, information and communication, choice of state of life, education. and equal protection of the law regardless of sex, nationality, color, or creed. The other parts are the rights pertaining to the family (nine articles), domestic rights of states (ten articles), and rights of states in the international community (thirteen articles).

This was a chapter of American Catholic history that was almost forgotten. After its initial impact,[17] no one seemed to remember or record

---

16. See "A Declaration of Human Rights. A Statement Just Drafted by a Committee Appointed by the National Catholic Welfare Conference," *The Catholic Action* 29 (February 1947) 4–5, 17; and "A Declaration of Rights. Drafted by a Committee Appointed by the National Catholic Welfare Conference," *The Catholic Mind* 45 (April 1947) 193–96. A German translation appeared in "Eine Charta der Menschenrechte: Eine Denkschrift der Katholiken Amerikas," *Die Furche* 8 (February 1947) 4–5. Both the original American and a German translation, along with an interesting analysis can be found in Gertraud Putz, *Christentum und Menschenrechte* (Innsbruck: Tyrolia, 1991) 322–30, 388–97.

17. Cf. "Basic Schedule of Rights," *Commonweal* 45 (February 14, 1947) 435; "NCWC on Human Rights," *The N.C.W.C. News Service* 86 (February 15, 1947) 538; Dies Villeneuve, "Recent Events," *Catholic World* 164 (March 1947) 562–63.

it, until 1990, yet this is a chapter of history that makes one proud of being an American Catholic. The American Catholic Church here took the lead in promoting human rights on a worldwide basis and probably had a significant influence in the drafting of the U.N.'s "Universal Declaration of Human Rights." This lost chapter of an American Catholic contribution to human rights and to democracy came to light when Dr. Gertraud Putz, an Austrian historian, noted how accidental and labyrinthine her discovery in 1990 of the 1947 American document was. She wrote that she had in her research come across an article in a 1947 Austrian periodical, *Die Furche*, with a German translation of what looked like an American Catholic Declaration of Human Rights, but with no reference to the original. She then wrote:

> The difficult search for the English text shall not remain hidden from the reader. Through a personal contact with Professor Johannes Schwartländer of the University of Tübingen, doubtless the most knowledgeable scholar of the history of human rights, I was directed to an American human rights expert, Professor Leonard Swidler in Philadelphia. The accident that he—who at first also knew nothing of the existence of this Declaration—is married to a historian with whom he discussed the matter made it possible that she then took up the search. In a letter dated April 18, 1990, she responded to my letter and explained the difficulty in finding the Declaration, for it had no listed author under which it could be indexed. However, the fact that Professor Arlene Swidler precisely at that time was giving a course on "American Catholic History" at Villanova University led her to search further, and she ended by writing: "However, I am quite sure I have found the important material by paging through the significant periodicals."[18]

Religion and State

Stating the Question

Union of religion and state? Separation of religion and state? These are two clear positions, each claiming to be the best for the creative welfare of humankind. At least in the mind of the masses, the first position appears to be represented by Islam, the second position by Christianity, and an ambiguous in-between by Judaism in the example of Israel. As with all popular perceptions, there is a substantial element of reality to it, but at the same time

---

18. Putz, *Christentum und Menschenrechte*, 325.

the reality is much more complex than is perceived by the masses—and by masses of intellectuals. Hence, it is important to look at least briefly at the complexity of the relationship between the state and religion in order to address the fundamental question about which relationship between religion and state is the most beneficial to humanity. This will be viewed at with Christianity and Islam as the two prime examples, though Judaism with Israel as a modern experiment will also be noted.

Union of Religion and State All-Pervading

In all past civilizations, religion has been an integral, constitutive element. Among other things, religion supplied the ethical basis on which the authority of the state and law was built. As a result, in all past civilizations there has been a very intimate relationship between religion and state. Very often that relationship was so close that one could speak of the union of religion and state. In that close relationship, religion at times tended to dominate the state, and at other times the state tended to dominate religion. We have seen both in recent times and still today. The Soviet state's domination of Orthodox Christianity was an example of the former; the Ayatollahs' and Mullahs' domination of the state in Iran, of the latter. The relationship of the separation of religion and state is a unique phenomenon in human history that occurred in the modern West—more about that below.

As discussed above, in the early centuries of Christianity in the Greco-Roman world Christian writers were strongly in favor of religious liberty. After the Constantinian embrace of the Christian religion in the fourth century, they quickly switched to the position that the state had the responsibility of seeing that the truth was protected and favored—and of course Christianity had the truth. In theory, no one was to be forced to accept Christianity, but not infrequently the theory was not translated into practice. With the development of medieval Christendom in the western half of the former Roman Empire, almost everyone became Christian, with the exception of the Jews, who for the most part were allowed to continue a separate existence, later often in ghettos.

The history of Islam was not very different. In theory, no individual or community was to be forced to embrace Islam, but in practice the *Jihad*, in the sense of a Holy War against non-Muslim states, not infrequently was launched aggressively. Although the *millet* system allowed non-Muslims within a Muslim-conquered state to practice their religion, the non-Muslims were clearly second-class citizens, which doubtless encouraged conversion to Islam, and surely not the contrary.

At various times during the intertwined history of Christianity and Islam one side or the other pointed, usually with justification, an accusing finger at the other as a brutal aggressor. In fact, neither Christianity nor Islam can claim to have been predominantly the victim and the other the aggressor; the acid of history dissolves any such claim from either side. *Jihad* and the Crusades easily match each other in gratuitous aggressiveness.

Development of the Separation of Religion and State

Something unique in human history, however, began to take place in Western Christianity, in Christendom: the gradual, painful move toward the separation of religion and state. Some might trace its beginnings to the Gregorian Reforms when Pope Gregory VII (1021–85 CE) attempted dramatically and substantially to separate the Church from the power of the Holy Roman Empire and other civil powers. No one at the time promoted the notion of the separation of church and state. Rather, each side attempted to wrest power to their side; witness the thirteenth-century "imperial interregnum" manipulated by the popes (when for fifty years the popes effectively prevented the election of a Holy Roman Emperor), followed soon by the imprisonment of that most authoritarian of all popes, Boniface VIII, by the king of France, Phillip the Fair, at the beginning of the fourteenth century.

It was precisely this mammoth power struggle that encouraged a weariness with the unquestioned assumption of the union of church and state. The Renaissance, with its shifting of interest from the divine to the human, provided a further basis for the gradual questioning of the wisdom of the union of church and state. This questioning manifested itself visibly in the so-called left wing of the sixteenth-century Reformation. The Anabaptists and related sects clearly and vigorously rejected the idea of the union of church and state, for which, of course, they were viciously persecuted by Catholics and mainline Protestants.

In the end, it was the pitting of Catholics and Protestants against each other that magnified the incipient weariness with the consequences of the union of church and state—induced by the earlier struggle between the pope and civil rulers—to the point of the full embrace of the principle of the separation of religion and state during the eighteenth-century Enlightenment. The U.S. Constitution for the first time gave a formal national articulation of the idea of separation of church and state. From that time it spread throughout the West in various juridical expressions and from there increasingly around the globe.

Developments in Islam

Like all previous civilizations, Islam (speaking now of Islam as a civilization, which has the religion Islam as its vital source) initially grew vigorously, plateaued for a time, then, as many Muslim scholars themselves have descried, went into decline. The decline became increasingly apparent from the eighteenth century onward. In the nineteenth and twentieth centuries much of the Islamic world fell under Western colonialism and was increasingly dominated by Christendom, now largely become "the West."

The observation of the decline and present inferiority of Islamic countries is not merely a reflection of Christian prejudice. Doubtless, many Christians unwarrantedly attribute the unprecedented advances of Western civilization mainly to Christianity, not recognizing that it is more the disengaging of Christianity (and all religions and ideologies) from the power of the state that is the main source of those ongoing advances. In fact, Muslim scholars have increasingly been articulate about the depressed state of Islamic countries. For example, in Seyed Othman Alhabshi's book,[19] which explains the background of the newly founded Institute of Islamic Understanding Malaysia, we find the following strong statement: "The Muslim world is currently plagued with almost nothing but negative attributes of a civilization." He then listed some of the "plagues": "underdevelopment, backwardness, poverty, inequitable income and wealth distribution, high inflation, acute illiteracy and serious unemployment, economic and political instability." If possible, even clearer was the comment: "Although eight hundred years was long enough to accumulate a wealth of experience to ward off various human ills, the Muslims declined almost without any rebound till this day."[20]

Recently, several Muslim nations, including Iran, Sudan, and Afghanistan, have tried to regain their former Islamic glory by reuniting religion and state through the embrace of "Islamism" (as noted above, the term that Muslim scholars use rather than the perhaps less accurate Western term, "fundamentalism"). The same goal is being sought by radical Islamists within other Muslim countries, such as Egypt, and in Syria/Iraq. This development took a quantum leap forward in the wake of the disastrous defeat of the anti-Israel Islamic nations in the 1967 Six-Day War with Israel. "An international theological debate was convened in Cairo's Al-Azhar University in the autumn of 1968, where the participants discovered that their failure was due not to Israel's superiority but to their neglect of Islam. A return to

---

19. Seyed Othman Alhabshi, *An Inspiration for the Future of Islam* (Kuala Lumpur: Institute of Islamic Understanding Malaysia, 1994) 8.

20. Ibid., 12.

the faith was urged not only as a source of solace and comfort in time of adversity and loss of orientation, in view of the mounting disillusionment with the West and modernity, but also as a source of inspiration for restoring the old glory."[21]

Unfortunately, rather than regaining former "Islamic Glory," the Islamists were thereby insuring that their nations will remain no more than third-class societies. That fact seems to be dawning slowly even on that bastion of Muslim religious conservatism, Iran—judging from recent struggle by many Iranians to turn away from Islamism and start gradually down the path toward democracy.

The Unique Quality of Western Civilization

When such historians as Arnold J. Toynbee survey the total history of humankind they find that there have been a number of civilizations that have come into existence, flourished, and then declined (Toynbee discerned twenty-six civilizations in human history). Many of them achieved admirable accomplishments, the Greco-Roman civilization being the one best known to Westerners. Its achievements were indeed so great that during the late Renaissance there was a lively debate about whether the Ancients (meaning the Greeks and Romans) or the then-moderns had attained greater cultural heights. However, the Greco-Roman accomplishments were in many regards matched, and in some surpassed, by the Chinese and Islamic civilizations.

However, it is no cultural hubris to be aware that the rising arc of Western civilization—largely derived from a synthesis of the Judeo-Christian tradition, the Greco-Roman tradition, the Germanic tradition, with a significant influence of medieval Islam, and modern science and thought—has reached far beyond where any of the other twenty-five civilizations have gone, in culture, science, politics, economic prosperity, technology, etc. Moreover, Western civilization has now become a global civilization in a way that had never occurred before, and the process of globalization appears to be intensifying in exponential fashion. This is not to discount Western-now-becoming-global civilization's defects, blind spots and seething problems, some of the most critical of which are largely a result of its very accomplishments, such as the population explosion (because of medical and agricultural advances), the ecological crisis (because of technological advances and the population explosion). But, even that illustrates the main

---

21. Raphael Israeli, *Muslim Fundamentalism in Israel* (London: Brassey's, 1993) 8.

point: Western civilization's greatest problems flow not from its weaknesses but from its even more awesome, unparalleled achievements.

The Separation of Religion and State a Vital Key

One of the *essential* elements in the advances of Western civilization in culture, science, politics, economic prosperity, and technology—the likes of which, for all of its massive problems were never before experienced in human history—is the separation of religion from the power of the state. Religion here includes any "ideology" that functions as a religion, such as atheistic Marxism. It is clear to see today in Eastern Europe and the former U.S.S.R. what disaster the union of state and the "religion" of Marxism led to.

Western civilization or, rather, Christendom in the Late Middle Ages began reaching the cultural level of the earlier Greek and Roman, and the then contemporary Islamic, civilizations. All historical data strongly suggest that Christendom would have plateaued at approximately that level for a longer or shorter period of time, and then gone into decline—as had all other civilizations before and as eventually the Islamic civilization did as well. That did not happen, however. One very fundamental reason was that—starting with the Gregorian Reforms, through the Renaissance, the Reformation, and on into the Enlightenment and beyond—religion and the state slowly and very painfully began to be separated. This separation broke the forced quality of religion/ideology, consequently freeing the human spirit and mind to pursue its limitless urge to know ever more, to solve every problem it confronts. This resulted in a series of what historians call revolutions in the West: the commercial revolution (sixteenth–seventeenth centuries), scientific revolution (seventeenth century), industrial revolution (eighteenth–nineteenth centuries), political revolution (epitomized in the eighteenth-century American and French Revolutions), and on into the nineteenth and twentieth centuries with myriads of revolutions of all sorts occurring at geometrically increasing speed and magnitude.

With these "exponential" advances in capabilities, the possibilities of destructiveness increased correspondingly—as the medieval philosophers said: The corruption of the best becomes the worst, *corruptio optimi pessima*. Nevertheless, because freedom is of the *essence* of being human, even though we may well destroy ourselves if we do not learn wisdom and live virtuously, we can never turn back to an unfree stage of human development.

Hence, those societies that try to reunite religion/ideology with the power of the state are doomed always to be third-class societies. New problems and challenges will always arise in human societies. Humans, however, have a virtually limitless capability of intellect, imagination, and spirit (which is another way of saying what the biblical book of Genesis meant by recording that God made humans in God's image, the *imago Dei*) with which to address and overcome those problems and challenges ever anew. Unfortunately, when that innate creative human spirit is imprisoned in a doctrinal straitjacket ("*ortho*doxy," "*straight*-doctrine," becomes in fact "*strait*-doctrine") imposed from above by the power of the state, it will die from spiritual circulation-strangulation, and then that society will fall behind, and perhaps even succumb to, those societies that retain their creativity.

That is why, for example, the present attempt of Islamists to reestablish the Muslim law, the *shar'ia*, in the Muslim world will condemn those countries *always* to be behind the "West." Given the Islamists' memory of the past medieval cultural glory and superiority of Islam over the West, it is precisely the present inferiority in almost every way of all Islamic countries vis-à-vis the West that infuriates them.

As noted earlier, one finds an acknowledgment of the present decline of Islamic civilization and a determination to do something positive about it, in certain leading Muslim circles, for example, in Malaysia: "None of the Muslim countries are considered to be developed or advanced, despite about ten are among the rich nations of the world." Perceptively the author noted that the Muslim countries "are so weak politically, economically, socially and even educationally . . . Muslims have become so weak and dependent on others in almost every field,"[22] and then quotes Malaysian Prime Minister Mahathir Mohamad: "We Muslims are backward in many fields."[23]

Of course, the same disastrous consequences would also result, for example, in India if the recently resurgent Hindu "fundamentalists" have their way—and North Korea will likewise always remain relatively "backward" as long as it maintains a union of ideology and state. Many Islamist apologists argue, however, that Islam is different from the West and its major religion, Christianity, because, unlike Christianity, Islam is a holistic religion that includes politics as well as all other aspects of life. In this, unfortunately, they are forgetting that Christendom was exactly the same for well over a millennium—the Constantinian Era. It is only when Christendom, the West, began to break out of that mischievous marriage of religion/ ideology and state

---

22. Alhabshi, *An Inspiration for the Future of Islam*, 14–15.

23. Prime Minister, Dato Seri Dr. Mahathir Mohamad at the opening of the International Youth Camp, Morib, Selangor, August 10, 1981, cited in ibid., 18.

(only allegedly virtuously "holistic") that it embarked on the path of human freedom with its limitless possibilities of creativity (and destruction).

Israel: An Example of Religion and State Impoverished

Not infrequently, one also hears from some Western Jews in dialogue with Christianity—afflicted by the same unconsciousness of the history of Christendom as most Muslims—an argument similar to that of many Muslims, namely, that, unlike Christianity, this time Judaism is a holistic religion that includes all aspects of life. In the West this line of argument does not extend to include politics in the form of a union of religion and state. However, it does expand to include a type of union of religion and state in the "Jewish State" of Israel—greatly to the detriment of both religion and state.

The sad fact is that the vast majority of Israelis are unconnected with any institutional form of Judaism. The forced choices are virtually between an observant Orthodoxy, which more than 80 percent of Jews the world over find unacceptable, and a completely secular lifestyle. Modern versions of Judaism—Reform, Conservative, and Reconstructionist Judaism, all vibrant in the world's largest Jewish community, U.S. Jewry—are restricted by Orthodox political maneuvering to a minuscule portion of the Israeli population. In brief, Israeli Jewish religious life as a result of the union of state and Orthodox Judaism is gravely impoverished.

Judaism, of course, is not the only religion in Israel. Even though religious liberty is proclaimed by Israeli law, there are many restrictions on religions other than Orthodox Judaism and numerous privileges granted only to Orthodox Judaism. Partly as a consequence, the other religions are also impoverished. For example, both Christianity and Islam in Israel tend to be highly traditional, largely opposed to any serious grappling with modernity. In so many ways, observing religious life in Israel, especially in Jerusalem, is like stepping back into a medieval time-warp. For example, one can read of murders because of "family honor," which are more or less accepted by the Arab population and met with a shoulder shrug by much of the Jewish population. As one instance (*Jerusalem Post*, July 15, 1994), a twenty-one-year-old Druze (an eleventh-century religion derived from Islam) shot his thirty-eight-year-old sister twenty times after she returned from New York for a visit, because she had bleached her hair and wore a short skirt, thus sullying the family and community honor. The Druze religious community registered no condemnation whatsoever, and the Israeli police were at pains to explain why the brother had gotten so angry.

That such horrible crimes happen in Israel is not the point (this occurred while O. J. Simpson was on trial for the murder of his former wife). Rather, it is the reaction, or lack thereof, by the specific religious community and the "well, what can you expect?" attitude by much of the larger community. The point is that the union of religion and state, with its Israeli continuation of the Turkish *millet* system, whereby each religious institution is given the legal power to control matters of "personal status," has doubtless contributed to the Druze community's remaining "medieval" in its acceptance of killings because of "family honor." To say the least, this is an impoverishment of religion. It also seriously cripples the state, for as a consequence many of its citizens are restricted and oppressed in ways that make them less effectively contributing citizens—and a state will flourish only to the extent that its citizens flourish.

This same point was made by a loyal Israeli Druze who was a longtime member of the Israeli Foreign Service and a Knesset Member: "The minute I live in a state which defines itself religiously or nationally as a Jewish state, as an Islamic state, or as a Christian state, then other communities should not expect any priorities or equality in that state. Once the State of Israel was defined as a Jewish state, the non-Jews in that Jewish state cannot expect equality."[24] This is not the view of only an Israeli minority. The former Rector of Haifa University and the Chair of the Governmental Advisory Commission on Druze Affairs wrote the following concerning certain minorities: "In fact there is no real equality of rights even though Israel is a democracy and genuinely tries to treat its citizens equally . . . There are different classes of citizens which unfortunately is not exactly the ideal of universal citizenship."[25]

The Challenge to Jews, Christians, and Muslims Together

As we know, however, the separation of religion and state at its best did not and does not mean hostility between religion and state. Rather, it frees each, religion and state, to fulfill its respective function untrammeled by, but closely related to, the other. For the state, that function can be described briefly as the responsibility "to organize society so as to protect the rights of

---

24. Zeidan Atashi, "A View from within the Druze Community," in *The Constitutional and Political Status of Minorities in Israel: The Druze Community* (New York: The Israel Colloquium, 1994) 23.

25. Gabriel Ben-Dor, "An Overview of Israeli-Druze Relations," in ibid., 16.

all, and promote the common good," and for religion, "to provide an explanation of the ultimate meaning of life and how to live accordingly."

Clearly, the West does not have the perfect solution to the question of the relation between religion and the state; it has many different imperfect solutions. The quite "anemic" condition of a Christianity not completely separated from the state in Germany, Scandinavia, England, and other European countries, vis-à-vis its turbulent but comparatively vital condition in the U.S. with its completely separate relationship of religion and state further bears out the thesis that the separate but creative relationship of religion and state is good for both religion and state and, hence, for humankind.

The validity of this insight can also be seen in Indonesia, the largest Muslim country in the world. With 90% of its two hundred ten million population being Muslim, Indonesia has more Muslims than all the Arab countries combined. In Indonesia there is still a solid commitment to the "Five Principles" (*Pancasila*), which include both of the key "Western" notions of democracy and religious liberty; Islam is not designated as the state religion. Before the turmoil precipitated by the Asian economic meltdown, a visit to Indonesia revealed a country rapidly moving out of the ranks of developing countries with a booming economy, rapidly rising educational standards, and harmonious, actively creative relations with the other religious communities in and outside the country.[26] For example, there were, and still are, cooperative ties between some of the Islamic theological institutes and Christian and Buddhist universities, and several nongovernmental organizations promote interreligious dialogue, such as "Interfidei: Institute for Inter-Faith Dialogue in Indonesia," "International Forum Indonesia," "Paramadina," and "Madia." We hear about the religious violence in various parts of Indonesia, but we do not often hear is that it is largely promoted by renegade elements of the military and former supporters of the dictator Soeharto in order to destabilize the new democratic government in an attempt to retain their old abusive power and money—and by the influx of money from Wahabi (fundamentalist) Islam in Saudi Arabia.

The "perfect" solution of the relationship of religion and state lies only in an "infinite" future, toward which humans are always striving. The West—and countries such as Indonesia, Japan, etc., inspired by the principles of democracy and religious liberty—has shown that separation of religion and state is *essential* to the true, full functioning of both religion and state and to human progress to "infinity." The separation of religion and

---

26. For an excellent overview of Islam in Indonesia, see Franz Magnis-Suseno, "Indonesischer Islam: Wohin?" *Asien* (October 1993).

the state is a *necessary*, though not *sufficient*, cause of the unending creative development of humanity.

As seen above, clearly not all Muslim thinkers and leaders are Islamists, despite the great show of force released by the radical Khomeinis of Iran, Turabis of the Sudan, and Taliban of Afghanistan. Contemporary critical-thinking Muslim scholars and leaders such as Indonesia's former President Wahid and Foreign Minister Shihab—but others as well—were/are fully aware of the dangers of Islamism, of the history of the results of the union of religion and state, and of the need to move to a relationship of a creatively cooperative, pluralistic separation of religion and state.

The great challenge to Jewish and Christian thinkers and leaders is to work together with such Muslims, and men and women of other religions and ideologies, to develop jointly relationships between religion and state that will maintain both the essential separation between the two and the needed cooperative spirit.

The Relationship among Religion (Ideology), Ethics, and the State

Christianity and Islam are the two most populous, geographically widespread, and powerful religions today (as they have been for centuries and will be for the foreseeable future). They, along with Judaism, must lead the way in developing and spreading a creative relationship between religion (ideology), ethics, and the power of the state. Though small in numbers today, the significance of Judaism in the past—remember, it comprised almost a tenth of the population of the Roman Empire (eight to ten million out of one hundred million) at the time of Jesus—was immense through its decisive influence in the shaping of Western civilization; in an almost baffling way it has today once again become immensely significant through the tiny state of Israel and particularly in its relationship to the West (former Christendom) and Islam. Thus Judaism, Christianity, and Islam have a special responsibility to take the lead in developing and furthering a creative relationship among religion, ethics, and the state.

No society can flourish without having a cohesive basic ethic at its foundation. The foundation of this essential societal ethic has in the past been provided by various religions. This was and is true for Western civilization as well, in that at its ethical basis there lies the Judeo-Christian religious tradition, though increasingly "rationalized" and "secularized" in recent centuries. Indeed, even in the most powerful nation of Western civilization, the U.S., there is scholarly consensus on the existence at its core, and on the importance of, a "civil religion," which is precisely this "quasi-deistized" Judeo-Christian tradition.

Each society will have to develop, maintain, and constantly update for itself such a fundamental ethic if it is to survive and flourish, but in the new millennium it will increasingly have to do so within the context of "modernity," with its growing focus on freedom, human rights, religious/cultural pluralism, and separation of religion and state. All of these foci, of course, have their necessary correlatives, that is, responsibility, human obligations, religious/ cultural mutual respect and dialogue, and respect and cooperation between religion and state.

Underlying all of these and other elements of modernity, with which each society will have to come to terms in conjunction with their own traditions and in their own creative way, is the global fact that no society can live in even relative isolation today in the third millennium. Ours is already "one world"—global communications, global transportation, global economics—and holding it all together will have to be a global ethic, with freedom/ responsibility, human rights/ obligations, religious pluralism/dialogue, and separation/respect between religion and state. This global ethic must, and can, be arrived at and constantly extended by consensus through unending dialogue among women and men of all religious and ethical persuasions. Those with the greatest power and influence have the greatest responsibility to lead the way in this consensus-building through dialogue and consequent action: Jews, Christians, and Muslims.

Law and Ethics[27]

The Meaning of Ethics and Law

Human beings are persons, that is, beings who can know endlessly, choose freely, and love. Hence, when we speak of ethics, we are talking about the principles of behavior of free beings, of humans. We do not speak of our animal pets as having ethics or complain that trees do not follow their ethics. Because only we humans have freedom, only we can choose whether or not to act in a certain way. This is what we mean when we talk about ethics: the principles by which free beings, humans, choose to act one way or another.

When we speak of law in the most general sense, we are talking about the operation of the principle of cause and effect. Thus, we speak of the

---

27. The initial form of this chapter was a lecture I delivered before the International Senate of the Union Internationale des Avocats, in the Eschenbach Palace, Vienna, on "The Relationship between the Law and a Global Ethic," February 21, 1998.

laws of nature, the law of gravity, and the like. Step out a tenth storey window, and the law of gravity operates to dash us to the ground at a certain rate of acceleration and a certain force—with the consequences being quite predictably smashing. Cause: stepping out the tenth storey window; effect: being dashed to the ground—unless, of course, something intervenes, such as a strong awning appropriately placed on the ninth floor.

When the term "law" is used in a societal context, the same fundamental notion applies. Commit murder (cause), and we are punished by incarceration or execution (effect)—again, unless something intervenes, such as not being found out. In a way, the same basic principle of cause and effect operates in the field of ethics as well. We say in English that we "ought" to choose good and avoid evil; we speak of being "obliged" to choose the good. Our English word "obliged" comes from a Latin root, "*ob-ligare*," "to be bound to." Hence, we are bound to, obliged to, do the good, which will bring about a good result. If, however, we as free beings choose instead to do evil, we are likewise "bound to" suffer the evil consequences—again, unless something intervenes, such as being forgiven by the person offended. It is worth noting again that the Latin root of the term "religion" is fundamentally the same as that of "oblige," that is, "*re-ligare*," "to be bound back."

The Relationship between Ethics and Law

Fundamentally, the relationship between law and ethics in human society is that the law is a public expression of an ethical requirement; law also operates in the external forum, while ethics operates in the internal forum. Thus, all law is a particular, overt specification of some aspect of ethics. Ethics is the broader category. Everything required by law is required by ethics, but not everything required by ethics is required by law.[28]

Most often in human history, the law of a society has largely reflected the ethics of a particular portion of the society, which in a variety of ways dominated the rest of the society, with whose ethics theirs was at variance.

---

28. Many cultures have spoken of all human law as (or that should be) a reflection the Divine Law. Such a notion is at the foundation of Confucianism, as in the tenet of *T'ien-ming*, the "Mandate of Heaven." It is found as well in Roman thinkers such as first-century BCE Cicero: "Law is the highest reason, implanted by Nature which commands what ought to be done and forbids the opposite . . . Law is not a product of human thought, nor is it any enactment of peoples, but something eternal which rules the whole universe by its wisdom in command and prohibition. Thus they have been accustomed to say that Law is the primal and ultimate mind of Jupiter" (*De legibus*, in Donald S. Greenberg, *Classics of Western Thought*, 4th ed. (New York: Harcourt, Brace Jovanovich, 1988) 1:434–35.

In that case, "might made right." A prevailing societal ethics, of course, is ultimately determined by the fact that all government exists at the sufferance of the governed. Even in those extremely savage dictatorships in which the "elite," operating according to their "ethics," killed right and left, the abused population for the time accepted the "ethics" of the elite as the lesser of evils—but it accepted it rather than rebel to the point of their utter self-destruction.

In such situations, there obviously exists a kind of schizophrenia, a splintered society wherein the freedom, and hence creativity, of the majority of the population is greatly restricted rather than given rein and fostered. Obviously, such a "split-personality" condition is at least as destructive for a society as it is for an individual person. Just as for the good of the individual, so also for the good of whole society, such a split needs to be overcome. The freedom and creativity of both the individual and society need to be released and encouraged.

Clearly, those persons concerned about the welfare of not only individual persons but also of human society in general must/will commit themselves to overcoming that societal split and promoting the freedom and creativity of all. In fact, the long stretch of human history shows clearly that this process is well underway. The move of humankind from a primitive tribal state to the gradual founding of civilizations, to the fantastic relatively simultaneous "great leap forward" of the "Axial Period" (800–200 BCE) in China, India, the Near East, and Europe,[29] to the breakthrough of Modernity in the eighteenth-century Western Enlightenment, and now to the dawning of the "Age of Global Dialogue,"[30] creating a new global civilization. Freedom and responsible self-governance, that is, democracy, for all was not even a dream or *desideratum* until the Enlightenment. Now it is becoming a reality for rapidly increasing numbers around the globe. People can be suppressed today, but they cannot be satisfied. Humankind is "coming of age," becoming adult—with all the agonies and ecstasies of that process of maturation.

In this new age, the continued imposition by law of the ethics of a privileged "elite" is no longer acceptable. The age-old way of dominance by the few is waning. The age-old striving for freedom and responsibility for

---

29. See Karl Jaspers, *Vom Ursprung und Ziel der Geschichte* (Zurich: Artemis, 1949) 19–43; E.T.: Michael Bullock, *The Origin and Goal of History* (New Haven: Yale University Press, 1953).

30. See Leonard Swidler, "The Age of Global Dialogue," *Marburg Zeitschrift fur Religionswissenschaft* 1/2 (July 1996); available at http://www.unimarburg.de/fb11/religionswissenschaft/journal/swidler.html.

the many is waxing. Law now is increasingly expected to reflect the ethics of freedom and responsibility of all.

The Nature of Religion and the Validation of Society's Ethics

In those situations where a law is contrary to the ethical principles of the many, the claim is made that law does not oblige ethically, as was noted already by Thomas Aquinas in his treatise *"De lege,"* and even far earlier by Cicero.[31] However, the sanction, the "effect," of the "cause" of an ethically invalid law may still be carried out if the law is violated—as in the case of Martin Luther King, Jr.'s being jailed when nonviolently disobeying U.S. racial segregation laws—or not carried out if successfully avoided by flight, force, etc.

The question then arises: Where does the "effect," the sanction, resulting from violating an *ethical* principle come from? It arises from what we in the West have called "religion," or its functional equivalent, an "ideology," for example, atheistic Marxism. For example, in the Abrahamic religions traditionally understood, good behavior merits continued existence after death in the "Kingdom of Heaven." In Indian religions, Hinduism, Buddhism, etc., traditionally understood, the law of "karma" operates: Every human action has its consequences in a future existence. Some similar cause-and-effect procedure exists in every religion and ideology, including very "critical-thinking" modern versions of each older religion.

Whence, then, comes the validation of a religion? The answer lies in the nature of religion. As detailed above, religion is an "explanation of the ultimate meaning of life and how to live accordingly, based on some notion of the Transcendent," normally with the four "C's": Creed, Code, Cult, Community-structure.[32] From the very constitutive structure of religion/ideology, the validation of its ethics flows: A religion's ethics are the necessary behavioral principles resulting from the religion's "explanation of the ultimate meaning of life." There will, then, be a basically one-to-one rela-

---

31. Thomas Aquinas, *Summa Theologiae*, I,II, q.90,a.3. See also Cicero, *De legibus*, where he wrote: "Laws were invented for the safety of citizens, the preservation of States, and the tranquillity and happiness of human life . . . and when such rules were drawn up and put into force, it is clear that men called them 'laws.' From this point of view it can be understood that those who formulated wicked and unjust statutes for nations, thereby breaking their promises and agreements, put into effect anything but 'laws'" (in Greenberg, *Classics of Western Thought*, 1:437–38.

32. Besides above, pg. 36, see Swidler and Mojzes, *Study of Religion*, for greater detail.

tionship between the law and the ethics of the society—in the sense that all laws will/should be ethically acceptable—that is, if there is but one religion or ideology pervading that society. But, what of a society in which there are several influential religions and/or ideologies? What will the relationship be between the law and the ethics flowing from the disparate religions and/or ideologies?

Global Civilization and "Religions (Ideologies)-in-Dialogue"

In past history the answer to that question was basically that one religion/ideology and its ethics prevailed, with minor concessions reluctantly granted to the other religions/ideologies. This condition began to change radically with the Enlightenment, as reflected simultaneously in the 1789 American "Bill of Rights" and the French "Declaration of the Rights of Man." Still, at the beginning of this period of religious liberty, the ethics that shaped the laws of America and France were predominantly Christian—Protestant and Catholic, respectively. Only gradually have the ethics, and resultant laws, opened themselves to the influence of other religions and ideologies. That process is one that proceeds by way of dialogue, and it is unending.

As the third millennium moves forward, it is evident to all that humankind as a whole is rapidly moving into a global civilization made up of many cultures. As noted earlier, in 1993, Harvard University Professor Samuel Huntington wrote of the coming clash of civilizations, cultures.[33] He was partially accurate. We have seen the violent clash of cultures: Catholicism-Protestantism in Northern Ireland, Islam-Catholicism-Orthodox Christianity in Bosnia, Islam-Orthodox Christianity in Azerbaijan-Armenia, Buddhism-Hinduism in Sri Lanka, Judaism-Islam in the Near East, etc. All previous civilizations have had a religion (or, in recent modern times, occasionally its functional equivalent, an ideology, such as Marxism in the Soviet Union) at its heart, shaping and reflecting its understanding of the ultimate meaning of life and the outflowing values. But, what now of the burgeoning global civilization? What religion or ideology will be at its heart? It, too, will need a spiritual, life-giving vision and consequent values—otherwise it will die aborning.

The heart of the emerging global civilization will be no particular religion or ideology. Rather, it will be "religions/ideologies-in-dialogue." This heart began to take shape at the beginning of the twentieth century with the launching of the intra-Christian ecumenical movement in 1910,

---

33. See Samuel P. Huntington, "Clash of Civilizations?" *Foreign Affairs* 73 (Summer 1993) 22–49.

gradually drawing the myriad Christian churches into intense dialogue. It was further developed in the 1960s by the initiation of widespread interreligious/interideological dialogue, led especially by the Catholic Church in its watershed event of Vatican II.

Global Law and a Global Ethic

Both intra-Christian and interreligious/ideological dialogues have increased at a geometric rate, shifting unto another level once more in 1991 when Küng and I issued a call for the drafting and eventual adoption of a "Universal Declaration of a Global Ethic."[34] That project is proceeding apace. See the next chapter for greater detail.

What ought the relationship be between the developing a global ethic and the law on the global level? Global law needs faithfully to reflect a global ethic; global law should also contribute to the shaping of a global ethic. To fulfill both parts of its responsibility, the global law profession needs to have its experts in global law be in close and constant dialogue with the other major shapers of a global ethic. This will include all disciplines, professions and walks of life, but in an especially intense way it will concentrate on the dialogue with thinkers and scholars of religious and philosophical ethics.

Toward a Global Ethic[35]

It is beyond the borders of sanity that Catholics and Protestants were for decades blowing each other up in Northern Ireland, that Hindus and Buddhists wantonly murdered each other in Sri Lanka, that Jews and Muslims are always teetering on the abyss of war in the Near East, that Sikhs and Hindus terrorize each other in the Punjab, that in Kashmir Muslims and Hindus are always in a state of unrest with hands on their guns, that various factions of Christians and Muslims made the "Switzerland of the Near East," Lebanon, a roiling charnel house, that fundamentalist Hindus in India murder Christians and Muslims—and on and on. Our religions and ideologies must put a stop to these perversions of religion and ideology!

---

34. See Swidler, *For All Life*.

35. I am grateful to Hans Küng for this programmatic insight from his books. *Projekt Weltethos* (Munich: Piper, 1990); and *Global Responsibility: In Search of a New World Ethic* (New York: Crossroad, 1991). He has since then founded an institute for Global Ethic (http://www.weltethos.org/dat_eng/index_e.htm), and published several other books on a global ethic. See also Swidler, *For All Life*.

Horrendous as the bombings of Hiroshima and Nagasaki were, imagine if Hitler had had a nuclear bomb with which to tip his V-2 rockets that he rained down on London (and could have most anywhere else in the world) in the last months of World War II. The real horror is that he was only a few months away from his goal when the Allied armies marched into the secret laboratory in a mountain cave in the tiny southwest German village of Haigerloch in late April, 1945. The same is true of Saddam Hussein; had the Israelis not destroyed his nuclear plant in 1985 he would by 1990 have had a nuclear bomb to fit on his SCUD missiles—which, remember were fired not only at the Jews in Israel but also at other Muslims and the Allied forces from thirty-four countries in Saudi Arabia.

The world does not have the luxury of waiting patiently for a global ethic. When the fact of the epistemological revolutions leading to the growing necessity of interreligious, interideological, intercultural dialogue is coupled with the fact of all humankind's interdependency—such that any significant part of humanity could precipitate the whole of the globe into a social, economic, nuclear, environmental, or other catastrophe—there arises the pressing need to focus the energy of these dialogues on not only how humans perceive and understand the world and its meaning but also on how they should act in relationship to themselves, to other persons, and to nature, within the context of reality's undergirding, pervasive, overarching source, energy, and goal, however understood. In brief, humankind needs increasingly desperately to engage in a dialogue on the development of not a Buddhist ethic, a Christian ethic, a Marxist ethic, etc., but of a global ethic—and I believe a key instrument in that direction will be the shaping of a "Universal Declaration of a Global Ethic."

What a Universal Declaration of a Global Ethic Is

I say ethic in the singular rather than ethics in the plural, because what is needed is not a full-blown global ethics in great detail—indeed, such would not even be possible—but a global consensus on the fundamental attitude toward good and evil and the basic and middle principles to put it into action. Clearly also, this ethic must be global. It will not be sufficient to have a common ethic for Westerners or Africans or Asians, etc. The destruction, for example, of the ozone layer or the loosing of a destructive gene mutation by any one group will be disastrous for all.

I say also that this "Universal Declaration of a Global Ethic" must be arrived at by consensus through dialogue. Attempts at the imposition of a unitary ethics by various kinds of force have been had aplenty, and they have inevitably fallen miserably short of globality. The most recent failures can be seen in the widespread collapse of communism and in an inverse way in the resounding rejection of secularism by resurgent Islamism. That the need for a global ethic is most urgent is becoming increasingly apparent to all; humankind no longer has the luxury of letting such an ethic slowly and haphazardly grow by itself, as it willy nilly will gradually happen. It is vital that there be a conscious focusing of energy on such a development. Immediate action is necessary.

When a "Universal Declaration of a Global Ethic" is finally drafted—after multiple consultations, revisions, and eventual acceptance by the full range of religious and ethical institutions—it will then serve as a minimal ethical standard for humankind to live up to, much as the U.N.'s "Universal Declaration of Human Rights." Through the former, the moral force of the world's religious and ethical institutions can be brought to bear especially on those issues that are not very susceptible to the legal and political force of the latter. Such an undertaking by the religions and ideologies of the world would be different from, but complementary to, the work of the U.N.

Principles of a Universal Declaration of a Global Ethic

I will first offer some suggestions of the general notions that I believe ought to shape a "Universal Declaration of a Global Ethic," and then offer a tentative draft constructed in their light.

1. The Declaration should use language and images that are acceptable to all major religions and ethical groups; hence, its language ought to be "humanity-based," rather than from authoritative religious books; it should be from "below," not from "above."

2. Therefore, it should be anthropocentric, indeed more, it must be anthropocosmocentric, for we cannot be fully human except within the context of the whole of reality.

3. The affirmations should be dynamic in form, in the sense that they will be susceptible to being sublated; that is, they might properly be reinterpreted by being taken up into a larger framework.

4. The Declaration needs to set both inviolable minimums and open-ended maximums to be striven for; but maximums may not be required, for they might violate the freedom-minimums of some persons.

5. It could well start with—though not limit itself to—elements of the so-called "Golden Rule": Treat others as we would be treated.

6. As humans ineluctably seek ever more knowledge/truth, so, too, they seek to draw what they perceive as the good to themselves (that is, they love). Usually, this self is expanded to include the family and then friends. It needs to continue its natural expansion to the community, nation, world, and cosmos—and the source and goal of all reality.

7. But, this human love necessarily must start with self-love, for one can love one's "neighbor" only as one loves oneself; but, since one becomes human only by interhuman mutuality, loving others fulfills one's own humanity, and thus is also the greatest act of authentic self-love.

8. Another aspect of the "Golden Rule" is that humans are always to be treated as ends, never as mere means, that is, as subjects, never as mere objects.

9. Yet another implication of the "Golden Rule" is that those who cannot protect themselves ought to be protected by those who can.

10. A further ring of the expanding circles of the "Golden Rule" is that nonhuman beings are also to be reverenced and treated with respect because of their being.

11. It is important that not only basic but also middle ethical principles be spelled out in this Declaration. Although most of the middle ethical principles that need to be articulated in this Declaration are already embedded in juridical form in the "Universal Declaration of Human Rights," it is vital that the religions and ethical traditions expressly state and approve them. Then, the world, including both adherents and outsiders of the various religions and ethical traditions, will know to what ethical standards all are committing themselves.

12. If a "Universal Declaration of a Global Ethic" is to be meaningful and effective, however, its framers must resist the temptation to pack too many details and special interests into it. It can function best as a kind of "constitutional" set of basic and middle ethical principles from which more detailed applications can constantly be drawn.

Such general suggestions need to be discussed, confirmed, rejected, modified, supplemented. Beyond that, it is vital that all the disciplines contribute what from their perspectives ought to be included in the Declaration, how it should be formulated, what is to be avoided—and this is beginning to happen. The year 1993 was the 100th anniversary of the 1893 World Parliament of Religions, which took place in Chicago and marked the beginning of what became worldwide interreligious dialogue. As a consequence, a number of international conferences took place, and at the center of them was the launching and developing of a "Universal Declaration of a Global Ethic."

A Plan of Action

The first was held in New Delhi, India, in February, 1993; the second in August of the same year in Bangalore, India; and the third that year in September in Chicago. For that huge (over 6,000 participants) September, 1993, Chicago "Parliament of the World's Religions" Küng drafted a document titled "Declaration toward a Global Ethic," which the Parliament adopted.[36]

Beyond that, the text given below—after having been commissioned by the January 1993 meeting in Graz, Austria, of the ISAT was drafted by myself and submitted to and analyzed at the January, 1994, meeting of ISAT in Jerusalem. It was focused on during the Spring, 1993, semester graduate seminar I held at Temple University "Global Ethics-Human Rights-World Religions," and it was also a major focus of the "First International Conference on Universalism" in August, 1993, in Warsaw. A Consultation of the American Academy of Religion in November, 1993, in Washington DC, was devoted to the topic; the sixth ISAT in January, 1994, concentrated for a second year on the Universal Declaration; in May, 1994, and it was the subject of a conference sponsored by the "International Association of Asian Philosophy and Religion—IAAPR" in Seoul, Korea. The World Conference on Religion and Peace in part focused on it in its Fall, 1994, World Assembly in Rome/Riva del Garda, Italy; and it was the subject of a conference in San Francisco in honor of the "Fiftieth Anniversary of the Founding of the United Nations," on "Celebrating the Spirit: Towards a Global Ethic," held June 20–21, 1995.

In March, 1997, in Paris, the Philosophy and Ethics Division of UNESCO held the first meeting of its newly established committee to work toward a "Universal Ethic." Its second meeting was held December, 1997 in Naples in conjunction with the Instituto Italiano degli Studii Filosofici. Both of the above drafts (as well as the one described next) were submitted to this UNESCO committee.

Somewhat later, Küng drafted a third text, this time within the context of the InterAction Council, titled "A Universal Declaration of Human Responsibilities." The InterAction Council is a committee of former heads of states, chaired by retired Chancellor Helmut Schmidt of Germany. All three texts have been subjected to numerous consultations and comments

---

36. Hans Küng and Karl-Josef Kuschel, eds., *A Global Ethic* (New York: Continuum, 1993).

by scholars and thinkers from multiple philosophical, religious, and other backgrounds.

To summarize, it is imperative that various religious and ethical communities, ethnic groups, and geographical regions work on discussing and drafting their own versions of a "Universal Declaration of a Global Ethic," that is, *what they consider their own basic ethical principles, which they at the same time believe people of all other religious and ethical traditions could also affirm.* The three existing drafts should certainly be utilized in this process, but all communities and regions need to make their own contributions to the final Declaration. In the process of wrestling with the issue and forging the wording, they will make the concern for a global ethic their own and will thus better be able to mediate it to their "constituents" and enhance the likelihood of the Declaration's being adhered to in practice.

What needs to be stressed is that such a project cannot be carried out only by the scholars and leaders of the world's religious and ethical communities, though obviously the vigorous participation of these elements is vital. The ideas and sensitivities must also come from the grassroots. It is also at the grassroots, as well at the levels of scholars and leaders, that consciousnesses must be raised on the desperate need for the conscious development of a global ethic, and, once drafted and accepted, the conviction of its validity must be gained. The most carefully thought out and sensitively crafted Declaration will be of no use if those who are to adhere to it do not believe in it. A global ethic must work on all three levels: scholars, leaders, grassroots. Otherwise it will not work at all. Hence, it is vital that:

> First, all religious, ethical, ethnic, and geographical communities and organizations (either alone or in concert with others, but always in a dialogic spirit)—and most especially the myriad NGOs of the world—need to move seriously but quickly to the drawing up of their own Draft of a "Universal Declaration of a Global Ethic."
>
> Second, these groups need to strategize on how to maneuver their drafts to gain the greatest influence in all the theaters in which each operates: the U.N., other NGOs, scholarly groups, religious groups, the vast world of the internet, myriads of grassroots organizations—in short, wherever aroused imaginations will lead.
>
> Third, each group should send their Draft of a "Universal Declaration of a Global Ethic" to the Center for Global Ethics, c/o Prof. Leonard Swidler, *Journal of Ecumenical Studies*, Temple University (062-56), 1700 N. Broad St., Philadelphia, PA 19121-0843, USA; e-mail: dialogue@temple.edu; Fax: 215-204-4569),

and/or to Prof. Hans Küng at his Foundation: Stiftung Weltethos, Waldhäuser Strasse 23, Tübingen 72076, Germany; Fax: 49-7071-61-01-40; email: office@weltethos.org—which will serve first as collection and distribution centers, and, when the time is appropriate, facilitators in the process of synthesizing a final draft and devising in as democratic manner as possible a process of worldwide adoption.

In sum, having studied, listened and thought, all are challenged to take up this vital task and act.

Draft of a Universal Declaration of a Global Ethic

Rationale

We women and men from various ethical and religious traditions commit ourselves to the following Universal Declaration of a Global Ethic. We speak here not of "ethics" in the plural, which implies rather great detail, but of "ethic" in the singular, that is, the fundamental attitude toward good and evil, and the basic and middle principles needed to put it into action.

We make this commitment not despite our differences but arising out of our distinct perspectives, recognizing nevertheless in our diverse ethical and religious traditions common convictions that lead us to speak out *against* all forms of inhumanity and *for* humaneness in our treatment of ourselves, one another, and the world around us. We find in each of our traditions: (a) grounds in support of universal human rights, (b) a call to work for justice and peace, and (c) concern for conservation of the earth.

We confirm and applaud the positive human values that are, at times painfully slowly but nevertheless increasingly, being accepted and advocated in our world: freedom, equality, democracy, recognition of interdependence, and commitment to justice and human rights. We also believe that conditions in our world encourage, indeed require, us to look beyond what divides us and to speak as one on matters that are crucial for the survival of and respect for the earth. Therefore, we advocate movement toward a global order that reflects the best values found in our myriad traditions.

We are convinced that a just global order can be built only upon a global ethic that clearly states universally recognized norms and principles and that such an ethic presumes a readiness and intention on the part of people to act justly—that is, a movement of the heart. Second, a global ethic requires a thoughtful presentation of principles that are held up to open investigation and critique—a movement of the head.

Each of our traditions holds commitments beyond what is expressed here, but we find that within our ethical and religious traditions the world community is in the process of discovering elements of a fundamental minimal consensus on ethics that is convincing to all women and men of good will, religious and nonreligious alike, and that will provide us with a moral framework within which we can relate to ourselves, each other, and the world in a just and respectful manner.

In order to build a humanity-wide consensus we find it is essential to develop and use a language that is humanity-based, though each religious and ethical tradition also has its own language for what is expressed in this Declaration.

Furthermore, none of our traditions, ethical or religious, is satisfied with minimums, vital as they are; rather, because humans are endlessly self-transcending, our traditions also provide maximums to be striven for. Consequently, this Declaration does the same. The maximums, however, clearly are ideals to be striven for, and therefore cannot be required, lest the essential freedoms and rights of some thereby be violated.

Presuppositions

As a Universal Declaration of a Global Ethic, which we believe must undergird any affirmation of human rights and respect for the earth, this document affirms and supports the rights and corresponding responsibilities enumerated in the 1948 Universal Declaration of Human Rights of the United Nations. In conjunction with that first U.N. Declaration we believe there are five general presuppositions which are indispensable for a global ethic:

a. Every human possesses inalienable and inviolable dignity; individuals, states, and other social entities are obliged to respect and protect the dignity of each person.

b. No person or social entity exists beyond the scope of morality; everyone—individuals and social organizations—is obliged to do good and avoid evil.

c. Humans are endowed with reason and conscience—the great challenge of being human is to act conscientiously; communities, states and other social organizations are obliged to protect and foster these capabilities.

d. Communities, states, and other social organizations that contribute to the good of humans and the world have a right to exist and flourish; this right should be respected by all.

   e. Humans are a part of nature, not apart from nature; ethical concerns extend beyond humanity to the rest of the earth, and indeed the cosmos. In brief, this Declaration, in reflection of reality, is not just anthropocentric, but cosmoanthropocentric.

A Fundamental Rule

We propose the Golden Rule, which for thousands of years has been affirmed in many religious and ethical traditions, as a fundamental principle upon which to base a global ethic: "What you do not wish done to yourself, do not do to others," or, in positive terms, "What you wish done to yourself, do to others." This rule should be valid not only for one's own family, friends, community, and nation, but also for all other individuals, families, communities, nations, the entire world, the cosmos.

Basic Principles

1. Because freedom is of the essence of being human, every person is free to exercise and develop every capacity, as long as it does not infringe on the rights of other persons or express a lack of due respect for things living or nonliving. In addition, human freedom should be exercised in such a way as to enhance both the freedom of all humans and due respect for all things, living and nonliving.

2. Because of their inherent equal dignity, all humans should always be treated as ends, never as mere means. In addition, all humans in every encounter with others should strive to enhance to the fullest the intrinsic dignity of all involved.

3. Although humans have greater intrinsic value than nonhumans, all such things, living and nonliving, do possess intrinsic value simply because of their existence and, as such, are to be treated with due respect. In addition, all humans in every encounter with nonhumans, living and nonliving, should strive to respect them to the fullest of their intrinsic value.

4. As humans necessarily seek ever more truth, so, too, they seek to unite themselves, that is, their "selves," with what they perceive as the

good; in brief, they love. Usually, this "self" is expanded/transcended to include their own family and friends, seeking the good for them. In addition, as with the Golden Rule, this loving/loved "self" needs to continue its natural expansion/transcendence to embrace the community, nation, world, and cosmos.

5. Thus, true human love is authentic self-love and other-love, corelatively linked in such a way that ultimately it is drawn to become all-inclusive. This expansive and inclusive nature of love should be recognized as an active principle in personal and global interaction.

6. Those who hold responsibility for others are obliged to help those for whom they hold responsibility. In addition, the Golden Rule implies: If we were in serious difficulty wherein we could not help ourselves, we would want those who could help us to do so, even if they held no responsibility for us; therefore we should help others in serious difficulty who cannot help themselves, even though we hold no responsibility for them.

7. Because all humans are equally entitled to hold their religion or belief—that is, their explanation of the ultimate meaning of life and how to live accordingly—as true, every human's religion or belief should be granted its due freedom and respect.

8. In addition, dialogue—that is, conversation whose *primary* aim is to learn from the other—is a necessary means whereby women and men learn to respect the other, ceaselessly to expand and deepen their own explanation of the meaning of life, and to develop an ever-broadening consensus whereby men and women can live together on this globe in an authentically human manner.

Middle Principles

The following "Middle Ethical Principles" are those which underlie the U.N. Universal Declaration of Human Rights, formally approved by almost every nation in the world:

1. *Legal Rights/Responsibilities:* Because all humans have an inherent equal dignity, all should be treated equally before the law and provided with its equal protection. At the same time, all individuals and communities should follow all just laws, obeying not only the letter but most especially the spirit.

2. *Rights/Responsibilities concerning Conscience and Religion or Belief:* Because humans are thinking, and therefore essentially free-deciding beings, all have the right to freedom of thought, speech, conscience, and religion or belief. At the same time, all humans should exercise their rights of freedom of thought, speech, conscience, and religion or belief in ways that will respect themselves and all others and strive to produce maximum benefit, broadly understood, for both themselves and their fellow humans.

3. *Rights/Responsibilities concerning Speech and Information:* Because humans are thinking beings with the ability to perceive reality and express it, all individuals and communities have both the right and the responsibility, as far as possible, to learn the truth and express it honestly. At the same time everyone should avoid cover-ups, distortions, manipulations of others, and inappropriate intrusions into personal privacy; this freedom and responsibility is especially true of the mass media, artists, scientists, politicians, and religious leaders.

4. *Rights/Responsibilities concerning Participation in All Decision-making Affecting Oneself or Those for Whom One Is Responsible:* Because humans are free-deciding beings, all adults have the right to a voice, direct or indirect, in all decisions that affect them, including a meaningful participation in choosing their leaders and holding them accountable, as well as the right of equal access to all leadership positions for which their talents qualify them. At the same time, all humans should strive to exercise their right, and obligation, to participate in self-governance as to produce maximum benefit, widely understood, for both themselves and their fellow humans.

5. *Rights/Responsibilities concerning the Relationship between Women and Men*: Women and men are inherently equal, and all men and women have an equal right to the full development of all their talents as well as the freedom to marry, with equal rights in living out or dissolving marriage. At the same time, all men and women should act toward each other outside of and within marriage in ways that will respect the intrinsic dignity, equality, freedom, and responsibilities of themselves and others.

6. *Rights/Responsibilities concerning Property:* Because humans are free, bodily, and social in nature, all individual humans and communities have the right to own property of various sorts. At the same time, society should be so organized that property will be dealt with respectfully,

striving to produce maximum benefit not only for the owners but also for their fellow humans, as well as for the world at large.

7. *Rights/Responsibilities concerning Work and Leisure:* Because to lead an authentic human life all humans should normally have both meaningful work and recreative leisure, individuals and communities should strive to organize society so as to provide these two dimensions of an authentic human life both for themselves and for all the members of their communities. At the same time, all individuals have an obligation to work appropriately for their recompense, and, with all communities, to strive for ever more creative work and recreative leisure for themselves, their communities, and other individuals and communities.

8. *Rights/Responsibilities concerning Children and Education:* Children are first of all not responsible for their coming into existence or for their socialization and education; their parents are. Where for whatever reason they fail, the wider community, relatives, and civil community have an obligation to provide the most humane care possible, physical, mental, moral/spiritual and social, for children. Because humans can become authentically human only through education in the broad sense, and today increasingly can flourish only with extensive education in the formal sense, all individuals and communities should strive to provide an education for all children and adult women and men that is directed to the full development of the human person, respect for human rights and fundamental freedoms, the promotion of understanding, dialogue, and friendship among all humans—regardless of racial, ethnic, religious, belief, sexual, or other differences—and respect for the earth. At the same time, all individuals and communities have the obligation to contribute appropriately to providing the means necessary for this education for themselves and their communities, and beyond that to strive to provide the same for all humans.

9. *Rights/Responsibilities concerning Peace:* Because peace as both the absence of violence and the presence of justice for all humans is the necessary condition for the complete development of the full humanity of all humans, individually and communally, all individuals and communities should strive constantly to further the growth of peace on all levels—personal, interpersonal, local, regional, national, and international—granting that (a) the necessary basis of peace is justice for all concerned; (b) violence is to be vigorously avoided, being resorted to only when its absence would cause a greater evil; and (c) when peace is ruptured, all efforts should be bent to its rapid restoration,

on the necessary basis of justice for all. At the same time, it should be recognized that peace, like liberty, is a positive value that should be cultivated constantly, and therefore all individuals and communities should make the necessary prior efforts not only to avoid its breakdown but also to strengthen its steady development and growth.

10. *Rights/Responsibilities concerning the Preservation of the Environment:* Because things, living and nonliving, have an intrinsic value simply because of their existence, and also because humans cannot develop fully as humans, or even survive, if the environment is severely damaged, all individuals and communities should respect the ecosphere within which "we all live, move, and have our being," and act so that (a) nothing, living or nonliving, will be destroyed in its natural form except when used for some greater good, as, for example, the use of plants/animals for food; and (b) if at all possible, only replaceable material will be destroyed in its natural form. At the same time, all individuals and communities should constantly be vigilant to protect our fragile universe, particularly from the exploding human population and increasing technological possibilities that threaten it in an ever-expanding fashion.[37]

Education: Deep-Dialogue and Critical-Thinking

Whatever content and skills education should impart, at its foundation it needs to foster a mentality of Deep-Dialogue (briefly, a method of entering other perspectives and returning mutually transformed) and Critical-Thinking (briefly, raising our *pre*suppostions from the *un*conscious to the conscious level so that we can rationally reflect on and decide concerning them, and asking at least the three "*W*" questions: *What* precisely are we talking about? *Whence*, that is, the source of the claim? *Whither* do the implications lead?

The renovation of education—from the cradle to the grave—needs to be based on a global ethic, within an emerging global civilization (*not* a monolithic one, but one that is a "Unity in Diversity": *E Pluribus Unum*, "Out of Many, One"). Deep-Dialogue and Critical-Thinking are core human competencies that function at the foundation of all human life and experience. This key flows from the insight that Reality itself, and therefore

---

37. June 14, 1995, revision. Send suggestions and revisions to Prof. Leonard Swidler, J.E.S., Temple University (062-56), 1700 N. Broad St., Philadelphia, PA 19121-0843, USA; Fax: 215-204-4569; E-mail: dialogue@temple.edu.

also our thinking about it, is a dynamic, unified field of interrelations—a profound dialogic process in which all things are interconnected.

Deep-Dialogue and Critical-Thinking are two sides of the coin of humanity. Hence, it needs to permeate all aspects of education: the cognitive, linguistic, moral, political, and esthetic.

Formation of Deep-Dialogue/Critical-Thinking

Deep-Dialogue is a powerful transformative process—which eventually must become a *habit of mind and spirit*, traditionally known as a *virtue*—grounded in classical philosophical and spiritual traditions in a global context. It has been experimentally developed and distilled over many years through a wide range of interworld encounters (interreligious, intercultural, interideological, etc.). It is a method of entering other worlds or perspectives and returning mutually transformed, having gained a deepened sense of one's own worldview and an awakened awareness of the worldview of others. Through this awakening power of Deep-Dialogue, individuals and communities are able to experience common ground between worlds and across differences and thus achieve deeper personal integrity and community-building.

At the same time, in order to open oneself to Deep-Dialogue, it is vital to develop the skills of thinking carefully and clearly, that is, of Critical-Thinking (*critical*, from the Greek, *krinein*, to choose, to judge). We need to learn how to understand what we—and others—really mean when we say something and why we say it, in order to "choose," to "judge" where we believe the truth lies. Critical-Thinking, thus, entails at least these three elements:

> 1. That we work to raise our *pre*suppostions from the unconscious level—where by definition they reside—to the conscious level. Only then can we deal with them fully humanly, that is, rationally reflect on and decide for, against, or partly-partly concerning them.
>
> 2. That we learn to understand all statements, whether from ourselves or others, in *their* context, that is, a text can be correctly understood in *its con*text. Only then will we be able to translate the original core of the statements/texts into *our* context.
>
> 3. That we learn to probe with great precision *every* statement, first of our own, but also of all others, to learn *precisely* what they *really* mean. This is particularly important to do concerning

simple statements, terms, and cliches because very often unconscious presuppositions lie beneath them.

This process of Critical-Thinking obviously entails a mental dialogue within our own mind. Thus, at its root Critical-Thinking is dialogic—and Deep-Dialogue at its root entails clear, critical thought. They are two sides of the coin of humanity. They must become virtues, habits of mind and spirit. It has become increasingly clear that one of the greatest challenges facing contemporary cultures and all levels of education is coping creatively with the powerful forces that arise when diverse worldviews and perspectives encounter one another. The most chronic, intractable, and devastating problems facing cultures today center on the breakdown of human relations in the collision of worldviews and differences in all aspects of our lives.

The Insights of Deep-Dialogue/Critical-Thinking

I am convinced that Deep-Dialogue and Critical-Thinking are core human competencies that function at the foundation of all human life and experience. From a wealth of cultural experience through the ages there has emerged the realization that human reason, Critical-Thinking, is dialogical at its core. Deep-Dialogue is thus the heart of our rational capacity to negotiate Reality, to be in touch with the ever-changing worlds around us. Together, Deep-Dialogue and Critical-Thinking are vital in the art of being human.

This insight that the dynamics of dialogue permeate our life in every way is reflected in the ancient, perennial awareness that we humans ourselves play a vital role in co-shaping our living realities. Now, the most advanced research has made it clear that we humans inhabit worlds that we ourselves shape (and that reciprocally shape us) through our thought processes. We humans inhabit worldviews that we make through dialogical processes of conceptualization, interpretation, imagination, construction, revision—all of which are integral to the rational enterprise.

In this way every aspect of our life, our experience, and the world around us arises in the context of a worldview or complex of lifeworlds that we inhabit and that inhabit us. It has become clear that at the core of this human art of world-making, which shapes *all* our experience, there is a fundamental dialogic dynamic between the self, or subject, and the realities that surround us. At the very foundation of our life we are situated in an interrelational structure of self and other (subject and object), which always involves modes of dialogue, interpretation, and critical thought.

Thus, it may be said that we humans are dialogical/rational beings, world-makers, interpretive beings who directly co-shape and participate in all phenomena that appear to us. In this deeper and expanded sense of the rational enterprise we can see that natural reason is essentially our capacity to shape our lifeworlds, to make our experience, to analytically recognize and clarify differences, and to cope with multiplicity and diversity. At the same time, it is also a capacity synthetically to discern fundamental unities and common ground, to harmonize differences into coherent order, and to negotiate complex factors in the forging of our individuality, personal identity, and integrity.

Further, the dialogic structure of humanity entails not only thinking and speaking dialogically, but likewise acting toward and with others—persons and things—in ways that are also dialogic. Since the principles on which we base our actions are called "ethics," and given that we are living increasingly in a single world, we are correspondingly moving toward a common basis, a global ethic, which shapes how we treat ourselves, each other, and the world we all inhabit.

These fundamental skills and competencies in the art of being a person exhibit diverse dimensions in the dynamics of Deep-Dialogue/Critical-Thinking. In this respect the virtues of Deep-Dialogue/Critical-Thinking are at work in every aspect of our lives—in our passions, emotions, and feelings, in our cognition, understanding, judgment, and deliberations, in our relations with self, others, and ecology. In the art of becoming a Person, an integral being (an *in*dividual, that is, undivided), it is now more urgent than ever for us to cultivate core competencies in the dynamics of Deep-Dialogue/Critical-Thinking, for these skills not only enable us to become whole Persons, integral beings, who can harmonize a boundless diversity of worldviews, perspectives, and identities into a coherent inner life, but who can also negotiate our outer life, our ethics, in peaceful and nonviolent ways of communion and community with others and with ecology.

Renovating the Foundation of Integral Education

Foundation

Since the capacities and skills of Deep-Dialogue/Critical-Thinking operate at the foundation of all our experience, they are the key ingredients in the advancement of the educational process. How we conduct our minds is all-important in the quality of our life. When we proceed in the ways of Deep-Dialogue/Critical-Thinking we promote a more meaningful, coherent, and integral life. When we do not, the result is increased fragmentation, turbulence, and loss of meaning. The dynamics of Deep-Dialogue/Critical-Thinking affect every aspect of the conduct of our mind. There is no area of our experience that does not, for example, involve some mode of interpretation: to exist, to be in the world, to experience, to feel is to be in some form of "thinking" and interpretation.

In this respect, every subject, every discipline in the school curriculum, indeed, in life itself—involves the art of "thinking" and interpretation. Since Deep-Dialogue/Critical-Thinking skills are at play in every dimension of thinking, it is not surprising that we now perceive that these core competencies are at work—or certainly should be—in all dimensions of experience, in every subject and discipline, in every aspect of our life, and, hence, in the educational curriculum as well. Therefore, we are now able to integrate diverse dimensions of experience and the curriculum that could not be brought together in systematic unity before.

Here we see that globalization is directly connected with the dynamics of Deep-Dialogue/Critical-Thinking: The dynamic of globalization involves the growing encounter of diverse worldviews and perspectives in a shared space. This is why Deep-Dialogue is also global dialogue—global in the sense of embracing not just physical space but also all worldviews and cultures. Thus, the renovation of the space of education in a pluralistic meeting of diverse worlds, cultures, disciplines, perspectives, and narratives calls for the innovations of the global classroom. The core competencies and skills in Deep-Dialogue/Critical-Thinking thus enable us to reorganize and systematically integrate diverse dimensions of the curriculum, including the areas of life and education that follow.

Reasoning and Critical-Thinking: The Knowing Arts

Here, I am speaking of all ways that we humans can know—our multiple ways of "knowing." Our art of reasoning is taken to deeper, more powerful levels through Deep-Dialogue/Critical-Thinking—the art of interpretation, of making sense of things, of understanding, of judgment, of inference are all expanded in the skills of negotiating between worlds. It is one thing to process meaning and understanding within a given worldview. It is vastly more challenging to gain access to multiple alternative worlds (diverse and widely variant systems of meaning) *and* to hold them together in dialogical consciousness.

The capacity to negotiate multiple alternative perspectives, worldviews, ideologies, narrative forms—to think critically between worlds—is an area of education that has been underdeveloped. In our dramatically globalizing cultures it becomes urgent to globalize our rational capacities, to inculcate the Deep-Dialogue/Critical-Thinking habit of thinking and reasoning between worlds. It is now increasingly recognized that the activities of open inquiry, truth-seeking, and cognition essentially involve the capacities to mediate and negotiate between multiple alternative perspectives and narrative worlds. Here we need to expand and develop the areas of discursive dialogue, deliberative dialogue, diversity dialogue, and integral dialogue.

Discursive dialogue develops and augments all areas of discursive reason, within a given worldview and between worldviews. *Deliberative dialogue* enhances the skills in deliberating between and among diverse perspectives or ideologies in the art of decision-making. *Diversity dialogue* augments the analytical skills of discerning and respecting real differences within and between worlds. One vital aspect of Deep-Dialogue/Critical-Thinking is the capacity to recognize real differences and appreciate true diversity without losing the common ground and unities that hold creative diversity together. Thus, these skills heighten both the analytic and synthetic abilities of discursive thought. *Integral dialogue* focuses on those virtues of Deep-Dialogue/Critical-Thinking that bring out underlying unities, relations, identities, and common ground across widely variant differences within and between worlds.

Moving between Worlds in the Language Arts

Wherever there is thought and meaning, we find language and the language arts in play. In this respect all of the knowing arts listed above are relevant to all aspects of the mastery of the language arts. One key area that has been neglected in the traditional curriculum is mastering the skills of moving between worlds, between religions, cultures, ideologies, and diverse structures of meaning. All of the skills of creative thinking, writing, discussion, and conversation are taken to a new level through Deep-Dialogue/Critical-Thinking. In the area of literature, where widely diverse narrative forms are involved, the capacities of Deep-Dialogue/Critical-Thinking enable thoughtful readers to gain ever deeper appreciation of the differences and commonalities between shifting narrative contexts and forms.

Cognitive Development and Awakening Scientific Understanding

It becomes immediately apparent that the concern for truth and knowledge is profoundly affected when we are faced with very different worldviews, narrative accounts, conceptual frameworks, and divergent paradigms of interpretation and theory-making. The older ways of seeking truth and gaining coherent scientific understanding have not been adequate in the scientific search for truth between worldviews and widely variant paradigms of interpretation. It becomes clear that the highest virtues of scientific understanding and the scientific experimental method are those of the dynamics of Deep-Dialogue/Critical-Thinking. Indeed, the cultural advance to scientific methods of inquiry are celebrations of certain skills of Deep-Dialogue/Critical-Thinking. The creative interplay, for example, between forming a theory and experimentally testing it with an openness to ongoing revision is a virtue of Deep-Dialogue/Critical-Thinking. However, now scientific inquiry and truth seeking between worldviews, between and across divergent paradigms of world making, advance scientific method to its higher globalized form.

5. Mindfulness Education: Rational Awakening and Becoming Integral: It is more obvious now that as the higher powers of mind are activated through the awakening energy of Deep-Dialogue/Critical-Thinking, the skills in becoming a whole and integral Person are greatly augmented and accelerated. When people are exposed to diverse worlds and perspectives, when they inhabit multiple worlds and are inhabited by diverse worldviews, something profound happens in the structure of their inner lives. Their identity and sense of self can become fractured and broken across the diverse world contexts in which they find themselves situated.

Here, it is clear that the skills of Deep-Dialogue/Critical-Thinking enable humans to cultivate inner deep dialogue and clarifying critical thought to negotiate the experience within. In globalizing the space of the inner self to encounter creatively all the cultures of the globe through Deep-Dialogue/Critical-Thinking, we are better able to become integral, whole Persons. In this respect, these skills are essential to human flourishing in our emerging global civilization. We now begin to see the essential connection between rational awakening, personal integrity, and moral education.

The classical view of education rightly understood that educating the whole person is essentially tied to the awakening of moral education. Now we see further that this rational awakening is at the same time becoming a more fully aware being, one with a deeper capacity to enter with full presence into the present moment. Thus, to enter this sacred space of Deep-Dialogue is to develop Critical-Thinking, to deepen our rational awareness, to activate our higher moral and spiritual powers, to enter a deeper form of cognitive and scientific awareness, to achieve greater wellbeing in becoming a more whole and integral individual—a *Person*.

Moral and Political Education: Global Citizenship and Community

Today there is not only a deeper awakening of the inner life and of personal wellbeing, but this is now also seen to be directly connected with the awakening of our outer life in the wider context. As the space of culture becomes increasingly globalized, multiple worlds encounter one another in a pluralistic marketplace. The core habits of mind and spirit of Deep-Dialogue/Critical-Thinking are more essential than ever for democratic and civil discourse. The key to good citizenship involves the skills of deep listening, clear thinking, and speaking across and between diverse worldviews and perspectives. Moral Deep-Dialogue and Critical-Thinking are vital in cultivating such virtues as respect for others and for differences, indeed, for all the moral virtues. Thus, the dynamics of Deep-Dialogue/Critical-Thinking are at the heart of the quality of our inner life (*intra*personal) and outer life (*inter*personal). In this respect it is essential that we raise our youth with the skills of Deep-Dialogue/Critical-Thinking; they are vital in humanizing our shared corporate space.

In awakening the virtues of Deep-Dialogue/Critical-Thinking we tap the foundations of global ethics and open the common ground for genuine communication across and between worldviews. In thus humanizing the space of culture it becomes possible to find the long sought union of unity and diversity. Deep-Dialogue and Critical-Thinking create common ground in which individuals may flourish and multiplicity and diversity may be appreciated and respected, while at the same time the common origin of our diverse worlds is honored and celebrated. This is why Deep-Dialogue and Critical-Thinking are key to global ethics, global citizenship, and civic democracy.

Peace Studies: Coexistence Education–Unity and Diversity Awakening

We now see more readily that diverse attempts in recent years to help our youth cope creatively with issues of identity, multiplicity, diversity, difference, and unity all converge on mastering the skills of Deep-Dialogue/Critical-Thinking. Such diverse attempts as "diversity training," "sensitivity training," "tolerance education," "coexistence work," "community building," "peace studies," "conflict resolution" are all more localized attempts to tap the powers of Deep-Dialogue/Critical-Thinking. The capacity to listen deeply to others who inhabit different worlds and perspectives, the ability to recognize and honor genuine difference, the competence to truly enter other worlds and resist reducing the Other to one's own worldview—are all vital in the awakening of nonviolent forms of being a self and being in culture. Here, too, the skills of "mediation" and "negotiation" between polarized and mutually estranged views are developed. By activating the core competencies of Deep-Dialogue/Critical-Thinking we tap the foundations of the many initiatives to humanize the corporate space of our shared lives. Thus, Deep-Dialogue and Critical-Thinking are vital in fostering a culture of nonviolence and of peaceful sharing of corporate space.

Awakening Esthetic Experience: Creative Imagination and the Arts

It comes as no surprise that the awakening powers of Deep-Dialogue/Critical-Thinking should also be at the heart of our esthetic life. It has become more obvious in the twentieth, and now the twenty-first, century that our deepest esthetic creativity and capacity for esthetic experience turns on our openness to an ever-deeper encounter with works of art in the diverse media. Whether the appreciation of poetics and literature in the language arts, or the esthetic encounter with music, visual, or lively arts—the core competencies of Deep-Dialogue/Critical-Thinking foster the awakening of our esthetic capacities. Esthetic dialogue helps to deepen and enrich the fundamental structures of all our experience (between the Subject and the Other—that is, the Object appearing to it). This esthetic enrichment in turn affects everything we encounter in our lives.

Integral Education and the Foundation of the Liberal Arts

It should now be apparent that the introduction of Deep-Dialogue/Critical-Thinking into the core of the Liberal Arts will have profound implications for revisioning and restructuring our current educational priorities and practices. It is now more obvious that interdisciplinary (intercultural, inter-world) education is not a secondary or derivative form of education but a *primary* dimension of human understanding. The classical ideal of realizing a truly integral education for whole persons becomes more attainable with the introduction of Deep-Dialogue/Critical-Thinking into our educational life. It is now possible to detect deeper connections and common ground among all areas of the liberal arts, especially among the natural sciences, the social sciences, and the humanities, as well as with the professions.

Transformation of Consciousness—Transformation of the World

Humanity's move in the third millennium BCE from mere tribal existence to the Age of Civilizations (from the Latin *civis* for "city," wherein higher human capacities developed) involved a radical transformation of human consciousness. A similar radical transformation in human consciousness took place in the first millennium BCE (referred to as the Axial Period, when the great primary religions and philosophies appeared around the globe). Now, at the beginning of the third millennium CE, humanity is entering into a third phase of radical transformation of consciousness, the Age of Global Dialogue, which will be characterized by globalization and Deep-Dialogue and its obverse Critical-Thinking.

Just as the earlier broad development of a sense of personal responsibility with the inbreaking of the Axial Age and just as the claim of the universal validity of democracy and human rights in political life with the Enlightenment transformed the world for all subsequent centuries, now at the dawn of the Age of Global Dialogue the dramatic spreading of Deep-Dialogue/Critical-Thinking will utterly and creatively transform the world *ad infinitum*.

Seven Stages of Deep-Dialogue Applied to Teaching: The Total Learning Process

These seven stages of Deep-Dialogue applied to teaching were adapted by Launa Ellison on October 22, 2000, at a training session conducted by the Global Dialogue Institute after having the Seven Stages of Deep-Dialogue, as presented and discussed above.

Stage 1: Radical Encountering of Difference; Self Faces the Other

Self faces an Other way of teaching, a different view of what is possible, a different view of teacher behavior. This Other disrupts my settled patterns of interpretation. This Other represents a different way of making sense of learning, a different way of experiencing students, a different way of experiencing important classroom processes. This new Other is disconcerting. I feel vulnerable and challenged. I must make a decision to move forward toward the change—or draw back.

Stage 2: Crossing Over, Letting Go and Entering the World of the Other: Self Transformed through Empathy

This new view of "Total Learning Processes" is very different from my own. I feel challenged to inquire, investigate, engage. I realize that I need to stand back and distance myself from my former habits and patterns of minding my teaching practices. I begin to realize that these new teaching processes organize and process the world very differently from my way. I realize that I must learn new habits and ways of interpretation to make sense of "Total Learning Processes." I must translate my practices into a different form of teaching that sees education and student learning differently.

Stage 3: Inhabiting and Experiencing the World of the Other; Self Transformed into the Other

I begin to feel a new, deep connection—empathy—for these new ways. I want to let myself go, to grow in this new way of "Total Learning Processes." I hold on to my prior views as much as I can, but I do advance in a conservative fashion. I experience an excitement in discovering, in inhabiting a new and different view of the teaching-learning process.

Stage 4: Crossing Back with Expanded Vision; Self Returns Home with New Knowledge

I return to my classroom, bringing back new knowledge of how to think and act—and may even wish to adopt/adapt some of it for myself. As a result of my experience, I now realize that there are other ways of understanding the teaching-learning process. I am therefore open to rethinking how I see myself, my students, and the "Total Learning Process." My encounter with these new ways challenges my former identity, and everything begins to appear in a new light. There now begins a dramatic deepening of my sense of Self. There is no return to my former unilateral way.

Stage 5: The Dialogical/Critical Awakening: A Radical Paradigm Shift; Self Inwardly Transformed

As a result of the "Total Learning Process," I can no longer return to my former ways with the students. I begin to realize that my encounter with the "Total Learning Process" has shaken the foundation of my former view of learning and classroom management, my former identity as teacher. Now that I am mindful of the living reality of other ways of teaching/learning, of other perspectives, I can no longer return to my former identity and forget these new ways. I begin to realize there are other ways of teaching, other perspectives that surround me. I now open to a plurality of other views and perspectives on teacher-student relationships and feel that this irrevocably changes my sense of self.

Stage 6: The Global Awakening: The Paradigm Shift Matures; Self Related to Self, Others, the World

I have a new sense of Self and "Total Learning Processes" that are inseparably bound together in a boundless interrelational web. This diversity enriches my self and my teaching. I now see that all worlds are situated in a common ground of reality and that radical differences are nevertheless situated in a field of Unity. I experience three related dimensions of global dialogical awakening:

(a) I become aware of a deep inner dialogue within my self. In this inner dialogue I feel increasingly more deeply rooted and grounded while I teach. My identity is enriched as I experience a more potent sense of my uniqueness and celebrate the uniqueness of each of my students. (b) As my new inner dialogue and reflective thinking evolve, I find myself in new and transformed relations with my students, parents, and school culture. This new phase of relations with my peers can be disorienting and disconcerting, for as I now dramatically grow in my new role I find myself at an estranged distance from many of my peers. I face a new turbulence—miscommunication and misunderstanding with my colleagues—and a challenging and dramatic dialogue unfolds. (c) As this inner/outer dialogue matures, I realize that my understanding of "Total Learning Processes" enters a new light. Dialogues abound in all directions. I have a new sense of reality and dynamic ever-deepening relations. I have a new attitude toward life and teaching.

Stage 7: Personal and Global Transforming of Life and Behavior; Self Lives and Acts in a New Global Dialogical Consciousness

As my new understanding of "Total Learning Processes" becomes a habit of life, I find that my behavior and disposition with myself, with my students, and with my school community have changed. I realize that the deepest care for my self essentially involves my care for others and my school environment. I have a deeper sense of belonging to my world and to my community—and with this a boundless sense of responsibility in all of my conduct. I now realize that I have been transformed in the deepest habits of mind and behavior.

6

Dialogue Attempted

A Christian Experiment in "Ecumenical Esperanto"

Perhaps the problems and promises of the most pressing dialogues have been sufficiently outlined, and the goals and the suggested means to the goals are now about as clear as they can be made in a purely theoretical way. The next step is to try to put the theory into action. I as a Christian theologian need to attempt to reflect on my Christian faith in an "ecumenical Esperanto," which is "from below" and "from within" that can claim to be recognizably Christian and at the same time make room for non-Christians to recognize their own faith or ideology therein—somehow to feel included in that language. This will be a difficult undertaking for both sides since, as I have indicated, both the new language and the new consciousness to be able to hear and understand the new language need to be forged by us together. Both sides need to stretch ourselves as far as we can to meet and understand our dialogue partner *in optimam partem*, the most sympathetic manner possible, while still staying in integral touch with our own sources. To my non-Christian sisters and brothers I must say: Let us help each other. Let us try together.

The "I" and Radical Openness

Granted, the dialogic character of the contemporary Christian's affirming, appropriating, and acting on Christian belief that moves dialectically between the Christian tradition (with Yeshua as its primary standard) and contemporary experience, it is in the final analysis, "I," right now—and "I" includes looking to the past and the future, includes me in context and community, and therefore is really an "I-we," deciding within the horizon of the Ultimate Meaning of life—who am the final decider on what is proper to affirm intellectually, trust emotionally-spiritually, and act on. That great beacon of Western theology, St. Thomas Aquinas, said as much when he wrote: "All things are subject to divine providence, but rational creatures are so in a superior way. For they are under divine providence by participating in it, for they are called to in some way *be* divine providence for themselves and for others."[1] The contemporary Catholic moral theologian Franz Böckle made a similar point: The human being "however would also not be free if these norms were laid upon him from the outside, as for example by a biblical or natural law positivism. He must set them himself— again, however, not arbitrarily but freely. It is precisely his freedom that reveals itself to him as a task."[2]

To paraphrase John Henry Newman, after all the agonizing is over, it is conscience first and pope second. That is eminently true even when we decide that pope—or tradition, or whatever—is first, for in reality it is precisely that which *our conscience* tells us is proper in that case. In other words, all talk in religion, indeed, all talk about God, is ultimately really talk about ourselves (though not necessarily only so), for all religion is about the ultimate meaning of *our* lives; we know God only insofar as God is related to *us*. Even talk about God *in se* is really positive or negative extrapolation of talk about God *ad nos*, "facing us."[3] That is why many persons, religious and would-be religious, become impatient over theological speculation that does not rather clearly have a soteriological aim, that is, that leads us to what we are convinced is the purpose of life—whether it is called redemption, the Reign of God, *moksha, nirvana*, or whatever.

Catholic theologian Quentin Quesnell made essentially the same point:

> The Christian message . . . meaning specifically those parts of the Bible and of early Christian monuments and history which happen, under a particular interpretation, to appeal to the person who is talking. This is inevitable. It is nothing to be ashamed

---

1. *Summa Theologiae*, I–II, Q. 91, a. 2: "Inter cetera autem rationalis creatura excellentiori quondam modo divinae providentiae subiacet, inquantum et ipsa fit providentiae particeps, sibi ipsi et aliis providens."

2. Franz Böckle, "Theonome Autonomie in der Begrundung der Menschenrechte," in Johannes Swartländer, ed., *Modernes Freiheit Ethos und christlicher Glaube* (Munich: Kaiser, 1981) 306.

3. Wilfred Cantwell Smith commented: "We thought all religious orientations fundamentally anthropological; we have found that this demolishes some myths, at least superficially, but makes others much more intelligible than they were, and in turn this makes anthropology, one's doctrine of man, turn out to be in effect religious, at least potentially" (Wilfred Cantwell Smith, *Toward a World Theology* [Philadelphia: Westminster, 1981], 146).

of. But it must be recognized, and that is what the subject-conscious, self-aware new paradigm of theology is all about . . . What then is the foundation? . . . in brief (as Lonergan explains at length) the foundation is the theologian's own *self.* There can be no other . . . Theologians in pre-self-conscious theology could speak as if they were able to appeal to God, God's mind, God's will, as their norm, criterion, or measure. But a norm, criterion, or measure must be something at our disposal . . . A subject-aware theology knows its unity comes from God not as from a norm but as from an aspiration.[4]

Everyone searching for religious meaning and truth, no matter how convinced by and committed to a particular tradition or position, if they would act with integrity, must have a "radical" openness and openness "in principle." For example, they must be willing to say with total seriousness that for the sake of integrity it is possible in the future that they might have to cease being Christian or Muslim or theist or Marxist—at least as they now understand it. It may not seem at all likely, but they must be open to the possibility.[5] This is the risk spoken of above in dialogue.

   4. Quentin Quesnell, "On Not Negotiating the Self in the Structure of Theological Revolutions," typescript at January 3–11, 1984, conference in Honolulu on "Paradigm Shifts in Buddhism and Christianity: Cultural Systems and the Self," 13, 15.
   5. Some time after writing this section, I came across very strong corroboration in the writings of two Catholic theologians, Bernard Lonergan and Walter E. Conn. In speaking about conversion first of all in the intellectual sphere, Conn—here following Lonergan—wrote that "its really crucial significance is found in the kind of personal, existential self-appropriation that we have been discussing, the appropriation of oneself as a free, responsible, and self-constituting originator of value, who in one's own self-transcending judgments and choices is the criterion, of the real and the truly good" (Conn, *Conscience*, 192). Elsewhere, Conn—also picking up on the paradigm shift in the radical involvement of the thinker in truth statements discussed above—wrote of "the possibility of cognitive conversion: the critical recognition of the constitutive and normative role of one's own judgment in knowing reality and therefore value. A person who experiences such critical understanding of self as knower ceases to look beyond the self somewhere 'out there' for a criterion of the real or the valuable. For cognitive conversion consists precisely in discovering that criterion in one's own realistic judgment" (Conn, "Conversion," 325–6). Lonergan, speaking of the move from intellectual to moral conversion, wrote: "Moral conversion goes beyond the value, truth, to values generally. It promotes the subject from cognitional to moral self-transcendence. It sets him on a new, existential level of consciousness and establishes him as an originating value" (Bernard Lonergan, *Method in Theology* [New York: Herder & Herder, 1972], 241). The notion of "radical openness" is also confirmed by Conn: "It is right that each person should be able to take a stand on his or her own conscience, uncoerced by external force. But everyone who does so should also recognize that appeals to conscience do not automatically or necessarily make one right, that some consciences are more authentic than others, and that one's commitment to his or her 'conscience' must always remain critical. Sincerity to what one feels deeply about, or spontaneously 'thinks best,'

If I may add a personal note: When I was younger I suffered great anxieties, at times, agonies, whenever my well-learned beliefs were seriously challenged by doubts. I very slowly learned to find ever-deeper, ever more complex, yet simpler, explanations. The deeper the challenge, the more profound the resultant clarification when it finally came. I eventually realized that if I were like Faust, "*immer strebend*" (*aber sanft*, I would add), those resolutions always did come. So, now maintaining a radical openness not only fills me with no anxiety, but it fills me instead with an inner calm, trust, even joy of anticipation.

Stages of Faith Development and Interreligious, Interideological Dialogue

Earlier, it was pointed out that authentic dialogue occurs only when each partner comes primarily to learn from the other, when each therefore assumes that they do not have the fullness of truth; consequently, they meet each other fundamentally as equals, *par cum pari*. This clearly cannot happen if the partners do not share in some significant ways a deabsolutized understanding of truth-statements. When the partners do not hold some sort of relational understanding of truth-statements, but an absolute one, then interreligious, interideological encounters with them can only be prolegomena to authentic dialogue. Of course, it is absolutely vital that these prolegomena be worked through so as to arrive at authentic dialogue one day.

However, it is extremely helpful to note that there is a relationship between an individual's cognitional, moral judgment, and one's faith-ideology development. These relationships have been worked out by pioneer scholars such as Erikson, Piaget, Kohlberg, and Fowler.[6] The relationship might be summed up in the two words, "prerequisites" and "stages." Cognitional capacities and psychosocial experiences must reach certain minimums before the individual can advance to the next level of moral judgment and/or faith-ideology. The advance does not necessarily occur, but, without the presence of the prerequisite capacities and experiences, it cannot occur. Moreover, a more advanced level of moral judgment and/or faith-ideology cannot be attained without passing through the lower stages.

---

in other words, is not enough. Sincerity must be fully and continually self-critical if it is to be authentic. For such self-criticism, of course, a radical openness to other viewpoints is a prerequisite; and such openness seems to have its necessary condition in a deep sense of humility" (Conn, *Conscience*, 207).

6. The work of the first three is admirably summed up in Fowler, *Stages of Faith*.

Kohlberg and his colleagues developed a schema of three pairs of stages of moral judgment development; he called them pre-conventional, where the standard for moral judgment tends to be the self—conventional where the standards come from the outside society, and post-conventional where the standards tend to go beyond societal patterns to general principles.[7] (It should be noted also that in all these various advancements, the attainment of the previous stages is not rejected, but they are taken up into the next higher stage and transformed.) Fowler, building on the work of Piaget and Kohlberg and adding to it that of Erikson with his emphasis on the psychosocial dimension of human development, has built an impressive body of field research and analysis, on the basis of which he formulated his theory of six stages of faith-ideology development.

What has special bearing on the matter of interreligious, interideological dialogue are the characteristics Kohlberg and colleagues have found in what they call the post-conventional stages, five and six, and what Fowler and colleagues have found in his stages five and six of faith-ideology development. Faith, as used by Fowler, clearly is not restricted to "religious" faith, but includes all grounding explanations of life, that is, religions and ideologies. Kohlberg comments on the move from conventional to post-conventional moral reasoning as follows: "The rejection of conventional moral reasoning begins with the perception of relativism, the awareness that any given society's definition of right and wrong, however legitimate, is only one among many, both in fact and theory."[8] Thus, it would seem necessary for a person to have moved to Kohlberg's stage five in moral reasoning in order to engage in authentic interreligious, interideological dialogue.

In writing about his stage five in faith-ideology development, Fowler has some startlingly pertinent things to say:

> Stage 5 accepts as axiomatic that truth is more multidimensional and organically interdependent than most theories or accounts of truth can grasp. Religiously, it knows that the symbols, stories, doctrines and liturgies offered by its own or other traditions are inevitably partial, limited to a particular people's experience of God and incomplete. Stage 5 also sees, however, that in the relativity of religious traditions what matters is not

---

7. The work of Kohlberg was to some extent challenged by his co-worker Carol Gilligan with her argument that he did not take women into account in his surveys. See Carol Gilligan, *In a Different Voice* (Cambridge: Harvard University Press, 1982). However, that problem does not arise in the work of Fowler, for his interviews are fifty-fifty women and men.

8. Lawrence Kohlberg and Carol Gilligan, "The Adolescent as a Philosopher: The Discovery of the Self in a Postconventional World," *Daedalus* 100 (Fall 1971) 1072.

their relativity to each other, but their relativity—*rela*tivity—to the reality to which they mediate relation. Conjunctive faith [Fowler's stage 5], therefore, is ready for significant encounters with other traditions than its own, expecting that truth has disclosed and will disclose itself in those traditions in ways that may complement or correct its own. Krister Stendahl is fond of saying that no interfaith conversation is genuinely ecumenical unless the quality of mutual sharing and receptivity is such that each party makes him or herself vulnerable to conversion to the other's truth. This would be Stage 5 ecumenism. This position implies no lack of commitment to one's own truth tradition. Nor does it mean a wishy-washy neutrality or mere fascination with the exotic features of alien cultures. Rather, Conjunctive faith's radical openness to the truth of the other stems precisely from its confidence in the reality mediated by its own tradition and in the awareness that that reality overspills its mediation. The person of Stage 5 makes her or his own experience of truth the principle by which other claims to truth are tested. But he or she assumes that each genuine perspective will augment and correct aspects of the other, in a mutual movement toward the real and the true.[9]

Again, it would seem clear that Stage 5 faith-ideology is a prerequisite for authentic interreligious, interideological dialogue. Before that, interreligious, interideological encounters would be prolegomena to authentic interreligious, interideological dialogue.

The age pattern of the appearance of Stage 5 faith-ideology also has a bearing on this issue. According to Fowler, transitional Stage 4–5 does not appear until the twenties, and then only in relatively small numbers when covering the whole spectrum of U.S. society. However, of those adults over thirty that his team interviewed in depth (359 persons over eight years), a third of them attained transitional Stage 4–5 or higher, meaning that a third of the population (if the sample is truly representative) over thirty is capable of authentic dialogue. It should also be noted that with higher levels of education the percentage of more advanced faith-ideology stages proportionally increases. Since by the very nature of the enterprise, those persons most likely to be interested in interreligious, interideological dialogue will also tend to have higher than average education levels, the percentage of persons participating in formal interreligious, interideological dialogue who are at Stage 4–5 faith-ideology development and, hence, capable of authentic

---

9. Fowler, *Stages of Faith*, 186–87.

dialogue should be considerably higher than 33 percent—though statistics are not available to indicate precisely how much.

Thus, it is important to know at what stage potential participants in interreligious, interideological dialogue are, so as to avoid unwarranted expectations—and subsequent disillusionments. Being forewarned about what stage potential dialogue participants are at, a sensitive person should be able to assist all concerned to work their way through the necessary prolegomena more helpfully and perhaps even more rapidly. Obviously, much work needs to be done in correlating faith-ideology development and the practice of interreligious, interideological dialogue.

This research also speaks to the concern expressed to Knitter when he advanced his interreligious "pluralist" Christology.[10] He was at great pains to stress the consequent need to develop "reception" of this "deabsolutized" theology by the masses of the faithful. He was correct in the need for this emphasis, but Fowler's research indicates that there is a much greater base for such reception than one might have presumed. It would seem that many of the sheep of the flock are far ahead of the shepherds. It is the latter who are perhaps often the greatest hindrances—resisting the new paradigm.

What also needs even more research and thought is the correlation between stages of faith-ideology development and interreligious, interideological dialogue on the level of the group and culture. Lonergan raised the issue when speaking about the educational process, "in the difference between the child beginning kindergarten and the doctoral candidate writing his dissertation. But the difference produced by the education of individuals is only a recapitulation of the longer process of the education of [hu]mankind, of the evolution of social institutions and of the development of cultures. Religions . . . all had their rude beginnings, slowly developed, reached their peak."[11]

One need only think of the official stance of the Catholic Church toward dialogue with non-Catholic Christians, let alone non-Christians, before and after Vatican II. The former was vigorously negative, and the latter just as vigorously positive. Vatican II was clearly a conversion experience on the level of a whole religious institution, clearly based on the attainment, officially, of a new level of cognitive capacity, which allowed the institution also to advance to Stage 5 in faith development. Again, one need only do a comparative study of the Vatican documents in regard to the limitations on absolute claims resulting from an awareness of history, or in regard to

10. Paul F. Knitter, "Toward a Liberation Theology of Religions," in Hick and Knitter, *Myth of Christian Uniqueness*, 184–85.

11. Bernard Lonergan, *Collection*, ed. F. E. Crowe (New York: Herder & Herder, 1967) 254.

the possibility of learning from other religions, both before Vatican II (for example, *Mortalium animos*, 1928, *Humanae generis*, 1950) and during and after the Council. The transition from Stages 3 and 4, ideology-centered, to Stage 5, dialogue-oriented, is very apparent. Of course the implementation of the official transition has been anything but smooth and painless; the resistance on the part of those Catholic officials in positions of power who personally have not yet themselves made the transition is intense.

Fortunately for Catholicism, the dreary, depressing decades of the backward-looking pontificates of John Paul II and Benedict XVI (1978–2013) are followed by one open, committed to the Vatican II vision, Pope Francis.

Moreover, I am in agreement with Fowler's statement: "Careful theological work is required in a faith tradition to determine the normative images of adulthood which that tradition envisions. By normative images of adulthood I mean to ask, what developmental trajectory into mature faith is envisioned and called for by a particular faith tradition, at its best? While unable to speak for others, I am convinced that the normative image of adulthood envisioned in Christian faith leads out toward Universalizing faith Stage 6 [Fowler's final state]." I also agree with the further statement: "The modal developmental level is the average expectable level of development for adults in a given community . . . The operation of the modal level in a community sets an effective limit on the ongoing process of growth in faith. My observations lead me to judge that the modal developmental level in most middle-class American churches and synagogues is best described in terms of Synthetic-Conventional faith [Stage 3, ideology-centered] or perhaps just beyond it [that is, we are right, the others are wrong]."[12]

What of the 33 percent of the over-thirty population who are at transitional 4–5 stage or higher? Have they left the churches? Various surveys strongly suggest that as many as a third of U.S. Catholics have left the Catholic Church. Are they often frustrated and underutilized by them? If they were mostly present and active and not restricted, it would seem there would be a great deal more creative interreligious, interideological dialogue occurring on the grassroots level and above than seems to be. What of those church members at Stages 2 and 3 who are held back rather than encouraged to advance to their full capabilities? The potential for good within the churches is immense; the actuality is much less so. Might the situations in other Western religions, and ideologies be similar?

What the facts are in non-Western cultures and religious and ideological traditions requires careful work. The importance of such work for

---

12. Fowler, *Stages of Faith*, 107

interreligious, interideological dialogue, for theology, for ideology, for religions in general, and human life on this globe can hardly be overemphasized. Fortunately, Fowler and his colleagues are beginning seriously to investigate his findings and analyses cross-culturally.

"Reconciling the World to God through Christ"

After these prolegomena, let me finally try as a Christian to theologize in "Ecumenical Esperanto." Although I have argued that the historical Yeshua ought to be the primary standard for what is considered Christian, at the same time I do not want to give the impression that I wish to dismiss everything that was said "about" Yeshua by the New Testament writers. Their words have often been precious and insightful to me. Hence, I would like to reflect on a very key notion found in the New Testament that has been formative of much of subsequent Christian history and at the same time the source of tremendous difficulties for non-Christians, as well as all critical thinkers.

Let me begin by posing the problem this way: Does the Pauline statement that the world is reconciled to God through Christ (cf. Rom 5:10–11; 2 Cor 5:19–20) have to be understood in a way that is unacceptable, even not understandable, to the modern critical mind, and also antithetic to the possibility that other world religions are valid, authentic ways of humanity's being "reconciled to God"? I believe it does not. Paul here is obviously talking about something that far transcends the everyday life experience that we have of reality. Clearly, he is not going to be able to use language in its normal, everyday sense. However, like all human beings, he will nevertheless have to use the one language that we have, namely, human language, with all its limitations, formed by the everyday experience we have—and then perhaps, at most, extend it out from that everyday experience to lend it additional variations of meaning.[13]

---

13. The careful word studies by Friedrich Buchsel in Gerhard Kittel, *Theological Dictionary of the New Testament* (Grand Rapids: Eerdmans, 1968) 1:254–55, and by other scholars in various reference works, really do not resolve the problem as we have posed it. It is clear from these studies that the word used by Paul (and he is only one who uses it in the New Testament), *katallassein*, and its variant *katallagenai*, fundamentally means to change, and in this case to change the relationship between God and humanity in a positive direction, that is, to reconcile. *Theos en en Christo kosmon katallasson heauto* is how Paul put it in 2 Cor 5:19. Jerome translated it: *Deus erat in Christo mundum reconcilians sibi*. The very notion of reconciliation in whatever language is perforce on the transphysical, "metaphorical" plane; it is not used to describe material, physical things but the relationship between beings on the mental or psychological level. The word studies tend not to point out that obvious fact—perhaps because it is

Although Paul necessarily used everyday language, he sometimes used it in a way that was quite common in his time in order to convey meanings that went far beyond our everyday experience of things. Such use of language very often is called mythic, that is, the use of a connected set of images that points to a meaning beyond the surface meaning—like a metaphor. That is what Paul is doing here. Thus, his language will *sound* as if he were describing in a very empirical, perhaps even physical, ontological, manner what he understood *really* to have happened on a different level in the relationship between the world and God in the Christ event. The image that is projected by Paul is as if somehow the world—meaning mainly humanity—was in a way pointed in the wrong direction, namely, away from God—who existed in a transcendent fashion, that is, outside of the world. Then, God worked through Christ, who, as it were, reached his huge hand up and grasped the world by the scruff of its neck and turned it around so that it was facing God once again. Thus, there was a sort of ontological, cosmic "reconciling of the world with God through Christ."

Of course, this is a transphysical, mythic, metaphorical image. Paul was not so naive as to think that he was in fact empirically describing the way things really are physically with this language in the same way that he might have described the various parts of a tent, how they were related to each other, what materials they were made of, etc. (as a professional tentmaker, he presumably must have done this, often quite well). Rather, he was attempting to communicate some insight that would contribute to an "explanation of the meaning of life." This is what mythic stories are supposed to do. Just what was this insight contributing to the "explanation of the meaning of life" that Paul was trying to communicate with this mythic image? It seems to me that it can be explained as follows.

Paul obviously had a profound experience of Jesus Christ, even though he never met him personally while Yeshua was alive on earth. This experience of Jesus Christ was for Paul quite obviously a breakthrough kind of experience, a "turn-around," a *metanoia*, or conversion experience. Through it he felt that he now had a profoundly positive kind of relationship with the ultimate meaning of life for him, which he called God—and this new, profoundly positive relationship for him came through his encounter with Jesus Christ. For Paul, Jesus Christ provided the opportunity, the occasion, the means to have this positive relationship with the ultimate meaning of life, God. Paul was much more interested in soteriology than in Christology; he

---

such an obvious given. But, when the theologians go to work on the meaning of Paul's statements, they often seem to be oblivious of this fact.

was much more concerned about "Christ's incarnation in Christians" than in "God's incarnation in Christ."[14]

In similar fashion, for other Christians Jesus Christ has also been this means of attaining a profoundly positive relationship with the ultimate meaning of life, God. From Jesus Christ or, more precisely, Yeshua, Christians learn that the ultimate meaning of life is to stand in the center of one's being and turn and reach outward; it is to love, that is, to reach out beyond oneself to the good, to being, to all that exists. For human beings this means primarily other persons, but it also includes all beings, and ultimately the Source, Sustainer, and Goal of all being, whom Christians and many others call God. Nontheists, such as Theravada Buddhists, may prefer to use such terms as "universe" or "nature"—perhaps not unlike that school of Western thought following the Jewish philosopher Spinoza that spoke of "God, that is, Nature," *Deus sive Natura*. This is not in any way self-destructive, for as was noted above and pointed out by Yeshua when he cited from the Hebrew Bible, we are to love our neighbor *as* our self. We can love our neighbor, that is, others, only to the extent that we truly love ourselves. Authentic self-love and authentic love of the other are not only not mutually exclusive, they are necessarily mutually inclusive.

There is much more to the further understanding of the living out of this central insight that Christians claim to find in the life of Yeshua. As remarked above, Christians believe—that is, they are convinced—that, in this man Yeshua of Nazareth, this central insight into the meaning of human life and the attendant insights and implications were so fully exemplified and lived out to the point of a self-emptying, agonizing death for the sake of his friends that they feel compelled to use language that speaks of the meeting of the human and the divine in him. At any rate, by looking at Yeshua, by encountering him, Christians claim that they are thereby enabled to have a profound positive relationship with God. In other words, they are "reconciled to God."

Christians, further, are convinced that the inflow of insights as to the meaning of life was so overwhelming in Yeshua that to express this perception they had to turn to hyperbolic language, language that was metaphorical, poetic, for this kind of language normally is what human beings must use when trying to express something that transcends everyday language. This is the same point made earlier when speaking of Paul's use of what I called mythic language. Catholic theologian David Tracy expressed the same idea when he used the term "limit-language": "All authentic limit-language seems to be initially and irretrievably a symbolic and metaphorical

---

14. See Joseph A. Fitzmyer, "Jesus the Lord," *Chicago Studies* 17 (1978) 91.

one. Insofar as the hidden dimension of an ultimate limit is not merely hidden but not even expressible in the language of the everyday (as no-*thing*, no object in the world alongside other objects), that language retains the linguistic structure of metaphor and symbols . . . even *explicitly* religious language (for example, the language of the scriptures or of the Christian myths) is intrinsically symbolic and metaphorical limit-language."[15]

Hence, recalling what was said earlier, Christians eventually began to speak of Yeshua of Nazareth as the meeting point of the divine and the human, so that later, in the fourth and fifth centuries when Christianity had become the state religion of the Roman Empire and had largely embraced the Hellenistic thought world and means of conceptualization, orthodox Christians began to speak of the "God-man." Unfortunately, for subsequent Christians and for the rest of the world the profound insight that the first Christians had in their liberating encounter with Yeshua of Nazareth was now translated out of its poetic, metaphorical language into Hellenistic empirical, ontological language in a manner that took the original language also to be empirical, ontological. It was a profound misjudgment not to perceive that almost all the original language of the first Christians as expressed in the New Testament was in fact poetic, metaphorical, when speaking in its most ecstatic terms about the significance and meaning of Yeshua of Nazareth.[16]

Paul, the great preacher of the "proclaimed *Christos*," made it crystal clear that for the most part he—necessarily—used metaphorical language when speaking of *Christos* and his relationship to God (*ho theos*) when, in his first letter to the Corinthians, he noted that in the end *Christos* (here referred to as "the son," *ho huios*) would not stand supreme over all, as if he himself were God, *ho theos*, but would submit himself to God: "The son himself (*autos ho huios*) will submit (*hypotagesetai*) to him who submitted

---

15. David Tracy, *Blessed Rage for Order* (New York: Seabury, 1979) 108.

16. See the discussion above on pg. 288. It is ironic that two Christian scholars, one a moderate Protestant and the other a moderate Catholic, should both use modern critical analysis—here, mainly audience criticism (i.e., learning how the original audience would have understood words and phrases used to determine their meanings as intended by the New Testament authors)—to arrive at slightly differing conclusions, which, when taken together, document solidly that *all* the New Testament writers were using language metaphorically when speaking of Yeshua in divinizing terms. The first, James D. G. Dunn, argued that this was the case everywhere, except in some Johannine texts—specifically excluding the Pauline texts (see James D. G. Dunn, *Christology in the Making* [Philadelphia: Westminster, 1980], 210–11). The second, Edward Schillebeeckx, argued that this was the same everywhere, except in some Pauline texts—specifically excluding the Johannine texts (Schillebeeckx, *Jesus*, 556–57).

all things to him so that God may be all things in all (*ina e ho theos panta en pasin*)" (1 Cor 15:28).

Küng spoke in a different but nevertheless similar manner in writing that Yeshua "*is* in human form God's "Word," "Will," "Son." However, this statement must not be misunderstood. Even New Testament talk about the Father and the Son must not be understood as a two-god teaching, a bitheism, and then tritheism. "No, God is for Jesus and thus also for Christians of all times always the one and only. There is, even in the Bible, no other god outside of God! . . . The Son in not God the Father, and God the Father is not the Son . . . The historical person of Jesus Christ stands for God, manifests him, definitively reveals him."[17]

However, given the difference between the Semitic and Hellenistic thought worlds, perhaps such a misperception was unavoidable. The Hellenistic Christians had to try to understand the meaning of Yeshua in their own thought categories. Since the Hellenistic world did not have a historical, relational view of truth but an absolutist one, it was almost impossible for it to conceive of authentically valid statements about the meaning of life in categories other than their own absolutist, ontological ones, assuming that all true statements about the meaning of life could be properly expressed only in such categories. Of course, in today's mental world, with its historical, relational understanding of truth, we need not, *may not*, remain thus limited. We must attempt to recapture the original "historical," significance of what Yeshua thought, taught, and wrought and express that in contemporary historical, deabsolutized, critical-thought categories.[18]

---

17. Küng, *Christentum un Weltreligionen*, 187.

18. There are many issues that will need to be aired and resolved at this point; Christian scholars need to get on with this vital task. One of the objections likely to be raised by traditionalists is that this description of the meaning of Jesus Christ, i.e., Christology, is simply that of nineteenth-century liberal Protestantism. First of all, it is precisely the traditionalists who should know that merely pointing out that something has been said before does not thereby make it false. Moreover, given the huge advances in the scriptural sciences in the past hundred years, despite surface similarities, the differences between the two positions will also be significant. As to the problem of immutably fixing the interpretation of the scriptural Gospel message in ontological language in the fourth and fifth centuries in Hellenistic Christianity, it should be remembered that—assuming that my argument and that of many other scholars is correct—that radical shift from metaphorical to metaphysical language was made once between the first and the fourth centuries, between the Semitic and Hellenistic milieu. *Ab esse ad posse*—if it happened, it is possible; i.e., if it happened once, why not twice, or more times?

A solemn decree from an ecumenical council can never be changed? Compare the following statements from two councils recognized to be fully ecumenical by the Catholic Church: The 16th Ecumenical Council, Constance (1414–18): "This synod declares first that, being legitimately convoked in the Holy Spirit, forming a general council and representing the universal Church, it has immediate power from Christ, which every

Even in the New Testament, however, the early Christians spoke of Yeshua as if he were not only *a* possible way to learn the meaning of human life and thereby to become reconciled with God, but they also felt that, in comparison with all other possibilities, he was so vastly far in advance, so radically better than the others, that they spoke of him in absolute language. Or, at least, they did so at times. Again, it becomes apparent that they were speaking in hyperbolic terms—just as when Yeshua said of the eye that scandalized one that one should pluck it out, everyone understood him not to mean an actual physical destruction of one's eye; this was a metaphorical way of communicating a profoundly important religious message. It must be recalled that the very central notions and insights that Yeshua was communicating, for example, those of love of God and love of neighbor as the two greatest commandments, were not exclusively his but were precisely the central pillars not only of the ancient Israelite religion but also quite specifically those of Pharisaic Judaism. Hence, in other words, Yeshua and his followers, including the writers of the New Testament, were Jews who thought and spoke Jewishly, that is, metaphorically, rather than ontologically.

Logically, one would have to ask then, what of other great religious leaders in the history of humankind? For example, are not many of the insights found in the core teachings of the "Fathers" of Rabbinic Judaism very helpful to everyone in leading them to understand more fully the meaning of human life, that is, to "be reconciled to God"? Cannot similar things be said of the profoundly beautiful and insightful teachings of Moses, Mohammed, Gautama, Confucius, and others? To be sure, one would have to say, yes—which is precisely what was also said by the Muslim Hasan Askari: "As far as the subjects of the finality claim (Gautama, Jesus, or *Mohammed*) are concerned . . . if they point to themselves (which they cannot do in terms of

---

state and dignity, even if it be the papal dignity, must obey in what concerns faith, the eradication of the mentioned schism [there were three Popes at that time, the so-called Western Schism], and the reformation of the said Church in head and members. Likewise, it declares that whoever of whatever condition, state, dignity, even the papal one, refuses persistently to obey the mandate, statutes and orders of prescripts of this sacred synod and of any other general council legitimately convened, above set out, or what pertains to them as done or to be done, will be penalized and duly punished with recourse if necessary to other means of law." Vatican Council I (1870), however, stated: "All the faithful of Christ are bound to believe that the holy apostolic See and the Roman pontiffs have the primacy over the whole world . . . that the judgment of the apostolic See, whose authority has no superior, can be reviewed by none; and that no one is allowed to judge its judgments. Those, therefore, stray from the straight way of truth who affirm that it is lawful to appeal from the judgments of the Roman pontiffs to an ecumenical council—as to an authority superior to the Roman pontiff" (quoted in Leonard Swidler, *Freedom in the Church* [Dayton, OH: Pflaum, 1969], 92–93). Again, if it happened once, it can happen again.

the metaphor they employ, for that will involve contradiction), all of them are false; and if they point to the Beyond (which is precisely what the metaphor is all about), all of them are true."[19]

Nevertheless, Christians are persuaded that in Yeshua of Nazareth one finds the full explanation, the living out, of the meaning of life—a reconciliation with God. They claim that all human beings *could* find the meaning of life through Yeshua of Nazareth. Therefore, they make a universal claim that Yeshua of Nazareth provides salvation for all human beings, that is, he provides a way to "be reconciled with God" for all human beings. However, at the same time, one must also recognize that not all human beings have been, are, or will be in a position to receive this insight, to be "reconciled with God through Christ." They may have other paths by which they come to this insight, to this "reconciliation."

What, then, of the claim of the early Christians about the universal salvific significance of Jesus Christ? Could it not be understood to be a *potentially* universal salvific significance? The insights and exemplification of how to live an authentic human life in a proper relationship to God given by Yeshua are believed by Christians to be the true way to be fully human, to be in a right relationship to God, the ultimate meaning of life. But, is it not possible that there could be various ways in which to express these insights, not only in terms of ideas, teachings, stories, etc., but also in various practices, patterns of social relationship, and the like? That would mean there would be all sorts of ways of teaching and passing on these profound insights into the meaning of life. These would then coalesce around certain outstanding teachers and form various social patterns or structures that we call religions or ideologies. This is not to say, of course, that everything taught and practiced in every religion or ideology is necessarily authentically human, authentically a "reconciliation of the world with God," as Christians believe that they find in Yeshua. This is not any more likely than that everything Christians have taught and practiced in the past two thousand years has been authentic in its expression of the meaning of life or has been true to the insights and example given by Yeshua.

There are a number of other considerations that lead to the same conclusions. For example, it should be noted that "christological statements should be regarded as belonging not to the language of philosophy, science or dogmatics, but rather to the language of confession and testimony."[20] Or, to use the terminology of Krister Stendhal, they are in "religious language

---

19. Hasan Askari, "Within and Beyond the Experience of Religious Diversity," in Hick and Askari, *Experience of Religious Diversity*, 209.

20. Frances Young, "A Cloud of Witnesses," in John Hick, ed., *The Myth of God Incarnate* (Philadelphia: Westminster, 1977) 13.

... love language, caressing language."²¹ One can attempt to translate love language into philosophical language, poetry into prose (though there will be an inevitable loss), but it would be a gross error and distortion to treat love language, poetry itself, as if it were actually philosophical prose. That has happened too often in Christianity (and other religions as well?), with the all-too-frequent fateful result that the message is distorted, and even destroyed; that has been especially true of the statements of the first followers of Yeshua.²²

Furthermore, as noted, the ancient world lived within the mentality of classicist culture where the view of truth was static, absolute, exclusivistically either-or. Hence, if they believed something about Yeshua was true, it therefore *had* to be unchanging, absolute, exclusive, for that was the nature of truth, as they understood it. But, with the paradigm or model shift in the modern critical world view to the historical, praxis, perspectival, interpretative, dialogic views of truth, critical Christians are now able to, *must*, affirm the salvific, "reconciling," truth about Yeshua without being absolutistic and exclusivistic. Knitter pointed out that the early Christians were certainly aware that there were many truth-claims in the world around them. However, "they felt that if any one of these claims really were true, it had to either conquer or absorb the others. That is what truth did. Unavoidably, then, when they encountered the overwhelming truth of Jesus, they would have to describe it as the only or the final truth." But, Knitter added, in today's world of historical consciousness, "coupled with a new experience of pluralism it seems possible for Christians to feel and announce the saving truth about Jesus and his message without the requirements of classicist culture, that is, without having to insist that Jesus' truth is either exclusive or inclusive of all other truth."²³

Still further, it must be remembered that the world of the Way (*Hodos*) of Yeshua was a world of Jewish eschatological apocalypticism: The end of

---

21. Krister Stendhal, "Notes for Three Bible Studies," in Gerald Anderson and Thomas Stransky, eds., *Christ's Lordship and Religious Pluralism* (Maryknoll, NY: Orbis, 1981) 14–15.

22. Knitter has a helpful comment on the issue of the kind of language used and the understanding of its truth content: "This is not to imply that there was no metaphysical truth in what the early Christians said or that they were conscious of this distinction between metaphysical and confessional language. If they could have made such a distinction, they most likely would have said that the cognitive or metaphysical content of their confessional language was that there was no one else like Jesus. I am suggesting that given the nature of their language, such metaphysical claims are not intrinsic to that language. Today, Christians can hear and use the same language with different metaphysical content" (Knitter, *No Other Name?*, 261).

23. Ibid., 183.

the world was imminent, as was also the "second coming." The Reign of God that Yeshua preached was about to be fulfilled through him. As a result, one of the earliest community reflections on the meaning of Yeshua was a "Maranatha Christology."[24] Hence, there could have been no thought at all about the possibility of other saviors; there was no time for them to happen. Quick, get ready now! When the final end of this world by its transformation into the Reign of God through the "second coming" of Yeshua did not happen, the finality of the *end-time* was shifted to the *center* of history, as was analyzed by Rosemary Ruether.[25] Yeshua as the *final*, eschatological prophet was simply moved to be the *center* of history: a shift from an apocalyptic to a classicist worldview. Again, with the passing of both worldviews, the saving significance of Yeshua can, must, be expressed without its absolutistic and exclusivistic "protective coloring."

If there is any validity in these reflections, it should be apparent that Christians need not, should not, take a condemnatory attitude toward non-Christians, particularly those who are adherents of other religions or ideologies, for fear that they would be disloyal to their Christian commitment. Rather, they would be disloyal to their Christian commitment (that is, *effectively* to preach the Good News to today's critical-thinking world in a language that is dynamic and dialogic) if they did not seek to recognize the same truths, the same insights, wherever they find them. This immediately implies that Christians ought to take a stance not of debate but of dialogue with non-Christians. In this dialogue they will doubtless learn that there are many valuable insights in their own Christian traditions that they had overlooked, or suppressed or distorted, and they will have been brought to this rediscovery of their own treasures through finding those very same insights held forth in another religion or ideology in exemplary fashion.

Moreover, is it not also possible that they will discover in another religious, ideological tradition insights that do not seem to have been expressed in their own Christian tradition? If they can resist the temptation to be doctrinaire and triumphalistic, they will have to say, yes, it is possible; we can hope to gain truly new insights into the meaning of life.

What does this do to the Christian notion that Yeshua the Christ is somehow the fullness of what it means to be human? For one thing, it would be said that presumably none of the new insights gathered would run contrary to what had already been exemplified ("revealed," to use theological language, "from above") in Yeshua the Christ. Further, one can speak of a development, an unfolding, an evolution. One can take the language of a

---

24. See Schillebeeckx, *Jesus* (New York: Seabury, 1979) 405–6.
25. See Rosemary Ruether, *To Change the World* (New York: Crossroad, 1981).

Teilhard de Chardin and speak of moving from the Alpha to the Omega point. Is it not the case that even the early Christians spoke of *another* coming of the Christ? Surely, another coming is not going to be identical with the first coming. If it were, it would not be another coming; it would be the first coming. There will be profound similarities, but if it is to be another, then there must also be some differences. Might not these "new insights" constitute part of these differences?

If Christians come to be persuaded that Mohammed and Marx, for example, provided some "new insights," might they not be seen as part of the "other coming"? Does the second coming of Christ have to be seen and understood only in terms of being at a specific time at the end of history? Obviously, that is not necessary, for here we are clearly again dealing with metaphorical, hyperbolic, poetic, mythic language. Talk of the eschaton is clearly beyond our everyday experience. However, cannot the events within history be taken to be stages toward, even constitutive elements leading to, that eschaton, that Omega point, to again use Teilhardian language? If so, then there need be no opposition ultimately between the Christian understanding of how the world is "reconciled to God through Christ" and how many people will in fact experience this reconciliation to God, this learning of the ultimate meaning of human life, through means other than Yeshua the Christ.

An Open Christology or a "Realitology"?

John Cobb has pointed out that until the nineteenth century it was assumed that Yeshua expressly affirmed his own divinity. However, "the creative transformation that is the history of New Testament scholarship step by step removed from our understanding of the real Jesus all such claims about himself. It participated centrally thereby in the radical humanization of the Christian image of Christ that has dominated the recent history of the understanding of incarnation."[26] That has led to the possibility—and I would argue, the necessity—of making the historical Yeshua, the fully human being, the standard of what it means to be Christian. However, the power of the impact of Yeshua on his followers was so great that "it gave rise to a profusion of images in its explication rather than to any consistent theory."[27] As noted above, the term "*Meshiach*," among others, was applied to Yeshua by his followers. Its meaning was inwardly transformed and gradually ex-

---

26. John B. Cobb Jr., *Christ in a Pluralistic Age* (Philadelphia: Westminster, 1975) 132.

27. Ibid., 115.

panded. Eventually, it came to be filled with the notion of divinity. That clearly was not the understanding of Yeshua himself or of his first followers, as can be seen in the early layers of the Synoptic Gospels. Whether it was the understanding even in the later writings of the New Testament is now disputed. Be that as it may, if what Yeshua thought, taught, and wrought is taken as the ultimate measure of Christian doctrine, and he did not claim himself to be God or understand the term "*Meshiach*" to be infused with the notion of divinity when his contemporary followers were using it to refer to him, does that mean that Christians must abandon the traditional term "Christ"? Obviously not, as long as it is not given a meaning that stands in contradiction to how Yeshua would have understood it—if it is to be identified with Yeshua exclusively.

However, there are a number of contemporary Christian theologians who have used the term "Christ" in a way that is *not* exclusively identified with Yeshua of Nazareth. Cobb, for example, wrote that "'Christ' is therefore a name for the Logos . . . It refers to the Logos *as* incarnate."[28] Elsewhere he also rightly linked the *Logos* with the Hebrew *Hokmah/Sophia*, when he said, "I myself wish that the Johannine prologue had spoken of Sophia instead of Logos, and I propose that, despite the predominance of Word in the tradition, we speak today of Wisdom."[29] But he also made the notion of Christ much broader than the manifestation of the *Logos* in Yeshua of Nazareth. Rather, Christ is "the process of creative transformation in and of the world . . . All authentic thinking and speaking embodies this creative transformation as does all sensitivity of feeling and free imagination. Indeed life itself is the continuing expression of the Logos as creative transformation . . . God or the Logos as incarnate is Christ."[30]

In a way, the *Logos* is God *in se.* and Christ is God *ad extra*, though the notions of incarnation and creative transformation also play central roles in Cobb's thought here. He then spoke of Yeshua being so one with the incarnate manifestation of the *Logos*, that is, with Christ, that Christ "co-constitutes with the personal past the very selfhood of"[31] Yeshua. He pointed out, however, that "there is no *a priori* basis for determining whether others have participated in this structure of existence. That remains an open question."

---

28. Ibid., 76.

29. John B. Cobb Jr., "Toward a Christocentric Catholic Theology," a lecture delivered at the conference "Toward a Universal Theology of Religion," held at Temple University, October 17–19, 1984, published in Swidler, ed., *Toward a Universal Theology of Religion*, 86–100.

30. Cobb, *Christ in a Pluralistic Age*, 77.

31. Ibid., 142.

But "so far as we know, Jesus is unique."[32] Cobb wrote similarly elsewhere that, although "this Wisdom is incarnate in Jesus cannot mean that Jesus is the only channel through which God is present in the world . . . Jesus is the center of history for Christians."[33]

The key thing to notice here is that while on the one hand the Christian tradition is reaffirmed in that Yeshua is said to be a unique incarnation of the *Logos* and that he is consequently the center of history, on the other hand he is explicitly said not to be the only incarnation of the *Logos* and is the center of history *for Christians*. Cobb then argued for an "open Christology," or open Christocentrism: "Now the problem with that story is not, as some suppose, that Jesus is at the center, but that the circumference is far too narrow."[34] Although Christianity should be centered on Yeshua, it is to be open to all religious and secular values and to allow itself to be inwardly transformed by them—because all creative transformations are manifestations of the *Logos*. Eventually, Cobb also asked: "In order to include these stories, too, is it necessary to give up the centrality of Jesus and seek some other principle of organization or revelation for the larger whole? Should I, after all, give up my Christocentric catholic project in favor of the universal

---

32. Ibid. Hick expressed a similarly cautious view: "Whether he incarnated self-giving love more than anyone else who has ever lived, we cannot know. But we do know that his actual historical influence has been unique in its extent" (Hick, *God Has Many Names*, 28). Judging from the description of the life and teaching of Yeshua and their subsequent influence, it would seem that Yeshua was uniquely "love-filled," "God-filled," in that sense. It is highly unlikely, though not certainly so, that such a life could have been lived elsewhere without having had similar effects. Moreover, even if we conclude from the lack of similar effects from other lives in the past, we cannot *a priori* exclude that possibility from the future. Metaphorically speaking, that would be to try to lock God in the box of human history, human past. See Dennis Nineham, "Epilogue," in Hick, *Myth of God Incarnate*, 186–204, where as a New Testament scholar he argues that the historical documentary evidence available is inadequate to claim moral perfection for Yeshua. More recently Sanders summed up this view: "We cannot say that a single one of the things known about Jesus is unique . . . The combination can doubtless be called 'unique', but that shows that he was an individual and not a two-dimensional representative of a type . . . We cannot even say that Jesus was a uniquely good and great man . . . History, in fact, has grave difficulty with the category 'unique'. . . It is, rather a fault of New Testament scholarship that so many do not see that the use of such words as 'unique' and 'unprecedented' shows that they have shifted their perspective from that of critical history and exegesis to that of faith. We can accept without argument Jesus' greatness as a man, but we must stop well short of explaining his impact by appeal to absolutely unique personal qualities. What is unquestionably unique about Jesus is the result of his life and work" (Sanders, *Jesus and Judaism*, 319–20).

33. Cobb, "Toward a Christocentric Theology."

34. Ibid.

theology of religion?"³⁵ He, tentatively, answered, no. I think the answer should be both no and yes, as I will detail below.

Cobb is a Protestant theologian. This problem was also wrestled with by the Catholic theologian Raimundo Panikkar, who also spoke of Christ in a way not unlike Cobb's "creative transformation": "The thesis of the *Unknown Christ* is that ... there is something in every human being that does not alienate Man but rather allows Man to reach fullness of being. Whether the way is transformation or some other process ... this ... principle exists. Christians have called it Christ, and rightly so."³⁶ Clearly, for Panikkar, too, the term "Christ" is understood very broadly, including all the manifestations of the divine. Problems arise with the exclusive identification of Christ with Yeshua of Nazareth. To this issue Panikkar says that "the Christ we are speaking of is by no means the monopoly of Christians, or *merely* Jesus of Nazareth."³⁷ He is so certain of this position that he wrote: "That the historical name Christ should not be confined to the thus-named historical Jesus hardly needs mentioning here."³⁸ Panikkar, too, affirmed that Yeshua is key for Christians, for it is through him that they come to God but, not only is the latter more important than Yeshua, so also is the world-pervasive manifestations of God, Christ: "My suggestion is that they [Christians] should not give it [the term "Christ"] up too lightly and be satisfied simply with Jesus—however divinized. It is in and through Jesus that Christians have come to believe in the reality that they call Christ, but this Christ is the decisive reality."³⁹

In Panikkar's thought there is nothing of the exclusive identifying of Christ with Yeshua, as in the narrowly ontologically understood propositions that had become traditional in much of Christian thought. Christ for Panikkar (and Cobb) is a metaphor, a symbol—which gives the term not less but more importance; only a "materialistically" minded thinker would argue otherwise: "Christ has been and still is one of the most powerful symbols of humankind, though ambivalent and much-discussed."⁴⁰ But, if Christ is an ambivalent symbol, why does Panikkar nevertheless focus on it? He wrote that, "Christ is still a living symbol for the totality of reality: human, divine and cosmic. Most of the apparently more neutral symbols such as God, Spirit, Truth and the like truncate reality and limit the centre

---

35. Ibid.
36. Panikkar, *Unknown Christ*, 29.
37. Ibid., 49.
38. Ibid., 27.
39. Ibid., 29.
40. Ibid., 26–27.

of life to a disincarnate principle, a nonhistorical epiphany, and often an abstraction." He added that, in his book, "Christ stands for that centre of reality, that crystallization-point around which the material can grow. Rama may be another such name, or Krishna, or (as I maintain) Isvara, or Purusha, or even Humanity. But God, Matter, Consciousness or names such as Future, Justice, Love are not the living symbols that our research required."[41]

What does such an approach do to the Christian doctrine of the incarnation? Hick addressed this question directly and argued that, whenever in Christian history "theologians have tried to spell out its meaning in literal, factual terms the result has been heretical . . . And all attempts to treat the incarnation as a factual hypothesis have likewise been rejected by the church because they have failed to do justice either to Jesus' full humanity or to his full deity." He added that "one may say that the fundamental heresy is precisely to treat the incarnation as a factual hypothesis! For the reason why it has never been possible to state a literal meaning for the idea of incarnation is simply that it has no literal meaning." Hick insisted that the incarnation "is a mythological idea, a figure of speech, a piece of poetic imagery. It is a way of saying that Jesus is our living contact with the transcendent God . . . Thus reality is being expressed mythologically when we say that Jesus is the Son of God, God incarnate, the Logos made flesh."[42]

This "new" way of understanding statements about Yeshua and Christ is in many ways reminiscent of the "old" way of understanding, namely, the "Jewish" way of Yeshua and his contemporaries discussed earlier. What are the chances that this metaphorical, symbolic way of understanding of these statements will be widely accepted outside of a coterie of theological experts? I am in substantial agreement with Hick when he said that the Christian mind will almost inevitably come to see the doctrines of the incarnation and the Trinity in a new way, "no longer as precise metaphysical truths but as imaginative constructions giving expression—in the religious and philosophical language of the ancient world—to the Christian's devotion to Jesus as the one who has made the heavenly Father real to him." He noted that, in physiological-psychological categories, "This is the kind of development which the intellectual part of the Christian mind (appropriately, in the human brain, the left hemisphere!) is likely to undergo, while its more emotional other half perhaps continues to use the traditional language of Christian mythology without raising troublesome questions about its meaning."[43]

41. Ibid., 27.
42. Hick, *God Has Many Names*, 74–75.
43. Ibid., 125–26.

Rudolf Bultmann a number of decades ago launched the project of demythologization. He argued that the religious truths of the Bible (and he mainly restricted himself to the New Testament) were expressed in the language that was current in that culture, namely, mythological language—and in this he surely was right. He then said these truths had to be translated out of the original mythological language into a language understood by contemporary men and women, and he did so in the categories of existentialist philosophy.

There is much of enduring value in this Bultmannian project. The first is to see that the language of the Bible, as well as of every other text, is culture-bound and that if its content is to be useful it must be translated out of that language into ones living people understand and can make use of. There is also something of enduring value in his having chosen existentialist philosophical categories into which to translate the biblical message, for existentialist philosophy does in many ways profoundly penetrate into the perennial human reality. However, even those categories are not profound enough or broad enough to reach all human beings living today adequately. In many ways they are severely culture-bound—although the fact that they have struck such responsive cords in such an "alien" religious culture as Japanese Buddhism does indicate that they also often penetrate to the very heart of humanness. As discussed before, doubtless no one language would be broad enough to reach all human beings today. The cultural, sociological, and psychological contexts of people are much too varied to allow such. Moreover, with the continued passing of time, even the multifarious conditions for the present world will constantly change further so that, if such a single all-purpose language were designable for today, it would no longer be adequate for tomorrow.

Does that mean that an "Ecumenical Esperanto" is really an undoable and even undesirable project? No, rather, I think it means that it is an unending and a limited project. That it must be unending, though cumulative, is clear enough, I believe. I have already stipulated above that it must also be thought of as a limited—but not therefore less valuable—project to serve as a supplementary language that could be understood eventually by humans from all cultures and religions because it is radically humanity-based. It is not to be thought of as an eventual replacement for the various religious languages, although as it becomes more penetrating it would also transformingly influence the different religious languages. Rather, it would allow persons of differing religious traditions to communicate effectively with each other, especially in situations of more than bilateral conversations.

For example, when the notion of an open Christocentrism was expounded by Cobb, it was responded to by a Buddhist hailing it as an advance and simultaneously counter-proposing "an analogous position for Buddhism, i.e., a Buddhocentrism."[44] Both such moves within their respective religious cultures are to be applauded in that they move from a closed to an open stance. Also, it must be said that something like those moves would have to be made for the sake of self-understanding of each tradition. The Christian, for example, must make sense out of what it means to be a Christian in a way that will take into account the major elements of the Christian tradition, and that means, among other things, utilizing and making sense of Christian symbols, language, etc. That is sufficient, and necessary, for religious conversation *ad intra*, but not *ad extra*, especially if it engages more than one partner. What is the Jew, Muslim, Hindu, etc., going to say when confronted with open Christocentric and Buddhocentric thinkers who invite them to dialogue together? Should they simply add their own "centrisms" to the dialogue? Hardly, if any understanding and mutual transformation is to be hoped for. A humanity-based "Ecumenical Esperanto" that is soteriology-centered must be developed.

If a Christocentrism, Buddhocentrism, etc., is adequate and even necessary *ad intra*, what is to be the "center," the "logy" of an "Ecumenical Esperanto"? No obvious term suggests itself, such as Christ or Buddha. There are several possibilities. In choosing one, however, care will have to be taken that it be broadly inclusive, excluding at least none of the major religious and ideological traditions. Likewise, we should not be unduly attached to the chosen term, for we are clearly in an experimental period, and here pragmatism should definitely rule, that is, that term that works best should be employed. We will also have to reckon with the possibility, even probability, that such a term will not have the lively "vibrations" of older, more particular terms (which is why Panikkar, for example, chose to stay with "Christ" and tried to broaden its meaning—to say nothing of the *ad intra* intention of much of his writing), but I believe there is a better chance that such a term will gradually grow to be suffused with profound meanings for people of differing religious traditions than that an older particular term will be sufficiently broadened and come to be accepted by "foreigners" without stimulating negative "vibrations." In this important issue I believe Cobb and Panikkar are mistaken in the judgment that their magnificently open Christologies are not only properly directed *ad intra*, but also *ad extra*.

In trying to deal with the finalities of the various major religions of the world, I have often spoken about "Ultimate Reality." Other theologians

---

44. Kenneth K. Inada, "Comments on 'Toward a Christocentric Catholic Theology' by John Cobb Jr.," a response delivered at the conference, "Toward a Universal Theology of Religion," at Temple University, October 17–19, 1984; published in Swidler, ed., *Toward a Universal Theology of Religion*, 104–13.

have done the same. I would propose that this be at least one of the ways we develop our "Ecumenical Esperanto," by speaking not of Christ, Buddha, or God when referring to the Final as dealt with by all the religions and ideologies but, rather, by speaking of "Ultimate Reality," or some variant. Hence, the body of reflection on "Ultimate Reality" might well be called "Realitology." Such a neologism of course has many problems. The very fact that it is a neologism puts many persons off; it is abstract and lacks the vitality of a history or tradition. But, does not "Buddhology" sound like a neologism to the majority of the world? Except for Christians, will a modern-language transliteration of a Greek translation of a Hebrew term meaning the anointed one—"Christology"—be anything more than a confused abstraction? Do the names Rama or Krishna, which Panikkar also offers as possibilities, have the vitality of a history or tradition for any but a handful outside of the subcontinent of India? So, perhaps "Realitology" is relatively no worse off than the particular possibilities that are suggested. If it does not, for example, carry the positive qualities from the past history of Christ and Christology, it also is not freighted with all of its negative qualities from the history of Christian Antisemitism and religious imperialism, which have left deep, indelible marks throughout the world.

Conclusion

This is my initial statement in the dialogue. I am persuaded that my theological reflection here is in integral touch with the source of my Christian faith on this matter—in fact, I believe that it is in much closer touch than many other attempted interpretations have been for a very long time. Of course, I need to be in dialogue with my fellow Christians on this contention—the *intra*religious dialogue dimension. I also hope that in this reflection I have moved toward the shaping of an "Ecumenical Esperanto" in which modern critical thinkers—Jews, Muslims, Hindus, Confucians, Buddhists, Humanists, Marxists, etc.—will be able to say that they can "understand" the insight I am struggling to express and that they somehow feel included in those concepts, terms, images, etc. If I have succeeded at all, regardless of the modifications that will be necessary as a result of the subsequent dialogue, we will have taken one step toward the forging of a "universal theology of religion-ideology."

It is within this new paradigm of understanding, this matrix of interreligious, interideological dialogue that, I am convinced, future creative systematic reflection, "theologizing," will have to take place. What Knitter has said in this regard about Christians is, I believe, true, *mutatis mutandis*, of adherents of all religions and ideologies: "If [all religious persons], trusting God and respecting the faith of others, engage in this new encounter with other traditions, they can expect to witness a growth or evolution such as [religion] has not experienced since its first centuries. This growth will paradoxically both preserve the identity of [every religion] and at the same time transform it. Such paradox is no mystery; we are acquainted with it in our own personal lives as well as in nature."[45]

Our Understanding of Ultimate Reality Shapes Our Actions

Most people do not understand themselves as philosophers or theologians. Rather, they think of themselves as practical persons who want to get on with living a good life, however they understand what a good life is. Hence, philosophical/theological questions about the Ultimate Reality seem to most not only very abstract—and therefore both difficult to understand and uninteresting—but also totally impractical. This is a serious error. How we conceive of reality determines how we will act. Whether I think, for example, that my child's illness is because of the *karma* of a previous life, or because someone is sticking pins in a doll image of her, or because she has had contact with some bacteria, determines how I act in response—and doubtless whether or not my child lives. Thus, philosophy and theology—how I understand reality ultimately—are profoundly practical.

I want to look relatively briefly at some of the major families of attempts to conceive and name Ultimate Reality. Of course there can be other ways of grouping these attempts—including the attempt that claims that such an attempt is the chasing of a chimera—but this grouping has, I believe, a certain plausibility that I wish to pursue. I will also be interested in how others might group them differently. Then I want to suggest a candidate for this perennial attempt to conceive and name Ultimate Reality that will not negate all previous attempts but will make a Copernican turn in helping to bring them together in their quest: in dialogue, in Deep-Dialogue.

The attempts at conceiving and naming Ultimate Reality can be grouped in several "families" by their ultimate vision: (a) Polytheism (Many), (b) Hinduism (One and Many), (c) Judaism and Islam (One), (d) Zoroastrianism and Manicheism and Yin-Yang (Two), (e) Christianity (One and Three), (f) Buddhism (Nothing), and (g) Confucianism/Taoism (Harmony).

---

45. Knitter, *No Other Name?*, 230.

Polytheism: The Many

Many scholars of religion are convinced that the earliest human reflection on Ultimate Reality came up with multiple sources of existence. A few have argued that the initial thought was that there was one ultimate source but that this primal notion then disintegrated into polytheism. Perhaps henotheism (the idea that there are many gods, but one chief god over them all) was a stopping place either on the way down from monotheism or the way up to it or both.

In any case, the polytheistic understanding of Ultimate Reality focuses on the obvious reality that there is an immense diversity out there. It seems, from one point of view, that the more we learn, the greater appears the variety in the cosmos. In the distant past, humans lived in a very circumscribed geographical area, so had only a limited knowledge of the variety even here on Earth. With the advance of the means of knowledge, movement, and communication, we humans constantly learn more and more about the seemingly limitless variety on Earth, let alone the cosmos with its billions of galaxies, each of which contains billions of stars, and who knows how many circling planets. To paraphrase the Bible, Reality, thy name is legion.

For the polytheist, this gargantuan multiplicity can come only from a like source, that is, from an endless multiplicity of Ultimate Reality. Thus, even for "pure" polytheists, untempered by henotheism, all existence flows from plural sources, the gods. The insight that polytheism captures for us is that there really are many, many things, and that this manyness is somehow reflective of their source(s).

Hinduism: The One and the Many

As noted earlier, many think of Hinduism as simply polytheism, but this is a serious mistake. On the popular level, doubtless many Hindu devotees are polytheistic, but for the most part Hinduism stresses that there are many manifestations (*avatara*) of the one Ultimate Reality (*Brahman*), often called upon with the sacred word *Aum* (or *Om*). The main goal in mainstream Hinduism is for each individual "self" (as noted briefly above: *atman*—the Sanskrit word for "breath," as in the English cognate "atmosphere," and like the English "spirit," coming from the Latin *spiritus*, "breath") ultimately to be united with the one Source of all reality, *Brahman*. Sometimes *Brahman* is named *Atman*, so that the goal of human life is for the *atman* to be united with *Atman*.

Thus, in mainstream Hinduism there is an acknowledgment of the Many *avatara* and *atmana* on the one hand and the One Source and Goal, *Brahman* or *Atman*, on the other. This is true whether one looks at the more extreme "semi-monist" doctrine of Advaita Vedanta of Shankara (788–820 CE) or the more moderate "semi-dualist" position of Ramanuja (1017–1137 or 1077–1157 CE). For Shankara all reality is ultimately one, so that all that we humans perceive as multiplicity is finally *maya*, illusion. Nevertheless, for us humans there really is *maya*, which finally is taken up into Ultimate Oneness—there is both Many (though *maya*) and One. For the vastly more popular position of Ramanuja (even if his name may not be known), there clearly is both the Manyness of diversity and Ultimate Oneness.

There is a profound attractiveness to this position of the One and the Many, for it corresponds to the human combination of our senses (which are many) and our intellect, which abstracts from the many what we humans see as the inherent oneness in things. For example, we see numberless dogs, but at the same time do not hesitate to name the many animals with a single word, dog. Even in the latest cosmology, the countless billions of stars are seen to have all come from a single "Big Bang" 13.8 billion years ago. Thus, Hinduism in a preeminent way preserves the doctrine of the One and the Many by seeing it in One God with many manifestations, which corresponds to our many human experiences of oneness and manyness, as with many sense images of one concept: *e pluribus Unum*.

Judaism/Islam: The One

The blazing insight of Judaism is seen in the image of the One God in the Burning Bush that was not consumed, who named Godself *Yahweh*, "I Will Be Who I Will Be," a both unitive and processive self-naming. There was no manyness expressed here, only the "I" of *Yahweh*. This personal name of the Hebrew Ultimate Reality is clearly singular. However, there was a certain ambiguity about the Hebrew general name most often used for god, *elohim*. The root of the term is *el*, as is often found in names of humans and angels—Michael, Gabriel, Ezekiel, Emmanuel, Israel—even though *el* was originally a Canaanite male god (at times in the Bible the female form *eloah* is also used to refer to the one true God.) The suffix *im* denotes the plural of a noun and is at times matched in the plural form of verbs, as in: "Let us make humankind in our image" (Gen 1:26) and "Look, they [the man and woman] have become like one of us, knowing good and evil" (Gen 3:22).[46] It is most

---

46. For a more detailed discussion of the questions of number and gender of God in the Bible, see Leonard Swidler, *Biblical Affirmations of Woman* (Philadelphia:

likely that the Hebrews started out in ancient prehistoric imes as polytheists, then moved on to being henotheists (see the first commandment of the Decalogue: "I am Yahweh your god . . . you shall have no other gods before (or beside, *ahl* in Hebrew) me" (Exod 20:1), that is, there were other gods, but they were not to be revered before or beside Yahweh. In any case, no scholar disputes that the Hebrews uniquely in history (primeval prehistory might be disputed by some scholars) held to pure monotheism, certainly by the sixth century BCE. The Pharaoh Ikhnaton in thirteenth-century BCE Egypt may have been a monotheist, but his belief, however understood, was quickly eradicated after his death.

Thus, there came into the world an extremely strong stress on Ultimate Oneness. In contrast to all the other creation stories—and there are myriads of such stories, for every culture and subculture had one—the Hebrews were unique in their emphasis on the unique origin of all reality. The first chapter of Genesis at the beginning of the Bible makes it clear that everything that exists was created by the one God and that everything that God created was *tov* and that all of creation together was declared by God to be *mod tov*.

Much of the history of the Hebrew people (named "Israel" after the "nickname" of the third patriarch, Jacob, whose twelve sons generated the "Twelve Tribes of Israel," and after whom the Jew Yeshua's twelve closest followers were named the "Twelve Apostles") is about Israel's worshiping and obeying—or not—the one God Yahweh. According to the Bible, when Israel believed in and obeyed the one true God, all went well with them, but when it strayed into polytheism or in any way drifted from the oneness of God and God's teaching (*Torah*), it suffered terribly. The oneness of Ultimate Reality was and is the central focus of the Israelite people and one of its subsequent "religions," Judaism (named after Judah, one of the twelve sons of Jacob), as is reflected in the central Jewish prayer, the *Schema Israel*: "Hear oh Israel, Yahweh your God is one (*echad*)!" (Deut 6:4).

Islam followed hard on the heels of Judaism in its stress on the oneness of God and even surpassed it in some ways. The oneness of God is the cornerstone (and almost the whole building) of the Muslim credo, the *Shahada* (Arabic, "testimony"): *la ilaha illa 'llahu* ("there is no god but God." (*'llahu*, pronounced *allahu*, is simply the generic Arabic word for "god.") Many use it as a proper name, like Yahweh in Judaism, which, of course, it is not. ("*l*" or "*al*" is the Arabic parallel to the Hebrew "*el*"—both being Semitic languages—meaning god.) To the above statement about there being only one God, the *Shahada* adds only "and Mohammed is his prophet."

Westminster, 1978), especially 35–36.

Islam went further than Judaism in stressing the oneness of God, as is reflected in the doctrine of *Tawhid* (Arabic, "making one"). Here, not only is it claimed that there is only one God but also that there is total oneness in the very reality of this one and only God. The negative doctrine matching that of *Tawhid* is *Shirk* (Arabic, "associating"—see Qur'an 4, 51, where it says that *Shirk* is an unforgivable sin). Both *Tawhid* and *Shirk* are aimed by Islam at any kind of associating of any one or thing with God, for God is One. That is, they clearly were aimed at polytheism, which was widespread in Mecca at the time of Mohammed, and even at the Christian doctrines of the Trinity (wherein God is mysteriously Three Persons in One God) and of the Incarnation (wherein Jesus is said to be the Son of God become human).

Perhaps ironically, this notion of *Tawhid* led within Islam to a stress on the part of many Sufi Muslims on the oneness of all, eliminating the distance between Creator and creature (*Fana'*, Arabic, "fading away"), melting in its extreme form into a kind of pantheism. The most (in)famous of such Sufi mystics were Bistami (d. 874 CE), and al Hallaj (858–922 CE), both Persians. They were so profoundly moved by their experience of oneness with God that the former declared: "Glory to me, how great is my mystery"; and the latter: "When you see me, you see God." Both were condemned, and al Hallaj was tortured and put to death, for such "heretical" understandings of Oneness.

Thus, the oneness of Ultimate Reality was the major focus of both Judaism and Islam. This oneness was/is understood in both transcendent and imminent forms. The more "orthodox" versions of both Judaism and Islam stress the radical separation between one Creator and creation on the one hand, and the more "mystical" versions emphasize the unity between Creator and creation on the other; both in their own ways stress Ultimate Reality's oneness. Once again, even in modern subatomic and cosmological physics, there seems to be looming a kind of ultimate oneness with the interchangeability of matter and energy, all rushing out of the one Big Bang.

Thus, both Judaism and Islam capture the insight of the Oneness of Ultimate Reality and that all creation is good, flowing from the one Good Source.

Zoroastrianism/Manicheism/Yin-Yang: The Two

It is normally obvious to humans that there are basically two kinds of reality, matter and spirit—that which occupies space and can be apprehended by the senses, and that which does not occupy space and can be apprehended only by the abstract intellect. Such a metaphysics is called "dualism." Ultimate

Reality was then also thought by some to be two. Hence, Zoroaster (Greek, in his original Persian, Zarathustra, 628–551 BCE), who affirmed a single supreme creator God, *Ahura Mazda* (the God of Light), also posited an evil principle, *Ahriman* (the Principle of Darkness), which is the source of evil in the world. Although in Zoroaster's teaching *Ahura Mazda* would triumph in the end, there was a certain ambivalence, so there was a tendency among later followers to move toward a full dualism of good and evil.

This tendency became full blown much later in another Persian, Mani (216–74 CE), who taught that there were two Ultimate Principles, the "Father of Greatness" and the "Prince of Darkness." Here, clearly, body was bad and spirit good; the soul was imprisoned in the body, and therefore asceticism, mortification of the flesh, was the path to salvation. Manicheism thus can be called "extreme dualism." It had a large impact in later Christianity, especially through St. Augustine, perhaps the most influential thinker in Christian history, for he was a Manichee before becoming a Christian and carried many of his dualist ideas with him into Christianity

Quite unrelated causally is a third dualist emphasis on the twoness of Ultimate Reality, namely, the Yin-Yang Principle of China, stemming from the fourth century BCE. Yin is the female, negative, dark principle, and Yang the male, positive, light principle. However, the Yin-Yang doctrine does not set up antitheses of good *vs.* evil, as in Zoroastrianism or Manicheism. Rather, Yin is the power of the Earth and Yang the power of Heaven, and all life comes from the harmony of these two forces (more of Harmony below).

One could also point to the contrasting views of Ultimate Reality via their epistemologies in the two greatest Greek philosophers, Plato (428–348 BCE) and his student Aristotle (84–322 BCE). Plato came close to a Oneness viewpoint by insisting that it is the Ideas (for example, "Dogness") that are the really real and our experience of Manyness (many dogs) was only of "shadows" on the wall of the cave of our human life. Aristotle argued instead that there is nothing in the intellect (the Oneness of the Idea) except what first came through the senses (Manyness).

In any case, these religions focus on the twoness found in the cosmos, and therefore also, they argue, in Ultimate Reality, the source of the cosmos. They lift up, thereby, an insight into reality and its Source that must not be lost sight of—the bipolarity of the world we live in: positive-negative, light-dark, male-female, body-soul, in-out, up-down.

Christianity: The One and the Three

The "founder" of Christianity was the very devout and learned Jew, Yeshua (whose name means "Yahweh Saves"). He naturally deeply believed in the oneness of God. And, much like the later Muslim Sufi mystics, he also spoke of himself and God as one, which also got him in trouble and, according to the Gospel narratives, was the tearing point leading to his condemnation before the court of the High Priests—though it obviously was the political concern of Yeshua's being thought of as a king that led the man with the power, the Roman Pontius Pilate, to execute him in typical Roman fashion, on a cross.

Nevertheless, it is also true that Yeshua spoke of God as Father (in a way typical of Galilean holy men and the Pharisees) and spoke of the spirit of God, as was also typical of the whole biblical tradition, starting from the very first verse of the Bible: "And the spirit of God brooded over the abyss." For Yeshua and his first followers, as good Jews, such talk was naturally understood as typically Jewish metaphorical language, as picture language, not as abstract, philosophical, empirical, ontological language (such thought patterns and language—as the very terms "philosophical," "empirical," "ontological" reflect—were typical of Greeks, not Semites).

Later followers of Yeshua, now known in the Greek (*Iesous*) or Latin (*Jesus*) form, along with the Greek form (*Christos*) of the Hebrew title *Meshiach*, or Messiah, were apparently unaware of this profound difference in the use of language. These later followers, now calling themselves Christians, more and more came exclusively from the Greek-speaking world and, hence, tended to think as Greeks: philosophically, empirically, ontologically. By the fourth century the Father, Son, and Spirit were ontologized in Christian thought, leading to the doctrine of the Trinity, declared at the first Ecumenical Council held under the aegis of the first Christian emperor, Constantine, in 325 CE in Nicaea, a suburb of his new city, Constantinople.

It is clear to me that the Greek Christians misunderstood what the Jews of the Bible were saying, that the Jews who wrote the Bible and Yeshua would not only have been shocked at the "answers" that the Greeks came up with, but would have been even more utterly puzzled at their "questions." As noted before, for Yeshua and the Jews in general the big question was not what to think but what to do. The "ontological" questions seemed perfectly obvious to the Greeks to ask, though to the ancient Jews of two thousand years ago they were nonstarters. The Jew Yeshua made it clear that it was not what one thought, but what one did that saved or condemned one: "Giving drink to the thirsty, food to the hungry, clothe the naked, visit the sick and those in prison . . . what you did to the least of these, you did to me" (Matt 25:31–40).

As a result of asking Greek ontological questions, fourth-century Christians came up with an amazing understanding of Ultimate Reality. They reaffirmed the oneness of Ultimate Reality, of God, but at the same time affirmed the threeness of God as well. At first this might seem like just a slight variation of the One and the Many understanding of Ultimate Reality. However, it really is something more profound.

There are three unique relationships at the beginning of the infinite list of numbers. Not only is each unique in itself, but all of them together are radically differentiated from all other numbers. After zero, one, two, and three, the relationships between each other number and the rest are basically the same; they are simply the Many. However, think, first, of the incredible difference between zero and one, between *no*thing and *some*thing. Then, there is the unique relationship between one and two—it moves from one, aloneness, to more, togetherness. As Hegel pointed out, one cannot think of being, without relating it to nonbeing. Or, in more everyday fashion, it makes no sense to speak of female, without there also being male.

Then there is the fascinating, unique relationship of three. For example, when we move from two dimensions to three, we move from the "unreal" world of the picture or drawing to the "real" world of things, which is made up of length, width, and height. Here is our everyday experience of a Oneness in Threeness. Or, think of the relationship between two subjects, two persons. First, each is aware of her or himself; second, each is then also aware of the other; third, both are then aware that each is aware of the other. This third level of awareness reaches a third, qualitative difference from each of the first two. The awareness—or the love—between the two persons now becomes a third reality. This triadic relationship is also reflected in fundamental interpersonal relationships when a man and a woman each becomes aware of/loves her/himself, then becomes aware of/loves the other, and lastly their awareness of/love for each other moves to the third dimension in the embodiment of that awareness of/love for each other in the child.

We find this triadic structure in many other places in our experience. A further fundamental example is human knowledge. Knowing is fundamentally a triadic relationship: There is the knower, the known, and their merging, the "knowing." Put into a seven-syllable mantra: subject, object, then knowing. Hegel saw a similar triadic pattern in all reality, and especially human history; thesis, antithesis, synthesis is how he put it.

So, it apparently "felt" right to those early Greek Christians to think and speak of Ultimate Reality as trinitarian, that is, Threeness in Oneness. Because they were of Greek mentality, they were profoundly interested in ontological questions, in the same way that the first Semitic followers of Yeshua were profoundly interested in ethical questions (this is not to say that neither had any interest in the other's major questions, but only where each's main mental focus was).

Here was Yeshua being referred to by some of his followers as the son of God (the Greeks were apparently unaware that for the Jews this simply meant that the person lived according to God's teaching, *Torah*). Here, Yeshua was referring to God as Father (as did many other Jews of Yeshua's time). Finally, here was the Bible's frequent speaking of the spirit (*ruach*) of God, indeed, the holy spirit (*ruach ha kadosh*) of God. Presumably not realizing that, to the Jewish mentality, all this was metaphorical picture language—not abstract, philosophical, ontological Greek language—the Greek Christians put those terms together with their broad human experience of threeness and declared that Ultimate Reality, God, was also Three in One. After all, humanity—man, woman, and eventually child—was made in God's image (*imago Dei*, Gen 1:6). The Creator God's inner reality would, of course, be reflected in God's creation; so, finding Threeness-in-Oneness at the heart of so much of creation naturally led to the conclusion that creation's Threeness-in-Oneness was a mirror of the one Creator's Threeness-in-Oneness—a triune, Three-in-One, Ultimate Reality.

The psychological/physical human pattern of relationship as the *imago Dei* led Augustine to develop at great length his reflection on the Trinity, explaining that in the One God the Father knows, and therefore loves, himself, this self being the perfect image of himself, the Son, and the love for each other being embodied in the Spirit.

It should be added that this Threeness-in-Oneness of creation as a reflection of Ultimate Reality manifests itself in at least three other major world religions, though not with such centrality of position as in Christianity. In Hinduism there is the trinity of Ultimate Reality, the *Trimutri: Brahma, Vishnu,* and *Shiva.* In Taoism there is the *T'ai I* (Grand Unity), *T'ien I* (Heavenly Unity), and *Ti I* (Earthly Unity). In Mahayana Buddhism there is the *Trikaya:* The threefold body of the Buddha, that is, of Ultimate Reality. In this doctrine the three bodies are named, first, the manifestation body, *Nirmana-kaya*; second, the heavenly body, *Sambhoga-kaya*; and third, *Dharma-kaya*—in ascending order, as it were. The *Nirmana-kaya* is like the various human manifestations of Ultimate Reality, for example, Moses, Yeshua, Buddha, Mohammed. The *Sambhoga-kaya* is like the several personal Gods affirmed by the various traditions, for example, Yahweh, the Holy Trinity, Allah, Ishvara, Amida (of Pure Land Buddhism), who have various virtues, characteristics, names, etc. At the highest point is Ultimate

Reality itself, *Dharma-kaya*, which Zen Buddhist Abe described as "formless Emptiness or boundless Openness."[47]

Thus, Christianity preeminently, and other major religious streams in lesser ways, lifted up another key insight into our cosmos, its unity in threeness in oneness—thesis-antithesis-synthesis, length-width-height, man-woman-child, etc.—and concluded that it was at least a faint mirror image of the Threeness in Oneness of Ultimate Reality.

Buddhism: Ultimate Nothing

To begin with, Siddhartha Gautama (563–483 BCE), the Buddha, was not interested in Ultimate Reality. He thought of himself as a physician of the soul. The essence of Gautama's teaching is found in his Four Noble Truths, which were only about how correctly to understand human life and live accordingly—nothing about Ultimate Reality. Nevertheless, Gautama's followers did develop a doctrine about Ultimate Reality, a very unusual one. Gautama rejected the idea that there were separate independent existing beings. Rather, all beings were ultimately a web of relations.

It was in the nontheistic, nonpersonal, relational process mode of thought that Gautama and early Buddhism thought and taught, with the result that, when they eventually spoke of Ultimate Reality, they developed the key concept of "Emptiness," *Sunyata*, another name for the Buddhist doctrine of *Pratitya Samutpada*, "Dependent Co-origination," which means that nothing exists as a self-subsisting, isolated thing; rather, everything is ultimately a net of relationships and consequently is always in flux, is "becoming."

It was the second-century CE Nagarjuna, the second patriarch of Mahayana Buddhism, who developed the doctrine of *Sunyata*. He clearly denied that there were any self-subsisting substances but insisted that whatever "is" at any moment of space-time consisted of conditions or relationships, and these, too, were dependently co-originated: "The 'originating dependently' we call 'emptiness.'" "Emptiness *is* dependent co-origination."[48] Thus, *Sunyata* does not mean simply the lack of everything but has the quite positive meaning of being the Ultimate Source of all reality, and *Sunyata*'s very "nature" is that of unspecified relatedness in process.

In a way, the Mahayana Buddhist doctrine of Ultimate Reality's being understood as Emptiness, as *Sunyata*, is like an inverse version of the Aristotelean and Thomistic doctrine of Ultimate Reality, where God is Being

---

47. Abe, "Dynamic Unity," 163–90.
48. Nagarjuna, cited in ibid.

Itself, Pure Actuality, *Actus Purus*; the Buddhist version, rather than being positive, is negative: Ultimate Reality was Emptiness, Pure Potentiality, *Potentia Pura*. It is also a little like the Hindu description of Ultimate Reality as *Brahman Nirguna*, Ultimate Reality with no attributes or specifications, as distinct from *Brahman Saguna*, which is Ultimate Reality with attributes. Recall here the earlier-mentioned analogy, and also recalling that analogies always limp, and hence must not be taken any farther than is helpful: Electricity can take the form of heat as in a stove, or light as in a lamp, or locomotion as in a trolley; but ultimately it has no particular form originally when it exists in its source in the dynamo (*Sunyata*).

Thus, there is expressed in the doctrine of *Sunyata* the insight that in Ultimate Reality there are no limitations, no particularities; all is possible, infinite possibilities.

Confucianism/Taoism: Ultimate Harmony

Confucianism has had a long history of over two-and-a-half millennia and consequently has gone through many transformations. It became so dominant in China that it grew somnolent and rigid by the beginning of the twentieth century so that it was violently rejected (May Fourth Movement, 1919—though, ironically, that also dates the beginnings of is revival in the New Confucianism Movement).[49] Until then no one spoke of Confucianism's not being a religion; everyone realized that it was. As discussed above, from even pre-Confucius (551–479 BCE) times, in the Shang period (1766–1123 BCE) the term *Shang-Ti* (Lord on High) or *Ti* (Lord) was used to refer to the highest of the gods and eventually to a transcendent being, perhaps even a creator god. In the Chou period (1122–249 BCE) the term most often used for God was *T'ien* (Heaven), symbolized by a large human head. After the Chou conquered the Shang, both *Ti* and *T'ien* were used to refer to God, understood as a personal God.[50] To Confucius, Ultimate Reality was still personal, but by the tenth century CE, if not long before, *T'ien* tended to be understood more nonpersonally. Nevertheless, *T'ien* was affirmed as real, and its laws were to be followed. The fundamental belief was that humans (*Ren*) needed to pattern themselves after God or Heaven:

---

49. See Umberto Bresciani, *Reinventing Confucianism: The New Confucian Movement* (Taipei: Taipei Ricci Institute for Chinese Studies, 2001), and Shu-hsien Liu, John Berthrong, Leonard Swidler, eds., *Confucianism in Dialogue Today: West, Christianity, and Judaism* (Philadelphia: Ecumenical, 2005).

50. Cf. Ching in Küng and Ching, *Christentum und Chinesische Religion*, 42.

T'ien ren he yi, "The Unity of Heaven and Human." The fundamental law, thus, was *He*, Harmony.

"There is harmony when we have certain things which are mutually different, but which still find a way of relating to each other meaningfully. *Harmony is the foundation of the existence of all beings in the universe.*"[51] This expresses the core Confucian doctrine of *Tai He*, the Great Harmony, or as one contemporary mainland Chinese scholar put it, the Universal Harmony: In Confucian thought, the concept of *Tai He* actually comprises four levels: harmony within nature, harmony between humans and nature, harmony among humans themselves (that is, harmony in social life), and harmony within a person (harmony of body and mind, of inside and outside). In these four elements we basically have the structure of "universal harmony."[52]

Here the *He*, Harmony, between *T'ien* and *Ren* has been "smoothed out" in Marxist fashion so that Ultimate Reality is folded into nature, but another mainland Chinese scholar of the Chinese Academy of Science makes it clear that "A Confucian strove to obey *T'ien Ming*, the Will of Heaven, and to practice his religious teachings in social life . . . In every moment he felt that *Shangti* was at his side watching. The sincere piety of a Confucian toward *Shangti* was not inferior to that of a believer of any other religion."[53]

The ancient Confucian ideal of *He*—Harmony among all things, and finally with Ultimate Reality—is best expressed on the contemporary scene by Fang Dongmei's (1899–1977) Philosophy of Comprehensive Harmony, which, while built on the core of Confucian thought, harmonizes with it the Taoist thought of Laotsu as well as the thought of Mohtsu, India, and the West:

> The distinctive traits of the life of the Chinese nation are represented in Laotsu, Confucius, and Mohtsu. Laotsu expresses the mysterious working of the *Tao*; Confucius describes the archetypal principle of cosmic change; Mohtsu expounds the holy feeling of love. The one who unites Laotsu and Mohtsu [who taught the love for all] and teaches the Middle Path is but Confucius. Only the *Tao* of the school of the peerless sage Confucius is the most balanced . . . It not only can digest and amalgamate Laotsu and Mohtsu, and even the latecomer, Buddhist thought. It can as well absorb the wisdom of Greece, of Europe, and of India, and create an immensely broad sphere of "creativity and

---

51. Qian Xun, as paraphrased in Bresciani, *Reinventing Confucianism*, 441; emphasis added.

52. Tang Yijie, quoted in ibid., 442.

53. Li Shen, quoted in ibid., 444.

harmony," where the finite living human being is able to experience the *infinite being* and value.[54]

The whole thrust of Taoism is that the human should learn the Way (*Tao*) of Reality and follow the Way, should harmonize with it. For Laotsu and Taoism the *Tao* is transcendent, for "the *Tao* that can be known is not the *Tao*."

Thus, there is at the heart of Chinese religious thought and practice the stress on the Middle Way (as also with Gautama's *Majjhima Patipada* [Middle Path] and Aristotle's *In medio stat virtus* [virtue lies in the middle]), a stress on the human need to learn the structure of Reality and to align, to harmonize her/himself with it. And this Ultimate Structure is *T'ien*, transcendent and dynamic, as is reflected in the very term used, the Way, and in our human experience of the ever-moving cosmos.

Summary of Insights from World Religions

There are, thus, at least these seven key insights into how to conceive and name Ultimate Reality, which, of course then has enormous consequences on how we humans see the world and live our lives. In brief they are:

1. The Many: There really are many, many things in the cosmos, and this manyness is somehow reflective of their source(s).

2. The One and the Many: Thus, Hinduism in a preeminent way preserves the doctrine of the One and the Many by seeing it in One God with many manifestations, which corresponds to our many human experiences of oneness and manyness, as with many sense images of one concept: *e pluribus Unum*.

3. The One: Thus, both Judaism and Islam capture the insight of the Oneness of Ultimate Reality and that all creation is good, flowing from the one Good Source, and that underneath the variety of beings there is Being.

4. The Two: The dualist traditions lift up an insight into reality and its Source, which must not be lost sight of—the bipolarity of the world we live in: positive-negative, light-dark, male-female, body-soul, in-out, up-down, etc.

5. The One and the Three: Christianity preeminently, and other major religious streams in lesser ways, lifted up another key insight into our

---

54. *Zhexue san hui* (Taipei, 1970) 6, quoted in ibid., 295; emphasis added.

cosmos, its threeness in oneness: thesis-antithesis-synthesis, length-width-height, man-woman-child—and its imaging of the Threeness in Oneness of Ultimate Reality.

6. Ultimate Nothing: There is expressed in the doctrine of *Sunyata* the insight that in Ultimate Reality there are no limitations, no particularities; all is possible, infinite possibilities—an inverse of All is One.

7. Ultimate Harmony: There is at the heart of Chinese religious thought and practice a stress on the human need to learn the structure of Reality and to align, to harmonize oneself with it. This Ultimate Structure is *T'ien*, transcendent and dynamic: *T'ien ren he yi*, "The Unity of Heaven and Human."

The Move to Deep-Dialogue

There are often specific names behind each of these worldviews, and though each has something significant to contribute to the perennial human effort of conceiving and naming Ultimate Reality, they are, as worldviews, mutually incompatible. The very fact that they are each *world*views tell us that they are totalizing, encompassing the whole world. We can, of course, see many similarities, but never complete congruity; otherwise, they would not be *different* worldviews. Moreover, some of the positions taken regarding Ultimate Reality are mutually exclusive. For example, the polytheistic, Islamic and Buddhist positions seem at first blush to be not just contrary but even contradictory. What to do?

In the past several thousand years, we humans have tended to deal with these differences with indifference, aggression, or absorption. Given the contemporary, rapidly accelerating process of globalization, we can no longer be indifferent to those with different worldviews; they are becoming our neighbors in numberless ways. Aggression (the reaction of choice of Christianity, Islam, and modern Ideologies) is increasingly found to be unacceptable, for it violates the Other's human rights, and human rights are being insisted upon worldwide. Absorption (the reaction of choice of Hinduism, Buddhism, and Taoism) is likewise increasingly found wanting, for it is seen to hide a hidden superiority sense, a smugness.

As noted earlier, humankind is with blinking eyes staggering out of the darkness of the Age of Monologue (wherein we talked only with ourselves, that is, persons who thought like us—or should) into the dawning Age of Global Dialogue (wherein we want to talk with those who think differently from us so *we* can learn). All the adherents of the several families of religions listed above, with their varying views and naming of Ultimate Reality, have something to learn from the others, without abandoning their particular insight—in fact, enriching it. This is happening through dialogue, through transformative Deep-Dialogue.

Deep-Dialogue, let us recall, is something far beyond mere conversation between two or more persons. It means to stand on our position and at the same time seek self-transformation through opening ourselves to those who think differently. Together with its counterpart, Critical-Thinking, it is a whole new way of thinking. To open ourselves to Deep-Dialogue, however, we must at the same time also develop the skills of thinking carefully and clearly, of Critical-Thinking (recall that "critical" is from the Greek, *krinein*, to choose, to judge). Deep-Dialogue and Critical-Thinking are necessarily two sides of one reality. Further, however, beyond being a whole new way of thinking, I see the dialogical principle at the very basis of all reality at the heart of a Cosmic Dance of Dialogue.

The Continuum Principle: All reality is dialogic, operating on a continuum:

Destructive Dialogue →	**Disinterested Dialogue** →	**Dialogical Dialogue** →	**Deep-Dialogue**
Elements are polarized against each other	Elements are tolerant of each other	Elements learn from each other	Elements are mutually transformed

The Reality-Is-Dialogic Principle

All reality is fundamentally interactive, mutual, "dialogic." This dialogic structure is present from the subatomic to the cosmic (where on both levels matter and energy are convertible; further, a growing number of thinkers believe that the binary structure of computers—that is, an endless series of 1's and 0's in "dialogue" with each other—is reflective of the fundamental nature of all reality), through the *intra*personal to the *inter*personal, still further to the intercommunal, and ultimately the global—and beyond to the Source and Goal of all reality.

The Integrative Principle

Not only is all reality "dialogic," but it is also integrative. This "dialogue" of all reality oscillates in polar tension between the destructive and the integrative. For example, when the dialogic relationship among the electrons, protons, neutrons and other "particles" and "waves" in an atom is not "integrated," when the centrifugal and centripetal forces are not balanced in creative polar tension, the atom will "disintegrate" into either a black hole or a nuclear explosion. As matter becomes ever more complex, the integration of the "dialogue" becomes more and more that of a delicately balanced network, which makes a qualitative leap when it reaches living matter and a still greater leap when it arrives at reflexive, rational/intuitive, affective, "spiritual" human beings.

The Knowing-Is-Dialogic-Integrative Principle

All knowing is interactive, mutual, dialogic, and integrative between the known and the knower, for knowing is a kind of unifying of the object and the subject—a kind of "integration." For example, the surface of a table becomes one with, "integrated with," the surface of my fingers. The interactive, mutual, unifying, dialogic-integrative character is doubly true when the knower is also the known, as in my learning about what it means to be human. This is very especially true when *I* learn what it means *for me* to be human. That dialogic-integrative character, then, is endlessly, infinitely, true of all knowing: From (a) when the known and the knower are separate object and subject, through (b) when the known and knower are *inter*personal, further through (c) when the known and knower are communities of persons, ultimately to (d) when they embrace the whole globe—and beyond to (e) the Source/Goal of all reality.

Deep-Dialogue and Ultimate Reality

This fundamental advance in human consciousness, Deep-Dialogue/Critical-Thinking, opens the way to think in nonexclusive ways about Ultimate Reality. This is a Copernican turn, the "dialogical-critical turn" in human evolution. It opens the way to a global consciousness that can build bridges between worldviews and perspectives. This awakened global dialogical/critical perspective between worlds is a profound revolution in how we see, experience, and process reality in every aspect of our life.

Beginning especially in the early nineteenth century with the growth of a strong sense of history, followed by the development of a series of "hermeneutics of suspicion," it has become increasingly clear that all statements about reality, including Ultimate Reality, are necessarily limited: spoken always in particular contexts, addressing particular questions, utilizing particular thought categories, employing particular kinds of language, viewing all from particular viewpoints of social place, gender, religious conviction, etc. However, there cannot be *only* particular views, for then we would have no way to speak with an Other; we can speak to each other only on the basis of what we have in common (beginning with our common language), of what unites us. There clearly is also an underlying commonality; otherwise, we would not even be able to discern that there was difference—difference from what? The very fact that we can differ is built on a fundamental commonality, a unity, within which context we can perceive differences, particularities.

To be fully human, then, it is vital that we be aware, as noted earlier, of both the limited, particular character of all statements *and* at the same time of the underlying unity within which differences can even appear. Therefore, because no single narrative, no single name can fully comprehend or name the Final First (thus recognizing the particularity of all language), we humans must also be in endless dialogue with each other in order to approach endlessly the infinite Ultimate Principle as an ever visible, yet ever-receding, horizon (thus recognizing the underlying unifying dialogic context within which all language should ultimately be placed).

Thus, I am speaking about the "concept" *Dia-Logos* (Greek: "reason/word") as a global expression of the Ultimate Principle. Therefore, when speaking English or another Indo-European language, I use the "term" *Dia-Logos*. Other languages will use their own corresponding terms to express the concept, for example, Chinese *dui hwa*.[55]

---

55. The Chinese equivalent for the English word "dialogue" is "*dui hua.*" (1) *Dui* in the phrase "*dui hua*" corresponds to *dia* in the English word "dialogue." *Dui*, as a prepositional verb, means "to confront, to face," or "being toward"; as a noun, it means "a pair, a couple of," which is composed of two things, referring to the "togetherness" of beings; further, it might refer to the primordial state of beings in the world, in which human beings always already find themselves in the world of beings. (2) *Hua* in the phrase "*dui hua*" corresponds in some sense to *logue* in the English word "dialogue." *Hua* means words spoken or written, or speech. This word is composed of two separate characters that are combined. The radical part or root-meaning one is "to speak, to say" (*yan* in Chinese), which, in ancient Chinese, as a verb, is not used by itself, but always together with another verb "*to tao,*" in the form of "*yan dao.*" As a noun, *yan* means the words, (or the language). The phonetic or sound-giving part of the word "*hua*" is that for "tongue." Thus, the word "*dui hua*" in Chinese might be used to refer to the comportment of human beings, even in their very early primordial state of being together

We know that from subatomic physics, to astronomical cosmology, to the inner and inter workings of humanity, all reality is not static (Greek: *stasis:* standing still), but dynamic (*dynamis:* movement, energy). Hence, at the foundation of all reality is not just *Logos*, as expressed in the specific Greek and Christian cultural languages, but on a global intercultural, interlanguage level: *Dia-Logos*.

It is vital here to recall that, as a global name for "what is first," *Dia-Logos*, does not compete with or displace the many primal names that have emerged across time and cultures. Rather, the force of *Dia-Logos* helps us to be mindful that the Ultimate Principle inherently generates alternative primal names, each of which has unique creative force. Thus, *Dia-Logos* designates the *plurality* that must resonate: *Tao, Aum, Sunyata, Hohmah, Logos, Nomo, Energy Field*—the boundless range of genuine primal names. Nor does this suggest that these diverse primal names for the Ultimate Principle are "synonymous" or "equivalent" in any naive or uncritical sense. Rather, *Dia-Logos* opens space for diversity—which nevertheless co-arises in Unity. This "unity in plurality," *e pluribus unum*, is the power of *Dia-Logos*.

Thus, we might say that *Dia-Logos* is the matricial concept and term within which all the culturally specific concepts and terms for Ultimate Reality can be found, appreciated, and brought into interminable and always fruitful Deep-Dialogue, leading to an emerging and always expanding global ethic,[56] forming the framework within which we all will live our lives.

Conclusion

We humans more and more do not understand and speak of Reality, Ultimate Reality, in absolutist, exclusivist concepts and terms but within a dialogic mental framework—not giving up our particular convictions, but also increasingly becoming aware that they can be only a partial picture of Reality. What will this do to how we act in the world? Because our perception of Reality sets the mental framework within which we decide what is right and wrong, good and evil—our ethics—our behavior will gradually become more open, dialogic, nuanced. It will also become more humble, because the "richer" our knowledge becomes, the more we will realize how limited our knowledge really is. Thus, humanity will tend to emulate Socrates, who realized that the wise person is the one who knows that he does not know.

---

with each other in the world, or as a means of expressing the self as being in the world, or expressing the self "toward others" in the world (Guan Ping).

56. See above as well as Swidler, *For All Life*.

7

Final Conclusion

The basic drive for physical survival is something humanity shares with the other living beings, but it is not what makes women and men human. Humans are beings who can know and love and act freely with knowledge. In fact, humans not only can, but also must, know-love-act-freely-with-knowledge if they are to be something more than a beast, if they are to be at all human. But, once humans have started on the path of knowing-loving-acting-freely-with-knowledge, they will not be satisfied with knowing-loving-freely-acting-knowingly just a little or even a lot. Human nature is directed at an open-ended, endless, infinite, all-embracing, comprehensive knowing and loving and freely acting knowingly. That total knowing-loving-freely-acting-knowingly that humans, both individually and communally, have created over the centuries is religion—and the culture that matches it.

In the past, individuals and their various cultures have tended to live in relative isolation from each other. Only a few extraordinary individuals truly crossed over into alien cultures, but such isolation is no longer possible in the world at the beginning of the third millennium. Although cultures remain distinct, they can no longer remain untouched by others. All of our different cultures must now live within a global culture.

The situation is similar for religions. Several of the world religions and ideologies have attempted to dominate the world, and four of them have had rather remarkable success: Buddhism, Christianity, Islam, and Marxism. Only the first never tried to expand by the force of arms; it took the path of a "passive imperialism." The other three tried the "aggressive imperialist" approach, but it is clear from experience that no one of these, or any other, religions/ideologies will be completely triumphant and destroy all the rest. Rather, just as the various cultures of the world must now live within a global culture, so also the religions of the world must now live within a global dialogue. Hence, our way forward is by way of Deep-Dialogue, consciously entering into the Cosmic Dance of Dialogue.

Come, let us dialogue!

Index

After the Absolute, xi, xii, 46, 73, 294
Age of Global Dialogue, ix, xi, 4, 7,
    43–44, 46, 48, 239, 261, 274,
    338, 362, 404
Aristotle, 5, 16, 134, 313, 396, 400, 403
Abe, Masao, 65–67, 81, 284, 400
Agobard, 198
Akiba, Rabbi, 148, 161
Anicca, 48
An-Na'im, Abdullah, 219, 220
Antisemitism, 169, 182, 197, 199, 201,
    390
Aquinas, Thomas, 16, 22, 48, 52, 59,
    72–73, 124, 242, 283, 286–87,
    315, 339, 367
Arkoun, Mohammad, 217, 218
Askari, Hassan, 65, 221, 379, 380
Association for the Rights of Catholics
    in the Church, 86, 323
Atman, 47, 63, 244, 292, 393
Axial Period, 39–41, 43–45, 338, 363

Baeck, Leo, 203–5
Baha'ism, 58
Balic, Smail, 216–17
Basileia tou Theou, 48, 132, 252–53,
    255, 257
Being, 9, 16–17, 24, 26, 29–31, 39, 45,
    47–48, 55, 61–63, 66, 68, 71–73,
    75, 77–79, 83, 100, 103, 123–25,
    138–39, 142, 164, 184–86, 189–
    90, 244–45, 266, 284–86, 288,
    292, 309, 353, 376, 386, 398,
    400–403, 407–8
Ben Chorin, Schalom, 203, 204
Benedict XV, Pope, 91, 135

Benedict XVI, Pope, x, 46, 311, 373
ben Zakkai, Yohanan, Rabbi, 148,
    154–55, 158
Berthrong, John, 70, 259, 261, 264–65,
    401
Bhagavad-Gita, 246, 248
Bodhisattva, 31, 44, 58, 254, 273, 286
Boniface VIII, Pope, 19, 327
Boszormenyi-Nagy, Ivan, 26, 32
Brahman, 47, 59, 61–63, 65, 163, 242,
    244–45, 247, 291, 392–93, 401
Brown, Robert McAfee, 88
Buddhism, xi, 4, 5, 38–39, 44, 47–48,
    56–59, 63–68, 77, 101, 103–4,
    118, 121, 135, 137–38, 193, 195–
    96, 208, 240, 249–51, 255–56,
    258–60, 278–80, 284–86, 290–
    91, 293, 339–40, 368, 388–89,
    391, 399, 400, 404, 408
Bultmann, Rudolf, 179–80, 388, 409

Capra, Frijof, 18, 97
Catholic-Communist
    Collaboration in Italy, xi
Catholicism, x–xii, 7, 14, 19
Ching, Julia, 69, 27, 259
Christian-Marxist dialogue, x, xi
Christology, 3, 164, 168–72, 177,
    179–80, 182–83, 186, 188, 190,
    192–93, 195, 216, 250, 252, 255,
    279, 288, 372, 375, 377–78,
    382–83, 385, 390
Chrysostom, St. John, 198
Cicero, 337, 339
Cobb, John B., Jr., 126, 249, 294, 383–
    86, 388–89

Competitive-Cooperation, xii
Confucian-Christian Dialogue, 70, 259, 275, 306
Communism, ix, xi, 48–49, 58, 74–75, 77–78, 103, 121, 251, 264, 273, 295, 297, 299, 300–301, 303–4, 307, 343
Confucianism, xi, 56, 59, 69–71, 101, 135, 240, 259, 260–66, 268–74, 305–6, 310, 312, 337, 391, 401–2
Confucianism, New, 261, 263, 270, 401
Conn, Walter E. 28, 30, 31, 368, 369
Cosmic Dance of Dialogue, 7–10, 405
Cotroneo, Margaret, 32

Creed, 1, 6, 36, 80, 130, 184–85, 200, 221, 279, 289, 324, 339
Critical-Thinking, ix, xii, 3, 5, 71, 129–130, 139, 141–44, 193, 215, 221, 235, 266, 287–88, 335, 353–62, 382, 405–6

Dabar, 61, 191, 243, 291
de Bary, William Theodore, 264, 270–71
Deep-Dialogue, ix, xii, 4, 140–44, 215, 234–35, 353–62, 391, 404–6, 408–9
De Lange, Nicolas, 203
Dia-Logos, 144, 407, 408
Dialogue Decalogue, xii, 97, 129
Demythologization, 249, 276, 388
Dukkha, 48, 64, 252, 278
Dunne, John S, 100, 108
Duran, Khalid, 112, 221–23, 231

Ecumenical Esperanto, 2, 3, 7, 112, 114–18, 366, 374, 388–89, 390
Ecumenical Vanguard, x, 91, 227
Ecumenism, 86, 91–94, 118–19, 228, 299, 371
Eggfelden, Bavaria, 60
Einstein, Albert, 4, 8, 17–18, 47
Emotional-Intelligence, xii
Enlightenment, 17–18, 40, 47, 107, 114, 118, 178, 187–88, 194, 210, 270, 282, 317, 320–21, 330, 338, 340, 362
Epistemology, 17–18, 25, 126
Erikson, Erik, 26–29, 369–70

Ethics, 1, 7, 12, 32–34, 36, 58, 104, 144, 160–61, 184, 226, 235, 271, 279–80, 286, 312, 335–42, 345–48, 356, 360

Falk, Harvey, 151, 153, 158
Feminism, 281
Fowler, James W., 26–27, 30, 46, 369–74
Francis, Pope, 46, 86, 373
Francis (of Assisi), St., 31–32
Fu, Wei-Hsun Charles, 268
Fuchs-Kreimer, Nancy, 159, 239
Full human life, 105, 122, 125, 130, 132

Gadamer, Hans-Georg, 21, 98, 176, 185
Garaudy, Roger, 49, 73–78, 80, 126, 251, 299, 301, 310–11
Gilbert, Arthur, x
Global Ethic, 140, 145, 231–32, 269, 336, 341–49, 353, 356, 360, 408
Golden Rule, 55–58, 98, 269, 272, 343–44, 348, 350
Golubovic, Zagorka, 78–80, 311
Greco, Bernardino, 32
Gryson, Roger, 282

Halacha, 38, 71, 101, 165, 184, 280
Halifax, Lord (Edward Wood), 91
Hassan, Riffat, 223–24, 231
Havener, Ivan, 180
Hellwig, Monika, 169, 294
Hermeneutics, 19, 21, 42, 98, 114, 118, 167, 183, 407
Hick, John, 46, 62, 65–66, 96, 104–5, 110, 127, 145, 192–93, 221, 245, 372, 375, 380, 385, 387
Hilberg, Raul, 199, 200
Hillel, 57, 148, 150–51, 153–55, 157–58, 269, 272
Hinayana, 47, 56, 59
Hindu-Christian Dialogue, 240
Hinduism, xi, 38, 47, 60–63, 66, 99, 101, 111, 118, 122, 135, 206, 208, 240–42, 244–45, 247–48, 259, 280, 290, 339–40, 391–93, 399, 403–4
Historicism, 18–19, 42, 114, 168
Hokmah, 59–61, 63, 191, 242–243, 245–246, 284

Household codes, 269, 313
Hulsbosch, Ansfried, 186
Human nature, 7, 46, 50–53, 59, 71, 74, 123, 186, 267, 305, 318
Human rights, xi, 7, 78, 102, 123, 125, 139, 212, 220–25, 269, 280–81, 303, 307, 311–22, 324–25, 336, 343–45, 347–48, 350, 362, 404
Huntington, Samuel, xi, 340

International Scholars Abrahamic Trialogue, 112, 222, 226, 236
Interreligious dialogue, ix–xii, 13, 16, 95, 97–99, 104–5, 108, 136–37, 192–93, 206, 210, 215, 220–21, 224, 228, 238–39, 241, 249, 258, 269, 293, 296, 334, 344
Islam, 1, 35, 38, 48, 57, 59, 61, 63, 95, 99, 101, 103, 118, 122, 127, 129, 135, 139, 140, 157, 167, 185, 202, 205, 207, 209–25, 227, 229, 231, 237–42, 248–50, 259–60, 280, 283, 285, 301, 325–35, 340, 343, 391, 393–95, 403–4, 409
Islamism, 211, 214, 223, 328–29, 335, 343
Israel, 56, 102, 133, 145, 149, 158–62, 164–65, 172, 175, 188–89, 191, 203, 205, 210, 212, 225, 227, 232–33, 275, 280, 291, 293, 325–26, 328–29, 332–33, 335, 342, 379, 393–94
Jack, Homer A., 51
Jaspers, Karl, 39, 45, 338
Jihadism, 211, 214
John XXIII, Pope, 92, 103, 221, 295, 298, 319–22
John Paul II, Pope, 46, 85, 322
Josephus, 151, 155
Journal of Ecumenical Studies, x, xii, 39, 68, 88, 97, 112, 150, 158, 164, 203, 215–16, 220–21, 223, 226, 238, 269, 294, 297, 301–2, 307, 346
Judaism, xii, 32, 38–39, 48, 55, 57, 59, 63, 83, 95–96, 101, 117–118, 122, 135, 145–56, 159–61, 167, 174–76, 178, 182, 184–85, 189–90, 193, 195, 197, 198, 202–205, 207–8, 210, 229, 232, 240, 248–50, 252, 258–60, 280, 283, 285, 292–93, 325–26, 332, 335, 340, 379, 385, 391, 394–95, 401, 403

Kant, Immanuel, iix, 26, 57–58, 65, 185
Klostermeier, Klaus, 97
Kelly, Joseph G., 164, 178–79, 252
King, Martin Luther, Jr., 102, 339
Kittel, Gerhard, 61, 146, 243, 374
Knitter, Paul F. 16, 25, 104–5, 108–9, 116, 119, 127, 193, 231, 256, 294, 372, 381, 390–91
Kohlberg, Lawrence, 26–28, 30, 369–70
Kuhn, Thomas, 4
Küng, Hans, x, 14, 43–44, 64–65, 67–68, 70–73, 76, 86, 167, 169–75, 180–81, 219, 226, 247, 250–51, 259–60, 263–64, 266, 271, 273–74, 286, 311, 341, 345, 347, 378, 401

Lapide, Pinchas, 168, 180, 203–5, 229, 231
Law, 7, 23, 26, 54–55, 57–58, 64, 78–79, 84, 86, 101, 123, 133, 139–40, 145–48, 151–52, 155–60, 164, 181–82, 189, 191, 198, 207, 217, 220, 223–24, 229, 254, 273, 278–80, 290, 297, 308, 312–13, 315–17, 320, 324, 326, 331–32, 336–41, 350, 367, 379, 401–2
Lee, Bernard J., 166, 180
Lee, Jung Young, 68
Leo XIII, Pope, 91, 92, 103
Logos, 40, 61, 63, 144, 191, 243, 245, 279, 384–85, 387, 407–408
Logos theology, 191ff.
Lonergan, Bernard, 21, 23, 26, 29–30, 74, 368, 371–72
Luther, Martin, 51–52, 200–201
Lutheranism, 13, 88, 90, 93, 95, 208

Magdalen, Mary, 162
Magnis-Suseno, Franz, 334
Mahayana, 44, 64–65, 67, 250, 284, 286, 291, 399–400
Malines Conversations, 91

INDEX

Mannheim, Karl, 20, 21, 176
Marechal, Joseph, 76–77
Marxism, x–xi, 1, 6–7, 13, 34, 36, 49, 59, 73–80, 96, 99, 102–103, 106–7, 109, 112, 116–19, 121–22, 139, 208, 211, 240, 251, 271, 274, 291, 295–311, 330, 339–40, 342, 368, 383, 390, 402, 409
Matteo, Anthony, 77, 70
Maya, 148, 303
McNamara, Martin, 151–52
Mekilta, 149
Memra, 191
Mencius, 51, 262, 265, 269
Mercier, Cardinal Désiré, 91
Messiah, 157, 160–61, 164, 167–68, 204, 208, 223, 229–230, 290, 397
Metzger, Max, 91
Mishnah, 148, 151–53, 158
Mojzes, Paul, xi, 222, 231, 235–36, 238–39, 265, 297–99, 301–302, 304, 307–8, 310, 339
Mou Tsung-san, 69–71
de Mun, Albert, 103
Murphy-O'Connor, Jerome, 188
Mussner, Franz, 146, 166, 181, 203

Nagarjuna, 67, 400
Neusner, Jacob, 150–51, 155
Neville, Robert C., 261
Newbigin, Lesslie, 12
Niebuhr, H. Richard, 26
Nirvana, 38, 47–48, 50, 63–64, 132, 163, 253, 255, 257, 286, 288, 290, 367
Niwano, Nikkyo, 137

Obama, Barack, 187
Osman, Fathi, 215–16, 231

Panikkar, Raimundo, 60, 62–63, 98, 107–10, 116–17, 242, 244–45, 268, 386, 389–90
Pantheism, 72, 246, 395
Paradigm shift, 4, 5, 16, 29, 43–44, 67, 118, 142–44, 256, 274, 294, 364, 368
Paul of Tarsus, xi, 19, 155, 157–59, 161–63, 165, 171, 175, 178, 180, 182, 188–91, 193, 205, 270, 279, 289, 313, 374–77
Paul VI, Pope, 12, 83, 103, 135, 137, 210, 294, 321–22
Peace, 41, 64, 85, 91, 102, 124, 164, 210, 212, 218, 225–27, 229, 231, 236, 255, 257, 290, 296, 308–9, 319, 322, 347, 352–53, 356, 360–61
Pharisees, 149–53, 155, 157–58, 163, 165, 189, 252, 281, 293, 397
Philo, 147, 150, 184
Philosophy, 5, 6, 9, 16, 17, 22, 25–27, 29, 37, 39, 40, 48, 54, 57, 67, 70, 71, 74, 76, 78, 80, 97, 105, 109–11, 117, 121, 126, 140, 169, 184–85, 201, 216–17, 241, 246–48, 251, 254, 260–62, 264, 266, 268, 279, 282–83, 291–92, 295, 297, 300–306, 309, 316, 330, 341, 345–46, 354, 362, 370, 376, 380–81, 388, 391, 396–97, 399, 402
Piaget, Jean, 26, 27, 28, 369–70
Pieris, Aloysius, 104
Pius XI, Pope, 91, 103, 135, 165
Pius XII, Pope, 135, 265
Polytheism, 184, 246, 278, 280, 313–14, 390–92, 394–95, 404
Pratitya samutpada, 67, 400
Pregeant, Russell, 164, 169
Presbyterianism, 1, 36, 90, 93, 95, 228
Pseudepigrapha, 147

Q, 22, 52, 180–81
Quesnell, Quentin, 4, 367–68
Qumran, 153, 155
Qur'an, 110, 185, 207–8, 216–20, 222–24, 229–30, 248, 250, 255, 258, 395

Rabbi, x, 36, 38, 48, 57, 59, 63, 87, 145–56, 158–62, 203, 205, 220, 229, 239, 242, 250–55, 257–58, 275, 280, 379
Rabin, Yitzak, 210
Rahman, Fazlur, 185, 216, 218–19, 221
Rahner, Karl, 76–77, 301
Ramanuja, 247–48, 393
Ratzinger, Joseph, x, 46

Realitology, 383, 390
Reimarus, Hermann Samuel, 174
Relationality, 15–17, 19–20, 22–24, 26–28, 32, 34, 68, 103, 137, 143
Religious liberty/freedom, 84, 220–23, 225, 304, 314–21, 326, 332, 334, 340
Religion-State relations, 233–34
Ressourcement, 250–51, 258
Ricci, Matteo, 69, 262, 264–65, 401
Riceour, Paul, 21
Rissho Kosei-Kai, 137, 286
Rivkin, Ellis, 151–52, 155, 157
Roosevelt, Eleanor/Franklin, 318–19, 324
Rosemont, Henry, 23, 117
Ruether, Rosemary Radford, 382

Sagnier, Mark, 103
Salvation, 12, 19, 49, 81, 133, 152, 158, 164, 173, 177, 180, 193, 195, 207, 226, 250, 252, 255, 257, 267, 283, 380, 396
Samartha, Stanley, 16, 127, 241
Sanders, E. P. 146, 155, 159, 174, 176, 182, 189, 191, 385
Scheler, Max, 20
Schillebeeckx, Edward, 166, 171–73, 175, 180–81, 186–87, 191, 219, 377, 382
Schoonenberg, Piet, 186, 191
Schwartländer, Johannes, 123, 318, 325
Self-love, 55, 58, 271, 273, 344, 350, 376
Sengupta, Santos Chandra, 66, 111, 246–48
Shalom, 257
Shammai, 148, 150–51, 154–55, 158, 293
Shankara, 61, 244, 246–47, 393
Shar'ia, 38, 71, 101, 140, 185, 280, 331
Sigal, Phillip, 147–50, 153–56, 158–59
Sikhism, 57, 295, 341
Sivaraksa, Sulak, 103, 136
Sloyan, Gerard, 181
Smith, Wilfred Cantwell, 99, 110–11, 367
Sociology of Knowledge, 18, 20, 42, 118, 168, 183

Stendhal, Krister, 380–81
Sunyata, 64–67, 75, 77, 121, 138, 258, 284, 286, 400–401, 404
Suttee, 121–22
Swidler, Leonard, x, xi, xii, 12, 31, 46, 78, 85–86, 91, 110, 112, 140, 146, 150, 173, 203, 216, 220, 222–23, 227, 231, 239, 259, 269, 281, 294, 299, 303–304, 323, 325, 338, 346, 353, 379, 393, 401

Taha, Mahmud Muhammad, 219–20
Takizawa, Katsumi, 193
Talbi, Mohamed, 220–21
Talmud, 57, 102, 148–49, 151, 153, 158, 199, 253, 255
Tang Yi, 67, 100, 105, 121, 251, 402
Tanha, 47–48, 253
Taoism, 18, 38, 39, 56, 59, 62, 67, 69, 71–73, 97, 99–101, 104–5, 121, 135, 206, 240, 245, 251, 259, 260, 264, 268, 280, 284, 286, 291, 295, 304, 391, 399, 401–4, 408
Teilhard de Chardin, Pierre, 74, 77, 186, 383
Theologia negativa, 65–66
Thomas Aquinas. *See* Aquinas, Thomas
Torah, 38, 57, 59, 73, 96, 146–50, 155–61, 164, 171, 182, 191, 228, 242, 255, 257–58, 271, 280, 394, 399
Toynbee, Arnold J., 329
Tracy, David, 109, 113, 181, 376–77
Trialogue, xi, 112, 206, 209, 216, 222–23, 226–28, 230–39
Truth, 4, 7, 8, 10–12, 15–25, 29–30, 34, 38, 44, 48, 62, 66, 74–75, 83–86, 88, 96–97, 100–101, 119, 121, 125–28, 136, 157, 169, 181, 183, 208, 210–12, 215, 219–21, 230, 244, 249, 252, 294, 297, 308, 310, 320, 326, 344, 349, 351, 354, 358, 359, 368–71, 378–79, 381–82, 386–88, 400
Tu Wei-ming, 70 261

Ultimate Reality, 4, 7, 37, 46–48, 52, 54, 59, 61–62, 65–68, 72–73, 80–81, 111, 127, 133, 138, 145, 184, 230, 241–48, 258, 282–87, 291–92, 294, 389–96, 398–408
Una Sancta Movement, x, 91, 92

Vatican Council II, x, 12, 13, 45, 84, 86, 92, 119, 210
Vermes, Geza, 152–56, 174–75, 178, 189–190, 379

Way, 37–39, 71, 72, 80, 87, 100, 108, 160–61, 165–66, 168, 179, 220, 279–80, 284, 381, 403

Wilkens, Ulrich, 252–53
World Council of Churches, 6–7, 16, 89, 105, 241
World Parliament of Religions, 344

Yagi, Seiichi, 30–31, 132, 193–94
Yeshua, 38, 57, 63, 65, 83, 87, 145–89, 192–97, 201–204, 207–9, 246, 249–55, 257–58, 269–70, 272, 274–83, 285, 287–90, 293–94, 366, 374–87, 394, 397, 399
Yin-Yang, 73, 391, 395–96
Yorubism, 57

Zoroaster, 55, 391, 395–96

www.ingramcontent.com/pod-product-compliance
Lightning Source LLC
Chambersburg PA
CBHW071227290426
44108CB00013B/1318